Microsoft®
Office XP

Introductory Course

Pasewark and Pasewark

COURSE
TECHNOLOGY
—————★—————
™
THOMSON LEARNING

Australia • Canada • Mexico • Singapore • Spain • United Kingdom • United States

THOMSON

COURSE TECHNOLOGY

Microsoft® Office XP Introductory Course™

by Pasewark and Pasewark*

William R. Pasewark, Sr., Ph.D.
Professor Emeritus, Texas Tech
University

**William R. Pasewark, Jr.,
Ph.D., CPA**
Professor, Accounting
Texas Tech University

Carolyn Pasewark Denny, M.Ed.
National Computer Consultant,
Reading and Math Certified
Elementary Teacher
Certified Counselor, K-12

Scott G. Pasewark, B.S.
Occupational Education
Computer Technologist

Jan Pasewark Stogner, MBA
Financial Planner

Frank M. Stogner, MBA, CPA
International Business

Beth Pasewark Wadsworth, B.A.
Graphic Designer

Dave Lafferty
Senior Product Manager

Kim Ryttel
School Marketing Manager

Robert Gaggin
Product Manager

Jodi Dreissig
Associate Product Manager

GEX Publishing Services
Production Services

CEP Inc.
Developmental Editor

*Pasewark and Pasewark is a trademark of the Pasewark LTD.

Experience Office for the Future!
With these exciting new products
from South-Western Computer Education!

Our exciting new **Microsoft Office XP** books will provide everything needed to master
this software. All titles are MOUS certified for both core and expert level in
all applications:

NEW! **Microsoft Office XP Introductory Course** by Pasewark and Pasewark
*75+ hours of instruction for beginning through intermediate features on Word, Excel,
Publisher, Access, PowerPoint, FrontPage, and Windows.*

0-619-05843-9   Textbook, Hard Spiral Cover, Core MOUS Certification
0-619-05844-7   Textbook, Soft Cover
0-619-05847-1   Activities Workbook
0-619-05845-5   Instructor's Resource Kit (IRK) CD-ROM Package
0-619-05935-4   Annotated Instructor Edition

NEW! **Microsoft Office XP Advanced Course** by Cable, Morrison, and CEP Inc.
*75+ hours of instruction for intermediate through advanced features on Word, Excel,
Access, PowerPoint, and Outlook.*

0-619-05848-X   Textbook, Hard Spiral Cover, Expert MOUS Certification
0-619-05849-8   Textbook, Soft Cover
0-619-05852-8   Activities Workbook
0-619-05850-1   Instructor's Resource Kit (IRK) CD-ROM Package
0-619-05936-2   Annotated Instructor Edition

NEW! **Microsoft Word 2002** by Pasewark and Pasewark and Morrison

0-619-05890-0   Complete Textbook, Soft Spiral Cover, Expert MOUS Certification, 35+ hours
0-619-05893-5   Introductory Textbook, Soft Spiral Cover, Core MOUS Certification, 12+ hours

NEW! **Microsoft Excel 2002** by Pasewark and Pasewark and Cable

0-619-05878-1   Complete Textbook, Soft Spiral Cover, Expert MOUS Certification, 35+ hours
0-619-05894-3   Introductory Textbook, Soft Spiral Cover, Core MOUS Certification, 12+ hours

NEW! **Microsoft PowerPoint 2002** by Pasewark and Pasewark and CEP, Inc.

0-619-05886-2   Complete Textbook, Soft Spiral Cover, Comprehensive MOUS Certification,
                 35+ hours
0-619-05895-1   Introductory Textbook, Soft Spiral Cover, Comprehensive MOUS Certification,
                 12+ hours

NEW! **Microsoft Access 2002** by Pasewark and Pasewark and Cable

0-619-05883-8   Complete Textbook, Soft Spiral Cover, Expert MOUS Certification, 35+ hours
0-619-05896-X   Introductory Textbook, Soft Spiral Cover, Core MOUS Certification, 12+ hours

Join Us On the Internet **http://www.course.com**

How to Use this Book

What makes a good computer instructional text? Sound pedagogy and the most current, complete materials. That is what you will find in *Microsoft® Office XP: Introductory Course*. Not only will you find an inviting lay-out, but also many features to enhance learning.

Objectives—
Objectives are listed at the beginning of each lesson, along with a suggested time for completion of the lesson. This allows you to look ahead to what you will be learning and to pace your work.

SCANS—
(Secretary's Commission on Achieving Necessary Skills)—The U.S. Department of Labor has identified the school-to-careers competencies. The eight workplace com-petencies and foun-dation skills are identified in exer-cises where they apply. More informa-tion on SCANS can be found on the *Instructor Resource Kit* CD-ROM.

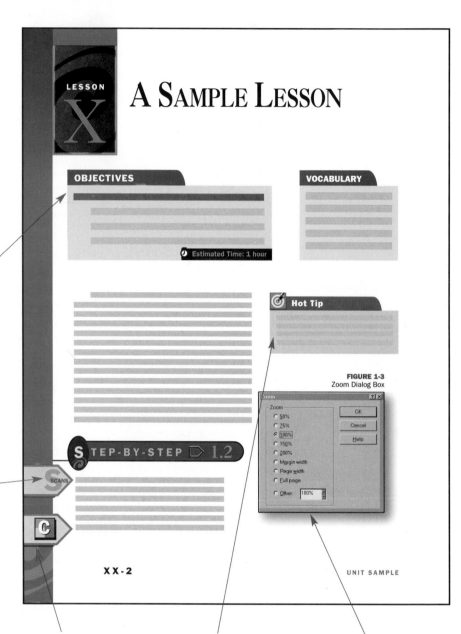

A SAMPLE LESSON

LESSON X

OBJECTIVES

Estimated Time: 1 hour

VOCABULARY

Hot Tip

FIGURE 1-3
Zoom Dialog Box

STEP-BY-STEP 1.2

SCANS

C

XX-2

UNIT SAMPLE

Certification Icon—
This icon is shown wherever a criteria for Microsoft Office User Specialist (MOUS) certification is cov-ered in the lesson. A correlation table with page numbers is pro-vided in Appendix A of this book and on the *Instructor Resource Kit* CD-ROM.

Marginal Boxes—
These boxes provide additional information for Hot Tips, fun facts Did You Know? fun facts, Computer Concepts, the Internet, Extra Challenges activities, and Teamwork ideas.

Enhanced Screen Shots—Screen shots now come to life on each page with color and depth.

How to Use this Book

Summary—At the end of each lesson, you will find a summary to prepare you to complete the end-of-lesson activities.

Vocabulary/Review Questions—Review material at the end of each lesson and each unit enables you to prepare for assessment of the content presented.

Lesson Projects—End-of-lesson hands-on application of what has been learned in the lesson allows you to actually apply the techniques covered.

Critical Thinking Activities—Each lesson gives you an opportunity to apply creative analysis and use the Help system to solve problems.

Command Summary—At the end of each unit, a command summary is provided for quick reference.

End-of-Unit Projects—End-of-unit hands-on application of concepts learned in the unit provides opportunity for a comprehensive review.

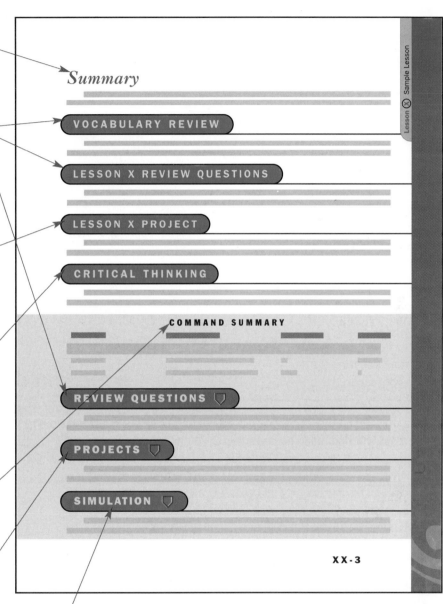

Summary

VOCABULARY REVIEW

LESSON X REVIEW QUESTIONS

LESSON X PROJECT

CRITICAL THINKING

COMMAND SUMMARY

REVIEW QUESTIONS

PROJECTS

SIMULATION

XX-3

Simulation—A realistic simulation runs throughout the text at the end of each unit, reinforcing the material covered in the unit.

Capstone Simulation—Another simulation appears at the end of the text, to be completed after all the lessons have been covered, to give you an opportunity to apply all of the skills you have learned and see them come together in one application.

Appendices—Appendices cover the Microsoft Office User Specialist Program, Windows Basics, Computer Concepts, and Microsoft Office Speech Recognition.

PREFACE

There are three versions of Office XP. They are described in the chart below. The chart shows which of the programs are in each version. Instructions for all versions are in this book.

NAME OF PROGRAM	OFFICE XP STANDARD	OFFICE XP PROFESSIONAL	OFFICE XP PROFESSIONAL SPECIAL EDITION*
Word 2002	X	X	X
Excel 2002	X	X	X
Outlook 2002	X	X	X
PowerPoint® 2002	X	X	X
Access 2002		X	X
FrontPage 2002			X
Publisher 2002			X
*Limited-time version			

You will find much helpful material in this introductory section. The *How to Use This Book* pages give you a visual summary of the kinds of information you will find in the text. The *What's New* section summarizes features new in this version of Microsoft Office. Be sure to review *Guide for Using This Book* to learn about the terminology and conventions used in preparing the pages and to find out what supporting materials are available for use with this book. If you are interested in pursuing certification as a Microsoft Office User Specialist (MOUS), read the information on *The Microsoft Office User Specialist Program*.

An Ideal Book for Anyone

Because computers are such an important subject for all learners, instructors need the support of a well-designed, educationally sound textbook that is supported by strong ancillary instructional materials. *Microsoft® Office XP: Introductory Course* is just such a book.

The textbook includes features that make learning easy and enjoyable—yet challenging—for learners. It is also designed with many features that make teaching easy and enjoyable for you. Comprehensive, yet flexible, *Microsoft® Office XP: Introductory Course* is adaptable for a wide variety of class-time schedules.

The text includes a wide range of learning experiences from activities with one or two commands to simulations and projects that challenge and sharpen learners' problem-solving skills. This book is ideal for computer courses with learners who have varying abilities and previous computer experiences. A companion text, *Microsoft® Office XP: Advanced Course*, is available for a second course.

The lessons in this course contain the following features designed to promote learning:

- Objectives that specify goals students should achieve by the end of each lesson.
- Concept text that explores in detail each new feature.
- Screen captures that help to illustrate the concept text.
- Step-by-Step exercises that allow students to practice the features just introduced.
- Summaries that review the concepts in the lesson.
- Review Questions that test students on the concepts covered in the lesson.
- Projects that provide an opportunity for students to apply concepts they have learned in the lesson.
- Critical Thinking Activities that encourage students to use knowledge gained in the lesson or from the application's Help system to solve specific problems.

Each unit also contains a unit review with the following features:

- A Command Summary that reviews menu commands and toolbar shortcuts introduced in the unit.
- Review Questions covering material from all lessons in the unit.
- Projects that give students a chance to apply many of the skills learned in the unit.
- A simulation that proposes real-world jobs a student can complete using the skills learned in the unit.

Acknowledgments

The authors gratefully thank Rhonda Davis for coordinating the preparation of manuscript and for using her business experiences to write several segments of Office XP. We also thank Laura Melton for her contribution to this book.

All of our books are a coordinated effort by the authors and scores of professionals working with the publisher. The authors appreciate the dedicated work of all these publishing personnel and particularly those with whom we have had direct contact:

- Course Technology: Melissa Ramondetta, Robert Gaggin, Kim Wood, and Jodi Dreissig
- Custom Editorial Productions (CEP) Inc.: Betsy Newberry, Rose Marie Kuebbing, Virginia Ewbank, and Anne Chimenti.

Many professional Course Technology sales representatives make educationally sound presentations to instructors about our books. We appreciate their valuable work as "bridges" between the authors and instructors.

Authors' Commitment

In writing *Microsoft® Office XP: Introductory Course*, the authors have dedicated themselves to creating a comprehensive and appealing instructional package to make teaching and learning an interesting, challenging, and rewarding experience.

With these instructional materials, instructors can create realistic learning experience so learners can successfully master concepts, knowledge, and skills that will help them live better lives—now and in the future.

About the Authors

Pasewark LTD is a family-owned business. We use Microsoft® Office in our business, career, personal, and family lives. Writing this book, therefore, was a natural project for seven members of our family who are identified on the title page of this book.

The authors have written more than 100 books about computers, accounting, and office administration.

Pasewark LTD authors are members of several professional associations that help authors write better books.

The authors have been recognized with numerous awards for classroom teaching.

AWARD-WINNING BOOKS BY THE PASEWARKS

The predecessor to this book, *Microsoft® Office 2000: Introductory Course*, by the Pasewarks, won the Text and Academic Authors Association *Texty Award* for the best el-hi computer book for the year 2000.

In 1994, the Pasewarks also won a *Texty* for their Microsoft Works computer book. Their book, *The Office: Procedures and Technology,* won the first William McGuffey Award for Textbook Excellence and Longevity. The Paseworks' book *Microsoft® Works 2000 BASICS* won the Texty Award for the best computer book for the year 2001.

WHAT'S NEW

Microsoft Office XP has many features that help you to be more productive and to enjoy using your computer. Some of the new features covered in this Introductory Course are listed below. Other features are identified and taught in the companion book, *Microsoft® Office XP: Advanced Course*.

- Software is easier to install, use, and manage.

- Office XP identifies and corrects installation and operating errors.

- The task pane, which opens automatically in all of the Office applications, contains commonly used commands that can help a user work more efficiently.

- In Word, the Mail Merge Wizard is simplified and easier to use.

- It is easy for Word users to share and collaborate on documents by using the Track Changes feature, Compact and Merge feature, and improved options on the Reviewing toolbar.

- In Outlook, a user can choose to see a single reminder window for all appointment or task reminders.

- The Contacts window in Outlook includes a Display As field for e-mail names. The recipient's name appears in the To: box when you create an e-mail, instead of the e-mail address.

- The Print Preview option in PowerPoint enables the user to preview how a presentation will look when printed.

- In PowerPoint, a user can send a presentation to someone else for review. After viewing any changes made to the presentation, the user can choose to merge the changes back into the orginal document.

- In PowerPoint's Normal view, a user can also view a presentation in an outline or thumbnail format. These miniature slides in thumbnail form allow a user to view slides without advancing through the entire presentation.

- Speech Recognition allows a user to dictate text and select menu, toolbar, and dialog box items.

START-UP CHECKLIST

HARDWARE

Minimum Configuration

✓ PC with Pentium 133 MHz or higher processor. Pentium III recommended.

✓ RAM requirements

   ✓ Windows 98 and Windows 98 Second Edition – 24 MB of RAM plus 8 MB for each application running simultaneously.

   ✓ Windows Me, Windows NT Workstation 4.0, or Windows NT Server 4.0 – 32 MB of RAM plus 8 MB for each application running simultaneously.

   ✓ Windows 2000 Professional – 64 MB of RAM (128 MB RAM recommended) plus 8 MB for each application running simultaneously.

✓ Hard disk with 245 MB free for typical installation

✓ CD-ROM drive

✓ Super VGA monitor with video adapter. (800 x 600) or higher-resolution. 256 colors or more required.

✓ Microsoft Mouse, IntelliMouse, or compatible pointing device

✓ 14,000 or higher baud modem

✓ Printer

Recommended Configuration

✓ Pentium III PC with 128 MB RAM or higher

✓ 56,000 baud modem

✓ Multimedia capability

   Accelerated video card
   Audio output device

✓ For e-mail, Microsoft Mail, Internet SMTP/POP3, or other MAPI-compliant messaging software

SOFTWARE

✓ Windows 95, 98, Me, or NT Workstation 4.0 with Service Pack 6.0 installed, or Windows 2000

✓ For Web collaboration and Help files, Internet Explorer 5 browser or Windows 98

GUIDE FOR USING THIS BOOK

Please read this Guide before starting work. The time you spend now will save you much more time later and will make your learning faster, easier, and more pleasant.

Terminology

This text uses the term *keying* to mean entering text into a computer using the keyboard. *Keying* is the same as "keyboarding" or "typing."

Text means words, numbers, and symbols that are printed.

Conventions

The different type styles used in this book have special meanings. They will save you time because you will soon automatically recognize from the type style the nature of the text you are reading and what you will do.

WHAT YOU WILL DO	TYPE STYLE	EXAMPLE
Text you will key	**Bold**	Key **Don't litter** rapidly.
Individual keys you will press	**Bold**	Press **Enter** to insert a blank line.

WHAT YOU WILL SEE	TYPE STYLE	EXAMPLE
Filenames in book	**Bold upper and lowercase**	Open **IW Step2-1** from the data files.
Glossary terms in book	***Bold and italics***	The ***menu bar*** contains menu titles.
Words on screen	*Italics*	Highlight the word *pencil* on the screen.
Menus and commands	**Bold**	Choose **Open** from the **File** menu.
Options/features with long names	*Italics*	Select **Normal** from the *Style for following paragraph* text box.

Review Pack CD-ROM

All data files necessary for the Step-by-Step exercises, end-of-lesson Projects, end-of-unit Projects and Jobs, and Capstone Simulation exercises in this book are located on the *Review Pack* CD-ROM. Data files for the *Activities Workbook* are also stored on the *Review Pack* CD-ROM.

Data files are named according to the first exercise in which they are used and the unit of this textbook in which they are used. A data file for a Step-by-Step exercise in the Introductory Microsoft Word unit would have a filename such as **IW Step1-1**. This particular filename identifies a data file used in the first Step-by-Step exercise in Lesson 1. Other data files have the following formats:

- End-of-lesson projects: **IW Project1-1**
- End-of-unit projects: **IW Project2**
- Simulation jobs: **IW Job3**

Instructor Resource Kit CD-ROM

The *Instructor Resource Kit* CD-ROM contains a wealth of instructional material you can use to prepare for teaching Office XP. The CD-ROM stores the following information:

- Both the data and solution files for this course.

- ExamView® tests for each lesson. ExamView is a powerful testing software package that allows instructors to create and administer printed, computer (LAN-based), and Internet exams. ExamView includes hundreds of questions that correspond to the topics covered in this text, enabling learners to generate detailed study guides that include page references for further review. The computer-based and Internet testing components allow learners to take exams at their computers, and also save the instructor time by grading each exam automatically.

- Electronic *Instructor's Manual* that includes lecture notes for each lesson, answers to the lesson and unit review questions, and references to the solutions for Step-by-Step exercises, end-of-lesson activities, and Unit Review projects.

- Instructor lesson plans as well as learner study guides that can help to guide students through the lesson text and exercises.

- Copies of the figures that appear in the student text, which can be used to prepare transparencies.

- Grids that show skills required for Microsoft Office User Specialist (MOUS) certification and the SCANS workplace competencies and skills.

- Suggested schedules for teaching the lessons in this course.

- Additional instructional information about individual learning strategies, portfolios and career planning, and a sample Internet contract.

- Answers to the *Activities Workbook* exercises.

- PowerPoint presentations showing Office XP features for each unit in the text.

Additional Activities and Questions

An *Activities Workbook* is available to supply additional paper-and-pencil exercises and hands-on computer applications for each unit of this book.

SCANS

The Secretary's Commission on Achieving Necessary Skills (SCANS) from the U.S. Department of Labor was asked to examine the demands of the workplace and whether new learners are capable of meeting those demands. Specifically, the Commission was directed to advise the Secretary of Labor on the level of skills required to enter employment.

SCANS workplace competencies and foundation skills have been integrated into *Microsoft® Office XP: Introductory Course*. The workplace competencies are identified as 1) ability to use resources, 2) interpersonal skills, 3) ability to work with information, 4) understanding of systems, and 5) knowledge and understanding of technology. The foundation skills are identified as 1) basic communication skills, 2) thinking skills, and 3) personal qualities.

Exercises in which learners must use a number of these SCANS competencies and foundation skills are marked in the text with the SCANS icon.

THE MICROSOFT OFFICE USER SPECIALIST PROGRAM

APPROVED COURSEWARE

What Does This Logo Mean?

It means this courseware has been approved by the Microsoft® Office User Specialist Program to be among the finest available for learning Microsoft Office XP, Microsoft Word 2002, Microsoft Excel 2002, Microsoft PowerPoint® 2002, Microsoft Access 2002, and Microsoft Outlook® 2002. It also means that upon completion of this courseware, you may be prepared to become a Microsoft Office User Specialist.

What is a Microsoft Office User Specialist?

A Microsoft Office User Specialist is an individual who has certified his or her skills in one or more of the Microsoft Office desktop applications of Microsoft Word, Microsoft Excel, Microsoft PowerPoint®, Microsoft Outlook®, or Microsoft Access, or in Microsoft Project. The Microsoft Office User Specialist Program typically offers certification exams at the "Core" and "Expert" skill levels.* The Microsoft Office User Specialist Program is the only Microsoft approved program in the world for certifying proficiency in Microsoft Office desktop applications and Microsoft Project. This certification can be a valuable asset in any job search or career advancement.

More Information

To learn more about becoming a Microsoft Office User Specialist, visit *www.mous.net*. To purchase a Microsoft Office User Specialist certification exam, visit *www.DesktopIQ.com*.

* The availability of Microsoft Office User Specialist certification exams varies by application, application version, and language. Visit *www.mous.net* for exam availability.

TABLE OF CONTENTS

UNIT INTRODUCTION

UNIT INTRODUCTORY MICROSOFT WORD

UNIT INTRODUCTORY MICROSOFT POWERPOINT

UNIT INTRODUCTORY MICROSOFT OUTLOOK

UNIT INTRODUCTORY MICROSOFT PUBLISHER & MICROSOFT FRONTPAGE

NTRODUCTION

UNIT

lesson 1   1.5 hrs.

**Microsoft® Office XP
Basics and the Internet**

Estimated Time for Unit: 1.5 hours

LESSON
1

MICROSOFT® OFFICE XP BASICS AND THE INTERNET

Introduction to Office XP

Office XP is an integrated software package. An *integrated software package* is a program that combines several computer applications into one program. Office consists of a word processor application, a spreadsheet application, a database application, a presentation application, a schedule/organization application, a desktop publishing application, and a Web page application.

Internet

For more information on Microsoft Word and other Microsoft products, visit Microsoft's Web site at *http://www.microsoft.com.*

The word processor application (Word) enables you to create documents such as letters and reports. The spreadsheet application (Excel) lets you work with numbers to prepare items such as budgets or to determine loan payments. The database application (Access) organizes information such as addresses or inventory items. The presentation application (PowerPoint) can be used to create slides, outlines, speaker's notes, and audience handouts. The schedule/organization application (Outlook) increases your efficiency by keeping track of e-mail, appointments, tasks, contacts, events, and to-do lists. The desktop publishing application (Publisher) helps you design professional looking documents. The Web page application (FrontPage) enables you to create and maintain your own Web site.

Hot Tip

If the Microsoft Office Shortcut Bar is installed, you can use it to open an Office application and create a blank document at the same time.

Because Office is an integrated program, the applications can be used together. For example, numbers from a spreadsheet can be included in a letter created in the word processor or in a presentation.

Starting an Office Application

An Office application can be started from the Programs menu on the Start menu or directly from the Start menu.

OPENING AN OFFICE APPLICATION FROM THE PROGRAMS MENU

To open an Office application from the Programs menu, click the Start button, select Programs, and then click the name of the application you want to open.

OPENING AN OFFICE APPLICATION FROM THE START MENU

To open an Office application and create a new blank document within the application at the same time, click the

Computer Concepts

You can also open a new file from within an application by choosing **New** on the **File** menu. The New dialog box appears, which is very similar to the New Office Document dialog box.

Start button. Then, click New Office Document on the Start menu. When the New Office Document dialog box appears, click the General tab (see Figure 1-1), and then double-click the icon for the type of blank document you want to create. The application for that type of document opens and a new blank document is created. For example, if you double-click the Blank Database icon, Access will open and a blank database will be displayed on the screen.

FIGURE 1-1
General tab in the New Office Document dialog box

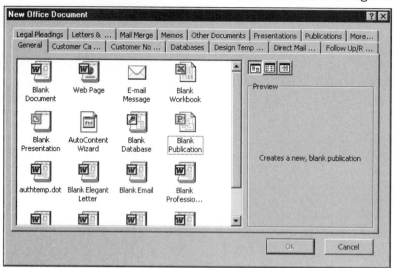

STEP-BY-STEP ▷ 1.1

1. Click the **Start** button to open the Start menu.

2. Click **New Office Document** and the New Office Document dialog box appears, as shown in Figure 1-1.

3. Click the **General** tab, if it is not already selected.

4. Double-click the **Blank Presentation** icon. PowerPoint starts and a blank presentation appears.

5. Click the **Close** button on the right side of the menu bar to close the blank presentation. The PowerPoint program will remain open.

6. Click the **Start** button again.

7. Point to **Programs**, and then **Microsoft Word**. Word starts and a blank document appears, as shown in Figure 1-2. Leave Word and PowerPoint open for use in the following Step-by-Steps.

Understanding the Opening Screen

Look carefully at the parts of the opening screen for the Word program labeled in Figure 1-2. These basic parts of the screen are similar in all of the Office programs and are discussed in Table 1-1.

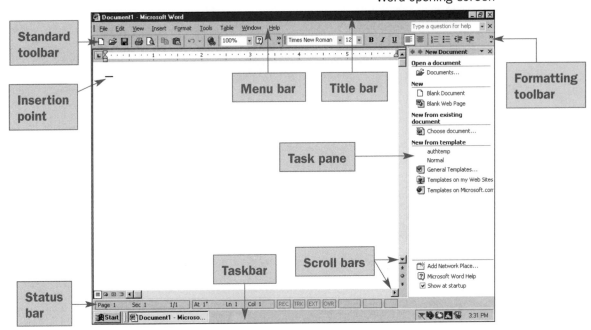

FIGURE 1-2
Word opening screen

TABLE 1-1
Understanding the opening screen

ITEM	FUNCTION
Title bar	Displays the names of the Office program and the current file.
Menu bar	Contains the menu titles from which you can choose a variety of commands.
Standard toolbar	Contains buttons you can use to perform common tasks.
Formatting toolbar	Contains buttons for changing formatting, such as alignment and type styles.
Insertion point	Shows where text will appear when you begin keying.
Scroll bars	Allow you to move quickly to other areas of an Office application.
Status bar	Tells you the status of what is shown on the screen.
Taskbar	Shows the Start button, the Quick Launch toolbar, and all open programs.
Task pane	Opens automatically when you start an Office application. Contains commonly used commands that pertain to each application.

The *task pane* is a separate window on the right-hand side of the opening screen, as shown in Figure 1-2. It opens automatically when you start an Office application and contains commonly used commands that can help you work more efficiently. To close the task pane, simply click the Close button. To view the task pane, select Task Pane from the View menu.

Using Menus and Toolbars

A **menu** in an Office application is like a menu in a restaurant. You look at the menus to see what the program has to offer. Each title in the menu bar represents a separate **pull-down menu**. By choosing a command from a pull-down menu, you give the program instructions about what you want to do.

When you first use a program, each menu displays only basic commands. To see an expanded menu with all the commands, click the arrows at the bottom of the menu. As you work, the program adjusts the menus to display the commands used most frequently, adding a command when you use it and dropping a command when it hasn't been used recently. Figure 1-3 compares the short and expanded versions of the Edit menu.

FIGURE 1-3
Short menu vs. expanded menu

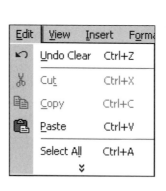

Toolbars provide another quick way to choose commands. The toolbars use **icons**, or small pictures, to remind you of each button's function. Toolbars can also contain pull-down menus. Unless you specify otherwise, only the Standard and Formatting toolbars are displayed, but many more are available. To see a list of the toolbars you can use, right-click anywhere on a toolbar.

As with the menus, toolbars initially display buttons only for basic commands. To see additional buttons, click Toolbar Options (the button with two right arrows >>) on the toolbar and choose from the list that appears, as shown in Figure 1-4. When you use a button from the list, it is added to the toolbar. If you haven't used a button recently, it is returned to the Toolbar Options list.

FIGURE 1-4
Toolbar Options list

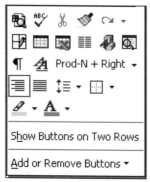

Opening, Saving, and Closing Office Documents

In Office applications, you *open*, *save*, and *close* files the same way. Opening a file means loading a file from a disk onto your screen. Saving a file stores it on a disk. Closing a file removes it from the screen.

OPENING AN EXISTING DOCUMENT

To open an existing document, you can choose Open in an application's File menu, or choose the option to open an existing document from the task pane. In Word, you would choose the Documents option in the Open a document section of the task pane. For either option, the Open dialog box appears (see Figure 1-5). You can also choose Open Office Document on the Start menu, which displays the Open Office Document dialog box.

FIGURE 1-5
Open dialog box

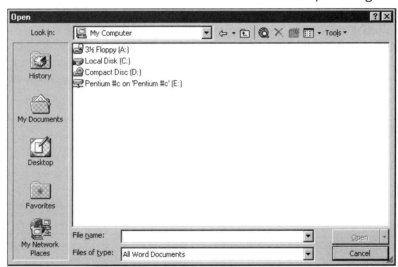

The Open (or Open Office Document) dialog box enables you to open a file from any available disk or folder. The Look in box, near the top of the dialog box, is where you locate the disk drive that contains the file you want to open. Below that is a list that shows you the folders or resources that are on the disk. Double-click a folder to see what files and folders are contained within. To see all the files or office documents in the folder instead of just those created with a particular application, choose All Files or Office Files from the Files of type drop-down list box located near the bottom of the dialog box. The bar on the left side of the dialog box provides a shortcut for accessing some of the common places to store documents.

When you have located and selected the file you want to open, click the Open button. If you click the down arrow next to the Open button, a menu is displayed as shown in Figure 1-6. You can choose to open a copy of the document or open the document in your browser if it is saved in Web page format.

FIGURE 1-6
Open menu

S TEP-BY-STEP ▷ 1.2

1. With Word on the screen, choose **More documents** in the Open a document section of the task pane. The Open dialog box appears, as shown in Figure 1-5. (You may have to select **Document** in the Open a document section of the task pane if it is the first time this program has been opened.)

2. Click the down arrow to the right of the **Look in** box to display the available disk drives.

3. Click the drive that contains your data files and locate the **Employees** folder, as shown in Figure 1-7.

4. Double-click the **Employees** folder. The folders within the Employees folder appear (see Figure 1-8).

5. Double-click the **Sarah** folder. The names of the Word files in the Sarah folder are displayed.

6. Click the down arrow at the right of the **Files of type** box and select **All Files**. The names of all files in the Sarah folder are displayed.

7. Click **Schedule Memo** to select it and then click **Open** to open the file. Leave the file open for the next Step-by-Step.

FIGURE 1-8
Contents of the Employees folder

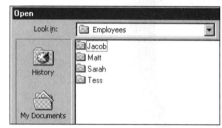

FIGURE 1-7
Employees folder

You can see how folders help organize and identify documents. The Sarah folder also contains a spreadsheet with the work schedule for the first two weeks in September. In the next Step-by-Step, you will start Excel, the Office spreadsheet application, and open the spreadsheet that goes with the memo.

S TEP-BY-STEP ▷ 1.3

1. Click the **Start** button.

2. Click **Open Office Document**.

3. Click the down arrow at the right of the **Look in** box and click the drive that contains the data files, if necessary.

4. Double-click the **Employees** folder; then double-click the **Sarah** folder.

5. Double-click **September Schedule** to open the file. Excel opens and **September Schedule** appears on the screen as shown in Figure 1-9. Leave the file open for the next Step-by-Step.

FIGURE 1-9
September Schedule file

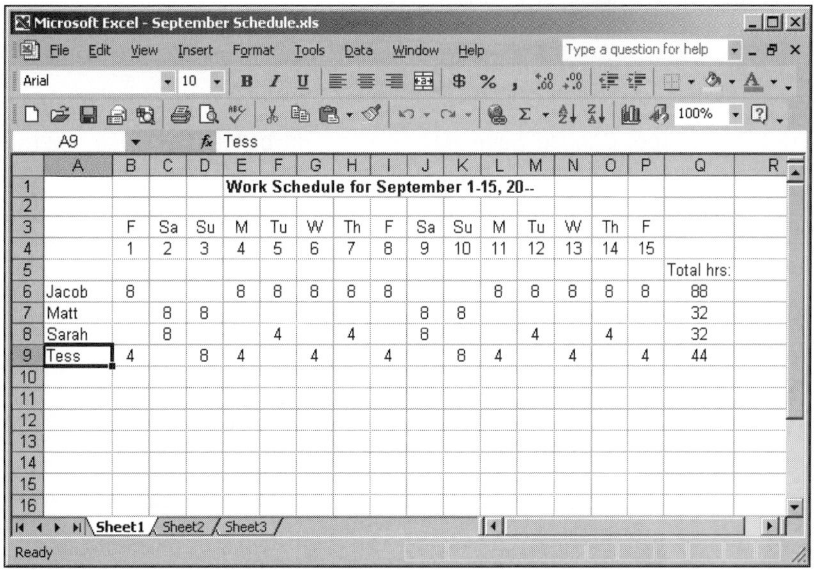

Saving a File

Saving is done two ways. The Save command saves a file on a disk using the current name. The Save As command saves a file on a disk using a new name. The Save As command can also be used to save a file to a new location.

FILENAMES

Unlike programs designed for the early versions of Windows and DOS, filenames are not limited to eight characters. With Windows, a filename may contain up to 255 characters and may include spaces. However, you will rarely need this many characters to name a file. Name a file with a descriptive name that will remind you of what the file contains, such as Cover Letter or Quarter 1 Sales. The filename can include most characters found on the keyboard with the exception of those shown in Table 1-2.

TABLE 1-2
Characters that cannot be used in filenames

CHARACTER	NAME	CHARACTER	NAME
*	asterisk	<	less than sign
\	backslash	.	period
[]	brackets	;	semicolon
:	colon	/	slash
,	comma	"	quotation mark
=	equal sign	?	question mark
>	greater than sign	|	vertical bar

1. *September Schedule* should be on the screen from the last Step-by-Step. Choose **Save As** on the **File** menu. The Save As dialog box appears, as shown in Figure 1-10.

2. In the File name box, key **Sept Work Sched**, followed by your initials.

3. Click the down arrow to the right of the Save in box and choose where you want to save the file.

4. Choose **Save** to save the file with the new name. Leave the document open for the next Step-by-Step.

FIGURE 1-10
Save As dialog box

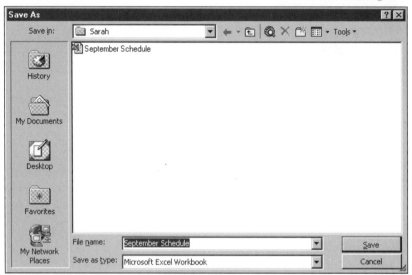

Closing an Office Document

You can close an Office document either by choosing Close on the File menu or by clicking the Close button on the right side of the menu bar. If you close a file, the application will still be open and ready for you to open or create another file.

1. Choose **Close** on the **File** menu. *Sept Work Sched* closes.

2. Click the **Microsoft Word** button on the taskbar to make it active. *Schedule Memo* should be displayed.

3. Click the **Close** button in the right corner of the menu bar to close *Schedule Memo*. Leave Word open for the next Step-by-Step.

Shortcuts for Loading Recently Used Files

Office offers you two shortcuts for opening recently used files. The first shortcut is to choose Documents from the Start menu. A menu will open listing the fifteen most recently used documents similar to that shown in Figure 1-11. To open one of the recently used files, double-click the file you wish to open.

The second and third shortcuts can be found on each Office application's File menu and task pane. The bottom part of the File menu and the Open a document section of the task pane show the filenames of the four most recently opened documents, with the most recently opened first as shown in Figure 1-12. When a new file is opened, each filename moves down to make room for the new most recently opened file. To open one of the files, you simply choose it as if it were a menu selection. If the document you are looking for is not on the File menu, use Open to load it from the disk.

Hot Tip

When you first use an Office application, the menus only display the basic commands. To see an expanded menu with all the commands, click the arrows at the bottom of the menu. As you work, the menus are adjusted to display the commands used most frequently, adding a command when you choose it and dropping a command when it hasn't been used recently.

Hot Tip

If the file is on a floppy disk, you must be sure that the correct disk is in the drive.

FIGURE 1-11
Most recently used files

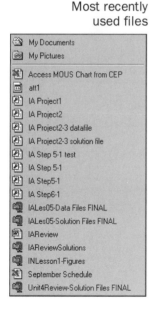

FIGURE 1-12
Most recently used files on the File menu and task pane

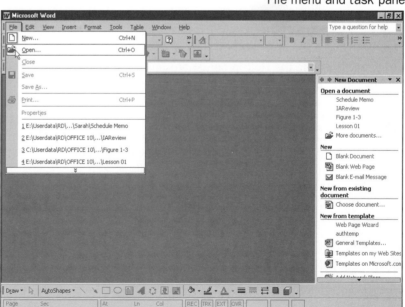

Office Help

This lesson covers only a few of the many features of Office applications. For additional information, use the Office Help system as a quick reference when you are unsure about a function. To get specific help about topics relating to the application you are using, access help from the Help menu on the application's menu bar. Then, from the Help dialog box, shown in Figure 1-13, you can choose to see a table of contents displaying general topics and subtopics, key a question in the Answer Wizard, or search the Help system using the Index.

FIGURE 1-13
Microsoft Word Help

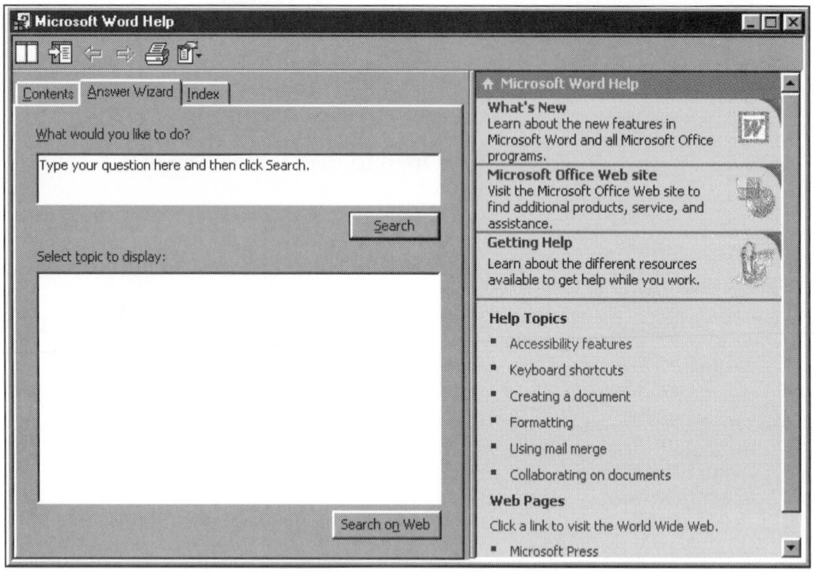

Many topics in the Help program are linked. A *link* is represented by colored, underlined text. By clicking a link, the user "jumps" to a linked document that contains additional information about that topic.

Clicking the buttons on the toolbar controls the display of information. The Hide button removes the left frame of the help window from view. The Show button will restore it. Back and Forward buttons allow you to move back and forth between previously displayed help entries. Use the Print button to print the help information displayed. The Options button offers navigational choices, as well as options to customize, refresh, and print help topics.

The Contents tab is useful if you want to browse through the topics by category. Click a book icon to see additional help topics. Click a question mark to display detailed help information in the right frame of the help window.

STEP-BY-STEP ▷ 1.6

1. Open the Word Help program by choosing **Microsoft Word Help** on the **Help** menu.

2. Click the **Hide** button on the toolbar to remove the left frame.

3. Click the **Show** button to display it again.

4. The Answer Wizard tab is displayed and the right frame displays the Microsoft Word Help screen. Your screen should appear similar to Figure 1-13.

5. Click the **Accessibility features** link in the right frame.

6. Read the contents of the Help window and leave it open for the next Step-by-Step.

Hot Tip

If the Office Assistant appears, turn it off by clicking **Options** in the balloon, clearing the Use the Office Assistant check box, and clicking **OK**.

Using the Answer Wizard tab, you can key in a question about what you would like to do. Then click one of the topics that appear in the box below to display the information in the right frame.

When you want to search for help on a particular topic, use the Index tab and key a word. Windows will search alphabetically through the list of help topics to try to find an appropriate match, as shown in Figure 1-14. Double-click a topic to see it explained in the right frame of the help window.

FIGURE 1-14
Index tab of the Help system

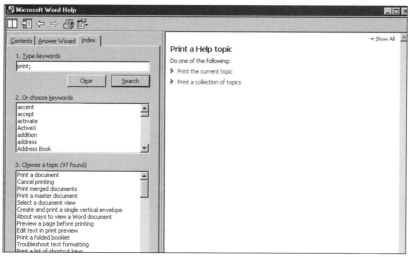

1. Click the **Index** tab.

2. Key **print** in the Type keywords box and click **Search**.

3. In the Choose a topic box, search through the list until you find **Print a Help topic**. Click it to display information in the right frame, as shown in Figure 1-14.

4. In the right frame, click **Print the current topic** and then **Print a collection of topics**. The information on both topics will display.

5. Read the information, then print the information by following the instructions you read.

6. Click the **Back** button to return to the previous help entry.

7. Click the **Forward** button to advance to the next help entry.

8. Close the Help program by clicking the **Close** button.

Office Assistant

The Office Assistant is a feature found in all the Office programs that offers a variety of ways to get help. The Assistant, shown in Figure 1-15, is an animated character that offers tips, solutions, instructions, and examples to help you work more efficiently. The default Office Assistant character is a paperclip. A *default* setting is the one used unless another option is chosen.

Hot Tip

You can change the way the Office Assistant provides help by clicking **Options**, choosing the **Options** tab, and making selections.

FIGURE 1-15
Default Office Assistant

The Office Assistant monitors the work you are doing and anticipates when you might need help. It appears on the screen with tips on how to save time or use the program's features more effectively. For example, if you start writing a letter in Word, the Assistant pops up to ask if you want help, as shown in Figure 1-16.

FIGURE 1-16
Office Assistant automatically volunteering assistance

If you have a specific question, you can use the Office Assistant to search for help. To display the Office Assistant if it is not on the screen, choose Show the Office Assistant from the Help menu. Key your question and click Search. The Assistant suggests a list of help topics in response.

STEP-BY-STEP ▷ 1.8

1. Choose **Show the Office Assistant** from the **Help** menu. The Office Assistant appears. If necessary, click the **Office Assistant** to display the text box.

2. Key **How do I use the Office Assistant?** in the text box.

3. Click **Search**. A list of help topics is displayed, as shown in Figure 1-15.

4. Click the down arrow next to the **See More ...** option, and choose **Guidelines for searching for Help**. The Microsoft Word Help box appears.

5. Click the **Using the Index to narrow your scope** link.

6. Read about the Index and print the information.

7. Click the **Close** box to remove the Help window from the screen.

8. Open a new Word document.

9. Key **Dear Zack,** and press **Enter**. A message from the Office Assistant appears, asking if you want help writing your letter, as shown in Figure 1-16.

10. Click **Just type the letter without help**.

11. Close the Word document without saving. Leave Word on the screen for the next Step-by-Step.

Quitting an Office Application

The Exit command on the File menu provides the option to quit Word or any other Office application. You can also click the Close button on the right side of the title bar. Exiting an Office application takes you to another open application or back to the Windows desktop.

STEP-BY-STEP ▷ 1.9

1. Open the **File** menu. Notice the files listed toward the bottom of the menu. These are the four most recently used files mentioned in the previous section.

2. Choose **Exit**. Word closes and Excel is displayed on the screen.

3. Click the **Close** button in the right corner of the title bar. Excel closes and the desktop appears on the screen. The taskbar shows an application is still open.

4. Click the **PowerPoint** button on the taskbar to display it on the screen. Exit PowerPoint. The desktop appears on the screen again.

Accessing the Internet

The *Internet* is a vast network of computers linked to one another. The Internet allows people around the world to share information and ideas through Web pages, newsgroups, mailing lists, chats, e-mail, and electronic files.

Connecting to the Internet requires special hardware and software and an Internet Service Provider. Before you can use the Internet, your computer needs to be connected and you should know how to access the Internet.

The *World Wide Web* is a system of computers that share information by means of hypertext links on "pages." The Internet is its carrier. To identify hypertext documents, the Web uses addresses called *Uniform Resource Locators (URLs)*. Here are some examples of URLs:

http://www.senate.gov
http://www.microsoft.com
http://www.course.com

Computer Concepts

There are two basic types of Internet connections. Dial-up access uses a modem and a telephone line to communicate between your computer and the Internet. Most individual users and small businesses have dial-up access. Direct access uses a special high-speed connection between a computer network and the Internet. This access is faster but more expensive than dial-up access. Many businesses and institutions have direct access.

The Web toolbar, shown in Figure 1-17, is available in all Office programs. It contains buttons for opening and searching documents. You can use the Web toolbar to access documents on the Internet, on an *intranet* (a company's private Web), or on your computer. To display the Web toolbar in an application, choose View, Toolbars, Web.

FIGURE 1-17
Web toolbar

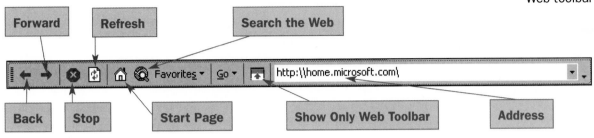

The Back button takes you to the previous page and the Forward button takes you to the next page. Click the Stop button to stop loading the current page. The Refresh button reloads the current page. Click the Start Page button to load your *home page*, the first page that appears when you start your browser. The Search the Web button opens a page in which you can type keywords and search the Web. The Favorites button shows a list to which you can add your favorite sites so that you can return to them easily. From the Go button's menu, you can choose to go to different sites or key in an address using the Open command. Click Show Only Web Toolbar when you want to hide all the toolbars except the Web toolbar. When you know the specific address you want to jump to, key it in the Address box.

To view hypertext documents on the Web, you need special software. A *Web browser* is software used to display Web pages on your computer monitor. Microsoft's *Internet Explorer* is a browser for navigating the Web that is packaged with the Office software. When you click the Start Page button, Search the Web button, or key an URL in the Address box of the Web toolbar, Office automatically launches your Web browser. Depending on your type of Internet connection, you may have to connect to your Internet Service Provider first. Figure 1-18 shows a Web page using Word as a browser.

Hot Tip

Toolbars display buttons for basic commands only. To see additional buttons, click More Buttons on the toolbar and choose from the list that appears. When you use a button from the list, it is added to the toolbar. If you haven't used a button recently, it is added to the More Buttons list.

Hot Tip

You can display the Web toolbar in any Office application and use it to access the World Wide Web.

FIGURE 1-18
Web browser

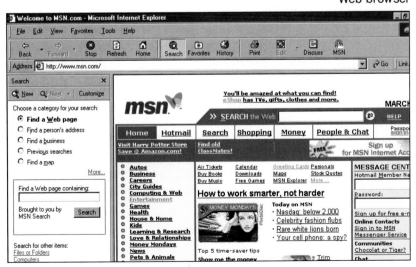

1. Connect to your Internet Service Provider if you're not connected already.

2. Open **Word**. Choose **Toolbars** on the **View** menu, and **Web** from the submenu if the Web toolbar isn't displayed already.

3. Click the **Start Page** button on the Web toolbar. The Start Page begins loading, as shown in Figure 1-18. Wait a few moments for the page to load. (Your start page may be different from the one shown.)

4. Close Internet Explorer by clicking its **Close** button, and return to Microsoft Word.

5. Click the **Search the Web** button on the Web toolbar. In Internet Explorer, click the Search button on the toolbar if necessary to display the Search pane on the left side of the screen.

6. Key **weather** in the *Find a Web page containing* box.

7. Click **Search** and a list of weather-related Web sites appear.

8. Click one of the Web sites to display more information on the weather.

9. Click the **Back** button until you return to the Start page.

10. Close Internet Explorer. Close all the Word windows that are open. If a message appears asking you if you want to save changes, click **No**.

11. Disconnect from your Internet Service Provider.

Computer Concepts

To search for topics on the Web using Microsoft's Search page, key your topic in the Search box, choose a search engine, and click **Search**.

Summary

In this lesson, you learned:

- Microsoft Office XP is an integrated software package that consists of a word processor application, a spreadsheet application, a database application, a presentation application, a schedule/organizer application, a desktop publishing application, and a Web page application. The documents of an integrated software package can be used together.

- Office applications can be started from the Programs menu and from the Start menu.

- Most Office tasks are done in the opening screen of each application. The basic parts of the opening screen are similar in all of the Office programs. The task pane is a separate window on the right-hand side of the opening screen. The task pane contains commonly used commands that can help you work more efficiently.

- Each title in the menu bar represents a separate pull-down menu. When you first use a program, each menu displays only basic commands. As you work, the program adjusts the menus to display the commands used most frequently, adding a command when you choose it and dropping a command when it hasn't been used recently.

- Toolbars provide another quick way to choose commands. The toolbars use icons, or small pictures, to remind you of each button's function. Toolbars can also contain pull-down menus.

- You can open an existing document from the File menu, from the task pane, or from the Start menu. The Open dialog box will be displayed enabling you to open a file from any available disk or directory.

- No matter which Office application you are using, files are opened, saved, and closed the same way. Filenames may contain up to 255 characters and may include spaces.

- Recently used files can be opened quickly by choosing the filename from the bottom of the File menu or from the task pane. You can also click the Start button, and select Documents to list the 15 most recently used files. To exit an Office application, choose Exit from the File menu or click the Close button on the title bar.

- The Office Help program provides additional information about the many features of the Office applications. You can access the Help program from the menu bar and use the Contents, Answer Wizard, and Index tabs to get information.

- The Office Assistant is a help feature found in all Office applications. It offers tips, advice, and hints on how to work more effectively. You can also use it to search for help on any given topic.

- The Web toolbar contains buttons for opening and searching documents on the Internet, on an intranet (a company's private Web), or on your computer.

- A Web browser is software used to display Web pages on your computer. Microsoft Internet Explorer is a browser for navigating the Web that is packaged with the Office software.

VOCABULARY REVIEW

Define the following terms:

Close

Default

Home page

Icon

Integrated software package

Internet

Internet Explorer

Intranet

Link

Menu

Open

Pull-down menu

Save

Task pane

Toolbar

Uniform Resource Locators
(URLs)

World Wide Web

Web browser

LESSON 1 REVIEW QUESTIONS

WRITTEN QUESTIONS

Write a brief answer to the following questions.

1. List four of the applications that are included in Office.

2. What is one way to start an Office application?

3. What is the difference between the Save and Save As commands?

4. If the Web toolbar is not on the screen, how do you display it?

5. What is the location and the function of the title bar, menu bar, status bar and taskbar?

TRUE/FALSE

Circle T if the statement is true or F if the statement is false.

T F 1. In all Office applications, you open, save, and close files in the same way.

T F 2. A read-only file is a printed copy of a document.

T F 3. The Office Assistant is available in all Office programs.

T F 4. The Web uses addresses called URLs to identify hypertext links.

T F 5. As you work in Office, the menus are adjusted to display the commands used most frequently.

PROJECT 1-1

You need to save a copy of September's work schedule in Jacob, Tess, and Matt's folders.

1. Use the **New Office Document** command to open a new Word document.

2. Use the **Open Office Document** command to open the **September Schedule** Excel file from the **Sarah** folder in the data files.

3. Use the **Save As** command to save the file as **Sept Work Sched**, followed by your initials, in Jacob's folder.

4. Repeat the process to save the file in Tess and Matt's folders as well.

5. Close **Sept Work Sched** and exit Excel.

6. Close the Word document without saving and exit Word.

PROJECT 1-2

1. Open Word and access the Help system.

2. Click the **Index** tab.

3. Key **tip** in the Type keywords box to find out how to show the **Tip of the Day** when Word starts.

4. Print the information displayed in the right frame.

5. Click the **Answer Wizard** tab.

6. In the What would you like to do? box, key **What do I do if the Office Assistant is distracting?**

7. Click **Search**.

8. In the Select topic to display box, select **Troubleshoot Help**.

9. In the right frame, click on the link **The Office Assistant is distracting**.

10. Print the information about what to do if the Office Assistant is distracting.

11. Close the Help system and exit Word.

PROJECT 1-3

1. Connect to your Internet Service Provider.

2. Open your Web browser.

3. Search for information on the Internet about Microsoft products.

4. Search for information about another topic in which you are interested.

5. Return to your home page.

6. Close your Web browser and disconnect from the Internet.

Extra Challenge

If you are using Microsoft Internet Explorer as your Web browser, choose **Web Tutorial** on the **Help** menu and use the tutorial to learn more about the Internet.

CRITICAL THINKING

ACTIVITY 1-1

Describe how you would use each of the Office applications in your personal life. Imagine that you are a business owner and describe how each of the Office applications would help you increase productivity.

ACTIVITY 1-2

Use the Office Help system to find out how to change the Office Assistant from a paper clip to another animated character. Then find out how you can download additional Assistants.

ACTIVITY 1-3

Open your Web browser. Compare the toolbar of your browser with the Web toolbar shown in Figure 1-13. Use the Help system if necessary and describe the function of any buttons that are different. Then describe the steps you would take to print a Web page.

INTRODUCTORY MICROSOFT® WORD

UNIT

lesson 1 — 1 hr.
Word Basics

lesson 2 — 1 hr.
Basic Editing

lesson 3 — 1 hr.
Helpful Word Features

lesson 4 — 1 hr.
Formatting Text

lesson 5 — 1 hr.
Formatting Paragraphs and Documents

lesson 6 — 2 hrs.
Desktop Publishing with Word

lesson 7 — 2 hrs.
Working with Documents

lesson 8 — 3 hrs.
Increasing Efficiency Using Word

Estimated Time for Unit: 12 hours

LESSON 1

WORD BASICS

OBJECTIVES

Upon completion of this lesson, you should be able to:

- Create a new document.
- Understand the four ways to view your document on the screen.
- Identify the parts of the Normal view screen.
- Enter text.
- Navigate through a document.
- Save a document.
- Locate and open an existing document.
- Preview a document.
- Print a document.
- Print in landscape orientation.

 Estimated Time: 1 hour

VOCABULARY

Landscape orientation

Normal view

Portrait orientation

Print preview

Task pane

Word processing

Word wrap

Introduction to Word Processing

W*ord processing* is the use of computer software to enter and edit text. Using word processing software such as Word, you can easily create and edit documents such as letters and reports. You can even create documents that can be published as Web pages. These documents can be used at school, home, and work.

The Word lessons in this unit contain step-by-step exercises for you to complete using a computer and Word. After completing all of the exercises, you will be able to create and revise your own word processing documents.

Creating a New Word Document

Start Word by clicking the Start button and choosing Microsoft Word from the Programs menu. A screen displaying copyright information will appear briefly, followed by a blank page where documents are created and edited, as shown in Figure 1-1.

FIGURE 1-1
Document in Normal view

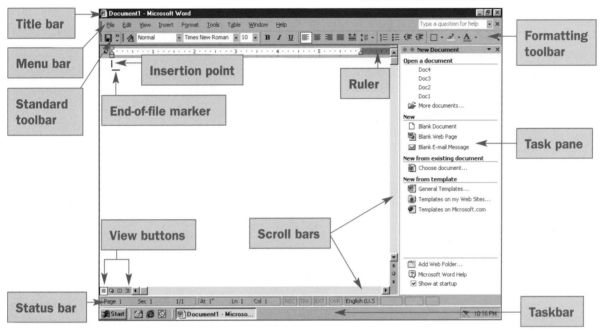

S TEP-BY-STEP ▷ 1.1

1. With Windows running, click **Start** on the taskbar.

2. Choose **Microsoft Word** from the **Programs** menu. A blank page appears, as shown in Figure 1-1.

3. Leave the blank Word document open for the next Step-by-Step.

Viewing the Document Screen

You have four ways to view a document on the screen: Normal, Web Layout, Print Layout, and Outline. The table below describes the features of each view and when you will want to use them.

TABLE 1-1
Document screen views

VIEW	DESCRIPTION	
Normal	Shows a simplified layout of the page so you can quickly key, edit, and format text. Headers and footers, page boundaries, and backgrounds are not displayed.	☰
Web Layout	Simulates the way a document will look when it is viewed as a Web page. Text and graphics appear the way they would in a Web browser, and backgrounds are visible.	
Print Layout	Shows how a document will look when it is printed. You can work with headers and footers, margins, columns, and drawing objects, which are all displayed.	▤
Outline	Displays headings and text in outline form so you can see the structure of your document and reorganize easily. Headers and footers, page boundaries, graphics, and backgrounds do not appear.	

To switch between views, choose the view you want from the View menu or click one of the view buttons at the bottom left of the document window.

Understanding the Normal View Screen

Most text entry and formatting tasks will be done using the Normal view screen. *Normal view* is a simplified page layout that allows you to enter and format text quickly. Look carefully at the parts of the Normal view screen labeled in Figure 1-1, and find them on your screen. Many of these elements appear in other Office applications as well and have already been discussed in the *Introduction* unit. Some of the important features of the Normal view screen are described in Table 1-2, and discussed below.

TABLE 1-2

Lesson ① Word Basics
Understanding the Normal view screen

ITEM	FUNCTION
Standard toolbar	Contains buttons you can use to perform common tasks, such as printing and opening documents.
Formatting toolbar	Contains buttons for changing character and paragraph formatting, such as alignment and type styles.
Ruler	Used to change indents, tabs, and margins.
End-of-file marker	Shows the end of the document.
Insertion point	Shows where text will appear when you begin keying.
View buttons	Allow you to change views quickly.
Status bar	Tells you what portion of the document is shown on the screen and the location of the insertion point. It also displays the status of certain Word features.

The *task pane* is a separate window on the right-hand side of the document window. It opens automatically when you start Word. The task pane contains commonly used commands that can help you work more efficiently. To close the task pane, simply click the Close button. To view the task pane, select task Pane from the View menu.

The mouse pointer looks like an I-beam in the text area of the window, but when you move it out of the text area toward the toolbars, it turns into an arrow to allow you to point and click easily on toolbar buttons and menu names.

Text Entry and Word Wrap

To enter text in a new document, you begin keying at the insertion point. As you key, the insertion point moves to the right and data in the status bar changes to show your current position on the line. If the text you are keying extends beyond the right margin, it automatically moves to the next line. This feature is called *word wrap* because words are "wrapped around" to the next line when they do not fit on the current line.

Press Enter only once to end a line at a specific place or to start a new paragraph. To insert a blank line, press Enter twice.

1. If it is visible, close the task pane by clicking the **Close** button on the task pane.

2. Switch to Normal view by clicking the **Normal View** button.

3. Key the text from Figure 1-2, and watch how the words at the ends of lines wrap to the next line as they are keyed.

4. If you key a word incorrectly, just continue keying. You will learn how to correct errors later in this lesson. Leave the document open for the next Step-by-Step.

FIGURE 1-2

Each day you should take time to plan and organize the day's work. You can avoid wasted effort and meet your goals when a daily time plan is made.

When making a daily time plan, list all tasks you need to complete that day and rank the tasks in order of importance. Record tasks on a calendar and draw a line through each task as it is completed.

Weekly and monthly time plans also can help you organize your schedule and avoid wasting time. These time plans can be made following the same steps as those you used for completing a daily time plan.

Navigating Through a Document

In order to correct errors, insert new text, or change existing text, you must know how to relocate the insertion point in a document. You can move the insertion point in a document using the mouse or using keyboard commands. For short documents, it might be faster to move the insertion point using the mouse. To relocate the insertion point, place the I-beam where you want the insertion point and then click the left mouse button. The blinking insertion point appears.

When working with a long document, it is faster to use the keyboard to move the insertion point. Table 1-3 shows the keys you can press to move the insertion point.

TABLE 1-3
Keyboard shortcuts for moving the insertion point

PRESS	TO MOVE THE INSERTION POINT
Right arrow	Right one character
Left arrow	Left one character
Down arrow	To the next line
Up arrow	To the previous line
End	To the end of a line
Home	To the beginning of a line
Page Down	To the next page
Page Up	To the previous page
Ctrl+right arrow	To the next word
Ctrl+left arrow	To the previous word
Ctrl+End	To the end of the document
Ctrl+Home	To the beginning of the document

STEP-BY-STEP ▷ 1.3

1. Move the mouse pointer to the end of the first line in the first paragraph. Click once. The insertion point moves to the end of the line.

2. Move the insertion point to the end of the document by pressing **Ctrl+End**.

3. Move the mouse pointer to the left of the first letter of the first word in the document (the mouse pointer should remain in I-beam form).

4. Click once to place the insertion point before the first letter.

5. Move to the fourth word in the first line by pressing **Ctrl+right arrow** three times.

6. Click **End** to move to the end of the sentence.

7. Click the down arrow to move to the next line.

8. Click **Ctrl+Home** to move to the beginning of the document. Leave the document open for the next Step-by-Step.

Saving a File

When you save a file for the first time, you can choose Save As on the File menu or click the Save button on the toolbar. The Save As dialog box appears, as shown in Figure 1-3. This is where you name your file and choose where to save it.

The next time you want to save changes to your document, simply choose Save. Word saves the document by overwriting the previous version. After you have already saved a file, you can use Save As to save it again using a different name or to save it to a new location.

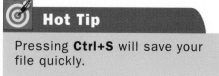

Hot Tip

Pressing **Ctrl+S** will save your file quickly.

FIGURE 1-3
Save As dialog box

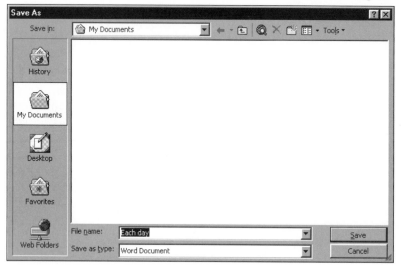

Folders can help you organize files on your disks. To create a new folder within your current folder, click the Create New Folder button in the Save As dialog box. A New Folder dialog box appears, as shown in Figure 1-4. Give the folder a name. After you click OK, Word automatically opens the new folder so you can store your current document in it if you wish.

FIGURE 1-4
New Folder dialog box

STEP-BY-STEP ▷ 1.4

1. Click the **Save** button on the toolbar. The Save As dialog box appears, as shown in Figure 1-3.

2. Click the down arrow at the right of the **Save in** box to display the available disk drives.

3. Choose the drive where you want to save the file.

4. Click the **Create New Folder** button. The New Folder dialog box appears, as shown in Figure 1-4.

5. In the Name box, key **Lesson 1**. Click **OK**.

6. In the File name box, select the name of the file, and key **Time Plan** followed by your initials.

7. Click **Save**. Word saves the file in the folder you created.

8. Word returns you to the Normal view screen. Choose **Close** from the **File** menu to close the document.

Locating and Opening an Existing Document

With Word on the screen, you can open an existing document by choosing Open on the File menu or clicking the Open button on the Standard toolbar. This displays the Open dialog box, as shown in Figure 1-5, where you can open a file from any available disk and folder. You can also open documents by using the task pane.

Hot Tip

You can also open a file by double-clicking it in the Open dialog box.

FIGURE 1-5
Open dialog box

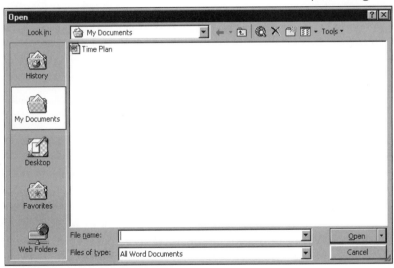

1. With Word on the screen, choose **Open** on the File menu. The Open dialog box appears.

2. Click the down arrow to the right of the **Look in** box to display the available disk drives.

3. Select the drive and/or folder in which you saved the file **Time Plan**.

4. Select the file and click **Open**. Leave the document open for the next Step-by-Step.

Previewing Your Document

The ***Print Preview*** command enables you to look at a document as it will appear when printed. You can access the Print Preview command on the File menu, or you can click the Print Preview button on the toolbar. The preview window looks similar to the one shown in Figure 1-6. The pointer changes to a magnifying glass with a plus (+) sign in the middle. Simply position the magnifying glass where you want to view text up close and click. The text will be enlarged. The magnifying glass changes to a minus (-) sign. When you click the document again, it will return to the size that fits in the window.

FIGURE 1-6
Print Preview

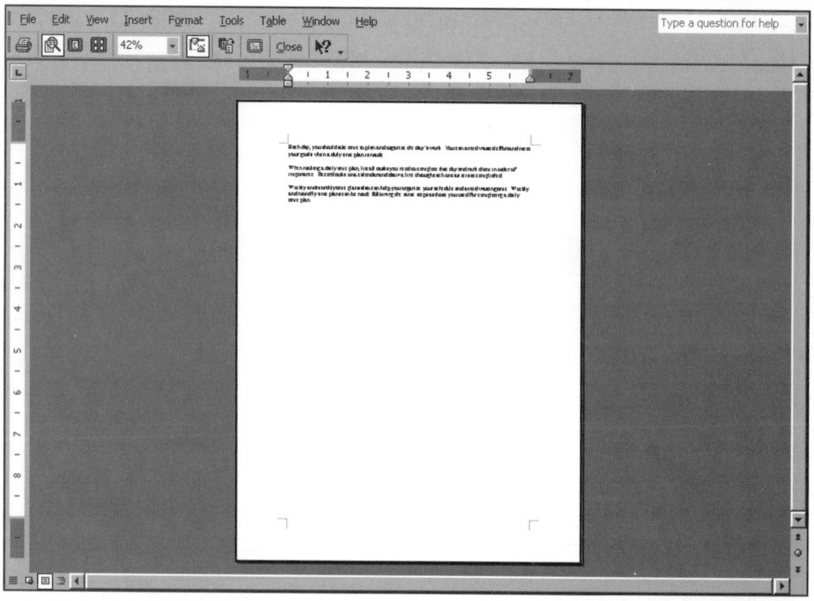

The Print Preview toolbar, shown in Figure 1-7, contains options for looking at your document. You can print your document, view one page or multiple pages of your document, control the percentage of zoom, display the ruler, shrink text to fit a page, show the full screen, close Print Preview, and use Help. Refer to Table 1-4 for a description of the functions of each item on the Print Preview toolbar.

FIGURE 1-7
Print Preview toolbar

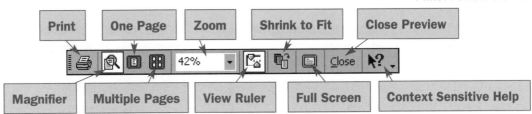

TABLE 1-4
Print Preview Toolbar buttons

ITEM	FUNCTION
Print button	Prints the document using the default settings.
Magnifier	Lets you zoom in and out on a section of the document.
One Page button	Shows one page in Print Preview.
Multiple Pages button	Shows up to six pages in Print Preview.
Zoom button	Controls the percentage of magnification in which to view the document.
View Ruler button	Displays rulers along the left and top of the Print Preview screen.
Shrink to Fit button	Changes the font size of a document so that more text will fit on a page.
Full Screen button	Maximizes the window so you can view an entire page on the screen at a larger percentage of magnification than the regular Whole Page view.
Close Preview button	Closes the Print Preview window and returns you to your document view.

STEP-BY-STEP ▷ 1.6

1. Click the **Print Preview** button on the toolbar.

2. Click the text part of the page with the plus sign magnifying glass. The page is enlarged.

3. Click with the minus sign magnifying glass. The page returns to full-page view.

4. Click the **View Ruler** button. The rulers appear (or disappear).

5. Click the **Full Screen** button. The window is maximized.

6. Click the **Close Full Screen** button. You are returned to full-page view.

7. Click the down arrow on the **Zoom** box. Click **50%**.

8. Click the down arrow again and click **150%**.

9. Click the down arrow again, and click **Whole Page**. You are returned to full-page view.

10. Click the **Close** button on the toolbar to return to the Normal view screen. Leave the document open for the next Step-by-Step.

Printing Your Document

At any time, you can print a full document, a single page, or multiple pages from a document on the screen. The Print dialog box, shown in Figure 1-8, appears when you choose Print on the File menu.

You can also print by clicking the Print button on the Standard toolbar or on the Print Preview toolbar, but the Print dialog box won't appear. Clicking the button causes Word to skip the Print dialog box and begin printing immediately using the default settings, which are to print all pages.

FIGURE 1-8
Print dialog box

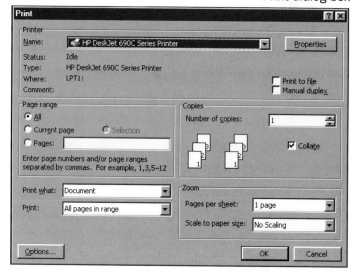

1. Choose **Print** on the **File** menu. The Print dialog box appears.

2. Print the document using the default settings by clicking **OK**.

3. Choose **Close** on the **File** menu to close the document. (Click **Yes** to save any changes if you are prompted.)

Selecting a Page Orientation

Word gives you two ways to print text on a page. Documents printed in ***portrait orientation***, as shown in Figure 1-9, are longer than they are wide. By default, Word is set to print pages in portrait orientation. In contrast, documents printed in ***landscape orientation***, as shown in Figure 1-10, are wider than they are long. Most documents are printed in portrait orientation. Some documents, however, such as documents with graphics or numerical information, look better when printed in landscape orientation.

You can change the orientation of the document you want to print by choosing Page Setup on the File menu. The Page Setup dialog box appears, as shown in Figure 1-11.

FIGURE 1-9
Portrait orientation

Professional Dress Style Show

Tuesday, April 2
at 6 p.m.
Monarch Hotel
Tickets are $10
Proceeds benefit the
Businesswomen's Club Scholarship Fund

FIGURE 1-10
Landscape orientation

Join us for the
Time Management Techniques Seminar

Easy to use time saving techniques for those who want to learn to set priorities and defeat procrastination.

February 3, 8:00 a.m. to 12:00 p.m., Conroe Building—Room 110
Business Council of Rapid City

FIGURE 1-11
Page Setup dialog box

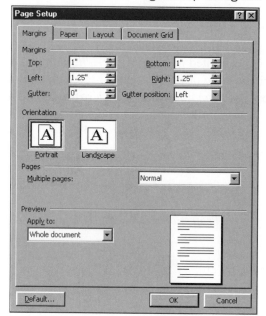

STEP-BY-STEP ▷ 1.8

1. Open **IW Step1-8** from the data files.

2. Save the document as **Workshop** followed by your initials.

3. Choose **Page Setup** on the **File** menu. The Page Setup dialog box appears.

4. Click the **Margins** tab if it is not already selected.

5. In the Orientation section, choose the **Landscape** option. Click **OK**.

6. Use Print Preview to preview the document.

7. Save, print, and close the document.

Summary

In this lesson, you learned:

■ Word is a word processing program that can be used to create documents such as letters, memos, forms, and even Web pages.

■ You can view the document screen in Normal view, Web Layout view, Print Layout view, and Outline view.

■ The key elements of the Normal view screen are the Standard and Formatting toolbars, ruler, end-of-file marker, insertion point, view buttons, and status bar.

■ When text is entered, the word wrap feature automatically wraps words around to the next line if they will not fit on the current line.

■ When corrections or additions need to be made, the insertion point can be placed anywhere within a document using the keyboard or mouse.

■ When you save a document for the first time, the Save As dialog box appears. This is where you name your file and choose where to save it.

■ You can locate and open an existing document through the Open dialog box.

■ The Print Preview command allows you to see a document as it will appear when printed.

■ You can print a document by choosing the Print command from the File menu or by clicking the Print button on the Standard toolbar.

■ You can use the Page Setup dialog box to change the page orientation to portrait orientation or landscape orientation.

VOCABULARY REVIEW

Define the following terms:

Landscape orientation	Print preview	Word processing
Normal view	Task pane	Word wrap
Portrait orientation		

MULTIPLE CHOICE

Select the best response for the following statements.

1. The Normal view screen contains all of the following except:
   A. title bar
   B. view buttons
   C. Save in box
   D. insertion point

2. What dialog box do you use to save a file for the first time?
   A. Save
   B. Locate File
   C. Save As
   D. Save File

3. Clicking the Print button on the toolbar causes Word to
   A. begin printing immediately using default settings.
   B. display the Print dialog box.
   C. switch to the Print Preview screen.
   D. show the document on the screen as it will appear when printed.

4. To move the insertion point to the end of the document, press
   A. the down arrow.
   B. End.
   C. Page Down.
   D. Ctrl+End.

5. Which of the following is *not* a method for opening an existing document?
   A. Click the Print Preview button on the Standard toolbar.
   B. Choose Open on the File menu.
   C. Click the Open button on the Standard toolbar.
   D. Use the task pane.

FILL IN THE BLANK

Complete the following sentences by writing the correct word or words in the blanks provided.

1. _____ view allows you to enter and format text quickly.

2. To insert a blank line in a document, press the _____ key twice.

3. Documents printed in _____ orientation are wider than they are long.

4. The blinking _____ shows where text will appear when you begin keying.

5. _____ can help you organize files on your disks.

LESSON 1 PROJECTS

PROJECT 1-1

Match the description in the right column to the correct term in the left column.

_____ 1. Right arrow

_____ 2. Left arrow

_____ 3. Down arrow

_____ 4. Up arrow

_____ 5. End

_____ 6. Home

_____ 7. Page Down

_____ 8. Page Up

_____ 9. Ctrl+right arrow

_____ 10. Ctrl+left arrow

_____ 11. Ctrl+End

_____ 12. Ctrl+Home

A. To the previous line

B. To the next word

C. To the end of the document

D. To the beginning of a line

E. To the previous word

F. To the beginning of the document

G. Right one character

H. To the end of a line

I. To the next screen

J. Left one character

K. To the previous screen

L. To the next line

PROJECT 1-2

Create a flyer announcing an upcoming program at the planetarium.

1. Open **IW Project1-2** from the data files.

2. Save the document as **Planetarium** followed by your initials.

3. Place the insertion point at the end of the sentence beneath the graphic, and key the following text:
   The third program entitled "Our Mother Earth" will be presented by Dr. Don Everett, Ph.D.

4. Insert a blank line after Green Hills Park Planetarium; then key the following:
   Thursday, May 8, 7 p.m. - 8 p.m.

5. Change the orientation of the document to landscape.

6. Preview the document.

7. Save, print, and close the document.

PROJECT 1-3

Write a letter thanking Dr. Everett for the presentation.

1. Choose **New** on the **File** menu, then **Blank Document** on the task pane to create a new Word document.

2. Key the following text:

```
Dear Dr. Everett,

Thank you so much for participating in the Thursday Night
Lectures. Your presentation, "Our Mother Earth," was entertaining
as well as informative. All who attended now know much more about
their home planet. Because of your involvement, the lecture
program continues to be a great success.
Sincerely,
```

3. Insert four blank lines after *Sincerely*, and key your name.

4. Save the document as **Thank You Letter** followed by your initials.

5. Print and close the document.

PROJECT 1-4

Create an advertisement for a department store sale. Before printing the advertisement, you need to add some text and change the orientation.

1. Open **IW Project1-4** from the data files.

2. Save the document as **Sale** followed by your initials.

3. Place the insertion point between the two sentences at the end of the document, and key this text: **Hurry down to Wilmore's to take advantage of our low prices on holiday merchandise.**

4. Place the insertion point at the end of the last sentence, and key this text: **Don't miss your chance!**

5. Change the orientation of the document to portrait.

6. Preview the document

7. Save, print, and close the document.

CRITICAL THINKING

ACTIVITY 1-1

A friend mentions to you that there is a helpful feature in Word called Click and Type, and you want to find out more about it. Use the Help system to print information about the feature, and answer the following questions:

■ What does Click and Type enable you to do?

■ How do you turn on the Click and Type feature?

■ In which views can you use Click and Type?

ACTIVITY 1-2

With Windows, a filename may contain up to 255 characters and include spaces. You should use a descriptive filename that will remind you of what the file contains, making it easy to retrieve.

Read each item below. From the information given, develop a filename for each document. Key the filename beside the appropriate number in a new Word document. Each file must have a different name. Strive to develop descriptive filenames. Choose a filename for the document you created. Print and close.

1. A letter to Spinnaker Publishing Company requesting a catalog.

2. A report entitled "Changing Attitudes Concerning Bird Sanctuaries" written by the wildlife preserve company, Future Dreams. The report will be used to develop a grant proposal.

3. A letter that will be enclosed with an order form used to place an order with Spinnaker Publishing Company.

4. A letter of complaint to Spinnaker Publishing Company for sending the wrong merchandise.

5. An announcement for a reception to be given in honor of a retiring executive, Seth Alan Grey.

6. A memorandum to all employees explaining job openings and salary increases within the national company, Canyon Enterprises.

7. Minutes of the May board of directors' meeting of Towering Insurance Company.

8. A press release written by Future Dreams to the media about a one-day event called Live in Harmony with Nature.

9. A mailing list for sending newsletters to all employees of Canyon Enterprises.

10. An agenda for the June board of directors' meeting of Towering Insurance Company.

BASIC EDITING

Selecting Text

Selecting is highlighting a block of text. Blocks can be as small as one character or as large as an entire document. After selecting a block of text, you can edit the entire block at once. You can select text using the mouse, using the keyboard, or using the keyboard in combination with the mouse.

To select text with the mouse, position the I-beam to the left of the first character of the text you want to select. Hold down the left button on the mouse, drag the pointer to the end of the text you want to select, and release the button. To remove the highlight, click the mouse button. Table 2-1 summarizes other ways to select text.

 Hot Tip

You can also select text items that are not next to each other. Simply select the first item you want, and press and hold down the **Ctrl** button; then select the other items you want.

TABLE 2-1
Selecting blocks of text

Lesson ② Basic Editing

TO SELECT THIS	DO THIS
Word	Double-click the word.
Line	Click one time in the left margin beside the line.
Line (or lines)	Click one time in the left margin beside the line, and then drag the mouse downward to select the following lines. Or Position the insertion point at the beginning of a line, press and hold down Shift, and press the down arrow once to select one line or several times to select more lines.
Sentence	Press and hold down Ctrl, and click in the sentence.
Paragraph	Triple-click anywhere in the paragraph. Or Double-click in the left margin of the paragraph.
Multiple paragraphs	Double-click in the left margin beside the paragraph; then drag to select following paragraphs.
Entire document	Triple-click in the left margin. Or Hold down Ctrl, and click one time in the left margin. Or Choose Select All from the Edit menu.

STEP-BY-STEP ▷ 2.1

1. With Word open, click **More documents** in the New Document task pane. If the task pane is not visible, choose **Task Pane** from the **View** menu. The Open dialog box appears.

2. Open **IW Step2-1** from the data files.

3. Save the document as **Time Plan2** followed by your initials.

4. Click one time in the margin to the left of the word *Each* to select the first line.

5. Click one time anywhere in the document to remove the highlight.

6. Double-click the word **Each** to select it.

7. Click anywhere to remove the highlight.

8. Triple-click anywhere in the first paragraph to select it.

9. Remove the highlight.

10. Position the insertion point before the *y* in the word *you* in the first sentence. Click and drag to select the words *you should take time*.

11. Remove the highlight.

12. Choose **Select All** from the **Edit** menu to select the entire document.

13. Remove the highlight. Leave the document open for the next Step-by-Step.

Using the Backspace and Delete Keys

You might find that you need to delete characters or words. There are two ways to delete characters: using the Backspace key or using the Delete key. Pressing Backspace deletes the character to the left of the insertion point. Pressing Delete removes the character to the right of the insertion point. You can also easily remove a number of characters or words by selecting them and then pressing either Backspace or Delete.

S TEP-BY-STEP ▷ 2.2

1. Place the insertion point after the word *should* in the first sentence of the document.

2. Press **Backspace** until the words *you should* and the extra blank space following the comma disappear.

3. Place the insertion point before the word *can* in the first sentence of the last paragraph.

4. Press **Delete** until the word *can* and the blank space after it disappear.

5. In the first sentence of the second paragraph, select the words *that day*.

6. Press **Delete**. The words disappear.

7. Use **Backspace** and **Delete** to correct any additional mistakes you may have made. Save the document, and leave it open for the next Step-by-Step.

Using Overtype

In *Overtype mode*, the text you key replaces, or types over, existing text. Overtype mode is especially useful for correcting misspelled words or for replacing one word with another word of the same length. For example, you can replace the *ie* in *thier* with *ei* to correct the spelling of *their* without having to insert or delete any letters or spaces.

You can turn Overtype on or off by double-clicking OVR on the status bar, as shown in Figure 2-1, or by pressing the Insert key. When Overtype is on, OVR will be shown in black. After replacing text, turn off Overtype mode by double-clicking OVR or pressing the Insert key so you do not key over any text you want to keep.

FIGURE 2-1
Overtype mode

STEP-BY-STEP ▷ 2.3

1. Position the insertion point after the period at the end of the second paragraph.

2. Insert a blank line to start a new paragraph. Key the following text:

```
As you mark off each performed
task, you will feel a sense of
accomplishment, which will motivate
you to complete more tasks.
```

3. Double-click **OVR** on the status bar. OVR appears in black, as shown in Figure 2-1.

4. Move the insertion point back to the left of the *f* in the word *feel* in the sentence you just keyed. Key **gain**.

5. Move the insertion point to the *p* in *performed* in the same sentence. Key **completed**.

6. Double-click **OVR** in the status bar to turn off the Overtype mode.

7. Save the document, and leave it open for the next Step-by-Step.

Using Undo and Redo

When working on a document, you will sometimes delete text accidentally or change your mind about editing or formatting changes you made. This is when the Undo command is useful. The Undo command will reverse a number of recent actions. To use the Undo command, click the Undo button on the toolbar or choose Undo from the Edit menu. The Undo command on the menu will include a description of your most recent action, such as Undo Clear or Undo Typing.

You can keep choosing the Undo command to continue reversing recent actions, or you can click the down arrow next to the Undo button on the toolbar to see a drop-down list of your recent actions. The most recent action appears at the top of the list, as shown in Figure 2-2. Choose the action you want to undo. Word will undo that action and all the actions listed above it.

FIGURE 2-2
Undo list

Similar to the Undo command is the Redo button on the toolbar or the Redo command on the Edit menu. Use this command to reverse an Undo action. As with the Undo command, when you click the down arrow next to the Redo button, a list of recent actions appears.

1. Click the arrow on the **Undo** button on the toolbar. A drop-down list appears, as shown in Figure 2-2.

2. Scroll down the list—all choices will be highlighted as you scroll—and choose **Typing c**. (The description should read *Undo 9 actions*.) The word *completed* changes back to *performed*.

3. Click the down arrow on the **Redo** button on the toolbar. A drop-down list appears.

4. Scroll down the list and choose **Typing d**. (The description should read *Redo 9 actions*.) The word *performed* changes back to *completed*.

5. Select the word **accomplishment**.

6. Press **Delete**.

7. Choose **Undo Clear** from the **Edit** menu. The word *accomplishment* reappears.

8. Save the document, and leave it open for the next Step-by-Step.

Hot Tip

If the **Redo** button is not visible, you can display it by clicking **More Buttons** (>>) on the toolbar; then choose it from the list of buttons.

Moving and Copying Text

At some point when you are editing a document, you will probably want to move or copy text to a different location. The feature that makes these moving and copying operations so easy is the Office Clipboard. The **Clipboard** is a temporary storage place in the computer's memory. You send text to the Clipboard by using either the Cut command or the Copy command from the Edit menu or by clicking the Cut or Copy button on the toolbar. Then you can retrieve that text by using the Paste command or the Paste button. The Clipboard is displayed in the task pane, as shown in Figure 2-3.

FIGURE 2-3
Office Clipboard in the task pane

Moving Text

You use the Cut and Paste commands to move text from one location to another. The **Cut** command removes the selected text from your document and places it on the Clipboard. When you **paste** the text, it is copied from the Clipboard to the location of the insertion point in the document. Moving text in this manner is often referred to as cutting and pasting.

The Paste Options button appears in the lower right-hand corner of the pasted text. By clicking on this button, you can choose formatting options without clicking a toolbar or opening a dialog box.

1. Display the Clipboard by choosing **Office Clipboard** from the **Edit** menu. If necessary, resize the task pane to view the document.

2. Click the **Clear All** button to clear any items that are on the Clipboard.

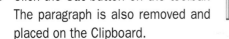

3. Select the last sentence of the document.

4. Choose **Cut** from the **Edit** menu. The sentence you selected disappears from the screen. It has been placed on the Clipboard.

5. Select the first paragraph.

6. Click the **Cut** button on the toolbar. The paragraph is also removed and placed on the Clipboard.

7. Position the insertion point at the end of the last paragraph.

8. Insert a blank line.

9. Move your pointer to the top icon on the Clipboard. Click the icon. The paragraph and the **Paste Options** button appear at the insertion point.

10. Hover the pointer over the **Paste Options** button. A down arrow appears.

11. Click the down arrow on the **Paste Options** button to view the options available for pasting text. Click outside the list to close it without changing the selected option.

12. Save the document, and leave it open for the next Step-by-Step.

Copying Text

The Copy command is similar to the Cut command. When you choose the *Copy* command, however, a copy of your selected text is placed on the Clipboard while the original text remains in the document. As before, you retrieve the copied text from the Clipboard.

> **Hot Tip**
>
> You can also access the Cut, Copy, and Paste commands by right-clicking the mouse button on the selected text and choosing the commands from the shortcut menu.

1. Select the first sentence of the last paragraph, which begins *Each day.*

2. Click the **Copy** button on the toolbar.

3. Position the insertion point at the beginning of the first paragraph.

4. Click the **Paste** button on the toolbar. The sentence is copied.

5. Save the document, and leave it open for the next Step-by-Step.

Using Drag and Drop to Move or Copy Text

When copying or moving text a short distance within a document, you can use a quick method called ***drag and drop***. Select the text you want to move, and then place the mouse pointer on the selected text. Click and hold down the mouse button. A small box will appear below the pointer. Using the mouse, drag the text to the location where you want to move it. As you begin dragging, a dotted insertion point appears. Place the dotted insertion point where you want the text, and release the mouse button.

To use the drag-and-drop method to copy text, perform the same steps as when moving text but hold down Ctrl while dragging. A box with a + (plus) sign beside it appears below the pointer. When you release the mouse button, the text is placed at the dotted insertion point location while the originally selected text remains unchanged. Just as with the Cut and Paste commands, the Paste Options button will appear when you use the drag-and-drop method to move or copy text.

STEP-BY-STEP ▷ 2.7

1. Select the last sentence of the document, which begins *You can avoid*.

2. Position the pointer over the selected text.

3. Click and hold. A dotted insertion point will appear at the pointer, and a box will appear below the pointer.

4. Drag the pointer to the end of the second paragraph. Position the pointer after the period ending the paragraph, and release the mouse button. The sentence is moved.

5. Select the first sentence of the second paragraph, which begins *As you mark*.

6. Position the pointer over the selected text, and click and hold.

7. Hold down **Ctrl**, and drag to place the dotted insertion point after the word *work* at the end of the last paragraph. Release the mouse button and then **Ctrl**. The sentence is copied.

8. Delete the last paragraph.

9. Select the last sentence, which begins *Weekly and monthly*, and click the **Cut** button on the toolbar.

10. Display the Clipboard, which now has four items. Clear the clipboard.

11. Close the Clipboard. Adjust spacing as necessary between sentences and paragraphs.

12. Save, print, and close the file.

Did You Know?

You can use the Office Clipboard in other Office programs, such as Excel. For example, you can copy a chart you created in Excel to a report you are writing in Word.

Summary

In this lesson, you learned:

■ You can speed operations by selecting blocks of text.

■ You can delete text using Backspace and Delete. Overtype mode allows you to replace existing text with the new text that is keyed. Overtype is especially useful for correcting misspelled words.

■ You can undo recent actions by using the Undo command. When you click the down arrow next to the Undo button, a drop-down list of your recent actions appears. You can redo an action using the Redo button.

■ You can send text or graphics to the Clipboard by using either the Cut or Copy command from the Edit menu or toolbar. Then you can retrieve that text or graphic by using the Paste command.

■ When copying and moving text a short distance, you can use a quick method called drag and drop.

VOCABULARY REVIEW

Define the following terms:

Clipboard	Drag and drop	Paste
Copy	Overtype mode	Selecting
Cut		

LESSON 2 REVIEW QUESTIONS

TRUE/FALSE

Circle T if the statement is true or F if the statement is false.

T F 1. You can edit an entire block of text by selecting it.

T F 2. Pressing Backspace deletes the character to the right of the insertion point.

T F 3. Use Overtype mode to reverse a recent action.

T F 4. Click the down arrow next to the Undo button to see a drop-down list of the most recent actions in Word.

T F 5. The Clipboard provides long-term storage, just as saving a file does.

Write a brief answer to the following questions.

1. How do the Cut and Copy commands differ?

2. What is the drag-and-drop method for copying text?

3. What are the three ways to select an entire document?

4. When is the Undo command useful?

5. What are the two ways to delete characters?

LESSON 2 PROJECTS

PROJECT 2-1

Create a checklist to send to candidates for a summer language workshop. The checklist should include the items missing from their applications.

1. Open **IW Project2-1** from the data files.

2. Save the document as **SLW Checklist** followed by your initials.

3. Key the following paragraph between the title and the first paragraph. Use the editing skills you have learned in this lesson to correct any mistakes.

   ```
   We are pleased that you have applied to be part of the Summer Language
   Workshop at Granville University. The six-week program gives qualified high
   school juniors and seniors an opportunity to study a foreign language and
   earn college credits.
   ```

4. Move the items on the checklist to place them in alphabetic order.

5. Copy the entire document, and place it at the bottom of the page, leaving four blank lines between documents.

6. Preview the document. Print from the Print Preview window.

7. Save and close.

PROJECT 2-2

Your business, Web Essentials, designs and creates Web pages. You have developed some tips for companies that now have Web sites. However, the document needs to be corrected before being distributed.

1. Open **IW Project2-2** from the data files.

2. Save the file as **Web Site** followed by your initials.

3. Make the corrections indicated by the proofreader's marks in Figure 2-4.

FIGURE 2-4

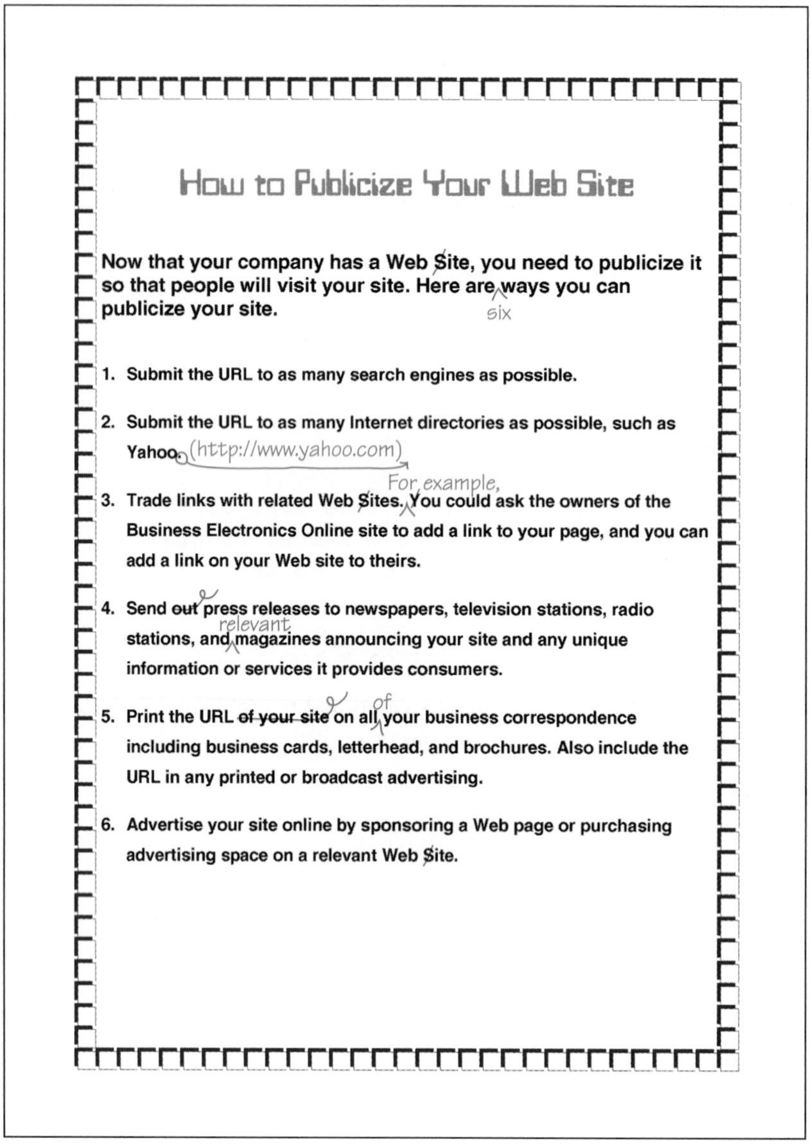

How to Publicize Your Web Site

Now that your company has a Web Site, you need to publicize it so that people will visit your site. Here are ~six~ ways you can publicize your site.

1. Submit the URL to as many search engines as possible.

2. Submit the URL to as many Internet directories as possible, such as Yahoo (http://www.yahoo.com)

3. Trade links with related Web Sites. *For example,* You could ask the owners of the Business Electronics Online site to add a link to your page, and you can add a link on your Web site to theirs.

4. Send out press releases to newspapers, television stations, radio stations, and *relevant* magazines announcing your site and any unique information or services it provides consumers.

5. Print the URL ~of your site~ on all *of* your business correspondence including business cards, letterhead, and brochures. Also include the URL in any printed or broadcast advertising.

6. Advertise your site online by sponsoring a Web page or purchasing advertising space on a relevant Web Site.

4. Save, print, and close.

PROJECT 2-3

Your business is sponsoring a golf tournament to benefit the local food bank. Key an information sheet to post on the bulletin board.

1. Open **IW Project2-3** from the data files.

2. Save the document as **Golf Tournament** followed by your initials.

3. Insert a blank line after the first paragraph, and key the following text. Use what you've learned to correct errors as you key.

```
Where: Forest Hills Golf Club
When: June 22-23
Time: Tee times begin at 8 a.m.
Cost: $50 entry fee per person
Register at the Forest Hills Pro Shop or at Shade's Auto Dealership.
```

4. Use Overtype to replace **When:** with **Date:**.

5. Select and delete the word **Where** and key **Location**.

6. Undo the change.

7. Move the last sentence of the first paragraph to the end of the last paragraph.

8. Save, print, and close the document.

PROJECT 2-4

The Career Placement Center is preparing informational pamphlets as a resource for people seeking employment. Edit the following page of the pamphlet.

1. Open **IW Project2-4** from the data file.

2. Save the document as **Interview** followed by your initials.

3. Use Overtype to replace the word *candid* in the fourth sentence in the first paragraph with the word *honest*.

4. Use cut and paste to move the second paragraph to the end of the document, creating a new paragraph.

5. Use drag and drop to move the last sentence of the first paragraph to the end of the second paragraph.

6. Delete the word **Third** and the comma following it in the last sentence of the second paragraph, and key **It is also a good idea to**.

7. Save, print, and close the document.

SCANS

ACTIVITY 2-1

You are opening a new T-shirt shop in the mall and will be hiring several employees. You need to adopt employee policies so new employees will know the rules of the company. Your policies will cover tardiness, absenteeism, dress code, employee evaluations, telephone answering procedures, and use of the telephone for personal calls. Choose three of those issues (or choose your own issues), and write a paragraph about each one. Be sure to include penalties for not following the policies. Use the editing skills you have learned in this lesson to make any needed corrections.

SCANS

ACTIVITY 2-2

A co-worker asks you the following questions about using the Clipboard to copy and paste items. Use Help to answer the questions.

■ What happens when the Clipboard is full and I try to copy an additional item?

■ How do I reset the count on the Clipboard so that it will display automatically again?

■ Which other Office programs can I use the Clipboard to paste items into?

HELPFUL WORD FEATURES

OBJECTIVES

Upon completion of this lesson, you should be able to:

- Use AutoFormat As You Type, AutoComplete, and AutoText.

- Make corrections using AutoCorrect, automatic spell checking, and automatic grammar checking.

- Check the spelling and grammar of a document.

- Insert the date and time.

- Use the Thesaurus.

- Find specific text and replace it with other text.

⏱ **Estimated Time: 1 hour**

VOCABULARY

AutoComplete

AutoCorrect

AutoFormat As You Type

Automatic grammar checking

Automatic spell checking

AutoText

Spelling and Grammar Checker

Thesaurus

Automatic Features

W ord offers many types of automated features that can help you create documents. *AutoCorrect* corrects errors as you enter text, *AutoFormat As You Type* applies built-in formats as you key, *AutoComplete* guesses words as you are keying, and *AutoText* inserts frequently used text. Word also has automatic features that check your spelling and grammar.

AutoCorrect

AutoCorrect corrects common capitalization, typing, spelling, and grammatical errors. AutoCorrect is also useful for inserting text quickly. For example, you can specify that when you key the letters *nyc,* they will always be replaced with *New York City*. Figure 3-1 illustrates the AutoCorrect options available.

 Hot Tip

Smart tags, indicated by purple dotted lines, identify and label text on which you can perform actions that would normally require you to open another program.

FIGURE 3-1
AutoCorrect dialog box

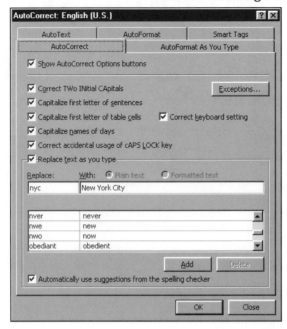

If you hover the mouse pointer over text that has been automatically corrected, a small blue box, called the *AutoCorrect Options button*, will appear, as shown in Figure 3-2. If you point to the button, it will change to an icon with a down arrow next to it, as shown in Figure 3-3. Clicking the down arrow will display options for changing the AutoCorrect action. In this way, Word "learns" what you want it to do in the future.

Computer Concepts

The AutoCorrect features allow you to customize Word to your needs. Long, difficult names can be inserted with just a few keystrokes, keying errors that you normally make can be corrected as you type, and text Word recognizes as incorrect can be accepted as correct by clicking the **Exceptions** button.

FIGURE 3-3
AutoCorrect Options menu

FIGURE 3-2
AutoCorrect
Options button

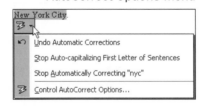

S TEP-BY-STEP ▷ 3.1

1. Open **IW Step3-1** from the data files.

2. Save the document as **NYC Trip** followed by your initials.

3. Place the insertion point on the first blank line after the list of things to do on Day 1, and key the following (with the misspelled word *hte*): **dinner at hte hotel restaurant**. Press **Enter**. Notice that AutoCorrect automatically capitalized *Dinner* as the first word in the sentence immediately after you keyed it. AutoCorrect also recognized that you meant to key *the* and automatically changed *hte* to the correct spelling.

4. Choose **AutoCorrect Options** on the **Tools** menu.

5. In the Replace box, key your three initials in lowercase. Press **Tab** to move to the With box.

6. In the With box, key your full name. Click the **Add** button.

7. Click **OK** to close the AutoCorrect dialog box.

8. Select **Student's Name** beside *To.*

9. Key your initials in lowercase followed by a space. AutoCorrect replaces the initials with your full name.

10. Save the document, and leave it open for the next Step-by-Step.

AutoFormat As You Type

When you use the AutoFormat As You Type feature, Word automatically applies built-in formats to text as you type. For example, if you type the number 1, a period, press Tab, and then key text, Word automatically formats the text for a numbered list. Similarly, if you type a bullet, press Tab, and key text, Word formats that text as a bulleted list. Word also changes fractions and numbers as you key, such as *3/4* to ¾ and *31st* to *31ˢᵗ*.

To choose which automatic formatting options you want, choose AutoCorrect from the Tools menu and then click the AutoFormat As You Type tab, as shown in Figure 3-4.

FIGURE 3-4
AutoFormat As You Type options

1. Place the insertion point at the end of the first item under *Day 1*, press the **spacebar**, and key **(Remember: Measurements for carry-on baggage are 25 1/2" x 22".)** Note that AutoFormat As You Type changes the fraction from *1/2* to *½* after you key it.

2. Place the insertion point on the blank line below *Day 5*. Key the following text:

`1. Tour Empire State Building`

3. Press **Enter**. Notice that AutoFormat As You Type automatically formats the next number in the list. Key the following text beside number 2:

`2. Shop on 5th Avenue`

4. Note that AutoFormat As You Type changes *5th* to *5th* after you key it. Press **Enter**. Key the following text beside number 3:

`3. 1 p.m. 1st bus departs for airport`

5. Observe that *1st* changes to *1st* after you key it.

6. Save the document, and leave it open for the next Step-by-Step.

AutoText

Using AutoText, you can store frequently used text, such as a name, an address, or a slogan, so you don't have to rekey the text each time. You can use the built-in AutoText entries that are available or create your own. To insert an entry, choose AutoText on the Insert menu. A submenu appears listing categories of common AutoText entries, such as Mailing Instructions and Salutation. Hovering on one of these items opens another submenu with the choices you can insert in your document, as shown in Figure 3-5.

FIGURE 3-5
AutoText menus

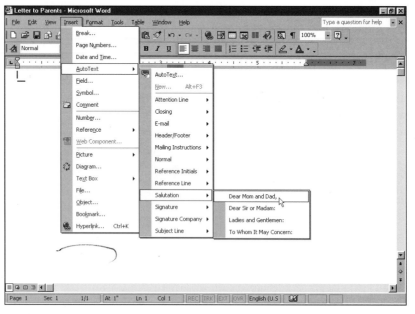

To create your own entry, choose AutoText from the Insert menu and then AutoText from the submenu. The AutoCorrect dialog box appears with the AutoText tab displayed, as shown in Figure 3-6. Key your entry and click Add. You can also add an entry to your document, delete an entry, or display the AutoText toolbar using this dialog box.

Hot Tip

Choose **View**, **Toolbars**, **AutoText** to display the AutoText toolbar and quickly access available AutoText entries, or create your own.

FIGURE 3-6
AutoText dialog box

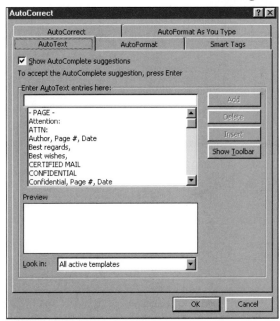

STEP-BY-STEP ▷ 3.3

1. Align the insertion point directly underneath the colon in *Date:* at the top of the memo.

2. Choose **AutoText** on the **Insert** menu and **Subject Line** on the submenu. Click **Subject:** and the text is automatically inserted in the document at the insertion point.

3. Choose **AutoText** on the **Insert** menu and **AutoText** on the submenu.

4. Key your name in the Enter AutoText entries here box.

5. Click **Add** to add your name to the AutoText entries. Click **OK** to close the dialog box.

6. Save the document, and leave it open for the next Step-by-Step.

AutoComplete

AutoComplete guesses certain words you are keying from the first few letters you key and then suggests the entire word. For example, if you key *Febr*, the word *February* appears in a ScreenTip above the insertion point, as shown in Figure 3-7. To accept the suggested word, press Enter, and the word *February* appears. To ignore the suggested word, just keep keying. Word can AutoComplete the days of the week, the months, and the current date as well as AutoText entries—including ones you have created.

FIGURE 3-7
ScreenTip

To: Student's Name
F February (Press ENTER to Insert) Coordinator
Date: 28 Febr
          Tentative Schedule for Trip to NYC

S TEP-BY-STEP ▷ 3.4

1. Delete your name beside *To*.

2. Begin keying your name in the same place. When the AutoComplete suggestion appears with your name, press **Enter** to accept it.

3. Select **Date**. Key **28 Febr**, and press **Enter** to accept the AutoComplete suggestion when it appears.

4. Select **Day 1**. Key **Mond** and press **Enter** to accept the AutoComplete suggestion when it appears.

5. Replace each of the other *Day* headings with the consecutive days of the week, accepting each AutoComplete suggestion when it appears.

6. Save the document, and leave it open for the next Step-by-Step.

Automatic Spell Checking

Automatic spell checking identifies misspellings and words that are not in Word's dictionary by underlining them with a wavy red line immediately after you key them. To correct a misspelled word that is underlined, position the pointer on the word and click with the right mouse button. A shortcut menu appears with a list of correctly spelled words. Click with the left mouse button on the suggestion that you want, and it replaces the misspelled word. The automatic spell checker can be turned on and off or adjusted by accessing the Spelling & Grammar tab of the Options dialog box (see Figure 3-8) through the Tools menu.

 Did You Know?

The automatic spell checker sometimes incorrectly identifies words as being misspelled, such as proper names. This is because the spell checker could not find the word in its dictionary.

FIGURE 3-8

Spelling & Grammar tab in the Options dialog box

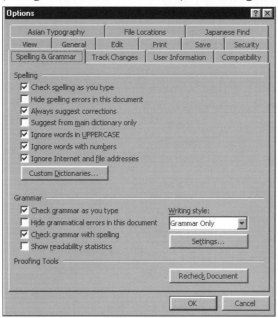

STEP-BY-STEP ▷ 3.5

1. Choose **Options** on the **Tools** menu. Click the **Spelling & Grammar** tab.

2. In the Spelling section, click the **Check spelling as you type** box if the box is not already checked.

3. Click **OK**.

4. Place the insertion point between the words *Street* and *District* in the second item under *Thursday*.

5. Key the misspelled word **Financal** followed by a space. The automatic spell checker detected the misspelled word and underlined it in red.

6. Position the I-beam on the underlined misspelled word, and click the *right* mouse button. A shortcut menu appears, as shown in Figure 3-9.

7. With the left mouse button, click **Financial**, the correct spelling. The misspelled word is replaced with the correctly spelled word, and the wavy red underline disappears.

8. Save the document, and leave it open for the next Step-by-Step.

FIGURE 3-9

Shortcut menu

Automatic Grammar Checking

Similar to the automatic spell checker feature, *automatic grammar checking* checks your document for grammatical errors. When it finds a possible error, Word underlines the word, phrase, or sentence with a wavy green line. To see the suggested corrections, right-click the word or phrase. Choose a suggestion from the shortcut menu, or choose Grammar to learn more about the particular grammar error that has been identified.

The automatic grammar checker looks for capitalization errors, commonly confused words, misused words, passive sentences, punctuation problems, and other types of grammar problems. You can tell Word to check for these and other common mistakes by selecting or deselecting options in the Grammar Settings dialog box, as shown in Figure 3-10. You access Grammar Settings by clicking the Settings button on the Spelling & Grammar tab in the Options dialog box.

FIGURE 3-10
Grammar Settings dialog box

S TEP-BY-STEP ▷ 3.6

1. Choose **Options** on the **Tools** menu. In the Options dialog box, click the **Spelling & Grammar** tab.

2. In the Grammar section, click the **Check grammar as you type** box if it is not already checked. In the Writing style box, select **Grammar & Style**. Click **OK**.

3. Create a fourth item under *Friday,* and key the following passive sentence:

   Guaranteed: a great time will be had by all!

4. Press **Enter** twice after you key the sentence. The grammar checker automatically identifies the sentence as a problem and underlines it in green.

5. Position the I-beam on the green underlined part of the sentence, and click the *right* mouse button. A shortcut menu appears, as shown in Figure 3-11.

6. Choose the suggested change at the top of the shortcut menu, **all will have a great time**. The sentence is corrected.

7. Save, print, and close the document.

FIGURE 3-11
Automatic grammar checker

Using the Spelling and Grammar Checker

In addition to checking your spelling as you type and making some corrections automatically, you can also check a document's spelling and grammar after you finish keying by using the *Spelling and Grammar Checker*. You can check an entire document or portions of a document by clicking the Spelling and Grammar button on the toolbar or by choosing the Spelling and Grammar command from the Tools menu.

The options in the Spelling and Grammar dialog box change depending on the nature of the error. When a spelling error is detected, the Spelling and Grammar dialog box appears, as shown in Figure 3-12. Figure 3-13 shows the Spelling and Grammar dialog box as it appears when a grammar error is identified. Table 3-1 and Table 3-2 explain each of the available options in the Spelling and Grammar dialog box.

FIGURE 3-12
Spelling and Grammar dialog box (Spelling)

FIGURE 3-13
Spelling and Grammar dialog box (Grammar)

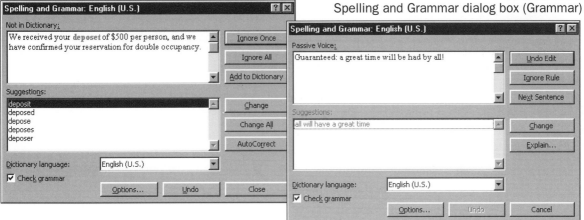

TABLE 3-1
Spelling and Grammar dialog box options (Spelling)

OPERATION	ACTION
Ignore Once	Ignores only the word displayed in red. The button changes to Resume if you click in the document.
Ignore All	Ignores all instances of the same word.
Add to Dictionary	Adds the selected word to the custom dictionary.
Change	Corrects only the selected word.
Change All	Corrects all instances of the same misspelling.
AutoCorrect	Adds the word and its correction to your AutoCorrect list.
Suggestions	Displays a list of proposed spelling changes.
Options	Allows you to change default spelling and grammar check settings.
Undo/Undo Edit	Reverses your last spelling change.
Cancel/Close	Before you make a spelling change, Cancel stops the spelling check. At the end of a spell check, Close stops the spelling check and saves all the changes you have made. After your first spelling change, the button name Cancel changes to Close.

TABLE 3-2
Spelling and Grammar dialog box options (Grammar)

OPERATION	ACTION
Ignore Once	Ignores only the grammar error displayed in green. The button changes to Resume if you click in the document.
Ignore Rule	Ignores all instances of the same occurrence of the rule.
Next Sentence	Accepts the manual changes you made to a document and continues with the spelling and grammar check.
Change	Corrects only the displayed grammar error.
Explain	Provides an explanation of the grammar or style rule being applied.
Suggestions	Displays a list of proposed spellings or grammar changes.
Options	Allows you to change default spelling and grammar check settings.
Undo	Reverses your last grammar change.
Cancel/Close	Before you make a grammar change, Cancel stops the grammar check. At the end of a grammar check, Close stops the grammar check and saves all the changes you have made. After your first grammar change, the button name Cancel changes to Close.

S TEP·BY·STEP ▷ 3.7

1. Open **IW Step3-7** from the data files.

2. Save the document as **Trip Letter** followed by your initials.

3. Press **Ctrl+Home** to move the insertion point to the beginning of the document.

4. Click the **Spelling and Grammar** button on the toolbar.

5. The word *deposet* is displayed in red type in the dialog box. Note that suggested words are listed in the Suggestions box.

6. Click the word **deposit,** if not already selected.

7. Click **Change**. Word replaces the misspelled word and continues checking.

8. The word *has* is displayed in green. The word *have* is in the Suggestions box. Click **Change**.

9. The word *vald* is displayed in red. The word *valid* is in the Suggestions box. Click **Change**.

10. The word *arive* is displayed in red. The word *arrive* is in the Suggestions box. Click **Change**.

11. The word *departur* is displayed in red. The word *departure* is displayed in the Suggestions box. Click **Change All**. Word replaces the error each time it occurs in the document and continues checking.

12. The word *a* is displayed in green. Click **Change** to change it to *an*.

13. The word *Cassaundra* is displayed in red because Word cannot find it in the dictionary. Click **Ignore All**.

14. The message *The spelling and grammar check is complete* appears.

15. Click **OK**. The insertion point returns to the beginning of the document.

16. Save the document, and leave it open for the next Step-by-Step.

Inserting the Date and Time

You can easily insert the current date and time into a word processing document. Choose Date and Time from the Insert menu to display the Date and Time dialog box, shown in Figure 3-14. Select one of the many different formats available. You can choose a different language and also whether or not the date will be updated automatically each time you open a document. When creating a letter or memo, you would want the date to remain fixed for record-keeping purposes. However, if you were inserting the date in a template or a report issued on a regular basis, you would probably want to have the current date displayed each time you opened the document.

Hot Tip

To automatically insert the current date using AutoComplete, begin keying the name of the current month. When a box pops up, press **Enter** to insert the month. Key a space. A box then pops up with the current date. Press **Enter** to insert the entire date in the document.

FIGURE 3-14
Date and Time dialog box

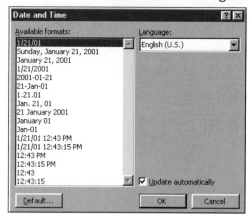

STEP-BY-STEP ▷ 3.8

1. Place the insertion point on the first blank line of the document.

2. Choose **Date and Time** on the **Insert** menu.

3. Click on the format similar to *25 September 2003.*

4. Make sure **English (U.S.)** is chosen in the Language box. There should *not* be a check in

the Update automatically box.

5. Click **OK**. The current date is inserted in the letter.

6. Save the document, and leave it open for the next Step-by-Step.

Using the Thesaurus

Computer Concepts

Even synonyms can have different shades of meaning. Be sure a synonym makes sense in context before replacing a word with it.

The **Thesaurus** is a useful feature for finding a synonym (a word with a similar meaning) for a word in your document. For some words, the Thesaurus also lists antonyms, or words with opposite meanings. Use the Thesaurus to find the exact word to express your message or to avoid using the same word repeatedly in a document. To use the Thesaurus, select the word you want to look up and choose Language from the Tools menu and Thesaurus from the submenu. The Thesaurus dialog box appears, as shown in Figure 3-15. In the Meanings box, click the word that best describes what you want to say. Then choose from the words listed in the Replace with Synonym box and click Replace. Table 3-3 describes the buttons in the Thesaurus dialog box.

Lesson 3 Helpful Word Features

FIGURE 3-15
Thesaurus dialog box

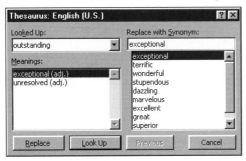

Thesaurus dialog box options

BUTTON	ACTION
Replace	Click to replace the original word with the word in the Replace with Synonym box.
Look Up	Click to show a listing of possible synonyms and meanings.
Cancel	Click to close the dialog box.
Previous	Click to show the last word you looked up in the current Thesaurus session.

S TEP-BY-STEP ▷ 3.9

1. Select the word **outstanding** in the first paragraph.

2. Choose **Language** on the **Tools** menu, and choose **Thesaurus** on the submenu. The Meanings box contains a list of the meanings of *outstanding*.

3. The meaning *exceptional (adj.)* should be selected. The box under *Replace with Synonym* contains a list of synonyms for *outstanding* using the *exceptional* meaning.

4. Click **wonderful**.

5. Click **Replace**. The word *outstanding* is replaced with the word *wonderful* in the document. Don't forget to change the preceding *an* to *a*.

6. Select the word **recommend** in the last sentence of the second paragraph.

7. Choose **Language** on the **Tools** menu, and choose **Thesaurus** on the submenu.

8. Using the *advocate (v.)* meaning, replace *recommend* with the synonym *advise*.

9. Save the document, and leave it open for the next Step-by-Step.

Using Find and Replace

Find and Replace are useful editing commands that let you find specific words in a document quickly and, if you wish, replace them instantly with new words. Both commands are chosen from the Edit menu. The Find and Replace dialog box appears as shown in Figure 3-16. (Click More to see the expanded dialog box.)

FIGURE 3-16
Find and Replace dialog box

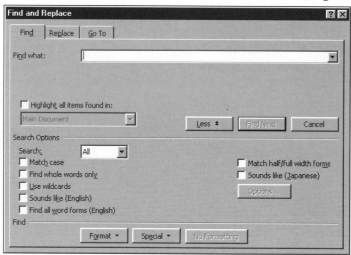

The Find Command

Using the Find command, you can quickly search a document for every occurrence of a specific word or phrase you key in the Find what box. The Find command moves the insertion point from its present position to the next occurrence of the word or phrase for which you are searching.

Find can locate whole or partial words. For example, it can find the word *all* or any word with *all* in it, such as *fall, horizontally,* or *alloy.* You can display options by clicking the More button in the Find and Replace dialog box to narrow your search criteria. The options in the Find and Replace dialog box are explained in Table 3-4.

You can use wildcards to broaden your search. A wildcard is a special character, such as a question mark or an asterisk, that represents a character or string of characters. Wildcards are useful when you are not sure of the spelling of the word you are looking for or if you are looking for words with similar spellings. Table 3-5 has more examples of how you can use wildcards. For a complete list of wildcards and their functions, click Special in the Find and Replace dialog box.

TABLE 3-4
Find dialog box options

OPERATION	ACTION
Search	Lets you search from the location of the insertion point up, from the location of the insertion point down, or all (the entire document).
Match case	Searches for words with the same case as that keyed in the Find what box.
Find whole words only	Finds only the word specified—not words containing the specified word.
Use wildcards	Makes it possible to search for words using special characters, such as a question mark or an asterisk, along with a word or characters in the Find dialog box.
Sounds like	Locates words that sound alike but are spelled differently. For example, if you key the word *so*, Word would also find the word *sew*.
Find all word forms	Lets you find different forms of words. For example, if you search for the word *run*, Word would also find *ran*, *runs*, and *running*.
Find Next	Goes to the next occurrence of the word.
Cancel	Stops the search and closes the dialog box.
More/Less	Displays the Find and Replace options/Hides the options.
Format	Lets you search for formatting, such as bold, instead of searching for a specific word. It also allows you to search for words with specific formatting, such as the word *computer* in bold.
Special	Lets you search for special characters that may be hidden, such as a paragraph mark, or special characters that are not hidden, such as an em dash (—).

TABLE 3-5
Using wildcards

TO FIND	KEY
Both *Caleb* and *Kaleb*	?aleb
Any five-letter word beginning with *a* and ending with *n*	a???n
June and *July*	Ju*
Kindness, tenderness, selfishness	*ness

C

1. Place the insertion point at the beginning of the document.

2. Choose **Find** on the **Edit** menu. The Find and Replace dialog box appears.

3. Click the **More** button.

4. In the Find what box, key **con***.

5. In the Search Options section, check the **Use wildcards** option.

6. Click **Find Next**. Word selects and stops on the word *confirmed*. (If the Find and Replace dialog box is covering the word *confirmed*, click on the title bar and drag the box down until the word is displayed.)

7. Click **Find Next**. Word stops on the word *consult*.

8. Click **Cancel**.

9. Move the insertion point to the beginning of the document.

10. Choose **Find** on the **Edit** menu.

11. Key **trip** in the Find what box.

12. Click the **Use wildcards** option to remove the check mark.

13. Click the **Find whole words only** option.

14. In the Search box, choose **All** if necessary.

15. Click **Find Next**. The word *trip* is selected. (You may need to move the dialog box to view the selected word.)

16. Click **Find Next** again. The second occurrence of the word *trip* is selected.

17. Click **Find Next** again. The message *Word has finished searching the document* appears. Click **OK**.

18. Click **Cancel**. The Find and Replace dialog box disappears.

19. Save the document, and leave it open for the next Step-by-Step.

The Replace Command

The Replace command is an extended version of the Find command. Replace has all the features of Find. In addition, the Replace command, shown in Figure 3-17, allows you to replace a word or phrase in the Find what box with another word or phrase you key in the Replace with box. The replacements can be made individually using the Replace button, or all occurrences can be replaced at once using the Replace All button.

FIGURE 3-17
Replace tab in the Find and Replace dialog box

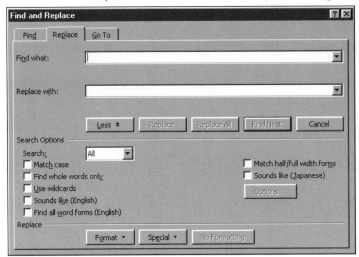

STEP-BY-STEP ▷ 3.11

1. Press **Ctrl+Home** to move the insertion point to the beginning of the document.

2. Choose **Replace** on the **Edit** menu.

3. Key **April** in the Find what box.

4. Key **June** in the Replace with box.

5. Click the **Find whole words only** option in the **Search Options** section. In the Search box, choose **All**, if necessary.

6. Click **Replace All**. The following message appears: *Word has completed its search of the document and has made 1 replacement.*

7. Click **OK**.

8. Key **trip** in the Find what box.

9. Key **tour** in the Replace with box.

10. Click **Replace All**. The following message appears: *Word has completed its search of the document and has made 2 replacements.*

11. Click **OK**.

12. Click **Close** to close the Find and Replace dialog box.

13. Save, print, and close the document.

Summary

In this lesson, you learned:

- AutoCorrect automatically corrects common capitalization and spelling errors as you type. The AutoFormat As You Type feature automatically applies built-in formats to text as you type. You can use AutoText to store frequently used text so you don't have to rekey the text each time. AutoComplete guesses certain words you are keying from the first few letters and then suggests the entire word.

- Automatic spell checking identifies misspellings and words that are not in Word's dictionary by underlining them in red immediately after you key them.

- Automatic grammar checking automatically checks your document for grammatical errors. When Word finds an error, it underlines the word, phrase, or sentence with a wavy green line.

- The Spelling and Grammar dialog box contains options that allow you to check the spelling and grammar of words, ignore words, make changes, and add words to your own custom dictionary.

- The Date and Time command is especially useful when including the date in a letter or memo.

- The Thesaurus is a useful feature for finding a synonym (a word with a similar meaning) for a word in your document. For some words, the Thesaurus also lists antonyms.

- The Find command moves the insertion point from its present position to the next occurrence of the word or phrase for which you are searching. Replace has all the features of Find. In addition, Replace allows you to replace a word or phrase in the Find what box with another word or phrase you key in the Replace with box.

VOCABULARY REVIEW

Define the following terms:

AutoComplete
AutoCorrect
AutoFormat As You Type

Automatic grammar checking
Automatic spell checking
AutoText

Spelling and Grammar Checker
Thesaurus

LESSON 3 REVIEW QUESTIONS

FILL IN THE BLANK

Complete the following sentences by writing the correct word or words in the blanks provided.

1. Checking the Update automatically box will display the _____ date each time you open the document.

2. A wavy green underline in a document indicates a possible _____ error.

3. Press _____ to accept a word suggested by AutoComplete.

4. Click _____ on the Tools menu to access the Thesaurus.

5. The Replace command is an extended version of the _____ command.

MATCHING

Match the correct term in the right column to its description in the left column.

____ 1. Ignores only the word displayed in red or green

____ 2. Changes fractions and numbers as you key, such as *3/4* to ¾

____ 3. Quickly searches a document for every occurrence of a specific word

____ 4. Uses a wavy red underline

____ 5. A wildcard

A. exclamation point

B. Ignore

C. automatic grammar checking

D. AutoFormat As You Type

E. Find

F. automatic spell checking

G. asterisk

H. Ignore All

LESSON 3 PROJECTS

PROJECT 3-1

Your company is preparing guidelines for proofreading outgoing correspondence. You need to make some additions to the document.

1. Open **IW Project3-1** from the data files.

2. Save the document as **Guidelines** followed by your initials.

3. Insert a blank line at the end of the document, and key the heading **Check Spelling** in the same format as the other headings.

4. Key the following text underneath the heading:

   The following words are commonly misspelled:

   business

address

environment

manual

column

February

calendar

grammar

noticeable

receive

5. Notice that AutoCorrect automatically capitalized each word. Use automatic spell checking to correct any words you misspelled while keying.

6. Use the Thesaurus to replace the word *helpful* in the second paragraph with a word that makes sense in context.

7. Replace all occurrences of the word *paper* with the word *document*.

8. Save, print, and close the document.

PROJECT 3-2

You are the assistant for Marina Bay Business and Professionals Association and need to make some changes to the minutes before submitting them at the upcoming meeting.

1. Open **IW Project3-2** from the data files.

2. Save the document as **Marina Minutes** followed by your initials.

3. Check the document's spelling and grammar, and correct any errors.

4. Insert the current date on the blank line beneath *Minutes of the Business Meeting*.

5. Using AutoComplete, insert your name at the beginning of the list of members who attended the meeting.

6. Replace all occurrences of *club* with the word *association*.

7. In the Old Business paragraph, find a synonym for the word *aim* that makes sense in context.

8. In the first New Business paragraph, find a synonym for the word *help* in the third sentence that makes sense in context.

9. In the Announcements paragraph, complete the first sentence by keying **the 27th of next month**.

10. Save, print, and close.

PROJECT 3-3

1. Open **IW Project3-3** from the data files.

2. Save the document as **Museum** followed by your initials.

3. Use the Thesaurus to change as many words as you can without changing the meaning of the text.

4. Save, print, and close the document.

CRITICAL THINKING

ACTIVITY 3-1

Word has many helpful editing features. Some Word features are more helpful as you key your text, and some are more useful after you have finished keying. Make a list of the Word features you would use as you key a document; make another list of Word features you would use after you finished keying the document. When you have finished, save the file with a filename of your choice; then print and close the file.

ACTIVITY 3-2

You work for Candlelight Time, a regional chain of candle stores. A new store will be opening soon, and your supervisor asks you to key a letter to potential customers announcing the grand opening and offering a free candle to the first 100 customers. Make the letter at least three paragraphs long. Use any helpful automatic features. Insert the current date, check the spelling and grammar, and hyphenate the document.

ACTIVITY 3-3

You recently started working for a publishing company where each manuscript is checked for readability statistics. Use the Help system to find out how to determine the reading level of a document and which readability scores are used.

FORMATTING TEXT

OBJECTIVES

Upon completion of this lesson, you should be able to:

- Apply different fonts and font styles to your text.
- Change the size and color of your text.
- Use different underline styles and font effects.
- Highlight text.
- Change the case of your text.
- Copy formats using the Format Painter.

⏱ **Estimated Time: 1 hour**

VOCABULARY

Font size

Font style

Fonts

Formatting

Highlight

Points

Toggling

Formatting Text

Once you have keyed text into your document, Word provides many useful tools to change the appearance of the text to make an impact on the reader. Arranging the shape, size, type, and general makeup of a document is called *formatting*. To format your document, you can use the Format command from the menu or use the buttons on the Formatting toolbar, as shown in Figure 4-1.

Hot Tip

If the Formatting toolbar on your screen does not show all of the buttons in Figure 4-1, click the down arrow at the end of the toolbar; then choose the **Add or Remove Buttons** option. Select **Formatting** and a drop-down list of available buttons appears. Click to choose the buttons you want added to or removed from the toolbar.

FIGURE 4-1
Formatting toolbar

Using Fonts

Designs of type are called *fonts*. Just as clothing comes in different designs, fonts have different designs. Like clothing, fonts can be dressy or casual. When you are creating a document, you should consider what kind of impression you want the text to make. Do you want your document to look dressy and formal? Or do you want it to look casual and informal? Using the fonts shown in Figure 4-2 would result in very different looking documents.

FIGURE 4-2
Different fonts

If you look closely at the F on the left in Figure 4-3, you can see small lines on the tips of the characters. These lines are called serifs. If a font has these serifs, it is called a serif font. If a font does not have serifs, like the F on the right, it is called a sans serif font. Serif fonts are generally considered to be "dressier" and easier to read than sans serif fonts and are often used for the body of a document. Sans serif fonts are often used for titles, headings, and page numbers.

 Did You Know?

The Chinese were printing texts as early as the second century A.D. and were using movable type by the eleventh century. Johannes Gutenberg is generally credited with inventing the printing press in the middle of the fifteenth century.

FIGURE 4-3
Serif versus sans serif font

Changing the Font

You can apply a new font by selecting it in the Font dialog box, as shown in Figure 4-4, or by using the Font box on the Formatting toolbar, as shown in Figure 4-5. To display the Font dialog box, choose Font on the Format menu. Click the Font tab to access the Font section of the dialog box. The Font box shows the current font. Click the down arrow to see other available fonts. Click on the font you want. The text in the Preview box will change to the chosen font.

To change the font using the Font box on the Formatting toolbar, simply click the down arrow at the right of the box, scroll to the font of your choice, and click it, as shown in Figure 4-5.

You can change the font of text already keyed by selecting it first and then choosing a new font. To change the font of text not yet keyed, first choose the font and then key the text.

FIGURE 4-4
Font dialog box

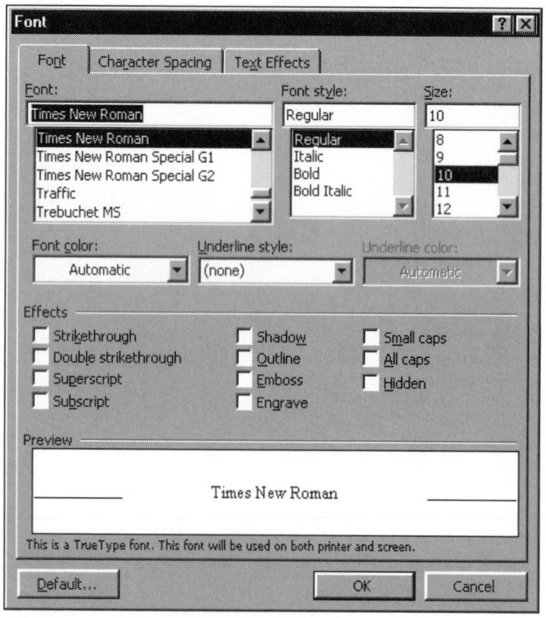

FIGURE 4-5
Font list box

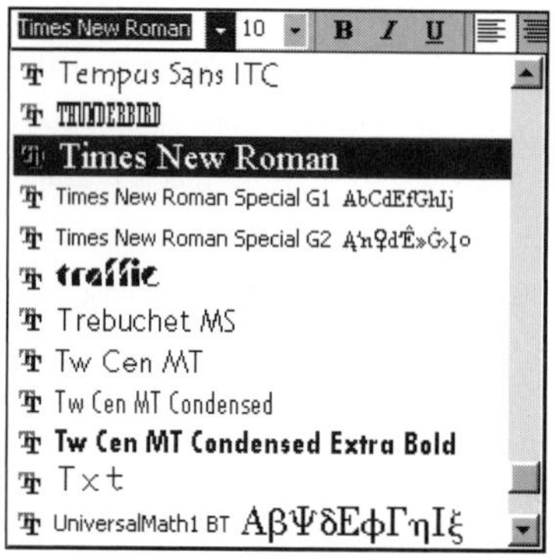

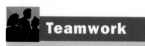

STEP-BY-STEP 4.1

1. Open **IW Step4-1** from the data files.
2. Save the document as **Diet** followed by your initials.
3. Choose **Select All** from the **Edit** menu to select all the text.
4. Choose **Font** from the **Format** menu. The Font dialog box appears, as shown in Figure 4-4. Click the **Font** tab if necessary.
5. In the Font box, scroll down and click **Times New Roman**. Notice the Preview box shows text in the new font.
6. Choose **OK**. The text in your document changes to Times New Roman.
7. Click anywhere in the document to remove the highlight.
8. Select the title of the document, *Reducing Fat in the American Diet.*

Teamwork

One of the most popular font types today is Times New Roman. With a partner, research the question of how this font got its name.

9. Click the down arrow on the **Font** button on the Formatting toolbar. A list of fonts appears.

10. Choose **Arial** from the list of fonts. The title appears in the selected font. Click the mouse button to remove the highlight.

11. Save the document, and leave it open for the next Step-by-Step.

Changing Font Style

Font style is a set of formatting features you can apply to text to change its appearance. Common font styles are bold, italic, and underline. These styles can be applied to any font. Figure 4-6 illustrates some of the styles applied to the Times New Roman font.

Hot Tip

A faster way to access the Font dialog box is by right-clicking in your document and choosing **Font** from the shortcut menu or by pressing **Ctrl+D**.

FIGURE 4-6
Different font styles

This is Times New Roman regular.
This is Times New Roman bold.
This is Times New Roman italic.
This is Times New Roman bold italic.
This is Times New Roman regular and underlined.

The easiest way to change font style is to select the text and click the Bold, Italic, or Underline buttons on the Formatting toolbar. To remove a style from the selected text, simply click the corresponding style button on the toolbar. Clicking a toolbar button to turn a feature on or off is called *toggling*.

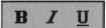

Styles can also be applied by selecting them from the Font style list box in the Font dialog box or by using the keyboard shortcuts shown in Table 4-1.

TABLE 4-1
Font style keyboard shortcuts

TO APPLY THIS STYLE	PRESS
Bold	Ctrl+B
Italic	Ctrl+I
<u>Underline</u>	Ctrl+U

1. Select the title.

2. Choose **Font** from the **Format** menu. In the Font Style box, click **Bold**.

3. Click **OK**. The title changes to bold style.

4. Select the first sentence in the first paragraph.

5. Click the **Italic** button on the Formatting toolbar. The text changes to italic.

6. Save the document, and leave it open for the next Step-by-Step.

Changing Font Size

Font size is determined by measuring the height of characters in units called *points*. There are 72 points in an inch. A standard font size for text is 12 points. The higher the point size, the larger the characters. Figure 4-7 illustrates the Arial font in 10, 14, and 18 point. You can change font size by using the Font Size box on the toolbar or the Font dialog box.

> **Hot Tip**
>
> Some of the formatting buttons may not be visible if the **Show Standard and Formatting toolbars on two rows** option is disabled. To enable this option, choose **Customize** from the **Tools** menu. In the Options section, click the **Show Standard and Formatting toolbars on two rows** check box to place a check mark in it.

FIGURE 4-7
Different font sizes

This is Arial 10 point.

This is Arial 14 point.

This is Arial 18 point.

Changing the Color of Text

You can change the color of text in order to emphasize certain words or data. Simply select the text, click the arrow on the Font Color button on the Formatting toolbar, and choose the color you want to apply from the palette, as shown in Figure 4-8.

FIGURE 4-8
Font Color palette

You can also use the Font dialog box to change the color of text on your screen. Select the text, and choose Font from the Format menu. Click the down arrow to the right of the Font color box, and choose the color you want.

Hot Tip

If you are not sure of the color on the Font Color palette, hover the pointer over the color box and the name of the color will appear.

STEP-BY-STEP ▷ 4.3

1. Select the entire document.

2. Choose **Font** from the **Format** menu. In the Size box, scroll down and click **14**.

3. Click **OK**. Remove the highlight.

4. Select the title.

5. Click the arrow on the **Font Size** button on the Formatting tool-bar. A list of font sizes appears.

6. Choose **18**. The title appears in 18-point size.

7. With the title still selected, choose **Font** from the **Format** menu. The Font dialog box appears.

8. Click the **Font color** list arrow. A palette of colors appears. Click **Green**. Notice the text in the Preview box changes to green.

9. Click **OK**. Remove the highlight. The title appears in green.

10. Save the document, and leave it open for the next Step-by-Step.

Changing Underline Style and Color

In the Font dialog box, you can choose an underline style from the Underline style list by clicking the down arrow. See Table 4-2 for some examples of underlining options. You can also change the color of the underline by clicking the Underline color down arrow and selecting a color from the palette.

TABLE 4-2
Underline styles

UNDERLINE STYLES	
Single Line	Dotted Line
Double Line	Wavy Line
Thick Line	Dot/Dash Line

Changing Font Effects

Word offers font effects to help you enhance your text. These font effects are shown in Table 4-3. To select a font effect, choose one of the options in the Effects section of the Font dialog box.

TABLE 4-3
Font effects

FONT EFFECT	RESULT
Strikethrough	~~No turning back~~
Double strikethrough	~~Caution: Hot~~
Superscript	The mountain is ^{high}.
Subscript	The pool is $_{deep}$.
Shadow	By invitation only
Outline	Thursday
Emboss	December 18
Engrave	Jack and Claire
Small caps	CALYPSO STREET
All caps	GLENMERLE
Hidden	Part of this text is

STEP-BY-STEP ▷ 4.4

1. Select the title.

2. Choose **Font** from the **Format** menu.

3. Under Effects, choose **Shadow**.

4. Click **OK**. The words now have a shadow effect. Remove the highlight.

5. Select the heading *Introduction*.

6. Right-click the heading, and choose **Font** from the shortcut menu to display the Font dialog box.

7. Click the **Underline style** list arrow. Choose the double-line style from the list.

8. Click the **Underline color** list arrow. Choose blue from the palette.

9. Click **OK**. The heading is now double-underlined in blue.

10. Save the document, and leave it open for the next Step-by-Step.

Extra Challenge

Open a new document. Key the words *happy*, *sad*, *angry*, *afraid*, *confident*, *excited*, and *bored*. Select each word, and change the font, size, style, color, and effect to reflect the meaning of the word.

Highlighting

To emphasize an important part of a document, you can *highlight* it in color. To highlight text or graphics, select the item and click the down arrow next to the Highlight button on the Formatting toolbar. Then choose the color you want from the palette that appears, as shown in Figure 4-9. Or if the Highlight button is already the color you want, click it and then select the text or graphics to be highlighted.

FIGURE 4-9
Highlight color palette

Changing Case

Uppercase letters are capitalized, while lowercase letters are not capitalized. This is referred to as the text case. To convert the case of text, simply select the text and choose Change Case from the Format menu. The Change Case dialog box appears, as shown in Figure 4-10, listing choices for changing case.

Sentence case changes selected text to look like a sentence, capitalizing the first letter of the first word. The lowercase option lets you change all selected text to lowercase. The UPPERCASE option lets you change all selected text to uppercase. The Title Case option changes selected text to initial caps—the first letter of each word in the title is capitalized. The tOGGLE cASE option reverses the case of the selected text: All capital letters are changed to lowercase, and all lowercase text is changed to uppercase. To choose a case option, click the appropriate option button.

FIGURE 4-10
Change Case dialog box

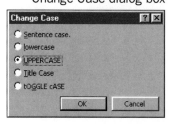

STEP-BY-STEP 4.5

1. Select the last sentence of the document that begins *Everybody needs*.

2. Click the down arrow on the **Highlight** button on the toolbar.

3. Choose the middle color on the top row, Turquoise. The selected text changes to the turquoise color.

4. Select the title.

5. Choose **Change Case** from the **Format** menu.

6. Choose **Title Case**.

7. Click **OK**. All words begin with a capital letter.

8. Select the words **In The** in the title.

9. Choose **Change Case** from the **Format** menu, and choose **lowercase** in the Change Case dialog box.

10. Click **OK**. The capital letters change to lowercase letters.

11. Save the document, and leave it open for the next Step-by-Step.

Copying Format and Style

Often you will spend time formatting a paragraph with indents, tabs, or styles such as bold and italic and then find that you need the same format in another part of the document. The Format Painter button on the toolbar allows you to copy the format and style of a block of text rather than the text itself. You can use the command to quickly apply a complicated format and style to text. To use the Format Painter command, select the formatted text you want to copy. Then click the Format Painter button, and select the text you want to format. The text changes to the copied format.

STEP-BY-STEP ⟹ 4.6

1. Select the heading **Introduction**. Change the font size to **16**.

2. With the heading still selected, click the **Format Painter** button on the toolbar. The pointer changes to a paintbrush and I-beam.

3. Scroll down and select the heading **Federal Dietary Guidelines**. The font size, underline style, and underline color formatting that were copied are applied.

4. Copy the same formatting to the headings *Recommended Dietary Guidelines for Americans* and *Fat in the American Diet*.

5. Save, print, and close the document.

Hot Tip

To apply a format multiple times, double-click the **Format Painter** button. When you're finished, click the **Format Painter** button one time to return the insertion point to an I-beam, which deactivates the command.

Summary

In this lesson, you learned:

- Serif fonts are generally considered to be easier to read than sans serif fonts and are often used for the text portion of a document. Sans serif fonts are often used for titles, headings, and page numbers.

- Common font styles are bold, italic, and underline. These styles can be applied to any font.

- Font size is measured in points. A point is about 1/72nd of an inch. The higher the point size, the larger the characters.

- You can change the color of text, style of underline, color of underline, and font effects from the Font dialog box.

- Changing case changes the selected text from uppercase to lowercase and vice versa.

- You can easily copy the format and style of blocks of text using the Format Painter.

VOCABULARY REVIEW

Define the following terms:

Font size	Formatting	Toggling
Font style	Highlight	
Fonts	Points	

LESSON 4 REVIEW QUESTIONS

MATCHING

Match the correct term in the right column to its description in the left column.

____ 1. Small lines at the ends of characters

____ 2. Single line, thick line, wavy line

____ 3. Strikethrough, Shadow, Engrave

____ 4. First letter of the first word in a sentence is capitalized

____ 5. First letter of each word is capitalized

A. title case

B. format

C. font size

D. font effects

E. serifs

F. toggle case

G. underline styles

H. sentence case

Write a brief answer to the following questions.

1. What are serif and sans serif fonts?

2. What are three common font styles?

3. What are five ways to change the appearance of text using the Font dialog box?

4. What are two ways to emphasize text?

5. What are two quick ways to open the Font dialog box?

LESSON 4 PROJECTS

PROJECT 4-1

You have been asked to prepare a certificate for the employee of the month at the hospital where you work.

1. Open **IW Project4-1** from the data files.

2. Save the document as **Certificate** followed by your initials.

3. Change all text to Baskerville Old Face, 20 point, Teal. If the font is not available, choose another appropriate font.

4. Change the font effect of all text to Emboss.

5. Change *Employee of the Month* to 36 point, bold, small caps.

6. Change *Joe Harrington* to Arial, 28 point, uppercase.

7. Change *June 2003* to 28 point, bold, italic.

8. Change page orientation to Landscape.

9. Save, preview, print, and close.

PROJECT 4-2

Make changes to the guidelines for proofreading outgoing correspondence so the document is more appealing to read.

1. Open **IW Project4-2** from the data files.

2. Save the document as **Guidelines2** followed by your initials.

3. Change the text font to Footlight MT Light, 12 point. If the font is not available, choose another appropriate font.

4. Change the title font to Tahoma, 16 point, bold, red, with a doublewavy underline.

5. Change the heading *Check Facts* to Tahoma, 14 point, italic, and blue.

6. Copy the format of the heading *Check Facts* to the other three headings.

7. Highlight the second sentence in the second paragraph in yellow.

8. Save, preview, print, and close.

PROJECT 4-3

In Lesson 2, you began preparing an informational pamphlet for people seeking employment. You are now ready to make more changes to the document.

1. Open **IW Project4-3** from the data files.

2. Save the document as **Interview2** followed by your initials.

3. Change the text font to Arial, 14 point.

4. Change the title font to Poster Bodoni, 18 point, and underline. If the font is not available, choose another appropriate font.

5. Highlight the second sentence in the first paragraph with Gray-25% from the color palette.

6. Save, preview, print, and close.

CRITICAL THINKING

ACTIVITY 4-1

An effective way to capture a reader's attention is to animate text. Use the Help system to figure out how to animate text, how to remove animation from text, and how to display or hide animation.

ACTIVITY 4-2

You work for a photo lab. In addition to film developing, the lab also offers reprints, enlargements, slides, black and white prints, copies and restorations, posters, and passport photos. Your manager wants to include a list with each customer's order of services available, and he asks you create it. List each service, how much it costs, and how much time it takes to complete. Make effective use of fonts, font sizes, styles, colors, and effects. Save the document as **Photo Lab**. Print and close the document.

FORMATTING PARAGRAPHS AND DOCUMENTS

OBJECTIVES

Upon completion of this lesson, you should be able to:

- Set the margins of a document.
- Align text.
- Adjust indents and line spacing.
- Change vertical alignment.
- Use Click and Type.
- Set and modify tabs.
- Apply bullet and numbering formats.
- Create an outline numbered list.
- Sort text.

⏱ **Estimated Time: 1 hour**

VOCABULARY

Alignment

Bullet

Indent

Leaders

Line spacing

Margins

Outline numbered list

Sorting

Tabs

Vertical alignment

Formatting Documents

Just as you apply formatting to text, you can also use Word features to format a document. Formatting presents a consistent and attractive style throughout a document, allowing your readers to understand your message more easily.

Setting Margins

Margins are the blank areas around the top, bottom, and sides of a page. Word sets predefined, or default, margin, settings, which you may keep or change. To change margin settings, choose Page Setup on the File menu, then click the Margins tab, as shown in Figure 5-1.

Did You Know?

Word measures margin settings in inches. You can change the measurement units to centimeters, millimeters, points, or picas. Choose the option you want from the Measurements box on the View tab in the Options dialog box, which is accessed through the Tools menu.

FIGURE 5-1
Page Setup dialog box

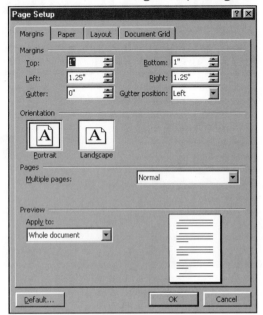

STEP-BY-STEP ▷ 5.1

1. Open the **IW Step5-1** document from the data files. You will recognize this as the document *Diet* from Lesson 4.

2. Save the document as **Diet2** followed by your initials.

3. Preview the document to see the existing margins. Close Print Preview.

4. Choose **Page Setup** on the **File** menu. Click the **Margins** tab if necessary.

5. Change the top margin to 1.25 inches by keying **1.25**.

6. Press **Tab** to go to the bottom margin setting. Notice that the margins of the sample document change as you press Tab.

7. Key **.75** as the bottom margin setting.

8. Key **1** as the left and right margin settings.

9. Click **OK**.

10. Preview the document to see the new margins. Close Print Preview.

11. Save and leave the document open for the next Step-by-Step.

Aligning Text

*A**lignment* refers to the position of text between the margins. As Figure 5-2 shows, you can choose left-aligned, centered, right-aligned, or justified for your text alignment.

Left-aligned and justified are the two most commonly used text alignments in documents. For invitations, titles, and headings, select Centered as the alignment for your text. Right alignment occurs frequently for page numbers and dates.

FIGURE 5-2
Text alignment

This text is left-aligned.
This text is centered.
This text is right-aligned.
This text is justified because the text is aligned at both the left and right margins. This text is justified because the text is aligned at both the left and right margins.

To align text, choose Paragraph on the Format menu. In the Paragraph dialog box, shown in Figure 5-3, choose an alignment from the Alignment drop-down list. You can also change alignment by clicking the alignment buttons on the Formatting toolbar, shown in Figure 5-4.

FIGURE 5-3
Paragraph dialog box

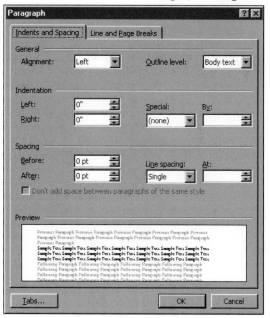

FIGURE 5-4
Alignment buttons

Align Left button

Center button

Justify button

Align Right button

S TEP-BY-STEP ▷ 5.2

1. Select the title.

2. Choose **Paragraph** on the **Format** menu.

3. Click the **Alignment** list arrow and click **Centered**.

4. Click **OK**. The title is centered.

5. Select the date above the title.

6. Click the **Align Right** button on the toolbar. (If the button is not displayed, choose it from the **More Buttons** menu.) The date is right-aligned.

7. Insert two blank lines between the date and the title.

8. Select the paragraph that begins *Today*.

9. Click the **Justify** button on the toolbar. The paragraph is justified.

10. Save and leave the document open for the next Step-by-Step.

Changing Indents and Spacing

An *indent* is the space you insert between text and a document's margin. You can indent text either from the left margin, from the right margin, or from both the left and right margins. You indent text by using the indent markers on the horizontal ruler, shown in Figure 5-5. To indent text, position the insertion point in the text you want to indent and drag one of the indent markers to the desired point on the ruler.

FIGURE 5-5
Indent markers

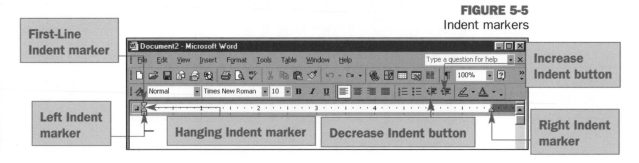

First-Line Indent marker

Increase Indent button

Left Indent marker

Hanging Indent marker

Decrease Indent button

Right Indent marker

Clicking the Decrease Indent or Increase Indent buttons on the Formatting toolbar is another way to indent text quickly.

Setting a First-Line Indent

The paragraph format where the first line indents more than the following lines is a first-line indent. Using the first-line indent marker, you can indent paragraphs as shown in Figure 5-6. After you set a first-line indent in one paragraph, all subsequent paragraphs you key will have the same first-line indent.

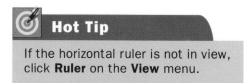

Hot Tip

If the horizontal ruler is not in view, click **Ruler** on the **View** menu.

FIGURE 5-6
First-line indent

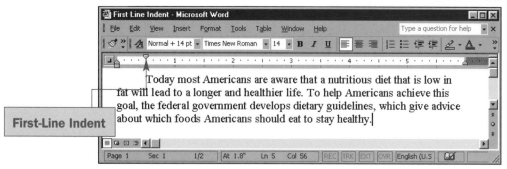

Setting a Hanging Indent

You can also create hanging indents in which the first full line of text is not indented but the following lines are, as shown in Figure 5-7. To set a hanging indent, drag the hanging indent marker to the right of the first-line indent marker. Hanging indents appear commonly in lists and documents such as glossaries.

FIGURE 5-7
Hanging indent

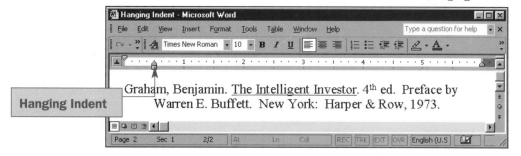

Indenting from Both Margins

Indenting from both margins, as shown in Figure 5-8, sets off paragraphs from the main body of text. You might use this type of indent for long quotations.

FIGURE 5-8
Indent from both margins

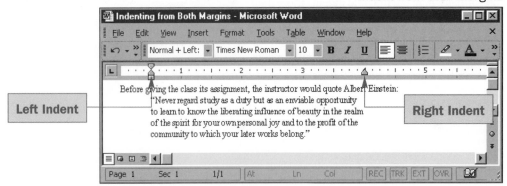

Left Indent

Right Indent

STEP-BY-STEP ▷ 5.3

C

1. With Diet2 open, position the insertion point anywhere in the first paragraph.

2. Click on the first-line indent marker, and drag it to the 0.5-inch mark, as shown in Figure 5-6. You have created a first-line indent.

3. Select the paragraph after the heading *Federal Dietary Guidelines*.

4. Click and drag the hanging indent marker to the 0.5-inch mark. You have created a hanging indent.

5. In the next paragraph, place the insertion point after the space following *1980,* and press **Enter**.

6. Now place the insertion point after the space following *eat."* and press **Enter**.

7. Select the quotation.

8. Click the left indent marker, and drag both the first-line indent and hanging indent markers to the 0.5-inch mark. You have created a left indent.

9. With the paragraph still selected, drag the right indent marker to the 6-inch mark. You have created a right indent.

10. Save and leave the document open for the next Step-by-Step.

Adjusting Line Spacing

Line spacing refers to the amount of space between lines of text. By default, Word single-spaces text. Single-spacing has no extra space between each line. To make text more readable, you can add space between lines of text. The 1.5 lines option adds half a line of space between lines. Double-spaced text has a full blank line between each line of text. (Figure 5-9 illustrates different spacing options.)

FIGURE 5-9
Line spacing options

The line spacing of this paragraph is single.
This paragraph is single-spaced.

The line spacing of this paragraph is 1.5 lines.
This paragraph is 1.5-spaced.

The line spacing of this paragraph is double.

This paragraph is double-spaced.

Change line spacing by choosing Paragraph on the Format menu and selecting the Indents and Spacing tab. Select options from the Line spacing drop-down list box (see Figure 5-3). You can also change line spacing by clicking the Line Spacing button on the Formatting toolbar (you may need to add the button to the toolbar). Click the down arrow, and choose from the listed options.

Another way to increase the readability of a page is to add spaces between paragraphs. You can add space before or after paragraphs by accessing the Paragraph dialog box and changing the values in the Before or After box of the Spacing area.

STEP-BY-STEP ▷ *5.4*

1. Select the first paragraph of the document.

2. Choose **Paragraph** on the **Format** menu.

3. In the Spacing section, click the **Line spacing** list arrow.

4. Click **Double**. Notice the text under *Preview* changes to double-spaced.

5. Click **OK**. The paragraph is double-spaced.

6. Select the paragraphs under the heading *Federal Dietary Guidelines* up to *Recommended Dietary Guidelines for Americans.*

7. Choose **Paragraph** on the **Format** menu.

8. Click the up arrow in the **After** box in the Spacing section; 0 point should change to **6 point**.

9. Click **OK**. The extra space appears before each selected paragraph.

10. Save, print, and close the document.

Hot Tip

You can access the Paragraph dialog box quickly by right-clicking and choosing **Paragraph** from the shortcut menu.

Changing Vertical Alignment

Vertical alignment* refers to the position of text between the top and bottom margins of a page. You can align text with the top of the page, center the text, distribute the text equally between the top and bottom margins, or align the text with the bottom of the page. Choose Page Setup on the File menu, and the Page Setup dialog box appears. Click the Layout tab to select it, as shown in Figure 5-10. Click the down arrow on the Vertical alignment list box and choose Top, Center, Justified, or Bottom. Then click OK.

FIGURE 5-10
Layout tab in the Page Setup dialog box

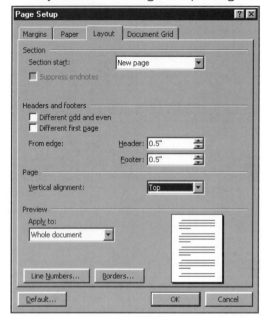

STEP-BY-STEP ▷ 5.5

1. Create a new Word document.

2. Key the following text:
Your name
Health and Nutrition 101
Reducing Fat in the American Diet

3. Center the text.

4. Change the font to **Arial** and the font size to **18**.

5. Choose **Page Setup** on the **File** menu.

6. Click the **Layout** tab to select it.

7. Click the **Vertical alignment** box list arrow, and choose **Center** from the list. Click **OK**.

8. Preview the document to see that the text aligns vertically.

9. Save the document as **Diet Title** followed by your initials.

10. Print and close the document.

Using Click and Type

Click and Type is a useful feature that you can use to insert text or other items into a blank area of a document. It saves you from having to enter blank lines or tabs manually in order to position the insertion point where you want it. Just double-click in the document where you want to insert text and begin keying.

To turn the feature on, choose Options on the Tools menu, click the Edit tab, and click the Enable click and type check box. Click and Type is available for use only in the Print Layout or Web Layout views. Click and type automatically applies formatting, such as centering text or right- or left-aligning paragraphs. You can see what formatting will be applied by watching the pointer as you move it to different areas of the document. Table 5-1 shows the different views of the pointer.

TABLE 5-1
Pointers in Click and Type

POINTER	FORMATTING
I⯗	Enters text at the insertion point left-aligned.
I̤	Enters text at the insertion point centered.
⯗I	Enters text at the insertion point right-aligned.

STEP-BY-STEP ▷ 5.6

1. Create a new Word document.

2. Switch to **Print Layout View**.

3. Scroll down until 4½ inches is visible on the left ruler.

4. With the pointer at the 4½-inch mark on the vertical ruler, move the pointer to the middle of the document (around the 3-inch mark on the horizontal ruler) and double-click.

5. Key the following text:
   Your name
   HD 1163
   Reducing Fat in the American Diet

6. Change the font to **Arial** and the font size to **18**.

7. Preview the document to see that the text appears centered horizontally and vertically, just as it was in the last Step-by-Step when you did it manually.

8. Close the document without saving.

Setting Tab Stops

Tab stops, or *tabs*, mark the place where the insertion point will stop when you press the Tab key. Tab stops are useful for creating tables or aligning numbered items. Text alignment can be set with decimal, left, right, or center tab stops, as shown in Figure 5-11. Left-aligned default tab stops are set in Word every half inch. See Table 5-2 for a description of these common tab stops.

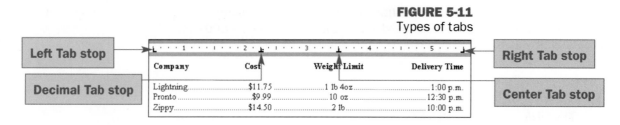

FIGURE 5-11
Types of tabs

Left Tab stop → | Right Tab stop
Decimal Tab stop | Center Tab stop

Company	Cost	Weight Limit	Delivery Time
Lightning	$11.75	1 lb 4oz	1:00 p.m.
Pronto	$9.99	10 oz	12:30 p.m.
Zippy	$14.50	2 lb	10:00 p.m.

TABLE 5-2
Common tab stops

Tab	Tab Name	Function
⌊	Left Tab stop	Left-aligns selected text at the point indicated on the horizontal ruler. This is the default tab.
⌐	Right Tab stop	Right-aligns selected text at the point indicated on the horizontal ruler. This is useful for aligning page numbers in a table of contents.
⊥	Center Tab stop	Centers selected text at the point indicated on the horizontal ruler. This is used with titles and announcements.
⊥	Decimal Tab stop	Aligns selected text on the decimal point at the point indicated on the horizontal ruler. This is helpful when preparing price lists, invoices, and menus.

To set tabs, select the text or place your insertion point in the paragraph and choose Tabs on the Format menu. The Tabs dialog box appears, as shown in Figure 5-12. Key the tab stop position, and choose the tab alignment you want. Click Set to set the tab.

Another way to set a tab stop is by clicking the tab box at the far left of the ruler. Each time you click, it changes to another type of tab—left, right, center, bar, or decimal. When it changes to the tab you want, click on the ruler at the place where you want to set the tab; the tab then appears. To remove a tab, drag it off the ruler.

FIGURE 5-12
Tabs dialog box

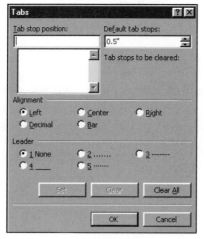

Solid, dotted, or dashed lines called *leaders*, which fill the blank space before a tab setting, may precede tabs. Sometimes these are used with tables of contents. To insert a leader, choose Tabs on the Format menu. In the Leader section, click to choose the leader option you want and click OK.

The Clear button allows you to clear a tab listed in the Tab stop position box. Use the Clear All button to clear all the tabs listed.

Computer Concepts

The tab box on the ruler also has options for additional tabs—bar, first-line indent, and hanging indent.

S TEP-BY-STEP ▷ 5.7

1. Open **IW Step5-7** from the data files.

2. Save the document as **Supplies** followed by your initials.

3. Display the ruler, if it is not showing already, by choosing **Ruler** on the **View** menu.

4. Select all data except the title.

5. If necessary, click the tab box on the ruler to display the left tab symbol. Click the **1.5**-inch mark on the ruler to insert a left tab. The first column of text aligns at the 1.5-inch mark.

6. Choose **Tabs** on the **Format** menu. The Tabs dialog box appears, as shown in Figure 5-12.

7. Click **Clear** to clear the -0.5 tab.

8. Select **1.5** in the Tab stop position box and key **5.75**.

9. In the Alignment section, click **Decimal** and in the Leader section, click **2**.

10. Click **Set**.

11. Click **OK**. The dialog box closes, and text in the second column lines up at the tab you set with leaders.

12. Save, print, and close the document.

Extra Challenge

You can practice setting tabs by creating a list of your own. Include three columns of information: the items, the approximate price of each item, and a phrase describing why you need each item. Use at least two different kinds of tabs.

Bulleted and Numbered Lists

Sometimes you may want to create a bulleted or numbered list in a document—for example, when it is difficult to distinguish between groups of items bunched together in a sentence. A numbered list is useful when items appear sequentially, such as instructions. A bulleted list often occurs when the order of items does not need emphasizing. A *bullet* is any small character that appears before an item. Pictures, symbols, and icons may all serve as bullets.

To create a bulleted or numbered list, click the Bullets button or Numbering button on the toolbar and begin keying.
Each time you press Enter, a new bullet or number automatically appears. To finish a list, press Enter twice. Alternatively, to convert existing text into a bulleted or numbered list, select the text and click the Bullets or Numbering button on the toolbar.

STEP-BY-STEP ▷ 5.8

1. Start a new Word document.

2. Key **To Do List** and press **Enter**.

3. Click the **Numbering** button on the toolbar. The number 1 appears and then a tabbed space so you can begin keying a numbered list.

4. Key **Go to the bank on Thur**. Press **Enter** to accept the AutoComplete word *Thursday*, and key a period to end the sentence.

5. Press **Enter**. Notice how Word automatically formats the next number in the list.

6. Key the remaining items in the to-do list as shown below.
```
2. Water the plants on Friday.
3. Key the February report.
```

7. After you key the third item, press **Enter** twice to stop the numbered list formatting.

8. Key **Items for Meeting** and press **Enter**.

9. Click the **Bullets** button on the toolbar. A bullet appears with a tabbed space so you can begin keying a bulleted list. Notice the bullet indents further than the numbered list. You will learn how to change this later.

10. Key **Murphy file**.

11. Press **Enter**. Notice how Word automatically continues formatting a bulleted list.

12. Key the remaining items under *Items for Meeting* shown below.
```
· Research report
· Notes from the meeting on
  January 13th
```

13. After keying the third item in the list, press **Enter** twice to stop the bulleted list formatting.

14. Save the document as **List** followed by your initials.

15. Print and close the document.

Outline Numbered List

An **outline numbered list** is a list with two or more levels of bullets or numbering. You can create multilevel lists, such as outlines, by choosing the Outline Numbered tab in the Bullets and Numbering dialog box. As shown in Figure 5-13, it contains predefined formats for multilevel lists. Click the format you want to use for your multilevel list and begin keying.

FIGURE 5-13
Outline Numbered tab

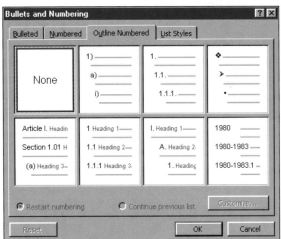

As you key a multilevel list, you will need to indent some items more than others. Click the Increase Indent and Decrease Indent buttons on the Formatting toolbar to help you build the hierarchy of your multilevel list.

> **Hot Tip**
>
> You can also press the **Tab** button to indent an item or press **Shift+Tab** to decrease the indent on an item.

STEP-BY-STEP ▷ 5.9

1. Open **IW Step5-9** from the data files.

2. Save the document as **Outline** followed by your initials.

3. Select the four items under *Payroll Deductions*.

4. Click the **Bullets** button on the Formatting toolbar. The items become a bulleted list.

5. Select the four items under *Income Sources*.

6. Click the **Numbering** button on the Formatting toolbar. The items become a numbered list. Do not worry if the bulleted list and numbered list do not align; you will learn how to change that later.

7. Place the insertion point on the blank line below the heading *Employment Benefits*.

8. Choose **Bullets and Numbering** on the **Format** menu. The Bullets and Numbering dialog box appears.

9. Click the **Outline Numbered** tab.

10. Click the second format on the top row and click **OK**. The number *1)* and an indent appear.

11. Key **Insurance** and press **Enter**.

12. Click the **Increase Indent** button. The indent is increased, and the letter *a)* appears.

13. Key **Medical** and press **Enter**.

14. Key **Life** and press **Enter**. Key **Dental** and press **Enter**.

15. Click the **Decrease Indent** button. The indent decreases, and the number *2)* appears.

16. Key the remaining items in the multilevel list below.

```
Employment Benefits
1) Insurance
   a) Medical
   b) Life
   c) Dental
2) Vacation
   a) Holidays
   b) Personal Days
3) Leave
   a) Sick
   b) Emergency
```

17. Save and leave the document open for the next Step-by-Step.

Changing and Customizing Lists

Using the Bullets and Numbering dialog box, you can change the appearance of lists the same way you chose a predefined format for the multilevel list. Select the list you want to change, and choose Bullets and Numbering on the Format menu to access the Bullets and Numbering dialog box. Click the Bulleted or Numbered tab, and click the format you want.

To change the appearance of a bulleted list, choose Bullets and Numbering on the Format menu. Choose the bullet style you want on the Bulleted tab, shown in Figure 5-14.

FIGURE 5-14
Bulleted tab

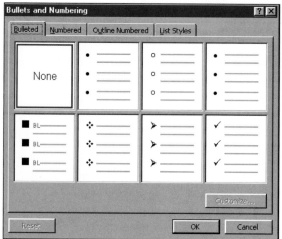

To customize a bulleted list, click the Customize button. As shown in Figure 5-15, you can change the bullet character, bullet position, or text position in the Customize Bulleted List dialog box. The Preview box shows how the list will look.

Computer Concepts

You can insert a picture or another bullet graphic by clicking **Picture** on the Bulleted tab of the Bullets and Numbering dialog box. Picture bullets occur frequently when creating documents for the Web.

FIGURE 5-15
Customize Bulleted List dialog box

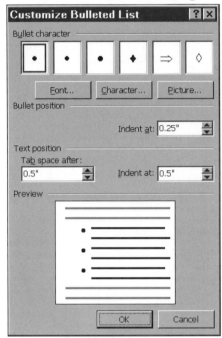

To change the appearance of a numbered list, click the Numbered tab, shown in Figure 5-16. Click the numbered style you want, and choose whether you want to restart the numbering or continue the previous list.

FIGURE 5-16
Numbered tab in the Bullets and Numbering dialog box

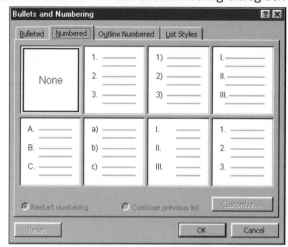

To customize a numbered list, click the Customize button. As shown in Figure 5-17, you can change the number format, number style, number position, and text position in the Customize Numbered List dialog box. The Preview box shows how the list will look.

FIGURE 5-17
Customize Numbered List dialog box

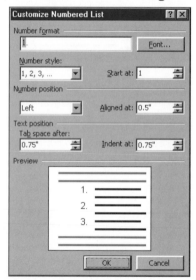

S TEP-BY-STEP ▷ 5.10

1. Select the four bulleted items under *Payroll Deductions*. (The bullets will not be selected.)

2. Choose **Bullets and Numbering** on the **Format** menu. The Bullets and Numbering dialog box appears.

3. Click the **Bulleted** tab if necessary.

4. Click the second bullet option on the second row and click **OK**. The bullets change character.

5. Select the four numbered items under *Income Sources.* (The numbers will not be selected.)

6. Choose **Bullets and Numbering** on the **Format** menu. The Bullets and Numbering dialog box appears.

7. Click the **Numbered** tab if necessary.

8. Click the first choice on the second row.

9. Click the **Customize** button. The Customize Numbered List dialog box appears.

10. In the Number position section, change the *Aligned at* setting to **0.25 inches**.

11. In the Text position section, enter **0** in the *Tab space after* box, and **0.5"** in the *Indent at* box.

12. Click **OK**. The numbered list changes to an alphabetic list and aligns with the bulleted list.

13. Save, print, and close the document.

 Extra Challenge

Open the **List** document you created in Step-by-Step 5.8. Change the bulleted list so that it aligns with the numbered list, and change the bullet character.

Sorting Text in a Document

S*orting* arranges a list of words in ascending order (*a* to *z*) or in descending order (*z* to *a*). Sorting can also arrange a list of numbers in ascending (smallest to largest) or descending (largest to smallest) order. Sorting is useful for putting lists of names or terms in alphabetic order.

To sort text in a document, choose Sort on the Table menu. The Sort Text dialog box appears, as shown in Figure 5-18. In this dialog box, you can choose the options for the sort.

FIGURE 5-18
Sort Text dialog box

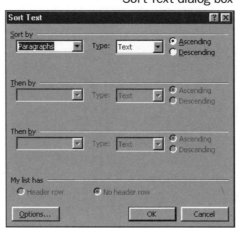

1. Open the **IW Step5-11** document from the data files. This is the *Supplies* document that you last used in Step-by-Step 5.7. Save the document as **Supplies2** followed by your initials.

2. Select the list if necessary. Do not select the title.

3. Sort the list in ascending order by price following these steps:
   a. Choose **Sort** on the **Table** menu. The Sort Text dialog box appears, as shown in Figure 5-18.
   b. In the Sort by box, choose **Paragraphs** if necessary.
   c. In the Type box, choose **Number**.
   d. Click **Ascending** if necessary.
   e. Click **OK**. The list sorts in ascending order by price.

4. Sort the list in alphabetic order following these steps:
   a. With the list still selected, choose **Sort** on the **Table** menu. The Sort Text dialog box appears.
   b. In the Sort by box, choose **Paragraphs** if necessary.
   c. In the Type box, choose **Text** if necessary.
   d. Click **Ascending** if necessary.
   e. Click **OK**. The list sorts in ascending alphabetic order.

5. Save, print, and close the document.

Summary

In this lesson, you learned:

- Margins are the blank areas around the top, bottom, and sides of a page. You can change the margin settings by choosing Page Setup on the File menu.

- You can align text by choosing Paragraph on the Format menu or by clicking the buttons on the Formatting toolbar. You can also change the vertical alignment in the Page Setup dialog box.

- You can indent text either from the left margin, from the right margin, or from both the left and right margins.

- Single-spacing has no extra space between each line. Double-spacing has one full line space between each line of text.

- Click and Type allows you to insert text or other items into a blank area of a document.

- Text alignment can be set with decimal, left, right, or centered tabs. Leaders can be used with any kind of tab.

- You can use the Bullets or Numbering buttons on the toolbar to create bulleted or numbered lists. To change the appearance of a list, choose Bullets and Numbering on the Format menu to access the Bullets and Numbering dialog box.

- Outline numbered lists contain two or more levels of text.

- You can sort text or numbers in ascending or descending order by choosing Sort on the Table menu.

NET TERMS REVIEW

Define the following terms:

Alignment	Line spacing	Tabs
Bullet	Margins	Vertical alignment
Indent	Outline numbered list	
Leaders	Sorting	

LESSON 5 REVIEW QUESTIONS

TRUE/FALSE

Circle T if the statement is true or F if the statement is false.

T   F   1. You can sort numbers and text using the Sort Text dialog box.

T   F   2. Tabs are useful for adding space before or after a paragraph.

T F 3. Documents are normally aligned left or justified.

T F 4. A hanging indent is when the first full line of text is followed by indented lines.

T F 5. Your document will have no margins unless you specify them.

MULTIPLE CHOICE

Select the best response for the following statements.

1. What type of text has a full blank line between each line of text?
    A. single-spaced
    B. indented
    C. double-spaced
    D. aligned

2. Which tab in the Bullets and Numbering dialog box contains predefined formats for multilevel lists?
    A. Numbered
    B. Bulleted
    C. Outline Numbered
    D. all of the above

3. The upper triangle at the left edge of the ruler indicates the
    A. first-line indent marker.
    B. decrease indent marker.
    C. hanging indent marker.
    D. left indent marker.

4. Text can be aligned using all of the following types of tab stops except
    A. justified.
    B. decimal.
    C. right.
    D. center.

5. Click and Type can be used in
    A. Normal view.
    B. Outline view.
    C. Print Layout view.
    D. all of the above.

LESSON 5 PROJECTS

PROJECT 5-1

1. Open **IW Project5-1** from the data files.

2. Save the document as **Porch Lights** followed by your initials.

3. Sort the paragraphs in ascending alphabetic order.

4. Create a numbered list from all the text (not including the headings).

5. Customize the list so the numbers align at 0" and the text indents at 0.25".

6. Change the line spacing of the text so 6-point spacing appears before each paragraph.

7. Change the left and right margins to 1 inch.

8. Save, print, and close the document.

PROJECT 5-2

1. Open **IW Project5-2** from the data files.

2. Save the document as **Shipping** followed by your initials.

3. Place the insertion point two lines below the paragraph.

4. Set left tabs at 1.75 inches, 3 inches, and 4.75 inches.

5. Key the headings **Company**, **Cost**, **Weight Limit**, and **Delivery Time** in bold using the tabs.

6. Press **Enter**. Clear all the current tabs.

7. Set a decimal tab with dot style leaders at 1.94 inches.

8. Set a center tab with dot style leaders at 3.5 inches.

9. Set a right tab with dot style leaders at 5.63 inches.

10. Using the tabs just set, key the following information in a table:

```
Lightning   $11.75    1 lb. 4 oz.    1:00 p.m.
Pronto      $9.99     10 oz.         12:30 p.m.
Zippy       $14.50    2 lbs.         10:00 a.m.
Speed Air   $12.95    none           3:00 p.m.
```

11. Sort the list alphabetically in ascending order.

12. Indent the first line of the first paragraph 0.5 inches.

13. Change the line spacing of the table to 1.5 inches.

14. Save, print, and close the document.

PROJECT 5-3

A friend of yours will be married soon. She has asked you to help her design the wedding invitations.

1. Open **IW Project5-3** from the data files.

2. Save the document as **Wedding** followed by your initials.

3. Set the font to Edwardian Script IT, 18 point, bold. If this font is not available, choose another appropriate font.

4. Center the text.

5. Vertically center the text.

6. Save, print, and close the document.

PROJECT 5-4

1. Open **IW Project5-4** from the data files. This is the *Interview2* document that you last used in Project 4-4.

2. Save the document as **Interview3** followed by your initials.

3. Key a colon after the words *such as* in the first sentence of the second paragraph, and then delete the rest of the sentence.

4. Insert a blank line, and key the following items as a bulleted list with the bullet character shown:

   ❖ Social Security card
   ❖ Names and addresses of former employers
   ❖ Names and addresses of references
   ❖ A copy of your resume
   ❖ School records

5. Double-space the first paragraph, and indent the first line 0.25 inches.

6. Sort the bulleted list in ascending alphabetic order, and change the spacing to 1.5.

7. Save, print, and close the document.

PROJECT 5-5

1. Open **IW Project5-5** from the data files.

2. Save the document as **Government** followed by your initials.

3. Number the items under *Executive Branch* using a format of your choice.

4. Bullet the items under *Judicial Branch* using a format of your choice. Customize the list so that the bullets align at 0.25". Set the **Tab space after** and **Indent at** settings to 0.50".

5. Key the remaining information in the outlined numbered list below.

```
Legislative Branch
1) Senators
   a) Direct Election-Statewide
   b) Term—Six Years

2) Representatives
   a) Direct Election-Congressional District
   b) Term—Two Years
```

6. Save, print, and close the document.

CRITICAL THINKING

ACTIVITY 5-1

You have keyed a bulleted list of items for a project at work, but the bulleted characters keep showing up as clock faces. Use Help to figure out what the problem is and how to solve it.

ACTIVITY 5-2

Make a list of your three favorite songs, your three favorite books, and your three favorite movies. Click Character in the Customize Bulleted List dialog box to search for just the right bullet character for each list. (*Hint:* The Webdings font has many fun characters you can use.) Use the Help feature to assist you.

DESKTOP PUBLISHING WITH WORD

OBJECTIVES

Upon completion of this lesson, you should be able to:

■ Format text into columns.

■ Add borders and shading.

■ Insert and scale clip art.

■ Wrap text around graphics.

■ Draw objects.

■ Select, resize, cut, copy, and paste objects.

■ Change the appearance of objects.

■ Add text to drawings.

■ Create and modify diagrams.

⏱ **Estimated Time: 2 hours**

VOCABULARY

Borders

Chart

Clip art

Desktop publishing

Diagram

Graphics

Scale

Selection rectangle

Shading

Sizing handles

What Is Desktop Publishing?

Desktop publishing is the process of combining text and graphics to create attractive documents. With desktop publishing, you can design a newsletter for a school organization, an advertisement for a business, or a program for a fund-raising event. Employers consider desktop publishing experience a valuable asset because it shows that you can use a computer to communicate information.

Creating Columns

C

Sometimes a document can be more effective if the text is formatted in multiple columns. A newsletter is an example of a document that often has two or more columns. Columns are easy to create in Word. Choose Columns on the Format menu. The Columns dialog box appears, as shown in Figure 6-1. In this dialog box, specify the number of columns you want and how much space you want between the columns. Unless you specify otherwise, all columns will be equal width. You can also specify whether you want a line separating the columns. You can convert existing text into columns or create the columns before keying text. Text that you key will fill up one column before flowing into the next.

To format a document into columns without accessing the Columns dialog box, click the Columns button on the toolbar. A drop-down menu, as shown in Figure 6-2, lets you choose the number of columns you want, up to four.

If you are in Normal view when you choose the Columns command, Word automatically switches to Print Layout view so the columns appear side by side.

Computer Concepts

You can create up to 14 even or uneven columns in a document.

FIGURE 6-1
Columns dialog box

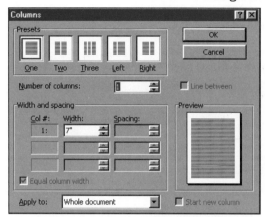

FIGURE 6-2
Columns drop-down menu

STEP-BY-STEP 6.1

1. Open **IW Step6-1** from the data files.

2. Save the document as **Hampton Hills** followed by your initials.

3. Choose **Columns** on the **Format** menu.

4. In the Presets box, choose **Two**.

5. In the Width and spacing section, click the up arrow on the **Spacing** box until it reads **0.6"**.

6. Click the **Line between** check box. Click **OK**.

7. Click **Print Preview** to view the columns. Close Print Preview.

8. Save and leave the document open for the next Step-by-Step.

Extra Challenge

You can delete or move columns just as you do text. Select the first column and press **Delete**. Undo the delete. Cut the text in the second column and paste it at the beginning of the first column. Undo the cut and paste operations.

Using Borders and Shading

C

Borders and shading add interest and emphasis to text. However, be sure to use them sparingly. Too many borders or too much shading on a page can make it look cluttered and hard to read.

Adding Borders to Paragraphs

Borders are single, double, thick, or dotted lines that appear around one or more words or paragraphs. You can specify whether the border appears on all four sides (like a box), on two sides, or on only one side of the paragraph. Other options include shadow, 3-D, and custom borders. Select the text you want to border and choose Borders and Shading on the Format menu. On the Borders tab of the Borders and Shading dialog box, shown in Figure 6-3, specify the border setting, style, color, and width of line. After selecting your options, you can see a sample in the Preview box.

FIGURE 6-3
Borders tab in Borders and Shading dialog box

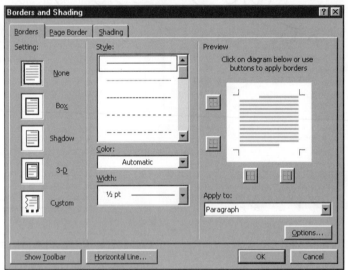

Adding Shading to Paragraphs

You can also add *shading*—grays or colors—or patterns, such as diagonal stripes, to paragraphs or lines to emphasize text. However, to maintain the readability of a paragraph that contains several sentences, add only light shading (25% or less) to text. Select the text you want to shade and access the Shading tab in the Borders and Shading dialog box, shown in Figure 6-4. Here you can choose the shading, pattern, and color you want. The Preview box shows you a sample of what your shading choices will look like.

FIGURE 6-4
Shading tab in Borders and Shading dialog box

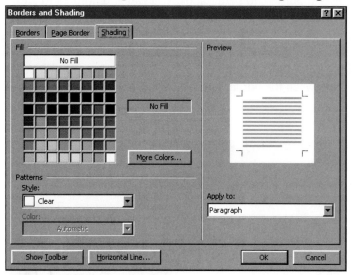

STEP-BY-STEP ▷ 6.2

1. Select the heading *Don't Forget to Pay Your Rent!*, the blank line, and the sentence below it.

2. Choose **Borders and Shading** on the **Format** menu.

3. Click the **Borders** tab if necessary.

4. In the Setting section, click the **Box** button.

5. Click the **Width** box arrow and choose the **1½ pt** width from the menu.

6. In the Color box, choose **Blue**.

7. Click the **Shading** tab. In the Fill section, choose **Light Yellow**. Choose **15%** from the **Style** list box.

8. Click **OK**. In addition to the border, the text now contains a blue border with light yellow 15% shading, as shown in Figure 6-5.

9. Save and close the document.

FIGURE 6-5
Text with border and shading

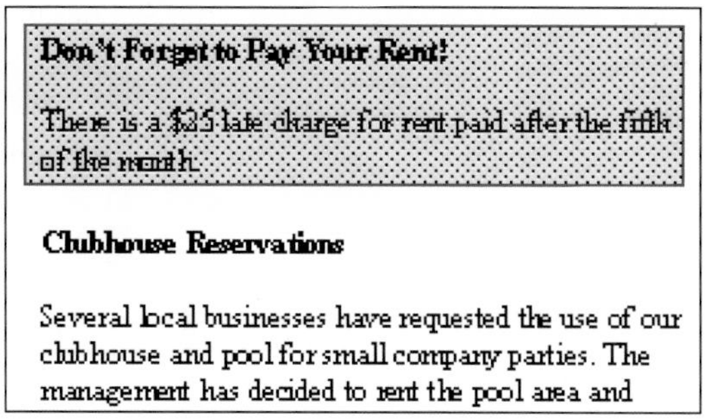

> **Don't Forget to Pay Your Rent!**
>
> There is a $25 late charge for rent paid after the fifth of the month.

Clubhouse Reservations

Several local businesses have requested the use of our clubhouse and pool for small company parties. The management has decided to rent the pool area and

Adding Borders to Pages

The same way you add borders to paragraphs, you can add borders to entire pages. In the Borders and Shading dialog box, choose the Page Border tab, as shown in Figure 6-6. Here you can choose the setting, line style, width, and color of the border you want. You can choose predefined art borders from the Art drop-down list box. You can add page borders to any or all sides of a page. Click the Options button and the Border and Shading Options dialog box appears, as shown in Figure 6-7. Here you can specify the amount of space between the border and the text or edge of the page.

FIGURE 6-6

Page Border tab in Borders and Shading dialog box

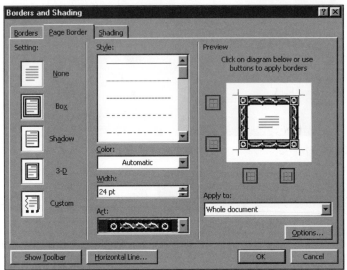

FIGURE 6-7

Border and Shading Options dialog box

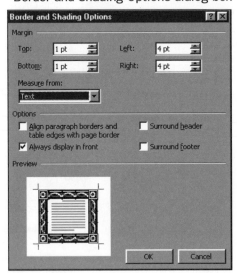

S TEP-BY-STEP ▷ 6.3

Pack

1. Open **IW Step6-3** from the data files. Save the file as **Wedding2** followed by your initials.

2. Choose **Borders and Shading** on the Format menu.

3. Click the **Page Border** tab. In the Setting section, click the **Box** button.

4. In the Color box, choose **Black**.

5. Click the arrow on the **Art** box, and choose a predefined art border appropriate for a wedding invitation. You can see a preview of how your document will look in the Preview section.

6. Click the **Options** button. The Border and Shading Options dialog box appears.

7. Click the arrow on the **Measure from** box and select **Text**. Click **OK** twice to close the dialog boxes.

8. Click the **Print Preview** button to see how your document will appear. Close Print Preview.

9. Save, print, and close the document.

Working with Graphics

W ord allows you to enhance documents by adding graphics. *Graphics* are pictures that help illustrate the meaning of the text and make the page more attractive. Word has predefined shapes, diagrams, and charts, as well as pictures. Word also includes drawing tools that enable you to create your own graphics and add them to your documents. To access Word's drawing tools, click the Drawing button on the Standard toolbar to display the Drawing toolbar, as shown in Figure 6-8. To work with graphics, you must be in Print Layout view.

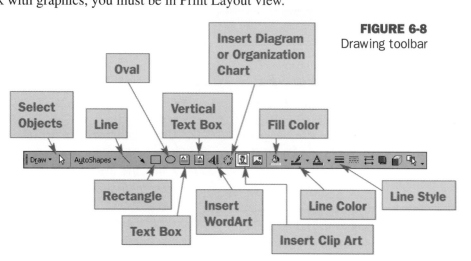

FIGURE 6-8
Drawing toolbar

Inserting Clip Art

Graphics that are already drawn and available for use in documents are called ***clip art***. Clip art libraries offer artwork of common objects that may improve the quality of your work. To insert clip art, choose Picture on the Insert menu and Clip Art on the submenu. The Insert Clip Art task pane appears, as shown in Figure 6-9. In the box under Search text, key a word or words that describe the kind of clip art you wish to insert. Word will search the installed clip art in the Media Gallery for images that match the search text you entered. When Word finds the images, it displays them in the task pane, as shown in Figure 6-10. Scroll to view the images and click the one you want. Word inserts the clip art at the insertion point in your document. You can also insert clip art by clicking the Insert Clip Art button on the Drawing toolbar.

Computer Concepts

The Media Gallery includes other media types besides clip art, such as photographs, movies, and sounds. You can also connect to the Web to access more images.

FIGURE 6-9
Insert Clip Art task pane

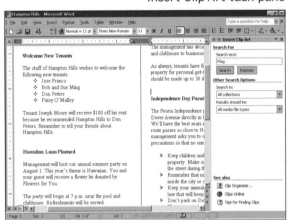

FIGURE 6-10
Clip art images in task pane

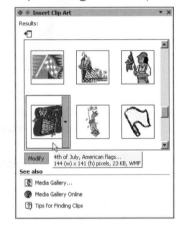

STEP-BY-STEP 6.4

1. Open the file **Hampton Hills** you last used in Step-by-Step 6.2.

2. In the second column, place the insertion point on the blank line above the *Independence Day Parade* heading.

3. Choose **Picture** on the **Insert** menu, and then click **Clip Art** on the submenu. The Add Clips to Organizer dialog box appears. Click **Later** to close the dialog box.

4. The Insert Clip Art task pane also appears. In the Search text box, key **flag**. Click **Search**.

5. Click the U.S. flag image of your choice. The clip art is inserted in your text.

6. Close the **Insert Clip Art** task pane.

7. Place the insertion point on the blank line after the *Hawaiian Luau Planned* heading.

8. Click the **Insert Clip Art** button on the Drawing toolbar. (If the Add Clips to Organizer dialog box appears, click **Later**.)

9. In the Search text box, key **palm tree**. Click **Search**.

10. Click the palm tree image of your choice. The clip art is inserted in your text.

11. Close the Insert Clip Art task pane.

12. Save and leave the document open for the next Step-by-Step.

Selecting Clip Art

Although clip art is already created, you can alter the way it appears on a page. To edit clip art, you must first select it. To select clip art, position the insertion point over the clip art and click. A box with eight small squares appears around the clip art, as shown in Figure 6-11. The box is called the *selection rectangle*. The squares are called *sizing handles*.

When the clip art is selected, the Picture toolbar appears, as shown in Figure 6-12. Using the buttons on the toolbar, you can change the image to black and white or grayscale, increase or decrease the contrast or brightness, crop the image, select a text wrapping style, or reset its original properties. You can also format clip art by clicking the Format Picture button on the toolbar. The Format Picture dialog box appears, as shown in Figure 6-13.

FIGURE 6-11
Selection rectangle with sizing handles

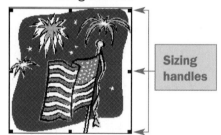

Sizing handles

FIGURE 6-12
Picture toolbar

Line Style button

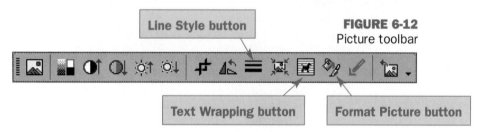

Text Wrapping button

Format Picture button

FIGURE 6-13
Format Picture dialog box

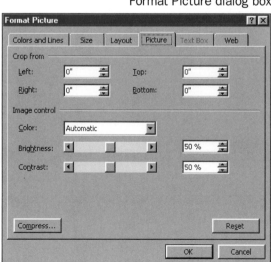

Resizing Clip Art

Once the clip art has been inserted, it can be resized to fit better in the text. To resize the clip art, first select it; then click on a sizing handle. The insertion point becomes a crosshair. Drag the handle inward or outward to make the object smaller or larger. After adjusting the clip art to the desired size, click anywhere in the window to deselect it.

To change the size, or *scale*, of a graphic so its proportions are precise, choose Picture on the Format menu. The Format Picture dialog box appears. In the Format Picture dialog box,

Hot Tip

You can quickly access the Format Picture command by selecting the object and then right-clicking the mouse button. Choose **Format Picture** on the shortcut menu.

click the Size tab, where you can key an exact size or a percentage of length and width scale, as shown in Figure 6-14. You can also scale clip art using the corner handles to drag inward or outward.

FIGURE 6-14

Size tab in Format Picture dialog box

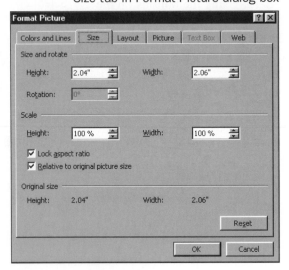

STEP-BY-STEP ▷ 6.5

1. Click the picture of the flag to select it.

2. Click the **Center** button on the Formatting toolbar. The flag clip art is centered in column 2.

3. With the clip art still selected, use the handles to resize it to approximately 2 inches tall by 2 ½ inches wide.

4. Deselect the clip art.

5. Click the picture of the palm tree to select it.

6. Choose **Picture** on the **Format** menu.

7. Click the **Size** tab. In the Scale section, click the **Height** down arrow until 35% appears in the box. Notice that the Width percentage and the Size measurements in inches also change.

8. Click **OK**. The clip art is smaller.

9. Save and leave the document open for the next Step-by-Step.

Wrapping Text around Clip Art

To save space and make a document look more professional, you may want to wrap text around the clip art. To do this, choose Picture on the Format menu. In the Format Picture dialog box, click the Layout tab to see the wrapping options, as shown in Figure 6-15. The Wrapping style samples show how the text will flow around the graphic. You can also click the Text Wrapping button on the Picture toolbar. Click the text wrapping style you want from the pull-down menu, as shown in Figure 6-16.

FIGURE 6-15
Layout tab in Format Picture dialog box

FIGURE 6-16
Text wrapping options

STEP-BY-STEP ▷ 6.6

1. Select the palm tree if it is not already selected.

2. Click the **Text Wrapping** button on the Picture toolbar.

3. Click **Square** on the submenu. Click anywhere in the window to deselect the palm tree. Your document should appear similar to the one in Figure 6-17.

4. Change the format of *Hampton Hills* to Imprint

MT Shadow, 28 point, green. If the font is not available, choose another appropriate font.

5. Change the format of *Newsletter* to 20-point, blue.

6. Preview the document. If the newsletter is more than one page, adjust spacing of the text or the size of the clip art.

7. Save, print, and close the document.

FIGURE 6-17
Text wrapping with clip art

Hawaiian Luau Planned

Management will host our annual summer party on August 1. This year's theme is Hawaiian. You and your guest will receive a fresh flower lei donated by Flowers for You.

Drawing Graphics

Word provides tools for you to create your own graphic images. The Drawing toolbar contains buttons for drawing and manipulating objects, such as lines, arcs, rectangles, circles, and free-form shapes. Table 6-1 summarizes the basic drawing tools that appear on the Drawing toolbar.

TABLE 6-1
Drawing tools

Button	Name	Function
▢	Rectangle	Draws rectangles and squares. To use, click and hold the mouse button; then drag to draw. To create a perfect square, hold down the Shift key as you drag.
╲	Line	Draws straight lines. To use, position the pointer where you want the line to begin; then click and hold the mouse button, and drag to where you want the line to end.
⬭	Oval	Draws ovals and circles. To use, click and hold the mouse button; then drag to draw the oval or circle. To create a perfect circle, hold down the Shift key as you drag.
▧	Select Objects	Lets you select and manipulate objects. To use, click on the arrow. The insertion point assumes the pointer shape.

STEP-BY-STEP ▷ 6.7

1. Open a new Word document.

2. Change the orientation to landscape.

3. If necessary, click the **Drawing** button on the Standard toolbar to display the Drawing toolbar.

4. Click the **Oval** button. The mouse pointer changes to a crosshair.

5. Position the pointer on the upper left side of the document.

6. Press and hold the mouse button. Drag to draw an oval about 1½ inches tall by 3 inches wide. Release the mouse button when your oval is approximately the same size and in the same position as the pond shown in Figure 6-18.

7. Click the **Line** button. The mouse pointer changes to a crosshair.

8. Position the pointer on the upper left corner of the document. Drag to draw a line from the upper left corner to the lower left corner. Release the mouse button when your line is positioned similar to *Dover Avenue* shown in Figure 6-18.

9. Use the Line button to create the other roads on the map. Be sure to click the **Line** button each time you draw a line.

10. Preview your document and compare it with Figure 6-18. Make any necessary adjustments.

11. Save the document as **Park Map** followed by your initials. Leave the document open for the next Step-by-Step.

FIGURE 6-18
Park map

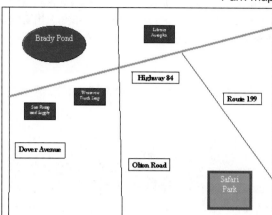

Editing Drawings

As with clip art, you can change the way your drawings appear in a document. To edit a drawing object, you must first select it. Position the insertion point over the object and click. Handles appear around the object, and a four-sided arrow appears with the arrow pointer. Drag one of the handles inward or outward to make the object smaller or larger. Click anywhere in the window to deselect the object. Select and press Delete or Backspace to delete an object.

You can cut, copy, and paste objects the same way you do text. The Cut and Copy commands place a copy of the selected image on the Clipboard. Pasting an object from the Clipboard places the object in your drawing. To move an object, select it, and then press and hold the mouse button while you drag the object to its new location.

S TEP-BY-STEP ▷ 6.8

1. Click the **Rectangle** button.

2. Position the pointer in the lower left corner of your document.

3. Drag to draw a rectangle similar to *Sun Pump and Supply* on the map. When you release the mouse button, the rectangle is selected.

4. Click the **Copy** button on the toolbar.

5. Click the **Paste** button. A copy of the rectangle appears.

6. Click the **Paste** button two more times. Two more copies of the rectangle appear.

7. The last rectangle you pasted is still selected. Place the pointer in the middle of the rectangle, and hold down the mouse button. Drag the rectangle to the right side of the document so it is in the same position as *Liberty Autoplex* on the map.

8. Select the next rectangle, and drag it to the same position as *Westview Truck Stop* on the map.

9. Select the last rectangle, and drag it to the same position as *Safari Park* on the map. Use the handles to create a square 1½ inches by 1½ inches. Deselect the square.

10. Save and leave the document open for the next Step-by-Step.

Adding Color and Style to Objects

Color adds life to your drawings. Word allows you to fill objects with color and change the color of lines. To change the color, select the object you want to fill or the line you want to change. Click the Fill Color button or the Line Color button on the Drawing toolbar. When you click the down arrow on one of these buttons, a color box appears, as shown in Figures 6-19 and 6-20. To choose a color from the color box, simply click the color you want. Your selected object appears in this color.

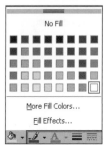

FIGURE 6-19
Fill Color button
with color box

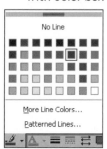

FIGURE 6-20
Line Color button
with color box

Another way to change the appearance of drawings is to change the line style. You can change the style of the line or lines that make up an object, such as a rectangle. Word gives you many choices for line styles, including thick and thin lines, dotted lines, and arrows. To change the line style, select the line you want to change and click the Line Style button on the Drawing toolbar. When you click the Line Style button, a menu of line styles appears, as shown in Figure 6-21. Click a line style, and your selected line or object's line changes to your choice.

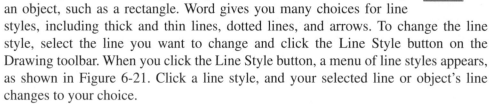

FIGURE 6-21
Line style menu

S**TEP-BY-STEP** ⬠ 6.9

1. Select the oval on the map.

2. Click the down arrow on the **Fill Color** button on the Drawing toolbar. The color box appears.

3. Click the **Blue** color square. The oval is filled with the color blue.

4. Select the square on your drawing.

5. Click the down arrow on the **Fill Color** button, and click the color **Lime**. The square is filled with the color lime.

6. Select each rectangle on your drawing, and fill them with the color **Brown.**

7. Select the line labeled *Highway 84* on your map.

8. Click the down arrow on the **Line Color** button on the Drawing toolbar. The color box appears.

9. Click the color **Red**.

10. With the line still selected, click the **Line Style** button. A menu of line styles appears.

11. Click the **4½ pt** thick line. The line on your drawing thickens.

12. Select the square, and click the arrow on the **Line Color** button. Click the color **Green**. The line around the square is now green.

13. Click the **Line Style** button. Click the **6 pt** thick line. The line around the square thickens. Deselect the square.

14. Save and leave the document open for the next Step-by-Step.

Adding Text to Your Drawings

Often your drawings will require labels. Word provides several ways to add text to a document. The easiest way is to right-click in the object and choose Add Text on the shortcut menu. Word places the insertion point inside the graphic. Key and format your text, and click outside the object to deselect it.

Another way to add text to your drawing is to insert text boxes. To add a text box, click the Text Box button on the Drawing toolbar or choose Text Box on the Insert menu. A crosshair pointer appears. Position the pointer where you want the text box to appear, and then click and drag to create a text box. An insertion point appears inside the text box so you can key the text you want. Text within a text box can be formatted like regular text.

Once a text box is inserted into a document, it can be treated similarly to a graphic. You can format, resize, or change the position of a text box using the same commands as you would with a drawing object. To format a text box, choose Text Box on the Format menu. To resize a text box, click the handles and drag. To move a text box, click and drag it to the location you want.

S TEP-BY-STEP ▷ 6.10

1. Select the pond. Right-click and choose **Add text** on the submenu to insert text.

2. Key **Brady Pond**. Format the text as Times New Roman, 18 point, centered, white.

3. Key **Sun Pump and Supply**, **Westview Truck Stop**, and **Liberty Autoplex** in the three small rectangles. Center the text and format it as Times New Roman, 10 point, centered, white.

4. Key **Safari Park** in the large square. Format as Times New Roman, 18 point, centered, white.

5. Click the **Text Box** button on the Drawing toolbar.

6. To create a label for Highway 84, place the crosshair below the red diagonal line, and to the right of the center line, as shown on the map in Figure 6-18. Click and drag the mouse to draw a text box approximately ½ inch tall and 2 inches wide. Release the mouse button.

7. With the insertion point in the text box, key **Highway 84**. Format as Times New Roman, 16 point, centered, bold.

8. Repeat steps 6 and 7 to insert the text boxes for Route 199, Dover Avenue, and Olton Road as shown on the map.

9. Preview the document. Make adjustments as needed.

10. Save, print, and close the document.

Creating Diagrams and Charts

Diagrams and *charts* organize information in illustrations so readers can better understand relationships among data. Word has several preset diagram types, which include Cycle, Radial, Pyramid, Venn, Target, and Organization Chart. To view these diagrams, choose Diagram on the Insert menu. A Diagram Gallery appears, as shown in Figure 6-22. When a diagram type is chosen, the diagram appears in the document with a drawing border around it. A Diagram toolbar also appears, as shown in Figure 6-23. Here you can add elements, or sections, and text to a diagram and change its size and color. You can also view the Diagram Gallery by clicking the Insert Diagram or Organization Chart button on the Drawing toolbar. When you are satisfied with your diagram, click outside the drawing border and the diagram will be placed in your document at the insertion point. To delete a diagram, select the diagram or organization chart and press Delete.

FIGURE 6-22
Diagram Gallery

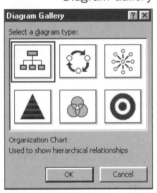

Insert Shape button

FIGURE 6-23
Diagram toolbar

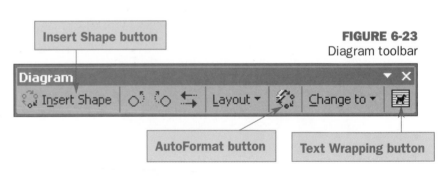

AutoFormat button   **Text Wrapping button**

STEP-BY-STEP ⟹ 6.11

1. Open **IW Step6-11** from the data files.

2. Save the document as **Diet3** followed by your initials.

3. Select the ten guidelines after the heading *Recommended Dietary Guidelines for Americans* and add bullets.

4. Place the insertion point after the last guideline and press **Enter** twice to insert a blank line.

5. Choose **Diagram** on the **Insert** menu. The Diagram Gallery appears.

6. Click the **Pyramid Diagram** button. Click **OK**. A pyramid diagram with a drawing border and three elements appears. The Diagram toolbar also appears.

7. Click the **Insert Shape** button on the Diagram toolbar. An element is added to the pyramid.

8. Click the **Insert Shape** button on the Diagram toolbar again. Another element is added to the pyramid.

9. Save and leave the document open for the next Step-by-Step.

Add Text and Design Styles to a Diagram

To add text to a diagram, click on the element where you want to insert the text. A drawing border appears around the element and the insertion point appears in the element. Key your text as you want it to appear in the diagram.

You can also use a preset design scheme to add color and design to your diagram. Click the AutoFormat button on the Diagram toolbar and the Diagram Style Gallery appears, as shown in Figure 6-24. Select a diagram style from the list in the left pane. A preview of the style appears in the right pane. After you select the style you want, click the Apply button.

FIGURE 6-24
Diagram Style Gallery

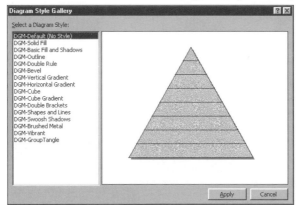

1. Click in the space near the pyramid to select it.

2. Click the second element from the top of the pyramid. Key **Use Sparingly**. Press **Enter** to start a new line. Key **Fats and Sweets**.

3. Click in the third element from the top. Key **2-3 Servings**. Press **Enter**. Key **Dairy and Meat Products**.

4. Click in the fourth element. Key **3-5 Servings**.

Press **Enter**. Key **Fruits and Vegetables**.

5. Click in the fifth element. Key **6-11 Servings**. Press **Enter**. Key **Cereals and Grains**.

6. Center the text in each element.

7. Bold the text in the first line of each element.

8. Click **AutoFormat** on the Diagram toolbar.

9. Select **Primary Colors**. Click **Apply**. The design scheme is applied to your diagram.

10. Save and leave the document open for the next Step-by-Step.

Resize a Diagram and Wrap Text

You resize your diagram by choosing Diagram on the Format menu. Click the Size tab; in the Scale section, adjust the percentage of the height or width scale of the diagram, as shown in Figure 6-25.

You wrap text around a diagram the same way you do clip art. Choose Diagram on the Format menu. Click the Layout tab and select a wrapping style. You can also press the Text Wrapping button on the Diagram toolbar.

FIGURE 6-25
Size tab in Format Diagram dialog box

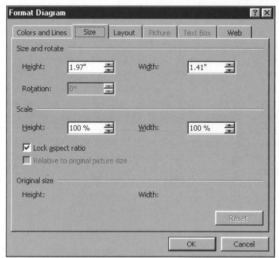

S TEP-BY-STEP ⟹ 6.13

1. Click to select the pyramid diagram if it is not already selected.

2. Click **Diagram** on the **Format** menu. The Format Diagram dialog box apears.

3. Click the **Size** tab. In the Scale section, click the **Height** arrow until **60%** appears in the box.

4. Click **OK**. The diagram is scaled down.

5. With the pyramid still selected, click the **Text Wrapping** button on the Diagram toolbar.

6. Select **Square** from the drop-down menu. The text appears to the right of the diagram. Deselect the pyramid.

7. Place the insertion point before the title *Fat in the American Diet*. Press **Enter** twice.

8. Save, print, and close the document. (*Note:* The text *Click to add text* that appears in the top element will not appear in the printed document.)

Summary

In this lesson, you learned:

- You can create documents with multiple columns. You can specify the number of columns and whether you want a line separating them.

- Borders and shading add interest and emphasis to text.

- You can insert clip art using the Microsoft Media Gallery and scale it to fit your document.

- To wrap text around an object, select the object and choose Picture on the Format menu.

- You can also draw grapics to add to word processing documents. The Drawing toolbar allows you to draw shapes such as lines, rectangles and ovals.

- Drawing objects can be resized, copied, and moved. To work with an object, click to select it.

- Text boxes can be created to contain special text. They can be formatted, resized, or moved just like drawing objects.

- Charts and diagrams organize your data in a manner that illustrates relationships among data. You can add text to charts and diagrams, as well as change the size and design style.

VOCABULARY REVIEW

Define the following terms:

Borders	Desktop publishing	Scale
Chart	Diagram	Selection rectangle
Clip art	Graphics	Shading
		Sizing handles

LESSON 6 REVIEW QUESTIONS

FILL IN THE BLANK

Complete the following sentences by writing the correct word or words in the blanks provided.

1. Choose the _____ tab in the Borders and Shading dialog box to add a border to an entire page.

2. Word will insert clip art at the _____ in the document.

3. The _____ toolbar contains tools you can use to draw and manipulate objects.

4. To add text to an object, right-click in the object and choose _____ on the shortcut menu.

5. To view the Diagram Gallery, click the _____ button on the Drawing toolbar.

MATCHING

Match the correct term in the right column to its description in the left column.

____ 1. Add a preset design to a diagram.   **A.** Format Picture button

____ 2. Format a document into columns.   **B.** Fill Color button

____ 3. Insert a border on four sides of a paragraph. **C.** Columns button

____ 4. Format clip art.   **D.** AutoShapes button

____ 5. Add color to an object.   **E.** AutoFormat button

F. Format Painter button

G. Box button

LESSON 6 PROJECTS

PROJECT 6-1

You volunteer at PAWS (Plains Animal Welfare & Shelter). The director has asked you to prepare a newsletter to be distributed to the community. She has given you some information and asked you to format it into a one-page newsletter.

1. Open **IW Project6-1** from the data files.

2. Save the document as **PAWS** followed by your initials.

3. Select the entire document and change the font to **Arial**.

4. Center the name, address, and telephone number.

5. Change the font of the name to 18 point, violet, bold. Change the font of the address and telephone number to 14 point, violet.

6. Place the insertion point in front of the word *About*. Format the document with two columns, with a line, and with 0.4-inch spacing between each column. Select the **This point forward** option from the Apply to drop-down list.

7. Format the headings *About PAWS* and *Choosing a Puppy* as 12 point, violet, bold. Center them in the columns.

8. Change the format of *Thank you for your help!* to 18 point, violet.

9. Apply bullets to the operating hours, the volunteer jobs available, and the list of needed items.

10. Apply the bold, italic, and underline styles to set off the items under *Choosing a Puppy*.

11. Place a 3 point violet border around the sentence beginning with *To volunteer.* Shade it with Aqua. Change the font size to 14.

12. Insert appropriate clip art above the title *Choosing a Puppy*. Key **dog** in the Search text box.

13. Preview the document. Adjust the spacing within the document if necessary.

14. Save, print, and close the document.

PROJECT 6-2

A friend is selling his house. He asks you to create a poster to accompany information sheets listing the features of the house.

1. Create the poster in Figure 6-26 using what you have learned in this lesson. Follow the instructions shown on the poster.

2. Save the document as **House Sale** followed by your initials.

3. Print and close the document.

FIGURE 6-26

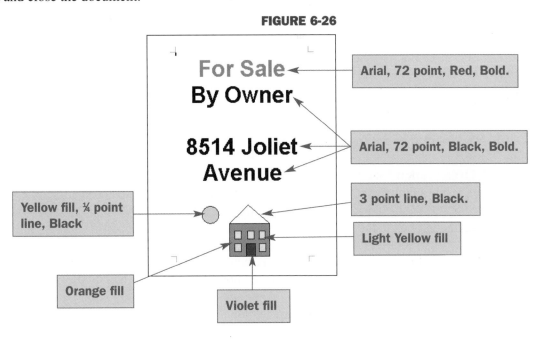

PROJECT 6-3

Your manager has asked you to create an invitation to the office holiday party.

1. Open **IW Project6-3** from the data files.

2. Save the document as **Holiday Invitation** followed by your initials.

3. Insert clip art with a holiday theme above the text. Resize and align the graphic to fit the document.

4. Change the text to a color, font, and size of your choice.

5. Apply an appropriate page border.

6. Save, print, and close the document.

PROJECT 6-4

You have been asked by the newly elected mayor of Monterey to prepare an organization chart of the city government. Use the outline shown in Figure 6-27 to label the chart.

FIGURE 6-27

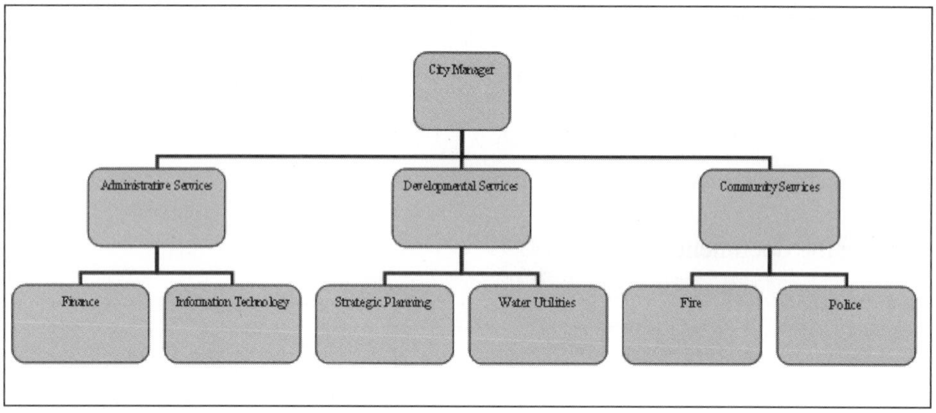

1. Open a new blank document.

2. Choose **Diagram** on the **Insert** menu.

3. Click **Organization Chart** if it is not already selected. Click **OK**. A blank organization chart appears inside a drawing border. The Organization Chart toolbar also appears.

4. Click in the first box in the second row to select it.

5. Click the down arrow on the **Insert Shape** button on the Organizational Chart toolbar. Click **Subordinate** to insert a box below the selected box.

6. Click the down arrow on the **Insert Shape** button again. Click **Subordinate** to insert another box below the selected box. There should now be two boxes below the first box on the second row.

7. Repeat steps 5 and 6 to insert two boxes below the second and third boxes on the second row.

8. Click the down arrow on the **Layout** button on the Organization Chart toolbar. Click Scale Organization Chart on the submenu to select the chart. Use the sizing handles to expand the chart to fit the page.

9. Click in the top box. Key **City Manager**.

10. Click in the first box on the second row. Key **Administrative Services**.

11. Key **Developmental Services** and **Community Services** in the second and third boxes in second row.

12. Key **Finance** and **Information Technology** in the subordinate boxes under Administrative Services.

13. Key **Strategic Planning** and **Water Utilities** in the subordinate boxes under Developmental Services.

14. Key **Fire** and **Police** in the subordinate boxes under Community Services.

15. Format text in all boxes as 10 point.

16. Preview your document. Close Print Preview.

17. Save your document as **Organization** followed by your initials.

18. Print (using landscape orientation) and close your document.

CRITICAL THINKING

ACTIVITY 6-1

SCANS

The computers in the office where you work are not currently networked. Next week a computer consultant is coming to install a network. Your supervisor wants to send him a layout of the computers in the office so he can get an idea of what is involved in the project. Use the drawing tools to create a layout of the office. Be sure to indicate where each computer and printer is located. Use fill colors and line colors to make the document more effective.

ACTIVITY 6-2

SCANS

Use the Help system to find out how to apply WordArt to a document. Use the PAWS newsletter created in Project 6-1 to apply WordArt to the organization's name.

WORKING WITH DOCUMENTS

OBJECTIVES

Upon completion of this lesson, you should be able to:

- Switch between documents.
- Copy and paste text between documents.
- Insert page breaks.
- Work with multipage documents.
- Insert headers and footers.
- Create footnotes and endnotes.
- Create a section with formatting that differs from other sections.
- Apply styles.
- Insert and format tables.
- Organize a document in outline view.

🕐 **Estimated Time: 2 hours**

VOCABULARY

Endnote

Footer

Footnote

Header

Page break

Pane

Section

Style

Table

Switching Between Documents

The ability to work in more than one document at a time is one of the most useful features of Word. Suppose, for example, you are creating a résumé in one document. While the résumé document is on the screen, you can create a new document where you can key the cover letter you will send with the résumé. You can even create a third document of a list of references. As you work, you can switch back and forth between the documents as often as needed.

Computer Concepts

All the programs in Office XP allow you to open new documents while you are working in other documents. You can even work in documents created in another Office program, such as Excel, while working in Word.

When you open or create a new document, Word displays it on top of the document that is already open. The new document window becomes the active window, and a button corresponding to the document is displayed on the taskbar, as shown in Figure 7-1. Moving back and forth between documents is easy. Just click the taskbar button for the document you want to display to make that document the active window. You can also choose the document you want from the Window menu, as shown in Figure 7-2.

FIGURE 7-2
Window menu
with files

FIGURE 7-1
Taskbar with buttons for open files

| Start | Cover Letter - Micros... | Resume - Microsoft Word | 10:26 PM |

Window	Help
New Window	
Arrange All	
Split	
1 Cover Letter	
✓ 2 Resume	

STEP-BY-STEP ▷ 7.1

1. Open **IW Step7-1** from the data files. Save the document as **Diet Final** followed by your initials.

2. Open **IW Step7-1a** from the data files. It becomes the active window. Save the document as **Diet Title2** followed by your initials.

3. Notice that buttons for both documents are displayed on the taskbar. Click the **Diet Final** button on the taskbar to make it the active window.

4. Click the **Window** menu. On the menu, you will see your two documents listed with a check mark beside **Diet Final**. Click **2 Diet Title2**. The menu will close, and **Diet Title2** will once again be the active window. Leave the Diet Title2 document on the screen for the next Step-by-Step.

Copying and Pasting Text Between Documents

Just as you can copy and move text within a document, you can copy and move text from one document to another. For example, in preparing cover letters to send with a résumé, you could copy the paragraphs discussing your general work experience from one cover letter to another, eliminating the need to rekey the same information for each letter.

STEP-BY-STEP ▷ 7.2

1. Click the **Diet Final** button on the taskbar to make that document active.

2. Select the date. Click the **Copy** button on the toolbar. A copy of the text is placed on the Clipboard.

3. Click **Diet Title2** on the taskbar to display the document.

4. Move the insertion point to a new line after the existing text. Click the **Paste** button on the toolbar. The text you copied from **Diet Final** is placed in **Diet Title2**.

5. Use the Format Painter to copy the format of the title page information to the date you just inserted.

6. Save, print, and close **Diet Title2**. Leave the **Diet Final** document open for the next Step-by-Step.

Inserting Page Breaks

When a document has more text than will fit on one page, Word must select a place in the document to end one page and begin the next. The place where one page ends and another begins is called a ***page break***. Word automatically inserts page breaks where they are necessary. You also can insert a page break manually. For example, you might want to insert a page break manually to prevent an automatic page break from separating a heading from the text that follows.

To insert a page break manually, choose Break on the Insert menu. Choose Page break in the Break dialog box that appears, as shown in Figure 7-3.

In Normal view, an automatic page break is shown as a dotted line across the page. A manual page break is also shown as a dotted line across the page, but it has the words *Page Break* in the middle, as shown in Figure 7-4. To delete manual page breaks, select the page break line and press Backspace or Delete.

FIGURE 7-3
Break dialog box

FIGURE 7-4
Manual page break

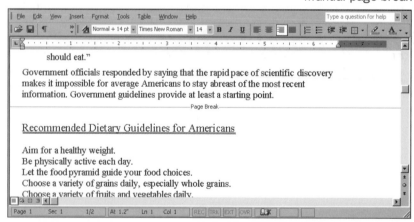

STEP-BY-STEP ▷ 7.3

1. Display the **Diet Final** document.

2. Switch to Normal view if necessary.

3. Place the insertion point in the blank line above the paragraph that begins *Recommended Dietary Guidelines.*

4. Choose **Break** on the **Insert** menu. The Break dialog box appears.

5. In the Break types area, **Page break** should be selected. Choose **OK**. The dotted line with the words *Page Break* in the middle indicates that a manual page break has been inserted. The heading and list now appear on page 2 of the document.

6. Save your changes, and leave the document open for the next Step-by-Step.

Hot Tip

Wait until you have finished keying and editing your document before inserting manual page breaks.

Working with Multipage Documents

When a document is only one page long, editing and formatting the text is easy. These tasks become more challenging in multipage documents because you cannot see the whole document on your screen at once. Word provides several useful tools for formatting and editing long documents.

Splitting Windows

Word lets you view two parts of a document at once by using the Split command on the Window menu. Suppose you want to see text at the beginning of a document while you are editing at the end of the document. By splitting the document, you can see both parts of the document. Each area of the document, called a *pane,* contains separate scroll bars to allow you to move through that part of the document. Figure 7-5 illustrates a split window.

FIGURE 7-5
Document divided with the Split command

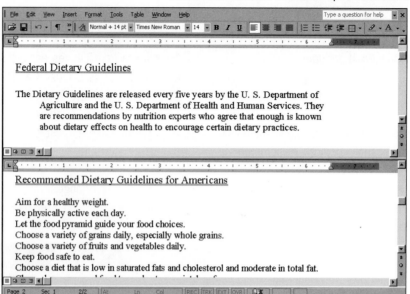

STEP-BY-STEP 7.4

1. Press **Ctrl+Home** to go to the beginning of the document.

2. Choose **Split** on the **Window** menu. A horizontal bar appears with the mouse pointer changing to a double-sided arrow as a positioning marker.

3. Position the bar so the document window is divided into two equal parts.

4. Click the mouse. The document window splits into two separate panes, each with independent scroll bars and rulers.

5. Press the down scroll arrow in the bottom pane of the split window. Notice that the document scrolls downward while the text in the upper pane remains still.

6. Choose **Remove Split** on the **Window** menu. The window returns to one pane. Leave the document open for the next Step-by-Step.

Using the Go To Command

One of the quickest ways to move through a long document is to use the Go To command. Go To allows you to skip to a specific part of a document. To skip to a specific page, choose Go To on the Edit menu. The Go To tab of the Find and Replace dialog box appears, as shown in Figure 7-6. Page is the default setting in the Go to what box, so in the Enter page number box, key the page number you want to move to. After you click Go To, Word will move the insertion point to the beginning of the page you specified.

Hot Tip

As you drag the vertical scroll box, a ScreenTip pops up and shows you the page number in relation to the position of the scroll box in the scroll bar.

FIGURE 7-6
Go To command

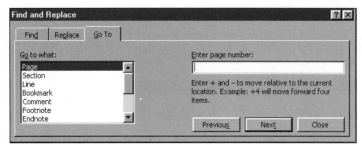

Another way to move through your document quickly is to use the Select Browse Object button, which is located at the bottom of the vertical scoll bar. Clicking the Select Browser Object button displays a menu of different options you can choose to look through, or browse, your document, as shown in Figure 7-7. By default, the browser option is set to browse by page. The up and down double arrows turn blue when an option other than page is selected. You can also access the Go To command by clicking the Go To button in the browse options menu.

FIGURE 7-7
Select Browser
Object options

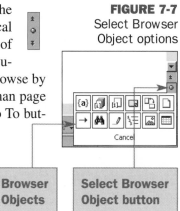

Browser Objects

Select Browser Object button

STEP-BY-STEP ▷ 7.5

1. Choose **Go To** on the **Edit** menu. The Find and Replace dialog box appears.

2. Click **Page** in the Go to what box.

3. In the Enter page number box, key **2** and click **Go To**. The insertion point moves to the beginning of page 2.

4. Click **Close**. The Find and Replace dialog box disappears. Keep the document open for the next Step-by-Step.

Viewing Hidden Characters

The Show/Hide ¶ command allows you to view hidden formatting characters, as shown in Figure 7-8. These are characters such as spaces, paragraph returns, and end-of-line marks. Being able to see these hidden characters can help you edit your text. The hidden formatting characters will not appear when you print your document.

FIGURE 7-8
Visible formatting characters

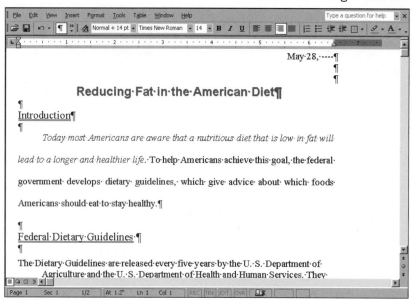

Using the Word Count Command

While you work on a document, you may want to know how many words it contains. The Word Count command quickly counts the pages, words, characters, paragraphs, and lines in your document. The insertion point can be located anywhere in the document when you use Word Count. You can count the words in a specific section of text by first selecting the text and then using Word Count. To use Word Count, choose Word Count on the Tools menu. A dialog box appears listing Word Count's findings, as shown in Figure 7-9. If you want to keep track of your word count, click the Show Toolbar button. A toolbar, shown in Figure 7-10, appears. Click Recount on the toolbar to display the current word count information.

FIGURE 7-9
Word Count dialog box

FIGURE 7-10
Word Count toolbar

STEP-BY-STEP ▷ 7.6

1. Press **Ctrl+Home** to go to the beginning of the document.

2. Click the **Show/Hide ¶** button on the toolbar unless it is already selected. Word makes the paragraph returns and spacebar characters visible.

3. Choose **Word Count** on the **Tools** menu. The Word Count dialog box appears. Note that the document has 452 words.

4. Click **Close**.

5. Click the **Show/Hide ¶** button. The characters are hidden.

6. Save your changes, and leave the document open for the next Step-by-Step.

Inserting Headers and Footers

Headers and footers allow you to include the same information, such as your name and the page number, on each page of a document. A ***header*** is text that is printed at the top of each page. A ***footer*** is text that is printed at the bottom of the page. Figure 7-11 shows both a header and a footer. Word has many header and footer options. You can even create separate headers and footers for even and odd pages.

FIGURE 7-11
Header and footer

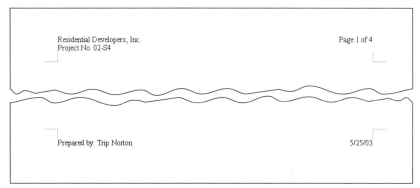

Insert headers and footers by choosing Header and Footer on the View menu. Headers and footers have their own formatting toolbar that appears when you choose the Header and Footer command. The toolbar, shown in Figure 7-12, contains formatting buttons you can use to insert the date, the time, and page numbers. Other buttons make it easy to access the Page Setup dialog box and to switch between the header and footer.

FIGURE 7-12
Header and Footer toolbar

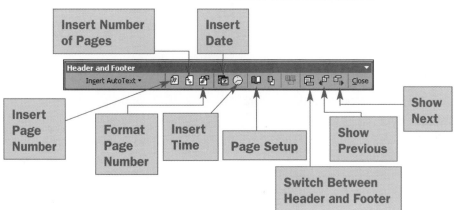

By default, Word assumes you want the same header and footer on all pages in a document. However, you can choose to have one header/footer on the first page with a different header/footer on all other pages. Choose Header and Footer on the View menu. Click the Page Setup button on the Header and Footer toolbar. In the Headers and footers box of the Layout tab, choose Different first page. Click OK and enter your headers and footers in the panes provided.

STEP-BY-STEP ▷ 7.7

1. Move the insertion point to the beginning of the document.

2. Choose **Header and Footer** on the **View** menu. Your document is changed to Print Layout view, and your insertion point is in the header pane. A Header and Footer toolbar appears.

3. Click the **Page Setup** button on the Header and Footer toolbar. The Page Setup dialog box appears.

4. Click the **Layout** tab. In the Headers and footers section, key **0.75** in the Footer box. Click **OK**.

5. Key your name in the header pane. Notice that the text is automatically formatted to 10-point Times New Roman.

6. Press **Tab**. Click the **Insert Date** button on the Header and Footer toolbar. The date appears.

7. Press **Tab**. Click the **Insert Page Number** button on the Header and Footer toolbar. The number 1 is inserted.

8. Switch to the Footer pane by clicking the **Switch Between Header and Footer** button. The insertion point appears in the footer pane.

9. Press **Tab** to move the insertion point to the centered tab.

10. Key **Reducing Fat in the American Diet**. Notice that the text is automatically formatted to 10-point Times New Roman.

11. Select the footer data you just keyed. Change the font to Courier New, 9 point.

12. Click the **Switch Between Header and Footer** button to go back to the header. Change the font of the header data to Courier New, 9 point.

13. Click the **Close** button on the Header and Footer toolbar.

14. Choose **Print Layout** on the **View** menu.

15. Scroll to the top and bottom of the page. The header and footer text you keyed is shown in light gray text.

16. Save your changes, and leave the document open for the next Step-by-Step.

Extra Challenge

Open a previously created document, and insert the page number right-aligned at the bottom of the page (in a footer). Experiment with the different number formats available.

You can also insert page numbers quickly into a header or footer by choosing Page Numbers on the Insert menu. The Page Numbers dialog box opens, as shown in Figure 7-13. Choose whether to display the page number in a header or footer, choose the alignment you want, and choose whether to show a page number on the first page. Your choices are reflected in the Preview box. To format the page number, click the Format button to open the Page Number Format dialog box, shown in Figure 7-14.

FIGURE 7-14
Page Number Format dialog box

FIGURE 7-13
Page Numbers dialog box

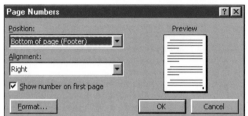

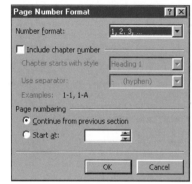

Creating Footnotes and Endnotes

FIGURE 7-15
Footnote and Endnote dialog box

A *footnote* or an *endnote* is used to document quotations, figures, or summaries or to provide other text you do not want to include in the body of a document. Footnotes are printed at the bottom of each page, and endnotes are printed at the end of the document.

To insert a footnote or an endnote, position the insertion point in the document where you need a reference. Choose Reference on the Insert menu and Footnote on the submenu. The Footnote and Endnote dialog box appears, as shown in Figure 7-15. Specify in the Location section whether you want a footnote or an endnote. In the Format section, choose to reference your footnote or endnote with a number or a custom mark. Click the Symbol button to choose a symbol. When you click Insert, the footnote or endnote pane opens, as shown in Figure 7-16. You can then key the footnote or endnote in the pane.

After you create a footnote, a number or the custom mark you chose will appear in the document. The corresponding footnote will print at the end of the page, or the endnote will print at the end of the document. You delete a footnote or an endnote by selecting the footnote number or symbol in the text and pressing Delete. The remaining footnotes/endnotes, if any, will be renumbered automatically.

Hot Tip

You can view footnotes you have created by choosing **Footnotes** on the **View** menu or by hovering the mouse pointer over the number or custom mark.

FIGURE 7-16
Footnote pane

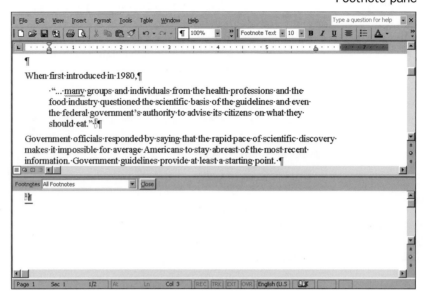

STEP-BY-STEP 7.8

1. Switch to **Normal** view. Place the insertion point after the quotation mark in the second paragraph under the heading *Federal Dietary Guidelines*.

2. Choose **Reference** on the **Insert** menu and **Footnote** on the submenu. The Footnote and Endnote dialog box appears.

3. Click **Insert** to accept the default options. The Footnote pane appears at the bottom of the document window with the insertion point blinking after the number 1.

4. Key "**Dietary Guidelines for Americans: Nononsense Advice for Healthy Eating,**" *FDA Consumer,* **November 1985, p. 14.** (Key the period.) The footnote may be shown in a different font; you will change it later.

5. Click **Close** in the Footnote pane.

6. Place the insertion point after the quotation mark in the last paragraph of the document.

7. Choose **Reference** on the **Insert** menu and **Footnote** on the submenu. Click **Insert**. The number 2 appears in the Footnote pane.

8. Key **U.S. Department of Agriculture and U.S. Department of Health and Human Services,** *Dietary Guidelines for Americans, 2000,* **5th edition, 2000, p. 30.** (Key the period.)

9. Select all text in the footnote pane. Change the font to Courier New, 9 point.

10. Click **Close** on the Footnote pane.

11. Switch to **Print Layout** view, and scroll to see the footnote at the bottom of each page.

12. Save, print, and close the document.

Computer Concepts

In Print Layout view, you can key a footnote directly at the bottom of a page without using the Footnote pane.

Creating a Section with Formatting That Differs from Other Sections

In Word, the default is the same page layout for an entire document. You can divide a document into two or more sections. A *section* is a part of a document where you can create a different layout from the rest of the document. For example, you might want to format only part of a page with columns. You can also have different headers and footers, page numbers, margins, print orientation, and other formatting features from section to section.

To create a new section, choose Break on the Insert menu. The Break dialog box appears, as shown in Figure 7-17. To start the new section on the next page, choose Next page. To start the new section on the same page, choose Continuous. To start the new section break on the next even-numbered or odd-numbered page, choose Even page or Odd page.

In Normal view, a section break is shown by a double dotted line across the page with the words *Section Break* in the middle, as shown in Figure 7-18. To delete section breaks, place the insertion point on the section break line and press Delete.

FIGURE 7-17
Break dialog box

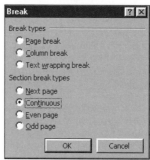

FIGURE 7-18
Section break

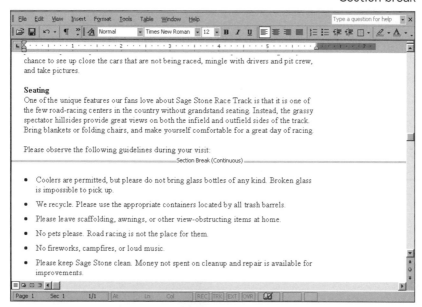

STEP-BY-STEP ▷ 7.9

1. Open **IW Step7-9** from your data files. Save the document as **Sage Stone** followed by your initials.

2. Switch to **Normal** view if necessary, and place the insertion point on the blank line before the bulleted list.

3. Choose **Break** on the **Insert** menu. The Break dialog box appears.

4. Click **Continuous** in the Section break types box.

5. Click **OK**. A double dotted line with the words *Section Break (Continuous)* in the middle indicates that a continuous section break is inserted.

6. Select the bulleted list.

7. Choose **Columns** on the **Format** menu. The Columns dialog box appears.

8. Format the list into two columns with 0.3" of space between them.

9. Click **OK**. Word switches to Print Layout view.

10. Save your changes, and leave the document open for the next Step-by-Step.

Applying Styles

In Word, a *style* is a predefined set of formatting options that have been named and saved. Applying styles to text can save time and add consistency to a document. For example, one particular style could specify 10-point, Arial, bold, and single line spacing. By applying that style, you can format text in one step instead of several and be certain that all text with that style looks the same. To apply a style, select text and choose an existing style from the Style box on the Formatting toolbar. You can also click the Styles and Formatting button to open the Styles and Formatting task pane or choose Styles and Formatting on the Format menu. The Styles and Formatting task pane appears, as shown in Figure 7-19, where you can see a preview and a description of each style.

FIGURE 7-19
Styles and Formatting task pane

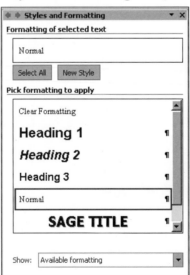

inward or outward to change the size of the table. To move a table manually, use the table move handle, also shown in Figure 7-22. To reposition a table in a document, hover the mouse pointer over the table move handle until it changes to a four-headed arrow. Click and drag the table to its new position.

Many of the commands on the Table menu are available on the Tables and Borders toolbar, shown in Figure 7-23. To display the toolbar, open the View menu, choose Toolbars, and then click Tables and Borders.

FIGURE 7-23
Tables and Borders toolbar

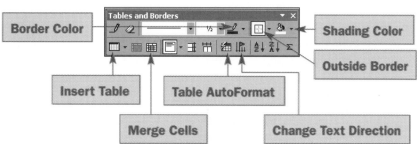

STEP-BY-STEP 7.12

1. Click to the left of *Precinct* (outside the table) to select the first row.

2. Click the **Center** button on the toolbar. All three of the headings are centered.

3. With the first row still selected, change the font size to 14 point, bold.

4. Position your pointer at the top of the Precinct column. When your pointer changes to a downward-pointing arrow, click to select the entire column.

5. Choose the **Center** button on the toolbar. The text in the entire column is centered.

6. With the first column still selected, choose **Insert** on the **Table** menu and **Columns to the Right** on the submenu. A new column is inserted to the right of the first column.

7. You decide you do not need this column after all. Click anywhere in the new column. Choose **Delete** on the **Table** menu and **Columns** on the submenu. The new column is deleted. Notice that the table structure also changes.

8. Drag the right border of the Precinct column to the left to reduce the column width. The column should be only slightly wider than the column heading.

9. Click to the left of the Precinct 4 row to select it.

10. Choose **Insert** on the **Table** menu and **Rows Below** on the submenu. A new row is inserted below the one you selected.

11. In the new row, key the following data:

    ```
    5, Lincoln Elementary School,
    900 Holly Avenue
    ```

12. Hover the mouse pointer over the table move handle until it changes to a four-headed arrow. Click and drag the table until it is centered.

13. Save your changes, and leave the document open for the next Step-by-Step.

Modifying Table Structure

You can make other modifications to the structure of a table using tools on the Tables and Borders toolbar. You can split cells to transform one column or row into two or more. You can merge cells to create one large cell out of several small cells. To split or merge cells, select the cells and click the Split Cells or Merge Cells button on the Tables and Borders toolbar.

The Table Properties dialog box, shown in Figure 7-24, gives you a number of other options for modifying a table. To open this dialog box, choose Table Properties on the Table menu. You can choose to wrap text around a table, change the cell and table alignment, and specify the height and width of columns and rows. To add interest to your table, you can rotate the text within a cell so the text reads vertically rather than horizontally. You can rotate text quickly by clicking the Change Text Direction button on the Tables and Borders toolbar or choosing Text Direction on the Format menu. In the Text Direction – Table Cell dialog box, shown in Figure 7-25, choose the orientation you want in the Orientation section and click OK.

FIGURE 7-24
Table Properties dialog box

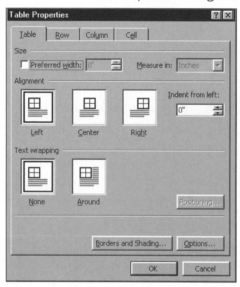

FIGURE 7-25
Text Direction – Table Cell dialog box

S TEP-BY-STEP ▷ 7.13

1. Choose **Toolbars** on the **View** menu, and then click **Tables and Borders** on the submenu.

2. Select the first row, and insert a row above it.

3. In the new first row, key **Cast Your Vote!**

4. Select the new first row, and click the **Merge Cells** button on the Tables and Borders toolbar. Center the text if necessary.

5. Select all the cells with numbers in them.

6. Choose **Text Direction** on the **Format** menu. The Text Direction - Table Cell dialog box appears.

7. In the Orientation box, choose the vertical text option on the left and click **OK**. The text changes to a vertical direction. The row heights also increase. Boldface the numbers.

8. Choose **Table Properties** on the **Table** menu. The Table Properties dialog box appears.

9. Click the **Row** tab.

10. In the Size section, key **0.35** in the Specify height box.

11. Click the **Table** tab.

12. In the Alignment section, click **Center**. Click **OK**.

13. Select all the data in the table (excluding headings).

14. Access the **Cell** tab of the Table Properties dialog box.

15. In the Vertical alignment section, choose **Center**. Click **OK**. The Table Properties dialog box closes.

16. Save your changes, and leave the document open for the next Step-by-Step.

Borders and Shading

You can change the borders and shading of one cell, one column or row, or the entire table. Select the Borders and Shading command on the Format menu, and then select a border or shading option.

STEP-BY-STEP 7.14

1. Select the table.

2. Choose **Borders and Shading** on the **Format** menu. Click the **Borders** tab if necessary.

3. Click the **All** button in the Setting section.

4. Click the down arrow on the **Color** box and choose **Red**. Click **OK**.

5. With the table still selected, click the arrow on the **Shading Color** button in the Tables and Borders toolbar and choose **Pale Blue** from the palette of colors. Click outside the table to deselect it.

6. Close the Tables and Borders toolbar. Save, print, and close the file.

Table AutoFormat

Word has many different predesigned formats that you can apply to your table. Place the insertion point in any cell in the table, and choose Table AutoFormat on the Table menu. The Table AutoFormat dialog box appears, as shown in Figure 7-26. You can also access the Table AutoFormat dialog box by clicking the Table AutoFormat button on the Tables and Borders toolbar.

FIGURE 7-26
Table AutoFormat dialog box

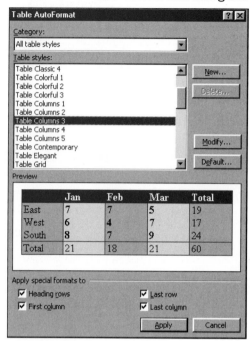

STEP-BY-STEP ▷ 7.15

1. Open **IW Step7-15** from the data files. Save the file as **Voting Memo2** followed by your initials.

2. Place the insertion point in the table.

3. Choose **Table AutoFormat** on the **Table** menu. The Table AutoFormat dialog box appears.

4. Choose **Table Contemporary** in the Table Style box. Click **Apply**.

5. Save, print, and close the file.

Organizing a Document in Outline View

Outlines are useful for creating a document with a hierarchical structure. To create an outline in Word, first switch to Outline view by clicking the Outline View button at the bottom left of the document window. When you do, the Outlining toolbar is displayed and an outline symbol appears so you can key a heading, as shown in Figure 7-27. A plus symbol (+) before a heading indicates that subheadings or body text are below the heading. A minus symbol (−) indicates that no subheadings or body text are below the heading.

FIGURE 7-27
Outlining toolbar

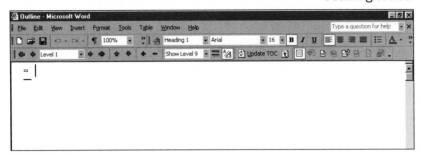

Creating an Outline

When you key the first heading and press Enter, Word formats the heading with the built-in heading style, Heading 1. The text formatting will not be visible while you are in Outline view. Word has nine built-in styles assigned for each different level of heading. As you key an outline, you can assign a heading to a different level. Click the Demote button on the Outlining toolbar to move a heading to the next lower level. Click the Promote button to move a heading to the next higher level. Click the Demote to Body Text button to style a heading as body text.

STEP-BY-STEP ⟹ 7.16

1. Create a new Word document, and switch to Outline view.

2. Key **Exercise** next to the minus symbol (-). The text is formatted as Heading 1.

3. Press **Enter**. Click the **Demote** button to move down a level, and key **Why Exercise?**

4. Press **Enter**. Press **Tab** to move down a level, and key **Feel better**.

5. Continue keying text as shown in Figure 7-28 using the Demote and Promote buttons to move up and down levels.

6. Save the document as **Exercise** followed by your initials. Leave the document open for the next Step-by-Step.

 Hot Tip

Pressing **Tab** will demote a heading to the next lower level, and pressing **Shift+Tab** will promote a heading to the next higher level.

FIGURE 7-28
Exercise outline

⬦ **Exercise**
   ⬦ *Why Exercise?*
      ⬦ Feel better
         ▫ **Increase energy**
         ▫ **Enhance self-esteem**
      ⬦ Look better
         ▫ **Lose weight**
         ▫ **Tone muscles**
      ⬦ Live longer
         ▫ **Lower cholesterol**
         ▫ **Lower high blood pressure**

Modifying an Outline

Once you have keyed an outline, you can easily modify it. Use the Up and Down buttons on the toolbar to move a heading to a different location. Or click the heading's outline symbol (+ or −), and drag it to a new location. When you move a heading that way, all the subordinate text underneath it moves too. Click the Expand or Collapse buttons to view only the headings you want and to make it easier to reorganize the outline. When you switch to a different view, outline indentations disappear but the style formatting for the headings is still visible.

STEP-BY-STEP ▷ *7.17*

1. Place the insertion point on the *Why Exercise?* heading, and click to select it. Then click the **Collapse** button to show only the headings.

2. Click the plus symbol (+) next to the *Look better* heading to select it.

3. Begin dragging the plus symbol up. As you do, a horizontal line appears. Drag until the line is between the headings *Why Exercise?* and *Feel better*. When you release the mouse button, the *Look better* heading is moved to the new location.

4. Place the insertion point on the *Why Exercise?* heading and click. Then click the **Expand** button. Notice that all the text underneath the *Look better* heading moved along with it.

5. Place the insertion point on the text *Lower high blood pressure* and click.

6. Click the **Move Up** button. The text moves up.

7. Click the **Show Formatting** button on the Outlining toolbar to display the document formatting.

8. Save, print, and close the document.

Computer Concepts

The outline symbols on the screen in Outline view show you the document's structure. They will not appear when you print.

Assigning Outline Levels to Paragraphs

When you work in Outline view, the built-in heading styles change the appearance of your text. However, sometimes you may want to impose a hierarchical structure on your document without any visible formatting. You switch to Print Layout view and select the paragraph. Choose Paragraph on the Format menu and then the Indents and Spacing tab. In the General section, click the level you want in the Outline level box. To see the outline formatting, click Outline view.

Hot Tip

If you want to work in a document without the outline formatting but want to see the outline structure, split the window. In one pane, choose **Print Layout** view; in the other, **Outline** view. As you work in either pane, the view in the other is updated automatically.

STEP-BY-STEP 7.18

1. Open **IW Step7-18** from the data files. Save the document as **Harris Clarke** followed by your initials.

2. Switch to **Print Layout** view if necessary.

3. Select the title **Harris Clarke Securities Online Service**.

4. Choose **Paragraph** on the **Format** menu, and choose the **Indents and Spacing** tab if necessary.

5. In the Outline level box, choose **Level 1** if necessary. Click **OK**.

6. Follow the same procedure to make *Getting Online* and *Online Information* into Level 2 headings.

7. Make *Activate*, *Login*, *Accounts*, and *Markets* into Level 3 headings.

8. Switch to **Outline** view. Your document should look similar to Figure 7-29.

9. Save, print, and close the document.

FIGURE 7-29
Harris Clarke outline

Harris Clarke Securities Online Service
   Using our Internet service, you have a financial management tool at your fingertips. You can access your account activity, get real-time stock quotes, and take advantage of our extensive market research. You can also contact your personal financial consultant or any of our customer service representatives.
   Getting Online
      Activate
         To activate your service, visit our Web site at www.hconline.com 24 hours a day.
      Login
         You will be assigned a ten-character password. You can save this password on the login screen so that you do not have to enter it each time you log on.
   Online Information
      Accounts
         You can customize how you view your account activity. You can view single or multiple transactions, switch between accounts, sort information, and specify a time range.
      Markets
         Market data is available at any time. You can chart securities, get expanded quote information, and access special reports.

Summary

In this lesson, you learned:

■ Moving back and forth between documents is easily done by clicking a document's icon in the taskbar.

■ You can copy and paste text between documents just as you can within a document.

■ Word automatically inserts page breaks where they are necessary. You also can insert a page break manually by choosing Break on the Insert menu and choosing Page break.

■ Several commands that are useful for formatting and editing long documents are: the Split command, the Go To command, the Show/Hide command, and the Word Count command.

■ Headers and footers have their own formatting toolbar that appears when you choose the Header and Footer command. The Header and Footer toolbar contains formatting buttons you can use to insert the date, the time, and page numbers.

■ A footnote or an endnote is used to document quotations, figures, or summaries or to provide other text that you do not want to include in the body of a document. Footnotes are printed at the bottom of each page, and endnotes are printed at the end of the document.

■ To create different page layouts within one document, divide the document into sections.

■ Styles are predefined sets of formatting options that add consistency to a document.

■ Tables are used to show data in columns and rows. They are usually easier to use than trying to align text with tabs. You can change the format of tables to best display your data.

■ Outlines are useful for creating a document with a hierarchical structure. You can work in Outline view and see the visible formatting or assign outline levels to paragraphs, which does not change the appearance of the document.

VOCABULARY REVIEW

Define the following terms:

Endnote	Header	Section
Footer	Page break	Style
Footnote	Pane	Table

LESSON 7 REVIEW QUESTIONS

MULTIPLE CHOICE

Select the best response for the following statements.

1. What command do you use to skip to a specific part of a document?
   A. Find
   B. Move To
   C. Go To
   D. Skip To

2. Using the Show/Hide ¶ command, you can view hidden
   A. buttons.
   B. formatting characters.
   C. window panes.
   D. bullets.

3. Which menu lists open documents?
   A. Window
   B. View
   C. Tools
   D. File

4. To create a table
   A. choose Table on the Insert menu.
   B. choose AutoFormat on the Format menu.
   C. choose Table Layout on the View menu.
   D. choose Insert on the Table menu.

5. In Outline view, which button moves a heading to a higher level?
   A. Plus
   B. Expand
   C. Promote
   D. Tab

FILL IN THE BLANK

Complete the following sentences by writing the correct word or words in the blanks provided.

1. When you open a new document, a button corresponding to the document is displayed on the _____.

2. The button for inserting a date in a header is found on the _____ toolbar.

3. To count words in a document, choose the Word Count command on the _____ menu.

4. To reposition a table manually in a document, use the _____.

5. A(n) _____ before a heading in Outline view indicates that subheadings or body text are below the heading.

LESSON 7 PROJECTS

PROJECT 7-1

1. Open **IW Project7-1** from the data files. Save the document as **Guidelines Final** followed by your initials.

2. Insert a manual page break before the *Check Spelling* heading.

3. Create a continuous section break, and format the list of words into two columns.

4. Open **IW Project7-1a** from the data files.

5. Select all the text and copy it.

6. Switch to the **Guidelines Final** document, and paste the text below the first paragraph under the *Be Consistent* heading.

7. Insert the page number right-aligned in a footer. In the Page Numbers dialog box, click the **Format** button. Specify that page numbers start with 1.

8. On the Layout tab of the Page Setup dialog box, key **.75** in the Footer box.

9. Save, print, and close the document. Close the **IW Project7-1a** document.

PROJECT 7-2

1. Open **IW Project7-2** from the data files. Save the document as **Porch Lights2** followed by your initials.

2. Create a header with the current date right-aligned.

3. Place the insertion point after the first sentence in #4. Create the following numbered footnote: **Call for more information on our Web hosting offer**.

4. Apply the Heading 2 style to the phrase *Constantly available information.*

5. Apply the Heading 2 style to the phrase that follows each number in the rest of the document.

6. Save, print, and close the document.

PROJECT 7-3

1. Open **IW Project7-3** from the data files. Save the document as **Sage Stone2** followed by your initials.

2. Insert a table with two columns and three rows below the bulleted items.

3. Key the data as shown in Figure 7-30.

4. Insert a new row below the first row in the table.

5. Key **Flag Day** in the first column and **Vintage Car Trade Show** in the second column.

6. Center the text in both columns.

7. Insert a new first row, key **Holiday Schedule**, and change the font size to 16.

8. Merge the cells in the first row, and center the title.

9. Choose **Table List 7** from the Table AutoFormat dialog box.

10. Save, print, and close the document.

FIGURE 7-30
Schedule

Memorial Day	Stock Classic Starter
Fourth of July	Sage Stone 500
Labor Day	Rip Cowen Stock Championship

PROJECT 7-4

1. In Outline view, create the outline shown in Figure 7-31.

2. Place the insertion point on **Recycling**, and collapse the outline.

3. Move the *Save landfill space* heading above the *Conserve natural resources* heading.

4. Expand the outline.

5. Move up the text *Oil kills freshwater organisms that fish eat.*

6. Save the document as **Recycle** followed by your initials.

7. Print and close the document.

FIGURE 7-31
Recycling outline

◊ **Recycling**
   ◊ *Conserve natural resources*
      ▫ Recycling paper products saves trees.
      ▫ Recycling aluminum saves energy that would be used
        to make new aluminum.
   ◊ *Save landfill space*
      ▫ Landfill space is becoming scarce.
      ▫ Recycled items do not take up space in landfills.
   ◊ *Avoid pollution*
      ▫ Oil dumped down sewers contaminates water.
      ▫ Oil kills freshwater organisms that fish eat.
      ▫ Litter is ugly and can be hazardous.

CRITICAL THINKING

ACTIVITY 7-1

You want to delete a footnote from a document. Then you decide to convert all the footnotes in a document to endnotes. Use the Help system to assist you.

ACTIVITY 7-2

You work for Alan's Tree & Garden Center, a retail nursery and tree farm that specializes in drought-tolerant plants. Since many customers are not sure what they should purchase when landscaping their yards, you mention to the manager that customers would appreciate having a brochure available with some basic information. He suggests that you create an outline of what should be included. Use Word to create an outline for a brochure that includes information about the business and the products and services offered, as well as information about trees, plants, shrubs, and soil.

ACTIVITY 7-3

Open **IW Activity7-3** from the data files. Use the document to create an outline of the material. Save the document as **Proofreading Outline**; then print and close the file.

INCREASING EFFICIENCY USING WORD

Using Templates and Wizards

Suppose you are a sales representative, and you must file a report each week that summarizes your sales and the new contacts you have made. Parts of this report will be the same each week, such as the format and the headings. Re-creating the document each week would be very time-consuming. Word solves this problem by allowing you to create a template or use an existing Word template for documents that you use frequently. A *template* is a file that already contains the basic elements of a document (such as page and paragraph formatting, fonts, and text) that you can customize to create a new document similar to but slightly different from the original. A report template would save all formatting, font choices, and text that do not change, allowing you to fill in only the new information each week.

Opening an Existing Template

Word contains many templates you can use to create documents. To open an existing Word template, choose New on the File menu. The New Document task pane opens, as shown in Figure 8-1. Click General Templates in the New from template section. The Templates dialog box opens. The Templates dialog box contains a number of tabs for document types, shown in Figure 8-2. Each tab contains several templates for that document type. You can use a template as is or modify it and save it as a new template.

FIGURE 8-1

New Document task pane

FIGURE 8-2

Templates dialog box

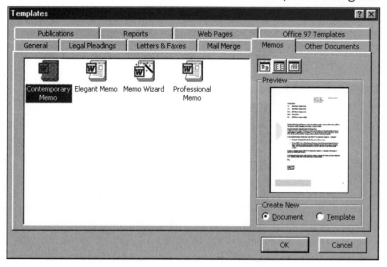

To open a template, click its icon and click OK. Word opens a new blank document with the settings and text specified by the template already in place. Replace the data in the template with your own data and save.

To open a template and modify it, click the template icon, click the Template option button in the Create New box, and click OK. After you have finished modifying the template, save it again with the same name or a new name.

STEP-BY-STEP ▷ 8.1

1. Choose **New** on the **File** menu.

2. Click **General Templates** in the New from template section in the New Documents task pane.

3. Click the **Memos** tab. Click **Contemporary Memo** to select it.

4. In the Create New box, choose **Document** if necessary.

5. Click **OK**. The Contemporary Memo template appears on your screen.

6. Switch to **Normal** view.

7. Click **[Click here and type name]** beside *To*, and key **Wyatt Brown, Marketing Assistant**.

8. Click **[Click here and type name]** beside *CC*, and key **Angela Holder, Bank Manager**.

9. Click **[Click here and type name]** beside *From*, and key **Joe Melton, Marketing Director**.

10. Click **[Click here and type subject]** beside *Re*, and key **New Account Campaign: Your First Checking Account**.

11. Select the text in the body of the memo and delete it. Key the following:

    ```
    Please have the first draft of the
    checking account pamphlet ready
    by Friday. I would like to pre-
    sent the final version at the
    directors' meeting next month.
    ```

12. Save the file as **Bank Memo** followed by your initials.

13. Print and close the document.

Creating a Template

As stated previously, you can create a template by modifying an existing one, or you can create a template from your own document. To create a template using a new blank document, open the Template dialog box. On the General tab, click Blank Document. Click the Template option in the Create New box and click OK. To create a template from an existing document, open the document and choose Save As on the File menu. In the Save As dialog box, key a filename and choose Document Template in the Save as type box. Your document will be saved as a template in the Templates folder of the Office folder on the hard drive. If you save a template somewhere other than this default location, it will not appear in the Templates dialog box when you want to use it.

STEP-BY-STEP ▷ 8.2

1. Choose **New** on the **File** menu. Click **General Templates** under New from template.

2. Click the **General** tab, and click the **Blank Document** icon to select it.

3. Click the **Template** option in the Create New box. Click **OK**. A blank document titled *Template1* appears on your screen.

4. Choose a font, and key the text from Figure 8-3. Center the text.

5. Place your insertion point to the left of the first line in the heading.

6. Choose **Picture** on the **Insert** menu. Click **Clip Art** on the submenu. The Insert Clip Art task pane appears. (If the Add Clips to Organizer dialog box appears, click **Later** to close it.)

7. In the Search text box, enter keys and click **Search**.

8. Click to insert one of the images of keys that is available.

9. Close the Insert Clip Art task pane.

10. Click on the image to select it. The Picture toolbar appears. Click the **Format Picture** button on the Picture toolbar. The Format Picture dialog box appears.

11. Click the **Size** tab if necessary. Scale the image to 40% so it will be the appropriate size for use in a letterhead. Click **OK**.

12. Change the top margin to 0.5 inches, the left and right margins to 1.75 inches, and the bottom margin to 1 inch.

13. When you finish creating the letterhead, move the insertion point below the letterhead.

14. Choose **Save As** on the **File** menu.

15. In the File name box, enter **Keys Template** followed by your initials; then click **Save**.

16. Close the file.

Hot Tip

If the Picture toolbar does not appear when you select an image, choose **Toolbars** on the **View** menu and **Picture** on the submenu.

FIGURE 8-3
Letterhead template

Keys Catering Service
309 Third Street
Churchville, NY 14428
Phone: 716-555-7534 Fax: 716-555-7536

Creating a Document Using a Template

You can use the template you created as many times as needed. To use a template, choose New on the File menu. In the New Document task pane, click General Templates in the New from template section. In the Templates dialog box, click the General tab; then click the template's icon, and click OK to bring up a copy of your template titled Document1. (Yours might be Document2 or Document3 depending on how many new documents you have created.) After you make changes to this document, choose Save As to save it to your data disk as a regular Word document with the .doc extension.

Computer Concepts

Word saves regular word processing documents with the *.doc* extension and saves template files with the *.dot* extension.

1. Choose **New** on the **File** menu. Click **General Templates** under New from template.

2. Click the **General** tab.

3. Click **Keys Template** to select it. Click **Document** in the Create new box if necessary. Click **OK**. A copy of the template opens, named **Document1**.

4. Save the document as **Keys Letter** followed by your initials.

5. Insert five blank lines below the letterhead, and key the letter shown in Figure 8-4 in Arial, 12 point.

6. Preview the document.

7. Save, print, and close the document.

8. Delete your template from the hard drive of your computer:
   a. Choose **New** on the **File** menu.
   b. Locate the **Keys Template** file.
   c. Right-click the **Keys Template** file.
   d. Click **Delete** on the shortcut menu.
   e. Click **Yes** in the Confirm File Delete dialog box. The template file is deleted. Close the Templates dialog box.

FIGURE 8-4
Text for Step-by-Step 8.3

March 6, 2003

Ms. Claire Denver
9007 Landridge Boulevard
White Plains, NY 10602-9007

Dear Ms. Denver:

Thank you for your request for more information about Keys Catering Service. I understand you are planning a reception for your son's engagement.

I have enclosed a brochure that describes our catering services. If you have any questions, please call me.

Sincerely,

Chris Keys
Owner

Enclosure

Using Wizards

A *wizard* is similar to a template, but it asks you questions and creates a document based on your answers. The word processing wizards available to you include memos, letters, faxes, reports, and Web pages. To start a wizard, choose New on the File menu. In the New Document task pane, click General Templates. In the Templates dialog box, click one of the tabs, click a document wizard, and click OK. A wizard dialog box opens, as shown in Figure 8-5. The Preview box shows a sample of what your document will look like. The wizard will begin by asking you a question or asking you to key information. Sometimes you will choose between two or more alternatives. When you click on a choice, an example is shown in the dialog box. Click Next to go to the next step. Click Back to go to the previous step. Click Finish at the end, and the wizard will create the document for you. Once you have created the document, you can add and modify text in your document.

FIGURE 8-5
Wizard dialog box

STEP-BY-STEP 8.4

1. Choose **New** on the **File** menu. Click **General Templates** under New from template.

2. Click the **Letters & Faxes** tab; then click the **Fax Wizard** icon to select it. Click **OK**. The Fax Wizard dialog box appears. Click **Next**.

3. Click the **Just a cover sheet with a note** option if necessary. Click **Next**.

4. Click **I want to print my document so I can send it from a separate fax machine** if necessary. Click **Next**.

5. In the Name box, key **Mr. Griffin Moss**.

6. In the Fax Number box, key **606-555-9163**. Click **Next**.

7. Choose the **Elegant** style. Click **Next**.

8. In the Name box, key **Isabelle Rose**.

9. In the Company box, key **Rose Investments**.

10. In the Mailing Address box, key the following:
    2016 Durham Street
    Dallas, TX 75295-2016

11. In the Phone box, key **214-555-3447**.

12. In the Fax box, key **214-555-8822**. Click **Next**.

13. Click **Finish**. The Wizard creates the document.

14. On the Company line, delete **[Click here and type company name]**.

15. On the Total No. of Pages Including Cover line, click **[Click here and type number of pages]** and key **2**.

16. On the Phone Number line, click **[Click here and type phone number]** and key **606-555-2382**.

17. On the Sender's Reference Number and Your Reference Number lines, delete **[Click here and type reference number]**.

18. On the Re: line, click and key **Investments**.

19. Double-click the **For Review** box.

20. Under Notes/Comments, click **[Click here and type any comments]** and key the following:

    Please consider the following
    investments. I will call you next
    week to discuss them.

21. Save the file as **Fax Cover Sheet** followed by your initials.

22. Print and close the document.

Extra Challenge

Use the Fax Wizard to create a personal fax cover sheet for yourself or for your school.

Workgroup Collaboration

The process of working together in teams, sharing comments, and exchanging ideas for a common purpose is called workgroup collaboration. When you work in groups, the different tasks are often divided among the team members. The team then meets to review each other's work, comment on it, and suggest changes. Word has several ways team members can collaborate.

Inserting and Viewing Comments

Word allows members to review documents without having to meet face-to-face. Comments can be made directly in the document on the computer.

To insert a comment, either position the pointer in the text where you wish to comment or select a word or words; then choose Comment on the Insert menu. If you are in Print Layout or Web Layout view, a text box will appear in the right margin where you can key your comments. The text box, or comment balloon, is connected to the text by a dashed line; the selected text is enclosed with brackets, as shown in Figure 8-6.

You can also click the New Comment button on the Reviewing toolbar. Choose Toolbar on the View menu; then choose Reviewing, as shown in Figure 8-7.

FIGURE 8-6
Comment balloon

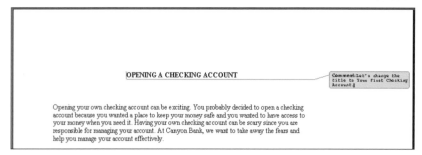

FIGURE 8-7
Reviewing toolbar

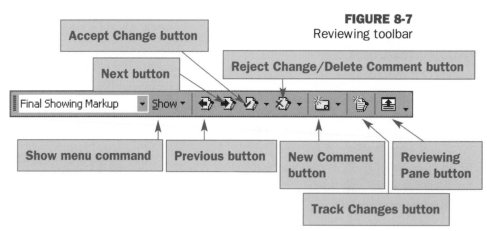

STEP-BY-STEP ▷ 8.5

C

1. Open **IW Step8-5** from the data files. Save it as **Checking Account** followed by your initials.

2. Switch to **Print Layout** view if necessary. Select the title.

3. Choose **Comment** on the **Insert** menu. In the comment balloon, key **Let's change the title to Your First Checking Account.**

4. In the first paragraph, select the sentence beginning with *Having your own checking account*.

5. Choose **Toolbars** on the **View** menu; then choose **Reviewing** if necessary. The Reviewing toolbar is displayed.

6. Click the **New Comment** button.

7. In the comment balloon, key **Change sentence to Owning your own checking account is a big responsibility.** (Key the period.)

8. In the first sentence of the second paragraph, select the word **teller**.

9. Click the **New Comment** button. In the comment balloon, key **Should be New Accounts Representative.** (Key the period.)

10. Select **$150** in the first sentence of the second paragraph.

11. Click the **New Comment** button. In the comment balloon, key **Should be $125.** (Key the period.)

12. Save your changes, and leave the document open for the next Step-by-Step.

Editing Comments

After you have inserted your comments into a document, you can go back and make changes to them. To move from comment to comment, click the Next button or Previous button on the Reviewing toolbar. To edit your comments, click inside the comment balloon and make your changes.

Another way to view and edit comments is to display the Reviewing pane, as shown in Figure 8-8. To show the Reviewing pane, click the Reviewing pane button on the Reviewing toolbar. To modify a comment in the Reviewing pane, click anywhere in the text of the comment and make the desired changes. When you are finished with your changes, click the Reviewing pane button again to close it.

FIGURE 8-8
Reviewing pane

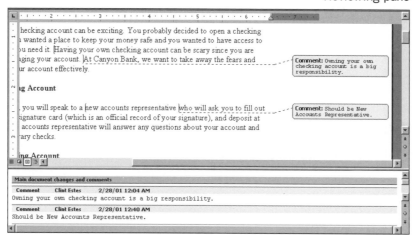

S TEP-BY-STEP ⟹ 8.6

1. With the document in Print Layout view and the Reviewing toolbar displayed, click to select the first comment balloon.

2. Position the insertion point at the end of the sentence. Key **Check with Robert to see if he wants to use this title in the pamphlet.**

3. Click the **Next** button on the Reviewing toolbar.

4. In the comment balloon, replace the words *your own* with **a**. The sentence should now begin *Change sentence to Owning a checking account.*

5. Click the **Next** button twice.

6. Click the **Reviewing pane** button on the Reviewing toolbar.

7. Scroll to the fourth comment in the Reviewing pane. Change $125 to **$100**. Note that the number also changes in the comment balloon.

8. Click the **Reviewing pane** button to close the Reviewing pane.

9. Hover the pointer over the comment balloon. A ScreenTip appears indicating who made the comment and when the comment was inserted.

10. Save, print, and leave the document open for the next Step-by-Step.

Hot Tip

In Normal view, only the Reviewing pane is displayed. The comment balloons are hidden.

Using Track Changes

Once a document is returned to you with a reviewer's comments and proposed changes, you have an opportunity to either accept or reject the changes and to add additional comments. Word provides a tool called *Track Changes* that keeps a record of any changes you or a reviewer makes in a document.

To activate the Track Changes feature, you can choose Track Changes on the Tools menu or you can click the Track Changes button on the Reviewing toolbar. Another way to activate Track Changes is to double-click TRK on the status bar. When Track Changes is activated, TRK will be shown in black.

In addition to comment balloons, which have already been discussed, Word also inserts revision marks and changed line marks directly into the text to indicate where a change has occurred.

Revision marks show text that has been added to or deleted from a document. Added text is indicated by underlines and a different color of text. Deleted text is indicated by strikethroughs and a different color of text. By default, revision marks are different colors for each reviewer. Changed line marks are vertical lines that appear in the left margin next to lines where the text was modified.

Hot Tip

To print a document with the comments and changes, open the Print dialog box from the File menu. In the Print what box, select **Print document showing markups** from the drop-down list.

TRK

S TEP-BY-STEP ⇒ 8.7

1. Display the Reviewing toolbar if necessary. Click the **Track Changes** button on the Reviewing toolbar to activate it.

2. Select **32 Holly Lane** in the address at the bottom of the page, and delete the line of text. A new comment balloon is created in the right margin showing the deleted text. A changed line mark also appears in the left margin.

3. Insert a blank line after the address, and key the following: **If you would like to learn more about other services available, contact the Customer Service Department at 909-555-BANK.** Note that the new text is underlined and shown in a different color.

4. Click to select the fourth balloon, which contains the text *Should be $100.* Click the **Reject Change/Delete Comment** button. The comment is deleted from the document.

5. Click the balloon containing the text *Deleted: 32 Holly Lane*. Click the **Accept Change** button.

6. Place your insertion point on the last sentence in the document. Click the **Accept Change** button. Note that the text changes to black.

7. Make all the changes suggested in the comment balloons.

8. Click the down arrow on the **Accept Change** button, and click **Accept All Changes in Document**.

9. Click the down arrow on the **Reject Change/Delete Comment** button, and click **Delete All Comments in Document**. The document should have no editing comments displayed.

10. Save the document as **Checking Account2** followed by your initials. Print and close the document.

Using Compare and Merge Documents

Compare and Merge is a useful way to view differences between documents. Suppose you send your document to several colleagues for review. They return their copies with changes and suggested revisions. Using the Compare and Merge feature, you can merge their comments and changes into one document for easy review.

To compare and merge documents, open an edited version of your document. Next, choose Compare and Merge Documents on the Tools menu. The Compare and Merge Documents dialog box appears, as shown in Figure 8-9. Select the original file you want to compare the edits to. To display the merge results in the original document, click Merge. To display the results in the current edited document, click Merge; then click Merge into current document. To display the results in a new document, click Merge; then click Merge into new document.

FIGURE 8-9
Compare and Merge Documents dialog box

C

1. Open **IW Step8-5** from the data files.

2. Choose **Compare and Merge Documents** on the **Tools** menu. The Compare and Merge Document window opens.

3. Click the down arrow on the **Look in** box. Locate and click **Checking Account2**.

4. Click the down arrow on the **Merge** button. Click **Merge into new document**. The results of the comparison are displayed in a new document.

5. Save as **Checking Account Merge** followed by your initials.

6. Print and close the document.

7. Close **IW Step8-5**.

Creating and Printing Envelopes

C

Addressing envelopes is easy using Word. Choose Letters and Mailings on the Tools menu and Envelopes and Labels on the submenu to display the Envelopes and Labels dialog box. On the Envelopes tab, shown in Figure 8-10, key the delivery address and return address. To change the envelope size or the font, choose Options to display the Envelope Options dialog box, shown in Figure 8-11.

FIGURE 8-10
Envelopes tab in Envelopes and Labels dialog box

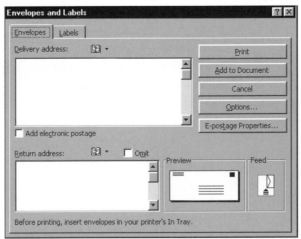

FIGURE 8-11

Envelope Options dialog box

STEP-BY-STEP ▷ 8.9

1. Create a new Word document.

2. Click **Letters and Mailings** on the Tools menu and **Envelopes and Labels** on the submenu. The Envelopes and Labels dialog box appears.

3. Click the **Envelopes** tab if necessary.

4. In the Delivery address box, key the following:

   Stephan Stordahl
   33 Wafarer Road
   Bozeman, MT 59715

5. In the Return address box, key your name and address.

6. Click the **Options** button. Click the **Envelopes Options** tab if necessary.

7. In the Delivery address box, click **Font** to display the Envelope Address dialog box.

8. Change the font to Comic Sans MS or another appropriate font and click **OK**. Click **OK** again to return to the Envelopes and Labels dialog box.

9. In the Envelopes and Labels dialog box, click **Print**. (Print the envelope on plain paper if desired.)

10. When a message appears asking if you want to save the new return address as the default return address, click **No**. Leave the blank Word document open for the next Step-by-Step.

Creating and Printing Labels

Creating labels is similar to creating envelopes. Click the Labels tab in the Envelopes and Labels dialog box, as shown in Figure 8-12. Key the address you want to appear on the labels. You can choose to print a full page of the same label or just one label. To choose a label type other than the one shown in the Label section, click the Options button to display the Label Options dialog box, shown in Figure 8-13.

FIGURE 8-12
Labels tab

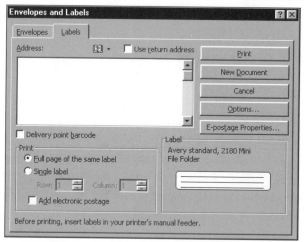

FIGURE 8-13
Label Options dialog box

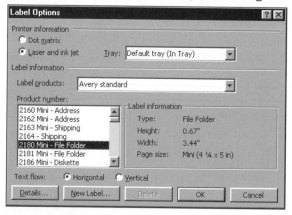

STEP-BY-STEP 8.10

1. Choose **Letters and Mailings** on the **Tools** menu and **Envelopes and Labels** on the submenu. The Envelopes and Labels dialog box appears.

2. Click the **Labels** tab.

3. In the Address box, key the following:

   ```
   Andrea Swan
   4040 Belmont Lane
   Chicago, IL 60646
   ```

4. Click the **Options** button to display the Label Options dialog box.

5. In the Product number box, scroll to choose **5160 - Address**. Click **OK**.

6. In the Envelopes and Labels dialog box, click **Print**. (Print the labels on plain paper.)

7. Close the document without saving.

Using Mail Merge

Mail merge is combining a document with information that personalizes it. For example, you might send a letter to each member of a professional organization. In each letter, the text is the same but the names of the recipients are different. A letter may begin *Dear Mr. Bradford* or *Dear Ms. Jansen*. The document with the information that does not change is called the ***main document***. The ***data source*** is the file containing the information that will vary in each document.

The Mail Merge Wizard will guide you through the mail merge process. Choose Letters and Mailings on the Tools menu and Mail Merge Wizard on the submenu. The Mail Merge task pane appears, as shown in Figure 8-14. Follow the directions in the Wizard to create the mail merge.

FIGURE 8-14
Mail Merge task pane

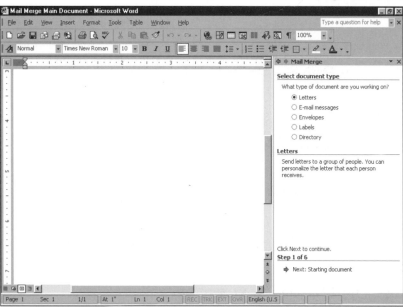

1. Open **IW Step8-11** from the data file. Save the document as **Keys Mail Merge** followed by your initials.

2. Choose **Letters and Mailings** on the **Tools** menu and **Mail Merge Wizard** on the submenu.

3. In the Mail Merge task pane under Select document type, click **Letters** if necessary.

4. Click **Next: Starting document**.

5. In the Select starting document box, click **Use the current document** if it is not already selected. Click **Next: Select recipients**.

6. Under Select recipients, click **Type a new list**.

7. Under Type a new list, click **Create**. The New Address List dialog box appears, as shown in Figure 8-15.

8. Key the following information in the New Address List dialog box:

```
Mr. Rudy Gardner
Ransom Resources, Inc.
613 Old Mill Road
Lynchburg, VA 24505
```

```
Ms. Diane Coffee
J & B Enterprises
925 Albany
Falls Church, VA 22046
```

```
Ms. Vivian Ogdon
Parkhill/Smith Consulting
3298 Jefferson Avenue
Virginia Beach, VA 23458
```

9. Click the **New Entry** button after keying the information for each contact. When you finish keying, click **Close**. The Save Address List dialog box appears.

10. Save the information you keyed as **Keys Contacts** followed by your initials. The Mail Merge Recipients list box appears.

11. Click the **Select All** button to place a check mark beside each name. Click **OK**.

12. Click **Next: Write your letter** in the Mail merge box. Place the insertion point where you want the recipient's name and address to appear in the document.

13. In the Mail Merge box under Write your letter, click **Address block**. The Insert Address Block dialog box appears.

14. Specify the address elements you want to appear in your letter. Click **OK**. The address block merge field is inserted into your document.

15. Insert two blank lines after the address block in your letter.

16. In the Mail merge task pane under Write your letter, click **Greeting line**. The Greeting Line dialog box appears.

17. Specify the greeting line format you want in your letter. Click **OK**. The greeting line merge field is inserted into your letter.

18. Click **Next: Preview your letters**.

19. In the Mail merge task pane under Preview your letters, click the arrows to preview your letters. Click **Next: Complete the merge**.

20. Click **Print** under Merge. The Merge to Printer dialog box appears.

21. Click the **Current record** option. Click **OK**.

22. The Print dialog box appears. Click **OK**. Your letter is printed.

23. Save and close the document.

FIGURE 8-15
New Address List dialog box

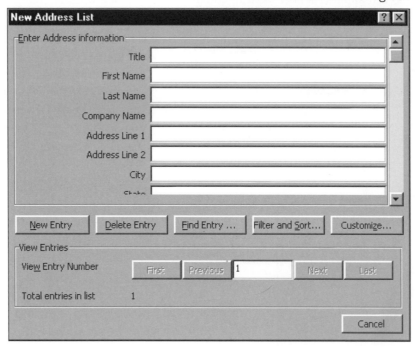

Creating a Web Page

A **Web page** is a document created with the programming language HTML (Hypertext Markup Language), which can be viewed by a Web browser, such as Internet Explorer. A Web browser is a program that translates HTML into the text, graphics, audio, and video you see displayed on your screen.

You can convert Word documents to Web pages without having to learn HTML. When you choose Save as Web Page on the File menu, Word converts your document to HTML format and supplies HTML tags for most common document features, such as tables and fonts.

To see what your document looks like when viewed by a browser, switch to Web Layout view. To actually preview a document in your browser, choose Web Page Preview on the File menu. The browser opens and displays your document.

STEP-BY-STEP ▷ 8.12

1. Open **IW Step8-12** from the data files.

2. Choose **Save as Web Page** on the **File** menu.

3. In the File name box, key **Porch Lights Web Page** followed by your initials. In the Save as type box, select **Web Page** from the drop-down list if necessary. Click **Save**.

4. Remove the date in the header.

5. Change the numbered list to a bulleted list.

6. Save your changes, and leave the document open for the next Step-by-Step.

A good way to enhance a Web page is to add a theme and text animation. A theme is a preformatted design that you can apply to a document to change its appearance without changing the content. A theme changes the color scheme, font, and formatting of your document to provide a new look. Choose Theme on the Format menu to open the Theme dialog box, shown in Figure 8-16.

FIGURE 8-16
Theme dialog box

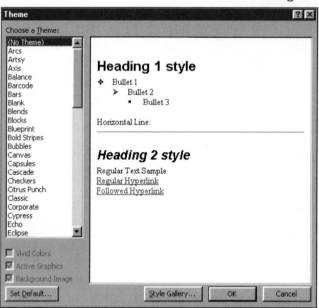

Text animation calls attention to a block of text by creating movement within or around the text. There are six animation effects, but only one effect can be applied at a time. To animate text, select the text, then choose Font on the Format menu. Click the Text Effects tab and choose an effect from the Animations box.

S TEP-BY-STEP ▷ 8.13

1. Choose **Theme** on the Format menu. The Theme dialog box appears.

2. In the Choose a Theme box, scroll down and choose **Cascade** or another appropiate theme. The preview box shows the design elements for that theme. Click **OK**. The Balance theme has been applied to your document.

3. Select the heading *Porch Lights Online*. Choose **Font** on the **Format** menu and click **Text Effects** tab.

4. Choose **Las Vegas Lights** in the Animations box. Click **OK**. The animation effect has been applied to the heading.

5. Choose **Web Page Preview** on the **File** menu. Your browser opens, and the document is displayed as a Web page, as shown in Figure 8-17. Click the **Maximize** button if necessary to view the Web page.

6. After viewing, close Web Page Preview.

7. Save, print, and close the document.

FIGURE 8-17
Web Page Preview

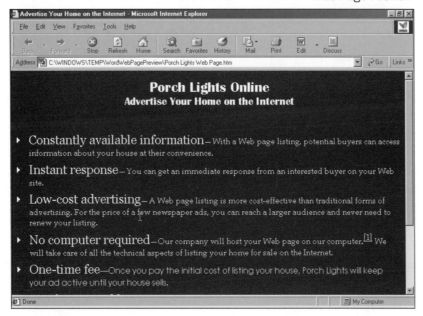

FIGURE 8-17
Web Page Preview

Using the Web Page Wizard

With the Web Page Wizard, you can create a single Web page or a whole Web site. A *Web site* is a collection of related Web pages connected by hyperlinks. *Hyperlinks* are the underlined and colored text you click on to go to a different location in your document or to an external location, such as a different Web page.

To start the Web Page Wizard, choose New on the File menu. In the New Document task pane, click General Templates under New from template. Click the Web Pages tab. Click the Web Page Wizard icon. If necessary, click to select Document under Create new; then click OK. The Web Page Wizard opens, as shown in Figure 8-18. Follow the directions in the wizard to create your own Web page.

FIGURE 8-18
Web Page Wizard

C

1. Choose **New** on the **File** menu. In the New Document task pane, click **General Templates** under New from template.

2. Click the **Web Pages** tab. Select the **Web Page Wizard** icon. Choose **Document** under Create New; then click **OK**.

3. The Web Page Wizard opens. Click **Next**.

4. In the Web site title box, key **Porch Lights Online Home Page** followed by your initials.

5. In the Web site location box, key the location indicated by your instructor. Click **Next**.

6. Click the **Vertical frame** option. Click **Next**.

7. In the Add Pages to Your Web site dialog box, select **Blank Page 1**. Click the **Remove Page** button. Click the **Remove Page** button again to delete **Blank Page 2**.

8. Click the **Add Existing File** button. The Open dialog box appears. Select **Porch Lights Web Page**, which you saved in the last Step-by-Step. Click **Open**. *Porch Lights Web Page* appears in the Current Pages in Web site box, indicating the document was added to your Web site. Click **Next**.

9. Select **Personal Web Page**. Click **Rename**. In the Rename Hyperlink dialog box, key **Porch Lights Online Home Page**, as shown in Figure 8-19. Click **OK**; then click **Next**.

10. Click **Add a Visual Theme** if necessary. Click **Browse Themes**. The Theme dialog box appears. Select a theme of your choice. Click **OK**; then click **Next**.

11. Click **Finish**. The Web Page Wizard automatically creates a Web site according to the instructions you gave. Your screen should appear similar to Figure 8-20.

12. If the Frames toolbar appears, close it.

13. Save the document as **Porch Lights Online Web Site** followed by your initials. Leave the document open for the next Step-by-Step.

Hot Tip

When you print your document, the background and text animation will not show up. They are designed to be viewed only on the screen.

FIGURE 8-19
Rename Hyperlink dialog box

FIGURE 8-20
Web site

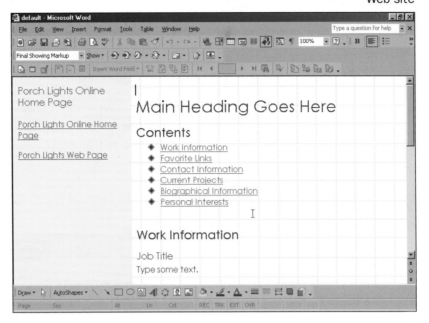

You now have the basic structure of your Web site in place, as shown in Figure 8-20. The left pane displays the contents of the Web site, while the right pane displays the body of the active Web page. What remains is for you to customize the Web page by replacing the existing text with your own. As with a template, you can delete text, add new text, and change text formatting to suit your needs.

STEP-BY-STEP ▷ 8.15

1. Select **Main Heading Goes Here**, and key **Porch Lights Online**.

2. Under Contents, delete **Work Information**, **Favorite Links, Biographical Information**, and **Personal Interests**.

3. Delete the headings *Work Information* and *Favorite Links* and their related text. The heading *Contact Information* should now be the first heading.

4. Delete *Biographical Information* and *Personal Interests* and their related text.

5. Insert a blank line under *Contact Information*, and key the following:

   ```
   Mike Garrett
   202 Deer Valley Drive
   Glendale, AZ 85306-5073
   ```

6. Select **Type some text** under *E-mail address*, and key **mgarrett@porchlight.com**.

7. Select **Type some text** under *Web address*, and key **www.porchlight.com**.

8. Select **Type some text** under *Office phone*, and key **800-555-6738**.

9. Under *Current Projects*, key the following addresses and prices:

```
210 Sunset Road ($79,950)
2112 70ᵗʰ Street ($149,500)
6306 York Place ($239,950)
```

10. Select **Date** after *Last revised,* and key today's date.

11. While holding down the **Ctrl** key, click the **Porch Lights Web Page** hyperlink to take you to the Porch Lights Web page.

12 While holding down the **Ctrl** key, click the **Porch Lights Online Home Page** hyperlink to return to the home page.

13. Choose **Web Page Preview** on the **File** menu to view your Web site in a Web browser. (You may need to click the **Maximize** button to view it.)

14. While in Web Page Preview, choose **Print** on the **File** menu. In the Print frames box, select **As laid out on screen**. Click **OK**. Close the Web browser.

15. Save your changes, and close the document.

Hot Tip

If the link is broken while keying (the blue text with a blue underline disappears), you can restore the hyperlink by selecting the text, and then choosing **Hyperlink** on the **Insert** menu. Click **OK**. The hyperlink should be restored.

Sending a Word Document via E-mail

You have two ways to send a document by e-mail with Word. You can e-mail a copy of a document directly from Word or e-mail a Word document as an attachment.

To send a document directly from Word, click the E-mail button on the Standard toolbar with the document open on your screen. An e-mail header appears where you fill in the recipient information. Then click the Send a Copy button. A copy of the document is e-mailed, but the original stays open so you can continue working on it.

To e-mail a document as an attachment, open or create a document and then choose Send To on the File menu. Choose Mail Recipient (as Attachment) on the submenu, enter the recipient information, and click Send.

Linking Data

As you have learned, Office is an integrated program. The word integration means combining parts into a whole. You can integrate data within a single application or among several applications. For example, in Word you can insert a hyperlink that connects two Word documents together. You can also copy a chart created in Excel to your Word document.

To insert a hyperlink into a document, select the text you want to make a hyperlink and choose Hyperlink on the Insert menu. The Insert Hyperlink dialog box appears, as shown in Figure 8-21. Choose whether you want to link to another document or to a Web page. Click OK and a hyperlink is inserted into the document. The text you selected is displayed in blue with a blue underline. Click it to go to the linked location.

FIGURE 8-21
Insert Hyperlink dialog box

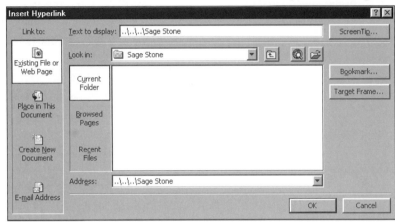

The *Paste Special* command allows you to connect data within Word or between Word and external sources, such as other Office programs. For example, you can copy a table from one document and choose Paste Special on the Edit menu to insert it into another document. In the Paste Special dialog box, shown in Figure 8-22, click Microsoft Word Document Object. When you choose the Paste link option, any changes you make to the original table file are updated in the document you pasted the table into.

FIGURE 8-22
Paste Special dialog box

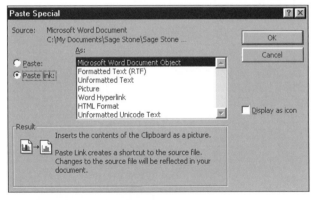

STEP-BY-STEP ▷ 8.16

1. Open **IW Step8-16** from the data files.

2. Save the document as **Sage Stone Link** followed by your initials.

3. In the second bulleted item, select the sentence **We recycle**.

4. Click **Hyperlink** on the **Insert** menu. The Insert Hyperlink dialog box appears.

5. Click the down arrow on the **Look in** box, and locate and click **IW Step8-16a** in the data files.

6. Click **OK**. The hyperlink is inserted into the document. The text you selected is blue with a blue underline.

7. While pressing **Ctrl**, click the hyperlink. The Recycling document opens.

8. Close the **Recycling** document.

9. Notice in the Sage Stone Link document that the hyperlink has changed color to indicate that it has been used. Save and minimize the document.

10. Open **IW Step8-16b** from the data files.

11. Save the file as **SS Table** followed by your initials.

12. Select the entire table and copy it.

13. Switch to the **Sage Stone Link** document.

14. Insert another blank line at the end of the document, and choose **Paste Special** on the **Edit** menu. The Paste Special dialog box appears.

15. Choose **Microsoft Word Document Object**, and click **Paste link**, as shown in Figure 8-22. Click **OK**. The table is pasted in the document.

16. Save the document.

17. Switch to the **SS Table** document. Move *Rip Cowan Stock Championship* so it is on Labor Day and *Stock Classic Starter* so it is on Memorial Day.

18. Save and close **SS Table**. Open **Sage Stone Link**. The changes you made in the table are reflected in the document.

19. Save, print, and close the document.

Summary

In this lesson, you learned:

- Templates allow you to save the format, font choices, and text of commonly produced documents. Wizards are similar to templates, but they ask you questions and create a document based on your answers.

- When working in a group, suggesting changes to a document is easily done by inserting comments.

- Changes made by each person can be identified and labeled by using the Track Changes feature.

- You can compare and merge various documents with comments and changes into one document for easy review.

- You can quickly create envelopes and labels by choosing the Letters and Mailings command on the Tools menu.

- Mail merge lets you insert changing information into a standard document.

- Choose Save as Web Page on the File menu to save a Word document as a Web page. Apply a theme to change the color scheme, font, and formatting.

- The Web Page Wizard helps you create a Web page or a Web site.

- You can insert a hyperlink into a Word document that links the document to another file or Web page.

- Paste Special allows you to move information from one document to another. Information changed in one document is automatically updated in the other.

VOCABULARY REVIEW

Define the following terms:

Data source

Hyperlink

Mail merge

Main document

Paste special

Template

Track changes

Web page

Web site

Wizard

LESSON 8 REVIEW QUESTIONS

WRITTEN QUESTIONS

Write a brief answer to the following questions.

1. How will using a template increase your efficiency?

2. What are three ways Word indicates that changes have been made in a document?

3. Under what circumstances would you use Mail Merge?

4. How do you insert a hyperlink into a document?

5. What are two ways to create a Web page?

TRUE/FALSE

Circle T if the statement is true or F if the statement is false.

T F 1. A template file can be used only once.

T F 2. The Compare and Merge feature allows you to merge two or more edited documents into one so the document can be reviewed easily.

T F 3. In a mail merge, the data source contains the information that stays the same.

T F 4. A theme links one document to another.

T F 5. You can change the size or font of an envelope in the Envelope Options dialog box.

LESSON 8 PROJECTS

PROJECT 8-1

1. Use the **Elegant Memo** template, and key the following:

    ```
    To: All Employees
    From: Jack Howard
    Subject: Job Shadow Day
    Date: [current date]
    CC: Norma Palmer, Twin Oaks High School
    ```

2. In the text part, key the following:

    ```
    Job Shadow Day

    Next Friday our company is participating in the Job Shadow program.
    Students from local high schools are given the opportunity to spend a day
    "shadowing" an employee at a participating business. If you are willing to
    be involved, please contact me by Monday.
    ```

3. Save the memo as **Job Shadows** followed by your initials.

4. Print and close the document.

PROJECT 8-2

1. Open **IW Project8-2** from the data files.

2. Save the document as **Journal Mail Merge** followed by your initials.

3. Create a mailing using mail merge and the following names and addresses:

    ```
    Mr. Ben Hodges
    Unisource Marketing, Inc.
    1908 Queens Street
    Los Angeles, CA 90025


    Mr. David Norris
    Pillar Shipping Company
    6421 Douglas Road
    Coral Gables, FL 33134
    ```

```
Ms. Charlotte Buckner

Accent Wireless

717 Pacific Parkway

Honolulu, HI 96813
```

4. Print one letter.

5. Create and print an envelope for Mr. Ben Hodges.

6. Save and close the documents.

PROJECT 8-3

1. Open **IW Project8-3** from the data files.

2. Save the document as a Web page named **Bank Web Page**.

3. Add a theme of your choice.

4. Select **other services available**, and create a link to **IW Project8-3a** in the data files.

5. Preview the Web page.

6. Save, print, and close the document.

CRITICAL THINKING

ACTIVITY 8-1

Your supervisor asks you to insert a graphic on an envelope and to attach the envelope to a document you are editing so she can print it later. Use the Help system to find out how to do as she has requested.

ACTIVITY 8-2

Use the Web Page Wizard to create a personal Web page about yourself. Include links to some of your favorite Web sites.

INTRODUCTORY MICROSOFT WORD

Introductory Microsoft Word

COMMAND SUMMARY

FEATURE	MENU COMMAND	TOOLBAR BUTTON	LESSON
Align Text	Format, Paragraph, Alignment	▤ ▤ ▤ ▤	5
AutoCorrect	Tools, AutoCorrect Options		3
AutoFormat As You Type	Tools, AutoCorrect Options, AutoFormat As You Type		3
AutoText	Insert, AutoText		3
Bold	Format, Font, Bold	**B**	4
Borders	Format, Borders and Shading	▦ ▾	6
Bullets	Format, Bullets and Numbering	▤	5
Case	Format, Change Case		4
Clip Art	Insert, Picture, Clip Art	▣	6
Close	File, Close	▣	1
Columns	Format, Columns	▤	6
Copy	Edit, Copy	▣	2
Copy Format and Style		◈	4
Create a New Document	File, New, Blank Document	▯	1
Cut	Edit, Cut	✂	2
Date and Time Insert	Insert, Date and Time		3
Delete Character	Backspace or Delete		2
Delete Page Break Line	Select page break line, Delete or Backspace		7
Drawing Graphics	View, Toolbars, Drawing	▨	6
E-mail	File, Send To	▣	8
Envelopes	Tools, Letters and Mailings, Envelopes and Labels	▤	8
Find	Edit, Find	▨	3
Font	Format, Font	Times New Roman ▾	4
Font Color	Format, Font	A ▾	4
Font Effects	Format, Font		4
Font Size	Format, Font	10 ▾	4

FEATURE	MENU COMMAND	TOOLBAR BUTTON	LESSON
Footnotes and Endnotes	Insert, Reference, Footnote		7
Go To	Edit, Go To		7
Grammar Check	Tools, Spelling and Grammar		3
Header and Footer	View, Header and Footer		7
Highlight			4
Hyperlink	Insert, Hyperlink		8
Indention	Format, Paragraph		5
Italic	Format, Font		4
Labels	Tools, Letters and Mailings, Envelopes and Labels		8
Line Spacing	Format, Paragraph		5
Mail Merge	Tools, Letters and Mailings, Mail Merge Wizard		8
Margins	File, Page Setup, Margins		5
Normal View	View, Normal		1
Numbering	Format, Bullets and Numbering		5
Open Existing Document	File, Open		1
Outline Numbered	Format, Bullets and Numbering		5
Outline View	View, Outline		1
Overtype		OVR	2
Page Breaks	Insert, Break		7
Page Numbers	Insert, Page Numbers or View, Header and Footer		7
Paste	Edit, Paste		2
Preview Document	File, Print Preview		1
Print Document	File, Print		1
Print Layout View	View, Print Layout		1
Redo	Edit, Redo		2
Remove Split Window	Window, Remove Split		7
Replace	Edit, Replace		3
Save	File, Save or Save As		1
Section Breaks	Insert, Break		7
Select Entire Document	Edit, Select All		4
Shading	Format, Borders and Shading		6
Show/Hide	Show/Hide	¶	7

FEATURE	MENU COMMAND	TOOLBAR BUTTON	LESSON
Sort	Table, Sort		5
Spell Check	Tools, Spelling and Grammar		3
Split a Window	Window, Split		7
Style	Format, Styles and Formatting	Normal	7
Table AutoFormat	Table, Table AutoFormat		7
Table Insert	Table, Insert, Table		7
Tabs	Format, Tabs		5
Text Box	Insert, Text Box		6
Theme for Web Page	Format, Theme		8
Thesaurus	Tools, Language, Thesaurus		3
Underline	Format, Font		4
Undo	Edit, Undo		2
Vertical Alignment	File, Page Setup		5
Web Layout View	View, Web Layout		1
Web Page	File, Save as Web Page		8
Word Count	Tools, Word Count		7

REVIEW QUESTIONS

MATCHING

Match the correct term in the right column to its description in the left column.

____ 1. List of options from which to choose   **A.** fonts

____ 2. Designs of type   **B.** default

____ 3. Text printed at the bottom of each page   **C.** taskbar

____ 4. Setting used unless another option is chosen   **D.** menu

____ 5. File that contains formatting and text you can customize   **E.** endnote

     F. footnote

     G. template

WRITTEN QUESTIONS

Write a brief answer to the following questions.

1. What are two ways to check the spelling in a document?

2. How do you align text? What are the four text alignment positions?

3. How do you resize an object?

4. What does the Split command do?

5. What is the Clipboard?

PROJECTS

PROJECT 1

1. Open **IW Project1** from the data files.

2. Save the document as **Island West** followed by your initials.

3. Check the document for spelling and grammar errors. Make changes as needed.

4. Find the word *Property*, and replace it with **Properties** each time it occurs in the document.

5. Move the heading *How do I get more information?* and the paragraph that follows to the end of the document.

6. Replace the word *excellent* in the second paragraph with a synonym that makes sense in context.

7. Change the line spacing of the document to **1.5**.

8. Change the orientation to landscape.

9. Change the title to Vineta BT, 28-point, Sea Green. If the font is not available, choose another appropriate font. *Center the title*

10. Center align the document vertically on the page.

11. Change each of the headings to the Heading 1 style.

12. Indent the last heading and paragraph 1 inch on each side, and center the heading.

13. Create a 3-point Indigo border around the last heading and paragraph filled with Light Green.

14. Save, print, and close the document.

PROJECT 2

1. Open **IW Project2** from the data files.

2. Save the document as **Baseball** followed by your initials. *Center Page vertically*

3. Insert a table with three columns and six rows after the first paragraph.

4. Key the data in the table as shown in Figure UR-1.

Date	Team	Time
April 10	A & B Muffler Eagles	3:00
April 17	Champion Sports Comets	12:00
April 24	Butler Plumbing Bulldogs	10:30
May 1	Harding Insurance Stars	12:00
May 8	Bruin Carpet Raiders	3:00

5. Center the three headings, and change the font size to 14 point.

6. Center the date and time columns.

7. Add a new row after *May 8*, and key the following data:

   ```
   May 22 Rapid Pager Cougars 10:30
   ```

8. Add a new row above the first row, and key **Reese Medical Center Mustangs**; merge the cells.

9. Apply AutoFormat Table **Colorful 3** to the table.

10. Highlight the sentence *If you have any questions*.

11. Insert baseball-related clip art above the title. Adjust the size if necessary.

12. Save, print, and close the file.

PROJECT 3

1. Open **IW Project3** from the data files. Save as **Verb Tense** followed by your initials.

2. Display the ruler if it is not already showing.

3. Center and bold the title. Increase the font size to 14.

4. Set the left tab to the 1.5-inch mark on the ruler.

5. Set a decimal tab with dash style leaders at 5 inches.

6. Center and bold the headings. Increase the font size to 12.

7. Insert a header with your name, the date, and the page number.

8. Save, print, and close the document.

PROJECT 4

1. Open **IW Project4** from the data files.

2. Save the document as **Bagel Mania** followed by your initials.

3. Change all the text to 12 point Times New Roman.

4. Center the title and change it to uppercase, Arial, 18 point, bold, orange with shadow effect.

5. Center the subtitle and change it to Arial, 14 point, italic.

6. Indent the first paragraph 0.5 inches.

7. Sort the list of bagels in alphabetic ascending order.

8. Insert a continuous section break before and after the list of bagels.

9. Format the list of bagels into three columns with 0.4 inches between them.

10. Change the Breakfast Bagels heading to 14 point, bold, small caps, dark teal, with an orange double underline.

11. Copy the format of the *Breakfast Bagels* heading to the *Lunch Bagels* heading.

12. Change the left and right margins to 1 inch.

13. Number the items in the breakfast and lunch bagel lists.

14. Change the line spacing of the first paragraph to 1.5, the types of bagels to double-spacing, and the breakfast and lunch lists to 6 points after spacing.

15. Align the prices in the breakfast and lunch lists at a 5.5-inch decimal tab.

16. Center, italicize, and change *Come again!* to 14 point.

17. Preview the document. Print from the Preview screen.

18. Save your changes, and close the document.

PROJECT 5

1. Open **IW Project5** from the data files.

2. Save the file as **Zephyr Theater** followed by your initials.

3. Make the numbered list into a bulleted list.

4. Select the heading **Performance Schedule** and all the text that follows.

5. Cut the selected text, and paste it in a new document.

6. Save the new document as **Performance Schedule** followed by your initials.

7. Change the theme to **Artsy** or another appropriate theme.

8. Save the document as a Web page with the filename **Schedule Web**. Minimize the document.

9. Switch to the **Zephyr Theater** document.

10. Change the theme to **Artsy** or another appropriate theme. Save the document as a Web page with the filename **Theater Web**.

11. Create a hyperlink to the **Schedule Web** file using the last line of text, *Schedule of Performances*.

12. Click the hyperlink to open the **Schedule Web** page.

13. Create a hyperlink to the Theater Web page using the last line of the text, *Back to Zephyr Theater Home Page*.

14. Click the hyperlink to return to the Theater Web page.

15. Preview the Web page in the browser. Print the page.

16. Close the preview. Save and close all files.

SIMULATION

You work at the Java Internet Café, which has been open only a few months. The café serves coffee, other beverages, and pastries and offers Internet access. Seven computers are set up on tables along the north side of the store. Customers can come in, have a cup of coffee and a Danish, and explore the World Wide Web.

Because of your Microsoft Office experience, your manager asks you to create and revise many of the business's documents.

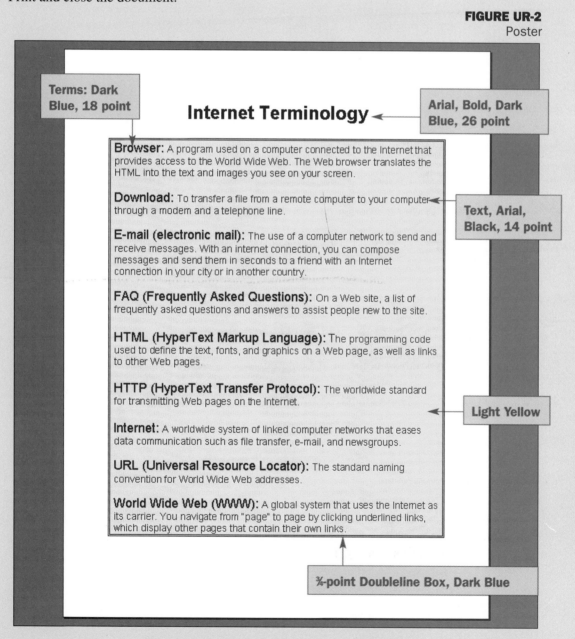

JOB 1

Many customers ask questions about the terms they come across while on the Internet. Your manager asks you to create a poster with definitions of the most common terms. A poster will hang near each computer.

1. Open a new Word document. *Set margins on 1 inch*

2. Create the poster shown in Figure UR-2.

3. Save the document as **Terms** followed by your initials.

4. Print and close the document.

FIGURE UR-2
Poster

JOB 2

Many customers become curious when they see computers through the window of the coffee shop. The café servers are often too busy to explain the concept to customers entering the store. Your manager asks you to revise the menu to include a short description of the café. These menus will be printed and placed near the entrance.

1. Open **IW Job2** from the data files.

2. Key the text below.

   ```
   The Java Internet Café is a coffee shop with a twist. As you can
   see, we have seven computers at the north side of the café. These
   computers provide high-speed Internet access to our customers.
   Whether you're a regular on the Net or a novice, our system is
   designed to allow you easy exploration of the World Wide Web.
   You've heard about it; now give it a try. Ask your server to help
   you get started.
   ```

3. Save the document as **Java Menu** followed by your initials.

4. Change the left and right margins to 1 inch.

5. Change the font of the paragraph you just keyed to Arial, 11 point if necessary.

6. Insert one blank line after the paragraph, and key the title **Menu** centered.

7. Change the font of *Menu* to Arial, 18 point, bold. You will paste the menu information from Excel later.

8. Insert and center the following footer:

   ```
   Sit back, sip your coffee, and surf the Net.
   ```

9. Change the font to Arial, 14 point, bold, centered.

10. Save, print, and close the document. Close Word.

INTRODUCTORY MICROSOFT® EXCEL

EXCEL BASICS

OBJECTIVES

Upon completion of this lesson, you should be able to:

■ Define the terms *spreadsheet* and *worksheet*.

■ Identify the parts of the worksheet.

■ Move the highlight in the worksheet.

■ Select cells and enter data in the worksheet.

■ Edit cells.

■ Find and replace data.

■ Zoom in and out in a worksheet.

■ Save a worksheet.

■ Print a worksheet.

🕐 **Estimated Time: 1.5 hours**

VOCABULARY

Active cell

Cell

Column

Formula bar

Highlight

Name box

Range

Row

Spreadsheet

Workbook

Worksheet

What Is Excel?

Excel is the spreadsheet application of the Office^XP programs. A ***spreadsheet*** is a grid of rows and columns containing numbers, text, and formulas. The purpose of a spreadsheet is to solve problems that involve numbers. Without a computer, you might try to solve this type of problem by creating rows and columns on ruled paper and using a calculator to determine results (see Figure 1-1). Computer spreadsheets also contain rows and columns, but they perform calculations much faster and more accurately than spreadsheets created with pencil, paper, and calculator.

FIGURE 1-1
Spreadsheet prepared on paper

Spreadsheets are used in many ways. For example, a spreadsheet can be used to calculate a grade in a class, to prepare a budget for the next few months, or to determine payments to be made on a loan. The primary advantage of spreadsheets is the ability to complete complex and repetitious calculations accurately, quickly, and easily. For example, you might use a spreadsheet to calculate your monthly income and expenses.

Besides calculating rapidly and accurately, spreadsheets are flexible. Making changes to an existing spreadsheet is usually as easy as pointing and clicking with the mouse. Suppose, for example, you have prepared a budget on a spreadsheet and have overestimated the amount of money you will need to spend on gas, electric, and other utilities. You can change a single entry in your spreadsheet and watch the entire spreadsheet recalculate the new budgeted amount. You can imagine the work this change would require if you were calculating the budget with pencil and paper.

Excel uses the term *worksheet* to refer to computerized spreadsheets. Sometimes you may want to use several worksheets that relate to each other. A collection of related worksheets is referred to as a *workbook*.

Starting Excel

Excel is started from the desktop screen in Windows. One way to start Excel is to click the Start button, select Programs, and then choose Microsoft Excel. When Excel starts, a blank worksheet titled Book1 appears on the screen. You will see some of the basic parts of the screen that you learned about in the Introduction: the title bar, the menu bar, and the toolbar. However, as shown in Figure 1-2, Excel has its own unique buttons and screen parts.

FIGURE 1-2
Excel opening screen

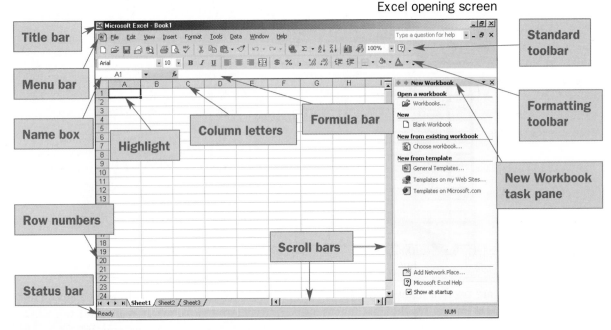

1. With Windows running, click the **Start** button, click **Programs**, and then choose **Microsoft Excel**.

2. Microsoft Excel starts and a blank worksheet titled *Book1* appears, as shown in Figure 1-2. Maximize the window, if necessary.

3. Leave the blank worksheet on the screen for use in the next Step-by-Step.

Parts of the Worksheet

Columns of the worksheet appear vertically and are identified by letters at the top of the worksheet window. *Rows* appear horizontally and are identified by numbers on the left side of the worksheet window. A *cell* is the intersection of a row and column and is identified by a cell reference, the column letter and row number (for example, C4, A1, B2).

The mouse pointer is indicated by a thick plus sign when it's in the worksheet. If you move the pointer up to the toolbars and menus, the pointer turns into an arrow. In Word, the insertion point indicates the point at which a character is keyed. In the worksheet the entry point is indicated by a *highlight*, which appears on the screen as a dark border around a cell.

The cell that contains the highlight is the ***active cell***, which is distinguished by a dark border. Your screen currently shows a border around cell A1, the active cell. You may change the active cell by moving the highlight from one cell to another. The ***formula bar*** appears directly below the toolbar in the worksheet and displays a formula when the cell of a worksheet contains a calculated value. On the far left side of the formula bar is the ***name box***, or cell reference area, that identifies the active cell.

Opening an Existing Worksheet

To open an existing worksheet, choose Open on the File menu, or click the Open button on the toolbar. In the Open dialog box, specify the file you want to open. When you start Excel, the program displays a new worksheet temporarily titled *Book1*. This worksheet is eliminated if you open another file.

Did You Know?

Excel has several template files that you may use to solve common spreadsheet problems (such as invoices, expense statements, and loan schedules). To open these files, choose General Templates in the New from template section of the New Workbook task pane. On the Spreadsheet Solutions tab, open the file that applies to the problem you would like to solve.

Hot Tip

The column letter and row number of the active cell highlighted in purple for easy reference.

STEP-BY-STEP ▷ 1.2

Suppose that you have volunteered to help a local environmental awareness group by conducting a census of species of birds. For the remainder of this lesson, you will complete a worksheet that accounts for each species of bird.

1. Click **Workbooks** in the New Workbook task pane. The Open dialog box appears.

2. In the **Look in** box, select the drive and/or folder containing the data files for this course. The files appear in the display window.

3. Double-click the filename **IE Step1-2**. The worksheet appears on the screen similar to Figure 1-3.

4. Leave the worksheet on the screen for the next Step-by-Step.

FIGURE 1-3

Opening a worksheet

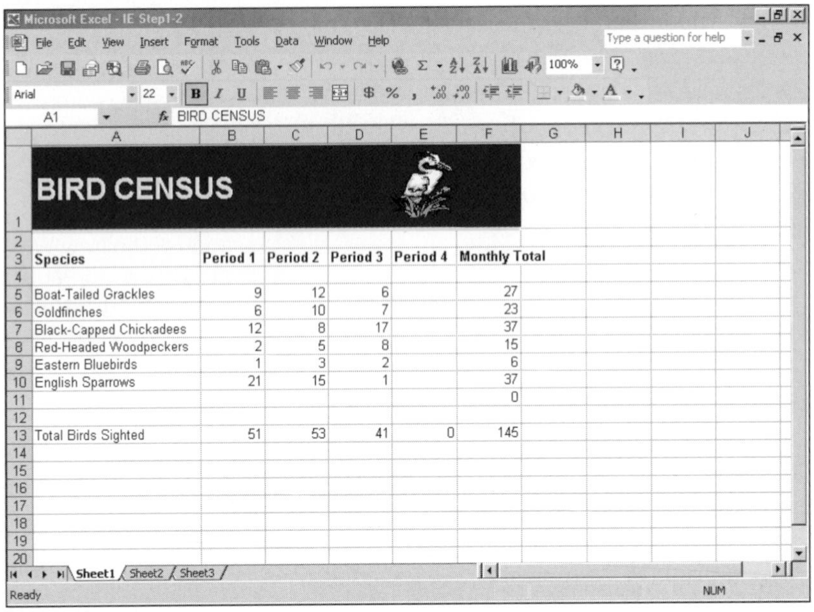

Moving the Highlight in a Worksheet

The easiest way to move the highlight to a cell on the screen is to move the mouse pointer to the cell and click. When working with a large worksheet, you may not be able to view the entire worksheet on the screen. You can scroll through the worksheet using the mouse by dragging the scroll box in the scroll bar to the desired position. You can also move the highlight to different parts of the worksheet using the keyboard or the Go To command in the Edit menu.

Using Keys to Move the Highlight

You can move the highlight by pressing certain keys or key combinations, as shown in Table 1-1. Many of these key combinations may be familiar to you if you use Microsoft Word. As in Word, when you hold down an arrow key, the highlight will move repeatedly and quickly.

TABLE 1-1
Key combinations for moving the highlight in a worksheet

TO MOVE	PRESS
Left one column	Left arrow
Right one column	Right arrow
Up one row	Up arrow
Down one row	Down arrow
To the first cell of a row	Home
To cell A1	Ctrl+Home
To the last cell containing data	Ctrl+End
Up one window	Page Up
Down one window	Page Down
To the previous worksheet in a workbook	Ctrl+Page Up
To the next worksheet in a workbook	Ctrl+Page Down

Using the Go To Command to Move in the Worksheet

You may want to move the highlight to a cell that does not appear on the screen. The fastest way to move to the cell is by choosing Go To on the Edit menu or by pressing the shortcut key, F5. The Go To dialog box appears, as shown in Figure 1-4. Key the cell reference in the Reference box and click OK. The highlight will move to the cell.

Did You Know?

You may also go to specific text or numbers in the worksheet by choosing the **Find** command on the **Edit** menu. The Find dialog box opens. In the Find what text box, key the data you would like to locate in the worksheet and then click **Find Next**. The highlight will move to the next cell that contains the data.

1. The highlight should be in cell A1.

2. Move to the last cell in the worksheet that contains data by pressing **Ctrl+End**. The highlight moves to cell F13 in the lower right side of the worksheet.

3. Move to the first cell of row 13 by pressing **Home**. The highlight appears in cell A13, which contains the words *Total Birds Sighted*.

4. Move up three rows by pressing the up arrow key three times. The highlight appears in cell A10, which contains the words *English Sparrows*.

5. Choose **Go To** on the **Edit** menu. The Go To dialog box appears as shown in Figure 1-4.

6. Key **B3** in the Reference box.

7. Click **OK**. The highlight moves to B3. Leave the worksheet on the screen for the next Step-by-Step.

FIGURE 1-4
Go To dialog box

Teamwork

Have a classmate call out cell references so you can practice moving the highlight to the correct cell using the methods you have learned.

Selecting a Group of Cells

Often, you will perform operations on more than one cell at a time. A selected group of cells is called a *range*. In a range, all cells touch each other and form a rectangle. The range is identified by the cell in the upper left corner and the cell in the lower right corner, separated by a colon (for example, A3:C5). To select a range of cells, place the highlight in the cell that is one corner of the range and drag the highlight to the cell in the opposite corner. As you drag the highlight, the range of selected cells will become shaded (except for the cell you originally selected). The column letters and row numbers of the range you select are highlighted in purple. If you select a range of cells that is too large to be entirely displayed on the screen, a ScreenTip appears diagonally to the last highlighted cell that tells how many rows and columns are included in the range, as shown in Figure 1-5.

FIGURE 1-5
Selecting a range of 19 rows and 7 columns

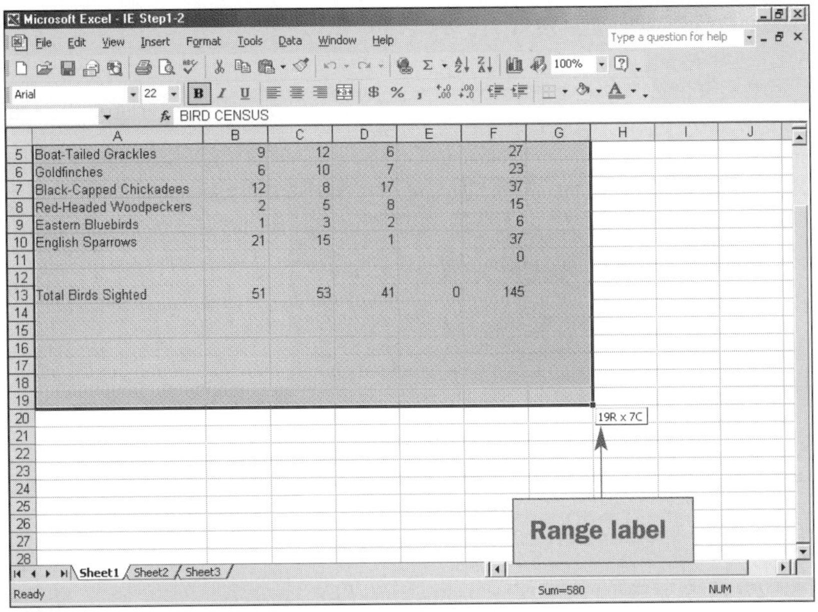

Range label

S TEP-BY-STEP ▷ 1.4

1. With the highlight in **B3**, hold down the left mouse button and drag to the right until **F3** is highlighted.

2. Release the mouse button. The range B3:F3 is selected. Notice that the column letters B through F and the row number 3 are shaded.

3. Move the highlight to **B5**.

4. Hold down the mouse button and drag down and to the right until **F13** is highlighted.

5. Release the mouse button. The range B5:F13 is selected. Leave the worksheet open for the next Step-by-Step.

Entering Data in a Cell

Worksheet cells may contain text, numbers, formulas, or functions. Text consists of alphabetical characters such as headings, labels, or explanatory notes. Numbers can be values, dates, or times. Formulas are equations that calculate a value. Functions are special formulas that place either values or characters in cells. (Formulas and functions are discussed in later lessons.)

You enter data by keying the text or numbers in a cell, and then either clicking the Enter button on the formula bar or pressing the Enter key on the keyboard. If you choose not to enter the data you have keyed, you can simply click the Cancel button on the formula bar or press Esc and the keyed data will be deleted.

If you make a mistake, choose Undo on the Edit menu or click the Undo button on the toolbar to reverse your most recent change. To undo multiple actions, click the down arrow to the right of the Undo button on the toolbar. A list of your previous actions is displayed and you can choose the number of actions you want to undo.

Hot Tip

The Enter and Cancel buttons will not appear unless you key data into a cell. You can click the Edit Formula button to edit a formula.

STEP-BY-STEP ▷ 1.5

1. Move the highlight to **E5** and key **15**. As you key, the numbers appear in the cell and in the formula bar.

2. Press **Enter**. The highlight moves to E6.

3. Key **4**.

4. Click **Enter** (the check mark) on the formula bar. Notice that the totals in F6, E13, and F13 change as you enter the data.

5. Undo the action by clicking the down arrow button to the right of the **Undo** button on the toolbar. A menu appears listing the actions you have just performed.

6. Choose **Typing '4' in E6** from the menu, as shown in Figure 1-6. The data will be removed from E6 and the data in F6 and E13 change back to the previous totals.

7. Now enter the following data into the remaining cells in column E:

Cell	Data
E6	5
E7	20
E8	4
E9	10
E10	16

8. In addition to the species above, you sighted a blue heron. Key **Heron** in cell **A11**.

9. Enter **1** in **E11**. Leave the worksheet on the screen for the next Step-by-Step.

Hot Tip

If you need help while working with any of Excel's features, use the Office Assistant. The Assistant is an animated character that offers tips, solutions, instructions, and examples to help you work more efficiently. It appears on the screen with tips on how to manage spreadsheet data and workbook files. If you have a specific question, you can use the Office Assistant to search for help. To display the Office Assistant if it is not on the screen, choose **Show the Office Assistant** on the **Help** menu. Click on the Office Assistant. Key your question and click **Search**. The Assistant displays a list of help topics in response.

FIGURE 1-6
Undo multiple actions by clicking the arrow to the right of the Undo button

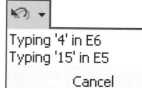

Changing Data in a Cell

As you enter data in the worksheet, you may change your mind about data or make a mistake. If so, you may edit, replace, or clear existing data in cells of the worksheet.

Editing Data

Editing is performed when only minor changes to cell data are necessary. Data in a cell may be edited in the formula bar by using the Edit key on your keyboard, F2. To edit data in a cell, select the cell by placing the highlight in the cell and pressing F2. An insertion point similar to the one in Word will appear in the cell and you can make changes to the data. Press Enter to reenter the data.

You may prefer to use the mouse pointer to edit a cell. First, click the cell you want to edit; then click in the formula bar at the place you want to change the data. After you have made the changes you need, click the Enter button.

Did You Know?

A worksheet is usually part of a collection of worksheets called a workbook. A tab near the bottom of the screen identifies a particular worksheet. You may move, copy, or delete a worksheet by right-clicking the worksheet tab and then selecting the operation you desire from the shortcut menu.

Replacing Data

Cell contents are usually replaced when you must make significant changes to cell data. To replace cell contents, select the cell, key the new data, and enter the data by clicking the Enter button (the check mark on the formula bar) or by pressing the Enter key.

Clearing Data

Clearing a cell will empty the cell of all its contents. To clear an active cell, you may either press the Delete key or Backspace key, or choose Clear on the Edit menu. Choosing Clear gives you a submenu allowing you to delete the format of the cell, the contents of the cell, or a note with the cell.

STEP-BY-STEP 1.6

1. Move the highlight to **D10**.

2. Press **F2**. An insertion point appears in the cell.

3. Make sure the insertion point is positioned after the 1 and key **8**.

4. Press **Enter**. The number 18 appears in the cell.

5. Move the highlight to **A11**.

6. Key **Blue Heron** and click the **Enter** button on the formula bar. The words *Blue Heron* replace the word *Heron* in the cell.

7. Move the highlight to **A3**.

8. Press the **Delete** key. The contents are cleared from the cell. Your screen should appear similar to Figure 1-7. Leave the worksheet on the screen for the next Step-by-Step.

FIGURE 1-7
Changing data in a cell

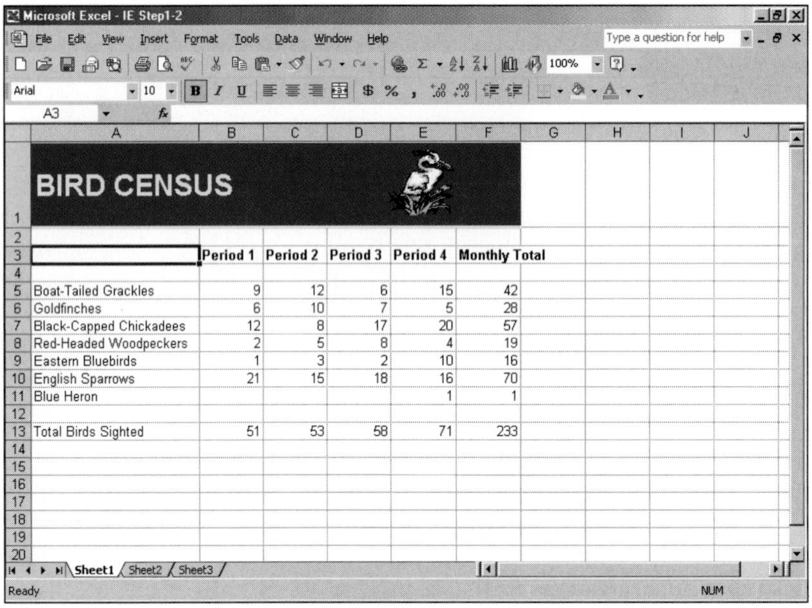

Microsoft Excel spreadsheet showing BIRD CENSUS data.

	A	B	C	D	E	F
3		Period 1	Period 2	Period 3	Period 4	Monthly Total
5	Boat-Tailed Grackles	9	12	6	15	42
6	Goldfinches	6	10	7	5	28
7	Black-Capped Chickadees	12	8	17	20	57
8	Red-Headed Woodpeckers	2	5	8	4	19
9	Eastern Bluebirds	1	3	2	10	16
10	English Sparrows	21	15	18	16	70
11	Blue Heron				1	1
13	Total Birds Sighted	51	53	58	71	233

Searching for Data

The Find command enables you to locate specific words or numbers in a worksheet. If you like, you may use the Replace command to change data you have found.

Finding Data

The Find command is used to locate data in a worksheet. It is particularly useful when the worksheet is large. When you choose Find in the Edit menu, the Find and Replace dialog box will appear. Table 1-2 specifies what actions may be specified in the Find and Replace dialog box.

The Find command can be used to locate words or parts of words. For example, searching for emp will find the words employee and temporary. In addition, searching for 85 will find 85, 850, and 385.

SEARCH OPTION	SPECIFIES
Find what box	the data you are looking for
Replace with box	the data that will be inserted in the cell
Format option	the format of the data you are looking for or inserting
Within list box	whether you will search the worksheet or the entire workbook
Search list box	whether the search will look across rows or down columns
Look in list box	whether the search will examine cell contents or formulas
Match case checkbox	whether the search must match whether the data is upper or lower case
Match entire cell contents checkbox	whether the search must match all contents of the cell

Replacing Data

The Replace command is an extension of the Find command. Replacement will substitute new data for data found. Replacement may be done by choosing the Replace command on the Edit menu or by clicking the Replace tab in the Find and Replace dialog box.

STEP-BY-STEP ▷ 1.7

1. Move the highlight to **A1**.

2. Choose **Find** on the **Edit** menu.

3. Key **Period** in the Find what box.

4. Click the **Find Next** button. The highlight will move to **B3**.

5. Click the **Replace** tab in the Find and Replace dialog box.

6. Key **Week** in the Replace with box.

7. Click **Replace**. The word *Period* will be replaced by *Week* in B3 and the highlight will move to **C3**.

8. Click **Replace All**. A message will appear indicating that Excel has completed the search and replaced all of the instances of the word *Period* with the word *Week* (in this case three replacements).

9. Click **OK**.

10. Click **Close** in the Find and Replace dialog box. Leave the worksheet on the screen for the next Step-by-Step.

Zoom View

Y ou can magnify or reduce the view of your worksheet by using the Zoom button on the Standard toolbar (or by using the Zoom command on the View menu). The default magnification is 100%. If you would like to get a closer view of your worksheet, select a larger percentage from the drop-down list. Reduce the view by selecting a smaller percentage from the drop-down list. If you would like a different magnification from those available on the drop-down list, you may key your desired percentage directly in the Zoom box.

Saving a Worksheet

Y ou save worksheets using the process you learned in the Introduction. The first time you save a worksheet, the Save As dialog box appears in which you name the worksheet. Once a worksheet has been saved, the Save command will update the latest version. The worksheet may also be saved by clicking the Save button on the Standard toolbar.

> **Did You Know?**
>
> **C** You may save a file in a new folder by clicking the **New Folder** button in the **Save As** dialog box. When the **New Folder** dialog box appears, key a name for the new folder and click **OK**.

1. Click the down arrow on the **Zoom** button on the Standard toolbar.

2. Click **200%**. The view of the worksheet will double in size.

3. Click the **Zoom** button's down arrow again, and then click **50%**. The view of the worksheet will shrink to half of its default size.

4. Click the **Zoom** button's down arrow once more, and then click **100%**. The worksheet will return to its default size.

5. Choose **Save As** on the **File** menu. The Save As dialog box appears.

6. Key **Bird Survey**, followed by your initials, in the File name text box.

7. Click **Save**. Leave the worksheet open for the next Step-by-Step.

Printing a Worksheet

You may print your worksheet by clicking the Print button on the Standard toolbar or by accessing the Print dialog box (see Figure 1-8). Use the Print dialog box to print part of a worksheet or change the way your printed worksheet looks. You will learn more about these options in Lesson 3. For now, you will print the entire worksheet using the default settings.

FIGURE 1-8
Printing a file

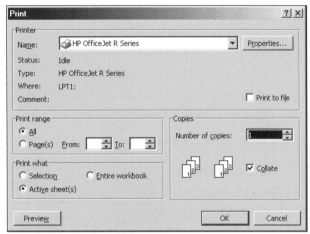

STEP-BY-STEP ▷ 1.9

1. Choose **Print** on the **File** menu. The Print dialog box appears.

2. Click **OK**. The worksheet begins printing.

3. Choose **Close** on the **File** menu. If you are asked to save changes, click **Yes**. The worksheet closes.

Summary

In this lesson, you learned:

- The purpose of a spreadsheet is to solve problems involving numbers. The advantage of using a spreadsheet is that you can complete complex and repetitious calculations quickly and easily.

- A worksheet consists of columns and rows intersecting to form cells. Each cell is identified by a cell reference, which is the letter of the column and number of the row.

- You can move to different cells of the worksheet by clicking on the cell with the mouse pointer, using a series of keystrokes, or scrolling with the mouse.

- Both text and numerical data may be entered into the worksheet. You can alter data by editing, replacing, or deleting.

- You can search for specific characters in a worksheet. You can also replace data you have searched for with specific characters.

- The Zoom box will enlarge the view of a worksheet on the screen.

- Changes in a worksheet are saved using the Save command in the File menu.

- A worksheet may be printed to provide a hard copy.

VOCABULARY REVIEW

Define the following terms:

Active cell	Highlight	X Spreadsheet
X Cell	Name box	Workbook
X Column	X Range	X Worksheet
Formula bar	Row	

LESSON 1 REVIEW QUESTIONS

TRUE/FALSE

Circle T if the statement is true or F if the statement is false.

T F 1. The primary advantage of the worksheet is to summarize text documents.

T F 2. A cell is the intersection of a row and column.

T F 3. The Go To command saves a file and exits Excel.

T F   4.   You may print a file by accessing the Print command in the File menu or by clicking the Print button on the Standard toolbar.

T F   5.   Once a worksheet has been saved under a new name, changes to a spreadsheet may be saved by clicking the Save button on the Standard toolbar.

WRITTEN QUESTIONS

Write a brief answer to the following questions.

1.   What term describes a cell that is ready for data entry?

2.   How are columns identified in a worksheet?

3.   What term describes a group of cells?

4.   What keys should be pressed to move the highlight to the last cell of the worksheet that contains data?

5.   What key is pressed to clear data from an active cell?

PROJECT 1-1

In the blank space, write the letter of the keystroke in the right column that matches the highlight movement in the left column.

____ 1. Left one column   **A.**   Ctrl+Home

____ 2. Right one column   **B.**   Page Up

____ 3. Up one row   **C.**   Right arrow

____ 4. Down one row   **D.**   Home

____ 5. To the first cell of a row   **E.**   Ctrl+Page Up

____ 6. To cell A1   **F.**   Left arrow

____ 7. To the last cell containing data   **G.**   Ctrl+End

____ 8. Up one window   **H.**   Up arrow

____ 9. Down one window   **I.**   Ctrl+Page Down

____ 10. To the previous worksheet in a workbook   **J.**   Down arrow

____ 11. To the next worksheet in a workbook   **K.**   Page Down

PROJECT 1-2

The file *IE Project1-2* contains information concerning the percent of home ownership in the United States. Make the following corrections and additions to the worksheet.

1. Open **IE Project1-2** from the data files.

2. Save the file as **Home Owner**, followed by your initials.

3. Enter **GA** in **A15**.

4. Enter **64.90%** in **B15**.

5. Enter **65.00%** into **C15**.

6. Edit the data in **A16** to be **HA**.

7. Edit the data in **B16** to be **53.90%**.

8. Delete the data in **A3**.

9. Save, print, and close the file.

PROJECT 1-3

Residential Developers, Inc., has developed a worksheet to help prospective homebuyers estimate the cost of homes in four different neighborhoods. The cost of homes within neighborhoods tends to fluctuate based on the square footage of the home. Each of the four neighborhoods tends to have a different cost per square foot.

1. Open **IE Project1-3** from the data files.

2. Save the file as **Development**, followed by your initials.

3. Enter the square footages in the following cells to estimate the home costs. The estimated home cost in each neighborhood will change as you enter the data.

Cell	Enter
C7	1250
C8	1500
C9	2200
C10	2500

4. After selling several houses in the Lake View neighborhood, Residential Developers, Inc., has figured that the cost per square foot is $67.00, rather than $65.00. Edit **B7** to show **$67.00**.

5. Save, print, and close the file.

PROJECT 1-4

1. Open **IE Project1-4** from the data files.

2. Save the file as **Surname**, followed by your initials.

3. Using the **Find** command, locate the name **Chavez**. Your highlight should appear in **A198**.

4. Press **Ctrl+Home** to return to **A1**.

5. Using the **Find** command, locate the name **Chang**. Your highlight should appear in **A691**. (*Hint*: The Find and Replace dialog box will remain on screen.) You may simply enter the new search in the Find what text box.

 Extra Challenge

See if you can find your last name, or the names of your friends, in the **Surnames** file you just created.

6. Close the Find and Replace dialog box and press **Ctrl+Home** to return to **A1**.

7. Using the **Find** command, locate the name **Forbes**. Your highlight should appear in **A987**.

8. Save and close the file.

ACTIVITY 1-1

SCANS

The purpose of a spreadsheet is to solve problems that involve numbers. Identify two or three numerical problems in each of the following categories that might be solved by using a spreadsheet.

1. Business

2. Career

3. Personal

4. School

ACTIVITY 1-2

SCANS

You have already selected a range of cells that is so large it extends to several screens. You realize that you incorrectly included one column of cells you do not want within the selected range.

To reselect the range of cells, you must page up to the active cell (the first cell of the range) and drag through several screens to the last cell in the range. You are wondering if there is a better way to reduce the selected range without having to page up to the original screen.

Use the Answer Wizard of the Help function of Microsoft Excel Help to learn how to select fewer cells without canceling your original selection. Using your word processor, write a brief explanation of the steps you would take to change the selected range.

CHANGING THE APPEARANCE OF A WORKSHEET

OBJECTIVES

Upon completion of this lesson, you should be able to:

- Change column width and row height.

- Position text within a cell by wrapping, rotating, indenting, and aligning.

- Change the appearance of cells using fonts, styles, colors, and borders.

- Designate the format of a cell to accommodate different kinds of text and numerical data.

- Apply and paint formats.

- Create and use styles.

- Find and replace cell formats.

⏱ **Estimated Time: 1.5 hours**

VOCABULARY

AutoFormat

Indented text

Rotated text

Style

Wrapped text

Changing the Size of a Cell

Worksheets are useful only when they are understandable to the user. It is important that data in a worksheet is accurate, but it is also important that data is presented in a way that is visually appealing.

Changing Column Width

Sometimes the data you key will not fit in the column. When data is wider than the column, Excel responds by doing one of the following:

- Displaying a series of number signs (######) in the cell.

- Cutting off the data (the right portion of the data will not be displayed).

- Letting the data run outside of the column.

- Converting the data to a different numerical form (for example, changing long numbers to exponential form).

You can widen the column by placing the mouse pointer on the right edge of the column heading (the column letter). The pointer then changes into a double-headed arrow. To widen the column, drag to the right until the column is the desired size. When you drag to change the width of a column, a ScreenTip appears near the pointer displaying the new measurements.

Another way to change column width is to use the Column Width dialog box, shown in Figure 2-1. Place the highlight in the column you would like to change. Then, choose Column on the Format menu and click Width on the submenu. In the Column Width dialog box, key the desired width and click OK.

FIGURE 2-1
Column Width dialog box

Changing Row Height

Change the row height by placing the mouse pointer below the row heading (the row number). The pointer then changes into a double-headed arrow. The row is increased in height by dragging downward until the row is the desired size. Also, the Row Height dialog box may be used to designate a specific row height. Place the highlight in the row you would like to change. Then, choose Row on the Format menu and click Height on the submenu. In the Row Height dialog box, key the desired height and click OK.

Hot Tip

You can change the width of several columns at a time by selecting the columns, and then dragging the right edge of one of the column headings. You may also change the height of several rows by selecting the rows, and then dragging the boundary below a selected row heading.

STEP-BY-STEP ▷ 2.1

1. Open **IE Step2-1** from the data files. Notice that the data in D3 extends partially into column E.

2. Save the worksheet as **3Q Budget**, followed by your initials.

3. Place the mouse pointer on the right edge of the column D heading. The pointer turns into a double-headed arrow.

4. Drag the double-headed arrow to the right until the ScreenTip reads *Width: 10.00 (75 pixels)*, as shown in Figure 2-2, and release the mouse button. The entire word *September* now fits within column D.

5. Select columns **B** through **D**.

6. Choose **Column** on the **Format** menu, and then choose **Width** on the submenu. The Column Width dialog box appears (see Figure 2-1).

7. Key **10** in the Column width text box.

8. Click **OK**. The widths of the selected columns have been changed to 10.

9. Scroll down one screen and place the mouse pointer on the bottom edge of the row 18 heading. The pointer turns into a double-headed arrow.

10. Drag the double-headed arrow down until the ScreenTip reads *Height 18.00 (24 pixels)*.

11. Save the file and leave the worksheet on the screen for the next Step-by-Step.

FIGURE 2-2
Column width measurement ScreenTip

Letting Excel Find the Best Fit

Suppose you have a column full of data of varying widths. You want the column to be wide enough to display the longest entry, but no wider than necessary. Excel can determine the best width of a column or the best height of a row. To determine the best fit for a column, place the highlight in the cell and choose Column on the Format menu, and then choose AutoFit Selection on the submenu. To determine the best fit for a row, place the highlight in the cell and choose Row on the Format menu, and then choose AutoFit on the submenu.

Hot Tip

Another way to find the best fit is to place the mouse pointer on the right edge of the column heading and double-click when the double-headed arrow appears.

STEP-BY-STEP ▷ 2.2

1. Place the highlight in cell **A20**. Notice that the words *Cumulative Surplus* are cut off.

2. Choose **Column** on the **Format** menu, and then choose **AutoFit Selection** on the submenu. Column A widens to show all the data in A20.

3. Save your work and leave the worksheet on the screen for the next Step-by-Step.

Positioning Text Within a Cell

Unless you specify otherwise, Excel enters text as left justified without wrapping. However, you may change the position of text within a cell in several ways (see Table 2-1).

TABLE 2-1
Positioning text within a cell

TEXT POSITION	FUNCTION	EXAMPLE OF USE
Wrapped	Begins a new line within the cell	Moves text to a new line when it is longer than the width of the cell
Rotated	Displays text at an angle	Turns the text so that it might be displayed in a narrower column
Indented	Moves the text several spaces to the right	Creates subheadings below primary headings
Left-Justified	Begins the text on the left side of the cell	The default justification for textual data
Centered	Places the text in the middle of the cell	Creates column headings
Right-Justified	Begins the text on the right side of the cell	The default justification for numerical data
Merge and Center	Merges multiple cells into one cell and places the text in the middle of the merged cell	Creates a title across the top of a worksheet

Text Wrap

Text that is too long for a cell will spill over into the next cell if the next cell is empty. If the next cell is not empty, the text that does not fit into the cell will not display. You can choose to have text wrap within a cell in the same way text wraps within a word-processing document using the text wrap option. The row height will automatically adjust to show all of the lines of text. This is referred to as *wrapped text*.

To turn on the text wrap option, select the cells in which you intend to wrap text. Then choose Cells from the Format menu. In the Format Cells dialog box, click the Alignment tab, as shown in Figure 2-3. In the Text control section click the Wrap text box to turn on the text wrap option.

 Hot Tip

You can also access the Format Cells dialog box by right-clicking an active cell or range and choosing **Format Cells** on the shortcut menu.

 S TEP-BY-STEP ▷ 2.3

1. Move the highlight to cell **A22**.

2. Choose **Cells** on the **Format** menu. The Format Cells dialog box appears.

3. Click the **Alignment** tab, if necessary.

4. Click the **Wrap text** box in the Text control section to insert a check mark (✓).

5. Click **OK**. The text wraps in the cell and the cell height adjusts automatically.

6. Save your work and leave the worksheet on the screen for the next Step-by-Step.

Rotating Text

Sometimes column headings are longer than the data in the columns. Excel allows you to save space by rotating the text to any angle. Using *rotated text* can also help give your worksheet a more professional look.

Computer Concepts

Rotated text can also be used when labeling charts.

To rotate text, select the cells containing the text you want to rotate and choose Cells on the Format menu. When the Format Cells dialog box appears, choose the Alignment tab, as shown in Figure 2-3. In the Orientation box, click a degree point, drag the angle indicator, or type the angle you want in the Degrees text box.

FIGURE 2-3

The Wrap text option on the Alignment tab in the Format Cells dialog box

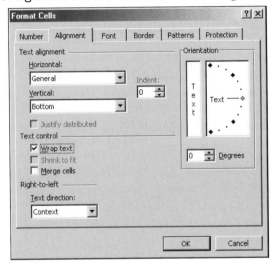

STEP-BY-STEP ▷ 2.4

1. Highlight **B3:D3**.

2. Choose **Cells** on the **Format** menu. The Format Cells dialog box appears.

3. Click the **Alignment** tab, if it is not already selected.

4. In the Orientation section, key **45** in the Degrees text box. The Text indicator moves to a 45-degree angle, as shown in Figure 2-4.

5. Click **OK**. The text in B3 through D3 is now displayed at a 45-degree angle.

6. Change the width of columns **B** through **D** to **8**.

7. Save your work and leave the worksheet on the screen for the next Step-by-Step.

FIGURE 2-4

Orientation section of Alignment tab in the Format Cells dialog box

Indenting Text

Indented text within cells can help distinguish categories or set apart text. Instead of trying to indent text by keying spaces, Excel allows you to click the Increase Indent button on the toolbar to accomplish this task easily. To move the indent in the other direction, click the Decrease Indent button.

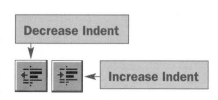

Aligning Text

You can align the contents of a cell several ways: left, centered, right, justified, and centered across several columns. Excel automatically left-aligns all text entries. All numbers are right-aligned unless a different alignment is specified.

To change the alignment of a cell, place the highlight in the cell and click one of the four alignment buttons on the toolbar.

For other alignment options, choose Cells on the Format menu, and then click the Alignment tab. In the Format Cells dialog box, click the alignment you want from the Horizontal or Vertical list boxes, and click OK.

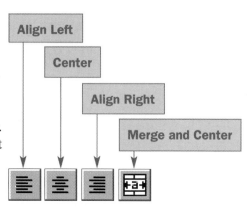

S TEP-BY-STEP ▷ 2.5

1. Move the highlight to **A5**.

2. Click the **Increase Indent** button on the toolbar.

3. Indent the text in **A6**.

4. Highlight **A10:A16** and indent the text.

5. Select **B3:D3**.

6. Click the **Center** button on the toolbar. The headings are centered.

7. Highlight **A7**.

8. Click the **Align Right** button. *Total Income* is aligned at the right of the cell.

9. Right align cells **A17**, **A19**, and **A20**.

10. Select **A1:D1**.

11. Click the **Merge and Center** button. *Asparagus Enterprises* is centered across cells A1 through D1.

12. Merge and center the *Third Quarter Budget* across **A2:D2**.

13. Save and leave the worksheet on the screen for the next Step-by-Step.

Computer Concepts

You can indent text in a cell up to 16 levels.

Changing Cell Appearance

T he appearance of a cell's contents may be changed to make it easier to read. You can alter the appearance of cell contents by changing the font, size, style, color, alignment, format, and borders.

Fonts and Font Sizes

The font and font size you choose may significantly affect the readability of the worksheet. The number, types, and sizes of fonts available depend largely on what fonts are installed on your computer. You can choose different fonts for different parts of a worksheet.

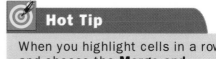

Hot Tip

When you highlight cells in a row and choose the **Merge and Center** button, the cells are merged and the contents are centered.

Changing fonts and sizes in a worksheet is similar to changing the fonts and sizes in a word-processing document. Highlight the cells you want to change and choose the font and size you want from the toolbar. You can also choose Cells on the Format menu. In the Format Cells dialog box click the Font tab. As shown in Figure 2-5, the Format Cells dialog box has options for changing the font, font style, font size, and color.

FIGURE 2-5
Font tab in the Format Cells dialog box

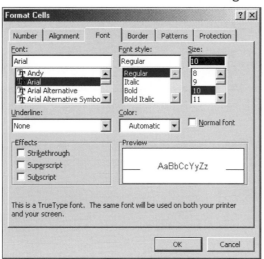

Style

Bolding, italicizing, or underlining can add emphasis to the contents of a cell. These features are known as font styles. To apply a font style, highlight the cell or cells you want to change and click the appropriate style button on the toolbar. To return the contents of the cell to a regular style, simply click the button again.

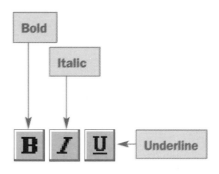

C

1. Select **B3:D3**.

2. Click the down arrow beside the **Font** box on the toolbar. Scroll down and choose **Times New Roman** (or a similar font).

3. Click the down arrow beside the **Font Size** box on the toolbar and choose **8**.

4. Move the highlight to **A1**.

5. Choose **Cells** on the **Format** menu. The Format Cells dialog box appears.

6. Click the **Font** tab.

7. In the Font list box, scroll down and click **Times New Roman**.

8. In the Font style list box, click **Bold**.

9. In the Size list box, scroll down and click **14**.

10. Click **OK**.

11. Highlight **A2**.

12. Click the **Bold** button on the toolbar.

13. Bold the following cells using the same procedure: **A4**, **A7**, **A9**, **A17**, **A19**, and **A20**.

14. Widen column **A** to **18**.

15. Select the range **B6:D6**.

16. Click the **Underline** button on the toolbar.

17. Underline **B16:D16**.

18. Select **A5:A6**.

19. Click the **Italic** button.

20. Italicize **A10:A16**.

21. Save your work and leave the worksheet on the screen for the next Step-by-Step.

Extra Challenge

Experiment by changing the font, size, and style of text in the worksheet. Use the **Undo** button to undo changes you make.

Color

Changing the color of cells or cell text is another way to add emphasis. To change the color of a cell using the toolbar, move the highlight to the cell and click the down arrow beside the Fill Color button on the toolbar. A menu of colors appears, as shown in Figure 2-6. Click the color you want, and the cell is filled with that color.

To change the color of text using the toolbar, move the highlight to the cell you want to change and click the down arrow beside the Font Color button. A menu of colors appears as shown in Figure 2-7. Click the color you want and the text is changed to your color choice.

FIGURE 2-6
Fill Color button color palette

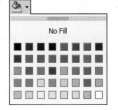

You can also change the color of cells and text using the Format Cells dialog box. Choose Cells on the Format menu, and then click the Patterns tab. Click on a color in the Cell shading section. You can also click the down arrow beside the Pattern box and choose a pattern from the menu.

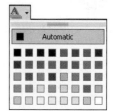

S TEP-BY-STEP ▷ 2.7

1. Select **A1:D1** (which is now merged into one cell).

2. Click the down arrow beside the **Font Color** button. A menu of colors appears.

3. Click the **Green** square in the second row of the color menu. (As you point to each square, a ScreenTip will tell you the color.) The title changes to green text.

4. With A1:D1 still selected, click the down arrow beside the **Fill Color** button. A menu of colors appears.

5. Click the **Gray-25%** square in the fourth row. The cell becomes light gray.

6. Save your work and leave the worksheet on the screen for the next Step-by-Step.

Extra Challenge

Change the text and cell color of all the headings.

Borders

You can add emphasis to a cell by placing a border around its edges. You can place the border around the entire cell or only on certain sides of the cell. You can add borders two ways. First, you can insert a border by highlighting the cell and choosing the Cells command on the Format menu. In the Format Cells dialog box, click the Border tab. Choose the border placement, style, and color (see Figure 2-8), and then click OK. In addition, you can insert a border quickly by clicking the down arrow of the Borders button on the Formatting toolbar. A box of border choices appears, as shown in Figure 2-9. Click one of the options to add the border you want.

S TEP-BY-STEP ▷ 2.8

1. Highlight **A4**.

2. Choose **Cells** from the **Format** menu. The Format Cells dialog box appears.

3. Click the **Border** tab.

4. In the Style box, click the thin, solid line (last choice in the first column).

5. In the Presets section, click the **Outline** button.

6. Click **OK**. When the highlight is moved, a border outlines the cell.

7. Highlight **A9**.

8. Click the down arrow beside the **Borders** button. From the menu that appears, choose **Outside Borders** (third choice on the last row).

9. Save your work and leave the worksheet on the screen for the next Step-by-Step.

Computer Concepts

Selecting cells and clicking the Borders button (instead of the down arrow) applies the last border that was chosen using the toolbar.

FIGURE 2-8
Border tab in the Format Cells dialog box

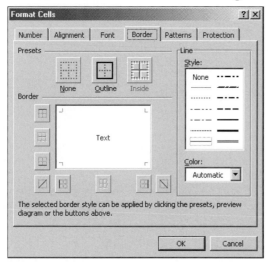

FIGURE 2-9
Borders button options

Cell Formats

Format affects the way data is shown in a cell. The default format is called General, which accommodates both text and numerical data. However, you can use several other formats (see Table 2-2). You can format a cell by highlighting the cell or range and choosing Cells on the Format menu. In the Format Cells dialog box, click the Number tab and select a format (see Figure 2-10) from the Category list, and then click OK. You can format data for currency, percentage, or commas, and to increase and decrease decimals, by clicking the appropriate button on the toolbar or in the Format Cells dialog box.

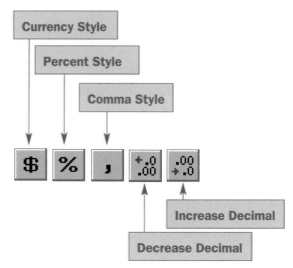

TABLE 2-2
Cell formats

FORMAT NAME	EXAMPLE	DISPLAY DESCRIPTION
General	1000	The default format; displays either text or numerical data as keyed
Number	1000.00	Displays numerical data with a fixed number of places to the right of the decimal point
Currency	$1,000.00	Displays numerical data preceded by a dollar sign
Accounting	$1,000.00 $ 9.00	Displays numerical data in a currency format that lines up the dollar sign and the decimal point vertically within a column
Date	6/8/02	Displays text and numerical data as dates
Time	7:38 PM	Displays text and numerical data as times
Percentage	35.2%	Displays numerical data followed by a percent sign
Fraction	35 7/8	Displays numerical data as fractional values
Scientific	1.00E+03	Displays numerical data in exponential notation
Text	45-875-33	Displays numerical data that will not be used for calculation, such as serial numbers containing hyphens
Special	79410	Displays numerical data that requires a specific format, such as zip codes or phone numbers
Custom	000.00.0	Displays formats designed by the user, including formats with commas or leading zeros

FIGURE 2-10
Number tab in the Format Cells dialog box

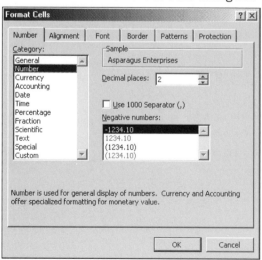

Using the Style Command

A *style* is a combination of formatting characteristics such as alignment, font, border, or pattern. Sometimes you will want to use a style on a consistent basis. For example, Excel has several styles that are predefined. On the other hand, you can create and name a style that you would like to use.

To apply a style that has already been created, select the cells to be formatted. Then, choose Style on the Format menu, and select the style you want from the Style name box. Click OK. To remove a style that has been applied, simply choose Style on the Format menu and choose Normal in the Style name box.

Did You Know?

If you know you will be using these styles again, you may want to define that style so you can apply it later. To define a style, select a cell that has the combination of formats you want. Choose **Style** on the **Format** menu, and name your style in the Style name box. Then click **Add** and **Close**.

Painting Formats

Format painting allows you to copy the format of a worksheet cell without copying the contents of the cell. For example, after formatting one cell for a percentage, you may format other cells for a percentage by painting the format.

To paint a format, begin by highlighting a cell that has the format you prefer. Click the Format Painter button on the toolbar, and then highlight the range of cells that you would like to format in the same manner.

STEP-BY-STEP ▷ 2.9

1. Select **B5:D5**.

2. Choose **Cells** on the **Format** menu. The Format Cells dialog box appears.

3. Click the **Number** tab.

4. Click **Currency** in the Category list box.

5. Click **OK**.

6. Change the width of columns **B** through **D** using AutoFit Selection.

7. Highlight **B5**.

8. Click the **Format Painter** button on the toolbar.

9. Drag from **B20** to **D20**. The format of B20:D20 will change to currency format.

10. Select the range **B6:D19**.

11. Open the Format Cells dialog box and click the **Number** tab, if necessary.

12. Click **Number** in the Category list box.

13. Click the **Use 1000 Separator (,)** box so that it is checked.

14. Click **OK**. Deselect the range. Your screen should look similar to Figure 2-11.

15. Save, print, and close the file.

Did You Know?

If you would like to paint the same format into several ranges, double-click the **Format Painter** button on the toolbar and then highlight as many ranges as you like.

FIGURE 2-11
By changing the appearance of a worksheet, you can make it easier to use

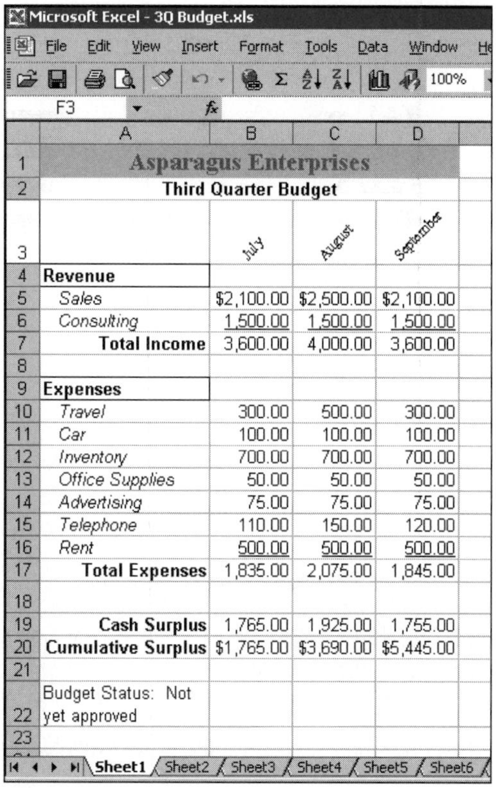

	A	B	C	D
1	Asparagus Enterprises			
2	Third Quarter Budget			
3		July	August	September
4	**Revenue**			
5	*Sales*	$2,100.00	$2,500.00	$2,100.00
6	*Consulting*	1,500.00	1,500.00	1,500.00
7	**Total Income**	3,600.00	4,000.00	3,600.00
8				
9	**Expenses**			
10	*Travel*	300.00	500.00	300.00
11	*Car*	100.00	100.00	100.00
12	*Inventory*	700.00	700.00	700.00
13	*Office Supplies*	50.00	50.00	50.00
14	*Advertising*	75.00	75.00	75.00
15	*Telephone*	110.00	150.00	120.00
16	*Rent*	500.00	500.00	500.00
17	**Total Expenses**	1,835.00	2,075.00	1,845.00
18				
19	**Cash Surplus**	1,765.00	1,925.00	1,755.00
20	**Cumulative Surplus**	$1,765.00	$3,690.00	$5,445.00
21				
22	Budget Status: Not yet approved			
23				

Clearing Cell Formats

You have learned how to change the appearance of a worksheet by bolding, italicizing, and underlining. You have also learned to add color and borders. You can remove the formats you apply to a cell or range of cells by selecting the cell or range, choosing Clear on the Edit menu, and then clicking Formats on the submenu. This removes the formatting *only*.

Applying an AutoFormat

An AutoFormat is a collection of font, patterns, and alignments that can be applied to a range of data. AutoFormats are applied by choosing the AutoFormat command on the Format menu.

STEP-BY-STEP 2.10

1. Open **IE Step2-10** from the data files.
2. Save the worksheet as **4Q Budget**, followed by your initials.
3. Select **A3:D20**.
4. Choose **AutoFormat** from the **Format** menu.
5. Click **Accounting 2** in the **AutoFormat** dialog box.
6. Click **OK**.

7. Click **A1**.

8. Choose **Clear** on the **Edit** menu, and then click **Formats** on the submenu. Notice that applied formats have now been removed.

9. Choose **Violet** (the second to last choice in row 3) from the **Font Color** box.

10. Click the **Bold** button.

11. Click **16** in the **Font Size** box.

12. Select **A1:D1**.

13. Click the **Merge and Center** button.

14. Save, print, and close the file.

Finding and Replacing Cell Formats

Previously you learned to find and replace data in a workbook. You may also find specific formats in a workbook and replace the format with another format. For example, it is possible to replace all italicized text with bolded text, or you might want to replace a cell filled with one color with another color.

STEP-BY-STEP ⇨ 2.11

1. Open **IE Step2-11** from the data files.

2. Save the worksheet as **Basketball Standings**, followed by your initials.

3. Choose **Replace** in the **Edit** menu.

4. Click the **Options** box.

5. In the **Format** drop-down box of the Find what line, choose **Choose Format From Cell**. The Find and Replace dialog box will disappear and an Excel pointer with a dropper will appear.

6. Click in **E5**. The Find and Replace dialog box will reappear.

7. Click the **Format** box of the **Replace with** line. The Replace Format dialog box will appear.

8. Click the **Number** tab if necessary.

9. Click **Number** in the **Category** box.

10. Key **3** in the **Decimal places** box.

11. Click **OK**.

12. Click **Replace All**. A message will appear stating that 24 replacements have been made.

13. Click **OK**.

14. Click **Close** in the Find and Replace dialog box.

15. Save, print, and close the file.

Summary

In this lesson, you learned:

■ Worksheet columns may be widened to accommodate data that is too large to fit in the cell.

■ You can use wrap, rotate, indent, or align features to change the position of text within the cells of a worksheet.

■ The appearance of cell data may be changed to make the worksheet easier to read. Font, font size, and style (bolding, italicizing, and underlining) may be changed. Color and borders may also be added.

■ The appearance of the cell may be changed to accommodate data in a variety of numerical formats.

■ A combination of formatting characteristics (such as alignment, font, border, or pattern) may be applied by using the Styles command.

■ Format painting is used to copy the format of a worksheet cell without copying the contents of the cell.

■ Various collections of fonts, patterns, and alignments can be applied to a range of data by using the AutoFormat command.

■ The Find and Replace command may be used to change cell formats.

VOCABULARY REVIEW

Define the following terms:

AutoFormat	Rotated text	Wrapped text
Indented text	Style	

LESSON 3 REVIEW QUESTIONS

TRUE/FALSE

Circle T if the statement is true or F if the statement is false.

T F 1. A series of number signs (######) appearing in a cell indicates that the data is wider than the column.

T F 2. Wrapped text will begin a new line within the cell of a worksheet when the data exceeds the width of a column.

T F 3. The Merge and Center button will combine several cells into one cell and place the text in the middle of the merged cell.

T F 4. You can place a border around the entire cell or only on certain sides of the cell.

T F 5. The default format for data in a cell is Text.

WRITTEN QUESTIONS

Write a brief answer to the following questions.

1. What cell format displays numerical data preceded by a dollar sign?

2. What is one way to let Excel determine the best width of a column?

3. What is one reason for rotating text?

4. What is the difference between the Fill Color and Font Color buttons?

5. What four cell alignment buttons are available on the toolbar?

LESSON 2 PROJECTS

PROJECT 2-1

Write the letter of the cell format option in the right column that matches the worksheet format described in the left column.

___ 1. Displays both text and numerical data as keyed   **A.** Accounting

___ 2. Displays numerical data with a fixed amount of   **B.** Time
places to the right of the decimal point

___ 3. Displays numerical data preceded by a dollar sign; however, dollar signs and decimal points do not necessarily line up vertically within the column

___ 4. Displays numerical data with dollar signs and decimal points that line up vertically within a column

___ 5. Displays text and numerical data as dates

___ 6. Displays text and numerical data as times

___ 7. Displays numerical data followed by a percent sign

___ 8. Displays the value of .5 as 1/2

___ 9. Displays numerical data in exponential notation

___ 10. Displays numerical data that will not be used for calculation, such as serial numbers containing hyphens

___ 11. Displays formats designed by the user

___ 12. Displays text in numerical format such as ZIP codes

C. Scientific

D. Fraction

E. Text

F. General

G. Date

H. Number

I. Percentage

J. Custom

K. Currency

L. Special

PROJECT 2-2

In this project, you will improve the appearance of a worksheet to better present your results.

1. Open **IE Project2-2** from the data files.

2. Save the file as **Bird Census**, followed by your initials.

3. Bold **A1**.

4. Bold the range **B3:F3**.

5. Rotate the text in **B3:F3** by 45 degrees.

6. Change the width of columns **B** through **E** to **6**.

7. Bold the range **A13:F13**.

8. Italicize the range **A5:A11**.

9. Right align **A13**.

10. Center align the data in cells **B3** through **F3**.

11. Change the font size in **A1** to **14**.

12. Merge and center cells **A1:F1**.

13. Place a single, thin line border around the heading *Bird Census*.

14. Save, print, and close the file.

PROJECT 2-3

The file *IE Project2-3* is a worksheet containing the inventory of The Pager Shop. The headings and numerical data have already been keyed in the worksheet. You are to make the spreadsheet easier to read and more attractive.

1. Open **IE Project2-3** from the data files.

2. Save the file as **Pager Shop**, followed by your initials.

3. Center the text in cells **B4:D5**.

4. Indent the text in **A7:A10**.

5. Change the width of columns **B**, **C**, and **D** to **10**.

6. Bold **B12** and **D12**.

7. Change the size of text in **A1** to **12** point. Merge and center **A1:D1**.

8. Change the size of text in **A2** to **11** point. Merge and center **A2:D2**.

9. Change the color of cells **A1:D1** to green using the Fill Color button (use the Green in the second row).

10. Change the color of cells in **A2:D2** to yellow (use the Light Yellow in the last row).

11. Format **C7:D10** and **D12** for **Currency** with two decimal places.

12. Change the color of text in **B12** and **D12** to the same green used to color the cells in A1:D1.

13. Save, print, and close the worksheet.

PROJECT 2-4

A college student would like to estimate her long-distance phone bill for calls she made to her home. Each time she makes a phone call, she notes the time of day and the number of minutes she spoke. She has prepared a worksheet to calculate the cost of the phone calls she has made. She must now format and print the worksheet.

1. Open **IE Project2-4** from the data files.

2. Save the file as **Long Distance**, followed by your initials.

3. Key **Estimate of Long Distance Bill** in **A1**.

4. Bold **A1**.

5. Change the size of the text in **A1** to **12** point.

6. Merge and center **A1:D1**.

7. Change the cell color of the range **A1:D1** to blue.

8. Change the color of the text in **A1** to white.

9. Underline the contents of **B3:C3**.

10. Center the contents of **B3:C3**.

11. Format **C4:D6** for **Currency** with two decimal places.

12. Format **D7** for **Currency** with two decimal places.

13. Underline the contents of **D6**.

14. Save, print, and close the file.

PROJECT 2-5

A balance sheet is a corporate financial statement that lists the assets (resources available), liabilities (amounts owed), and equity (ownership in the company). *IE Project2-5* contains the balance sheet of a large corporation, which needs to be formatted so that it is easier to read.

1. Open **IE Project2-5** from the data files.

2. Save the file as **Microsoft**, followed by your initials.

3. Change the column width of column **C** to **5**.

4. Change the size of the text in **A1** to **12** point.

5. Change the size of the text in **A2:A3** to **10** point.

6. Bold **A1**.

7. Merge and center **A1:E1**, **A2:E2**, and **A3:E3**.

8. Bold **A5**, **A6**, **A17**, **D5**, **D6**, **D15**, and **D19**.

9. Underline **B8**, **B12**, **B16**, **E11**, **E17**, and **E18**.

10. Format **B7**, **E7**, **B17**, and **E19** for Accounting with a dollar ($) symbol and no decimal places.

11. Format **B8:B16**, **E8:E13**, and **E16:E18** for **Accounting** with no decimal places and no symbol.

12. Save, print, and close the file.

PROJECT 2-6

The file *IE Project2-6* is a mileage chart between major cities in the United States. In this project you will make the data easier to read.

1. Open **IE Project2-6** from the data files.

2. Save the file as **Mileage**, followed by your initials.

3. Format **B2:O15** for **Number** with no decimal places and a comma separator.

4. Bold **B1:O1** and **A2:A15**.

5. Change the width of column **A** to **10**.

6. Rotate **B1:O1** to **-75** degrees.

7. Change the width of columns **B** through **O** to **5**.

8. Save, print, and close the file.

CRITICAL THINKING

ACTIVITY 2-1

To be useful, worksheets must be easy to view, both on screen and on the printed page. Identify ways to accomplish the following:

1. Emphasize certain portions of the worksheet.

2. Make text in the worksheet easier to read.

3. Distinguish one part of the worksheet from another.

4. Keep printed worksheet data from "spilling" onto another page.

ACTIVITY 2-2

You have been spending a lot of time formatting the bottom rows of worksheets when you enter new data. Your friend tells you that you could save some time by "extending" the formats that you have already created. She did not have time to explain how extending works so you are left curious.

Use the Help function in Excel to determine (1) how extended formatting works and (2) how to turn the extended formatting on and off.

ORGANIZING THE WORKSHEET

OBJECTIVES

Upon completion of this lesson, you should be able to:

- Copy data to other cells.
- Move data to other cells.
- Insert and delete columns and rows.
- Freeze titles.
- Use print options when printing a worksheet.
- Check the spelling of words in a worksheet.

⏱ **Estimated Time: 2 hours**

VOCABULARY

Filling

Freezing

Data in a worksheet should be arranged in a way that is easily accessed and observed. Data is rarely useful in its orginal format. You may reorganize data by moving it to another part of the work-sheet. You may also reduce data entry time by copying data to another part of the worksheet. If you decide that certain data is not needed you may delete entire rows or columns. If you would like to include additional information in a worksheet, you may insert another row or column.

Copying Data

When creating or enlarging a worksheet, you may want to use the same text or numbers in another part of the worksheet. Rather than key the same data over again, you can copy the data.

There are several ways to copy data in a worksheet. In this lesson, you will learn to copy and paste, use the drag-and-drop method, and fill cells. These operations can significantly decrease the amount of time needed to prepare a worksheet.

🎯 Hot Tip

Data copied into a cell will replace data already in that cell. Check your destination cells for existing data before copying.

Copy and Paste

Choosing the Copy command on the Edit menu or clicking the Copy button on the toolbar copies the contents of a cell or cells to the Clipboard. A revolving border appears around the selection, as shown in Figure 3-1. The Copy command will not affect the data in the original cell(s).

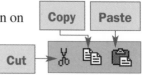

FIGURE 3-1
Copying data to another part of the worksheet

Next, place the highlight in the cell where you want the data to be copied. Then, choose Paste on the Edit menu or click the Paste button on the toolbar. The copied data will be pasted from the Clipboard to the cell or cells.

The data stored on the Clipboard will remain there until it is replaced with new data. If you would like to make multiple copies of that data, choose the Paste command again as many times as needed.

Hot Tip

If you are pasting a range of cells, it is not necessary to select the entire range; you need only highlight the upper left corner of the range into which data will be pasted.

STEP-BY-STEP ▷ 3.1

1. Start Excel, if necessary, and open **IE Step3-1** from your data files.

2. Save the file as **Utility**, followed by your initials.

3. Select the range **A3:D6**.

4. Choose **Copy** on the **Edit** menu. A revolving border surrounds the range.

5. Highlight **A8**.

6. Choose **Paste** on the **Edit** menu. The range of cells is copied from A3:D6 to A8:D11. (The border around A3:D6 will continue to revolve until you start the next step.)

7. Key **Natural Gas** in **A7**.

8. Key **100 cf** in **B7** to indicate the amount of cubic feet in hundreds.

9. Key **Cost / 100 cf** in **C7** to indicate the cost per hundred cubic feet.

10. Copy **D2** and paste it to **D7**.

11. Save the worksheet and leave it on the screen for the next Step-by-Step.

Using the Drag-and-Drop Method

Excel allows you to quickly copy data using the drag-and-drop method. First highlight the cells you want to copy. Then, move the pointer to the top border of the highlighted cells. The cross turns into an arrow pointer. While holding down the Ctrl key, drag the cells to a new location and release the mouse button. As you press the Ctrl key, a small plus sign (+) appears above the mouse pointer. As you drag the mouse pointer, a pop-up ScreenTip appears showing where the new location of the highlighted cells will be when you release the mouse button.

Computer Concepts

When you paste in Excel, a Paste options ScreenTip button with a list box arrow will appear on screen. You may use the list box to select from several paste options. For example, you may indicate whether you want the formatting to match the source or destination.

S TEP-BY-STEP ▷ 3.2

1. Select the range **A8:D11**.

2. Move the pointer to the top edge of cell A8 until it turns into an arrow pointer.

3. Press and hold down the **Ctrl** key. The plus sign appears.

4. Click and drag down until the pointer is in cell **A13** and the pop-up ScreenTip reads A13:D16.

5. Release the mouse button, and then the Ctrl key. The data is copied from A8:D11 to A13:D16.

6. Key **Water** in **A12**.

7. Key **1000 gallons** in **B12**.

8. Key **Cost / 1000 gal** in **C12** to indicate the cost per 1000 gallons of water.

9. Use the drag-and-drop method to copy **D7** to **D12**.

10. Bold the contents of cells **A7:C7** and **A12:C12**. Your screen should look similar to Figure 3-2.

11. Save and leave the worksheet on the screen for the next Step-by-Step.

The Fill Command

Filling copies data into adjacent cell(s). The Fill command on the Edit menu has several options on the submenu, including Down, Right, Up, and Left. Choose Down to copy data into the cell(s) directly below the original cell, as shown in Figure 3-3. Fill Up copies data into the cell(s) directly above the original cell.

Hot Tip

C Sometimes you may want to fill in a series of numbers or dates. For example, you might want a column to contain months such as January 2003, February 2003, March 2003, and so on. To fill cells with a series of data, begin by entering data in at least two cells. Then select the starting cells and drag the fill handle over the range of cells you want to fill.

FIGURE 3-2
Copying and pasting speed data entry

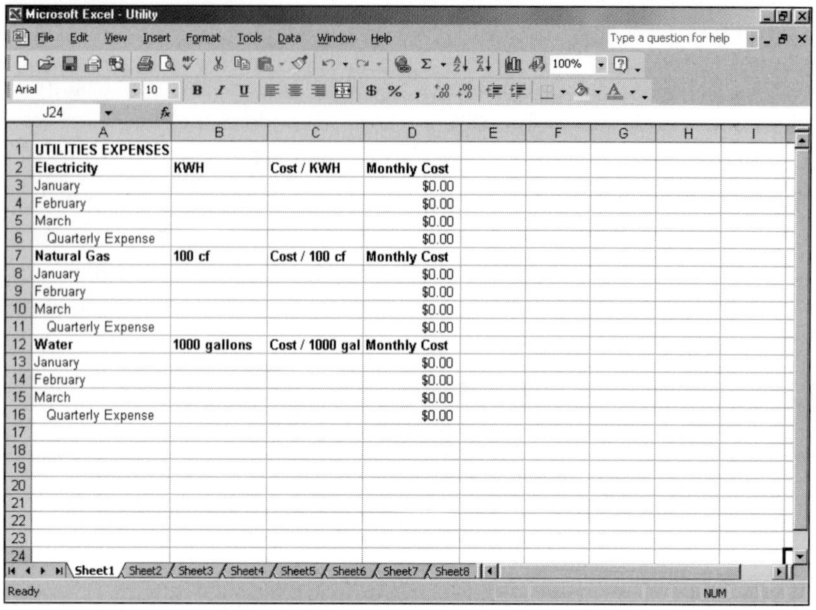

FIGURE 3-3
Fill Down copies data to adjacent cells below the original cell

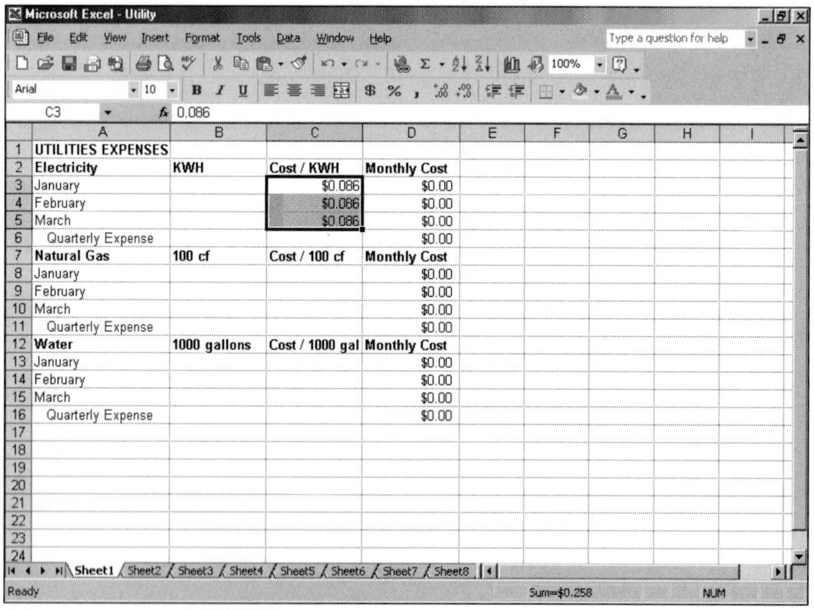

Fill Right and Fill Left copies data into the cell(s) to the right or left of the original cell. All options make multiple copies if more than one destination cell is selected. For example, the Down option can copy data into the next several cells below the original cell. Filling data is somewhat faster than copying and pasting because filling requires choosing only one command. However, filling can be used only when the destination cells are adjacent to the original cell.

STEP-BY-STEP 3.3

1. The cost of electricity for all three months is $0.086 per kilowatt hour. Enter **.086** in **C3**.

2. Drag from **C3** to **C5** to select the range to be filled.

3. Choose **Fill** on the **Edit** menu, then choose **Down** on the submenu. The contents of C3 are copied to cells C4 and C5.

4. Enter **.512** in **C8** to record the cost per 100 cubic feet of natural gas.

5. Use the **Fill Down** command to copy the data from **C8** to **C9** and **C10**.

6. Enter **.69** in **C13** to record the cost per 1000 gallons of water.

7. Use the **Fill Down** command to copy the data from **C13** to **C14** and **C15**.

8. Enter the following utility usage data into the worksheet:

Electricity	**KWH**
January	548
February	522
March	508
Natural Gas	**100 cf**
January	94
February	56
March	50
Water	**1000 gallons**
January	9
February	10
March	12

9. After completing the worksheet, notice that the monthly costs have been calculated based on the data you entered. Your screen should look similar to Figure 3-4.

10. Save and leave the worksheet on your screen for the next Step-by-Step.

FIGURE 3-4
Using the Fill Down command

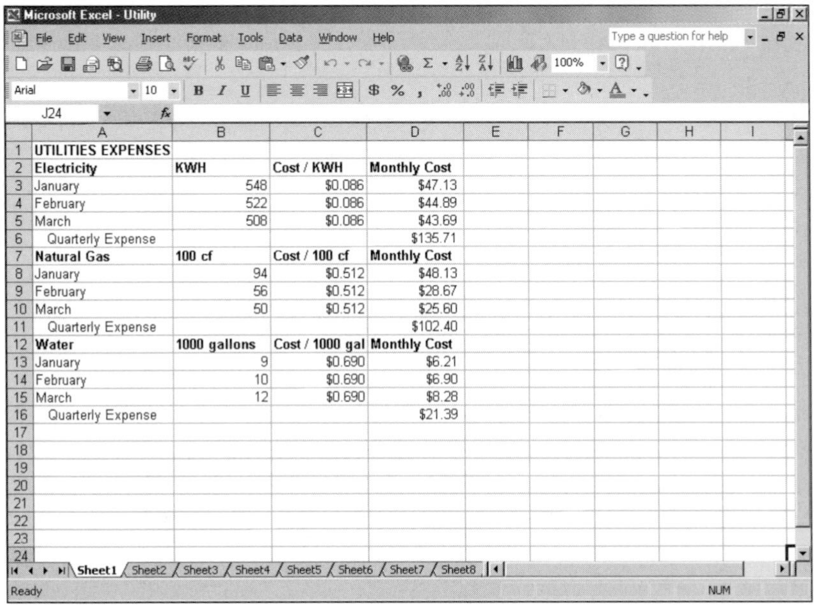

	A	B	C	D
1	UTILITIES EXPENSES			
2	Electricity	KWH	Cost / KWH	Monthly Cost
3	January	548	$0.086	$47.13
4	February	522	$0.086	$44.89
5	March	508	$0.086	$43.69
6	Quarterly Expense			$135.71
7	Natural Gas	100 cf	Cost / 100 cf	Monthly Cost
8	January	94	$0.512	$48.13
9	February	56	$0.512	$28.67
10	March	50	$0.512	$25.60
11	Quarterly Expense			$102.40
12	Water	1000 gallons	Cost / 1000 gal	Monthly Cost
13	January	9	$0.690	$6.21
14	February	10	$0.690	$6.90
15	March	12	$0.690	$8.28
16	Quarterly Expense			$21.39

Moving Data

There may be a time when you want to move data to a new location in a worksheet. You can move data two ways. The first method, cutting and pasting, is most appropriate when you want to move data to an area of the worksheet that is not currently in view on the screen. You've learned that the Copy command places a copy of the data on the Clipboard that can then be pasted into another area of the worksheet. The Cut command also places selected data on the Clipboard; however, the Cut command removes the data from its original position in the worksheet. After cutting data, place the highlight in the cell where you want the data to appear and choose Paste on the Edit menu or click the Paste button on the toolbar.

The drag-and-drop method can also be used to move data in the worksheet. The procedure is the same as you learned earlier in this lesson, except you do not hold down the Ctrl key as you would when you are copying data.

Computer Concepts

The drag-and-drop method is the easiest way to move data in a worksheet because you can do it without touching a key or using a menu.

S TEP-BY-STEP ▷ 3.4

1. Select the range **A12:D16**.

2. Click the **Cut** button on the toolbar. A revolving border surrounds the data in the range.

3. Highlight **A14**.

4. Click the **Paste** button on the tool-bar. The data moves to the range A14:D18.

5. Select the range **A7:D11**.

6. Move the pointer to the top edge of A7 until it turns into an arrow.

7. Click the mouse and drag down to **A8** until the pop-up ScreenTip reads A8:D12.

8. Release the mouse button. The data moves to the range A8:D12. Deselect the range. Your screen should look similar to Figure 3-5.

9. Save and leave the worksheet on the screen for the next Step-by-Step.

FIGURE 3-5

The Cut command moves data to another part of the worksheet

	A	B	C	D	E	F	G	H	I
1	UTILITIES EXPENSES								
2	Electricity	KWH	Cost / KWH	Monthly Cost					
3	January	548	$0.086	$47.13					
4	February	522	$0.086	$44.89					
5	March	508	$0.086	$43.69					
6	Quarterly Expense			$135.71					
7									
8	Natural Gas	100 cf	Cost / 100 cf	Monthly Cost					
9	January	94	$0.512	$48.13					
10	February	56	$0.512	$28.67					
11	March	50	$0.512	$25.60					
12	Quarterly Expense			$102.40					
13									
14	Water	1000 gallons	Cost / 1000 gal	Monthly Cost					
15	January	9	$0.690	$6.21					
16	February	10	$0.690	$6.90					
17	March	12	$0.690	$8.28					
18	Quarterly Expense			$21.39					
19									
20									
21									
22									
23									
24									

Inserting and Deleting Rows and Columns

You can also change the appearance of a worksheet by adding and removing rows and/or columns. In the previous Step-by-Step, you could have inserted rows between the types of utilities rather than move existing data.

To insert a row, choose Rows on the Insert menu. A row will be added above the highlight. To insert a column, choose Columns on the Insert menu. A column will be added to the left of the highlight.

When entering a long column of data, you may discover that you omitted a number at or near the top of the worksheet column. Rather than move the data to make room for the omitted data, it may be easier to insert a cell. Choose Cells on the Insert menu and the Insert dialog box opens. Designate whether you want existing cells to be shifted to the right or down.

When you want to delete a row or column, place the highlight in the row or column you want to delete. Then, choose Delete on the Edit menu. The Delete dialog box appears, as shown in Figure 3-6. Choose Entire row to delete the row, or choose Entire column to delete the column.

The easiest way to delete a row is to click on the row number to highlight the entire row. Then, choose Delete on the Edit menu. This process skips the Delete dialog box. You can easily delete a column the same way. Simply click the column letter to highlight the entire column, and then choose the Delete command. The Delete command erases all the data contained in the row or column. If you accidentally delete the wrong column or row, you can choose Undo to restore the data. Use Redo to cancel the Undo action.

You may also delete an individual cell by using the Delete command on the Edit menu. Suppose that you accidentally entered a number twice while

FIGURE 3-6

Delete dialog box

entering a long column of numbers. To eliminate the duplicate data, highlight the cell and choose Delete on the Edit menu. In the Delete dialog box (see Figure 3-6), click Shift cells up and then click OK. The cell is removed and the data in the cell below it is moved up one cell.

STEP-BY-STEP ▷ 3.5

1. Highlight any cell in row **2**.

2. Choose **Rows** on the **Insert** menu. Excel inserts a new, blank row 2. The original row 2 becomes row 3.

3. Highlight any cell in column **B**.

4. Choose **Columns** on the **Insert** menu. A blank column appears as column B. The original column B becomes column C.

5. Enter **Date Paid** in **B3**. Notice that it is automatically formatted like the other headings in that row.

6. Highlight any cell in column **B**.

7. Choose **Delete** on the **Edit** menu. The Delete dialog box appears as shown in Figure 3-6.

8. Click **Entire column** and click **OK**.

9. Click the row **3** number (left of *Electricity*). The entire row is selected.

10. Choose **Delete** on the **Edit** menu. Row 3 is deleted.

11. Click the **Undo** button on the toolbar. The row is restored.

12. Highlight **B17**.

13. Chose **Cells** on the **Insert** menu.

14. Click **Shift cells down** and click **OK**. The data in B17:B18 will be shifted to B18:B19.

15. Highlight **B17** if it is not currrently selected, and choose **Delete** on the **Edit** menu.

16. Click **Shift cells up** and click **OK**. The data in B18:B19 will be shifted back to B17:B18.

17. Save and leave the worksheet on the screen for the next Step-by-Step.

Freezing Titles

Often a worksheet can become so large that it is difficult to view the entire worksheet on the screen. As you scroll to other parts of the worksheet, titles at the top or side of the worksheet may disappear from the screen, making it difficult to identify the contents of particular columns. For example, the worksheet title *Utilities Expenses* in previous Step-by-Steps may have scrolled off the screen when you were working in the lower part of the worksheet.

Freezing will keep row or column titles on the screen no matter where you scroll in the worksheet. As shown in Figure 3-7, rows 1 and 2 are frozen so that when you scroll down, rows 3 through 13 are hidden. To freeze titles, place the highlight below the row you want to freeze or to the right of the column you want to freeze. Then, select Freeze Panes on the Window menu. All rows above the highlight and columns to the left of the highlight will be frozen. Frozen titles are indicated by a darkened gridline that separates the frozen portion of the worksheet from the unfrozen portion. To unfreeze a row or column title, choose the Unfreeze Panes command on the Window menu; the darkened gridline disappears and the titles will be unfrozen.

FIGURE 3-7
Freezing titles

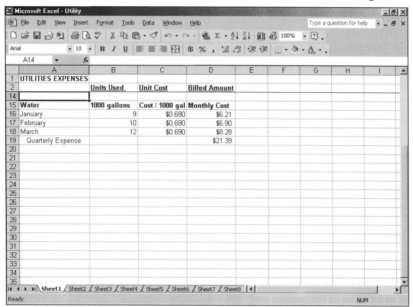

STEP-BY-STEP ▷ 3.6

1. Enter the following column titles into the designated cells:

Cell	Column Title
B2	Units Used
C2	Unit Cost
D2	Billed Amount

2. Underline and bold the contents of **B2**, **C2**, and **D2**.

3. Highlight **A3**.

4. Choose **Freeze Panes** on the **Window** menu. The title and column headings in rows 1 and 2 are now frozen. A darkened gridline appears between rows 2 and 3.

5. Scroll to the lower part of the worksheet to highlight cell **D19**. You will notice that the column headings remain at the top of the screen no matter where you move.

6. Choose **Unfreeze Panes** on the **Window** menu. The title and column headings are no longer frozen.

7. Save the file and leave it on the screen for the next Step-by-Step.

Printing Options

In Lessons 1 and 2, you printed a worksheet using the default settings. There are, however, other options for printing parts of a worksheet or changing the way a worksheet prints.

Printing Options in the Print Dialog Box

You can print part of a worksheet using the Print command. To define the part of the worksheet you want to print, select the range to be printed and choose Print on the File menu. When the Print dialog box appears (see Figure 3-8), click Selection in the Print what section.

FIGURE 3-8
Print dialog box

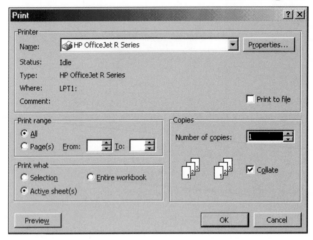

In the Print what section, you can also choose to print the active sheet(s), or the entire workbook. In addition, the Print dialog box lets you choose the number of copies to print. The Page range options let you specify whether you want to print all pages of the worksheet or certain pages.

Setting Page Breaks

If you are having difficulty placing data on a printed page in a way that is easily viewed, you may want to manually place page breaks in your worksheet. To force a page break above a selected cell, choose Page Break on the Insert menu. To remove a page break, select a cell below the page break and then choose Remove Page Break on the Insert menu.

Designing the Printed Page

The Page Setup command on the File menu allows you to set page margins and page lengths and widths, designate page numbers, and determine whether column letters, row numbers, and gridlines should be printed. The Page Setup dialog box is divided into four tabbed sections, shown in Figure 3-9. These sections are discussed on p. EI - 52.

FIGURE 3-9
Page Setup dialog box

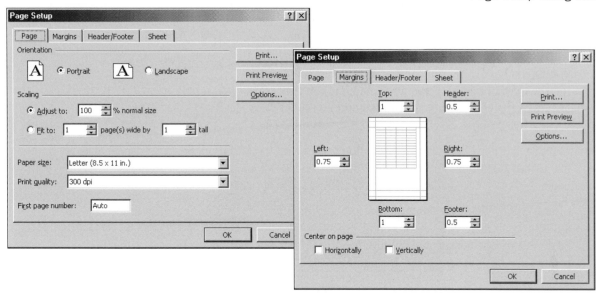

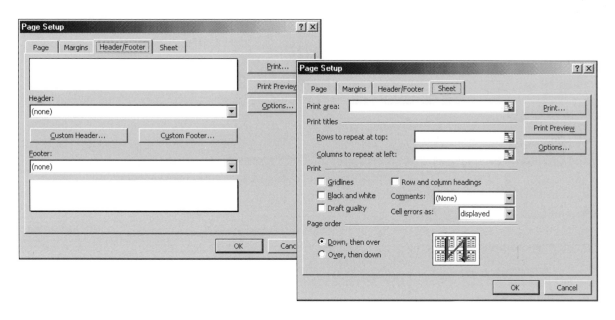

- **Page**. Page orientation (portrait or landscape), scaling, paper size, and print quality are designated under the Page tab. In addition, you can designate the page number of the first page of the worksheet.

- **Margins**. The Margins tab of the dialog box allows you to change the margins of the printed page by keying the margin size in the appropriate box. You can also choose to center the worksheet horizontally and/or vertically on the page.

- **Header/Footer**. Under the Header/Footer tab, you can key text to be printed at the top and bottom of each page.

- **Sheet**. Under the Sheet tab, you can set the print area and title of the worksheet. You can also choose whether gridlines, row headings, and column headings are printed.

Did You Know?

Sometimes you may want to print the same worksheet for different people with different information needs. A custom view will save print settings so that you may convert the spreadsheet to the view desired. To create a custom view, specify the page setup and print settings. Then select **Custom Views** on the **View** menu. Click **Add** in the Custom Views dialog box, and then key the name you would like to use for the custom view. Click **OK** to save the view format and settings. You may apply the customized view at any time by opening the Custom Views dialog box, selecting the view you want, and then clicking **Show**.

STEP-BY-STEP ▷ 3.7

C

1. Choose **Page Setup** on the **File** menu. The Page Setup dialog box appears.

2. Click the **Page** tab if it's not chosen already.

3. In the Orientation section, click the **Landscape** button. In the Scaling section, click the up arrow until **130** appears in the Adjust to box.

4. Click the **Margins** tab.

5. Click the down arrow on the Bottom box until **0.5** appears.

6. In the Center on page section, check **Horizontally** and **Vertically**.

7. Click the **Header/Footer** tab.

8. Click the down arrow on the **Header** text box.

9. Click **Utility, Page 1**.

10. Click the **Sheet** tab.

11. In the Print section, check **Gridlines** and **Row and column headings**.

12. Click the **Collapse Dialog** button at the right side of the **Print area** text box. The dialog box will disappear.

13. Drag from **A1** to **D19**.

14. Click the **Expand Dialog** button at the right side of the Page Setup — Print area dialog box. The Page Setup dialog box will appear and $A$1:$D$19 appears in the Print area text box.

15. Click **OK**.

16. Save and leave the worksheet on the screen for the next Step-by-Step.

Previewing a Worksheet before Printing

The Print Preview command shows how your printed pages will appear before you actually print them. To access the Print Preview screen (see Figure 3-10), choose Print Preview on the File menu or click the Print Preview button on the toolbar.

FIGURE 3-10
Print Preview screen

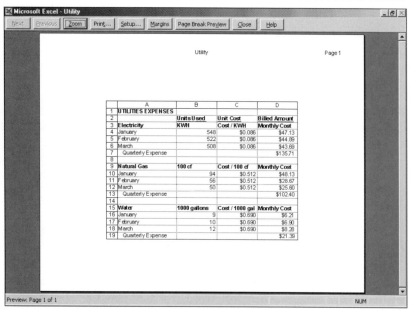

The buttons across the top of the screen provide options for viewing your worksheet. Choose Next and Previous to see other pages of your worksheet. Use the Zoom button or click the mouse pointer (which automatically turns into a magnifying glass in Print Preview) anywhere on the page to get a magnified view. Click the Margins button to change the margins of the worksheet, or click the Setup button to go to the Page Setup dialog box discussed earlier. Click Page Break Preview to adjust the page breaks and control what appears on each page when the worksheet is printed. When you have finished previewing the printed pages, you can return to the worksheet by choosing Close, or print the worksheet by choosing the Print button.

S TEP-BY-STEP ▷ 3.8

1. Select **A1:D19**.

2. Choose **Print** on the **File** menu. The Print dialog box appears.

3. Click **Selection** in the Print what box.

4. Click **OK**. The selection will print.

5. Click the **Print Preview** button on the toolbar. The Print Preview screen appears, as shown in Figure 3-10.

6. Click the **Zoom** button. A portion of the pre-viewed page becomes larger so that it can be examined in more detail.

7. Click **Setup**.

8. Click the **Sheet** tab, if it's not open already.

9. In the Print box, click the **Gridlines** box and the **Row and column headings** box to remove the check marks.

10. Click **OK**.

11. Click the **Print** button. The Print dialog box appears.

12. Print the active sheet by clicking **OK**.

13. Save and close the file.

Extra Challenge

Use the formatting commands you learned in Lesson 2 to make the spreadsheet more attractive.

Checking Spelling on a Worksheet

Excel has a dictionary tool that will check the spelling of words on a worksheet. Excel uses the same dictionary that is available in Microsoft Word. To spell-check a worksheet, select the Spelling command on the Tools menu, or click the Spelling button on the Formatting toolbar.

STEP-BY-STEP ⟹ 3.9

1. Open **IE Step3-9** from the data files, and save it as **Euro**, followed by your initials.

2. Click the **Spelling** button on the **Formatting** toolbar. The Spelling dialog box appears. The Spelling tool has correctly identified *Austia* as a misspelled word and has offered several suggestions for change.

3. Click **Austria** in the Suggestions box. Then, click **Change**. The Spelling tool will correct the change and move to the next word that is misspelled (*Finnland*).

4. Click **Finland**, and then click **Change**.

5. Next, the Spelling tool has identified *Markka* as a misspelled word. However, Markka is the correct spelling of the Finnish currency. (The term was identified as "Not in dictionary" because it is not a commonly used English word.)

WRITTEN QUESTIONS

Write a brief answer to the following questions.

1. What key do you press to copy data using the drag-and-drop method?

2. How do you make multiple copies of data that has been already copied to the Clipboard?

3. What should you do if you accidentally delete a column or row?

4. What command keeps the titles of a worksheet on the screen no matter where the highlight is moved?

5. Which menu contains the Spelling command?

LESSON 3 PROJECTS

PROJECT 3-1

Match the correct term in the right column to its description in the left column.

____ 1. You are tired of keying repetitive data.

____ 2. A portion of the worksheet would be more useful in another area of the worksheet.

____ 3. You forgot to key a row of data in the middle of the worksheet.

____ 4. You no longer need a certain column in the worksheet.

A. Print command or Print button

B. Fill command or Copy command

C. Rows or Columns command

IE-57

___ 5. Column headings cannot be viewed on the screen when you are working in the lower part of the worksheet.

___ 6. You want to be sure that all words are spelled correctly in the worksheet.

___ 7. Your boss would rather not view your worksheet on the screen and has requested a copy on paper.

___ 8. You would like to print only the selected area of a worksheet.

D. Spelling command

E. Cut command, Paste command

F. Selection option in the Print dialog box

G. Delete command

H. Freeze Panes command

PROJECT 3-2

IE Project3-2 contains a list of assets of Pelican Retail Stores. Perform the following operations to make the worksheet more useful to the reader.

1. Open **IE Project3-2** from the data files.

2. Save the file as **Pelican Stores**, followed by your initials.

3. Insert a column to the left of column **B**.

4. Widen column **A** to **45** spaces.

5. Move the contents of **D4:D17** to **B4:B17**.

6. Change columns **B** and **C** to **10** spaces.

7. Insert a row above row **4**.

8. Indent the contents of **A11**, **A15**, and **A18**.

9. Underline the contents of **B5:C5**.

10. Save, print, and close the file.

PROJECT 3-3

IE Project3-3 is a list of countries that trade with the United States. Because the spelling of some countries is complicated, you would like to check the spelling of the words in the worksheet.

1. Open **IE Project3-3** from the data files.

2. Save the file as **Import**, followed by your initials.

3. Freeze the column headings in rows **1** through **5**. (*Hint:* Place the highlight in **A6** before choosing the Freeze Panes command.)

4. Check the spelling of the countries listed in the worksheet.

5. Change the printed page so that the worksheet will be printed in portrait orientation.

6. Adjust the scaling of the printed page so that it is 80% of its original size.

7. Change the printed page so that the top and bottom margins are one-half inch.

8. Save, print, and close the file.

PROJECT 3-4

The file *IE Project3-4* accounts for the inventory purchases of a small office supply store. The worksheet is not currently organized by suppliers of the inventory.

1. Open **IE Project3-4** from the data files.

2. Save the file as **Supply Inventory**, followed by your initials.

3. Organize the worksheet so that it looks like the table below. The new worksheet should have inventory items organized by supplier, with proper headings inserted. Some of the data is out of order and needs to be moved. Remember to bold appropriate data.

Item	Ordering Code	Quantity
Mega Computer Manufacturers		
Mega X-39 Computers	X-39-25879	20
Mega X-40 Computers	X-40-25880	24
Mega X-41 Computers	X-41-25881	28
Xenon Paper Source		
Xenon Letter Size White Paper	LT-W-45822	70
Xenon Letter Size Color Paper	LT-C-45823	10
Xenon Legal Size White Paper	LG-W-45824	40
Xenon Legal Size Color Paper	LG-C-45825	5
MarkMaker Pen Co.		
MarkMaker Blue Ball Point Pens	MM-Bl-43677	120
MarkMaker Black Ball Point Pens	MM-Bk-43678	100
MarkMaker Red Ball Point Pens	MM-R-43679	30

4. The following inventory item has been accidentally excluded from the worksheet. Add the item by using the Fill Down command and then editing the copied data.

Item	Ordering Code	Quantity
MarkMaker Green Ball Point Pens	MM-G-43680	30

5. Delete the following items.

Item	Ordering Code	Quantity
Mega X-39 Computers	X-39-25879	20

6. Change the page orientation to landscape.

7. Save, print, and close the file.

PROJECT 3-5

1. Open **IE Project3-5** from the data files.

2. Save the file as **Time Record**, followed by your initials.

3. Delete rows **4** and **5**.

4. Insert the following information on the time record. (*Note:* The AutoComplete function may automatically enter some of the work descriptions for you as you begin to enter the data. To accept the data as it appears, press **Enter**.)

Date	From	To	Admin.	Meetings	Phone	Work Description
9-Dec	8:15 AM	12:00 PM		1.00	2.75	Staff meeting and call clients
10-Dec	7:45 AM	11:30 AM	2.00		1.75	Paperwork and call clients
11-Dec	7:45 AM	11:30 AM			3.75	Call clients
13-Dec	8:00 AM	12:00 PM	2.00	2.00		Mail flyers and meet w/KF

5. Freeze headings above row **8**.

6. Insert a blank row above row 16. Insert the following information:

Date	From	To	Admin.	Meetings	Phone	Work Description
12-Dec	7:45 AM	11:30 AM	2.00		1.75	Paperwork and call clients

7. Copy **D15** to **D16**.

8. Preview the worksheet and zoom in to see the total hours worked.

9. Change the orientation of the worksheet to landscape. Center horizontally and vertically on the page.

10. Save, print, and close the worksheet.

PROJECT 3-6

The file *IE Project3-6* contains the grades of several students taking Biology 101 during the spring semester. The instructor has asked that you, the student assistant, help maintain the grade records of the class.

1. Open **IE Project3-6** from the data files.

2. Save the file as **Class Grades**, followed by your initials.

3. Merge and center **A1:I1**. Merge and center **A2:I2**.

4. Column A contains the last names of students in the class.
   A. Add a column between the current columns **A** and **B** to hold the first names of the students.
   B. Enter **First Name** in **B3** of the new column.
   C. Enter the following names in the new column you created:

Row	Entry
4	Ashley
5	Kevin
6	Cindy
7	Raul
8	Haley
9	Cameron

5. Preview the worksheet.

6. Change the worksheet to landscape orientation and center it both vertically and horizontally on the page.

7. Remove the header.

8. Change the footer to read *Page 1*.

9. Save, print, and close the file.

PROJECT 3-7

You are a member of the Booster Club, an organization that raises money to purchase sports equipment for the local high school. You have been allocated $1,210 to purchase sports equipment for the school. You prepare a worksheet to help calculate the cost of various purchases. (*Note:* The AutoComplete function may enter some of the data for you as you begin to enter the data. To accept the data as it appears, press **Enter**.)

1. Open the file **IE Project3-7** from the data files.

2. Save the file as **Booster Club**, followed by your initials.

3. Bold and center the column headings in row **2**.

4. Insert a row above row **3**.

5. Freeze the column headings in row **2**.

6. Insert a row above row **8** and key **Bats** in **A8** (the new row).

7. Use the Fill Down command to copy the formula in **E4** to **E5:E11**. Do not copy the formula into E12.

8. Format the **Cost (D4:D11)** and **Total (E4:E12)** columns for currency with two decimal places.

9. Key the data for *Sport* and *Cost*, as given in the following table. Use the Fill Down command as needed to copy repetitive data. Widen the columns if necessary.

Item	Sport	Cost
Basketballs	Basketball	28
Hoops	Basketball	40
Backboards	Basketball	115
Softballs	Softball	5
Bats	Softball	30
Masks	Softball	35
Volleyballs	Volleyball	25
Nets	Volleyball	125

10. You have $1,210 to spend on equipment. The organization has requested you to purchase the items listed below. Any remaining cash should be used to purchase as many basketballs as possible.

Basketballs	5
Hoops	2
Backboards	2
Softballs	20
Bats	5
Masks	1
Volleyballs	7
Nets	1

11. Increase the number of basketballs and watch the dollar amount in the total. You should use $1,203.00 and have $7.00 left over.

12. Save, print, and close the file.

PROJECT 3-8

IE Project3-8 contains attendance data for a neighborhood swimming pool. Format the worksheet in a way that you find appealing. You may move data in the worksheet. You may also change the column width, color, alignment, borders, format, and font of the data. When you have finished, name and save the file as **Swimming Pool**, followed by your initials. Then print and close the file.

CRITICAL THINKING

C

ACTIVITY 3-1

As a zoo employee, you have been asked to observe the behavior of a predatory cat during a three-day period. You are to record the number of minutes the animal displays certain behaviors during the time that the zoo is open to visitors. Set up a worksheet that can be used to record the number of minutes that the cat participates in these behaviors during each of the three days.

■ Sleeping

■ Eating

■ Walking

■ Sitting

■ Playing

Make your worksheet easy to read by using bolded fonts, italicized fonts, varied alignment, and color.

WORKSHEET FORMULAS

Upon completion of this lesson, you should be able to:

■ Enter and edit formulas.

■ Distinguish between relative, absolute, and mixed cell references.

■ Use the AutoSum button and the point-and-click method to enter formulas.

■ Display formulas in the worksheet.

■ Perform immediate and delayed calculations.

🕐 **Estimated Time: 2.5 hours**

Absolute cell reference

Formulas

Mixed cell reference

Operand

Operator

Order of evaluation

Point-and-click method

Relative cell reference

What Are Formulas?

Worksheets can use numbers entered in certain cells to calculate values in other cells. The equations used to calculate values in a cell are known as *formulas*. Excel recognizes the contents of a cell as a formula when an equal sign (=) is the first character in the cell. For example, if the formula =8+6 were entered in cell B3, the value of 14 would be displayed in B3 of the worksheet. The formula bar displays the formula =8+6, as shown in Figure 4-1.

FIGURE 4-1
Formula result displays in the cell

Structure of a Formula

A worksheet formula consists of two components: operands and operators. An ***operand*** is a number or cell reference used in formulas. You can key cell references in uppercase (A1) or lowercase (a1). An ***operator*** tells Excel what to do with the operands. For example, in the formula =B3+5, B3 and 5 are operands. The plus sign (+) is an operator that tells Excel to add the value contained in cell B3 to the number 5. The operators used in formulas are shown in Table 4-1. After you have keyed the formula, enter it by pressing the Enter key or by clicking the check mark button on the formula bar.

As you enter cell references in the formula bar, you may notice that the reference will appear in a specific color. The cell referenced in the formula will be outlined in the same color. You may adjust the color-coded reference in the formula by moving or dragging the outlined cell in the worksheet.

TABLE 4-1
Formula operators

OPERATOR	OPERATION	EXAMPLE	MEANING
+	Addition	B5+C5	Adds the values in B5 and C5
-	Subtraction	C8-232	Subtracts 232 from the value in C8
*	Multiplication	D4*D5	Multiplies the value in D4 by the value in D5
/	Division	E6/4	Divides the value in E6 by 4
^	Exponentiation	B3^3	Raises the value in B3 to the third power

STEP-BY-STEP ▷ 4.1

1. Open **IE Step4-1** from the data files.

2. Save the worksheet as **Calculate**, followed by your initials.

3. Highlight **C3**.

4. Key **=A3+B3** and press **Enter**. The formula result 380 appears in the cell.

5. In **C4**, key **=A4-B4** and press **Enter**.

6. In **C5**, key **=A5*B5** and press **Enter**.

7. In **C6**, key **=A6/B6** and press **Enter**.

8. Check your results by comparing them to Figure 4-2. Save the worksheet and leave the file open for use in the next Step-by-Step.

FIGURE 4-2
Entering formulas

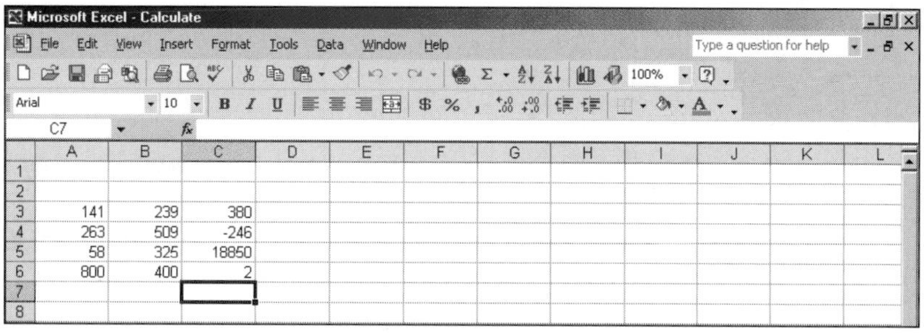

Order of Evaluation

Formulas containing more than one operator are called complex formulas. For example, the formula =C3*C4+5 will perform both multiplication and addition to calculate the value in the cell. The sequence used to calculate the value of a formula is called the *order of evaluation*.

Formulas are evaluated in the following order:

1. Contents within parentheses are evaluated first. You may use as many pairs of parentheses as you want. Excel will evaluate the innermost set of parentheses first.
2. Mathematical operators are evaluated in order of priority, as shown in Table 4-2.
3. Equations are evaluated from left to right if two or more operators have the same order of evaluation. For example, in the formula =20-15-2, the number 15 would be subtracted from 20; then 2 would be subtracted from the difference (5).

TABLE 4-2
Order of evaluation priority

ORDER OF EVALUATION	OPERATOR	SYMBOL
First	Exponentiation	^
Second	Positive or negative	+ or -
Third	Multiplication or division	* or /
Fourth	Addition or Subtraction	+ or -

STEP-BY-STEP ▷ 4.2

1. In **D3**, key **=(A3+B3)*20**. The values in A3 and B3 will be added, and then the result will be multiplied by 20.

2. Press **Enter**. The resulting value is 7600.

3. You can see the importance of the parentheses in the order of evaluation by creating an identical formula without the parentheses. In **E3**, key **=A3+B3*20**, the same formula as in D3 but without the parentheses.

4. Press **Enter**. The resulting value is 4921. This value differs from the value in D3 because Excel multiplied the value in B3 by 20 before adding the value in A3. In D3, the values in A3 and B3 were added together and the sum multiplied by 20.

5. Save the worksheet and leave it open for the next Step-by-Step.

Editing Formulas

Excel will not let you enter a formula with an incorrect structure. If you attempt to do so, a dialog box explaining the error appears. For example, if you enter a formula with an opening parenthesis but no closing parenthesis, a message describing the error and how to correct the error will appear. You can then correct the formula by editing in the formula bar. You can also edit formulas already entered in the worksheet. To edit a formula, highlight the cell, then press the Edit key (F2); or, click in the formula bar and key or delete data as necessary.

S TEP-BY-STEP ⟹ 4.3

1. Move the highlight to **E3**. The formula is shown in the formula bar.

2. Place the insertion point after the = in the formula bar and click.

3. Key **(**.

4. Press **Enter**. An error message appears asking whether you would like to accept a suggested change or correct the error yourself.

5. Choose **No** so that you may correct the error yourself. A dialog box describing the error appears.

6. Click **OK**.

7. Now move the insertion point in the formula bar between the 3 and the *.

8. Key **)**.

9. Press **Enter**. The value changes to 7600.

10. Save the file and leave it on the screen for the next Step-by-Step.

Relative, Absolute, and Mixed Cell References

Three types of cell references are used to create formulas: relative, absolute, and mixed. A *relative cell reference* adjusts to its new location when copied or moved. For example, in Figure 4-3, the formula =A3+A4 is copied from A5 to B5 and the formula changes to =B3+B4. In other words, this formula is instructing Excel to add the two cells directly above. When the formula is copied or moved the cell references change, but the operators remain the same.

FIGURE 4-3

Copying a formula with relative cell references

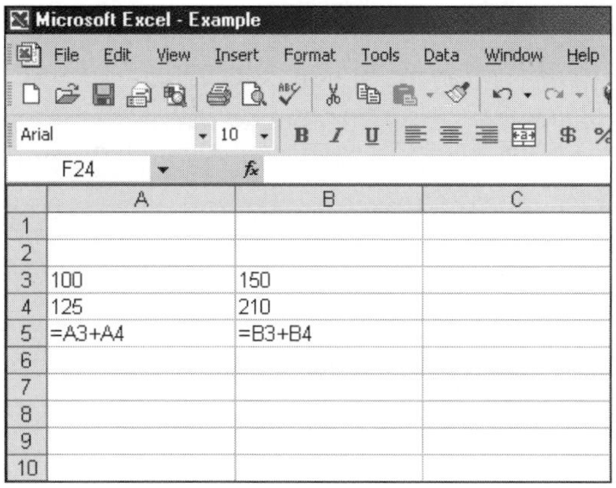

Absolute cell references do not change when moved or copied to a new cell. To create an absolute reference, you insert a dollar sign ($) before the column letter and/or the row number of the cell reference you want to stay the same. For example, in Figure 4-4, the formula =$A$3+$A$4 is copied from A5 to B7 and the formula remains the same in the new location.

FIGURE 4-4

Copying a formula with absolute cell references

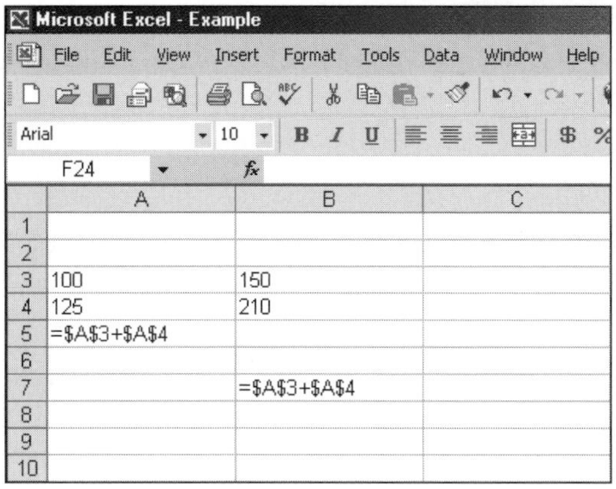

Cell references containing both relative and absolute references are called ***mixed cell references***. When formulas with mixed cell references are copied or moved, the row or column references preceded by a dollar sign will not change; the row or column references not preceded by a dollar sign will adjust relative to the cell to which they are moved. As shown in Figure 4-5, when the formula =A$3+A$4 is copied from A5 to B7, the formula changes to =B$3+B$4.

FIGURE 4-5
Copying a formula with mixed cell references

	A	B	C
1			
2			
3	100	150	
4	125	210	
5	=A$3+A$4		
6			
7		=B$3+B$4	
8			
9			
10			

STEP-BY-STEP ▷ 4.4

1. Place the highlight in **D3**. The formula =(A3+B3)*20 (shown in the formula bar) contains only relative cell references.

2. Use **Fill Down** to copy the formula in D3 to **D4**.

3. Place the highlight in **D4**. The value in D4 is 15440 and the formula in the formula bar is =(A4+B4)*20. The operators in the formula remain the same, but the relative cell references changed to reflect a change in the location of the formula.

4. Enter **=$A$3*($B$3-200)** in **D5**. The value in D5 is 5499. The formula contains absolute cell references, which are indicated by the dollar signs that precede row and column references.

5. Copy the formula in D5 to **D6**. The value in D6 is 5499, the same as in D5.

6. Move the highlight to **D5** and look at the formula in the formula bar. Now move the highlight to **D6** and look at the formula. Because the formula in D5 contains absolute cell references, the formula is exactly the same as the formula in D6.

7. Enter **=$A$4+B4** in **E4**. This formula contains mixed cell references (relative and absolute). The value in E4 is 772.

8. Copy the formula in E4 to **E5**. Notice the relative reference B4 changed to B5, but the absolute reference to A4 stayed the same. The value in E5 is 588.

9. Copy the formula in E5 to **F5**. Again, notice the relative reference changed from B5 to C5. The absolute reference to A4 stayed the same. The value in F5 is 19113.

10. Save, print, and close the file.

Creating Formulas Quickly

You have already learned how to create formulas by keying the formula or editing existing formulas. In this section, formulas are created quickly by using the point-and-click method and by clicking the AutoSum button.

Point-and-Click Method

Earlier, you constructed formulas by keying the entire formula in the cell of the worksheet. You can include cell references in a formula more quickly by clicking on the cell rather than keying the reference. This is known as the *point-and-click method*. The point-and-click method is particularly helpful when you have to enter long formulas that contain several cell references.

To use the point-and-click method to create a formula, simply substitute clicking the cell for keying a cell reference. For example, to enter the formula =A3+B3 in a cell, you first highlight the cell that will contain the formula. Next, press =, click cell A3, press +, click cell B3, and press Enter.

S TEP-BY-STEP ▷ 4.5

The manager of the Fruit and Fizz Shop would like to determine the total sales of juice and soda during the month, as well as to calculate the percentage of the total items sold for each type of juice and soda. Prices of individual servings are as follows:

	Large	Small
Juice	$1.50	$0.90
Soda	$0.80	$0.50

1. Open **IE Step4-5** from the data files.

2. Save the file as **Drinks**, followed by your initials.

3. Key **=(1.5*** in **D6** ($1.50 is the price for a large juice).

4. Click **B6**. (You will see that a moving colored border around the cell and the cell reference, in the same color, appears in the formula.)

5. Key **)+(.9*** ($0.90 is the price for a small juice).

6. Click **C6**.

7. Key **)**.

8. Press **Enter**. The amount $567.00 will appear in the cell.

9. Use **Fill Down** to copy the formula in D6 to **D7** and **D8**. The value in D7 is $393.90. The value in D8 is $142.50.

10. Key **=(.8*** in D9 ($0.80 is the price for a large soda).

11. Click **B9**.

12. Key **)+(.5*** ($0.50 is the price for a small soda).

13. Click **C9**.

14. Key **)** and press **Enter**. The value in D9 is $282.20.

15. Use **Fill Down** to copy the formula in D9 to **D10** and **D11**. Your screen should look similar to Figure 4-6.

16. Save and leave the file on your screen for the next Step-by-Step.

FIGURE 4-6
Inserting formulas using the point-and-click method

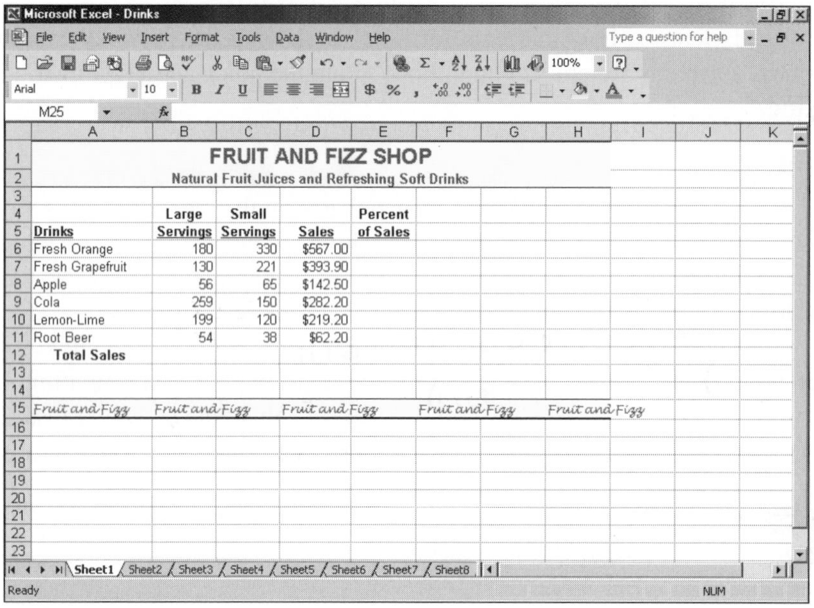

The AutoSum Button

Worksheet users frequently need to sum long columns of numbers. The AutoSum button on the toolbar makes this operation simple. The AutoSum button is identified by the Greek letter sigma (Σ). To use AutoSum, place the highlight in the cell where you want the total to appear. Click the AutoSum button, and Excel scans the worksheet to determine the most logical column or row of adjacent cells containing numbers to sum. Excel then displays an outline around the range it has selected. This range is identified in the highlighted cell. If you prefer a range other than the one Excel selects, drag to select those cells. Press Enter to display the sum in the cell.

The sum of a range is indicated by a special formula in the formula bar called a function formula. For example, if the sum of the range D5:D17 is entered in a cell, the function formula will be =SUM(D5:D17). The SUM function is the most frequently used function formula. Function formulas will be discussed in greater detail in the next lesson.

STEP-BY-STEP ▷ 4.6

1. Highlight **D12**.

2. Click the **AutoSum** button. The range D6:D11 is outlined. Excel has correctly selected the range of cells you would like to sum. The formula =SUM(D6:D11) appears in the formula bar.

3. Press **Enter**. D12 displays $1,667.00, the sum of the numbers in column D.

4. Highlight **E6**.

5. Press **=**.

6. Click **D6**.

7. Press /.

8. Key **$D$12** and press **Enter**.

9. Copy the formula in E6 to **E7:E12**. Your screen should look similar to Figure 4-7.

10. Save and leave the worksheet on your screen for the next Step-by-Step.

FIGURE 4-7
Using the AutoSum button

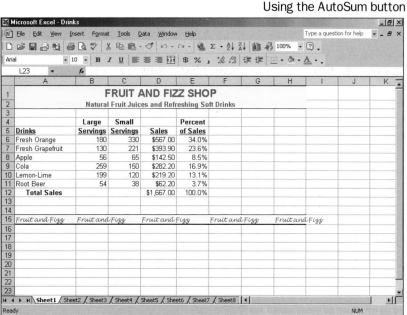

Previewing a Calculation

You may want to determine a calculated amount from worksheet data before entering a formula. By using a feature called Auto Calculation, you may determine, for example, the number of entries within a range or the average of amounts in a range. To use Auto Calculation to determine the sum of data contained in a range, select the range and then right-click on the status bar at the bottom of the screen. A menu will appear. By clicking Sum, the summation of data in the range will appear in the status bar.

 Hot Tip

Auto Calculation may also be used to determine the minimum or maximum value that lies within a range.

1. Select the range **B6:C6**.

2. Right-click anywhere in the status bar. A menu will appear.

	None
	Average
	Count
	Count Nums
	Max
	Min
✓	Sum

3. If it is not already checked, click **Sum** so that a check mark appears. The number of large and small orange juices served, 510, will appear in the status bar.

4. Select the range **B6:C11**. The total number of large and small drinks, 1,802, appears in the status bar. Click outside the range to deselect it and remain in this screen for the next Step-by-Step.

Formula Helpers

The Options dialog box, displayed by choosing Options on the Tools menu, contains several tabbed sections that define features in the worksheet. For example, the Formulas box in the Window options section on the View tab (see Figure 4-8) will replace the values in the cells of the worksheet with the formulas that created them. If a cell does not contain a formula, Excel displays the data entered in the cell. To display values determined by the formulas again, click to remove the check mark from the Formulas box. Another option of interest is the Manual button on the Calculation tab which will prevent worksheet formulas from calculating until you press the F9 key.

Hot Tip

Auto Calculation may be used to check the formula results. D12 contains a function formula that determines the sum of D6:D11. To check the results of the formula, right-click the status bar and click **Sum**. Then select D6:D11. The sum in the status bar should equal the value in D12.

FIGURE 4-8

View tab in the Options dialog box

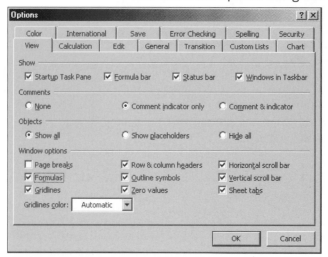

Showing Formulas on the Worksheet

In previous Step-by-Steps, you were able to view formulas only in the formula bar or in the cell as you were keying the formula. Cells of the worksheet contained the values determined by formulas rather than the formulas themselves. When creating a worksheet containing many formulas, you may find it easier to organize formulas and detect formula errors when you can view all formulas at once.

Hot Tip

You can also switch between viewing formulas and values by pressing Ctrl+` (the ` is located in the upper-left area of most keyboards).

Delayed Calculations

Values in the worksheet are usually calculated as a new formula is entered, but you can also calculate the formula at a specific moment. Delayed calculation (also called manual calculation) can be useful when you are working with a large worksheet that will take longer than usual to calculate; or you may want to view the difference in a particular cell after you have made changes throughout the worksheet.

To delay calculation, click the Manual button on the Calculation tab of the Options dialog box (see Figure 4-9) and then press F9 to start calculation. To return to automatic calculation, click the Automatic button in the Calculation section of the tab.

FIGURE 4-9
Calculation tab in the Options dialog box

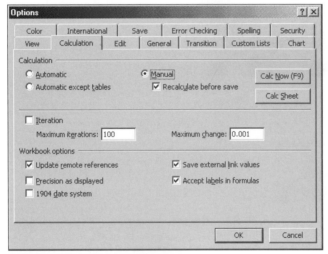

S TEP-BY-STEP ▷ 4.8

1. Choose **Options** on the **Tools** menu. The Options dialog box appears, as shown in Figure 4-8.

2. Click the **View** tab, if necessary.

3. In the Window options box, click the **Formulas** box so that a check mark appears.

4. Click **OK**. If the Formula Auditing toolbar appears, you may move it or close it.

5. Scroll to the right so that columns D and E appear on the screen. All formulas are now visible.

6. Press **Ctrl+`**. Cells with formulas now show values again.

7. Choose **Options** on the **Tools** menu.

8. Click the **Calculation** tab in the Options dialog box (see Figure 4-9).

9. Click the **Manual** button in the Calculation section.

10. Click **OK**. Calculation is now delayed.

11. Change the following values in the worksheet.
   a. Key **182** in **B6**.
   b. Key **220** in **C7**.
   c. Key **125** in **C10**.

12. While watching the screen press **F9**. Calculations occur as you press the key. The total sales in cell D12 should be $1,671.60.

13. Access the Options dialog box and the Calculation tab.

14. Click the **Automatic** button in the Calculation section and click **OK**.

15. Change the page orientation to landscape.

16. Save, print, and close the file.

Extra Challenge

Open the file you previously saved as Drinks. The current number of orange juices sold is 182. Determine how many large orange juices must be sold in order to achieve over $1,700 in sales by entering larger amounts in cell B5. When you have determined the amount, close the file.

Summary

In this lesson, you learned:

- Worksheet formulas perform calculations on values referenced in other cells of the worksheet.

- Relative cell references adjust to a different location when copied or moved. Absolute cell references describe the same cell location in the worksheet regardless of where they are copied or moved. Mixed cell references contain both relative and absolute cell references.

- Formulas may be created quickly by using the point-and-click method. This method inserts a cell reference by clicking on the cell rather than keying its column letter and row number.

- A group of cells may be summed quickly by using the AutoSum button on the toolbar. Excel will insert the SUM formula function and determine the most likely range to be summed.

- You may view the formulas used to create values in a worksheet by making selections in the Options menu.

- Calculation in a worksheet usually occurs as values or formulas are entered. You may delay calculation, however, by choosing Manual Calculation in the Options dialog box.

VOCABULARY REVIEW

Define the following terms:

Absolute cell reference	Operand	Point-and-click method
Formulas	Operator	Relative cell reference
Mixed cell reference	Order of evaluation	

LESSON 4 REVIEW QUESTIONS

TRUE/FALSE

Circle T if the statement is true or F if the statement is false.

T F 1. An operator is a number or cell reference used in formulas.

T F 2. In a complex formula, subtraction will be performed before multiplication.

T F 3. Operations within parentheses will be performed before operations outside parentheses in a formula.

T F 4. An absolute cell reference will change if the formula is copied or moved.

T F 5. Manual calculation is performed by pressing the F2 key.

Write a brief answer to the following questions.

1. Which operator has the highest priority in the order of evaluation in a worksheet formula?

2. What type of cell reference adjusts to its new location when it is copied or moved?

3. Write an example of a formula with a mixed cell reference.

4. Explain how to enter the formula =C4+B5+D2 using the point-and-click method.

5. Which keystrokes will display formulas in the worksheet?

LESSON 4 PROJECTS

PROJECT 4-1

Match the letter of the worksheet formula in the right column to the description of the worksheet operation performed by the formula in the left column.

____ 1.	Adds the values in A3 and A4	**A.**	=A3/(27+A4)
____ 2.	Subtracts the value in A4 from the value in A3	**B.**	=A3^27
____ 3.	Multiplies the value in A3 times 27	**C.**	=A3^27/A4
____ 4.	Divides the value in A3 by 27	**D.**	=A3+A4

____ 5. Raises the value in A3 to the 27th power

____ 6. Divides the value in A3 by 27, then adds the value in A4

____ 7. Divides the value in A3 by the result of 27 plus the value in A4

____ 8. Multiplies the value in A3 times 27, and then divides the product by the value in A4

____ 9. Divides 27 by the value in A4, then multiplies the result by the value in A3

____10. Raises the value in A3 to the 27th power, divides the result by the value in A4

E. =A3/27

F. =A3/27+A4

G. =(A3*27)/A4

H. =A3-A4

I. =A3*(27/A4)

J. =A3*27

PROJECT 4-2

1. Open **IE Project4-2** from the data files.

2. Save the file as **Formulas** followed by your initials.

3. Enter formulas in the specified cells that will perform the requested operations below. After you enter each formula, write the resulting value in the space provided.

Resulting Value		Cell	Operation
_____	a.	C3	Add the values in A3 and B3
_____	b.	C4	Subtract the value in B4 from the value in A4
_____	c.	C5	Multiply the value in A5 by the value in B5
_____	d.	C6	Divide the value in A6 by the value in B6
_____	e.	B7	Sum the values in the range B3:B6
_____	f.	D3	Add the values in A3 and A4, then multiply the sum by 3
_____	g.	D4	Add the values in A3 and A4, then multiply the sum by B3
_____	h.	D5	Copy the formula in D4 to D5
_____	i.	D6	Subtract the value in B6 from the value in A6, then divide by 2
_____	j.	D7	Divide the value in A6 by 2, then subtract the value in B6

4. Save, print, and close the file.

PROJECT 4-3

You are a fundraiser for Zoo America. Because winter is typically a slow time for the zoo, you decided to have a special fundraiser during the holidays. Zoo employees will set up booths at holiday events to sell T-shirts, sweatshirts, and coffee mugs. You have been asked to create a worksheet that calculates the bills of individuals who purchase these items. You are required to charge a sales tax of 7% on each sale. The file *IE Project4-3* is a worksheet lacking formulas required to calculate the bills. Complete the worksheet following these steps:

1. Open **IE Project4-3** from the data files.

2. Save the file as **Zoo** followed by your initials.

3. Enter formulas in **D6**, **D7**, **D8**, and **D9** that multiply values in column B times the values in column C.

4. Enter a formula in **D10** to sum the totals in **D6:D9**.

5. Enter a formula in **D11** to calculate a sales tax of 7% of the subtotal in **D10**.

6. Enter a formula in **D12** to add the subtotal and sales tax.

7. Change the worksheet for manual calculation.

8. Format **D6:D12** for currency with two places to the right of the decimal point.

9. Underline the contents of **D9** and **D11**. The worksheet is now ready to accept data unique to the individual customer.

10. A customer purchases two tiger T-shirts, three dolphin T-shirts, one sweatshirt, and four coffee mugs. Enter the quantities in column **C** and press **F9** to calculate.

11. Make sure that you have entered the formulas correctly. If any of the formulas are incorrect, edit them and recalculate the worksheet.

12. When you are confident that the worksheet is calculating as you intended, save the file.

13. Print the customer's bill and close the file.

PROJECT 4-4

Part 1

Alice Grant has been saving and investing part of her salary for several years. She decides to keep track of her investments on a worksheet. The file *IE Project4-4* contains the investments of Alice Grant. She owns several types of investments:

- **Money Market Account** — a bank savings account that does not require notification before money is withdrawn.

- **Stocks** — shares of ownership in a corporation.

- **Mutual Fund** — a collection of several stocks and/or bonds (borrowings) of corporations that are combined to form a single investment.

Alice's stock and mutual fund shares are sold on a major exchange and she may look up the value of the shares in the newspaper after any business day.

1. Open **IE Project4-4** from the data files.

2. Save the file as **Investments** followed by your initials.

3. In column D, calculate the values of the stocks by entering formulas in **D6** through **D8**. The formulas should multiply the number of shares in column B times the price of the shares in column C.

4. Also in column D, calculate the values of the mutual funds by entering formulas in **D10** and **D11**. Similar to the stocks, the formulas should multiply the number of shares in column B times the price of the shares in column C.

5. Enter a formula in **D12** that sums the values in **D4** through **D11**.

6. Alice wants to determine the percentage of each investment with respect to her total investments. Enter the formula **=D4/$D$12** in **E4**.

7. You may have noticed that the formula you entered in E4 contains an absolute cell reference. If this formula is copied into other cells, the absolute reference to D12 will remain the same. Copy the formula in **E4** to cells **E6** through **E8**, and cells **E10** through **E12**.

8. Save the file.

Part 2

After glancing at the newspaper, Alice realizes that the values of her investments have changed significantly. She decides to update the worksheet containing her investment records.

9. Change the worksheet to manual calculation.

10. Enter the following updated share price amounts:

Investment	Price
MicroCrunch Corp.	$16.00
Ocean Electronics, Inc.	$20.25
Photex, Inc.	$14.50
Prosperity Growth Fund	$ 5.50
Lucrative Mutual Fund	$13.00

11. Perform manual calculation by pressing **F9**.

12. Save and print the worksheet. Close the file.

PROJECT 4-5

Abundant Prairie Development is a housing development that is in the business of producing residential homes. One of the employees at the company has determined that housing prices in the Prairie Home neighborhood are primarily a function of the amount of square footage in the home, the number of bathrooms, and the number of car garages. Buyers are also willing to pay more for a house if it is on a cul-de-sac or if it has a swimming pool. You will use this information to develop a worksheet that estimates new home prices based on the variables that affect the home value.

1. Open **IE Project4-5** from the data files.

2. Save the file as **Home Price** followed by your initials.

3. Before considering other factors, the cost of a home is approximately $55 per square foot. Enter a formula in **D5** that multiplies the amount of square footage in **B5** times the value per square foot in **C5**.

4. The cost of a home is increased by $3,000 for each bathroom in the house. Enter a formula in **D6** that multiplies the number of bathrooms in **B6** by the value per bathroom in **C6**.

5. The cost of a home is increased by $2,500 for each car garage. Enter a formula in **D7** that multiplies the number of car garages in **B7** by the value per car garage in **C7**.

6. The cost of a home is increased by $2,000 if the house is located on a cul-de-sac. Enter a formula in **D8** that enters the increase in value in **C8** if a **1** is entered in **B8**.

7. The cost of a home is increased by $5,000 if the house has a swimming pool. Enter a formula in **D9** that enters the increase in value in **C9** if a **1** is entered in **B9**.

8. Use the AutoSum button to sum the numbers contained in **D5:D9** in **D10**.

9. A potential buyer inquires about the price of a home with the following qualities:

Square Feet	2,000 square feet
Number of Bathrooms	3
Number of Car Garages	2
On a Cul-de-Sac?	No
With a Swimming Pool?	Yes

Enter this data into **B5:B9** to determine the estimated price of the house.

10. Save, print, and close the file.

CRITICAL THINKING

ACTIVITY 4-1

You have been offered three jobs, each paying a different salary. You have been told the gross pay (the amount before taxes), but have not been told your net pay (the amount after tax has been taken out).

Assume that you will have to pay 10% income tax and 7% Social Security tax. Develop a spreadsheet with formulas that will determine the amount of net pay. The format should be similar to the following:

	A	B	C	D	E
1	DETERMINATION OF MONTHLY NET PAY				
2	Job Offer	Gross Pay	Income Tax	Social Security Tax	Net Pay
3		Job 1	$24,500		
4	Job 2	$26,600			
5	Job 3	$27,100			

Your worksheet should include:

■ Formulas in C3:C5 that multiply the gross pay in column **B** times **.10**.

■ Formulas in D3:D5 that multiply the gross pay in column **B** times **.07**.

■ Formulas in E3:E5 that subtract the amounts in columns **C** and **D** from the amount in column **B**. When you finish, save the file as **Job Offer**, followed by your initials, print, and close the file.

ACTIVITY 4-2

One of the most difficult aspects of working with formulas in a worksheet is getting them to produce the proper value after they are copied or moved. This requires an understanding of the differences between absolute and relative cell references.

If you experience difficulty after moving or copying formulas, you may not always have a text available to help you correct the problem. Use the Help system to locate an explanation of the differences between absolute and relative cell references. Print the explanation.

FUNCTION FORMULAS

Function Formulas

*F*unction formulas are special formulas that do not use operators to calculate a result. They perform complex calculations in specialized areas of mathematics, statistics, logic, trigonometry, accounting, and finance. Function formulas are also used to convert worksheet values to dates and times. In this section, you will learn the more frequently used function formulas. A more comprehensive explanation of many Excel functions appears in the *Excel Function Reference* at the end of this unit.

 Did You Know?

Excel has more than 300 function formulas.

Parts of Function Formulas

A function formula contains three components: an equal sign, a function name, and an argument. The equal sign tells Excel a function formula will be entered into the cell. The function name identifies the operation to be performed. The *argument* is a value, cell reference, range, or text that acts as an operand in a function formula. The argument is enclosed in parentheses after the function name. If a function formula contains more than one argument, commas separate the arguments. A colon separates the range of cells that make up the argument.

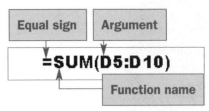

In the previous lesson, you created a function formula by using the AutoSum button. When pressed, the AutoSum button inserted an equal sign followed by the word SUM. The range of cells to be summed was designated within parentheses: for example, =SUM(D5:D10). In this function formula, the word *SUM* is the function name that identifies the operation. The argument is the range of cells that will be added together.

Function formulas may be entered in a worksheet in two ways. First, the function formula may be entered directly in a cell by keying an equal sign, the function name, and the argument. Function formulas may also be entered through dialog boxes by choosing Function on the Insert menu or by clicking the Insert Function button on the formula bar. The Insert Function and Function Arguments dialog boxes guide you through inserting a function in a cell (see Figure 5-1).

FIGURE 5-1
Insert Function and Function Arguments dialog boxes

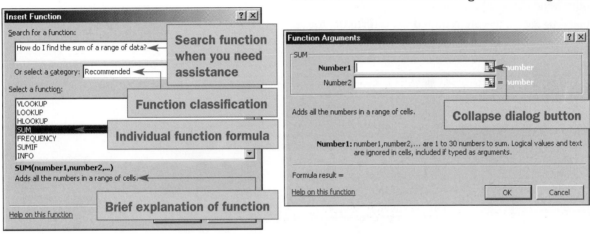

The Insert Function dialog box makes it easy to browse through all of the available functions to select the one you want. The dialog box also provides a brief explanation of any function you choose. Choose a function classification by clicking it in the Or select a category box. Then, choose an individual function formula within the category from the Select a function box. A description of the selected function formula appears near the bottom of the dialog box. Click OK to proceed to the Function Arguments dialog box.

In the Function Arguments dialog box, you may select a cell or range to appear in the argument. You can enter arguments in two ways. First, you can key the argument in the Function Arguments dialog box. Alternatively, you can click the Collapse dialog button at the end of the Number text boxes, and then select the cell or range directly from the spreadsheet. When you have finished specifying the argument, click the Expand Dialog button to restore the Function Arguments dialog box. When you have entered the desired argument, click OK, and your choices will be inserted as a function in the highlighted cell.

The Insert Function dialog box also contains a text box entitled Search for a function. By entering a brief description of what you want to do and clicking Go, Excel will suggest the functions best suited for the task you want to perform.

Entering a Range in a Formula by Dragging

Ranges are often included in function formulas. You may enter a range into a formula quickly by dragging on the worksheet. For example, suppose you want to enter the function formula =SUM(E5:E17). You would first enter =SUM(, then drag from E5 to E17. Complete the formula by keying the closing parenthesis and pressing Enter. Dragging can also be used when you are using the Function Arguments dialog box and collapse the dialog box. In this case, you simply select your range and then expand the dialog box—the function as well as the opening and closing parentheses are entered for you automatically.

Types of Functions

Mathematical and Trigonometric Functions

Mathematical and trigonometric functions manipulate quantitative data in the worksheet. Some mathematical operations, such as addition, subtraction, multiplication, and division, do not require function formulas. However, mathematical and trigonometric functions are particularly useful when you need to determine values such as logarithms, factorials, sines, cosines, tangents, and absolute values.

You already learned one of the mathematical and trigonometric functions when you used the AutoSum button to create SUM functions. One trigonometric function, the natural logarithm, and two other mathematical functions, the square root and rounding functions, are described in Table 5-1. Notice that two arguments are required to perform the rounding operation.

TABLE 5-1
Mathematical and trigonometric functions

FUNCTION	OPERATION
SQRT(number)	Displays the square root of the number identified in the argument. For example, =SQRT(C4) will display the square root of the value in C4.
ROUND(number,num_digits)	Displays the rounded value of a number to the number of places designated by the second argument. For example, =ROUND(14.23433,2) will display 14.23. If the second argument is a negative number, the first argument will be rounded to the left of the decimal point. For example, =ROUND(142.3433,-2) will display 100.
LN(number)	Displays the natural logarithm of a number. For example, =LN(50) will display 1.69897.

S TEP-BY-STEP ▷ 5.1

1. Open **IE Step5-1** from the data files.

2. Save the file as **Functions**, followed by your initials.

3. Highlight **B8**.

4. Enter **=SUM(B3:B7)**. (The same operation could have been performed using the AutoSum

button on the toolbar or by dragging to select the range.)

5. Highlight **B9** and choose **Function** on the **Insert** menu. The Insert Function dialog box appears, similar to Figure 5-1.

6. Click **Math & Trig** in the *Or select a category* box.

7. Scroll down and click **SQRT** in the *Select a function* box.

8. Click **OK**. The Function Arguments dialog box appears.

9. Enter **B8** in the Number text box. You will notice the value in B8, 2466, appears to the right of the Number box. The value that will appear in B9, 49.65883607, appears under the function (near the middle of the dialog box) as well as at the bottom of the dialog box next to *Formula result =*.

10. Click **OK**. The function formula in B9 is =SQRT(B8).

11. Highlight **B10**.

12. Click the **Insert Function** button on the formula bar. The Insert Function dialog box opens.

13. Click **Math & Trig** in the *Or select a category* box if it is not selected already.

14. Click **ROUND** in the *Select a function* box.

15. Click **OK**. The Function Arguments dialog box appears.

16. Enter **B9** in the Number box.

17. Enter **2** in the Num_digits box.

18. Click **OK**. The function formula in B10 is =ROUND(B9,2). Your screen should appear similar to Figure 5-2.

19. Save and leave the worksheet open for the next Step-by-Step.

FIGURE 5-2
Entering mathematical functions

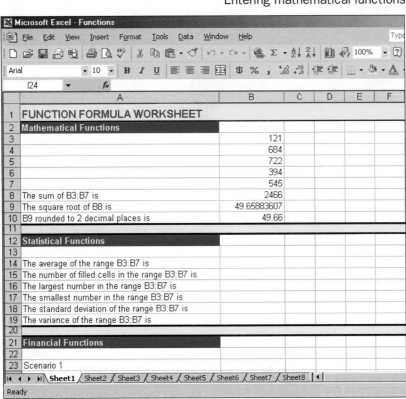

Statistical Functions

Statistical functions are used to describe large quantities of data. For example, function formulas can be used to determine the average, standard deviation, or variance of a range of data. Statistical functions can also be used to determine the number of values in a range, the largest value in a range, and the smallest value in a range. Table 5-2 shows some of the statistical functions available in Excel. Notice that all the statistical functions contain a range for the argument. The range is the body of numbers the statistics will describe.

TABLE 5-2
Statistical functions

FUNCTION	OPERATION
AVERAGE(number1,number2...)	Displays the average of the range identified in the argument. For example, =AVERAGE(E4:E9) displays the average of the numbers contained in the range E4:E9.
COUNT(value1,value2...)	Displays the number of cells with numerical values in the argument range. For example, =COUNT(D6:D21) displays 16 if all the cells in the range are filled.
MAX(number1,number2...)	Displays the largest number contained in the range identified in the argument.
MIN(number1,number2...)	Displays the smallest number contained in the range identified in the argument.
STDEV(number1,number2...)	Displays the standard deviation of the numbers contained in the range of the argument.
VAR(number1,number2...)	Displays the variance for the numbers contained in the range of the argument.

STEP-BY-STEP ▷ 5.2

1. To find the average of values in B3:B7, place the highlight in **B14**.

2. Click the **Insert Function** button on the formula bar. The Insert Function dialog box appears.

3. Click **Statistical** in the *Or select a category* box.

4. Click **AVERAGE** in the *Select a function* box.

5. Click **OK**. The Function Arguments dialog box appears.

6. Click the **Collapse Dialog** button at the right side of the Number1 text box.

7. Select **B3:B7** by dragging directly on the worksheet.

8. Click the **Expand Dialog** button on the right side of the formula bar.

9. Click **OK**.

10. To find the number of filled cells in B3:B7, highlight **B15**.

11. Access the Insert Function dialog box.

12. Click **Statistical** in the *Or select a category* box if it is not already selected, and click **COUNT** in the *Select a function* box.

13. Click **OK**.

14. Enter **B3:B7** in the Value1 box.

15. Click **OK**.

16. To find the largest number in B3:B7, highlight **B16**.

17. Enter **=MAX(B3:B7)**.

18. To find the smallest number in B3:B7, highlight **B17**.

19. Enter **=MIN(B3:B7)**.

20. To find the standard deviation of B3:B7, highlight **B18** and enter **=STDEV(B3:B7)**.

21. To find the variance of B3:B7, highlight **B19** and enter **=VAR(B3:B7)**. Your screen should look similar to Figure 5-3.

22. Save the worksheet and leave it open for the next Step-by-Step.

FIGURE 5-3
Entering statistical functions

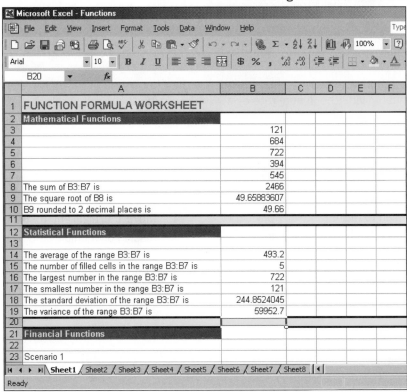

Financial Functions

Financial functions are used to analyze loans and investments. The primary financial functions are future value, present value, and payment, which are described in Table 5-3.

TABLE 5-3
Financial functions

FUNCTION	OPERATION
FV(rate,nper,pmt,pv,type)	Displays the future value of a series of equal payments (third argument), at a fixed rate (first argument), for a specified number of periods (second argument). (The fourth and fifth arguments are optional.) For example, =FV(.08,5,100) determines the future value of five $100 payments at the end of five years if you earn a rate of 8%.
PV(rate,nper,pmt,fv,type)	Displays the present value of a series of equal payments (third argument), at a fixed rate (first argument), for a specified number of payments (second argument). (The fourth and fifth arguments are optional.) For example, =PV(.1,5,500) displays the current value of five payments of $500 at a 10% rate.
PMT(rate,nper,pv,fv,type)	Displays the payment per period needed to repay a loan (third argument), at a specified interest rate (first argument), for a specified number of periods (second argument). (The fourth and fifth arguments are optional.) For example, =PMT(.01,36,10000) displays the monthly payment needed to repay a $10,000 loan at a 1% monthly rate (a 12% yearly rate divided by 12 months), for 36 months (three years divided by 12).*

* The rate and term functions should be compatible. In other words, if payments are monthly rather than annual, divide the annual rate by 12 to determine the monthly rate.

STEP-BY-STEP ▷ 5.3

Scenario 1: You plan to make six yearly payments of $150 into a savings account that earns 3.5% annually. Use the FV function to determine the value of the account at the end of six years.

1. Enter **.035** in **B24**. The value 3.5% appears in the cell.

2. Enter **6** in **B25**.

3. Enter **-150** in **B26**. The value $(150.00) appears in the cell. (A negative number is entered when you pay cash; positive numbers indicate that you receive cash. In this case, you are paying cash to the bank.)

4. Move the highlight to **B27**, and access the Insert Function dialog box.

5. Click **Financial** in the *Or select a category* box and click **FV** in the *Select a function* box.

6. Click **OK**.

7. Key **B24** in the Rate box.

8. Key **B25** in the Nper box.

9. Key **B26** in the Pmt box.

10. Click **OK**. The savings account will have grown to the amount shown in B27 after six years.

11. Save the file.

Scenario 2: You have a choice of receiving $1,200 now or eight annual payments of $210 that will be invested at your bank at 3% interest for the entire eight years. Use the PV function to determine which is the most profitable alternative.

1. Enter **.03** in **B29**.

2. Enter **8** in **B30**.

3. Enter **-210** in **B31**. (A negative number is entered when you pay cash. In this case, you are paying cash to the bank.)

4. Enter **=PV(B29,B30,B31)** in **B32**. The best decision is to take the delayed payments because the present value, $1,474.14, is greater than $1,200.

5. Save the file.

Scenario 3: You need to borrow $5,000. Your banker has offered you an annual rate of 12% interest for a five-year loan. Use the PMT function to determine what your monthly payments on the loan would be and how much interest you would pay over the life of the loan.

1. Enter **.01** in **B34**. (A 1% monthly rate [12% divided by 12 months] is used because the problem requests monthly, rather than annual, payments.)

2. Enter **60** in **B35**. (A period of 60 months [5 years times 12 months] is used because the problem requests monthly, rather than annual, payments.)

3. Enter **5000** in **B36**.

4. Enter **=PMT(B34,B35,B36)** in **B37**. The value ($111.22) will be red in the cell. The number is negative because you must make a payment. Under the conditions of this loan, you will pay a total of $1,673.20 ([$111.22 * 60 months] -$5,000 principal) in interest over the life of the loan. Your screen should look similar to Figure 5-4.

5. Save, print, and close the file.

FIGURE 5-4

Entering financial functions

	A	B	C	D	E	F
20						
21	**Financial Functions**					
22						
23	**Scenario 1**					
24	Rate	3.5%				
25	Periods	6				
26	Payment	$ (150.00)				
27	Future Value	$982.52				
28	**Scenario 2**					
29	Rate	3.0%				
30	Periods	8				
31	Payment	$ (210.00)				
32	Present Value	$1,474.14				
33	**Scenario 3**					
34	Rate	1.0%				
35	Periods	60				
36	Principal	$ 5,000.00				
37	Payment	($111.22)				
38						
39						
40						
41						
42						
43						

Date, Time, and Text Functions

Functions may also be used to insert dates and certain kinds of text into a worksheet. For example, date and time functions may be used to convert serial numbers to a month, a day, or a year. A date function may also be used to insert the current date or current time.

A text function can be used to convert text in a cell to all uppercase or lowercase letters. Text functions can also be used to repeat data contained in another cell. These functions are described in Table 5-4.

Did You Know?

 Lookup (LOOKUP, VLOOKUP, HLOOKUP) and reference (ADDRESS, COL-UMN, ROW) functions may be used to find cell contents or cell locations and use them as data in another part of the worksheet. For example, you might use the LOOKUP function to display the name of a person that you have located in a worksheet by entering a Social Security number.

TABLE 5-4
Date, time, and text functions

FUNCTION	OPERATION
DATE(year,month,day)	Displays the date in a variety of formats, such as *12/17/03* or *December 17, 2003.*
NOW()	Displays the current date or time based on the computer's clock. For example, =NOW() in a cell will display the current date and time, such as *5/23/03 10:05.*
REPT(text,number_times)	Displays the text (first argument) a specified number of times (second argument). For example, REPT(B6,3) will repeat the text in cell B6 three times.

S TEP-BY-STEP ▷ 5.4

1. Open **IE Step5-4** from the data files.

2. Replace the words *NEXT YEAR* in **A1** with next year's date (such as 2004).

3. Insert today's date in B13 by moving the highlight to **B13** and clicking the **Insert Function** button.

4. Click **Date & Time** in the *Or select a category* box.

5. Click **NOW** in the *Select a function* box.

6. Click **OK**. The Function Arguments dialog box appears.

7. Click **OK**. The function formula *=NOW()* appears in the formula bar. The current date and time appear in B13.

8. To format the date, choose **Cells** on the **Format** menu.

9. Click the **Number** tab if it is not selected already.

10. Click **Date** in the Category box if it is not selected already.

11. Choose the format that displays the day in numerical form and the month in abbreviated form, followed by the last two digits of the year, such as 14-Mar-01. Click **OK**.

12. Copy the contents of **B13** to **C13**.

13. With the highlight in **C13**, choose **Cells** on the **Format** menu to insert the current time.

14. Click the **Number** tab if it is not selected already.

15. Click **Time** in the Category box.

16. Choose the format that displays the time in numerical form followed by either AM or PM, such as 1:30 PM, and click **OK**. The time appears in C13.

17. To repeat the text from A1 in B14, place the highlight in **B14**.

18. Access the Insert Function dialog box.

19. Click **Text** in the *Or select a category* box and click **REPT** in the *Select a function* box.

20. Click **OK**.

21. Enter **A1** in the Text box, and enter **1** in the Number_times box.

22. Click **OK**. The title will be repeated in B14. If the title of the worksheet is changed, the text in B14 will instruct the user to rename the file.

23. Save the file under the name appearing in B14. Your screen should look similar to Figure 5-5.

24. Print and close the file.

FIGURE 5-5
Using function formulas to insert dates

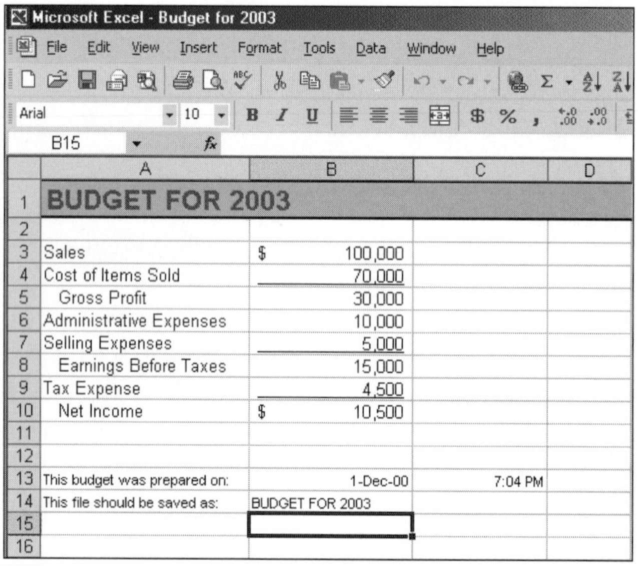

Logical Functions

Logical functions, such as the IF function, may be used to display text or values if certain conditions exist. In the IF function, the first argument sets a condition for comparison called a logical test. The second argument determines the value that will be displayed if the logical test is true. The third argument determines the value that will be displayed if the logical test is false.

For example, a teacher might use the IF function to determine whether a student has passed or failed a course. The function formula IF(C4>60,"PASS","FAIL") will display "PASS" if the value in C4 is greater than 60. The formula will display "FAIL" if the value in C4 is not greater than 60.

STEP-BY-STEP ▷ 5.5

Occidental Optical has noticed that its shipping costs have increased because retailers are asking for smaller amounts of optical solutions on a more frequent basis. To offset these costs, Occidental has decided to charge a $25 shipping fee for orders of less than 5 cartons. The company decides to use an IF function to determine whether or not the fee is applied to an order.

1. Open **IE Step5-5** from the data files, and save the file as **Optics** followed by your initials.

2. In cell **D6**, enter **=IF(B6<5,25,0)**.

3. Copy the function formula in **D6** to **D7:D15**. Your screen should appear similar to Figure 5-6.

4. Save, print, and close the file.

FIGURE 5-6
Using an IF function

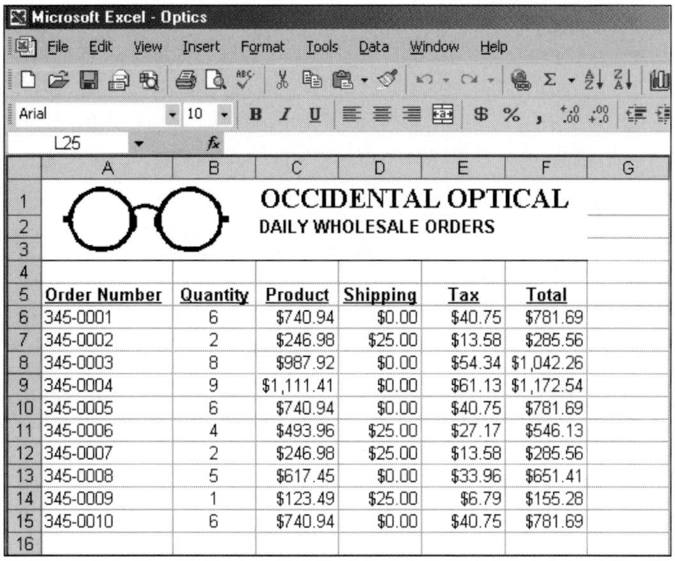

Order Number	Quantity	Product	Shipping	Tax	Total
345-0001	6	$740.94	$0.00	$40.75	$781.69
345-0002	2	$246.98	$25.00	$13.58	$285.56
345-0003	8	$987.92	$0.00	$54.34	$1,042.26
345-0004	9	$1,111.41	$0.00	$61.13	$1,172.54
345-0005	6	$740.94	$0.00	$40.75	$781.69
345-0006	4	$493.96	$25.00	$27.17	$546.13
345-0007	2	$246.98	$25.00	$13.58	$285.56
345-0008	5	$617.45	$0.00	$33.96	$651.41
345-0009	1	$123.49	$25.00	$6.79	$155.28
345-0010	6	$740.94	$0.00	$40.75	$781.69

Summary

In this lesson, you learned:

- Function formulas are special formulas that do not require operators.

- Excel has more than 300 function formulas.

- Function formulas may be used to perform mathematical, statistical, financial, and logical operations.

- Function formulas may also be used to format text and insert dates and times.

VOCABULARY REVIEW

Define the following terms:

Argument	Logical function	Statistical function
Financial function	Mathematical function	Trigonometric function
Function formula		

LESSON 5 REVIEW QUESTIONS

TRUE/FALSE

Circle T if the statement is true or F if the statement is false.

T F 1. Function formulas do not have operators.

T F 2. The AutoSum button creates the function formula =SUM in the highlighted cell.

T F 3. The SMALL function formula displays the smallest number contained in the range identified in the argument.

T F 4. You must use the Function Arguments dialog box to insert a function formula into a worksheet.

T F 5. The NOW() function will insert either the current date or current time into a spreadsheet cell.

FILL IN THE BLANK

Complete the following sentences by writing the correct word or words in the blanks provided.

1. The _____ is enclosed in parentheses in a function formula.

2. The _____ function formula is inserted in a cell when you click the AutoSum button.

3. You specify elements to be included in the function formula in the _____ dialog box.

4. _____ functions perform various operations, such as finding present and future values.

5. _____ functions describe large quantities of data, such as the average, standard deviation, or variance of a range of data.

LESSON 5 PROJECTS

PROJECT 5-1

Write the appropriate function formula to perform each of the described operations. You may refer to Tables 5-1 through 5-3 to help you prepare the function formulas.

_____ 1. Determine the smallest value in A4:A90.

_____ 2. Determine the standard deviation of the values in K6:K35.

_____ 3. Determine the average of the values in B9:B45.

_____ 4. Determine the yearly payments on a $5,000 loan at 8% for 10 years.

_____ 5. Determine the value of a savings account at the end of 5 years after making $400 yearly payments; the account earns 8%.

_____ 6. Round the value in C3 to the tenths place.

_____ 7. Determine the present value of a pension plan that will pay you 20 yearly payments of $4,000; the current rate of return is 7.5%.

_____ 8. Determine the square root of 225.

_____ 9. Determine the variance of the values in F9:F35.

_____ 10. Add all the values in D4:D19.

_____ 11. Determine how many cells in H7:H21 are filled with data.

_____ 12. Determine the largest value in E45:E92.

PROJECT 5-2

The file *IE Project5-2* contains a worksheet of student grades for one examination.

1. Open **IE Project5-2** from the data files.

2. Save the file as **Course Grades** followed by your initials.

3. Determine the number of students taking the examination by entering a function formula in **B26**.

4. Determine the average exam grade by entering a function formula in **B27**.

5. Determine the highest exam grade by entering a function formula in **B28**.

6. Determine the lowest exam grade by entering a function formula in **B29**.

7. Determine the standard deviation of the exam grades by entering a function formula in **B30**.

8. Format cells **B27** and **B30** for numbers with one digit to the right of the decimal.

9. Save, print and close the file.

PROJECT 5-3

Generic National Bank makes a profit by taking money deposited by customers and lending it to others at a higher rate. In order to encourage depositing and borrowing, you have developed a worksheet that informs depositors about the future value of their investments. Another portion of the worksheet determines the yearly payments that must be made on their loans. The incomplete worksheet is in *IE Project5-3*. Complete the worksheet by following these steps:

1. Open **IE Project5-3** from the data files.

2. Save the file as **Bank** followed by your initials.

3. Enter a PMT function formula in **B11** that will inform borrowers of the yearly payment. Assume that the loan principal (or present value) will be entered in B5, the lending rate will be entered in B7, and the term of the loan will be entered in B9. (*#DIV/0!*, indicating an error due to division by zero, will appear in the cell because no data is in the argument cell references yet.)

4. A potential borrower inquires about the payments on a $5,500 loan for four years. The current lending rate is 11%. Determine the yearly payment on the loan. (The number in B11 will be as a negative because it is an amount that must be paid.)

5. Print the portion of the worksheet that pertains to the loan (**A1:C14**) so that it may be given to the potential borrower.

6. Enter an FV function formula in **B24** informing depositors of the future value of periodic payments. Assume the yearly payments will be entered in B18, the term of the payments will be entered in B20, and the interest rate will be entered in B22. (*$0.00* will appear because no data is in the argument cell references yet.)

7. A potential depositor is starting a college fund for her son. She inquires about the value of yearly deposits of $450 at the end of 15 years. The current interest rate is 7.5%. Determine the future value of the deposits. (Remember to enter the deposit as a negative because it is an amount that must be paid.)

8. Print the portion of the worksheet that applies to the deposits (**A14:C26**) so that it may be given to the potential depositor.

9. Save and close the file.

PROJECT 5-4

The Tucson Coyotes have just completed seven preseason professional basketball games. Coach Patterson will soon be entering a press conference in which he is expected to talk about the team's performance for the upcoming season.

Part 1

Coach Patterson would like to be well-informed concerning player performance before entering the press conference. The file *IE Project5-4* contains scoring and rebound data for games against seven opponents. Complete the following spreadsheet so that Coach Patterson has information on player performance.

1. Open **IE Project5-4** from the data files.

2. Save the file as **Game Stats** followed by your initials.

3. Enter a formula in **J5** that sums the values in **B5:I5**.

4. Copy the formula in **J5** to **J6:J11**.

5. Enter a formula in **J18** that sums the values in **B18:I18**.

6. Copy the formula in **J18** to **J19:J24**.

7. Enter a function formula in **B12** that averages the game points in **B5:B11**.

8. Enter a function formula in **B13** that determines the standard deviation of the game points in **B5:B11**.

9. Enter a function formula in **B14** that counts the number of entries in **B5:B11**.

10. Copy the formulas in **B12:B14** to **C12:I14**.

11. Enter a function formula in **B25** that averages the rebounds in **B18:B24**.

12. Enter a function formula in **B26** that determines the standard deviation of the rebounds in **B18:B24**.

13. Enter a function formula in **B27** that counts the number of entries made in **B18:B24**.

14. Copy the formulas in **B25:B27** to **C25:I27**.

15. Save and print the file.

Part 2

Based on the worksheet you prepared, indicate in the blanks that follow the names of the players who are likely to be mentioned in the following interview:

Reporter: You have had a very successful preseason. Three players seem to be providing the leadership needed for a winning record.

Patterson: Basketball teams win by scoring points. It's no secret that we rely on (1), (2), and (3) to get those points. All three average at least 10 points per game.

Reporter: One of your players seems to have a problem with consistency.

Patterson: (4) has his good games and his bad games. He is a young player and we have been working with him. As the season progresses, I think you will find him to be a more reliable offensive talent.

(**Hint:** One indication of consistent scoring is the standard deviation. A high standard deviation may indicate high fluctuation of points from game to game. A low standard deviation may indicate that the scoring level is relatively consistent.)

Reporter: What explains the fact that (5) is both an effective scorer and your leading rebounder?

Patterson: He is a perceptive player. When playing defense, he is constantly planning how to get the ball back to the other side of the court.

Reporter: Preseason injuries can be heartbreaking. How has this affected the team?

Patterson: (6) has not played since being injured in the game against Kansas City. He is an asset to the team. We are still waiting to hear from the doctors on how soon he will be back soon.

Reporter: It is the end of the preseason, which is usually a time when teams make cuts. Of your healthy players, (7) is the lowest scorer. Will you let him go before the beginning of the regular season?

Patterson: I don't like to speculate on cuts or trades before they are made. We'll just have to wait and see.

1. _____

2. _____

3. _____

4. _____

5. _____

6. _____

7. _____

When you have finished filling in the blanks, close the file.

PROJECT 5-5

A golf coach has decided that a player must average a score of less than 76 to qualify for the team. In this project, you will indicate those who make the team by using an IF function.

1. Open **IE Project5-5** from the data files.

2. Save the file as **Golf Tryouts**, followed by your initials.

3. Enter a function formula in **I5** that displays "Made" if the average score in H5 is less than 76 and "Cut" if the the score is not less than 76. (*Hint:* The IF function has three arguments. The first argument is the logical test that determines whether the value in H5 < 76. The second argument is the text that appears if the statement is true. The third argument is the text that appears if the statement is false. Because the items to be displayed are words rather than numbers, they should be entered inside quotation marks.)

4. Copy the function formula from **I5** to **I6** through **I16**.

5. Enter a function formula in **B21** that will display today's date.

6. Choose the format that displays the month followed by the day and year, such as March 14, 2001.

7. Save and print the file.

PROJECT 5-6

You have worked for Xanthan Gum Corp. for several years and have been informed that you are now eligible for a promotion. Promotions at Xanthan are determined by supervisor ratings and a written examination. To be promoted, you must score an average of 80 or above in four categories:

- Supervisor rating of leadership potential
- Supervisor rating of understanding of duties
- Supervisor rating of willingness to work hard
- Written test score

After receiving your supervisor ratings, you decide to prepare a spreadsheet to determine the minimum written test score needed for promotion.

1. Open **IE Project5-6** from the data files.

2. Save the file as **Xanthan** followed by your initials.

3. In cell **B6**, enter **70** as the supervisor rating; in **B7**, enter **85**; and in **B8**, enter **80**.

4. Enter a formula in **B11** that determines the average of the values in **B6:B9**.

5. Format **B11** for a number with zero places to the right of the decimal.

6. Enter an IF function formula in **B12** that displays **PROMOTION** if the average score in B11 is greater than 80 and **NO PROMOTION** if the average score is less than 80.

7. Bold the contents of **B12**.

8. Enter the following possible test scores in B9: 75, 80, 85, 90, and 95. Which ones will result in a promotion?

9. Save, print, and close the file.

CRITICAL THINKING

ACTIVITY 5-1

You are considering the purchase of a car and would like to compare prices offered by several dealerships. Some dealerships have a car that includes the accessories you desire; others will need to add the accessories for an additional price. Prepare a worksheet similar to the following format:

	A	B	C	D
1	A COMPARISON OF PRICES BY DEALERSHIP			
2				
3	**Dealer**	**Base Price**	**Accessories**	**Total**
4	Bernalillo New and Used Cars	$16,300	$500	
5	Los Alamos Auto	$15,800	$400	
6	Mountain Auto Sales	$16,000	$400	
7	Sandia Car Sales	$17,100	$120	
8	Truchas Truck and Auto	$16,500	$550	
9				
10	Highest Price			
11	Lowest Price			
12	Average Price			

Perform the following operations to provide information that will be helpful in making the decision of where to buy the car.

- Enter formulas in **D4:D8** that will add the values in column **B** to the values in column **C**.

- Enter a function formula in **D10** that will determine the highest price in **D4:D8**.

- Enter a function formula in **D11** that will determine the lowest price in **D4:D8**.

- Enter a function formula in **D12** that will determine the average price in **D4:D8**.

When you have finished, save the file as **Car Purchase** followed by your initials, and print your results.

ACTIVITY 5-2

The Insert Function dialog box contains a text box entitled Search for a function. By entering a brief description of what you want to do and clicking Go, Excel will suggest functions best suited for the task you want to perform.

Suppose that you are preparing a large worksheet in which all cells within a range should contain data. You would like to enter a function formula near the end of a range that displays the number of cells in the range that are blank. If a number other than zero appears as the function result, you will know that you must search for the cell or cells that are empty and enter the appropriate data.

Open a blank worksheet and choose the Function command on the Insert menu. Then enter a description in the Search for a function text box that will find a function to count the number of empty cells in a range. If more than one function is suggested, choose each function in the Select a function text box and read the descriptions of the functions that appear below the text box. Then identify the function that is most appropriate to complete this task.

ACTIVITY 5-3

A manufacturing company prepares a budget each month. At the end of the month, a report is prepared that compares the actual amount spent to the budgeted amount as shown below.

	A	B	C	D	E
1	Manufacturing Expense Report				
2		Budgeted Amount	Actual Amount	Budget Variance	
3	Labor Expense	$54,000	$55,500	-$1,500	
4	Raw Material A Expense	$45,000	$44,000	$1,000	
5	Raw Material B Expense	$31,000	$32,000	-$1,000	
6	Overhead Expense	$100,000	$95,000	$5,000	
7					

How could an IF function formula be used to draw attention to a budget that has been exceeded?

MAKING THE WORKSHEET USEFUL

OBJECTIVES

Upon completion of this lesson, you should be able to:

■ Sort data in a worksheet.

■ Use the AutoFilter to extract needed data from the worksheet.

■ Hide worksheet columns or rows.

■ Use Draw in the worksheet.

■ Insert a picture in a worksheet.

■ Use Excel templates to format a worksheet.

■ Insert a hyperlink in a worksheet file.

■ Save an Excel file in a different format.

■ Add and edit comments.

■ Create and respond to discussion comments.

🕐 **Estimated Time: 2.5 hours**

VOCABULARY

AutoFilter

AutoFilter arrows

Clips Online

Comment

Discussion server

Drawing tool

Hiding

Hyperlink

Media clips

Sorting

Template

Web discussion

Sorting Data

Excel comes with a number of tools that make worksheets more useful. One of these, *sorting*, organizes data in an order that is more meaningful. In an ascending sort, data with letters will be in alphabetic order (A to Z) and data with numbers will be from lowest to highest. You may also sort in descending order in which data with letters will be sorted from Z to A and data with numbers will be sorted from highest to lowest.

If you have a column heading for data, you most likely will not want it to be sorted along with the data contained in the column. To prevent Excel from including the heading in the sort, select the Header row option in the Sort dialog box (see Figure 6-1).

FIGURE 6-1
Sort dialog box

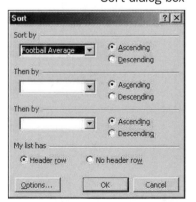

1. Open **IE Step6-1** from the data files, and save it as **NCAA**, followed by your initials.

2. Click **B3** to indicate that you want to sort by the data contained in column B.

3. Choose **Sort** on the **Data** menu. The Sort dialog box appears, similar to Figure 6-1. *Football Average* should appear in the Sort by box.

4. Click **Descending**.

5. Click **OK**. The data will be sorted from highest to lowest attendance. Your screen should appear similar to Figure 6-2.

6. Click **A3** to make *School* the new sort criterion.

7. Click the **Sort Ascending** button on the Standard toolbar. The data will be sorted alphabetically by school name.

8. Save the file and leave the worksheet open for the next Step-by-Step.

FIGURE 6-2
Sorting data in a worksheet

A	B	C
NCAA DIVISION 1 EVENT ATTENDANCE		
School	**Football Average**	**Basketball Average**
Michigan	110,822	11,023
Tennessee	107,595	15,561
Ohio St.	97,757	18,702
Penn St.	95,543	9,350
LSU	87,815	10,549
Florida	85,253	9,783
Georgia	84,487	6,777
Alabama	83,770	8,257
Auburn	82,435	10,500
Texas	82,216	10,878
South Carolina	81,904	9,497
Clemson	81,214	8,269
Florida St.	80,831	5,487
Notre Dame	80,302	8,770
Wisconsin	78,711	16,163
Nebraska	77,878	7,342
Texas A&M	77,579	4,906
Oklahoma	75,075	11,248
Michigan St.	74,023	14,659
Washington	71,629	7,861

AutoFilter

AutoFilter displays a subset of the data in a worksheet that meets certain criteria. Filtering will temporarily hide rows that do not meet the criteria you describe.

Choosing Filter from the Data menu and then choosing AutoFilter on the submenu starts the AutoFilter. When the AutoFilter is begun, *AutoFilter arrows* appear at the lower right corner of the column headings. By clicking the arrow, a drop-down list appears that allows you to display a specific row, the top ten items in the column, or a customized search or to restore all the data in the worksheet (see Figure 6-3).

Did You Know?

Unlike sorting, filtering will not rearrange the order of the data.

FIGURE 6-3
AutoFilter arrow and drop-down list

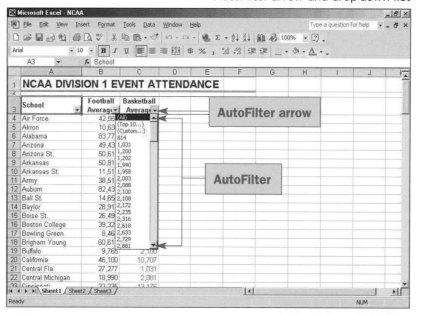

If the Top 10 feature is selected in the drop-down list, the Top 10 AutoFilter dialog box will appear (see Figure 6-4). In the Top 10 AutoFilter dialog box, you may specify the highest and lowest values in the column. For example, you might display rows with the ten largest values in that column of the worksheet. However, you can also change the specifications in the dialog box to display rows with other criteria. For example, you can display the highest tenth percentile or the lowest 50 items.

Hot Tip

When the AutoFilter of a particular column is in use, the AutoFilter arrow is blue. To restore all of the records, click the AutoFilter arrow and choose **All** in the drop-down list.

FIGURE 6-4
Top 10 AutoFilter dialog box

STEP-BY-STEP 6.2

1. Highlight **C3**.

2. Choose **Filter** from the **Data** menu, then choose **AutoFilter** from the submenu. AutoFilter arrows will appear in A3 through C3.

3. Click the AutoFilter arrow in **C3**. Your screen should appear similar to Figure 6-3.

4. Click **(Top 10...)**. The Top 10 AutoFilter dialog box will appear.

5. Click **OK**. The ten teams with the highest average basketball attendance appear.

6. Click the AutoFilter arrow in **C3** once more.

7. Scroll upward and click **(All)**. All of the data in the worksheet is restored.

8. Click the AutoFilter arrow in **B3**.

9. Click **(Top 10...)**. The Top 10 AutoFilter dialog box will appear.

10. Increase the number in the middle text box to **15**.

11. Click **Percent** in the right drop-down box.

12. Click **OK**. The teams with football attendance in the top 15th percentile appear.

13. Save, print, and close the file.

Hiding Columns and Rows

H*iding* temporarily removes a row or column from the screen. To hide a selected row or column, select either Row or Column on the Format menu, and then click Hide on the submenu. To redisplay a hidden row, select the rows on each side of the hidden rows you want to display. Then choose the Format menu, select Row, and click Unhide on the submenu. To display a hidden column, select columns on both sides of the hidden column, choose the Format menu, select Column, and then click Unhide on the submenu.

STEP-BY-STEP ⟹ 6.3

The Excel file *IE Step6-3* is a record of oil production for several wells over a six-month period. A manager has asked that you prepare two reports. The first report should tell the six-month production for each well in the field. The second report should summarize the production of the entire field for each of the six months.

1. Open **IE Step6-3** from the data files, and save it as **Combustion** followed by your initials.

2. Select columns **B** through **G**.

3. Choose **Column** on the **Format** menu, then choose **Hide** on the submenu. Columns B through G will be hidden.

4. Print the file.

5. Select columns **A** and **H**.

6. Choose **Column** on the **Format** menu, then choose **Unhide** on the submenu. Columns B through G will reappear.

7. Select rows **6** through **14**.

8. Choose **Row** on the **Format** menu, then choose **Hide** on the submenu. Rows 6 through 14 will be hidden.

9. Print the file.

10. Select rows **5** and **15**.

11. Choose **Row** on the **Format** menu, the choose **Unhide** on the submenu. Rows 6 through 14 will reappear.

12. Save the file and leave the worksheet open for the next Step-by-Step.

Using Draw in the Worksheet

The **_drawing tools_** in Excel can be used to insert lines and objects that help make a worksheet more informative. For example, you might use a text box to explain a value in the worksheet. Or you might use an object such as a rectangle or circle to create a corporate logo.

Creating Objects with Draw

Clicking the Drawing button on the Standard toolbar accesses the Drawing toolbar. The Drawing toolbar normally appears near the bottom of the screen.

STEP-BY-STEP ▷ 6.4

1. Click the **Drawing** button on the Standard toolbar. The Drawing toolbar appears near the bottom of the screen.

2. Click the **Text Box** button on the Drawing toolbar. The highlight turns into a ↓.

3. Drag from E18 to G20. A text box appears.

4. Key **Bad weather caused February production to be low.** in the text box.

5. Click the **3-D Style** button on the Drawing toolbar. A pop-up menu appears.

6. Click the upper left three-dimensional box that appears in the pop-up menu.

7. Click the **Arrow** button on the Drawing toolbar. The highlight turns into a +.

8. Drag from the left side of the text box to the contents of C15. Your screen should appear similar to Figure 6-5.

9. Save the file and leave it open for the next Step-by-Step.

Did You Know?

You can modify or delete lines and 3-D objects you have created in an Excel worksheet. To delete a line or object, click on it, and then press the **Delete** key. To change or modify a line or object, click on it, and then click the line, arrow, or 3-D button on the Drawing toolbar.

FIGURE 6-5
Using the drawing tools

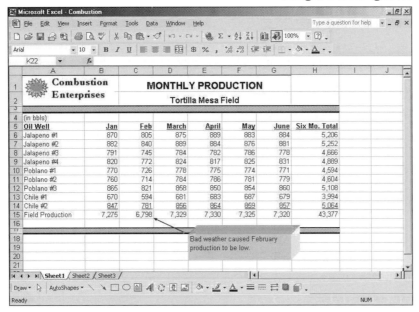

Editing Objects with Draw

Once objects have been created using the drawing tools, they may be changed. In most cases, clicking on the object and then using a button on the Formatting or Drawing toolbars allows you to make changes.

STEP-BY-STEP ▷ 6.5

1. Click the arrow that points to C15. Handles (small white circles) appear at the ends of the arrow.

2. Click the **Line Style** button on the Drawing toolbar. A submenu with different line thicknesses appears. Your screen should appear similar to Figure 6-6.

3. Click the **1½ point** line. The line thickness of the arrow will become thicker.

4. Click inside the 3-D box you created earlier. Handles will appear at each corner and side.

5. Click the **Shadow Style** button on the Drawing toolbar. A menu similar to the one in Figure 6-7 appears.

6. Click **Shadow Style 6** on the menu (second column, second row). The box will change from a 3-D box to a rectangle with a shadow along the lower right sides.

7. Select the text within the shadowed box.

8. Click the **Bold** button on the Formatting toolbar.

FIGURE 6-6
Line Style button options

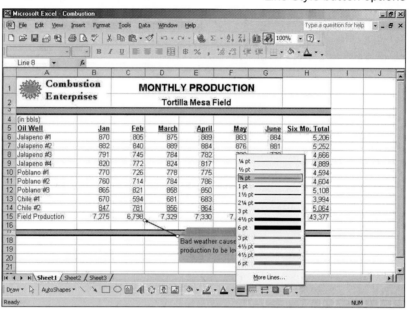

FIGURE 6-7
Shadow options

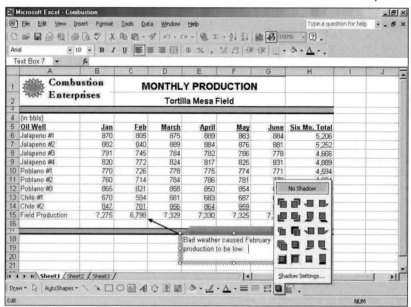

9. Click the down arrow to the right of the **Font Color** button on the Drawing toolbar, then click the orange-colored box. When you have finished, your screen should appear similar to Figure 6-8.

10. Click the **Drawing** button on the Standard toolbar to hide the Drawing toolbar.

11. Save, print, and then close the file.

FIGURE 6-8
Editing Drawing objects

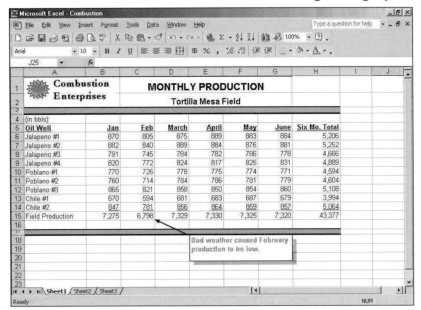

Adding a Picture to a Worksheet

You may want to change the appearance of a worksheet by adding a picture. For example, some corporations like to include their corporate logo on their worksheets. In addition, pictures are sometimes added to illustrate data contained in a worksheet. For instance, you might want to insert a smiley face into a worksheet, which would indicate good financial results (see Figure 6-9).

FIGURE 6-9
Pictures improve worksheet appearance

Inserting a Picture in a Worksheet

You may insert a picture from the media clips in the Office software, the **Clips Online**, or from a file that contains a picture. The **media clips** are a collection of clip art (as well as audio and video clips) that may be placed on your hard disk when Office is installed. To insert a picture from the media clips, select Picture on the Insert menu, and then select Clip Art on the submenu. The Insert Clip Art task pane, similar to Figure 6-10, appears on the right of the screen. Enter the type of picture you want in the Search text box and click Search. Excel will search for pictures that fit the search word. You may narrow the search by making specifications in the Other Search Options area of the task pane.

FIGURE 6-10
Insert Clip Art task pane

Did You Know?

You may expand the selection of clip art by accessing the clip art online. By clicking **Clips Online** at the bottom of the task pane, Office will access the Microsoft Design Gallery Live which is maintained by Microsoft on the Internet.

You insert a picture from a file by selecting Picture on the Insert menu, and then selecting From File on the submenu.

STEP-BY-STEP ▷ 6.6

1. Open **IE Step6-6** from the data files, and save it as **Botany** followed by your initials.

2. Choose **Picture** on the **Insert** menu, and then select **From File** on the submenu. The Insert Picture dialog box appears.

3. Choose **Rose** from the data files.

4. Click the **Insert** button. Your screen should appear similar to Figure 6-11. (You may also see the floating Picture Toolbar.)

5. Scroll down so that the lower sizing handles on the picture are visible.

6. Drag the middle lower sizing handle upward until the dark line at the bottom of row 6 is visible. (You may also see the Floating Picture Toolbar.)

FIGURE 6-11
Inserting a picture

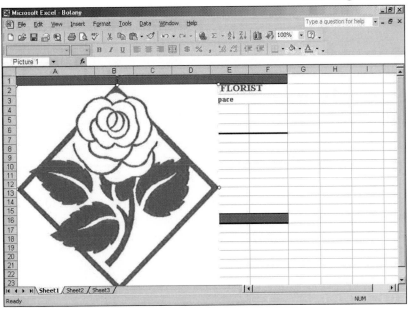

7. Drag the middle right sizing handle to the left until the edge of the picture is at the right side of column A. Your screen should appear similar to Figure 6-12.

8. Save the file and leave it open for the next Step-by-Step.

FIGURE 6-12

Dragging the sizing handles changes picture size

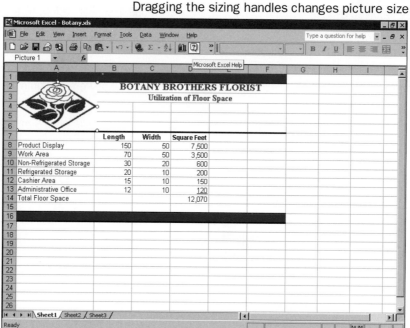

Editing a Picture

Once a picture has been inserted in a worksheet, you may move or edit it to fit your needs. Many of the edit functions are contained on the Picture toolbar (see Figure 6-13), which can be displayed by right-clicking on any toolbar and selecting Picture. Table 6-1 explains methods for editing pictures.

FIGURE 6-13

Picture toolbar

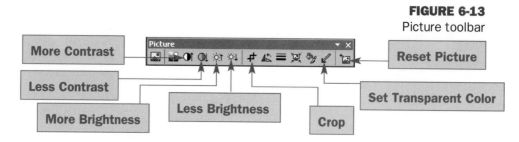

TABLE 6-1
Editing pictures

ACTION	SELECT THE PICTURE AND THEN:
Move the picture	Drag it to the desired position.
Restore the picture to the original format	Click the Reset Picture button on the Picture toolbar.
Resize the picture	Drag the sizing handles on the sides of the picture.
Crop the picture (trim the edges)	Click the Crop button on the toolbar and then drag the sizing handles.
Change the brightness of the picture	Click the More Brightness or Less Brightness button on the Picture toolbar.
Change the contrast of the picture	Click the More Contrast or Less Contrast button on the Picture toolbar.
Make a color in the picture transparent	Click the Set Transparent Color button on the Picture toolbar and then click a color in the picture.

STEP-BY-STEP ▷ 6.7

1. If the Picture toolbar is not already displayed, right-click on a toolbar and then click **Picture**.

2. After making sure the picture is selected, click the **Set Transparent Color** button on the Picture toolbar. The pointer will change to the set transparent color icon.

3. Click on a white part of the picture inside the diamond shape. You will now be able to see the gridlines of the worksheet behind the picture.

4. Click the **More Brightness** button on the Picture toolbar five times. The picture will change from a maroon to a pink color.

5. Close the Picture toolbar. Your screen should appear similar to Figure 6-14.

6. Save, print, and close the file.

FIGURE 6-14
A picture may be edited within a worksheet

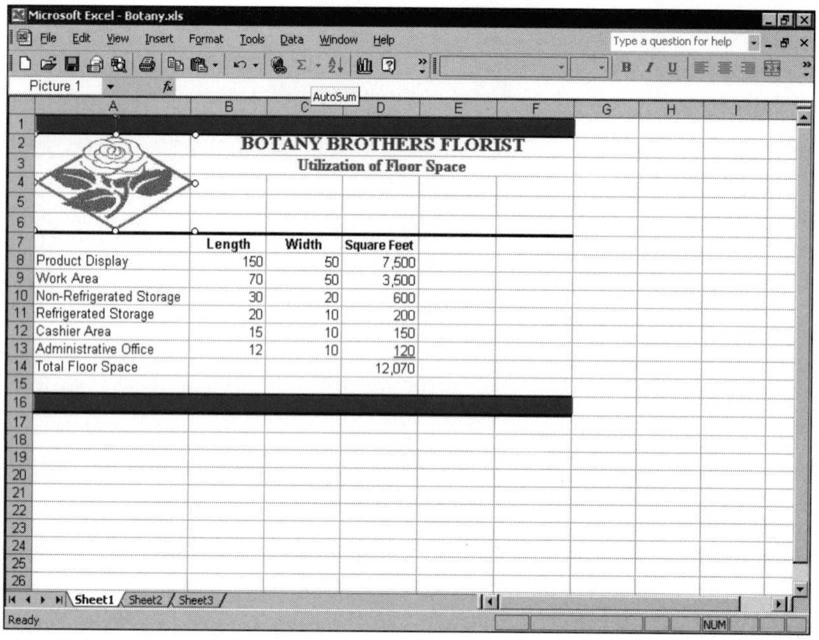

Using Templates

Templates automate tasks performed in Excel by creating a worksheet format that may be used more than once. For example, suppose you are required by your employer to submit a time record of your work each week. Each week you use the same worksheet format, but the number of hours that you enter into the worksheet changes from week to week. You may use a template file to save the portion of the worksheet that is the same every week. Then you need only add the data that is pertinent to each week.

Excel has several template files that may be saved to your computer when Office is installed. However, you may obtain additional templates by visting the Microsoft Office Template Gallery Web site (see Figure 6-15) by clicking Templates on Microsoft.com in the New Workbook task pane, or you may create your own template file.

FIGURE 6-15
The Microsoft Office Template Gallery Web site
provides templates that may be downloaded

Template files are accessed by clicking General Templates in the New from template area of the New Workbook task pane, as shown in Figure 16-6. When the Templates dialog box appears, click the Spreadsheet Solutions tab shown in Figure 6-17. The icons for template files differ slightly from normal Excel files, with a yellow strip across the top of the icon, as shown in Figure 6-18. After data has been entered into the template file, the file should be saved as a regular file.

FIGURE 6-16
Template files may be accessed from
the New Workbook task pane

FIGURE 6-17

Template files are located on the Spreadsheet Solutions tab of the Templates dialog box

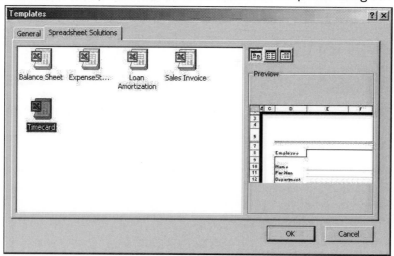

FIGURE 6-18
Excel file and Excel template file icons

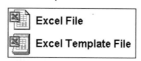

STEP-BY-STEP ▷ 6.8

In this Step-by-Step, you will access an Excel template to create a timesheet for the work performed in the last week.

1. Click **New** on the File menu. The New Workbook task pane will appear.

2. Click **General Templates** in the New from template area of the New Workbook task pane. The Templates dialog box will appear.

3. Click the **Spreadsheet Solutions** tab in the Templates dialog box.

4. Click the **Timecard** icon in the Templates dialog box.

5. Click **OK**. A template file entitled Timecard1 will appear.

6. Choose **Save as** from the **File** menu.

7. Be sure the proper drive has been selected and save the file as an Excel Workbook file (with the *.xls extension) named **Timecard1** followed by your initials.

8. Select **75%** in the Zoom box so that column R appears at the right side of the screen.

9. Enter the following data into the designated cells. When you are finished, your screen should look similar to Figure 6-19.

CELL	DATA	CELL	DATA
E10	Andrew Gaston	G16	9/5/2003
E11	Floor Salesperson	I10	0591
E12	Luggage	I11	591-03-8755
E16	9/1/2003	I12	Switzer

D19	Customer Contact	L19	10
I19	01-011	M19	8
J19	8	N19	5
K19	12		

10. Save, print, and close the file.

FIGURE 6-19
Template files make creating a new file easier

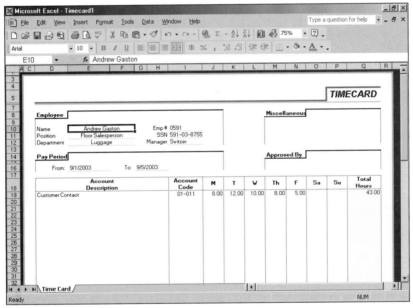

Inserting Hyperlinks in Files

You can insert *hyperlinks* in a worksheet that "jump" to other files or Web pages on the Internet. For example, you may want to create a link to another Excel file that contains the source data for information used in your current worksheet. You may also want to create a link to a Web page that contains information that relates to items contained in the worksheet.

To create a hyperlink, first select text or a graphic. Then click the Insert Hyperlink button on the toolbar (or right-click the item and select Hyperlink on the shortcut menu). When the Insert Hyperlink dialog box appears, key the filename or Web page address into the Type the file or Web page name text box. After you click OK, you will be returned to the spreadsheet and the pointer will appear as a pointed finger when it is passed over the linked item.

If you create a hyperlink to a file, that file will be opened when the text or graphic is clicked in the worksheet. If you create a hyperlink to a Web page, that page will be opened in your browser when you click the text or graphic that has been linked.

1. Open **IE Step6-9** from your data files.

2. Save the file as **Tax Estimate** followed by your initials.

3. Click **A15**.

4. Click the **Insert Hyperlink** button on the toolbar. The Insert Hyperlink dialog box appears.

5. Key **www.irs.gov** in the Address box of the Insert Hyperlink dialog box.

6. Click **OK**. The contents of A15 will become a hyperlink and will appear blue and underlined, as shown in Figure 6-20.

7. If you currently have Internet access, click the hyperlink in A15. The Internet site of the Internal Revenue Service should be displayed.

8. Exit your browser and return to the worksheet.

9. Save, print, and close the file.

FIGURE 6-20
Hyperlinks give access to other files or to the Internet

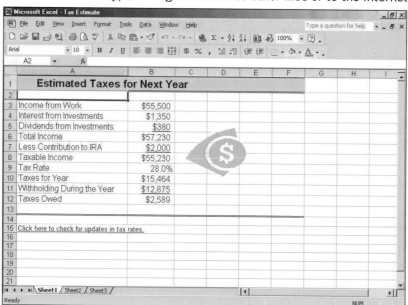

Saving Workbooks in Different Formats

Excel worksheets may be saved in different formats to be opened in different programs. For example, if you want to share data with a co-worker or friend who uses Lotus 1-2-3 or Quattro Pro spreadsheet programs, you may save your Excel file in a format that is readable by those programs. You may also save the file in a format that can be viewed as a Web page on the Internet. Excel can save files in the formats indicated in Table 6-2.

TABLE 6-2
Excel can save files in several formats

FILE TYPE	FILE CHARACTERISTIC
CSV	Data separated by commas
Formatted Text	Data separated by spaces
Microsoft Excel 97-2000 & 5.0/95 Workbook	Spreadsheet data created in an earlier version of Excel
Template file	Excel file used to create other similar files
Text	Data separated by tabs
Web Page	File to be displayed on the Internet
WK*	Spreadsheet data usable in LOTUS 1-2-3
WQ1	Spreadsheet data usable in Quattro Pro

S TEP-BY-STEP ▷ 6.10

The file *IE Step6-10* contains a worksheet used to report the expenses of a traveling salesperson. The company has several employees who use other spreadsheet programs. You have been asked to convert the Excel version of the file to one that is readable in Lotus 1-2-3. You have also been asked to save the Excel version of the file as a Web file so that it may be published and observed on the Internet.

1. Open **IE Step6-10** from the data files.

2. Save the file as **Excel Expense Report** followed by your initials.

3. Choose **Save as** from the **File** menu. The Save as dialog box appears.

4. Select **WK4 (1-2-3)(*.wk4)** in the Save as type drop-down list box.

5. Key **1-2-3 Expense Report** followed by your initials in the filename box.

6. Click **Save**. A dialog box will appear letting you know that all of the features of the worksheet may not be compatible with Lotus 1-2-3.

7. Click **Yes**. The file is saved as a file that may be opened in Lotus 1-2-3.

8. Close the file.

9. Open **Excel Expense Report** (saved with your initials).

10. Choose **Save as Web Page** from the File menu. The Save as dialog box appears.

11. Click **Publish**.

12. Select **Items on Expenses** in the Choose box if it is not selected already.

13. Click **Add interactivity with** check box in the Viewing options.

14. Select **Spreadsheet functionality** in the drop-down box in the Viewing options area if it is not selected already.

15. Key **Web Expense Report** followed by your initials and followed by the file extension **.htm** in the File name text box in the Publish as area. The filename should be preceded by the drive in which you store your files.

16. Make sure the **Open published web page in browser** check box is checked.

17. Click **Publish**. Your browser will open the file. The worksheet will appear as if it were published on the Internet. If you use Internet Explorer as your Internet browser, your screen should look similar to Figure 6-21. Notice that the workbook in the browser has full spreadsheet functionality, even though it is displayed in a Web browser.

18. Print the file from your browser.

19. Close your browser and all open files.

FIGURE 6-21
Excel files may be saved as Web files that can be viewed in an Internet browser

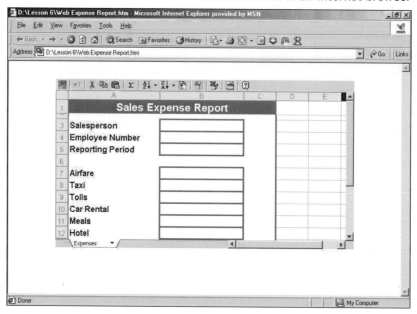

Viewing and Editing Comments

Inserting a Cell Comment

A cell *comment* is a message that explains or identifies information contained in the cell. For example, when abbreviations have been entered into cells, a cell comment can be used to spell out the words. In addition, comments can be used to explain the calculations in cells that contain formulas.

Most importantly, cell comments are used when one worksheet user wants to provide input to other users without altering the structure of the worksheet. For example, a supervisor might want to provide comments to an employee on how to improve the worksheet format.

Cell comments are inserted by choosing Comment on the Insert menu. A comment box appears with the user's name followed by a colon. Key the comment (see Figure 6-22), and then click outside the comment box to close it. A red triangle appears in the corner of the cell to indicate that the cell contains a comment. To read a cell comment, point to the cell that contains a red triangle and the comment is displayed.

Computer Concepts

You can view all the comments at once by choosing **Comments** on the View menu.

FIGURE 6-22
Comments inserted into a worksheet cell

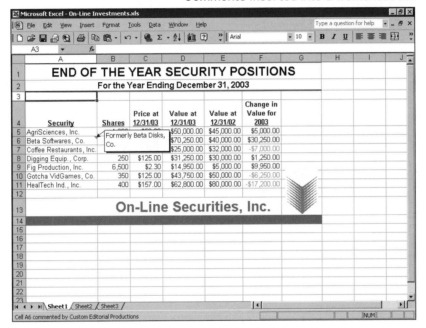

To edit a comment, select the cell that contains the comment and choose Edit Comment on the Insert menu. To delete a comment, choose Clear on the Edit menu and then choose Comments on the submenu.

Using Discussion Comments

Web discussions permit several worksheet users to view and comment on a worksheet that has been posted on the Internet. Discussions of Excel spreadsheets may take place either in Excel or in Microsoft Internet Explorer (versions 4.0 and later). In either application, accessing the Web Discussion toolbar starts Web discussions. In Excel, choosing Online Collaboration in the Tools menu and then clicking Web Discussions on the submenu access the Web discussion toolbar. In Microsoft Internet Explorer, clicking the Discuss button accesses the Web Discussion toolbar.

To be discussed on the Internet, a worksheet must first be posted on a *discussion server*. Both the file and the comments from the worksheet users will be processed on the discussion server.

If you have access to a discussion server, you may begin a Web discussion by choosing Online Collaboration from the Tools menu and then choosing Web Discussions on the submenu. When the Discussions toolbar appears, click Discussions and then Insert about the Workbook. You may then add discussion subjects and discussion text to which others can respond.

1. Open **IE Step6-11** from the data files.

2. Save the worksheet as **On-Line Investments** followed by your initials.

3. Highlight **A6**.

4. Choose **Comment** on the **Insert** menu. The cell comment box appears.

5. Key **Formerly Beta Disks, Co.** in the cell comment box, as shown in Figure 6-22.

6. Click outside the cell comment box. A small red triangle appears in the upper right corner of the cell, indicating that the cell contains a comment.

7. Point to cell **A6** with your mouse pointer. The cell comment appears on the screen.

8. Enter the following comments in the designated cells:

Cell   Comment

E9   Purchased on February 2, 2003.

A7   Sell if price reaches $13.00 per share.

A11   Analyst recommends buy.

9. Save, print, and close the file.

Summary

In this lesson, you learned:

- Data in a worksheet may be sorted in alphabetic or numeric order.

- The AutoFilter displays a subset of data in the worksheet that meets specific criteria.

- Rows and columns of a worksheet that are not needed may be hidden temporarily.

- The drawing tool in Excel may be used to insert objects into a worksheet.

- Pictures may be inserted in a worksheet to make its appearance more attractive.

- Templates are files with a basic design that may be used to create more than one worksheet.

- Hyperlinks in a worksheet permit the user to move to another file or to a Web page on the Internet.

- Excel worksheets may be saved in formats that can be read by other software programs.

- Comments are pop-up messages that may be added to cells to provide additional information.

VOCABULARY REVIEW

Define the following terms:

AutoFilter	Discussion server	Media clips
AutoFilter arrows	Drawing tool	Sorting
Clips Online	Hiding	Template
Comment	Hyperlink	Web discussion

LESSON 6 REVIEW QUESTIONS

TRUE/FALSE

Circle T if the statement is true or F if the statement is false.

T F 1. When sorting, the worksheet is always ordered with the smallest values listed first.

T F 2. The AutoFilter reorganizes data to place it in a different order.

T F 3. Hiding will temporarily remove a row or column from a worksheet.

T F 4. Pictures may be selected from the media clips using the Drawing tool.

T F 5. Excel files may be saved in formats that are readable by other software programs.

MATCHING

Match the correct term in the right column to its description in the left column.

_____ 1. Worksheet used to create other worksheets

_____ 2. Collection of clip art installed on your hard disk

_____ 3. Organizes data in an order that is more meaningful

_____ 4. Text or graphic that directs you to a file or Web page when clicked

_____ 5. Displays a subset of data that meets a certain criteria

A. AutoFilter

B. Template

C. Drawing tool

D. Filter arrows

E. Hyperlink

F. Template

G. Media clips

H. Sorting

LESSON 6 PROJECTS

PROJECT 6-1

The file *IE Project6-1* contains the salaries and annual ratings of Level 10 employees for Impact Corporation. Level 10 employees are currently paid between $30,000 and $35,000 per year. However, the management is concerned that salaries within that range do not relate to the level of performance of the individuals.

Part 1

In this part of the project, you will sort the data by the employee's annual rating. Then you will indicate one of two salary categories using the IF function formula. The salary categories are:

```
Salary Range              Salary Category
$30,000 to $32,5000       Low
$32,501 to $35,000        High
```

1. Open **IE Project6-1** from the data files.

2. Save the file as **Impact** followed by your initials.

3. Sort the data in **A6:E20** by the Annual Rating in descending numerical order.

4. Enter **=IF(D6<32500,"Low","High")** in **F6**.

5. Copy the formula in **F6** to **F7:F20**.

6. Save the file.

Part 2

If salaries are allocated based on annual ratings, employees with higher ratings should appear near the top of the worksheet and have *High* in column F. Those with lower ratings should appear near the bottom of the worksheet and have *Low* in column F. When a salary does not reflect an employee's annual rating, the word in column F may appear to be out of place.

Based on the worksheet you have prepared, determine which employees you believe are currently underpaid. Save, print, and close the file when you have completed the project.

PROJECT 6-2

The file *IE Project6-2* contains the top 100 grossing American films since 1997. The films are currently in alphabetical order by film name.

Part 1

Column D of *IE Project6-2* contains the number of dollars that the film grossed. Column E shows the amounts in column D in today's dollars (adjusted for inflation). Determine the most successful film in history by sorting the data.

1. Open **IE Project6-2** from the data files.

2. Save the file as **Movies** followed by your initials.

3. Sort the data in descending order by the Gross Adjusted for Inflation data.

4. Save and print the file.

Part 2

Suppose you would like to rent videotapes of successful movies that have been released in the last few years. Re-sort the data to show the most recently released movies at the top of the worksheet.

1. Sort the data by Release Date in descending order.

2. Save, print, and close the file.

PROJECT 6-3

The file *IE Project6-3* contains the facts on the 30 largest cities in the United States. Use the AutoFilter to answer the questions at the end of this project.

1. Open **IE Project6-3** from the data files.

2. Save the file as **Large Cities** followed by your initials.

3. Set the AutoFilter for the items in row 3.

4. Use the following AutoFilters in row 3 to answer the questions below. Remember to restore the records after each filter by choosing **All** in the drop-down list of the column with the blue AutoFilter arrow.

COLUMN	AUTOFILTER DROP-DOWN ITEM	AUTOFILTER CRITERION
B	Top Ten	Top 4 items
C	Top Ten	Bottom 3 items
D	Top Ten	Top 10 percent
G	0	Not needed

A. What are the four largest cities in the United States?

_____   _____   _____   _____

B. What are the three coldest cities in the U.S. during January?

_____   _____   _____

C. What cities are in the top 10 percentile of average July temperatures?

_____   _____   _____

D. How many of the 30 largest cities are at sea level (have altitudes of 0)?

_____

5. Save and close the file.

PROJECT 6-4

An employee of Paper Container Products would like to view the spreadsheet of the company's quarterly sales without the details of each geographic region and each quarter.

1. Open **IE Project6-4** from the data files.

2. Save the file as **Paper** followed by your initials.

3. Remove the quarterly data from view by hiding columns **B** through **E**.

4. Restore the quarterly data by unhiding columns **B** through **E**.

5. Remove the regional data by hiding rows **7** through **14**.

6. Print the summarized worksheet.

7. Restore the regional data by unhiding rows **7** through **14**.

8. Save and close the file.

PROJECT 6-5

1. Open the **Sales Invoice** template file from the General Templates menu under the Spreadsheet Solutions tab.

2. Save the file as **Sales Invoice1** followed by your initials.

3. Use the **Zoom** to adjust the file so that column N is near the right side of the screen.

4. Enter the following data into the worksheet:

CELL	CONTENT
C3	Cloth Crafts
M3	10001
D13	Anita Roberts
D14	4509 Lumpton Road
D15	New Orleans
D16	504-555-8796
F15	LA
H15	70145
M13	10/8/03
M14	100018
M15	013
M16	Dest
C19	5
D19	Fabric #515 per yard
L19	7.50
C20	10
D20	Fabric #440 per yard
L20	8.00
M37	5.00
L38	.05

5. Save, print, and close the file.

PROJECT 6-6

1. Open **IE Project6-6** from the data files.

2. Save the file as **School Bus Activity** followed by your initials.

3. Choose **Picture** on the **Insert** menu, and then select **From File** on the submenu. The Insert Picture dialog box appears.

4. Choose **School Bus** from the data files.

5. Click the **Insert** button.

6. Double-click the picture so that the Format Picture dialog box appears.

7. Click the **Size** tab.

IE-127

8. In the Scale area, change the Height and Width to **41%**. Click **OK**.

9. Drag the picture so that it fits within **E1:E3**.

10. Save, print, and close the file.

PROJECT 6-7

1. Open **IE Project6-7** from the data files.

2. Save the file as **Compact Cubicle** followed by your initials.

3. Insert the comment **Shut down for two hours for maintenance.** in cell **C8**.

4. Insert the comment **Production time increased two hours to make up for maintenance on machine 102.** in cell **C9**.

5. Insert the comment **Shut down for major repairs.** in cell **G9**.

6. Save, print, and close the file.

CRITICAL THINKING

ACTIVITY 6-1

Several template files are placed on your computer when you perform a typical installation of Excel. These template files are accessed by clicking General Templates in the New from template area of the New Workbook task pane. These template files include Balance Sheet, Expense Statement, and Loan Amortization. Open these files and give a brief description of their purpose. You may want to enter data in the worksheet to investigate the formulas contained in the template.

ACTIVITY 6-2

Clicking Clips Online in the Insert Clip Art task pane will access the Clips Online. If you have Internet access, use the Clips Online to locate the following clip art items:

- A Lion
- A valentine heart
- A plumber
- A cactus

WORKING WITH MULTIPLE WORKSHEETS

LESSON
7

Worksheets in a Workbook

A **workbook** is a collection of worksheets. **Sheet tabs** that appear at the bottom of the workbook window identify the worksheets within the workbook. The name of the sheet appears on the tab. Until the sheet is named, sheets are identified as Sheet1, Sheet2, etc., as shown in Figure 7-1.

FIGURE 7-1
Sheet tabs in a workbook

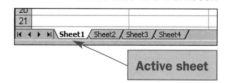

To work on a specific sheet, click on the tab of the worksheet. The sheet that appears on the screen is referred to as the **active sheet**. The sheet tab of the active sheet will be white.

Identifying Worksheets

Worksheets may be identified by naming them and by changing the color of their tabs.

Naming Worksheets

If you choose, you may change the default name (Sheet1, Sheet2,…) of a worksheet to a name that helps you identify the contents. To change the name, double-click the sheet tab, and then key the name you would like to identify the worksheet. (Alternatively, you may choose Sheet from the Format menu and then choose Rename from the submenu.)

Tab Colors

You may also identify a worksheet by changing its color. To change the tab color of the active sheet, choose Sheet from the Format menu and then choose Tab Color from the submenu. When the Format Tab Color dialog box appears, click the color that you want to appear on the tab.

STEP-BY-STEP ▷ 7.1

Continental Corporation currently consists of three divisions. A workbook has been prepared to summarize the sales of each division.

1. Open **IE Step7-1** from the data files.

2. Save the workbook as **Corporate Sales** followed by your initials.

3. Double-click the **Sheet3** tab. This worksheet will summarize the sales that appear on other worksheets.

4. Key **Corporate** and then press **Enter**. The word *Corporate* will appear on the third tab.

5. Change the name of Sheet1 to **Western**.

6. Change the name of Sheet2 to **Eastern**.

7. Change the name of Sheet4 to **Northern**.

8. Click the **Corporate** sheet tab.

9. Choose **Sheet** from the **Format** menu and then choose **Tab Color** from the submenu. The Format Tab Color dialog box will appear.

10. Click **black** in the upper left corner of the Format **Tab Color** dialog box.

11. Click **OK**. A black line will appear at the bottom of the Corporate sheet tab.

12. Click the **Northern** sheet tab. The Corporate sheet tab will turn black.

13. Change the color of the Northern, Western, and Eastern sheet tabs to yellow.

14. Click the **Corporate** sheet tab. Your screen should appear similar to Figure 7-2.

15. Save the file and leave the worksheet open for the next Step-by-Step.

FIGURE 7-2
Sheet tabs may be renamed and colored

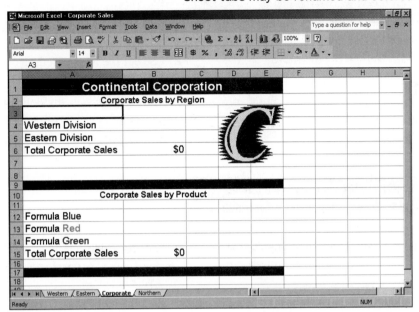

Positioning Worksheets in a Workbook

Inserting and Deleting Worksheets

Worksheets may be added to or deleted from a workbook. To insert a worksheet, click the tab of the worksheet that will follow the new sheet. Then click Worksheet on the Insert menu. A new worksheet will be inserted before the sheet you selected.

To delete a worksheet, select the worksheet and then click Delete Sheet on the Edit menu. Click OK to confirm the deletion. You can also right-click on any tab and select Insert or Delete on the shortcut menu.

> ### Hot Tip
>
> You may hide a worksheet in a workbook. Choose the worksheet you would like to hide, choose **Sheet** on the **Format** menu, and then click **Hide** on the submenu.

Modifying Worksheet Positions

Dragging the tab at the bottom of the workbook will change the position of a worksheet. When you click and hold on a tab, an arrow will appear at the left side of the tab. Drag the tab until the arrow appears in the desired position.

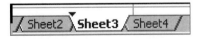

During the last year, the Northern Division, the smallest division, was combined with the Eastern Division. You are to delete the worksheet for the Northern Division. In addition, you would like to move the position of the Corporate worksheet so that it appears in the furthest right position.

1. Drag the tab of the **Corporate** sheet to the left until the arrow on the tab appears to the left of the Western tab and then release. The tab for the Corporate worksheet should now appear at the left side of the workbook.

2. Select the **Northern** division worksheet.

3. Choose **Delete Sheet** on the **Edit** menu. A message will appear warning that data may be permanently deleted.

4. Click **Delete**. The Northern worksheet tab should not appear at the bottom of the worksheet.

5. Save the file and leave the worksheet open for the next Step-by-Step.

Consolidating Workbook Data

In some cases you may need several worksheets to solve one numerical problem. For example, in a business that has several divisions, you may want to keep the financial results of each division on a separate worksheet. Then on a separate worksheet, you might want to combine the results of each division to show the combined results of all divisions.

Creating Links Between Worksheets

A *link* transfers data from one worksheet to another. To use data from one worksheet in another worksheet of a workbook, select the destination cell and then enter an = (or click the = button on the formula bar). Then click the sheet tab that contains the source data you would like to link, select the cell, or range of cells, and press Enter. The data will then be linked to the destination sheet. Any changes to the source data will also change the value in the destination cell.

Three-Dimensional References

Three-dimensional references are formula references that incorporate data from worksheets in an active worksheet. For example, in the active worksheet, you may want to add several numbers contained on other worksheets.

In a three-dimensional reference, the first part of the reference is the name of the worksheet, followed by an exclamation mark. The remaining part of the reference is the cell reference within the worksheet. For example, the reference Sheet2!B3 refers to the value contained in cell B3 on Sheet 2. Table 7-1 gives other examples of how three-dimensional references might be used.

Computer Concepts

You should be cautious when moving or copying worksheets in a workbook. For example, if you move a worksheet between other sheets, it might affect 3-D formula references in a workbook.

FORMULA	DISPLAYS
=Sheet4!D9	Inserts the value contained in D9 from the worksheet entitled Sheet4
=DivisionA!D10+DivisionB!D11	Adds the values in D10 of the worksheet entitled DivisionA and D11 of the worksheet entitled DivisionB
=SUM(Sheet2:Sheet4!D12)	Adds the values in D12 on Sheet2, Sheet3, and Sheet4
=SUM(Sheet2!D10:D11)	Adds the values in D10 and D11 of Sheet2

S TEP-BY-STEP ▷ 7.3

In this Step-by-Step, you will summarize values in the Eastern and Western Divisions in the Corporate worksheet.

1. Click the **Corporate** tab.

2. Select **B4** and key **=**.

3. Click the **Western** tab.

4. Select **B6**. The cell address preceded by the sheet name, =Western!B6, appears in the formula bar.

5. Press **Enter**. You are returned to the Corporate sheet, and $543,367 will appear in B4.

6. Select cell **B5**, if necessary, and key **=**.

7. Click the **Eastern** tab.

8. Select **B6**. The cell address =Eastern!B6 appears in the formula bar.

9. Press **Enter**.

10. Select **B12**, and enter **=**.

11. Click the **Western** tab.

12. Select **B3**. =Western!B3 appears in the formula bar.

13. Key **+**.

14. Click the **Eastern** tab.

15. Select **B3**. =Western!B3+Eastern!B3 appears in the formula bar.

16. Press **Enter**. You are returned to the Corporate sheet, and $306,744 will appear in B12.

17. Copy the formula in **B12** to **B13:B14**. When you are finished, the value in B15 should be the same as the value in B6 and your screen should appear similar to Figure 7-3.

18. Save the file and leave the worksheet open for the next Step-by-Step.

Did You Know?

You can place a background pattern in a worksheet. Choose **Sheet** on the **Format** menu and then click **Background** on the submenu. When the Sheet Background dialog box appears, select a picture that you would like placed in the background of the worksheet and then click **OK**.

FIGURE 7-3

Data from a workbook may be summarized on one worksheet

	A	B
1	**Continental Corporation**	
2	Corporate Sales by Region	
3		
4	Western Division	$543,367
5	Eastern Division	$516,001
6	Total Corporate Sales	$1,059,368
7		
8		
9		
10	Corporate Sales by Product	
11		
12	Formula Blue	$306,744
13	Formula Red	$566,399
14	Formula Green	$186,225
15	Total Corporate Sales	$1,059,368

Printing a Workbook

In previous lessons you learned to print selected areas of an active worksheet. You may also print an entire workbook, selected worksheets, or selected areas of a workbook. You designate the portion of the workbook to be printed in the Print what area of the Print dialog box (see Figure 7-4). The print area possibilities are shown in Table 7-2.

FIGURE 7-4
Printing alternatives are designated in the Print what area of the Print dialog box

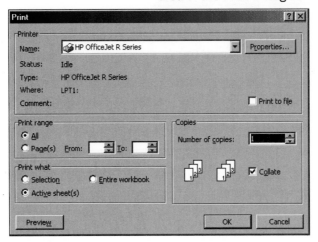

TABLE 7-2
Print area alternatives

PRINT WHAT SELECTION	PRINT RESULT
Selection	Prints range(s) selected within a single worksheet
Active sheet(s)	Prints the worksheet that appears on-screen, or will print additional worksheets that you have selected when you press Ctrl+the worksheet tab
Entire workbook	Prints all worksheets in a workbook

Printing Nonadjacent Selections of a Worksheet

To designate a print area in a worksheet, you typically select the print area, choose Print Area in the File menu, and then choose Set Print Area on the submenu. However, there may be times when you want to print selections in more than one part of a worksheet. For example, you may want to print the top and bottom part of worksheet, but not the middle portion of the worksheet.

To select more than one portion of a worksheet, begin by selecting the first portion that you would like to print. Then select additional portions by holding down the Ctrl key and dragging additional selections. Finally, in the Print dialog box, click Selection before clicking Print.

Printing More than One Worksheet

When printing more than one worksheet in a workbook, you may either print the entire workbook or selected worksheets in a workbook. To print an entire workbook, simply click Entire workbook in the Print what area of the Print dialog box (as shown in Figure 7-4).

To print only a few of the worksheets in a workbook, you must first select the worksheets to make them active. Additional worksheets can be made active by holding down the Ctrl key while clicking the worksheet tab. Then in the Print dialog box, select Active sheet(s) in the Print what area.

1. On the Corporate worksheet, select **A4:B6**.

2. While holding down the **Ctrl** key, select **A12:B15**.

3. Choose **Print** from the **File** menu. The Print dialog box will appear.

4. Click **Selection** in the Print what area.

5. Click **Preview**. Your screen should appear similar to Figure 7-5. The range A4:B6 will be printed on page 1 and A12:B15 will be printed on page 2.

6. Click **Print**. The selected areas will be printed.

7. Click the **Western** tab.

8. While holding down the **Ctrl** key, click the **Eastern** tab.

9. Choose **Print** from the **File** menu.

10. Make sure that **Active sheet(s)** is selected in the Print what area of the Print dialog box.

11. Click **Print**. The worksheets of the division will be printed, each on its own page.

12. Save and close the file.

FIGURE 7-5
Selected parts of a workbook may be printed

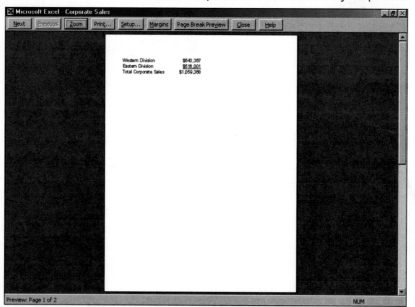

Summary

In this lesson, you learned:

- Worksheets are identified by naming and by changing the color of the worksheet tabs.

- Worksheets in a workbook may be inserted in and deleted from the workbook.

- Dragging the worksheet tab will change the position of a worksheet.

- Data in one worksheet may be linked to another worksheet.

- Three-dimensional references permit data from multiple worksheets to be used in formulas.

- Entire workbooks, selected worksheets, or selected areas of a workbook may be printed.

VOCABULARY REVIEW

Define the following terms:

Active sheet	Sheet tabs	Workbook
Link	Three-dimensional cell reference	

LESSON 7 REVIEW QUESTIONS

MATCHING

Match the correct formula result in the right column to its formula in the left column.

___ 1. =Sheet2!D10

___ 2. =Sheet2!D10+Sheet3!D11

___ 3. =SUM(Sheet2:Sheet4!D10)

___ 4. =SUM(Sheet2!D10:D11)

___ 5. =Sheet3!D10+Sheet3!D11

A. Adds the values in cell D10 on Sheet2, Sheet3, and Sheet4

B. Adds the values in D10 and D11 of Sheet3

C. Inserts the value in D10 of Sheet2

D. Adds the values in D10 of Sheet2 and D11 of Sheet3

E. Adds the values in D10 and D11 of Sheet2

FILL IN THE BLANK

Complete the following sentences by writing the correct word or words in the blanks provided.

1. _____ references are formula references that incorporate data from worksheets in an active worksheet.

2. A(n) _____ is a collection of worksheets.

3. _____ identify worksheets within a workbook at the bottom of a workbook window.

4. The sheet of a workbook that appears on the screen is the _____.

5. A(n) _____ tranfers data from one worksheet to another.

LESSON 7 PROJECTS

PROJECT 7-1

1. Open **IE Project7-1** from the data files.

2. Save the file as **Rainfall** followed by your initials.

3. Rename the sheets of the workbook and change the worksheet tab colors in the following manner:

EXISTING SHEET NAME	NEW SHEET NAME	TAB COLOR
Sheet1	Annual	Dark Blue
Sheet2	January	Blue
Sheet3	February	Light Blue
Sheet4	March	Pale Blue

4. Link the total rainfall recorded in **B34** of the **January** worksheet to **B3** of the **Annual** worksheet.

5. Link the total rainfall recorded in **B31** of the **February** worksheet to **B4** of the **Annual** worksheet.

6. Link the total rainfall recorded in **B34** of the **March** worksheet to **B5** of the **Annual** worksheet.

7. Save and print the **Annual** worksheet. Close the file.

PROJECT 7-2

1. Open **IE Project7-2** from the data files.

2. Save the file as **Voting** followed by your initials.

3. Rename the sheets of the workbook and change the worksheet tab colors in the following manner:

EXISTING SHEET NAME	NEW SHEET NAME	TAB COLOR
Sheet1	District 5	Red
Sheet2	P105	Orange
Sheet3	P106	Purple
Sheet4	P107	Green

4. Enter a formula in **D7** of the **District 5** worksheet that adds the values in **C5** of each of the precinct worksheets.

5. Enter a formula in **D9** of the **District 5** worksheet that adds the values in **C7** of each of the precinct worksheets.

6. Enter a formula in **D11** of the **District 5** worksheet that adds the values in **C9** of each of the precinct worksheets.

7. Enter a formula in **D13** of the **District 5** worksheet that adds the values in **C11** of each of the precinct worksheets.

8. Save and print the **District 5** worksheet. Close the file.

PROJECT 7-3

1. Open **IE Project7-3** from the data files.

2. Save the file as **Alamo Amalgamated** followed by your initials.

3. Change the worksheet tab colors in the following manner:

EXISTING SHEET NAME	TAB COLOR
Consolidated	Green
Alamogordo	Sea Green
Artesia	Light Green

4. Enter a formula in **C6** of the **Consolidated** worksheet that adds the values in **B6** of the **Alamogordo** and **Artesia** worksheets.

5. Enter a formula in **C7** of the **Consolidated** worksheet that adds the values in **B7** of the **Alamogordo** and **Artesia** worksheets.

6. Enter a formula in **C9** of the **Consolidated** worksheet that adds the values in **B9** of the **Alamogordo** and **Artesia** worksheets.

7. Enter a formula in **C10** of the **Consolidated** worksheet that adds the values in **B10** of the **Alamogordo** and **Artesia** worksheets.

8. Save and print all the worksheets in the workbook. Close the file.

PROJECT 7-4

1. Open **IE Project7-4** from the data files.

2. Save the file as **United Circuitry** followed by your initials.

3. Change the worksheet tab colors in the following manner:

EXISTING SHEET NAME	TAB COLOR
Year	Red
January	Light Orange
February	Gold
March	Tan

4. Link the total month production of Circuits 370, 380, and 390 recorded in **F4:F6** of the **January** worksheet to **B5:B7** of the **Year** worksheet.

5. Link the total month production of Circuits 370, 380, and 390 recorded in **F4:F6** of the **February** worksheet to **C5:C7** of the **Year** worksheet.

6. Link the total month production of Circuits 370, 380, and 390 recorded in **F4:F6** of the **March** worksheet to **D5:D7** of the **Year** worksheet.

7. Save and print the **Year** worksheet. Close the file.

CRITICAL THINKING

ACTIVITY 7-1

You have already learned how to link data in one worksheet to another worksheet within a workbook. Suppose that you wanted to link data from a worksheet in one workbook to a worksheet in a workbook contained in another Excel file. Use the Help function of Excel to determine how links might be established with other Excel files.

LESSON 8

WORKSHEET CHARTS

OBJECTIVES

Upon completion of this lesson, you should be able to:

- Identify the purpose of charting worksheet data.

- Identify the types of worksheet charts.

- Create a chart sheet and save a chart.

- Switch between charts and worksheets, zoom, and rename a chart.

- Preview and print a chart.

- Create an embedded chart.

- Edit a chart and change the type of chart.

⏱ **Estimated Time: 2.5 hours**

VOCABULARY

Axis

Chart

Chart sheet

Chart Wizard

Column chart

Data labels

Data series

Embedded chart

Image handles

Line chart

Pie chart

Scatter chart

What Is a Worksheet Chart?

A *chart* is a graphical representation of data contained in a worksheet. Charts make the data of a worksheet easier to understand. For example, the worksheet in Figure 8-1 shows the populations of four major U.S. cities for three years. You may be able to detect the changes in the populations by carefully examining the worksheet. However, the increases and decreases in the population of each city are easier to see when the contents of the worksheet are illustrated in a chart, such as the one shown in Figure 8-2.

FIGURE 8-1
This worksheet data could be shown in a chart

	A	B	C	D	E	F	G	H	I
1	**CITY POPULATIONS**								
2									
3	(in thousands)								
4		**1970**	**1980**	**1990**					
5	Boston	641	563	574					
6	Dallas	844	905	1,007					
7	Phoenix	584	790	983					
8	St. Louis	622	453	397					
9									
10									

FIGURE 8-2
A chart is a graphical representation of data in a worksheet

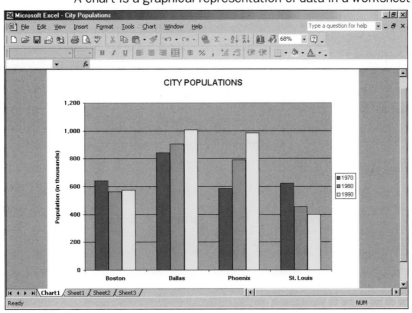

Types of Worksheet Charts

C ❯ In this lesson, you will create four of the most commonly used worksheet charts: column chart, line chart, pie chart, and scatter chart. These charts and several other types of charts are illustrated in Figure 8-3.

FIGURE 8-3
Charts available in Excel

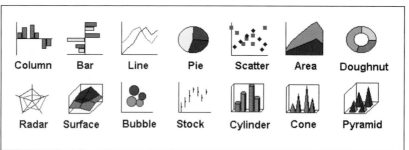

Column Chart

A *column chart* uses bars of varying heights to illustrate values in a worksheet and is useful for showing relationships among categories of data. For example, the column chart in Figure 8-2 has one vertical column to show the population of a city for each of three years and shows how the population of one city compares to populations of other cities.

Line Chart

A *line chart* is similar to the column chart except points connected by a line replace columns. The line chart is ideal for illustrating trends over time. For example, Figure 8-4 is a line chart that shows the growth of the U.S. federal debt from 1984 to 1998. The vertical axis represents the level of the debt and the horizontal axis shows the years. The line chart makes it easy to see how the federal debt has grown over time.

Did You Know?

Businesses often use column, bar, and line charts to illustrate growth over several periods. For example, the changes in yearly production or income over a 10-year period can be shown easily in a column chart.

FIGURE 8-4
A line chart is ideal for illustrating trends of data over time

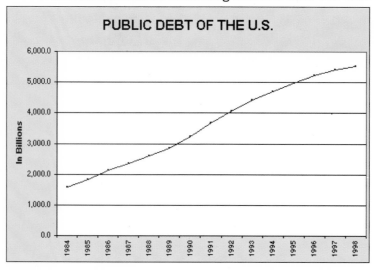

Pie Chart

Pie charts show the relationship of a part to a whole. Each part is shown as a "slice" of the pie. For example, a teacher could create a pie chart of the distribution of grades in a class, as shown in Figure 8-5. Each slice represents the portion of grades given for each letter grade.

Scatter Chart

Scatter charts, sometimes called XY charts, show the relationship between two categories of data. One category is represented on the vertical (Y) axis, and the other category is represented on the horizontal (X) axis. Connecting the data points with a line is not practical because points on a scatter chart usually do not relate to each other, as they do in a line chart. For example, the scatter chart in Figure 8-6 shows a data point for each of 12 individuals based on their height and weight. In most cases, a tall person tends to be heavier than a short person. However, because some people are tall and skinny, and others are short and stocky, the relationship between height and weight cannot be represented by a line.

Did You Know?

Businesses often use pie charts to indicate the magnitude of expenses in comparison to other expenses. Pie charts are also used to illustrate the company's market share in comparison to its competitors.

FIGURE 8-5
Each "slice" of a pie chart represents part of a larger group

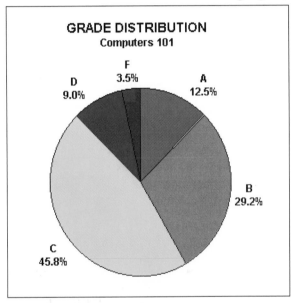

FIGURE 8-6
Scatter charts show the relationship between two categories of data

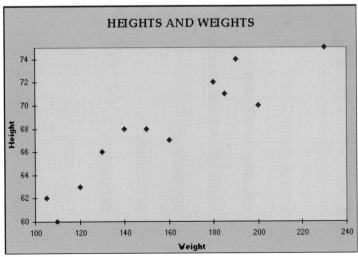

Creating a Chart from a Worksheet

You can create and display charts in two ways: by placing the chart on a chart sheet or by embedding the chart in the worksheet. A **chart sheet** is a separate sheet in the workbook on which you can create and store a chart. You can name the chart sheet to identify its contents and access it by clicking its tab. Use a chart sheet when you want to have the chart and data on the same screen or when you plan to create more than one chart from the same data.

An **embedded chart** is created within the worksheet. The primary advantage of an embedded chart is that it may be viewed at the same time as the data from which it is created. When you print the worksheet, the chart is printed on the same page.

Creating a Chart Sheet

Create a new chart sheet by first highlighting the data from the worksheet that is to be included in the chart. Then choose Chart on the Insert menu or click the Chart Wizard button on the toolbar. The **Chart Wizard**, an on-screen guide that helps you prepare a chart, appears. The Chart Wizard presents four steps for preparing a chart:

- **Step 1, Select the Chart Type**—Select a type of chart, such as column, line, or pie.

- **Step 2, Chart Source Data**—Confirm the range of data to be included in the chart. The range should also include the textual data that you plan to use as labels in the chart. You may also designate whether more than one series of data is to be charted. A **data series** is a group of related information in a column or row of a worksheet that will be plotted on a chart.

- **Step 3, Chart Options**—Designate the characteristics of the chart. The parts of a worksheet chart are identified in Figure 8-7. Table 8-1 describes the chart options that are specified under a separate tab in the Step 3 dialog box of the Chart Wizard.

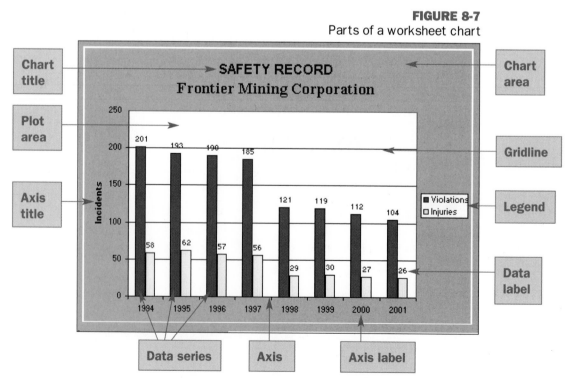

FIGURE 8-7
Parts of a worksheet chart

TABLE 8-1
Characteristics related to chart options

CHART OPTION TAB	OPTION FUNCTION
Titles	Headings that identify the contents of the chart or the axes in the chart; most charts have a chart title and titles for each axis
Axes	Lines that establish a relationship between data in a chart; most charts have a horizontal or X-axis and a vertical or Y-axis
Gridlines	Lines through a chart that relate the data in the chart to the axes
Legend	List that identifies patterns or symbols used in a chart
Data Labels	Text or numbers that identify the values depicted by the chart objects directly on the chart
Data Table	Data series values displayed in a grid below the chart

■ **Step 4, Chart Location**—Specify whether the chart will be embedded within the worksheet or appear on a separate sheet. When you create a chart on a separate sheet, it is identified by a name on a tab that appears near the bottom of the screen. The tab of the chart appears directly to the left of the tab of the worksheet from which the chart was created. If you do not name the chart in Step 4 of the Chart Wizard, Excel names the first chart sheet Chart1. If additional charts are created from the worksheet, they become Chart2, Chart3, and so on.

After you have completed these steps, a chart appears on-screen.

Hot Tip

To determine the name of a part of a chart, place the mouse pointer on that area. The name of the chart part will appear near the pointer.

Hot Tip

You can change options you selected in previous steps of the Chart Wizard by clicking the **Back** button at the bottom of the dialog box.

STEP-BY-STEP ▷ 8.1

1. Open **IE Step8-1** from the data files. Column A contains educational levels and Column B contains the median incomes of those with corresponding levels of education.

2. Select the range **A3:B8**. The highlighted items are the data to be included in the chart that you will create.

3. Choose **Chart** on the **Insert** menu. The Step 1 of 4 Chart Wizard dialog box opens, as shown in Figure 8-8.

4. Click **Column** in the Chart type list, if it is not already selected.

5. From the Chart sub-type options, click the first chart sub-type box if it is not already selected. The description will identify the selected chart as a "Clustered Column. Compares values across categories."

6. Preview the chart you are about to create by clicking and holding the **Press and Hold to View Sample** button.

7. Click **Next**. The Step 2 of 4 Chart Wizard dialog box appears. In this dialog box, Excel has created a sample chart.

8. Click **Next**. The Step 3 of 4 dialog box appears. The tabs at the top of the dialog box indicate options that may be changed in the chart.

9. Click the **Titles** tab if it is not selected already.

10. Key **YOUR EDUCATION PAYS** in the Chart title text box.

11. Key **Education Level** in the Category (X) axis text box.

12. Key **Median Income** in the Value (Y) axis text box. As you enter the titles, they will appear in the sample chart area on the right side of the dialog box. When you finish, the dialog box should appear similar to Figure 8-9.

13. Click the **Legend** tab.

14. Click the **Show legend** text box until no check mark appears in the box. This chart uses only one series of data and does not need a legend to distinguish among data.

15. Click **Next**. The Step 4 of 4 Chart Wizard dialog box appears.

16. Click **As new sheet**.

FIGURE 8-8
Step 1 of the Chart Wizard

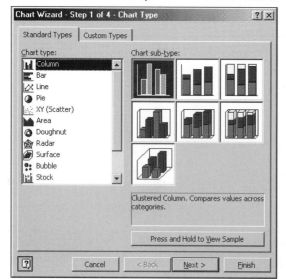

FIGURE 8-9
Enter chart titles on the Titles tab

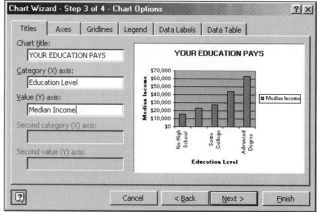

17. Enter **Column** in the text box. The dialog box should look similar to Figure 8-10.

18. Click **Finish**. Your screen displays a chart sheet with the chart you created. Near the bottom of

the page, a sheet tab titled Column appears. The chart should appear similar to Figure 8-11. Leave the file open for the next Step-by-Step.

FIGURE 8-10
Step 4 of the Chart Wizard

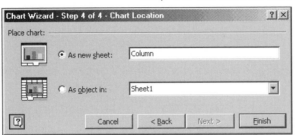

FIGURE 8-11
Finished chart sheet

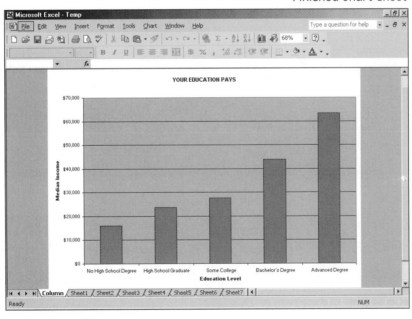

The chart illustrates the value of education in attaining higher income. Notice that the columns get higher on the right side of the chart, indicating that those who stay in school will be rewarded with higher incomes.

Excel may also display the Chart toolbar, which contains buttons that are useful in editing a chart. As you work more with charts you may want to use these buttons. To access the Chart toolbar, right-click anywhere in any existing toolbar and choose Chart from the pop-up menu that appears. If you do not want the Chart toolbar displayed, you can close it.

Saving a Chart

A chart is considered part of a workbook. When you save the workbook, you will also save the charts you have created. Save the worksheet and its chart(s) by choosing Save on the File menu. It does not matter if you are on the worksheet containing the data or the chart sheet.

1. Choose **Save As** on the **File** menu.

2. Save the file as **Education Pays** followed by your initials. Leave the file open for the next Step-by-Step.

Switching Between Chart Sheets and Worksheets

A chart sheet is closely related to the worksheet from which it is created. If you change the data in a worksheet, these changes will automatically be made in the chart created from the worksheet.

To return to the worksheet from which a chart was created, click the tab of the worksheet. The chart may be accessed once again by clicking the sheet tab with the chart name on it.

Zoom Command

You can use the Zoom command on the View menu to enlarge a chart sheet or worksheet to see it in greater detail or to reduce it to see more on your screen. You can use the preset zoom settings or key in your own between 10% and 400% of the actual size. When you choose the Fit Selection option, the sheet will automatically be sized to fit the screen. You can choose the Zoom command from the View menu or click the Zoom box on the toolbar.

STEP-BY-STEP ▷ 8.3

1. Click the **Sheet1** tab near the bottom of the screen. The worksheet appears.

2. Edit the contents of A5 to be **High School Degree**.

3. Click the **Column sheet** tab. The chart sheet appears. The label for the second column has changed.

4. To see the labels more closely, click the down arrow on the **Zoom** button. Click **75%**. Scroll to view all areas of the chart.

   `[ 50% ▼ ]`

5. To reduce the sheet to fit the screen, choose **Zoom** on the **View** menu. The Zoom dialog box appears.

6. Click **Fit selection** from the Magnification options. Click **OK**.

7. Save and leave the file open for the next Step-by-Step.

Renaming a Chart Sheet

Renaming a chart sheet is particularly useful after you have prepared several charts from one worksheet. These charts may become difficult to distinguish by their chart sheet number and are easier to recognize with more descriptive names. Change the name of the chart sheet by choosing the Sheet command on the Format menu and choosing Rename on the submenu. You may also change the name of the sheet by right-clicking the sheet tab and then clicking Rename on the shortcut menu (or you may double-click on the tab, which highlights the text, and then edit the name).

Hot Tip

You may delete chart sheets that are no longer needed by right-clicking the chart sheet tab, and clicking **Delete** on the shortcut menu.

STEP-BY-STEP ▷ 8.4

1. Right-click the **Column** sheet tab.

2. Click **Rename** on the shortcut menu.

3. Key **Income Chart** on the sheet tab.

4. Click outside the sheet tab.

5. Save and leave the file open for the next Step-by-Step.

Previewing and Printing a Chart

You preview and print a chart the same way you do a worksheet. You can click the Print Preview button to preview the sheet. You click the Print button to send the sheet directly to the printer.

STEP-BY-STEP ▷ 8.5

1. Click the **Print Preview** button. The chart appears in the preview window.

2. Click the **Print** button in the Print Preview window.

3. Click **OK**.

4. Save and close the file.

Creating an Embedded Chart

An embedded chart appears within a worksheet rather than on a separate sheet. An embedded chart is created the same way as a chart on a sheet, with one exception. In the last step of the Chart Wizard (step 4), you will click the As object in button rather than the As new sheet button, as shown in Figure 8-10.

In the next Step-by-Step, you will embed a pie chart into a worksheet. Pie charts compare items within one group to other items within the same group. For example, in a group of pet owners, you can show what percent owns dogs, cats, or fish. Pie charts differ from column and line charts because pie charts use only one series of numeric data. In the column chart

Computer Concepts

Embedded charts are useful when you want to print a chart next to the data the chart illustrates. When a chart will be displayed or printed without the data used to create the chart, a separate chart sheet is usually more appropriate.

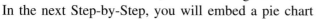

you created, you selected two columns of data to compare the level of education to median income. To create a pie chart, select a column of data, and then choose the Chart command on the Insert menu.

Because embedded charts are displayed directly on the worksheet, they may interfere with other worksheet data by covering it or by appearing in an area that is inconvenient for printing. You can move an embedded chart by dragging it to a different part of the worksheet. You can also change the size of an embedded chart by dragging the *image handles*, which are small black squares that appear at the corners and sides of an embedded chart.

S TEP-BY-STEP ▷ 8.6

Great Plains Grains is a company that sells a variety of agricultural products. The managers would like to determine which products make up the largest portion of their sales by illustrating the segment sales in a pie chart.

1. Open **IE Step8-6** from the data files.

2. Save the file as **Segment Sales** followed by your initials.

3. Select the range **A7:B10**.

4. Click the **Chart Wizard** button on the toolbar.

5. Click the **Pie** chart type.

6. Click the pie chart in the upper left corner of the Chart sub-type section if it is not already selected. The description will identify the selected chart as a "Pie. Displays the contribution of each value to a total."

7. Click **Next**. The Step 2 Chart Wizard dialog box appears.

8. Click **Next**. The Step 3 Chart Wizard dialog box appears.

9. Click the **Titles** tab if it is not selected already.

10. Key **Annual Sales by Segment** in the Chart title text box.

11. Click the **Legend** tab.

12. Make sure the **Show Legend** box is not checked.

13. Click the **Data Labels** tab.

14. Click the **Category name** and **Percentage** check boxes.

15. Click **Next**. The Step 4 Chart Wizard dialog box appears.

16. Click **As object in** if it is not already selected.

17. Click **Finish**.

18. Use the image handles to fit the chart within **C6:E14**. Your screen should look similar to Figure 8-12.

19. Save and print the file and leave the worksheet on your screen for the next Step-by-Step.

FIGURE 8-12
Creating an embedded pie chart

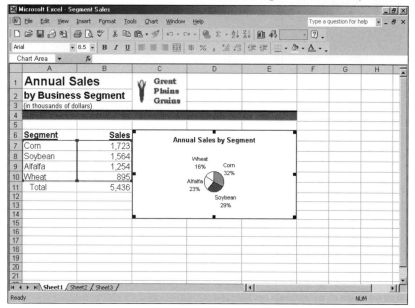

Creating Other Types of Charts

In previous Step-by-Steps you created a column chart and a pie chart. Now you will learn to create a three-dimensional chart and a scatter chart.

Three-Dimensional Charts

Excel allows you to make charts look as though they are three-dimensional. Area, bar, column, cone, cylinder, line, surface, pie, and pyramid charts are available in three-dimensional formats.

Hot Tip

You may print the chart with or without the worksheet data you used to create the chart. To print only the chart, select the chart by clicking on it and then choose **Print** on the **File** menu. To print the chart and the worksheet data, deselect the chart by clicking outside of it and then choose **Print** on the **File** menu.

1. Save the file as **Segment Sales 3D** followed by your initials.

2. Right-click the white space in the pie chart embedded in the worksheet. A shortcut menu appears.

3. Choose **Chart Type** on the menu. The Chart Type dialog box appears.

4. Click the middle chart in the top row of the Chart sub-type area. The chart description

"Pie with a 3-D visual effect" appears at the bottom of the dialog box.

5. Click **OK**. You are returned to the worksheet. Your screen should look similar to Figure 8-13.

6. Click outside the chart to deselect it.

7. Save, print, and then close the worksheet.

FIGURE 8-13
3-D pie chart

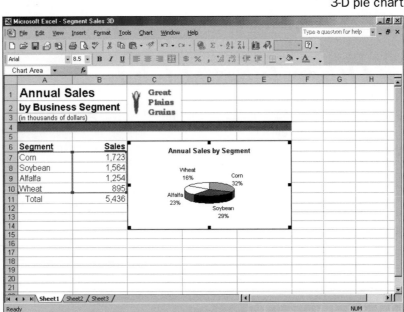

Scatter charts are sometimes referred to as XY charts because they place data points between an X- and Y-axis. Scatter charts can be difficult to prepare because you must designate which data should be used as a scale on each axis.

STEP-BY-STEP ▷ 8.8

Coronado Foundries produces manufactured goods. During the manufacturing process, a certain amount of scrap is produced. Management expects that as more goods are produced, more scrap is also be produced. They would like to create a chart to illustrate the expected relationship.

1. Open **IE Step8-8** from the data files.

2. Save the file as **Scrap Report** followed by your initials.

3. Select the range **B6:C16**.

4. Choose **Chart** on the **Insert** menu. The Step 1 Chart Wizard dialog box appears.

5. Click the chart type **XY (Scatter)**.

6. Click the first chart sub-type if it is not already selected. The description will identify the selected chart as a "Scatter. Compares pairs of values."

7. Click **Next**. The Step 2 Chart Wizard dialog box appears.

8. Click **Next**. The Step 3 Chart Wizard dialog box appears.

9. Click the **Titles** tab if it is not selected already.

10. Key **Production and Scrap Report** in the Chart title box.

11. Key **Units of Production** in the Value (X) axis box.

12. Key **Units of Scrap** in the Value (Y) axis box.

13. Click the **Legend** tab.

14. Make sure the **Show Legend** box is not checked.

15. Click **Next**. The Step 4 Chart Wizard dialog box appears.

16. Click **As new sheet** if it is not already selected.

17. Key **Scatter Chart** in the **As new sheet** text box.

18. Click **Finish**. A scatter chart appears on a chart sheet. You may be able to tell that factories with larger production also tend to generate more scrap. Notice that the data points are concentrated in the right portion of the chart. To spread the data out, you may adjust the scale of the chart.

19. To adjust the X-axis to the left, double-click the X (horizontal) axis. (A ScreenTip that reads **Value (X) axis** will appear when you have selected the appropriate axis.) The Format Axis dialog box appears.

20. Click the **Scale** tab.

21. Key **4000** in the Minimum box.

22. Click **OK**. The portion of the chart to the left of 4000 on the X-axis, which did not have any data points, has been removed.

23. To adjust the Y-axis downward, double-click the Y (vertical) axis. The Format Axis dialog box appears.

24. Click the **Scale** tab if it is not already chosen.

25. Enter **250** in the Maximum box.

26. Click **OK**. The portion of the chart above 250 has been removed. The chart sheet on your screen should look similar to Figure 8-14.

27. Save, print, and close the file.

FIGURE 8-14

Scatter charts can show labeled points between two axes

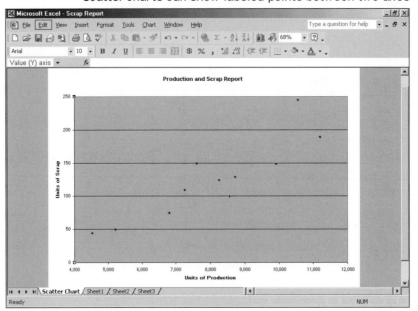

Editing a Chart

The Chart Wizard creates charts in a way that may be useful to many Excel users. However, you may want to edit the chart to suit your specific needs. For example, you may want to change a title font or the color of a column. Figure 8-15 shows six areas of the chart and some of the characteristics that may be changed. Clicking with the left mouse button selects the chart part. Double-clicking with the left mouse button produces one of the dialog boxes identified in Table 8-2. Within the dialog box, you can access tabbed areas to edit specific chart characteristics. Clicking the right mouse button produces a shortcut menu with options such as clearing data, inserting data, or changing chart types.

FIGURE 8-15
Six parts of the chart

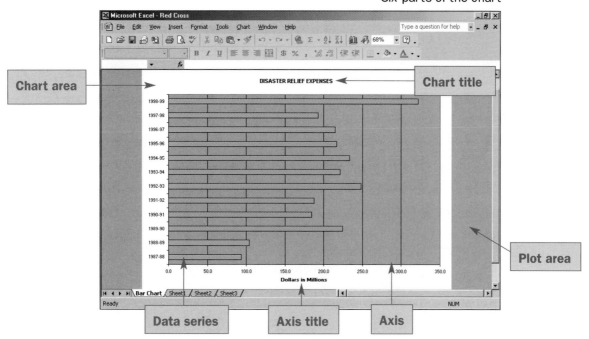

TABLE 8-2
Charts may be edited using one of six Format dialog boxes

FORMAT DIALOG BOX	TABBED AREAS OF THE DIALOG BOX
Format Chart Title	Patterns—designates the border and color of the chart title
	Font—designates the font, font size, and color of characters in the chart title
	Alignment—designates the justification and orientation of the chart title
Format Axis Title	Patterns—designates the border and color of the axis title
	Font—designates the font and font size of characters in the axis title
	Alignment—designates the justification and orientation of the axis title
Format Axis	Patterns—designates the border and color of the axis
	Scale—designates characteristics of the axis scale
	Font—designates the font and font size of characters in the axis
	Number—designates the format of numbers in the labels in the axis (for example, currency, text, date)
	Alignment—designates the orientation of the labels in the axis

TABLE 8-2

Charts may be edited using one of six Format dialog boxes (continued)

FORMAT DIALOG BOX	TABBED AREAS OF THE DIALOG BOX
Format Data Series	Patterns—designates the border and color of the data series
	Axis—designates whether the data is plotted on a primary or secondary axis
	X Error Bars and Y Error Bars—designate the treatment of points that extend beyond the scale of the chart
	Data Labels—designates the words or values that may appear on the points of a graph
	Series Order—designates which data series will appear first in clustered charts
	Options—designates the other characteristics unique to the chart type
Format Plot Area	Patterns—designates the border and color of the plot area
Format Chart Area	Patterns—designates the border and color of the chart background
	Font—designates the font and font size of characters in the chart area

STEP-BY-STEP ▷ 8.9

C

1. Open **IE Step8-9** from the data files. This is a worksheet containing the disaster services expenses of the American Red Cross.

2. Save the file as **Red Cross** followed by your initials.

3. Click the **Bar Chart** sheet tab. The sheet contains a chart that indicates the level of disaster services expense for each period.

4. To add a subtitle, click the chart title **DISASTER RELIEF EXPENSES**. A shaded border with handles surrounds the title.

5. Click to the right of the last *S* in the title. An insertion point appears.

6. Press **Enter**. The insertion point becomes centered under the first line of the title.

7. Key **American Red Cross**. The subtitle appears in the chart.

8. To change the font size of the horizontal axis labels, double-click the horizontal axis. The Format Axis dialog box appears.

9. Click the **Font** tab. The axis labels are currently 10 point.

10. Choose **12** in the Size box.

11. Click **OK**. You are returned to the chart sheet. The horizontal axis labels are now larger.

12. To change the color of the bars, double-click one of the bars. The Format Data Series dialog box appears.

13. Click the **Patterns** tab if it is not already selected.

14. Click any bright red in the Area box. A bright red color appears in the Sample box.

15. Click **OK**. You are returned to the chart sheet. The chart appears with bright red bars. Your screen should appear similar to Figure 8-16.

16. Save the file and leave the chart sheet open for the next Step-by-Step.

FIGURE 8-16
Modifying parts of the chart

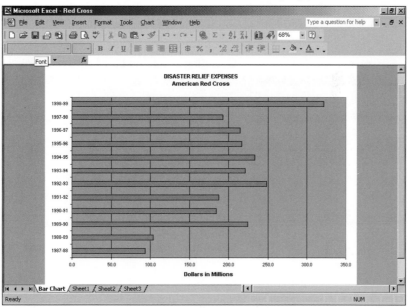

Changing the Type of Chart

After creating a chart, you can change it to a different type by choosing the Chart Type command on the Chart menu (or by clicking the chart area or plot area with the right mouse button and then choosing the Chart Type command). The Chart Type dialog box is the same dialog box that appears in the Step 1 Chart Wizard dialog box (see Figure 8-8).

Computer Concepts

Not all charts are interchangeable. For example, data that is suitable for a pie chart is often not logical in a scatter chart. However, most line charts are easily converted into column or bar charts.

1. Choose **Chart Type** on the **Chart** menu.

2. Click **Line** in the Chart type box.

3. Click the middle box in the first column of the Chart sub-type section if it is not already selected. The description will identify the selected chart as a "Line with markers displayed at each data value."

4. Click **OK**. The new line chart appears.

5. Rename the chart sheet as **Line Chart**. Your line chart should appear as shown in Figure 8-17.

6. Save, print, and close the file.

Extra Challenge

Convert the line chart you just created into a column chart.

FIGURE 8-17
Changing a column chart into a line chart

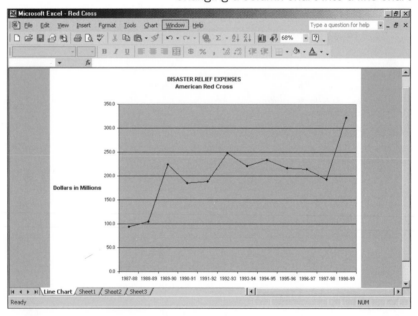

Summary

In this lesson, you learned:

■ A chart is a graphical representation of worksheet data. You can create several types of worksheet charts, including column charts, line charts, pie charts, and scatter charts. Several types of charts can also be created three-dimensionally.

■ Charts may be embedded within a worksheet or created on a chart sheet. A chart sheet is an area separate from the Excel worksheet in which a chart is created and stored. An embedded chart is created within a worksheet.

■ The Chart Wizard is a four-step on-screen guide that helps you prepare a chart from an Excel worksheet. The Chart Wizard is used to prepare a chart whether the chart is to appear in the worksheet or on a chart sheet.

■ A chart created from a worksheet is considered part of the workbook. When you save the workbook, you also save the charts you created from the worksheets.

■ You can edit your chart by clicking one of six areas of the chart that accesses a Format dialog box. You can change the type of chart in the Chart Type dialog box.

VOCABULARY REVIEW

Define the following terms:

Axis	Column chart	Image handles
Chart	Data labels	Line chart
Chart sheet	Data series	Pie chart
Chart Wizard	Embedded chart	Scatter chart

LESSON 8 REVIEW QUESTIONS

TRUE/FALSE

Circle T if the statement is true or F if the statement is false.

T F 1. A chart is a graphical representation of worksheet data.

T F 2. Column charts are the best way to represent data groups that are part of a whole.

T F 3. Line charts are a good choice for representing trends over a period of time.

T F 4. A scatter chart produces a "cloud" of data points not connected by lines.

T F 5. When the worksheet data changes, charts created from the worksheet also change.

FILL IN THE BLANK

Complete the following sentences by writing the correct word or words in the blanks provided.

1. A(n) _____ chart is represented by a circle divided into portions.

2. In a worksheet chart, the _____ shows patterns or symbols that identify the different types of data.

3. The _____ menu contains the command for renaming a chart sheet.

4. A(n) _____ chart is a chart that is created on the same sheet as the data being charted.

5. _____ represent the values depicted by chart objects such as data points or columns.

LESSON 8 PROJECTS

PROJECT 8-1

The file *IE Project8-1* contains the populations of the world's largest cities. Create a column chart to illustrate the data.

1. Open **IE Project8-1** from the data files.

2. Save the file as **Population** followed by your initials.

3. Create a column chart in a chart sheet from the data in **A5:B12**.

4. Title the chart **World's Largest Cities**.

5. Title the Y-axis **Population in Millions**. No X-axis title is needed.

6. Include major horizontal gridlines. (*Hint:* Gridlines are specified under the Gridlines tab in Step 3 of the Chart Wizard.)

7. Do not include a legend in the chart.

8. Name the chart sheet **Column Chart**.

9. Preview the chart.

10. Save, print, and close the file.

PROJECT 8-2

You have been running each morning to stay in shape. Over the past ten weeks you have recorded your running times in file *IE Project8-2*.

1. Open **IE Project8-2** from the data files.

2. Save the file as **Training** followed by your initials.

3. Create an embedded line chart with markers at each data value from the data in **A5:B14**.

4. Do not include a chart title.

5. Title the Y-axis **Time in Minutes**. No X-axis title is needed.

6. Include major horizontal gridlines in the chart.

7. Do not include a legend in the chart.

8. Use the chart handles to position the chart in the range **C3:I15** on the worksheet.

9. Save the file. Print the worksheet with the embedded chart, and close the file.

PROJECT 8-3

The file *IE Project8-3* contains the number of McDonald's hamburger restaurants in different regions of the world.

1. Open **IE Project8-3** from the data files.

2. Save the file as **McDonalds** followed by your initials.

3. Create a pie chart in a chart sheet from the data in **A6:B10**.

4. Title the chart **Systemwide Locations**.

5. Place a legend on the right side of the chart that identifies each geographic region.

6. Include percentages as data labels next to each slice.

7. Name the chart sheet **Pie Chart**.

8. Edit font sizes so the chart title is **24** points, the slice percentages are **18** points, and the legend is **18** points.

9. Switch to the worksheet. Edit the content of **A8** to be **Asia/Pacific** rather than *Asia*.

10. Switch back to the chart sheet to see that the legend has been updated with the edited data.

11. Save the file, print the chart, and close the file.

PROJECT 8-4

The file *IE Project8-4* contains the monthly cash flow of a young family. To better explain their expenses to family members, a member of the household decides to create a pie chart in which each slice represents an expense category that contributes to total expenses.

1. Open **IE Project8-4** from the data files.

2. Save the file as **Family Expenses** followed by your initials.

3. Create a three-dimensional pie chart on a chart sheet from the data in **A6:B13**.

4. Title the pie chart **Where Our Money Goes**.

5. Do not include a legend in the chart.

6. The pie chart should include the category names and percentages for each slice.

7. Name the chart sheet **3-D Pie Chart**.

8. Change the font size of the chart title to **18** points.

9. Change the font size of the data labels to **14** points.

10. Preview the chart, and determine in what areas you believe most spending occurs.

11. Save the file, print the chart, and close the file.

PROJECT 8-5

The file *IE Project8-5* contains the study time and examination scores for several students. The instructor is attempting to determine if a relationship exists between study time and examination scores.

1. Open **IE Project8-5** from the data files.

2. Save the file as **Study Time** followed by your initials.

3. Create a scatter chart without connecting lines in a chart sheet from the data in **B4:C21**.

4. Title the chart **Comparison of Exam Grades to Study Time**.

5. Title the X-axis **Hours of Study**.

6. Title the Y-axis **Examination Grades**.

7. Do not include gridlines, a legend, or data labels in the chart.

8. Name the chart sheet **Scatter Chart**.

9. Change the font size of the chart title to **20** points.

10. Change the font size of the axis titles to **14** points.

11. Change the font size of the axis labels to **12** points.

12. Change the minimum value of the vertical scale (Y-axis) to **50**.

13. Preview the chart and determine whether you believe a relationship exists between study time and examination results.

14. Save the file, print the chart, and close the file.

PROJECT 8-6

You operate the concession stand at the home baseball games of Mountain College, and have noticed a decrease in popularity of certain items as the season has progressed. The concession sales for each game have been kept on a worksheet. Now you would like to use the worksheet to create a chart that illustrates the change in sales levels for each product during the season.

1. Open **IE Project8-6** from the data files.

2. Save the file as **Concession Sales** followed by your initials.

3. Create a column chart on a chart sheet from the data in **A4:E9**.

4. Title the chart **Concession Sales**.

5. No X-axis title is needed. Title the Y-axis **Sales in Dollars**.

6. Include a legend at the right of the chart to identify the game number.

7. Name the chart sheet **Column Chart**.

8. Access the **Format Plot Area** dialog box, and change the color in the Area box to white.

9. Change the font of the chart title to **18** points.

10. Change the font size of the X (horizontal) axis labels to **14** points, and apply boldface to the labels.

11. Change the font size of the Y (vertical) axis labels to **12** points.

12. Change the font size of the Y-axis title to **14** points.

13. Change the font size of the legend labels to **12** points.

14. Preview the chart and determine which product has decreased in sales over the last four games.

15. Save the file, print the chart, and close the file.

PROJECT 8-7

The file *IE Project8-7* contains the income statement of Radiation Software Corporation for several years. You would like to illustrate the corporation's growth by charting the sales and income levels.

1. Open **IE Project8-7** from the data files.

2. Save the file as **Radiation** followed by your initials.

3. Create a line chart with markers in a chart sheet from the data in **A5:F7**.

4. Title the chart **Revenue and Income of Radiation Software Corporation**.

5. Title the Y-axis **(in Thousands)**. No X-axis title is needed.

6. Place a legend that distinguishes revenue from income at the bottom of the chart.

7. Name the chart sheet **Revenue Chart**.

8. Change the font size of the chart title to **18** points.

9. Change the font size of the X (horizontal) axis and Y (vertical) axis labels to **14** points.

10. Change the font size of the Y-axis title to **12** points.

11. Change the font size of the legend labels to **14** points.

12. Save the file and print the chart. As you view the printed chart, determine whether the company's sales have decreased, increased, or remained stable.

13. Change the type of chart to a clustered column chart.

14. Save the file, print the chart, and close the file.

PROJECT 8-8

1. Open **IE Project8-8** from the data files.

2. Save the file as **Temperature** followed by your initials.

3. Create a line chart with markers in a chart sheet from the data in **B3:M5**.

4. Title the chart **Temperatures for Chico, California**.

5. Title the Y-axis **Temperature in Fahrenheit**. No X-axis title is needed.

6. Place a legend on the right side of the chart that distinguishes the high and low temperatures.

7. Name the chart sheet **Line Chart**.

8. Change the font size of the chart title to **18** points.

9. Change the font size of the X (horizontal) axis and Y (vertical) axis labels to **14** points.

10. Change the font size of the Y-axis title to **16** points.

11. Change the font size of the legend labels to **14** points.

12. Double-click the high temperature line until the Format Data Series dialog box appears. Then make the following changes:
    A. Click the **Patterns** tab if necessary, and in the line area, change the weight to the heaviest line and the color to red.
    B. In the marker area, change the foreground to red and the background to red.

13. Click **OK** to exit the Format Data Series dialog box.

14. Double-click the low temperature line until the Format Data Series dialog box appears. Then make the following changes:
    A. In the line area (on the Patterns tab), change the weight to heavy and color to blue.
    B. In the marker area, change the foreground to blue and the background to blue.

15. Click **OK** to exit the Format Data Series dialog box.

16. Double-click the plot area of the chart until the Format Plot Area dialog box appears. In the Area part of the dialog box, change the color to white.

17. Click **OK** to exit the Format Plot Area dialog box.

18. Save the file, print the chart, and close the file.

CRITICAL THINKING

SCANS

ACTIVITY 8-1

For each scenario, determine what type of worksheet chart you believe is the most appropriate to represent the data. Justify your answer by describing why you believe the chart is most appropriate.

Scenario 1. A scientist gave different amounts of water to 200 potted plants. After 35 days, the height of each plant and the amount of water given to the plant were recorded in a worksheet.

Scenario 2. A corporation developed a new product last year. A manager in the corporation recorded the number of units sold each month. He noticed that sales in summer months were much higher than sales in the winter. He would like to prepare a chart to illustrate this information to other sales managers.

Scenario 3. A high school principal has students who come from five middle schools. She has recorded the name of the middle school and the number of students who came from each school. She would like to illustrate how some of the middle schools supply significantly more students than other middle schools.

Introduction to Microsoft Excel

UNIT REVIEW

COMMAND SUMMARY

FEATURE	MENU COMMAND	TOOLBAR BUTTON	LESSON
Align Data	Format, Cells, Alignment		2
Bold Data	Format, Cells, Font	B	2
Borders Around Cells	Format, Cells, Border	▦▾	2
Center Data Across Range of Cells	Format, Cells, Alignment, Center Across Selection	▤	2
Chart, Create a	Insert, Chart	▥	8
Chart, Preview a	File, Print Preview	▣	8
Color a Worksheet Tab	Format, Sheet, Tab Color		7
Column, Delete a	Edit, Delete, Entire Column		3
Column, Hide	Format, Column, Hide		6
Column, Insert a	Insert, Columns		3
Column, Unhide	Format, Column, Unhide		6
Column Width, Automatic	Format, Column, AutoFit Selection		2
Column Width, Specific	Format, Column, Width		2
Copy by Filling	Edit, Fill		3
Clip Art, Insert	Insert, Picture, Clip Art		6
Data, Color	Format, Cells, Font	A▾	2
Data, Copy	Edit, Copy	▣	3
Data, Filter	Data, Filter, AutoFilter		6
Data, Find	Edit, Find	▣	1
Data, Italicize	Format, Cell, Font	I	2
Data, Move	Edit, Cut, and then Edit, Paste	✂	3
Data, Paste	Edit, Paste	▣	3
Data Ascending, Sort	Data, Sort	A↓	6
Data Descending, Sort	Data, Sort	Z↓	6
Data, Replace	Edit, Replace		1
Data, Rotating	Format, Cells, Alignment		2
Data, Underline	Format, Cell, Font	U	2

FEATURE	MENU COMMAND	TOOLBAR BUTTON	LESSON
Data, Wrap	Format, Cells, Alignment, Wrap text		2
Decimal, Decrease	Format, Cells, Number		2
Decimal, Increase	Format, Cells, Number		2
Delay Calculations	Tools, Options, Calculation		4
Design a Printed Page	File, Page Setup		3
Drawing Toolbar, Display the	View, Toolbars, Drawing		6
Fill a Cell with Color	Format, Cells, Patterns		2
Font, Change a	Format, Cells, Font	Arial	2
Font Size, Change the	Format, Cells, Font	10	2
Format Painting			2
Formulas, Show	Tools, Options, View		4
Function Formula, Insert a	Insert, Function		5
Hyperlink, Insert a	Insert, Hyperlink		6
Indention, Decrease an	Format, Cells, Alignment		2
Indention, Increase an	Format, Cells, Alignment		2
Picture from a File, Insert	Insert, Picture, From File		6
Row, Delete a	Edit, Delete		3
Row Height, Change	Format, Row, Height		2
Row, Hide	Format, Row, Hide		6
Row, Insert a	Insert, Rows		3
Row, Unhide	Format, Row, Unhide		6
Spelling, Check	Tools, Spelling		3
Sum a Range (AutoSum)	Insert, Function	Σ	4
Titles, Freeze the	Window, Freeze Panes		3
Titles, Unfreeze	Window, Unfreeze Panes		3
Worksheet, Delete	Edit, Delete Sheet		6
Worksheet, Move	Edit, Move or Copy Sheet		7
Worksheet, Name a	Format, Sheet, Rename		6
Worksheet, Open a	File, Open		1
Worksheet, Preview a	File, Print Preview		3
Worksheet, Print a	File, Print		1
Worksheet, Save a Named	File, Save		1
Worksheet, Save an Unnamed	File, Save As		1
Zoom	View, Zoom	100%	1

TRUE/FALSE

Circle T if the statement is true or F if the statement is false.

T F   1. The active cell reference will appear on the toolbar.

T F   2. To select a group of cells, click each cell individually until all cells in the range have been selected.

T F   3. The Save As dialog box appears every time you save a worksheet.

T F   4. The formula =B$4+C$9 contains mixed cell references.

T F   5. A chart may be printed from the chart sheet.

MATCHING

Match the description in the right column with the text positioning function in the left column.

____ 1. Wrappping

____ 2. Rotating

____ 3. Indenting

____ 4. Justifying

____ 5. Merge and Center

A. Displays text at an angle

B. Aligns text to the right, left, or center

C. Combines several cells into one and places the contents in the middle of the cell

D. Begins a new line within a cell

E. Moves text several spaces to the right

FILL IN THE BLANK

Complete the following sentences by writing the correct word or words in the blanks provided.

1. A(n) _____ cell reference will remain the same when copied or moved.

2. The Manual button under the Calculation tab in the Options dialog box delays calculation until the _____ key is pressed.

3. The _____ toolbar button will add a range of numbers in a worksheet.

4. A(n) _____ chart uses bars to represent values in a worksheet.

5. The _____ tab in the Options dialog box is used to select to display formulas rather than values in the worksheet.

MATCHING

Match the correct result in the right column to the formula in the left column. Assume the following values appear in the worksheet:

Cell	Value
B2	5
B3	6
B4	4
B5	7

_____ 1. =10+B5

_____ 2. =B2*B4

_____ 3. =(B3+B4)/B2

_____ 4. =AVERAGE(B3:B4)

_____ 5. =SUM(B2:B5)

A. 2

B. 5

C. 17

D. 20

E. 22

PROJECTS

PROJECT 1

The worksheet in *IE Project1* is a daily sales report that is submitted by a gas station manager to the owner. Change the appearance of the worksheet to make it easier to read.

1. Open **IE Project1** from the data files.

2. Save the file as **Gas Sales** followed by your initials.

3. Change the size of the text in **A1** to **16** points.

4. Bold **A1**.

5. Change the width of column **A** to **20**.

6. Change the width of columns **B** through **D** to **15**.

7. Merge and center **A1:D1**.

8. Format **B2** for a **Date** in which the month is alphabetic and the day and year are numeric (Month XX, XXXX).

9. Enter **May 28, 2003** in B2.

10. Merge and center **B2:D2.**

11. Format **B3** for **Time** in which the hours and minutes are numeric and followed by AM or PM (XX:XX XM).

12. Enter **8:05 PM** in **B3**.

13. Merge and center **B3:D3**.

14. Change the size of the text in **A2:D8** to **14** points.

15. Wrap the text in **C5**.

16. Underline and center **B5:D5.**

17. Format **B6:B8** as a **Number** with a comma separator and no decimal places.

18. Format **C6:D8** for **Currency** with two decimal places.

19. Save, print, and close the file.

PROJECT 2

An income statement describes how profitable a company has been during a certain period of time. *IE Project2* is the income statement of Dole Food Company, Inc. Format the income statement in a way that makes it more readable to the financial statement user. The financial statement should have the following qualities:

■ The heading should be in a bold font that is larger than the font of the items in the body of the financial statement.

■ The heading should be separated from the body of the financial statement by at least one row.

■ Columns of the worksheet should be wide enough to view all of their contents.

■ The first (revenues) and last (net income) numbers in the financial statement should be preceded by dollar signs.

■ All numbers should use a comma as the 1,000 separator.

■ Color and borders should be added to make the file visually appealing.

When you have finished, save the file as **Dole** followed by your initials. Then print and close the file.

PROJECT 3

The file *IE Project3* is a worksheet that contains a list of members of the Computer Science Club
1 service points the members earned during the year. In preparation for the end-of-year banquet, the
b secretary would like to prepare a worksheet that identifies the exceptional members (those with ser-
e points exceeding 1000) and outstanding members (those with service points between 800 and
00). Format the worksheet with the following qualities:

Sort the data by column B, the number of service points, with those with the most points at the top
of the worksheet.

The title **Exceptional and Outstanding Members** should be inserted at the top of the worksheet.
The title should be made bold and in a font larger than the other text in the worksheet.

A bold subtitle **Exceptional Members** should be inserted above William Griffin's name.

A bold subtitle **Outstanding Members** should be inserted above Matthew Carcello's name.

A bold subtitle **Other Active Members** should be inserted above Mohamed Abdul's name.

The service points should be formatted as a Number with a comma separator and no decimal places.

The school colors are blue and red. Add these colors and bolding to make the worksheet visually
appealing.

When you have finished, save the file as **CSClub** followed by your initials. Then print and close the file.

PROJECT 4

The revenue and expenses of Escape Computer Network Corporation are recorded in *IE Project4*. You
uld like to illustrate the distribution of the corporation's costs for the year.

. Open **IE Project4** from the data files.

. Save the file as **Escape** followed by your initials.

. Create an exploded pie chart with three-dimensional effects in a chart sheet using the data in
A13:B19.

. Title the chart **Expenses for the Year**.

. Place a legend at the bottom of the chart to identify the slices.

. Include percentages next to each slice.

. Name the chart sheet **Pie Chart**.

. Edit font sizes so the chart title is **22** points, the slice percentages are **18** points, and the legend is
14 points.

. Preview the chart and determine the largest categories of expenses.

. Save the file, print the chart, and close the file.

You work at the Java Internet Café, which has been open a short time. The café serves coffee, other beverages, and pastries and offers Internet access. Computers are set up on tables in the store so customers can come in and have a cup of coffee and a Danish, and explore the World Wide Web. You are asked to create a menu of coffee prices and computer prices. You will do this by integrating Microsoft Excel and Microsoft Word.

JOB 1

1. Open a new Excel worksheet.

2. Key the data shown in Figure UR-1 into the worksheet, and format as shown.

FIGURE UR-1

	A	B	C	D
1	Coffee Prices			
2				
3	House coffee	$1.00	Café breve	$2.25
4				
5	Café au lait	$1.50	Café latte	$2.25
6				
7	Cappuccino	$1.75	Con panna	$2.50
8				
9	Espresso	$2.00	Espresso doppio	$2.75

3. Change the width of columns **A** and **C** to **29** and columns **B** and **D** to **9**.

4. Left-align data in columns **B** and **D**.

5. Change the font to **Arial, 14** points.

6. Format the data in columns **B** and **D** for currency, with two places to the right of the decimal.

7. Save the file as **Coffee Prices** followed by your initials.

8. Highlight and copy **A1** through **D9**.

9. Open Word and the **IE Simulation** document from the data files.

10. Insert one blank line below the **Menu** heading, and paste link the worksheet.

11. Save the document as **Java Café Menu** followed by your initials.

12. Switch to Excel.

13. Open **Computer** from the data files.

14. Rename and save it as **Computer Prices** followed by your initials.

15. Highlight and copy **A1** through **B11**.

16. Switch to Word and **Java Café Menu**.

17. Insert a blank line after the *Coffee Prices* menu listings.

18. Paste link the **Computer Prices** worksheet.

19. Preview the document. Adjust the placement of the data if necessary so that all data fits on one page.

20. Save, print, and close **Java Café Menu**.

21. Switch to Excel, and close **Computer Prices** and **Coffee Prices** without saving changes.

JOB 2

The menu you created has been very successful. However, your manager asks you to make a few changes.

1. Open the **Coffee Prices** and **Computer Prices** files you saved in Job 1.

2. Make the changes to the **Coffee Prices** and **Computer Prices** worksheets as shown in Figure UR-2.

Java Internet Café

2001 Zephyr Street
Boulder, CO 80302-2001
303.555.JAVA JavaCafe@Cybershop.com

The Java Internet Café is a coffee shop with a twist. As you can see, there are seven computers on tables at the north side of the café. These computers provide high-speed Internet access to our customers. Whether you're a regular on the Net or a novice, our system is designed to allow you easy exploration of the World Wide Web. You've heard about it; now give it a try. Ask your server to help you get started.

Menu

Coffee Prices

House coffee	$1.00 *(.75)*	Café breve	$2.25
Café au lait	$1.50	Café latte	$2.25
Cappuccino	$1.75 *(2.00)*	Con panna	$2.50
Espresso	$2.00	Espresso doppio	$2.75

Computer Prices

Membership fee -- includes own account with personal ID, password, and e-mail address	$10 per month
28,800 bps Internet access (members) -- includes World Wide Web, FTP, Telnet, and IRC plus e-mail	$4 per hour
28,800 bps Internet access (non-members) -- includes World Wide Web, FTP, Telnet, and IRC	$6 per hour
Color scanner -- includes Internet access, use of software and the CD-ROM library	$5 per 1/2 hour
Laser printer -- inquire about duplexing capabilities	$.25 per page

Sit back, sip your coffee, and surf the net.

3. Save and close **Coffee Prices** and **Computer Prices**. Exit Excel.

4. Switch to Word, and open **Java Café Menu**.

5. Notice the file has been updated since you made changes to the two worksheet files. Make the correction in the footer.

6. Save as **Java Café Menu 2** followed by your initials.

7. Print and close Excel. Exit Word.

TASK REFERENCE

Excel Function Reference

Hundreds of functions are available in Excel. This reference illustrates some of the more commonly used functions. The functions are grouped by the categories you see in the Paste Function dialog box. For each function there is an example of how it is used and how it should appear when entered in an Excel worksheet.

DATE AND TIME FUNCTIONS

FUNCTION	USE	TASK	EXAMPLE	
			THE FUNCTION FORMULA:	WILL DISPLAY:
DATE(year,month,day)	Displays the serial number of a date	Display the serial number for December 15, 2003	=DATE (2003,12,15)	37970 (in text format)
DATEVALUE(date_text)	Converts a text date to a serial number	Display the serial number for September 9, 2003	=DATEVALUE ("9/9/2003")	37873
DAY(serial_number)	Converts a serial number to a day of the month	Identify the day in October 9, 2003.	=DAY("10/9/2003")	9
HOUR(serial_number)	Converts portion of the serial number at the right of the decimal to an hour of the day at 7 p.m.	Display the hour of the day contained in a serial number for 12/15/2003	=HOUR(37240.8)	19
MONTH(serial_number)	Converts a serial number to a month	Display the month number contained in a serial number for 9/9/2003	=MONTH(37143)	9
NOW()	Displays the serial number of the current date and time	Display the serial number (assuming you are using the computer on December 15, 2003 at noon).	=NOW()	37970.5
TIME(hour,minute, second)	Displays the serial number of a time	Display the serial number of the 14th hour, 45th minute, 15th second.	=TIME(14,45,15) 0.601475	2:45 PM (in time format); (in text format)
TODAY()	Displays the serial number of today's date	Display the serial number of the day (assuming you are using the computer on December 15, 2003)	=TODAY()	37970 (in text format); 12/15/03 (in date format)

FUNCTION	USE	TASK	EXAMPLE	
			THE FUNCTION FORMULA:	WILL DISPLAY:
YEAR(serial_number)	Converts a serial number to a year	Display the year contained in a serial number for 9/9/2003	=YEAR(37873)	2003

Arguments

Date_text: date in text form (within quotations)

Day: day of the month stated as a number between 1 and 31

Month: month stated as a number between 1 and 12

Serial_number: Microsoft Excel uses a default date system in which dates are represented as the number of days after December 31, 1899. For example, January 3, 1900, is represented as 3, and February 7, 1999, is represented as 36198 when the cell is formatted for text. Numbers to the right of a decimal represent time. For example, 36198.5 indicates February 7, 1999, at 12:00 p.m.

Year: year stated as a number between 1900 and 9999

FINANCIAL FUNCTIONS

FUNCTION	USE	TASK	EXAMPLE	
			THE FUNCTION FORMULA:	WILL DISPLAY:
FV(rate,nper,pmt,pv, type)	Displays the future value of an investment	Find the value of 10, $1000 end-of-year payments invested at a 7% rate.	=FV(7%,10,1000,0,0)	$13,816.45
NPV(rate,value1, value2,…)	Displays the net present value of an investment	Find the net present value of an investment that requires a $10,000 outlay but pays $4,000 the first year, $3,000 the second, and $2,000 the third when an 8% rate is desired.	=NPV(8%,-10000, 5000,4000,2500)	$40.34
PMT(rate,nper,pv,fv,type)	Displays the periodic payment of an annuity	Find the end of year payment for a $100,000 loan at 8% for 10 years.	=PMT(8%, 10,10000,0,0)	($1,490.29)
PV(rate,nper,pmt,fv,type)	Displays the present value of an investment	Find the value of an investment that pays $5,000 at the end of every year for 30 years. Your expected rate of return is 8%.	=PV(8%,30,5000,0,0)	($56,288.92)

Arguments

Nominal_rate: the nominal (stated) rate of interest

Nper: the total number of payment periods in an annuity

Npery: the number of compounding periods per year

Pmt: the payment made each period

Pv: the present value

Fv: the future value

Type: 0 indicates payments at the end of the period, 1 indicates payments at the beginning of the period

FINANCIAL FUNCTIONS—DEPRECIATION FUNCTIONS

FUNCTION	USE	TASK	EXAMPLE	
			THE FUNCTION FORMULA:	WILL DISPLAY:
DB(cost,salvage,life, period,month)	Displays depreciation for a specified period using the declining balance method	Find the second year depreciation for a 6-year-old machine costing $10,000 with $1,000 salvage.	=DB(10000,1000, 6,2,12)	$2,172.39
SLN(cost,salvage,life)	Displays the straight-line depreciation for the period	Find the yearly depreciation for a 6-year-old machine costing $10,000 with $1,000 salvage.	=SLN(10000,1000,6)	$1,500.00
SYD(cost,salvage,life, period)	Displays the sum-of-years' digits depre-ciation for a period	Find the second year depreciation for a 6-year machine costing $10,000 with $1,000 salvage.	=SYD(10000, 1000,6,2)	$2,142.86

Arguments
Cost: initial cost of the asset
Month: the number of months in the first year of depreciation
Life: the number of periods an asset is depreciated
Period: the period in which depreciation is to be calculated
Salvage: the value of the asset at the end of its useful life

LOGICAL FUNCTIONS

FUNCTION	USE	TASK	EXAMPLE	
			THE FUNCTION FORMULA:	WILL DISPLAY:
AND(logical1,logical2,...)	Displays TRUE if all arguments are TRUE	Determine whether the value in B7 is both below 100 and above 50.	=AND(B7<100, B7>50)	TRUE (if the value in B7 is 78); FALSE (if the value in B7 is 120)
IF(logical_test,value_if _true,value_if_false)	Designates a logical test	Determine whether a student passes an examination by exceeding a score of 60. The grade is recorded in B7.	=IF(B7>60,"PASS", "FAIL")	PASS (if the value in B7 is 90); FAIL (if the value in B7 is 55)
NOT(logical)	Reverses the logic of an argument	Determine whether the value in B7 does not equal 0.	=NOT(B7=0)	TRUE (if the value in B7≠0); FALSE (if the value in B7=0)

FUNCTION	USE	TASK	EXAMPLE	
			THE FUNCTION FORMULA:	WILL DISPLAY:
OR(logical1,logical2,...)	Displays TRUE if any argument is TRUE	Determine whether the value in B7 is either below 100 or above 50.	=OR(B7>100,B7<50)	TRUE (if the value in B7 is 120 or 25); FALSE (if the value in B7 is 75)

Arguments

Logical: statement that may be evaluated as true or false
Logical_test: statement that may be evaluated as true or false
Value_if_false: the value displayed in the cell if the statement is false
Value_if_true: the value displayed in the cell if the statement is true

LOOKUP AND REFERENCE FUNCTIONS

In the statistical examples, assume the following range of cells in a worksheet:

	A	B	C
1	INCOME STATEMENT		
2		This Year	Last Year
3	Sales	$100,000	$90,000
4	Cost of Goods Sold	$45,000	$43,000
5	Administrative Expenses	$20,000	$15,000
6	Net Income	$35,000	$32,000

FUNCTION	USE	TASK	EXAMPLE	
			THE FUNCTION FORMULA:	WILL DISPLAY:
COLUMN(reference)	Displays the column number of a reference	Use the column number of cell B3 in a calculation.	=COLUMN(B4)	2 (because column B is the second column)
COLUMNS(array)	Displays the number of columns in a reference	Use the number of columns in a range in a calculation.	=COLUMNS(A2:C6)	3 (because the range contains three columns)
HLOOKUP(lookup_value,table_array,row_index_num,...)	Displays the value of an indicated cell in the top row of an array	Display the contents of the third row in a column	=HLOOKUP("This Year",A2:C6,3)	45000 (because this amount is in the third row of the range under "This Year")
ROW(reference)	Displays the row number of a reference	Use the row number of cell B4 in a calculation.	=ROW(B4)	4 (because row 4 is the fourth row)
ROWS(array)	Displays the number of rows in a reference	Use the number of rows in a range in a calculation.	=ROWS(A2:C6)	5 (because the range contains 5 rows)

Arguments
Array: an array (rectangular representation of a group of values) or range of cells
Col_index_num: the column number in the table_array
Lookup_value: value to be found in the first row or column
Table_array: the range or range name to be searched
Reference: cell address
Row_index_num: the row number in the table_array

MATHEMATICAL FUNCTIONS (SEE MATH & TRIG CATEGORY)

FUNCTION	USE	TASK	EXAMPLE THE FUNCTION FORMULA:	WILL DISPLAY:
ABS(number)	Displays the absolute value of a number	Determine the absolute value of the value in B7	=ABS(B7)	7 (if the value in B7 is either 7 or -7)
CEILING(number, significance)	Rounds a number to the higher multiple of significance	Round the price in B7 to the next highest dime.	=CEILING(B7,0.1)	$1.60 (if the value in B7 is either $1.59 or $1.51)
COS(number)	Displays the cosine of a number	Determine the cosine of the value in B7	=COS(B7)	.070737 (if the value in B7 is 1.5).
EXP(number)	Displays e raised to the power of a given exponent	Determine the base (e) when raised to the power of B7.	=EXP(B7)	4.481689 (if the value in B7 is 1.5)
FLOOR(number, significance)	Rounds a number to the lower multiple of significance	Round the price in B7 down to the next lower dime.	=FLOOR(B7,0.1)	$1.50 (if the value in B7 is either $1.59 or $1.51)
LN(number)	Displays the natural logarithm of a number	Determine the natural logarithm of the value in B7.	=LN(B7)	2.70805 (if the value in B7 is 15)
PI()	Displays the value of Pi	Determine the area of a circle with a radius length in B7.	=PI()*(B7^2)	78.5398 (if the radius value in B7 is 5)
POWER(number,power)	Displays the number raised to a power	Determine the cube of the value in B7.	=POWER(B7,3)	125 (if the value in B7 is 5)
PRODUCT(number1, number2,…)	Displays the product of the arguments	Determine the product of 7 times the value in B7.	=PRODUCT(B7,7)	35 (if the value in B7 is 5)
ROUND(number, num_digits)	Rounds a number to the specified digit	Round the price in B7 to the nearest dime.	=ROUND(B7,1)	$1.60 (if the value in B7 is $1.55); $1.50 (if the value in B7 is $1.54)
SIN(number)	Displays the sine of an angle	Determine the sine of the value in B7	=SIN(B7)	.997495 (if thevalue in B7 is 1.5)

FUNCTION	USE	TASK	EXAMPLE	
			THE FUNCTION FORMULA:	WILL DISPLAY:
SQRT(number)	Displays a positive square root	Determine the square root of the value in B7.	=SQRT(B7)	8 (if the value in B7 is 64)
SUM(number1, number2,...)	Adds the arguments	Determine the sum of the values in B7 and B8, plus 9.	=SUM(B7,B8,9)	20 (if the value in B7 is 5 and the value in B8 is 6)
TAN(number)	Displays the tangent	Determine the tangent of the value in B7.	=TAN(B7)	.969668 (if the value in B7 is .77)
TRUNC(number, num_digits)	Truncates a number to an integer	Truncate the value in B7 to the tenths digit.	=TRUNC(B7,1)	1.8 (if the value in B7 is 1.811 or 1.899)

Arguments

Number: any real number

Num_digits: the number of digits to be rounded (for example, 1 = tenths, 2 = hundredths)

Power: the exponent to which a base number is raised

STATISTICAL FUNCTIONS

In the statistical examples, assume the following range of cells in a worksheet:

	B
3	5
4	6
5	7
6	6
7	6
8	9

FUNCTION	USE	TASK	EXAMPLE	
			THE FUNCTION FORMULA:	WILL DISPLAY:
AVERAGE(number1, number2,...)	Displays the average of arguments	Determine the average of the range B3:B8.	=AVERAGE(B3:B8)	6.5
COUNT(value1, value2,...)	Displays the number of filled cells in a range	Determine the number of cells containing values in the range B3:B8.	=COUNT(B3:B8)	6
MAX(number1, number2,...)	Displays the maximum value in a data set	Determine the maximum value in the range B3:B8.	=MAX(B3:B8)	9
MEDIAN(number1, number2,...)	Displays the median of a range	Determine the median of the range B3:B8.	=MEDIAN(B3:B8)	6
MIN(number1, number2,...)	Displays the minimum value in a data set	Determine the minimum value in the range B3:B8.	=MIN(B3:B8)	5

FUNCTION	USE	TASK	EXAMPLE	
			THE FUNCTION FORMULA:	WILL DISPLAY:
MODE(number1, number2,…)	Displays the most common value in a data set	Determine the mode of the range B3:B8.	=MODE(B3:B8)	6
PERCENTILE(array,K)	Displays the percentile of values in a range	Determine the break for the 90th percentile of the range B3:B8.	=PERCENTILE (B3:B8,0.9)	8
STDEV(number1, number2,…)	Estimates the standard deviation	Determine the standard deviation of the range B3:B8.	=STDEV(B3:B8)	1.3784
VAR(number1, number2,…)	Estimates the variance	Determine the variance of the range B3:B8.	=VAR(B3:B8)	1.9

Arguments
number1,number2,…: group of numbers, an array, or a range
array: range of data
K: percent value between 0 through 1

TEXT FUNCTIONS

FUNCTION	USE	TASK	EXAMPLE	
			THE FUNCTION FORMULA:	WILL DISPLAY:
DOLLAR(number, decimals)	Converts a number to text in currency format	Convert the value in B7 to a dollar format rounded to cents.	=DOLLAR(B7,2)	$1,721.07 (if the value in B7 is 1721.0735)
EXACT(text1,text2)	Checks whether two text entries are identical	Compare the similarity of the word in B7 to the word in B8.	=EXACT(B7,B8)	FALSE (if the text in B7 is "there" and B8 is "their"); TRUE (if the text in B7 is "there" and B8 is "there")
LOWER(text)	Converts text to lowercase	Convert the text in B7 to lowercase.	=LOWER(B7)	Fall (if the text in B7 is "Fall" or "FALL")
PROPER(text)	Capitalizes the first letter in each word	Convert the text in B7 to proper case.	=PROPER(B7)	February (if the text in B7 is "february" or "FEBRUARY")
REPT(text,number_times)	Repeats text a designated number of times	Create a customized border.	=REPT("#-",5)	#-#-#-#-#-

FUNCTION	USE	TASK	EXAMPLE	
			THE FUNCTION FORMULA:	WILL DISPLAY:
UPPER(text)	Converts text to uppercase	Convert the text in B7 to uppercase	=UPPER(B7)	SELL! (if the text in B7 is "sell!" or "Sell!")

Arguments
Decimals: the number of digits to the right of the decimal point
Number: any real number
Number_times: the number of times an action will take place

INTRODUCTORY MICROSOFT® ACCESS

UNIT

Estimated Time for Unit: 9 hours

ACCESS BASICS

OBJECTIVES

Upon completion of this lesson, you should be able to:

- Understand databases.
- Start Access and open a database.
- Identify parts of the Access screen.
- Identify the database objects.
- Understand database terminology.
- Create a new database and a new table.
- Design, modify, name, and save a table.
- Navigate a database and enter records.
- Print a table and exit Access.

⏱ **Estimated Time: 1.5 hours**

VOCABULARY

Database management system

Datasheet view

Design view

Entry

Field

Field name

Primary key

Record

Database Basics

Access is a program known as a ***database management syatem***. A computerized database management system allows you to store, retrieve, analyze, and print information. You do not, however, need a computer to have a database management system. A set of file folders can be a database management system. Any system for managing data is a database management system. There are distinct advantages, however, to using a computerized database management system.

A computerized database management system (DBMS) is much faster, more flexible, and more accurate than using file folders. A computerized DBMS is also more efficient and cost-effective. A program such as Access can store thousands of pieces of data in a computer or on a disk. The data can be quickly searched and sorted to save time otherwise spent digging through file folders. For example, a computerized DBMS could find all the people with a certain ZIP code faster and more accurately than you could by searching through a large list or through folders.

Starting Access

To start Access, click the Start button on the taskbar. Select Programs, and then click the Microsoft Access icon to load Access. After a few moments, the Access startup screen appears, as shown in Figure 1-1. This screen gives you the option of opening an existing database or creating a new one. You can also choose to create a new database from an existing one or use a template to simplify the process of creating a database.

FIGURE 1-1
Access startup screen

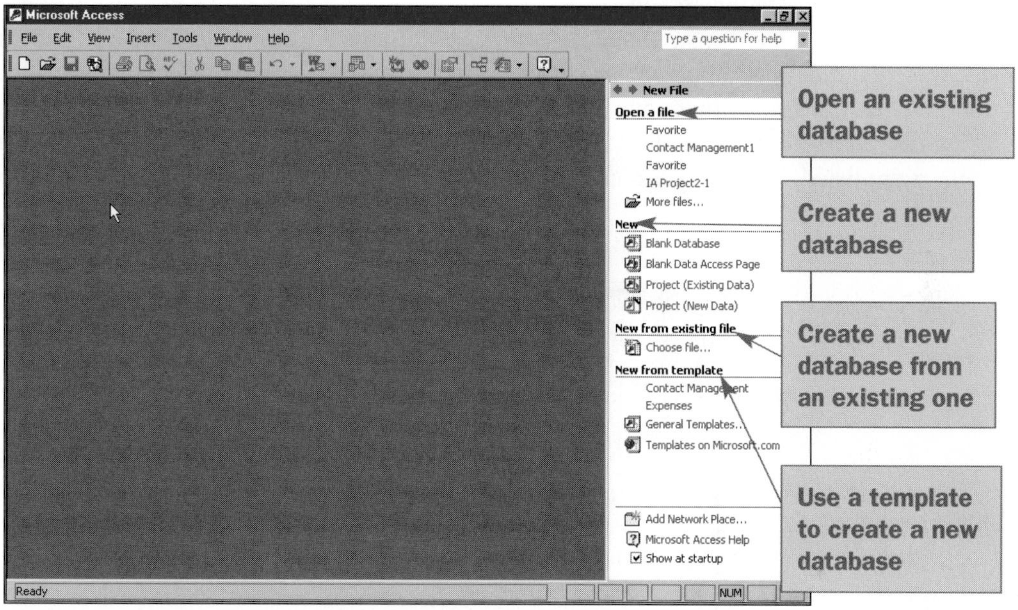

Open an existing database

Create a new database

Create a new database from an existing one

Use a template to create a new database

STEP-BY-STEP ▷ 1.1

1. With Windows 98 (or a later Windows program) running, click **Start** on the taskbar.

2. Point to **Programs** on the **Start** menu, and click **Microsoft Access**.

3. Access opens and the Access startup screen appears as shown in Figure 1-1. Leave this screen open for the next Step-by-Step.

Opening a Database

You can open an existing database from the File menu or from the New File task pane displayed on the right side of the screen. To open a database from the New File task pane, click either the *Files* or the *More files* option from the *Open a file* section and choose a database from the Open dialog box. To create a new database, click the *Blank Database* option from the *New* section. If you choose *Blank Database*, you must manually create the database. If you choose *Choose file* from the *New from existing file* section, you can create the new file from an existing one. If you choose an option from the *New from template* section, you will be guided through the creation of the database. You will learn more about creating databases later in this lesson.

When you open an existing database, the Database window appears, like that shown in Figure 1-2. The Objects bar on the left side of the window lists the types of database objects. The database objects window lists the various functions for creating the selected object as well as any objects that already exist. In Figure 1-2, for example, three functions for creating a table and one table named *service club members* are listed. You will learn about database objects later in this lesson.

FIGURE 1-2
Database window

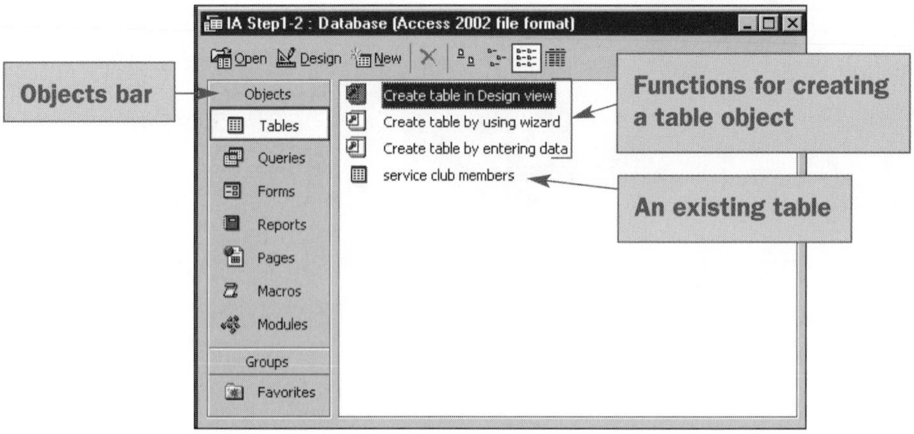

S TEP-BY-STEP ▷ 1.2

1. Click either the **Files** or the **More files** option in the *Open a file* section of the New File task pane. The Open dialog box displays. (You may need to click the **Files** option in the Open a file section if it is the first time that this copy of Access has been used.)

2. Open the file **IA Step1-2** from the data files. The Database window appears, as previously shown in Figure 1-2. Leave the database open for the next Step-by-Step.

The Access Screen

Like other Office applications, the Access screen has a title bar, menu bar, and toolbar. At the bottom of the screen is the status bar. If necessary, click the down arrow in the Objects bar to view the other objects. Figure 1-3 shows the Access screen with the *IA Step1-2* database open.

FIGURE 1-3
Access screen

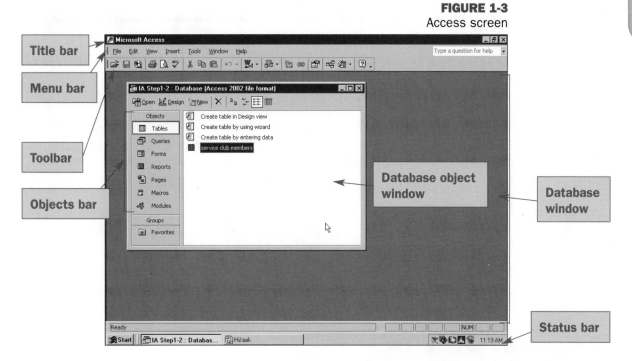

As you use Access, various windows and dialog boxes will appear on the screen. Unlike Word and Excel, Access does not have a standard document view. Instead, the screen changes based on how you interact with the database.

Database Objects

When a database is saved, the file that is saved contains a collection of objects. These objects work together to store data, retrieve data, display data, print reports, and automate operations. The Objects bar in the Database window displays a button for each type of object. If necessary, click the down arrow on the bar to view the additional objects.

Table 1-1 briefly explains the purpose of each type of object.

Did You Know?

As in other Office programs, you can access the Office Assistant for help. To display the Office Assistant, choose **Show the Office Assistant** on the **Help** menu. Key in a question and click **Search**.

TABLE 1-1
Database objects

OBJECT	DESCRIPTION
Table	Tables store data in a format similar to that of a worksheet. All database information is stored in tables.
Query	Queries search for and retrieve data from tables based on given criteria. A query is a question you ask the database.
Form	Forms allow you to display data in a custom format. You might, for example, create a form that matches a paper form.
Report	Reports also display data in a custom format. Reports, however, are especially suited for printing and summarizing data. You can even perform calculations in a report.
Page	Data access pages let you design other database objects so that they can be published to the Web.
Macro	Macros automate database operations by allowing you to issue a single command that performs a series of operations.
Module	Modules are like macros but allow much more complex programming of database operations. Creating a module requires the use of a programming language.

STEP-BY-STEP ▷ 1.3

1. Make sure **Tables** is selected on the Objects bar. Highlight the **service club members** table in the database objects window, and click the **Open** button. The table appears, as shown in Figure 1-4.

2. Choose **Close** on the **File** menu to close the table. The database objects window is visible again.

3. Click **Queries** on the Objects bar. There is one query object named *Lubbock*. This query locates members who live in Lubbock.

4. Click **Forms** on the Objects bar. There is one form object named *service members form*.

5. Choose **Close** on the **File** menu to close the database. Leave Access open for the next Step-by-Step.

FIGURE 1-4
Database table

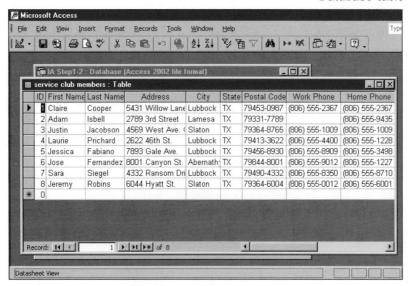

Database Terminology

Four terms are essential to know when working with databases. These terms relate to the way data is organized in a table. A record is a complete set of data. In the service club members table, each member is stored as a record. In a table, a record appears as a row, as shown in Figure 1-5.

Each record is made up of fields. For example, the first name of each member is placed in a special field that is created to accept first names. In a table, fields appear as columns. In order to identify the fields, each field has a field name. The data entered into a field is called an entry. In the service club members database, for example, the first record has the name Claire as an entry in the First Name field.

FIGURE 1-5
Records and fields

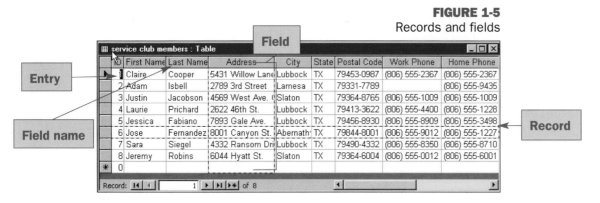

Creating a Database

The first step in creating a database is to create the file that will hold the database objects. To do this, you choose New on the File menu. The Access startup screen appears, as shown in Figure 1-6. In

IA - 7

the New File task pane on the right side of the screen, choose Blank Database and the File New Database dialog box appears. This is where you will name the file and store it with your other data files. Choose Create, and the Database window appears as shown in Figure 1-7. It will not contain any objects yet, because none have been created.

FIGURE 1-6
Access startup screen

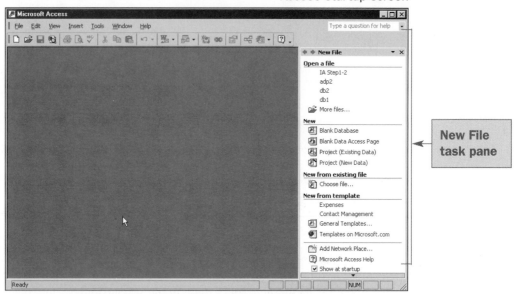

New File task pane

FIGURE 1-7
Database window

S TEP-BY-STEP ▷ 1.4

1. Choose **New** on the **File** menu. The Access startup screen appears, as shown in Figure 1-6.

2. In the New File task pane on the right side of the screen, choose **Blank Database** and the File New Database dialog box appears.

3. Save the database as **Favorite**, followed by your initials, and then click **Create**. Your Database window should look like that shown in Figure 1-7.

4. Double-click **Create table by entering data**. A new table appears in Datasheet view, as shown in Figure 1-8.

5. Choose **Close** on the **File** menu to go back to the Database window. Leave the window open for the next Step-by-Step.

 Extra Challenge

Create a new database using a database wizard. In the New File task pane, click **General Templates** and then the **Databases** tab. Select one of the database formats already designed for you and follow the screens to add your own information.

FIGURE 1-8
New table in Datasheet view

	Field1	Field2	Field3	Field4	Field5	Field6	Field7	

Record: 14 ◄ 1 ► ►I ►* of 21

Creating Tables

Because all other database objects rely on the existence of a database table, creating a table is the next step after creating a database. In many database management systems, data is stored using more than one table. To create a table, click Tables on the Objects bar. Click the New button and the New Table dialog box appears, as shown in Figure 1-9.

FIGURE 1-9
New Table dialog box

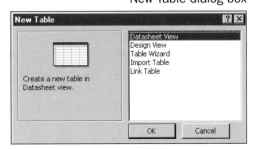

New Table

Create a new table in Datasheet view.

Datasheet View
Design View
Table Wizard
Import Table
Link Table

OK   Cancel

The New Table dialog box lists several ways to create a table. The most common way is to create the table in *Design view*. This is the view where you will design new tables and modify the design of existing tables. You can also create a table in Design view by double-clicking *Create table in Design view* in the Database window.

S TEP-BY-STEP ▷ 1.5

1. Click **Tables** on the Objects bar, if necessary, and then click **New**. The New Table dialog box appears, as shown in Figure 1-9.

2. Choose the **Design View** option and click **OK**. The Design view window opens. Leave the window on the screen for the next Step-by-Step.

Designing a Table

Now you are ready to design your table. You create the table's fields in the Design view window. As you can see in the window on your screen, each field into a table is divided into three sections: Field Name, Data Type, and Description. You will insert data in each of these three sections to create a table.

FIELD NAMES

First you have to decide what data you need to store. You should divide the data into categories to create fields. For example, suppose you want to create a database of your family members' birthdays. Some fields to include would be the person's name, address, and birthdate. An example of a record would be: Halie Jones (name), 3410 Vicksburg Ave., Dallas, TX 75224 (address), and 10/28/89 (birthdate).

Key the names of these fields in the Field Name column of the Table design window. It is helpful if you create meaningful field names that identify the types of data stored.

DATA TYPE

After keying the field name, press the Tab key to move to the Data Type column. Then determine the type of data to be stored in each field and choose an appropriate data type. The data type tells Access what kind of information can be stored in the field. Table 1-2 briefly describes the basic data types.

Choosing the correct data type is important. For example, you might think a telephone number or ZIP code should be stored in a field with a Number data type. However, you should use Number data types only when you intend to do calculations with the data. You won't be adding or subtracting ZIP codes. Numbers that will not be used in calculations are best stored as Text.

For a table of favorite restaurants, the name of the restaurant and its address would be stored in fields of Text type, which is the default data type. The typical meal cost is ideal for the Currency type. The date you last ate at the restaurant would be Date type, and a Yes/No data type could specify whether reservations are required. Use the Lookup Wizard to create a Lookup field that allows you to choose from a list the type of food the restaurant specializes in.

To choose a data type, click the arrow that appears in the Data Type column when the insertion point is in that column or when you key the first letter of the word. This button is called a drop-down arrow. A menu appears allowing you to choose a data type.

TABLE 1-2
Data types

DATA TYPE	DESCRIPTION
Text	The Text data type allows letters and numbers (alphanumeric data). A text field can hold up to 255 characters. Data such as names and addresses are stored in fields of this type.
Memo	The Memo data type also allows alphanumeric data. A memo field, however, can hold thousands of characters. Memo fields are used for data that does not follow a particular format. For example, you might use a Memo field to store notes about a record.
Number	The Number data type holds numeric data. There are variations of the Number type, each capable of storing a different range of values.
Date/Time	The Date/Time data type holds dates and times.
Currency	The Currency data type is specially formatted for dealing with currency.
AutoNumber	The AutoNumber data type is automatically incremented by Access for each new record added. Counters are used to give each record in a database a unique identification.
Yes/No	The Yes/No data type holds logical values. A Yes/No field can hold the values Yes/No, True/False, or On/Off.
OLE Object	The OLE Object data type is used for some of the more advanced features. It allows you to store graphics, sound, and even objects such as spreadsheets in a field.
Hyperlink	The Hyperlink data type is used to store a hyperlink as a UNC path or URL.
Lookup Wizard	The Lookup Wizard creates a field that allows you to choose a value from another table or from a list of values.

DESCRIPTION

The last step in designing a table is to key a description for each field. The description explains the data in the field. For example, a field for the *Restaurants* database named Last Visit could have a description such as Date I Last Ate at the Restaurant. The description clarifies the field name. It does not appear in a table, but does display in the status bar when you select the field.

C

1. Key **Name** in the first row of the Field Name column.

2. Press **Tab** (or **Enter**). The data type will default to Text, which is appropriate for the name of the restaurant.

3. Press **Tab** to move to the Description column.

4. Key **Name of restaurant** and press **Enter** to move to the next row.

5. Key the other fields and descriptions shown in Figure 1-10. All of the fields are Text data type.

6. Click in the **Data Type** box for the Specialty field. A down arrow will appear.

7. Click the arrow and choose **Lookup Wizard** from the drop-down menu that appears. The Lookup Wizard screen displays.

8. Choose **I will type in the values that I want** and click **Next**. A second Lookup Wizard screen displays.

9. Leave the *Number of Columns* at 1 and key the Lookup values as shown in Figure 1-11, using the Tab key to move down through the list. Click **Finish** when finished.

10. In the first blank row, key **Last Visit** in the Field Name column and press **Tab**.

11. Click the arrow in the **Data Type** field and choose **Date/Time** from the drop-down menu that appears.

12. Press **Tab**.

13. Key **Date I last ate at the restaurant** in the Description column. Press **Tab**.

14. Key **Reservations** in the Field Name column, choose **Yes/No** as the data type, and key **Are reservations required?** in the Description column. Leave the Design view window on the screen for the next Step-by-Step.

FIGURE 1-10
Defining fields in a table

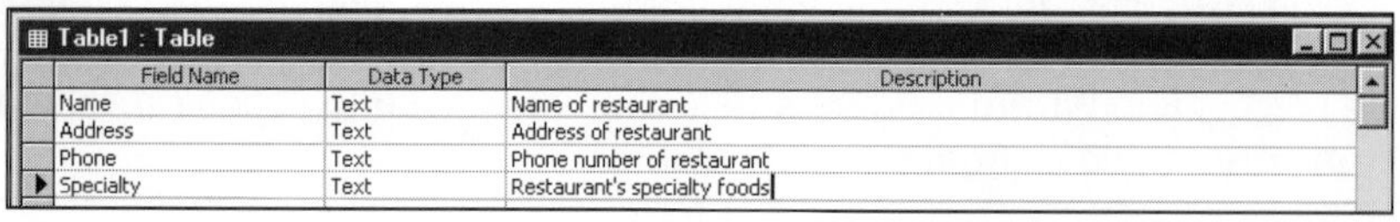

Field Name	Data Type	Description
Name	Text	Name of restaurant
Address	Text	Address of restaurant
Phone	Text	Phone number of restaurant
▶ Specialty	Text	Restaurant's specialty foods

Table1 : Table

Lookup Wizard screen

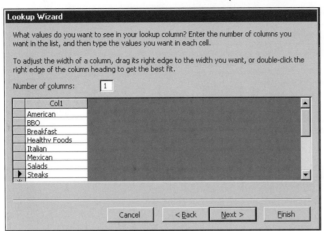

Naming and Saving a Table

After designing a table, you must give it a name and save the design. To save a table, choose Save on the File menu. The Save As dialog box appears, as shown in Figure 1-12. Key a name for the table and click OK. A message appears asking you if you want to create a *primary key*, which is a special field that assigns a unique identifier to each record. You can have Access create the primary key for you, in which case each record is automatically assigned a unique number. Or you can designate an existing field to be a primary key. For example, in a table containing the names and addresses of customers, you might create a field that contains a customer identification number. You could set this as the primary key, as it will be a unique number for each customer.

FIGURE 1-12
Save As dialog box

STEP-BY-STEP ▷ 1.7

1. Choose **Save** on the **File** menu. The Save As dialog box appears, as shown in Figure 1-12.

2. Key **Restaurants** in the Table Name box and click **OK**.

3. You will be asked if you want to create a primary key. Click **No**.

4. Choose **Close** on the **File** menu to close the Design view window and return to the Database window. Note that your *Restaurants* table now appears as an object, as shown in Figure 1-13. Leave the Database window open for the next Step-by-Step.

FIGURE 1-13

Database window showing *Restaurants* table as an object

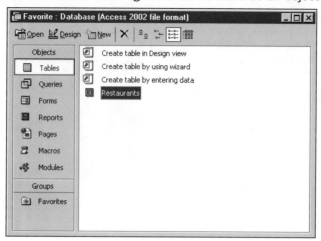

Modifying Tables

To modify the design of a table, you must be in Design view. Go to Design view by highlighting the name of the table in the Database window and clicking the Design button. In Design view, you can make changes to the names of fields, data formats, and descriptions.

You can add fields to the end of the list, or you can insert a new row for a field between existing fields. To insert a new row, place the insertion point in the row *below* where you want the new row to appear. Then, choose Rows on the Insert menu. You can delete a field by placing the insertion point in the row you want to delete and choosing Delete Rows on the Edit menu. You can also insert and delete rows by clicking the Insert Rows or Delete Rows button on the standard toolbar.

It is important to make sure you don't delete the wrong data in Design view; but if you do, you can click the Undo Delete button on the toolbar. The Undo Delete button reverses your last command.

You can delete an entire table by highlighting the table in the Database window and choosing Delete on the Edit menu.

When you finish changing fields, choose Save on the File menu or click the Save button on the toolbar.

> ### 💡 Did You Know?
>
> A primary key field is a unique identifier for a record. To set a field as a primary key, open the table in Design view and click the row selector for the desired field. Click the **Primary Key** button on the toolbar.

STEP-BY-STEP ▷ 1.8

1. Highlight the **Restaurants** table in the Database window if it's not selected already.

2. Click the **Design** button. The table appears in Design view.

3. Click in the first blank row's Field Name column to place the insertion point there. You may need to scroll down.

4. Key **Meal Cost** in the Field Name column. Press **Tab**.

5. Choose **Currency** as the data type. Press **Tab**.

6. Key **Typical meal cost** as the description.

7. Place the insertion point in the **Last Visit** field name.

8. Click the **Insert Rows** button on the toolbar. A blank row is inserted above the *Last Visit* field.

9. In the blank row, key **Favorite Dish** as the field name, choose **Text** as the data type, and key **My favorite meal** as the description.

10. Place the insertion point in the **Reservations** field name.

11. Click the **Delete Rows** button on the toolbar. The Reservations field is deleted.

12. Click the **Undo** button on the toolbar. The Reservations field reappears.

13. Click the **Save** button on the toolbar to save the design changes. Remain in this screen for the next Step-by-Step.

Navigating and Entering Records in Datasheet View

Once a table is created and designed, you can enter records directly into the table using *Datasheet view*. In Datasheet view, the table appears in a form similar to a spreadsheet, as you saw earlier in the lesson. As with a spreadsheet, the intersection of a row and a column is called a cell. To get to Datasheet view, select the table in the Database window and click the Open button, or click the View button on the toolbar while in Design view. You can switch back to Design view by clicking the View button again.

View, Datasheet

View, Design

The techniques used to enter records in the table are familiar to you. Press Enter or Tab to move to the anext field as you enter the data. Access will consider the data types as you enter data. For example, you must enter a valid date in a Date/Time field and you must enter a number in a Number field. If you don't, an error message appears.

After entering records in a table in Datasheet view, you do not need to save the changes. Access saves them for you automatically. Remember to always save changes to the table design in Design view.

You can use the mouse to move the insertion point to a particular cell in the table. You can also use the keys in Table 1-3 to navigate through a table.

Did You Know?

You can switch to the Datasheet or Design view using options on the View menu.

TABLE 1-3
Navigating in Datasheet view

KEY	DESCRIPTION
Enter, Tab, or right arrow	Moves to the following field.
Left arrow or Shift+Tab	Moves to the previous field.
End	Moves to the last field in the current record.
Home	Moves to the first field in the current record.
Up arrow	Moves up one record and stays in the same field.
Down arrow	Moves down one record and stays in the same field.
Page Up	Moves up one screen.
Page Down	Moves down one screen.

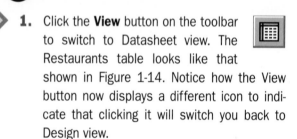

S TEP-BY-STEP ▷ 1.9

1. Click the **View** button on the toolbar to switch to Datasheet view. The Restaurants table looks like that shown in Figure 1-14. Notice how the View button now displays a different icon to indicate that clicking it will switch you back to Design view.

2. Key **Rosa's** in the Name field. Press **Tab**.

3. Key **8722 University Ave.** in the Address field. Press **Tab**.

4. Key **555-6798** in the Phone field. Press **Tab**.

5. Click the down arrow in the Specialty field and choose **Mexican** from the lookup list. Press **Tab**.

6. Key **Chicken Fajitas** in the Favorite Dish field. Press **Tab**.

7. Key today's date (XX/XX/20XX) in the Last Visit field. Press **Tab**. (If you do not key the year, it will be added automatically.)

8. The Reservations field has a check box in it. Click the check box or press the spacebar to place a check in the box. Press **Tab**.

9. Key **5.95** as the typical meal cost. Press **Tab**. Leave the database table open for the next Step-by-Step.

Extra Challenge

Create a database of your own favorite local restaurants. Use the fields from this *Restaurants* exercise, and any others that may apply.

FIGURE 1-14
Datasheet view

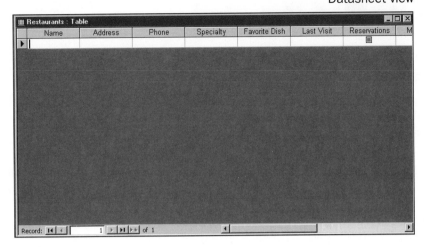

Printing a Table

You can print a database table in Datasheet view. Choose the Print command on the File menu to display the Print dialog box. As shown in Figure 1-15, you can choose to print all the records, only those selected, or for long tables you can specify the pages to print. Click the Setup button and the Page Setup dialog box appears, as shown in Figure 1-16. Here you can change the margins. To change the orientation, click the Properties button in the Print dialog box.

You can also click the Print button on the toolbar to print the database table. However, the Print dialog box will not appear for updates to the page setup.

FIGURE 1-15
Print dialog box

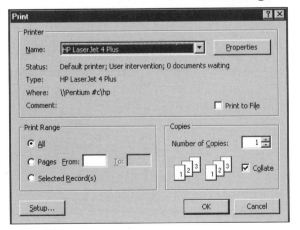

FIGURE 1-16
Page Setup dialog box

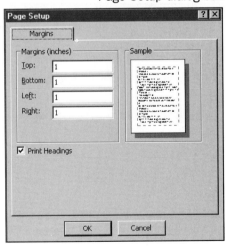

1. Choose **Print** on the **File** menu. The Print dialog box appears, as shown in Figure 1-15.

2. Click **Setup**. The Page Setup dialog box appears, as shown in Figure 1-16.

3. For the margins, key **.5** in the Left box and **.5** in the Right box.

4. Click **OK**.

5. In the Print dialog box, click **Properties**. The Properties dialog box appears.

6. Click on the Paper tab, if necessary.

7. From the Orientation options, click **Landscape**.

8. Click **OK**.

9. In the Print dialog box, click **All** from the Print Range options, if it isn't already selected. Click **OK**.

10. Close the table. The record has been saved in the table automatically.

Exiting Access

As in other Office programs, you exit Access by choosing the Exit command on the File menu. Exiting Access takes you back to the Windows desktop. Remember to remove any floppy disks, and properly shut down Windows before turning off the computer.

1. Choose **Close** on the **File** menu. The database closes.

2. Choose **Exit** on the **File** menu. The Windows desktop appears (assuming no other programs are open and maximized).

Summary

In this lesson, you learned:

- Access is a program known as a database management system. A computerized database management system allows you to store, retrieve, analyze, and print information. Start Access from the Programs menu.

- You can open an existing database from the File menu or from the New File task pane displayed on the right side of the screen. The Access screen has a title bar, menu bar, and toolbar. Access does not have a standard document view.

- A database is a collection of objects. The objects work together to store data, retrieve data, display data, print reports, and automate operations. The object types are tables, queries, forms, reports, macros, and modules.

- A record is a complete set of data. Each record is made up of fields. Each field is identified by a field name. The actual data entered into a field is called an entry.

- Creating a database creates a file that will hold database objects. To store data, a table must first be created. In Design view, you can create fields and assign data types and descriptions to the fields. Once a table has been created and designed, you can enter records in Datasheet view.

- As in other Office applications, you exit Access by choosing the Exit command from the File menu.

VOCABULARY REVIEW

Define the following terms:

Database management system	Entry	Primary key
Datasheet view	Field	Record
Design view	Field name	

LESSON 1 REVIEW QUESTIONS

TRUE/FALSE

Circle T if the statement is true or F if the statement is false.

T F 1. A computerized DBMS is more efficient than paper filing.

T F 2. Opening a database automatically displays the data in the table.

T F 3. Access has a standard document view that remains on the screen as long as a database is open.

T F 4. A database file is a collection of database objects.

T F 5. Fields are identified by field names.

WRITTEN QUESTIONS

Write a brief answer to the following questions.

1. Which window appears after you open a database?

2. List three types of database objects.

3. Which database object allows you to search for and retrieve data?

4. What is the term for the data entered in a field?

5. Which view is used to design tables?

LESSON 1 PROJECTS

PROJECT 1-1

1. Start Access.

2. Open the **IA Project1-1** database.

3. Open the **Restaurants** table in Datasheet view.

4. Insert the records shown in Figure 1-17.

5. Print the table in landscape orientation.

6. Close the table and database.

FIGURE 1-17

Name	Address	Phone	Specialty	Favorite Dish	Last Visit	Reservations	Meal Cost
Health Hut	3440 Slide Rd.	555-6096	Healthy foods	Fruit Delight	6/30/2000	☐	$5.50
Stella's	7822 Broadway	555-8922	Italian	Lasagna	7/6/2000	☑	$9.95
Tony's BBQ	2310 82nd St.	555-3143	BBQ	Baby Back Ribs	5/1/2000	☑	$10.95
Morning Glory	5660 Salem	555-6621	Breakfast	Daybreak Muffins	7/12/2000	☐	$2.95
Salads and Stuff	8910 Main St.	555-3440	Salads	Chicken Caesar Salad	4/29/2000	☐	$5.95
Saltlick Steakhouse	2100 Highway 281	555-6700	Steaks	Rib Eye	3/10/2000	☑	$13.50
Alamo Diner	451 San Jacinto	555-9833	American	Cheeseburger	8/4/2000	☐	$5.50

PROJECT 1-2

SCANS

1. Open the **IA Project1-2** database.

2. Create a new table named **Stores** using the field names, data types, and descriptions shown in Figure 1-18.

FIGURE 1-18

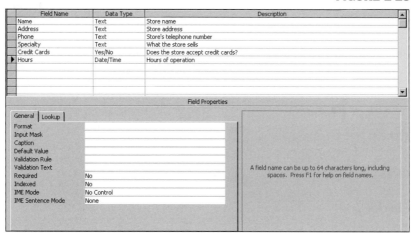

3. Save the table as **Stores** and close it. No primary key is necessary.

4. Open the table in Datasheet view and enter the record shown in Figure 1-19.

FIGURE 1-19

Name	Address	Phone	Specialty	Credit Cards	Hours
Electronics Plus	6443 Elgin St.	555-2330	Electronics	☑	10am to 6pm
				▨	

5. After keying the Hours field entry, a message appears telling you the value you entered isn't appropriate for the field. Click **OK** and delete the data in the Hours field.

6. Close Datasheet view and open the table in Design view.

7. Change the data type for the Hours field to **Text**.

8. Insert a new row above the Hours field and key a new field named **Checks** with the **Yes/No** data type, and **Does the store accept personal checks?** as the description.

9. Save the changes and close Design view.

10. Open the table in Datasheet view and click the check box (for *yes*) in the Checks field.

11. Key **10am to 6pm** in the Hours field.

12. Enter the records shown in Figure 1-20.

FIGURE 1-20

Name	Address	Phone	Specialty	Credit Cards	Checks	Hours
Music Master	2700 Canton	555-9820	Music-CDs	☑	☐	11am to 9pm
Rag Doll	2136 Quaker	555-4560	Ladies clothes	☑	☑	10am to 5:30pm
Vision Computers	6720 Data Drive	555-2300	Computers	☑	☑	10am to 7pm
Athletics X-Press	8904 Richmond	555-7811	Shoes	☑	☑	12pm to 7pm
College Clothiers	3340 University	555-3570	Clothes	☐	☑	12pm to 6pm

13. Change the left and right margins to **.5** inches and print the table.

14. Close the table and database.

PROJECT 1-3

1. Open the **IA Project1-3** database.

2. Open the **Stores** table in Design view.

3. Delete the **Checks** field.

4. Change the data type for the Credit Cards field to **Text**.

5. Save the changes and close Design view.

6. Open the table in Datasheet view.

7. Change the left and right margins to **.75** inches and print the table.

8. Close the table and database.

PROJECT 1-4

1. Create a new database named **Music**.

2. With the *Music* database open, create a new table named **Pop** using the field names, data types, and descriptions shown in Figure 1-21.

FIGURE 1-21

Field Name	Data Type	Description
Name	Text	Musical artist's name
Title	Text	Title of CD or tape
Year	Number	Year title was released
Type	Text	CD or tape?

Pop : Table

3. Save the table as **Pop**. No primary key is necessary.

4. Switch to Datasheet view and enter the records shown in Figure 1-22.

FIGURE 1-22

Name	Title	Year	Type
Dire Straits	Money for Nothing	1988	CD
Mariah Carey	Music Box	1993	CD
Van Morrison	Moondance	1970	Tape
Kenny G.	Silhouette	1988	CD
Natalie Merchant	Blind Man's Zoo	1989	CD
Billy Joel	Glass Houses	1980	Tape
		0	

5. Print the table.

6. Open the **Pop** table in Design view.

7. Delete the **Type** field.

8. Save the change.

9. Switch to Datasheet view and add the records as shown in Figure 1-23.

FIGURE 1-23

Name	Title	Year
Pretenders	The Isle Of View	1995
Jackson Browne	Looking East	1996
Genesis	Three Sides Live	1994
		0

10. Print the table.

11. Close the table and database.

ACTIVITY 1-1

Select a type of collection or a personal interest and create a database to organize it. Give the database a name that accurately reflects the data.

Create and design a table for your data using the Table Wizard. Carefully consider the fields your database will need.

To start the Table Wizard, double-click **Create table by using wizard** in the Database window and follow the screens to create your table. In the first screen, choose the Personal category and one of the Sample tables. In the Sample Fields column, select the fields for your new table. When finished with the first screen, click the **Next** button. In the second screen, enter the name of your table and click **Next**. On the third screen, choose **Enter data directly into the table** and click the **Finish** button. The table will appear in Datasheet view. Enter at least two records in the table. Change the margins if necessary and print the table. Close the table and exit Access.

ACTIVITY 1-2

When creating a database with many of the same types of fields, it is helpful to know how to copy the definition of a field. Use the Help feature and search for the steps to copy a field's definition within a table. Write down these basic steps.

MANIPULATING DATA

OBJECTIVES

Upon completion of this lesson, you should be able to:

- Edit a record and undo a change.
- Select records and fields.
- Delete a record.
- Cut, copy, and paste data.
- Change the layout of a datasheet.

⏱ **Estimated Time: 1.5 hours**

VOCABULARY

Field properties

Field selectors

Record pointer

Record selectors

Editing Records

To make editing records easier, Access provides navigation buttons on your screen. The navigation buttons are used to move around the datasheet. These buttons may not be necessary when working with databases as small as those you used in the previous lesson. As databases get larger, however, the navigation buttons become very useful. Figure 2-1 shows the locations of the navigation buttons.

FIGURE 2-1
Navigation buttons

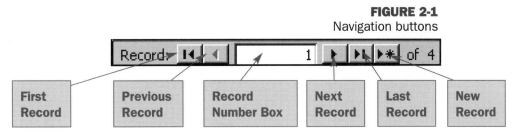

The First Record button is used to move quickly to the top of the table and the Last Record button is used to move to the bottom of the table. There are also buttons used to move to the next or previous record. To move to a specific record number, click the Record Number box and key the number of the record into the field. Press Tab to move to the specified record. To add a new record, click the New Record button.

An arrow to the left of the record indicates the current record. The computer keeps track of the current record using a *record pointer*. When you move among records in Datasheet view, you are actually moving the record pointer.

If you use the Tab key to move to a cell, Access highlights the contents of the cell. As in a spreadsheet, you can replace the contents of the cell by keying data while the existing data is highlighted. If you click a cell with the mouse, the insertion point appears in the cell, allowing you to edit the contents.

Undoing Changes to a Cell

There are three ways to undo changes to a cell. If you make a mistake keying data in a cell, you can choose Undo Typing on the Edit menu or click the Undo Typing button on the toolbar. This reverses your last action. If you have already entered the data in a cell and moved to the next cell (or any cell), choose Undo Current Field/Record on the Edit menu or click the Undo Current Field/Record button on the toolbar. You can also press the Esc button to restore the contents of the entire record.

STEP-BY-STEP 2.1

1. Start Microsoft Access and open **IA Step2-1** from the data files.

2. Open the **Calls** table in Datasheet view. The purpose of this table is to keep a log of telephone calls.

3. Click the **Last Record** button at the bottom of the table to move the record pointer to the last record.

4. Click the **First Record** button to move the record pointer to the first record.

5. Click the **Next Record** button to move the record pointer to the next record.

6. In the second record, the time is shown as 11:00 AM when it should be 10:30 AM. Press **Tab** until the Call Time field is highlighted.

7. Key **10:30** in the Call Time field and press **Tab**. (The field is formatted for AM.)

8. Move the mouse pointer to the Subject field in the third record. Click to place the pointer at the beginning of the field (where the pointer becomes a thick plus sign). The entire field will be highlighted.

9. Key **Computers** and press **Tab**.

10. Press **Esc**. The word *Computers* changes back to *Hardware*.

11. The entry in the Notes field of the third record is highlighted. Press **Delete**. The entry is deleted.

12. Click the **Undo** button on the toolbar. The Notes field entry reappears. Leave the table on the screen for the next Step-by-Step.

Selecting Records and Fields

You can quickly select records and fields by clicking the record or field selectors. *Field selectors* are at the top of a table and contain the field name. Figure 2-2 shows the Name field selected. *Record selectors* are located to the left of a record's first field. Clicking in the upper left corner of the datasheet selects all records in the database.

You can select more than one field by clicking the field selector in one field, holding down the Shift key, and clicking the field selector in another field. The two fields, and all the fields in between, will be selected. You can use the same method to select multiple records. You can also select multiple fields or records by clicking and dragging across the field or record selectors.

FIGURE 2-2
Record and field selectors

Selects all records

Record selector

Call ID	Name	Call Date	Call Time	Subject	Notes
1	Adam Hoover	9/16/03	10:10 AM	Proposal	Discuss planne
2	Claire Jones	9/16/03	10:30 AM	Lunch	Any plans for to
3	Joe Rodriguez	9/16/03	2:30 PM	Hardware	Can install next
4	Julie Hunter	9/17/03	8:30 AM	New employee	Call her to set u
*	(AutoNumber)				

Field selector

STEP-BY-STEP ▷ 2.2

1. Click the **Name** field selector to select the entire column.

2. Click the **Subject** field selector to select the entire column.

3. Select the **Name** field again.

4. Hold down the **Shift** key and click the **Call Time** field selector. The Name, Call Date, and

Call Time fields are selected, as shown in Figure 2-3.

5. Click the record selector of the **Claire Jones** record. The entire record is selected.

6. Select the **Julie Hunter** record. Leave the table on the screen for the next Step-by-Step.

FIGURE 2-3
Selecting multiple columns

Call ID	Name	Call Date	Call Time	Subject	Notes
1	Adam Hoover	9/16/03	10:10 AM	Proposal	Discuss planne
2	Claire Jones	9/16/03	10:30 AM	Lunch	Any plans for to
3	Joe Rodriguez	9/16/03	2:30 PM	Hardware	Can install next
4	Julie Hunter	9/17/03	8:30 AM	New employee	Call her to set u
*	(AutoNumber)				

Deleting Records

To delete an entire record, select the record and choose Delete Record on the Edit menu or press the Delete key. You can also click the Delete Record button on the toolbar. A message box appears, as shown in Figure 2-4, warning you that you are about to delete a record. Click Yes to permanently delete the record or No to cancel the deletion. Once you've deleted a record using the Delete Record command, you cannot use the Undo command or Esc key to restore it.

You cannot delete fields in Datasheet view the same way you delete records. As you learned in Lesson 1, you can delete fields in Design view.

Hot Tip

You can delete more than one record by holding down the **Shift** key, clicking the record selector in each field, and then selecting **Delete Record**.

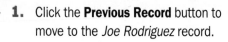

STEP-BY-STEP ▷ **2.3**

1. Click the **Previous Record** button to move to the *Joe Rodriguez* record.

2. Click the **Delete Record** button on the toolbar. A message appears, as shown in Figure 2-4, warning you that you are about to delete the record.

3. Click **Yes**. The record is deleted. Notice that the numbers in the Call ID field do not renumber when a record is deleted. The reason is that the number in the Call ID field is automatically assigned when the record is created and does not change. Leave the table on the screen for the next Step-by-Step.

FIGURE 2-4

Message warning you that you are about to delete a record

Cutting, Copying, and Pasting Data

The Cut, Copy, and Paste commands in Access work the same way as in other Office applications. You can use the commands to copy and move data within a table or between tables. To cut or copy an entire record, select the record and choose Cut or Copy on the Edit menu or click the Cut or Copy buttons on the toolbar.

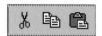

Using Cut, Copy, and Paste can sometimes be tricky. You must be aware that data pasted in a table will overwrite the existing data. If you want to cut or copy an entire record and paste it into a table as a new record, use the Paste Append command on the Edit menu. You can also highlight the blank record at the bottom of a table and choose Paste on the Edit menu or the Paste button on the toolbar. When you select a record and choose the Cut command, you will get the same message as when you use the Delete command. The difference is that with the Cut command, you can restore the record to the end of the table by using the Paste Append command.

Did You Know?

You can move and copy an entire object. In the Database window, select the object (table, query, form, or report) and choose **Cut** or **Copy** on the **Edit** menu. Open the database in which you want to paste the object and choose **Paste** on the **Edit** menu.

S TEP-BY-STEP ▷ 2.4

1. Select the **Adam Hoover** record.

2. Click the **Copy** button on the toolbar.

3. Click the **New Record** button. The new record appears at the bottom of the database. Click the **Paste** button on the toolbar to insert the information copied from Record 1.

4. Change the date and time of Record 4 to **September 17 at 5:00 pm**.

5. In the Notes field, delete the existing text and key **Proposal ready on Monday morning**.

6. Select the **Claire Jones** record.

7. Click the **Cut** button on the toolbar. The message saying that you are about to delete a record appears.

8. Click **Yes**.

9. Select the empty record at the end of the table.

10. Choose **Paste Append** on the **Edit** menu. The Claire Jones record appears as shown in Figure 2-5. Leave the table on the screen for the next Step-by-Step.

 Did You Know?

If you delete data or objects from a database, the database can become fragmented and use disk space inefficiently. Compacting rearranges how the database is stored on disk and optimizes the performance of the database. Access combines compacting and repairing into one process. Specify the database you want to compact and repair, choose **Database Utilities** on the **Tools** menu, and select **Compact and Repair Database**.

FIGURE 2-5
Using the Cut and Paste buttons to add a record

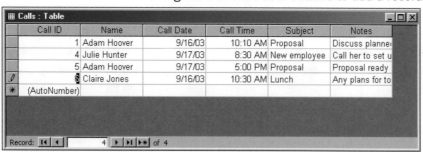

Changing Datasheet Layout

You can make many changes to the datasheet layout, including changing row height and column width, rearranging columns, and freezing columns.

Changing Row Height

You can adjust the row height in a datasheet, but the adjustment affects all the rows. To change the height, position the pointer on the lower border of a row selector, and it will turn into a double arrow, as shown in Figure 2-6. Using the double arrow, click and drag the row border up or down to adjust the row height.

You can also specify an exact row height. Choose Row Height on the Format menu and the Row Height dialog box appears, as shown in Figure 2-7. Key in a height in points (like font sizes) for the row.

FIGURE 2-6
Adjusting the
row height

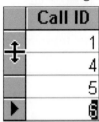

FIGURE 2-7
Row Height dialog box

STEP-BY-STEP ▷ 2.5

1. Position the mouse pointer on the lower border of the record selector for **Claire Jones**. You will know you have the pointer correctly positioned when it changes to a double arrow.

2. Drag the row border down slightly to increase the height of the row. When you release the mouse button, all rows are affected by the change.

3. Select the **Julie Hunter** record.

4. Choose **Row Height** on the **Format** menu. The Row Height dialog box, shown in Figure 2-7, appears.

5. Key **30** in the Row Height box and click **OK**. The row height increases to a height that allows the data in the Subject and Notes field to be read more easily. Leave the table on the screen for the next Step-by-Step.

Hot Tip

Instead of choosing **Row Height** on the **Format** menu, you can right-click the record selector and select **Row Height** on the shortcut menu that appears.

Changing Column Width

Often, the column widths provided by default are too wide or too narrow for the data in the table. Adjusting column width is similar to adjusting row height. To adjust the column width, place the mouse pointer in the field selector on the border of the column. The pointer changes to a double arrow. Click and drag to the width you want. Unlike rows, which must all have the same height, each field can have a different width.

When you choose Column Width on the Format menu, the Column Width dialog box appears, as shown in Figure 2-8. You can key a specific width or click the Best Fit button. The Best Fit button automatically selects the best width for the data in the column. Another way to choose the best fit is to place the mouse pointer on the field border and double-click when it turns into a double arrow.

Hot Tip

Instead of choosing **Column Width** on the **Format** menu, you can right-click the column and select **Column Width** on the shortcut menu that appears.

FIGURE 2-8
Column Width dialog box

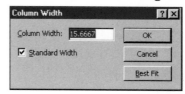

STEP-BY-STEP ▷ 2.6

1. Position the pointer on the right border of the **Notes** field selector.

2. Drag to make the column wide enough to allow all the information to fit in the field.

3. Select the **Call ID** field.

4. Choose **Column Width** on the **Format** menu. The Column Width dialog box appears, as shown in Figure 2-8.

5. Click **Best Fit**. The column narrows.

6. Use the Best Fit option to adjust the width of the **Call Date** field.

7. Select the **Call Time** field.

8. Choose **Column Width** on the **Format** menu. The Column Width dialog box appears.

9. Key **16** into the Column Width box and click **OK**.

10. Change the width of the **Subject** field to **25**.

11. Print the table in landscape orientation. Leave the table on the screen for the next Step-by-Step.

Rearranging Columns

In Datasheet view, Access allows you to rearrange fields by dragging them to a new location. First, select the field you want to move. Then click and hold down the mouse button on the field selector and drag the field to the new location. A vertical bar follows your mouse pointer to show you where the field will be inserted. Release the mouse button to insert the field in its new location.

STEP-BY-STEP ▷ 2.7

1. Select the **Call Date** field.

2. Click and drag the **Call Date** field to the left until the vertical bar appears between the Call ID and Name fields. Release the mouse

button. The Call Date column appears between the Call ID and Name columns, as shown in Figure 2-9. Leave the table on your screen for the next Step-by-Step.

FIGURE 2-9
Rearranging fields

Call ID	Call Date	Name	Call Time	Subject	Notes
1	9/16/03	Adam Hoover	10:10 AM	Proposal	Discuss planned budget
4	9/17/03	Julie Hunter	8:30 AM	New employee	Call her to set up 3 interviews
5	9/17/03	Adam Hoover	5:00 PM	Proposal	Proposal ready on Monday morning
6	9/16/03	Claire Jones	10:30 AM	Lunch	Any plans for today?
(AutoNumber)					

Record: I◄ ◄ 1 ► ►I ►* of 4

Freezing Columns

If a table has many columns, it might be helpful to freeze one or more columns, allowing them to remain on the screen while you scroll to columns that are not currently visible.

To freeze columns, select the column or columns you want to freeze and choose Freeze Columns on the Format menu. To unfreeze columns, choose Unfreeze All Columns on the Format menu.

STEP-BY-STEP ▷ 2.8

1. Select the **Call ID** field.

2. While holding down the **Shift** key, click the **Name** field. The Call ID, Call Date, and Name fields are all highlighted.

3. Choose **Freeze Columns** on the **Format** menu.

4. Click the horizontal scroll arrow at the bottom right of the table window to scroll to the Notes field. Notice that the frozen fields remain on the screen. (Note: If you do not have a horizontal scroll arrow, your screen is large enough to include all of the columns. Continue to Step 5.)

5. Choose **Unfreeze All Columns** on the **Format** menu.

6. Choose **Close** on the **File** menu. You will be asked if you want to save changes to the layout of the table.

7. Click **Yes**. The Database window is visible on the screen. Leave the database open for the next Step-by-Step.

Changing Field Properties

When you defined fields for a table in Lesson 1, you specified only the field name, data type, and description. Now that you have created and used fields in a variety of situations, it is time to learn about field properties. *Field properties* allow you to further customize a field beyond merely choosing a data type.

You can view and change field properties in a table or form's Design view. Figure 2-10 shows the field properties available for a Text data type; you will learn about the most common ones. The field properties available will vary depending on the field's selected data type.

FIGURE 2-10
Field properties in Design view

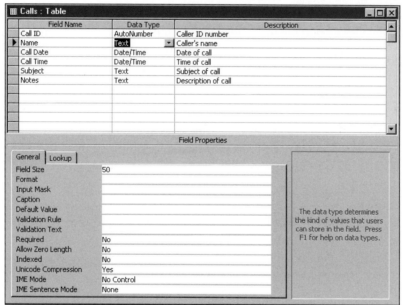

FIELD SIZE

One of the most common field properties is Field Size. In fields of Text type, the Field Size is merely the number of characters allowed in the field. You can specify that the field allow up to 255 characters. The default size is 50.

In fields of Number type, the Field Size allows you to specify the internal data type that Access will use to store the number. The available options are Byte, Integer, Long Integer, Single, Double, Replication ID, and Decimal. If you have computer programming experience, the available field sizes may be familiar to you. If the options mean nothing to you, don't worry. There is an easy way to select the appropriate field size. If your field is to store whole numbers only, use the Long Integer field size. If your field will store fractional numbers with decimal places, choose the Double field size.

FORMAT

Use the Format field property to specify how you want Access to display numbers, dates, times, and text. For example, the default format for dates is *10/28/03*. Using the Format property, you can change the format to *28-Oct-03* or *Tuesday, October 28, 2003*. You can also include the time with the date such as *10/28/03 11:54:30 AM*.

INPUT MASK

An input mask allows you to control the data pattern or format allowed in the field. You can also specify characters that will be put into the field automatically. For example, you can specify that a phone number be formatted with area code in parentheses, and the rest of the number split by a hyphen. When you key records, you won't have to key the parentheses or the hyphen; Access will put them in for you automatically. You can use the Input Mask Wizard to set the field's pattern or format for you.

CAPTION

The text you provide in the caption field property will be used *instead* of field names in forms, tables in Datasheet view, reports, and queries. For example, if the field name is *EmailName*, you could enter *E-mail address* in the caption field property. When you create a form that includes the field, the more descriptive name will appear as the field name.

DEFAULT VALUE

Another useful field property is Default Value. Use this field property when you have a field that usually contains the same value. For example, if most of the people in a database of names and addresses live in California, you can enter CA as the Default Value of the State field. The State field will automatically contain CA, unless you change it to another state.

REQUIRED

The Required field property specifies whether you must enter a value in the field. For example, in an employee database, you might specify that each field requires a telephone number. If you try to enter a record without including a telephone number, Access will alert you that you must enter one.

DECIMAL PLACES

Number and Currency fields have a field property called Decimal Places. This property usually adjusts automatically depending on the data in the field. You can specify a number of decimal places here to override the automatic setting.

STEP-BY-STEP ▷ 2.9

1. Open the **Calls** table in Design view.

2. Select the **Name** field.

3. Under the Field Properties section beside *Field Size*, double-click **50** to highlight it. Key **40**.

4. In the Caption box, key **Caller's Name**.

5. Click in the **Required** field property box. A down arrow will appear at the right end of the box.

6. Click the down arrow and choose **Yes** from the menu.

7. Select the **Call Date** field.

8. Click in the **Format** field property box. A down arrow appears.

9. Click the down arrow. A menu of date and time formats appears.

10. Choose **Medium Date**.

11. Click in the **Input Mask** field property box. Three periods appear on the right side of the box.

12. Click the three periods. The Input Mask Wizard screen appears with a list of date and time formats. (If a message box opens asking if you would like to install the Input Mask Wizard, click **Yes**.)

13. Choose **Medium Date**. Click **Finish**.

14. Choose **Yes** in the Required field property.

15. Select the **Notes** field.

16. Change the Field Size to **100**.

17. Save the table design. A message may appear stating that some data may be lost because you changed the setting for a field size to a shorter size. Click **Yes** to continue. Another message may appear asking if you want to test the changes. Click **Yes**.

18. Switch to Datasheet view to see the format changes to the Call Date field. Click in the **Call Date** field in the blank record at the bottom of the table to see the input mask you added. The Name field now contains the caption you entered. The other changes aren't visible.

19. Adjust the row height, if necessary, so you can see all the record data in each field. Print the table in landscape orientation.

20. Save and close the table and then close the database by clicking the **Close** button in the Database window.

Summary

In this lesson, you learned:

■ The navigation buttons are used to move around the datasheet. They allow you to move to the first record, the last record, the previous record, or the next record. You can also use a navigation button to add a new record.

■ There are three ways to undo changes to cells. If you make mistakes while keying data in a cell, you can click the Undo button. If you have already entered data and moved to the next cell, press Esc. To reverse all the changes to the previous record, choose Undo Saved Record on the Edit menu.

■ To delete a record, use the Delete Record command. Entire records and fields can be selected by clicking the record and field selectors. Cut, Copy, and Paste are available in Datasheet view to move and copy data. The Paste Append command pastes a record at the end of the database.

■ You can make many changes to a datasheet. You can change the row height and column width. You can also rearrange and freeze columns.

■ Field properties allow you to further customize a field beyond merely choosing a data type. Some of the more common field properties are Field Size, Input Mask, Caption, Default Value, Format, Required, and Decimal Places.

VOCABULARY REVIEW

Define the following terms:

Field properties   Record pointer
Field selectors   Record selectors

LESSON 2 REVIEW QUESTIONS

TRUE/FALSE

Circle T if the statement is true or F if the statement is false.

T F   1. If you click a cell with the mouse, the insertion point appears in the cell.

T F   2. Holding down the Alt key allows you to select more than one field.

T F   3. In Access, you can use the Cut, Copy, and Paste commands.

T F   4. Changing the height of one row changes the height of all datasheet rows.

T F   5. You can delete records and fields in Datasheet view.

WRITTEN QUESTIONS

Write a brief answer to the following questions.

1. What is the record pointer?

2. How do you delete a record in Datasheet view?

3. What does the Paste Append command do?

4. Why would you want to freeze columns in Datasheet view?

5. In what view do you change field properties?

PROJECT 2-1

1. Open the **IA Project2-1** database from the data files.

2. Open the **Employee Information** table in Datasheet view.

3. Go to record **7** and change the address to **4582 104th St**.

4. Go to record **11** and change the birthdate to **12/14/1961**.

5. Go to record **14** and change the first name to **Alex**.

6. Go to record **1** and change the last name to **Abraham**.

7. Undo your last change.

8. Delete record **5**.

9. Change the width of the **Address** field to **20** and the Zip Code field to **13**.

10. Change all other field widths using **Best Fit**.

11. Change the row height to **15**.

12. Change the left and right margins to **.5 inches** and print the table in landscape orientation.

13. Close the table. Click **Yes** if prompted to save changes to the layout of the table. Close the database.

PROJECT 2-2

1. Open the **IA Project2-2** database.

2. Open the **Employee Information** table in Datasheet view.

3. Copy record **4** and paste it at the bottom of the table.

4. In the pasted record, change the First Name to **Mike**, the SS Number to **343-26-9432**, the Title to **Account Executive**, the Birthdate to **9/28/61**, and the Salary to **2950**.

5. Move the **Birthdate** field to between the Zip Code and Department fields.

6. Freeze the **Employee Number**, **Last Name**, and **First Name** fields.

7. Scroll to the right until the **Birthdate** field is beside the **First Name** field.

8. Change the birthdate of Hillary Davis to **10/28/68**.

9. Unfreeze the columns.

10. Change the left and right margins to **.5 inches** and print the table in landscape orientation.

11. Close the table. Click **Yes** if prompted to save changes to the layout of the table. Close the database.

PROJECT 2-3

1. Open the **IA Project2-3** database.

2. Open the **Employee Information** table in Design view.

3. Format the **Salary** field for currency.

4. Select **Medium Date** from the Format field properties for the **Birthdate** field .

5. Select **Medium Date** from the Input Mask formats for the **Birthdate** field.

6. Key **Employee Number** as the Caption field property for the **Emp Number** field.

7. Make the **Zip Code** field **Required**.

8. Change the field size of the **Zip Code** field to **10**.

9. Save the table design. A message might appear asking if you want to continue. Click **Yes**. Another message might appear asking if you want to test the changes. Click **Yes**.

10. Switch to Datasheet view and insert the following records at the end of the table.

    16 Wells Wendy 404-76-5234 2610 21st St 79832-2610 15-Feb-72 Sales Executive Assistant **$2,150.00**

    17 Abbott Donna 372-98-2036 1824 Saratoga 79833-1900 12-Jan-59 Personnel Manager **$2,880.00**

11. Widen the **Salary** column and any other fields to show all data and column titles.

12. Change the left and right margins to **.3 inches** and print the table in landscape orientation.

13. Close the table. Click **Yes** if prompted to save changes to the layout of the table. Close the database.

 Internet

For information on careers, access the Occupational Outlook Handbook at *http://www.bls.gov/dolbls.htm*. Web sites and addresses change constantly. If you can't find the information at this site, try another.

ACTIVITY 2-1

Open the database you created for the Critical Thinking Activity in Lesson 1. Add two new records using the New Record button. Select a field and make a change to the data. Delete an entire record. Copy one record and paste it into the table as a new record. If necessary, increase the column width and row height to see all the data. Rearrange the columns. Print and close the table.

ACTIVITY 2-2

You can use the Office Clipboard to collect and paste multiple items from the various Office programs. The Office Clipboard automatically copies multiple items when you do any of the following:

1. Copy or cut two different items in succession in the same program.

2. Copy one item, paste the item, and then copy another item in the same program.

3. Copy one item twice in succession.

Using the Help system, find the steps to collect and paste multiple items. Briefly write down the steps in numbered order.

CREATING AND MODIFYING FORMS

OBJECTIVES

Upon completion of this lesson, you should be able to:

- Create and use forms.
- Modify forms.
- Create a calculated control on a form.
- Compact and repair a database.

🕐 **Estimated Time: 1.5 hours**

VOCABULARY

Bound control

Calculated control

Detail

Form Header

Form Footer

Unbound control

Creating Forms

Datasheet view is useful for many of the ways you work with a database table. Often, however, you may want a more convenient way to enter and view records. For example, the form shown in Figure 3-1 places all of the important fields from the Calls table into a convenient and attractive layout.

Forms can be created in Design view by placing fields on a blank form, arranging and sizing fields, and adding graphics. The Form Wizard makes the process easier by asking you detailed questions about the fields, layout, and format and then creates a form based on your answers. Creating a form in Design view gives you more flexibility, but the Form Wizard can create the form you need quickly and efficiently. You can also use the AutoForm feature which automatically creates a form that displays all the fields and records of the database table.

FIGURE 3-1
Forms can make entering and editing data easier

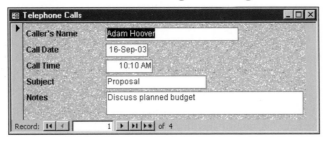

Using the Form Wizard

To create a form, click the Forms button on the Objects bar. Click the New button and the New Form dialog box appears, as shown in Figure 3-2. The New Form dialog box gives you several options for creating a form. In the next Step-by-Step, you will use the Form Wizard option. The New Form dialog box also asks you to specify the table or query to use as a basis for the form. In more complex databases, you may have to choose among several tables or queries.

You can also create a form using the Form Wizard by double-clicking Create form by using wizard in the Database window.

FIGURE 3-2
New Form dialog box

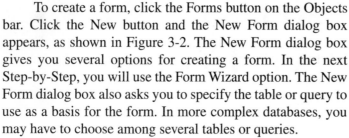

1. Open the **IA Step3-1** database from the data files. Click the **Forms** button on the Objects bar.

2. Click **New**. The New Form dialog box appears, as shown in Figure 3-2.

3. Choose the **Form Wizard** option and the **Calls** table from the drop-down list.

4. Click **OK**. The Form Wizard dialog box appears, as shown in Figure 3-3. Leave the Form Wizard dialog box on screen for the next Step-by-Step.

FIGURE 3-3
Form Wizard dialog box

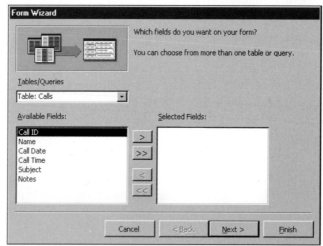

The next step is to choose the fields you want to appear on the form. To add a field to the form, click the field name in the Available Fields list and click the > button. To add all of the fields at once, click the >> button. If you plan to include almost all of the fields, click >> to include them all, then use the < button to remove the ones you do not want.

S TEP-BY-STEP ▷ 3.2

1. Click **>>**. All of the field names appear in the Selected Fields list.

2. Select the **Call ID** field in the Selected Fields list.

3. Click **<**. The **Call ID** field is moved back to the Available Fields list.

4. Click the **Next** button. The Form Wizard dialog box changes to ask you to select a layout for the form, as shown in Figure 3-4.

5. Leave the dialog box open for the next Step-by-Step.

FIGURE 3-4
Selecting a layout for a form

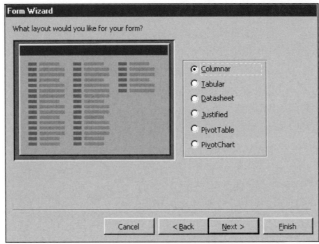

You have a choice of six different layouts for the form: Columnar, Tabular, Datasheet, Justified, PivotTable, and PivotChart. The Columnar layout is the most common type. The form in Figure 3-1 is an example of a Columnar layout. As data is entered, the insertion point moves down the fields.

The Tabular layout creates forms that look similar to a table in Datasheet view. The Tabular layout gives you the ability to make a more attractive Datasheet view. Figure 3-5 is an example of a form created using a tabular layout.

FIGURE 3-5
Tabular form layout

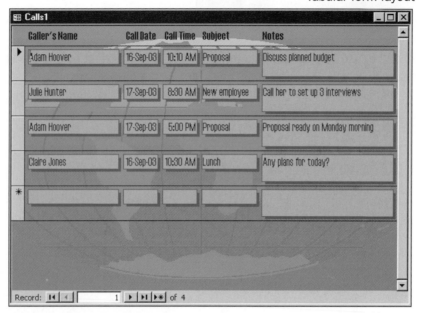

S TEP-BY-STEP ▷ 3.3

1. If not already selected, click the **Columnar** option.

2. Click **Next**. This dialog box asks you to choose a style, as shown in Figure 3-6.

3. Leave the dialog box open for the next Step-by-Step.

FIGURE 3-6
Choosing a style for a form

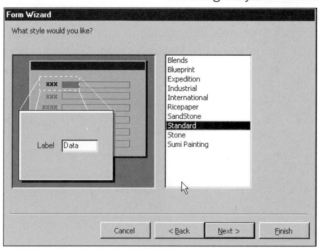

The style you select has no effect on the function of the form. Choosing a style allows you to personalize your form or give it flair. There are several styles from which to choose.

After you choose a style, you will be asked to name the form. The name you provide will appear in the Form section of the Database window. You are also given the option to begin using the form once it is created or to modify the form after the Form Wizard is complete.

STEP-BY-STEP ▷ 3.4

1. Choose the **Standard** style from the list. The preview box shows you what this form style looks like. It should look similar to Figure 3-6.

2. Click the other styles to see what they look like.

3. Choose the **SandStone** style and click **Next**. The final Form Wizard dialog box appears, as shown in Figure 3-7.

4. Key **Telephone Calls** in the title box.

5. Click the **Open the form to view or enter information** button if it's not chosen already.

6. Click **Finish**. Access creates the form, which should look like that shown in Figure 3-8.

7. Choose **Close** on the **File** menu to close the form. Leave the database open for the next Step-by-Step.

FIGURE 3-7
Naming the form

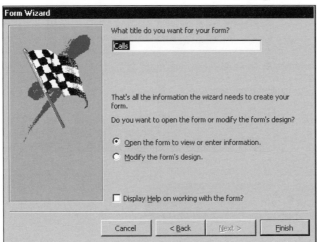

FIGURE 3-8
A custom form

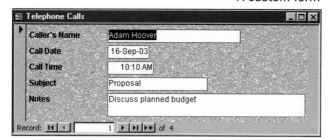

FIGURE 3-8
A custom form

Using the AutoForm Feature

The AutoForm feature automatically creates a form that displays all the fields and records of the database table. This is the quickest way to create a simple form since no detailed questions are asked about the fields, layout, or format.

To create a form using AutoForm, click the Forms button on the Objects Bar. Click the New button and the New Form dialog box appears, as shown in Figure 3-9. Choose one of the five AutoForm options listed that describe the name of the layout you want for the form. Specify the table or query to use as a basis for the form. The form is automatically created and displayed in the selected layout.

FIGURE 3-9
New Form dialog box

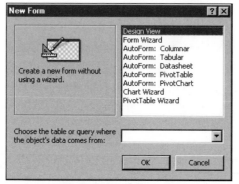

1. If not already selected, click **Forms** on the Objects bar.

2. Click **New**. The New Form dialog box appears, as shown in Figure 3-9.

3. Choose the **AutoForm: Columnar** option and the **Calls** table from the drop-down list.

4. Click **OK**. AutoForm creates the form with the columnar layout, as shown in Figure 3-10.

5. Click **Close** on the **File** menu. A message will appear asking if you want to save changes to the form.

6. Click **Yes**. The Save As dialog box appears.

7. Key **Calls AutoForm** into the **Form Name** box.

8. Click **OK**. Leave the database open for the next Step-by-Step.

FIGURE 3-10
Form created with the AutoForm feature

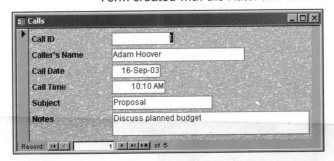

Using Forms

Using a form is basically the same as using Datasheet view. The same keys move the insertion point among the fields. You see the same set of navigation buttons at the bottom of the form, as shown in Figure 3-11. As with Datasheet view, you can move to a specific record by clicking in the Record Number box and entering the number of the record you want to see.

FIGURE 3-11
Navigation controls at the bottom of the form

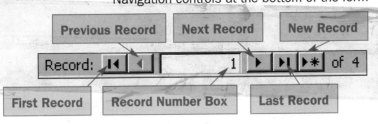

Table 3-1 summarizes the ways to move around when a form is displayed, including keyboard shortcuts.

TABLE 3-1
Navigating a form

TO MOVE TO THE...	BUTTON	KEYBOARD SHORTCUT
First record	First Record button	Ctrl+Home
Last record	Last Record button	Ctrl+End
Next record	Next Record button	Page Down
Previous record	Previous Record button	Page Up

To add a new record, click the Next Record button until the blank record at the end of the database appears, or click the New Record button. Key the new record. To edit an existing record, display the record and make changes in the fields of the form.

After entering or editing records in a form, you do not need to save the changes. Access saves them for you automatically. Remember to always save changes to the form design in Design view.

You can print forms much the same way you print tables. To print all the records in the form, choose Print on the File menu and the Print dialog box appears. In the Print dialog box, choose All from the Print Range options if you want to print all the records. Access will fit as many forms on each page as possible. To print only one record, display the record on the screen and choose Print on the File menu. Click the Selected Record(s) option from the Print Range options.

S TEP-BY-STEP ▷ 3.6

1. Open the **Telephone Calls** form.

2. Click the **New Record** button. A blank record appears in the form.

3. Enter the following information in the form:

   Caller's Name: Excel Travel Agency
   Call Date: 18-Sep-03
   Call Time: 10:21 AM
   Subject: Seattle trip
   Notes: Flight 412 Departs 7:40 AM/Arrives 1:30 PM

4. Click in the record number box. Delete the 5, key **4**, and press **Tab**.

5. Highlight the word **today** in the Notes field.

6. Key **Friday**.

7. Display record 5, and choose **Print** on the **File** menu. The Print dialog box appears.

8. Click the **Selected Record**(**s**) option from the Print Range options, and click **OK**. (The printed form may cut off the data in some of the fields.)

9. Choose **Close** on the **File** menu to close the form. Leave the database open for the next Step-by-Step.

Modifying Forms

Any form, whether created manually or with a Form Wizard, can be modified. You make changes to a form in Design view, which shows the structure of the form. To access Design view, select the form in the Database window, and then click the Design button. The form appears in Design view, as shown in Figure 3-12.

FIGURE 3-12
Design view

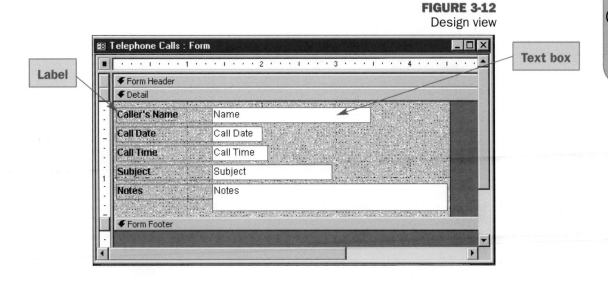

The form is divided into three sections: Form Header, Detail, and Form Footer. The **Form Header** section displays information that remains the same for every record, such as the title for a form. A Form Header appears at the top of the screen in Form view and at the top of the first page of the forms when printed. The **Detail** section displays records. You can display one record on the screen or as many as possible. A **Form Footer** section displays information that remains the same for every record, such as instructions for using the form. A form footer appears at the bottom of the screen in Form view or after the last detail section on the last page of the forms when printed.

The Toolbox, shown in Figure 3-13, which appears when you switch to Design view, has controls that you can use to modify and enhance the sections and objects on a form. The Label and Text Box tools are labeled in Figure 3-13 because they are used frequently. To determine the other controls available, you can hold your mouse over each of the icons on the Toolbox to view the ScreenTip. There are three types of controls: bound, unbound, and calculated. A **bound control** is connected to a field in a table and is used to display, enter, and update data. An **unbound control** is not connected to a field and is used to display information, lines, rectangles, and pictures. The Label control, which is an unbound control, allows you to add text as a title or instructions to a form. Look again at Figure 3-12. Notice that the field name is contained in a Label control, and the field entry is contained in the Text Box control. A Text Box control is tied to, or bound to a field in the underlying table, whereas the Label control is not.

In Design view, you can change the font, size, style, and other attributes of labels and text box data. Simply select the control, and use the buttons on the Formatting toolbar. Or, you can double-click a control to open its Properties dialog box and modify the attributes and other properties listed on the various tabs.

FIGURE 3-13
Toolbox

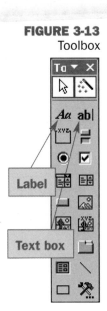

1. If not already selected, click **Forms** on the Objects bar. Choose the **Telephone Calls** form, and click the **Design** button. The form appears in Design view, as shown in Figure 3-12.

2. If necessary, display the Toolbox by clicking the **Toolbox** button. Click the **Line** button in the Toolbox.

3. Position the pointer in the **Detail** section between the Caller's Name label and the data field and click to place a line as shown in Figure 3-14.

4. Position the pointer at the right end of the line until a double arrow appears. Click and drag the right end of the line to the bottom of the form until it is vertical between the field labels and data fields as shown in Figure 3-15.

FIGURE 3-14
Inserting a line

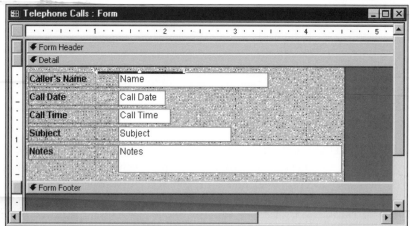

FIGURE 3-15
Repositioning the line object

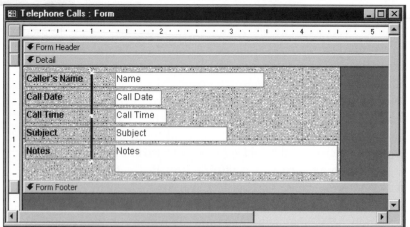

5. In the Detail section, double-click the **Caller's Name** label. The Label properties window opens, as shown in Figure 3-16. If necessary, select the **All** tab.

6. Change the caption to **Name** and close the Properties window.

7. Double-click the **Call Date** label and change the caption to **Date**. Double-click the **Call Time** label and change the caption to **Time**.

8. Position the pointer on the line between the **Form Header** section and **Detail** section until a double arrow appears as shown in Figure 3-17.

9. Click and drag the line down about a half-inch to increase the height of the Form Header section.

10. Click the **Label** button in the Toolbox.

11. Position the pointer in the **Form Header** section and click and drag to draw a text box as shown in Figure 3-18.

12. Key **TELEPHONE CALLS** at the insertion point that appears in the text box.

13. Click outside the text box to view the title. Double-click on the text box to display the Label properties dialog box.

FIGURE 3-16
The Label screen

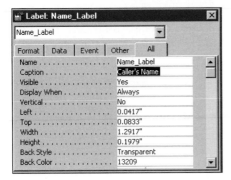

FIGURE 3-17
Resizing the Form Header

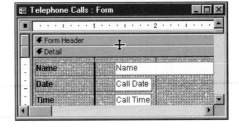

FIGURE 3-18
Inserting a text box

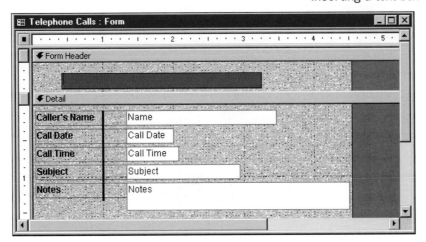

14. Scroll through the list of properties until you locate the *Font Name* and *Font Size* properties. Click in the **Font Name** text box, click the down arrow, and select **Arial Black**. Click in the **Font Size** box, click the down arrow, and change the size to **12**. Close the dialog box.

15. Position the pointer on the line at the bottom of the Form Footer section until a double arrow appears as shown in Figure 3-19. You may need to scroll down to view the Form Footer section.

16. Click and drag the line down about a half-inch to increase the height of the Form Footer section.

17. Click the **Check Box** button in the Toolbox.

18. Position the pointer in the Form Footer and click to place a check box as shown in Figure 3-20. Your text box to the right of the check mark will contain a different number from the one showing in the figure.

19. Double-click the text box to the right of the check mark. The Label properties dialog box appears.

20. Change the caption to **Return Call** and close the dialog box.

21. Click on the right border of the text box and drag to see all of the caption.

22. Choose **Close** on the **File** menu. A message appears asking if you want to save changes. Click **Yes**. You are returned to the Database window.

23. With the name of the form highlighted, click **Open**. The modified form appears on the screen.

24. If necessary, scroll to see all of the records. Go back to Record **1**, select **Print** on the **File** menu, make sure the **Selected Record(s)** option is selected, and click **OK**. Close the form and the database.

> ### Hot Tip
>
> To delete a line or other object on a form, make sure you are in Design view, click on the line or object to select it, and press the **Delete** key or choose **Delete** on the **Edit** menu.

FIGURE 3-19
Resizing the Form Footer

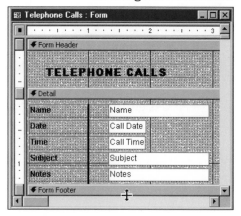

FIGURE 3-20
Form Footer with check box

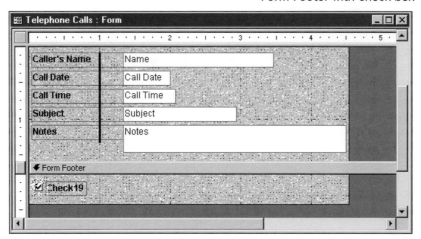

FIGURE 3-20
Form Footer with check box

Working with Calculated Controls

A *calculated control* on a form uses an expression to generate the data value for a field. For example, on an Orders form you might use the expression Unit Cost multiplied by Units Ordered or *=Unit Cost*Units Ordered*, to determine the value in the Total Cost field.

To create a calculated control on a form, open the Properties dialog box for the text box that will contain the calculation. The Properties dialog box will look like that shown in Figure 3-21. In the Control Source text box, key the expression for calculating the field value. You can also key a name for the calculated field in the Name text box, and determine the numerical format in the Format text box. Open the form and the value for the calculated field is calculated for each record.

FIGURE 3-21
Text Box properties dialog box

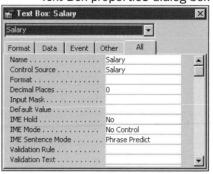

STEP-BY-STEP ▷ 3.8

1. Open the **IA Step3-8** database from the data files.

2. Click **Forms** on the Objects bar. Choose the **Employee Bonus** form and click the **Design** button. The form appears in Design view, as shown in Figure 3-22.

3. Position the pointer on the **Salary** text box as shown in Figure 3-22. Double-click to display the Text Box: Salary properties dialog box, as shown in Figure 3-21. If not already selected, choose the **All** tab.

4. Key **Bonus** in the **Name** box.

5. Key **=[Salary]*.10** in the **Control Source** box. The bonus field will be 10% of the employee's salary.

6. Click in the **Format** text box, click the down arrow, and choose **Currency**.

7. Close the properties dialog box. Double-click on the **Salary** label box which is to the left of the text box. The Label properties dialog box displays, as shown in Figure 3-23.

8. Change the **Caption** field to **Bonus** and close the dialog box. Switch to **Form** view by clicking the **View** button (on the Formatting toolbar).

9. If necessary, scroll to see all the records. Print the form for Record **2**. Close the form, save your changes and leave the database open for the next Step-by-Step.

FIGURE 3-22
Form in Design view

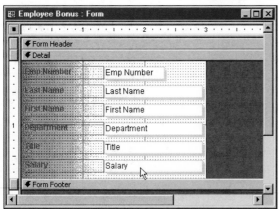

FIGURE 3-23
Label properties dialog box

Working with Hyperlinks

As you learned in Lesson 1, you can define a field in a database table as a hyperlink data type. This type of field actually stores the path to another database object or a specified file, or the address to a Web site.

You can also insert a hyperlink in a form (or the report or page objects in a database) that links you to another object in the database, another file, or a Web site. For example, you might have a form in a company database that you use to enter information regarding employees, such as their addresses, start dates, department, responsibilities, etc. You also maintain an Excel spreadsheet that tracks employees' salaries, bonuses, benefits, etc. You could insert a hyperlink in the database form that when clicked, immediately links you to the spreadsheet. The hyperlink provides you with an easy way to gain quick access to more information.

To insert a hyperlink, you must be in the form's Design view. Make sure the pointer is in the section of the form in which you want the hyperlink to appear, and then click the Insert Hyperlink button. In the Insert Hyperlink dialog box, select the file or Web page you want to link to, and then click OK.

Compacting and Repairing a Database

If you delete data or objects from a database, the database can become fragmented and use disk space inefficiently. Compacting rearranges how the database is stored on disk and optimizes the performance of the database. Access combines compacting and repairing into one process.

STEP-BY-STEP ▷ 3.9

1. Be sure no one else has the IA Step3-8 database open before continuing.

2. Choose **Database Utilities** on the **Tools** menu.

3. Click **Compact and Repair Database**.

4. When finished, close the table and database.

Hot Tip

You can also follow the steps in Step-by-Step 3.9 to compact and repair a database that is not open. Dialog boxes will display asking you to specify the database to compact and the new file name for the compacted database. If you use the same name, the original file will be replaced with the new compacted file.

Summary

In this lesson, you learned:

- Forms can be created in Design view by placing fields on a blank form, arranging and sizing fields, and adding graphics. The FormWizard makes the process of creating a form easier by asking you detailed questions about the fields, layout and format and then creates a form based on your answers. . You can also use the AutoForm feature which automatically creates a form that displays all the fields and records of the database table.

- Any form, whether created manually or with a Form Wizard, can be modified. You make changes to a form using Design view, which shows the structure of the form.

- The form in Design view is divided into three sections: Form Header, Detail, and Form Footer. The Form Header section displays information that remains the same for every record, such as the title for a form. A form header appears at the top of the screen in Form view and at the top of the first page of records when printed. The Detail section displays records. You can display one record on the screen or as many as possible. A Form Footer section displays information that remains the same for every record, such as instructions for using the form. A form footer appears at the bottom of the screen in Form view or after the last detail section on the last page of records when printed.

- The Toolbox has controls that you can use to modify and enhance the sections within a form. There are three types of controls: bound, unbound, and calculated. A bound control is connected to a field in a table and is used to display, enter, and update data. An unbound control is not connected to a field. A calculated control on a form uses an expression to calculate the data value for a field.

- If you delete data or objects from a database, the database can become fragmented and use disk space inefficiently. Compacting the database rearranges how the database is stored on disk and optimizes the performance of the database.

VOCABULARY REVIEW

Define the following terms:

Bound control	Detail	Form Footer
Calculated control	Form Header	Unbound control

LESSON 3 REVIEW QUESTIONS

TRUE/FALSE

Circle T if the statement is true or F if the statement is false.

T F 1. The style you select for a form has an effect on the function of the form.

T F 2. The Toolbox has tools that you can use to modify forms.

T F 3. You make modifications to a form in Datasheet view.

T F 4. If you delete data or objects from a database, the database can become fragmented and use disk space inefficiently.

T F 5. The AutoForm feature is the quickest way to create a simple form since no detailed questions are asked about the fields, layout, and format.

WRITTEN QUESTIONS

Write a brief answer to the following questions.

1. What are the six different layouts for a form?

2. How do you move to a specific record using a form?

3. What will happen if you use the same original name for a newly compacted database?

4.   What view is similar to a Tabular layout for a database?

5.   In what view do you change the properties for a control?

LESSON 3 PROJECTS

PROJECT 3-1

1.   Open the **IA Project3-1** database from the data files. Create a new form with the Form Wizard using the **Employee Information** table.

2.   Add the **First Name**, **Last Name**, **Department**, **Title**, and **Birthdate** fields.

3.   Use the **Columnar** layout and the **Standard** style.

4.   Title the form **Employee Birthdays** and open the form.

5.   Go to record **3**, Trent Broach, and change the title to **Director of Sales**.

6.   Go to record **16**, Donna Abbott, and change the Birthdate to **10-Jan-59**.

7.   Print record **16**.

8.   Close the form and leave the database open for the next project.

PROJECT 3-2

1.   Open the **Employee Bonus** form in Design view.

2.   Increase the size of the **Form Header** section to about ½ inch.

3.   Using the Label control, add a label box titled **EMPLOYEE BONUS**.

4. Change the Font Name to **Arial Black** and the Font Size to **12**.

5. Increase the size of the **Form Footer** section to about ½ inch.

6. Using the Check Box control, add a check box titled **Eligible for Stock Plan**. Increase the size of the text box to see all the title.

7. When finished, save the changes and switch to **Form** view.

8. Display and print record **6**.

9. Close the form and leave the database open for the next project.

PROJECT 3-3

1. Create a new form for the **Employee Information** table.

2. Use the **AutoForm: Columnar** option to create the form.

3. After the form is created, scroll through the records until you find the information on **Mark Mendoza**.

4. Print the information on **Mark Mendoza**. (Be sure the Selected Record(s) option is selected in the Print dialog box.)

5. Save the form as **Employee Data**.

6. Close the form.

7. Compact and repair the database. Close the database.

CRITICAL THINKING

ACTIVITY 3-1

Open the database you created for the Critical Thinking Activity 1-1 in Lesson 1. Use the Form Wizard to create a Tabular form that includes the fields of your database table. Choose an attractive style for the form. Add a record to the table using the new form. Print the record and close the form. Close the database.

ACTIVITY 3-2

Using the Help feature, look up the definition of a subform and how it works. Write down a short definition and provide an example of a form and subform relationship used in a business setting. Be sure to mention the name of the field used to link the form and subform.

LESSON 4

FINDING AND ORDERING DATA

OBJECTIVES

Upon completion of this lesson, you should be able to:

- Find data in a database.
- Query a database.
- Use filters.
- Sort a database.
- Index a database.
- Establish relationships in a database.
- Create a query from related tables.

⏱ **Estimated Time: 1.5 hours**

VOCABULARY

And operator

Ascending sort

Descending sort

Filter

Indexing

Multitable query

One-to-many relationship

Or operator

Primary key

Query

Referential integrity

Relationship

Search criteria

Subdatasheet

Using Find

The Find command is the easiest way to quickly locate data in a database. The Find command allows you to search the database for specified information. There are several options that allow you flexibility in performing the search. These options appear in the Find and Replace dialog box, shown in Figure 4-1.

You can access the Find and Replace dialog box by choosing Find on the Edit menu or by clicking the Find button on the toolbar. The Find command is available only when a datasheet or form is displayed.

FIGURE 4-1
Find and Replace dialog box

To search for the data in a particular field, place your insertion point in the field you want to search and click the Find button. The Find and Replace dialog box opens with the Look In box containing the field name to search. Key the data for which you are searching in the Find What box.

The Match text box has a drop-down list that lets you choose what part of the field to search. If you want to match exactly the entire contents of a field, choose Whole Field. More commonly, however, you will not want to enter the field's entire contents. For example, if you are searching a database of books for titles relating to history, you might want to search for titles with the word *history* anywhere in the title. In that case, you would choose Any Part of Field from the list. You can also specify that the search look only at the first part of the field by choosing the Start of Field option. For example, if you need to search a table of names for people whose last name begins with *Mc*, the Start of Field option would be convenient.

Hot Tip

Use the Find command when searching for one record at a time. Use the Filter tool when searching for multiple records. You will learn about filters later in this lesson.

Click the drop-down arrow for the Search text box to display a list in which you can specify whether you want to search up from the current record position, down from the current record position, or the entire table. The Match Case check box gives you the option of a case-sensitive search. Click the Search Fields as Formatted check box to search a field that has been formatted with a data pattern, such as an Input Mask.

Click Find Next to display the next record that matches the criteria you've specified. When the entire database has been searched, a message appears stating that the search item was not found.

STEP-BY-STEP ▷ 4.1

1. Open **IA Step4-1** from the data files. This database includes a table of products. The products represent the inventory of a small office supply store.

2. Open the **Products** table in Datasheet view.

3. Place the insertion point in the **Product Name** field of the first record.

4. Click the **Find** button. The Find and Replace dialog box appears.

5. Key **Fax Machine** in the Find What box.

6. Be sure the **Product Name** field appears in the **Look In** box.

7. Click the down arrow to the right of the **Match** box and choose **Any Part of Field** from the list.

8. Be sure **All** appears in the **Search** box. The Match Case and Search Fields As Formatted options should not be selected.

9. Click the **Find Next** button. Product 32 is selected, as shown in Figure 4-2.

10. Click **Find Next** again. A message appears telling you that the search item was not found. There is only one fax machine in the product line. Click **OK**.

> **Find Next**

11. Click **Cancel** to close the Find and Replace dialog box.

12. Close the table and leave the database open for the next Step-by-Step.

FIGURE 4-2
Finding data

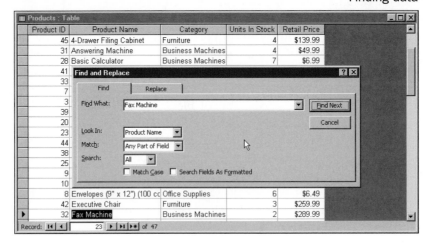

Using Queries

The Find command is an easy way of finding data. Often, however, you will need to locate data based on more complex criteria. For example, you may need to search for products with a value greater than $10. You cannot do that with the Find command. A special operation, called a *query*, will let you combine criteria to perform complex searches. For example, a query can locate products with a value greater than $10, of which fewer than three are in stock.

Queries allow you to "ask" the database almost anything about your data. In addition, you can create queries to display only the fields relevant to the search. For example, if you are querying a database of customers to locate those with a total purchased amount of $10,000 or more, you might want to display only the customers' names and total purchased amounts, rather than all the data in the table.

Creating a Query in Design View

The first step in creating a query is to open the appropriate database and click Queries on the Objects bar. Then click the New button to create a new query. The New Query dialog box appears, as shown in Figure 4-3. The New Query dialog box gives you the option of creating a query manually or using one of several Query Wizards. To create a query manually, use the Design View option in the New Query dialog box.

FIGURE 4-3
New Query dialog box

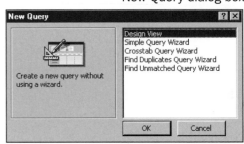

FIGURE 4-4
Show Table dialog box

STEP-BY-STEP ▷ 4.2

1. Click **Queries** on the Objects bar.

2. Click the **New** button. The New Query dialog box appears, as shown in Figure 4-3.

3. Choose **Design View**, if it is not already selected, and click **OK**. The Show Table dialog box appears from which you select a table to query, as shown in Figure 4-4. Leave the Show Table dialog box on the screen for the next Step-by-Step.

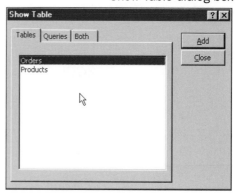

Because databases often include more than one table, you can choose the table you want to use in the Show Table dialog box. The Add button adds the fields from the highlighted table to your new query. After choosing a table and adding fields, click Close to close the Show Table dialog box. The fields you added now appear in a dialog box in the top pane of the query's design window, as shown in Figure 4-5.

The query window is divided into two parts. The top part of the window shows the available tables and fields (the Products table and its fields are shown in Figure 4-5).

FIGURE 4-5
Query window

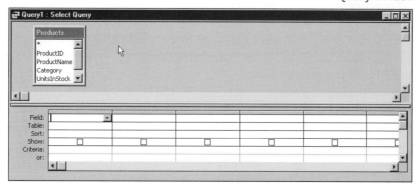

The bottom part of the window contains a grid that allows you to specify the information needed to create a query. To create a query, you must supply three pieces of information: the fields you want to search, what you are searching for (called the ***search criteria***), and what fields you want to display with the results. The Field row is where you select a field to be part of the query. Click the down arrow to display the available fields. To include more than one field in a query, click in the next column of the Field row and choose another field.

The Sort row allows you to sort the results of the query. The Show checkbox determines whether the field is to be displayed in the query results. Normally, this will be checked. Occasionally, however, you may want to search by a field that does not need to appear in the query results.

For the fields you want to search, enter search conditions in the Criteria row. For example, if you want to find only records that contain the words *Office Supplies* in the Category field, you would key

"Office Supplies" into the Criteria row of the Category field. When keying text into the *Criteria* row, always enclose it with quotation marks.

You can refine a search by using operators. For example, you might want to find all employees in a database table who make more than $30,000 a year, or you might want to search an inventory table for products of which there are less than five in stock. You can use the relational operators listed in Table 4-1 to conduct these types of searches.

TABLE 4-1
Relational operators

OPERATOR	DESCRIPTION
>	Greater than
<	Less than
=	Equal to
>=	Greater than or equal to
<=	Less than or equal to
<>	Not equal

You can also use the *And* or the *Or* operators. If you want to find records that meet more than one criteria, such as employees who make more than $30,000 a year *and* who have been with the company for less than two years, you would use the ***And operator***. Simply enter the criteria in the same Criteria row for the fields you want to search.

If you want to find records that meet one criteria or another, you would use the ***Or operator***. Enter the criteria in different rows for the fields you want to search.

After choosing the fields and entering search criteria, you should save the query by choosing Save on the File menu and keying in a name for the query. To run a query, click the Run button in the query's Design view. Or, you can run a query directly from the Database window. Select the query, and then click the Open button.

Hot Tip

To modify a query, open it in Design view. You can change the fields to be searched, the search criteria, and the fields to be displayed in the query results.

S TEP-BY-STEP ▷ 4.3

1. With the **Products** table selected in the Show Table dialog box, click **Add**. The fields of the *Products* table appear in the query window. Click **Close** to close the Show Table dialog box.

2. In the query grid, click the down arrow in the **Field** row of the first column and choose **ProductName**, as shown in Figure 4-6.

FIGURE 4-6
Selecting fields to query

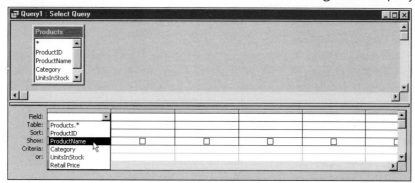

3. Click the in the **Field** row of the second column, click the down arrow, and choose **UnitsInStock** from the menu.

4. In the **Criteria** row of the **Units in Stock** column, key **<3**. This tells Access to display any records with fewer than 3 items in stock.

5. In the third column, choose the **Retail Price** field.

6. In the **Field** row of the fourth column, key **[Retail Price]*.90**.

7. Click in the **Table** row, click the down arrow, and choose **Products**.

8. Click in the **Field** row again and highlight **Expr1**. Replace *Expr1* by keying **Discount Price**. (Microsoft Access enters the default field name Expr1. Unless replaced by a more appropriate name this is the column heading you will see in Datasheet view.)

9. With the cursor in the Discount Price field box, right-click and choose **Properties** on the shortcut menu. The Field Properties dialog box will display.

10. Click in the **Format** box on the General tab, click the down arrow, and scroll down to click **Currency**. Close the dialog box.

11. Choose **Save** on the **File** menu. You are prompted for a name for the query.

12. Key in **Reorder Query** and click **OK**.

13. Choose **Close** on the **File** menu.

14. To run the query, highlight **Reorder Query** in the Database window and click **Open**. The results of the query appear, as shown in Figure 4-7.

FIGURE 4-7
Running a query

Reorder Query : Select Query			
Product Name	Units In Stock	Retail Price	Discount Price
Heavy Duty Stapler	2	$16.99	$15.29
Letter Sorter	2	$7.99	$7.19
Speaker Phone	2	$99.99	$89.99
Fax Machine	2	$289.99	$260.99
Cash Register	0	$269.99	$242.99
Photocopier	1	$699.00	$629.10
Typewriter	2	$129.99	$116.99
Computer Desk	2	$299.00	$269.10
Oak Office Desk	1	$399.00	$359.10
Bookshelf	2	$99.99	$89.99
Guest Chair	2	$159.00	$143.10

15. Choose **Print** on the **File** menu to print the table with the query applied. Click **OK**.

16. Choose **Close** on the **File** menu to close the results of the query. Leave the database open for the next Step-by-Step.

Hot Tip

You can display the down arrow menu in one step by clicking on the right side of the cell that you are accessing.

Using the Simple Query Wizard

You can also create a query using the Simple Query Wizard. The Simple Query Wizard asks you questions and then create a query based upon your answers. When creating a query using the wizard, you do not have as many options to choose from as when you create a query in Design view. For instance, you can choose the fields to display, but you cannot sort, group, or specify search criteria. To access the Simple Query Wizard, choose Queries on the Objects bar and then click New. In the New Query dialog box, choose Simple Query Wizard. Click OK and follow the screens to create the query.

Did You Know?

You can save a table, form, or query as a data access page, which allows you to view the database using the Web. To save an object as a data access page, choose **Save As** on the **File** menu. The Save As dialog box appears. Key the name of the data access page and choose **Data Access Page** as the type. Click **OK**.

1. Click **Queries** on the Objects bar.

2. Click the **New** button. The New Query dialog box appears.

3. Choose **Simple Query Wizard** and click **OK**. The Simple Query Wizard dialog box appears, as shown in Figure 4-8.

4. Click the down arrow on the **Tables/Queries** box and choose **Table: Products**. The fields from the Products table will appear in the Available Fields list.

5. In the Available Fields list, choose **ProductID** and click **>**. The field name will appear in the Selected Fields list.

6. Do the same for the **ProductName** and **Category** fields.

7. Click **Next**. The Simple Query Wizard dialog box changes to ask if you would like a detail or summary query. Choose **Detail** if not already selected.

8. Click **Next**. The Simple Query Wizard dialog box changes to ask you for a title, as shown in Figure 4-9.

FIGURE 4-8
Simple Query Wizard dialog box

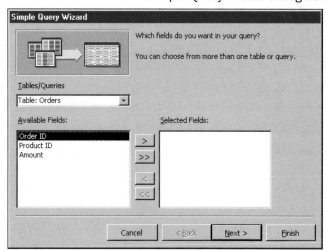

FIGURE 4-9
Keying a title for the query

9. If not already there, key **Products Query**. Be sure the option to open the query and view the information is selected.

10. Click **Finish**. The results of the query appear.

11. Choose **Print** on the **File** menu to print the results of the query. Click **OK**.

12. Choose **Close** on the **File** menu to close the results of the query. Leave the database open for the next Step-by-Step.

C ▷ Filters

Queries are very powerful and flexible tools. In many cases, however, less power is adequate. *Filters* provide a way to display selected records in a database more easily than using queries. Think of a filter as a simpler form of a query. A filter "filters out" the records that do not match the specified criteria. When you use a filter, all of the fields are displayed and the filter cannot be saved for use again later.

There are four types of filters: Filter By Form, Filter By Selection, Filter Excluding Selection, and Advanced Filter/Sort. The Filter By Form allows you to select records by keying the criteria into a form. To use Filter By Selection (the fastest and easiest option), you highlight a value or part of a value in a field as the criteria for the selection. The Filter Excluding Selection excludes the value you highlight as the criteria for the selection. To duplicate a query or create a more complicated selection use the Advanced Filter/Sort option.

To create a filter, a table must be open. Select Filter on the Records menu and then select one of the filter types from the submenu. If you select the Advanced Filter/Sort option, a Filter window like the one in Figure 4-10 appears. Notice that the Filter window is very similar to the query window. (Since there is only one table in this database, it's automatically added to the top part of the window.) Also notice that there is no *Show* row in the grid—all fields are displayed when you use a filter. In the grid, you select only those fields for which you want to enter criteria. When you have included all of the field specifications, choose Apply Filter/Sort on the Filter menu or click the Apply Filter button on the toolbar.

FIGURE 4-10
Design view for an advanced filter

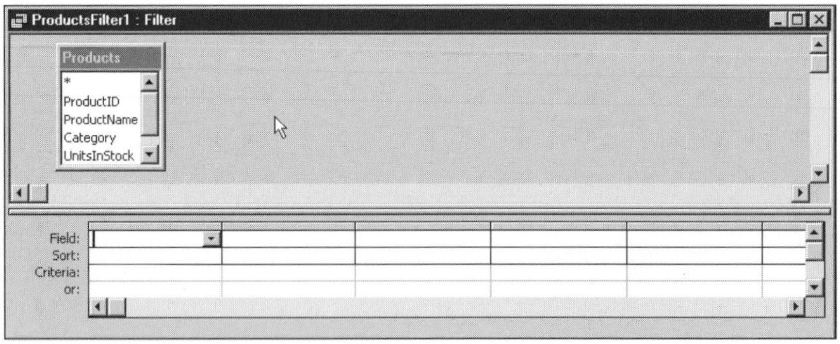

If you select Filter by Form, only the field names in the datasheet are displayed. When you click in a field, the filter arrow appears, as shown in Figure 4-11. Click the arrow and choose a data value from the list of all data values entered in the field. When finished, apply the filter. To create a filter by Selection you must first highlight the criteria in the table. Click Filter by Selection on the submenu and the filtered records display.

FIGURE 4-11
Filter by form

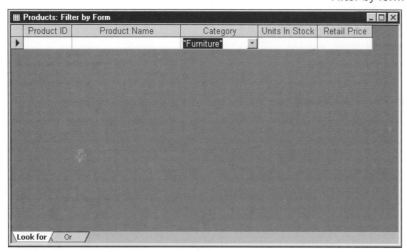

S TEP-BY-STEP ▷ 4.5

1. In the Database window, click **Tables** on the Objects bar.

2. Open the **Products** table in Datasheet view.

3. Choose **Filter** on the **Records** menu, then select **Advanced Filter/Sort** on the submenu. The Filter window appears, as shown in Figure 4-10.

4. Click the down arrow in the **Field** row of the first column and choose **Category** from the menu.

5. Key **"Furniture"** in the **Criteria** field of the first column. Include the quotation marks.

6. Click the **Apply Filter** button on the toolbar. The filter is applied, and only the products in the Furniture category are displayed, as shown in Figure 4-12.

7. Print the table with the filter applied.

FIGURE 4-12
A filter displaying the Furniture category

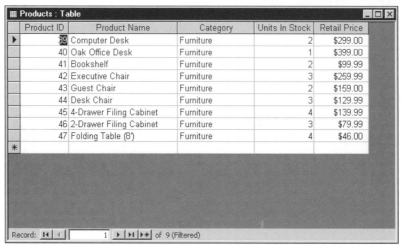

8. Click the **Remove Filter** button to remove the filter and display all records.

9. Choose **Filter** on the **Records** menu, then select **Filter by Form** on the submenu. A form appears, as shown in Figure 4-11.

10. Click the down arrow in the **Category** field. (Furniture was the criteria in the previous filter.)

11. Choose **Desk Accessories** from the list of options.

12. Click the **Apply Filter** button on the toolbar. The filter is applied, and only the products in the Desk Accessories category are displayed, as shown in Figure 4-13.

13. Print the table with the filter applied.

14. Click the **Remove Filter** button.

15. To create a Filter by Selection, highlight the word **Calculator** in the **Product Name** field for Product ID27.

16. Choose **Filter** on the **Records** menu, then select **Filter by Selection** on the submenu. The filter is applied, and only the calculator products are displayed, as shown in Figure 4-14.

17. Print the table with the filter applied.

18. Click the **Remove Filter** button. Leave the table on the screen for the next Step-by-Step.

FIGURE 4-13
A filter displaying the Desk Accessories category

Product ID	Product Name	Category	Units In Stock	Retail Price
22	Letter Tray	Desk Accessories	4	$2.99
23	Desk Accessory Set	Desk Accessories	3	$21.99
24	Letter Sorter	Desk Accessories	2	$7.99
25	Drawer Tray	Desk Accessories	5	$3.49
26	Rotary Card File	Desk Accessories	3	$25.99

FIGURE 4-14
A filter displaying the calculator products

Product ID	Product Name	Category	Units In Stock	Retail Price
27	Scientific Calculator	Business Machines	3	$19.98
28	Basic Calculator	Business Machines	7	$6.99
29	Printing Calculator	Business Machines	3	$29.99

Sorting

Sorting is an important part of working with a database. Often you will need records to appear in a specific order. For example, you may normally want a mailing list sorted by last name. But when preparing to mail literature to the entire mailing list, you may need the records to appear in ZIP code order. Access provides buttons on the toolbar to quickly sort the records of a table.

To sort a table, open the table and place the insertion point in the field by which you want to sort. Then click either the Sort Ascending or Sort Descending button. An ***ascending sort*** arranges records from A to Z or smallest to largest. A ***descending sort*** arranges records from Z to A or largest to smallest.

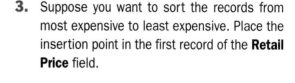

STEP-BY-STEP 4.6

1. The **Products** table should be open in Datasheet view. Suppose you want to sort the records from least in stock to most in stock. Place the insertion point in the first record of the **UnitsInStock** field.

2. Click the **Sort Ascending** button. The records appear in order by Units In Stock.

3. Suppose you want to sort the records from most expensive to least expensive. Place the insertion point in the first record of the **Retail Price** field.

4. Click the **Sort Descending** button. The products are sorted from most to least expensive.

5. Print the table and leave it open for the next Step-by-Step.

Sorting using the Sort Ascending and Sort Descending buttons is quick and easy. However, you will sometimes need to sort by more than one field. For example, suppose you want to sort the Products table by Category, but within each category you want the items to appear from most to least expensive. To perform this kind of sort, you must create a filter.

To use a filter to sort, create a filter as you normally do, but select an ascending or descending sort for the desired field or fields by clicking the down arrow in the Sort row. If the filter window has information left over from a previous sort or filter, you may need to click the cells with existing data and press the Backspace key to clear them.

STEP-BY-STEP 4.7

1. Choose **Filter** on the **Records** menu, and then choose **Advanced Filter/Sort** on the submenu.

2. Choose the **Category** and **Retail Price** fields as shown in Figure 4-15. Click the down arrow in the *Sort* row and choose **Ascending** for the Category field, and **Descending** for the Retail Price field. You may need to clear some existing data from the filter window.

3. Click the **Apply Filter** button.

4. Scroll through the datasheet to see that the records have been sorted according to the specifications in the filter.

5. Print the table with the filter applied. Leave the table and filter window open for the next Step-by-Step.

FIGURE 4-15
Sorting by more than one field

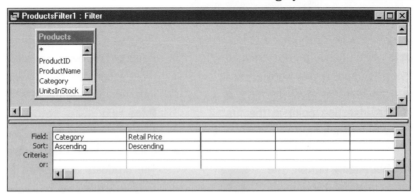

To filter and sort at the same time, add the information for both to the same filter window. Choose Filter on the Records menu and select Advanced/Filter Sort. In the Filter window select the field to which you want to apply a filter and the field to be sorted. Click the Apply Filter button on the toolbar.

S TEP-BY-STEP ▷ 4.8

1. Choose **Filter** on the **Records** menu, and then choose **Advanced Filter/Sort** on the submenu.

2. Suppose you want to display only the products with a retail price greater than $150. Key **>150** in the **Criteria** row of the **Retail Price** column. Leave the Category column as is.

3. Click the **Apply Filter** button. Only seven of the records meet the filter criteria and they

are sorted by retail price within the categories, as shown in Figure 4-16.

4. Print the table with the filter applied.

5. Click the **Remove Filter** button to remove the filter. All of the records appear again.

6. Close the table. If prompted to save the design of the table, click **No**. Leave the database open for the next Step-by-Step.

FIGURE 4-16
Filtering and sorting records

Product ID	Product Name	Category	Units In Stock	Retail Price
34	Photocopier	Business Machines	1	$699.00
32	Fax Machine	Business Machines	2	$289.99
33	Cash Register	Business Machines	0	$269.99
40	Oak Office Desk	Furniture	1	$399.00
39	Computer Desk	Furniture	2	$299.00
42	Executive Chair	Furniture	3	$259.99
43	Guest Chair	Furniture	2	$159.00

Record: 1 of 7 (Filtered)

Indexing

Indexing is an important part of database management systems. In small databases, indexes do not provide much benefit. Large databases, however, rely on indexing to quickly locate data. In an Access database, you can specify that certain fields be indexed. Access can find data in an indexed field faster than it can find data in a field that is not indexed.

For each field in Design view, you can specify whether you want the field to be indexed. To index a field, go to Design view and choose Yes for Indexed in the Field Properties section.

If indexing improves speed, why not index all of the fields? The reason is that each indexed field causes more work and uses more disk space. Before indexing a database, you should be sure that the benefit of indexing a field outweighs the negatives caused by indexing. As a general rule, index fields only in large databases, and index only those fields that are regularly used to locate records.

Setting a Primary Key

When you save a newly created table in a database, a message appears asking if you want to create a *primary key*, which is a special field that assigns a unique identifier to each record. You can have Access create the primary key for you, in which case each record is automatically assigned a unique number. Or, you can set the primary key to an existing field within the table. The existing field should contain a unique value such as an ID number or part number. Primary keys must be set before creating table relationships, which are covered in the next section.

To designate a field as the primary key, open the table in Design view. Choose the field you want to set as the primary key by clicking the row selector. Click the Primary Key button on the toolbar. A primary key icon now appears next to the primary key field.

S TEP-BY-STEP ▷ 4.9

1. In the **IA Step4-1** database, open the **Products** table in **Design** view.

2. Click the **row selector** for the **Product ID** field.

3. Click the **Primary Key** button on the toolbar. A key icon appears next to the **ProductID** field, as shown in Figure 4-17. Click the row selector for the field below to view the icon more clearly.

4. Close the table and a message appears asking you to save changes to the table. Click **Yes**. Leave the database open for the next Step-by-Step.

FIGURE 4-17
Setting the primary key

Field Name	Data Type	Description
ProductID	AutoNumber	
ProductName	Text	
Category	Text	
UnitsInStock	Number	
Retail Price	Currency	

Relationships

C

By defining **relationships** between the different tables within a database, you can create queries, forms, and reports to display information from several tables at once. You can create a relationship between tables that contain a common field. For example, you might have a table that contains the name, telephone number, and other data on real estate agents. A second table might contain information including the name of the listing agent or properties for sale. You could set up a relationship between the two tables by joining the fields containing the agents' names. Then you could create forms, queries, and reports that include fields from both tables.

The common fields must be of the same data type, although they can have different field names. In most relationships, the common field is also the primary key in at least one of the tables. It is referred to as the foreign key in the other table(s).

To ensure valid relationships between tables and prevent invalid data from being entered, Access utilizes **referential integrity** rules. These also help ensure that related data is not accidentally deleted or changed. To enforce referential integrity between tables, choose the Enforce Referential Integrity option when creating the relationship. If you break one of the rules with the related tables, Access displays a message and doesn't allow the change.

A **one-to-many relationship**, as illustrated in Figure 4-18, is the most common type of relationship. In a one-to-many relationship, a record in Table A can have matching records in Table B, but a record in Table B has only one matching record in Table A. In Figure 4-18, the ProductID field is the primary key in the Products table and the foreign key in the Orders table.

FIGURE 4-18
One-to-many relationship

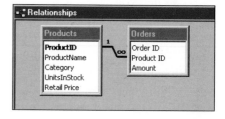

You define a relationship by clicking Relationships on the Tools menu or clicking the Relationships button on the toolbar. Add the tables you want to relate to the Relationships window. Next, drag the key field from one table to the key field in the other table.

STEP-BY-STEP ▷ 4.10

C

1. The **IA Step4-1** Database window should still be open. Click **Relationships** on the **Tools** menu or click the **Relationships** button on the toolbar. If the Show Table dialog box does not appear, as shown in Figure 4-19, click **Show Table** on the **Relationships** menu.

2. Choose the **Products** table and click **Add**. Repeat this step for the **Orders** table.

FIGURE 4-19
Show Table dialog box

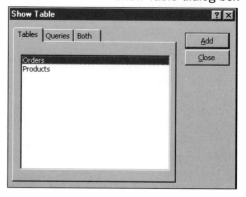

3. When finished, click **Close**. The Relationships window should appear as shown in Figure 4-20.

4. Click the **ProductID** field in the **Products** table. Drag and drop it on the **Product ID** field in the **Orders** table. (*Remember:* The common fields don't have to have the same field name; they just need to be of the same data type.) The Edit Relationships dialog box will appear as shown in Figure 4-21.

5. Check to be sure the Product ID field appears for both the Products and Orders tables. Click the **Enforce Referential Integrity** check box.

6. Click **Create**. The Relationships window appears as shown in Figure 4-22.

7. Close the Relationships window and a message appears asking if you want to save changes to the layout of Relationships. Click **Yes** to save the changes. Leave the database open for the next Step-by-Step.

FIGURE 4-20
Relationships window

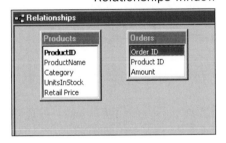

FIGURE 4-21
Edit Relationships dialog box

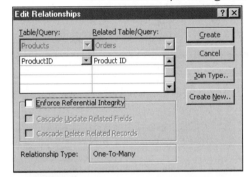

FIGURE 4-22
Table relationships

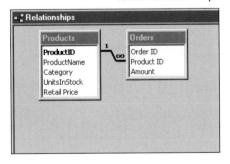

To print a database relationship, click Relationships on the Tools menu to display the Relationships window. Click Print Relationships on the File menu and a report listing the table relationships will display. Choose Print on the File menu or save the report for future reference.

1. With the **IA Step4-1** Database window open, click **Relationships** on the **Tools** menu. The Relationships window appears (see Figure 4-22).

2. Click **Print Relationships** on the **File** menu. A report listing the table relationships will display as shown in Figure 4-23.

3. Click **Print** on the **File** menu and the Print dialog box appears. Click **OK** to print the report.

4. Close the Report window. A message displays asking if you want to save changes to the design of the report. Click **No**.

5. Close the Relationships window. Leave the database open for the next Step-by-Step.

Viewing Related Records

To view the related records between two tables you can add a *subdatasheet*. To insert a subdatasheet, open the table with the primary key in Datasheet view, and choose Subdatasheet on the Insert menu. In the Insert Subdatasheet window, choose the related table and click OK. The table with the primary key will reappear. Click the expand indicator icon (+) to the left of each row to display a subdatasheet of related records.

FIGURE 4-23
Table relationships report

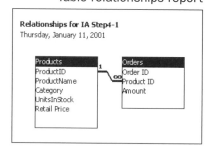

1. Open the **Products** table in Datasheet view.

2. Click **Subdatasheet** on the **Insert** menu. The Insert Subdatasheet dialog box will appear as shown in Figure 4-24.

3. Choose the **Orders** table and click **OK**. The Products table will reappear.

4. Click the expand indicator button (**+**) to the left of Product ID number **3** to display a subdatasheet of related records as shown in Figure 4-25.

5. Click the indicator button again to close the subdatasheet. Close the **Products** table. A message displays asking if you want to save

the changes to the Products table. Click **Yes** to save. Leave the database open for the next Step-by-Step.

FIGURE 4-24
Insert Subdatasheet dialog box

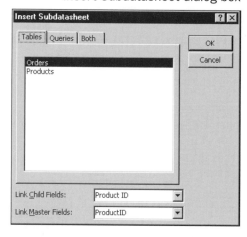

FIGURE 4-25
Subdatasheet of related records

		Product ID	Product Name	Category	Units In Stock	Retail Price
▶	+	1	Stick-On Notes	Office Supplies	112	$4.59
	+	2	Laser Paper (8.5" x 11")	Office Supplies	36	$22.99
	−	3	Colored paper assortment	Office Supplies	8	$5.99

	Order ID	Amount
	10002	3
	10003	4
✱	0	0

		Product ID	Product Name	Category	Units In Stock	Retail Price
	+	4	Fax paper	Office Supplies	7	$5.99
	+	5	Legal Pads (4 pack)	Office Supplies	21	$2.49
	+	6	Quadrille Pads (2 pack)	Office Supplies	9	$1.79
	+	7	Clipboard	Office Supplies	3	$1.29
	+	8	Envelopes (9" x 12") (100 cc	Office Supplies	6	$6.49
	+	9	Envelopes #10 (500 count)	Office Supplies	11	$11.99
	+	10	Envelopes #6.75	Office Supplies	5	$7.99
	+	11	3-ring binders (1")	Office Supplies	18	$1.49
	+	12	3-ring binders (2")	Office Supplies	9	$2.99
	+	13	File folders (1/3 cut) (100 co	Office Supplies	14	$6.49
	+	14	Standard Stapler	Office Supplies	6	$7.49

Record: ◀◀ ◀ 1 ▶ ▶◀ ▶✱ of 47

Creating a Multitable Query

After defining relationships in a database, you can create a ***multitable query*** to display the shared information from the related tables at once. For example, you might want to view customer information with the orders placed by the customers. To do this you would need data from both the Customers and Orders tables.

Except for a few additional steps, you will create a multitable query using the same procedure you've used to create queries. After opening the appropriate database, choose Queries on the Objects bar, and then click the New button to create a new query. The New Query dialog box appears. Choose the Design View option to create a query manually. In the Show Table dialog box, choose to add the related tables to the query. The fields in the related tables will appear in small boxes in the top part of the Select Query window, as shown in Figure 4-26.

In the lower pane of the query window, specify the information needed from both tables to create the query. After choosing the fields and entering the search criteria, save the query.

FIGURE 4-26
Query window

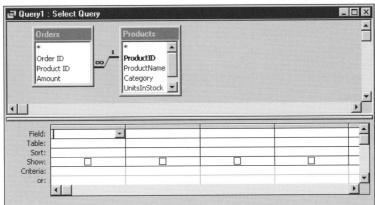

1. Click **Queries** on the Objects bar. Click the **New** button. The New Query dialog box appears.

2. Choose **Design View**, if it is not already selected, and click **OK**. The Show Table dialog box appears to allow you to choose the related tables for the query.

3. Select the **Orders** table, if necessary, and then click **Add**. The fields of the Orders table appear in the query window.

4. Select **Products** in the Show Table dialog box and click **Add**. The fields of the Products table appear in the query window.

5. Close the **Show Table** dialog box. The query window should look like Figure 4-26.

6. Click the down arrow in the **Field** row of the first column and choose **Orders.Order ID**, as shown in Figure 4-27.

7. Click the down arrow in the **Field** row of the second column and choose **Orders.Product ID**.

8. In the third column, choose **Products.Product Name**.

9. In the fourth column, choose **Orders.Amount**.

10. In the fifth column, choose **Products.Retail Price**.

11. Choose **Save** on the **File** menu, and enter **Invoice Query** as the name for the query. Click **OK**.

12. Click the **Run** button. The results of the query appear, as shown in Figure 4-28.

FIGURE 4-27
Select fields to display in the query results

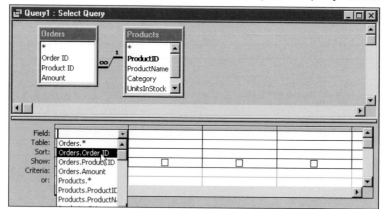

STEP-BY-STEP 4.13 CONTINUED

13. Choose **Print** on the **File** menu to print the table with the query applied. Click **OK**.

14. Choose **Close** on the **File** menu to close the query. Close the database.

FIGURE 4-28
Results of a multitable query

Invoice Query : Select Query

Order ID	Product ID	Product Name	Amount	Retail Price
10000	10	Envelopes #6.75	2	$7.99
10001	31	Answering Machine	1	$49.99
10001	24	Letter Sorter	1	$7.99
10002	46	2-Drawer Filing Cabinet	1	$79.99
10002	11	3-ring binders (1")	10	$1.49
10002	3	Colored paper assortment	3	$5.99
10003	25	Drawer Tray	2	$3.49
10003	17	3-hole punch	1	$9.99
10003	3	Colored paper assortment	4	$5.99
10004	32	Fax Machine	1	$289.99
10004	20	Date Stamp	2	$2.49
10005	26	Rotary Card File	1	$25.99
10005	4	Fax paper	3	$5.99

Record: 1 of 13

Summary

I n this lesson, you learned:

■ The Find command is the easiest way to locate data in the database. The Find command searches the database for specified information.

■ Queries allow more complex searches. A query allows you to search records using multiple and complex criteria and allows you to display selected fields. You can save a query and apply it again later.

■ A filter is similar to a query; however, it displays all fields and cannot be saved. A filter can be used to sort records, or records can be sorted directly in a table without the use of a filter. Using a filter to sort records allows you to sort by more than one criterion.

■ Indexing is an important part of database management systems. Indexing allows records to be located quickly, especially in large databases.

■ By defining relationships between the different tables within a database, you can create queries, forms, and reports to display information from several tables at once. Matching data in key fields sets up a relationship.

VOCABULARY REVIEW

Define the following terms:

And operator	Multitable query	Referential integrity
Ascending sort	One-to-many relationship	Relationship
Descending sort	Or operator	Search criteria
Filter	Primary key	Subdatasheet
Indexing	Query	

LESSON 4 REVIEW QUESTIONS

TRUE/FALSE

Circle the T if the statement is true or F if the statement is false.

T F 1. The Find command can search for data in all fields.

T F 2. The Find Next button in the Find dialog box finds the next record that matches the criteria you've specified.

T F 3. A query automatically displays all fields in the table.

T F 4. Filters cannot be saved for later use.

T F 5. An ascending sort arranges records from Z to A.

WRITTEN QUESTIONS

Write a brief answer to the following questions.

1. What is the easiest way to quickly locate data in a database?

2. What are the three pieces of information you must supply when creating a query?

3. What menu is used to access the command that creates a filter?

4. What button is used to sort records from largest to smallest?

5. What view allows you to index a field?

LESSON 4 PROJECTS

PROJECT 4-1

1. Open the **IA Project4-1** database file from the data files.

2. Open the **Houses** table in Datasheet view.

3. Use the **Find** command to locate the first house with wood exterior.

4. Use the **Find** command to locate any remaining houses with wood exterior.

5. Close the table.

6. Create a query that displays houses with two bedrooms. Have the query display only the Address, Bedrooms, and Price fields. Save the query as **2 Bedrooms**.

7. Run the query and print the results. Close the query. Leave the database open for the next project.

PROJECT 4-2

1. Open the **Houses** table in the **IA Project4-1** database in Datasheet view.

2. Sort the table so that the houses are displayed from most expensive to least expensive.

3. Change the column width to **Best Fit** for all the columns.

4. Print the results of the sort in landscape orientation.

5. Create a filter to display only the houses listed with **Brad Gray** as the agent. You do not have to sort the records.

6. Print the results of the filter in landscape orientation.

7. Remove the filter to show all the records in the table. Leave the database open for the next project.

PROJECT 4-3

1. With the **Houses** table in the **IA Project4-1** database open, create a filter that displays three-bedroom houses only, sorted from least to most expensive.

2. Print the results of the filter in landscape orientation.

3. Remove the filter to show all records in the table.

4. Create a filter that displays only houses with two-car garages and brick exterior.

5. Print the results of the filter in landscape orientation.

6. Remove the filter to show all records in the table. Leave the database open for the next project.

PROJECT 4-4

1. With the **Houses** table in the **IA Project4-1** database open, use the **Find** command to locate the houses that were listed during December.

2. Create a query that displays the houses listed with **Nina Bertinelli** or **John Schultz** as the agent. Have the query display only the **Address**, **List Date**, **Price**, and **Agent** fields and sort the **Price** field from most to least expensive. Save the query as **Bertinelli/Schultz**.

3. Run the query and print the results. Close the query.

4. Open the **Houses** table and create a filter that sorts the houses from most to least bathrooms and the price from least to most expensive.

5. Print the results of the filter in landscape orientation.

6. Remove the filter to show all records in the table.

7. Close the table and the database.

CRITICAL THINKING

ACTIVITY 4-1

You are a Realtor with three new clients who are ready to buy homes. List on paper each client's requirements in a home. For example, Buyer #1 might want a three-bedroom house with a brick exterior and the maximum price is $90,000.

Using the **IA Project4-1** database and the **Houses** table, create a filter or query to locate the information for each client and print the results.

ACTIVITY 4-2

Referential integrity is a set of rules that Access uses to check for valid relationships between tables. It also ensures that related data is not accidentally deleted or changed. Using the Help system, determine the conditions that must be met before you can enforce referential integrity. Write a brief essay that explains the importance of referential integrity in a relational database and why users of the database objects would benefit from it.

REPORTS AND MACROS

OBJECTIVES

Upon completion of this lesson, you should be able to:

- Create a report using a Report Wizard.
- Modify a report.
- Create and run a macro.

⏱ **Estimated Time: 1.5 hours**

VOCABULARY

Database report

Grouping

Macro

Reports

Databases can become large as records are added. Printing the database from Datasheet view may not always be the most desirable way to put the data on paper. Creating a *database report* allows you to organize, summarize, and print all or a portion of the data in a database. You can even use reports to print form letters and mailing labels. Figure 5-1 shows two examples of database reports. Database reports are compiled by creating a report object.

FIGURE 5-1
Database reports

Employees by Department

Department	Last Name	First Name	Salary
Advertising			
	Abernathy	Mark	$2,375.00
	Barton	Brad	$2,590.00
	Denton	Scott	$2,600.00
	Doss	Derek	$2,200.00
Marketing			
	Martinez	Christine	$1,780.00
	Powell	Lynne	$2,970.00
	Powers	Sarah	$1,500.00
Personnel			
	Davis	Lee	$2,680.00
Public Relations			
	Smith	Shawna	$2,950.00
Sales			
	Best	Trent	$2,600.00
	Broach	Margie	$2,450.00
	Collins	Greg	$2,750.00
	Collins	Dave	$2,620.00
	Davis	Hillary	$2,620.00
	Sims	Jennifer	$1,550.00
	West	Debbie	$3,100.00

Page 1 of 1

Products by Units in Stock — Tiffany Matthews

UnitsInStock	Product Name	Product ID	Category	Retail Price
0	Cash Register	33	Business Machines	$229.00
1	Oak Office Desk	40	Furniture	$399.00
	Photocopier	34	Business Machines	$599.00
2	Bookshelf	41	Furniture	$89.99
	Computer Desk	39	Furniture	$299.00
	Fax Machine	32	Business Machines	$249.99
	Guest Chair	43	Furniture	$199.00
	Heavy Duty Stapler	15	Office Supplies	$19.99
	Letter Sorter	24	Desk Accessories	$7.99
	Speaker Phone	30	Business Machines	$99.99
	Typewriter	35	Business Machines	$149.99
3	2-Drawer Filing Cabinet	46	Furniture	$89.99
	Clipboard	7	Office Supplies	$0.99
	Desk Accessory Set	23	Desk Accessories	$17.99
	Desk Chair	44	Furniture	$189.99
	Executive Chair	42	Furniture	$259.99
	Printing Calculator	29	Business Machines	$29.99
	Rotary Card File	26	Desk Accessories	$24.99
	Scientific Calculator	27	Business Machines	$19.98
	Surge Protector	37	Computer Supplies	$19.99
4	4-Drawer Filing Cabinet	45	Furniture	$149.99
	Answering Machine	31	Business Machines	$49.99
	Disk Storage Box	38	Computer Supplies	$6.99
	Folding Table (8')	47	Furniture	$44.99
	Letter Tray	22	Desk Accessories	$2.99
	Scissors	16	Office Supplies	$2.99
	Tape Dispenser	19	Office Supplies	$5.99
5	Drawer Tray	25	Desk Accessories	$2.99
	Envelopes #6.75	10	Office Supplies	$7.99
6	Envelopes (9" x 12") (10	8	Office Supplies	$5.99
	Standard Stapler	14	Office Supplies	$7.99
7	3-hole punch	17	Office Supplies	$9.99
	Basic Calculator	28	Business Machines	$3.99
	Date Stamp	20	Office Supplies	$1.99
	Fax paper	4	Office Supplies	$5.49
8	Colored paper assortme	3	Office Supplies	$4.99
9	3-ring binders (2")	12	Office Supplies	$2.99
	3.5" HD Diskettes (Box o	36	Computer Supplies	$8.99

Page 1 of 2

Printing a database from Datasheet view is a form of a report. Printing from Datasheet view, however, offers you much less flexibility than creating a report and printing it. In this lesson, you will learn how to create report objects.

Creating a Report

The report database object lets you create reports that include selected fields, groups of records, and even calculations. As with other Access objects, you can create a report object manually or use the Report Wizard. In this lesson, you will create a report using the Report Wizard.

To create a report, click Reports on the Objects bar and click the New button. The New Report dialog box appears, as shown in Figure 5-2.

In the New Report dialog box, choose the method to create the report. To use a Report Wizard, choose Report Wizard from the list. Click the down arrow to select the table or query Access will use to create a report. Choose a table if you want to include the entire table in the report. Choose a query to include only certain data in the report. In many cases, you will want to create a query before creating a report.

FIGURE 5-2
New Report dialog box

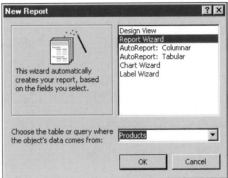

STEP-BY-STEP ▷ 5.1

1. Open **IA Step5-1** from the data files.

2. Click the **Reports** button on the Objects bar.

3. Click **New**. The New Report dialog box appears, as shown in Figure 5-2.

4. Choose **Report Wizard** from the list.

5. Click the down arrow and choose the table **Products** from the drop-down list. Click **OK**. The Report Wizard dialog box appears, as shown in Figure 5-3. Leave the Report Wizard dialog box on the screen for the next Step-by-Step.

FIGURE 5-3
Starting the Report Wizard

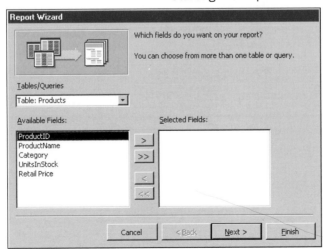

CHOOSING FIELDS FOR THE REPORT

Select fields for the report in the Report Wizard dialog box shown in Figure 5-3. You can select fields the same way you did when creating a form using the Form Wizard.

STEP-BY-STEP ▷ 5.2

1. Highlight **ProductName** in the Available Fields list. Click **>**. The ProductName field is now listed in the Selected Fields box.

2. The Category field is now highlighted in the Available Fields list. Click **>** three times to move the **Category**, **UnitsInStock**, and **Retail Price** fields to the Selected Fields box. Your screen should appear similar to Figure 5-4.

3. Click **Next**. The Report Wizard now gives you the option to group the report. Leave the Report Wizard dialog box on the screen for the next Step-by-Step.

FIGURE 5-4
Choosing fields

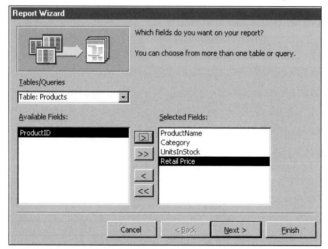

GROUPING AND SORTING THE REPORT

Grouping a report allows you to break it into parts based on the contents of a field. For example, you could organize a customers report into parts that group the customers by city. In the report you are creating now, you will group the report by product category. To group a report, choose the field(s) you want grouped from the Report Wizard dialog box shown in Figure 5-5.

Hot Tip

The >> button moves all fields in the Available Fields list to the Selected Fields list.

FIGURE 5-5
Grouping a report by fields

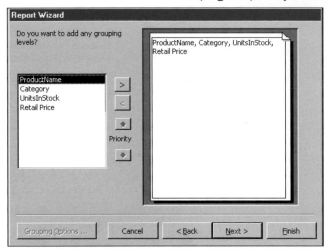

You can group by more than one field. When you group by more than one field, however, you must prioritize the fields. For example, you could group customers by state first, then by city within each state.

Sorting the report goes hand-in-hand with grouping. The dialog box shown in Figure 5-6 allows you to specify fields by which the report will be sorted. As you can see, you can sort by multiple fields. Sorting orders the records in a group based on the chosen field(s). For example, you could group a customers report by city and then sort it by company name. The records for each city would be listed in alphabetic order by company name.

FIGURE 5-6
Sorting a report

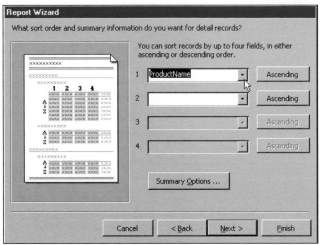

1. Highlight **Category** and click **>**. Your screen should appear similar to Figure 5-7.

2. Click **Next**. The Report Wizard asks you which fields you want to sort by, as shown in Figure 5-6.

3. Choose **ProductName** as the first sort field by clicking the down arrow next to the number 1 box. For this report, you will sort by one field only. Leave the Report Wizard dialog box displayed for the next Step-by-Step.

FIGURE 5-7
Report grouped by product category

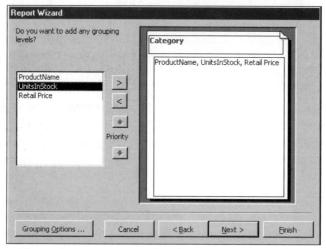

SUMMARY OPTIONS

One of the most useful features of reports is the ability to create summaries within them. Each group of records in a report can be followed by totals, averages, or other summary information. The Summary Options dialog box allows you to specify summaries for fields in the report.

1. Click the **Summary Options** button. The Summary Options dialog box appears.

2. For the **UnitsInStock** field, click the **Sum** option. The report will total the UnitsInStock field.

3. For the **Retail Price** field, click the **Min** and **Max** options.

4. Choose the **Calculate percent of total for sums** option. (Access takes the total UnitsInStock for each category and calculates a percentage of the Grand Total.) Your screen should appear similar to Figure 5-8.

FIGURE 5-8
Summary Options dialog box

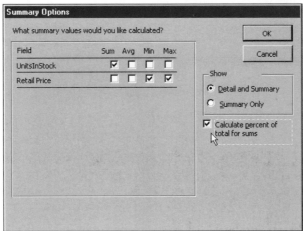

5. Click **OK** to close the Summary Options dialog box.

6. Click **Next**. The Report Wizard asks you to choose a layout and page orientation. Leave the Report Wizard dialog box on the screen for the next Step-by-Step.

LAYOUT, ORIENTATION, AND STYLE

Next, you'll choose the layout and orientation for your report, as shown in Figure 5-9. The layout options let you choose how you want data arranged on the page. When you choose a layout, a sample is shown in the preview box on the left side of the dialog box. Choose from Landscape or Portrait orientation and click Next.

FIGURE 5-9
Layout options

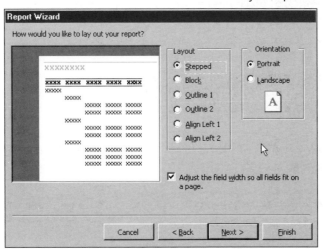

The next dialog box, shown in Figure 5-10, allows you to choose a style for the report. The style options are designed to give you some control over the report's appearance. The style you choose tells the reader of the report something about the data being presented. Some reports may call for a formal style, while others benefit from a more casual style. When you choose a style, a sample is shown in the preview box.

FIGURE 5-10
Style options

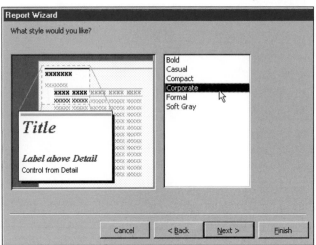

S TEP-BY-STEP ▷ 5.5

1. Choose the **Outline 2** layout. The sample layout is shown in the preview box. Click the other options to look at the other layouts. When you have seen all of the available options, choose **Stepped** as the layout.

2. Choose **Portrait** as the page orientation, if it is not already selected. Make sure the **Adjust the field width so all fields fit on a page** box is checked.

3. Click **Next**.

4. Choose the **Casual** style. The sample style is shown in the preview box. Click on the other options to look at the other styles. When you have seen all of the available options, choose **Corporate** as the style.

5. Click **Next**. The final Report Wizard dialog box appears. Leave the Report Wizard dialog box on the screen for the next Step-by-Step.

NAMING THE REPORT

The final step is naming the report, as shown in Figure 5-11. Use a name that gives an indication of the report's output. A report name can be up to 64 characters including letters, numbers, spaces, and some special characters. For example, if a report from a database of customers prints only the customers with companies in your city, you might name the report Local Customers.

FIGURE 5-11
Naming the report

In addition to naming the report, this dialog box presents you with options for what you want displayed when the Report Wizard completes its work. Most of the time you will want to preview the report you have created, so Preview the report is the default option. After Access creates the report, it is shown on your screen in Preview mode. You can instead choose to make modifications to the report. You will get a brief look at how modifications are made later in this lesson.

After creating a report, you do not need to save it. Access saves it for you automatically with the title you entered into the Report Wizard. You will, however, need to save any modifications made later to the design of the report.

> **Did You Know?**
>
> You can create a chart in either a form's or a report's Design view. Click **Chart** on the **Insert** menu. On the form or report, click where you want the chart to appear. Follow the steps in the Chart Wizard to create the chart based on the tables and the fields you select.

STEP-BY-STEP ▷ 5.6

1. Key **Category Report** as the title of the report.

2. Make sure the option to preview the report is selected and click **Finish**. The report appears in a window, as shown in Figure 5-12.

3. Scroll through the report to see the various categories.

4. Click the **Print** button to print the report.

5. Choose **Close** on the **File** menu. The report will be saved automatically. Leave the Database window open for the next Step-by-Step.

FIGURE 5-12
Previewing a report

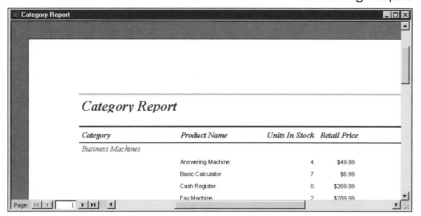

Modifying a Report

Any report, whether created manually or with the Report Wizard, can be modified. Make changes to a report using Design view, which shows the structure of a report. To open a report in Design view, select the report in the Database window, and then click the Design button. Figure 5-13 shows a report in Design view.

 Did You Know?

To add a graphic to a report, open it in Design view and click the **Image** button in the Toolbox. Click where you want to place the graphic in the report and the Insert Picture dialog box displays. Select the file where the picture is located. When finished, click **OK**. Access creates an image control that will display the graphic.

FIGURE 5-13
A report in Design view

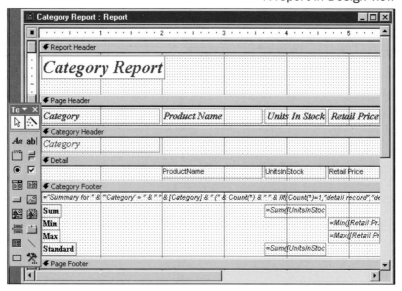

Like a form, the report is divided into sections, each identified by a band. Each section controls a part of the report and can be modified. Table 5-1 summarizes the purpose of each of the sections in the report.

TABLE 5-1
Report sections

SECTION	DESCRIPTION
Report Header	Contents appear at the top of the first page of the report.
Page Header	Contents appear at the top of each page of the report.
Category Header	Contents appear at the top of each group. Because your report is grouped by Category, the band is called Category Header.
Detail	Specifies the fields that will appear in the detail of the report.
Category Footer	Contents appear at the end of each group. The summary options appear in this band.
Page Footer	Contents appear at the end of each page of the report.
Report Footer	Contents appear at the end of the report.

Like a form, the sections in a report contain controls that represent each object on the report. These objects include field names, field entries, a title for the report, or even a graphical object, such as a piece of clip art. You can modify the format, size, and location of the controls in Design view to enhance the appearance of the data on the report.

In Design view, you can change the font, size, style, and other attributes of labels and text box data. Simply select the control and use the buttons on the Formatting toolbar. Or you can double-click a control to open its Properties dialog box, and then change attributes and other properties.

The Toolbox, shown in Figure 5-14, has tools that you can use to modify reports. The Label tool, for example, allows you to add text. (The buttons in the Toolbox may appear in three columns instead of the two shown in Figure 5-14.)

FIGURE 5-14
Toolbox

STEP-BY-STEP 5.7

1. If not already selected, click **Reports** on the Objects bar. Choose the **Category Report** and click the **Design** button. The report appears in Design view, as shown in Figure 5-13.

2. Click the **Label** button in the Toolbox. (If the Toolbox is not displayed, *right-*click on the report and choose **Toolbox** on the shortcut menu.)

3. In the **Report Header**, position the pointer to the right of the *Category Report* text, and click and drag to draw a text box as shown in Figure 5-15.

4. Key your name at the insertion point that appears in the text box. Click outside the text box to view the text.

5. Double-click the text box to display its properties dialog box, as shown in Figure 5-16. If not already selected, click the **All** tab. (*Note*: The label number that appears in your properties dialog box depends on the number of label controls you have added.)

6. Scroll through the list of properties until you locate the Font Name and Font Size properties. Click in the **Font Name** text box, click the down arrow, and select **Mistral** (or a comparable font). Then click in the **Font Size** text box, click the down arrow, and choose **14**. Close the properties dialog box.

7. Scroll down to the **Report Footer** section. Position the pointer on the **Grand Total** label box as shown in Figure 5-17, and double-click to open its properties dialog box. If not already selected, click the **All** tab.

FIGURE 5-15
Inserting text

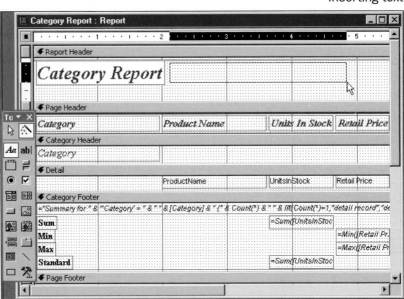

FIGURE 5-16
Label properties dialog box

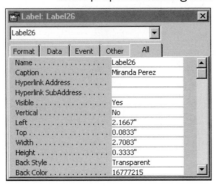

FIGURE 5-17
Modifying the Grand Total label

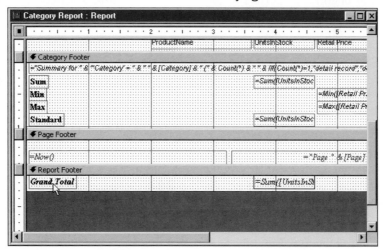

8. Change the **Caption** to **Total Units in Stock**. Change the **Font Size** to **12**. Close the dialog box.

9. With the **Total Units in Stock** label still highlighted, increase the label size by dragging the handle on the right border to the right until you see the entire caption.

10. In the **Detail** section, double-click the **Retail Price** box to open its properties dialog box, as shown in Figure 5-18. If not already selected, choose the **All** tab.

11. Click in the **Name** text box and key **Discount Price**. Then close the dialog box.

12. In the **Page Header** section, double-click the **Retail Price** label box to open its properties dialog box.

13. Change the Caption to **Discount Price** and close the dialog box.

14. With the **Discount Price** label still highlighted, increase the label size by dragging the handle on the right border to the right until you see the entire caption.

15. Click **Save** on the **File** menu.

FIGURE 5-18
Text Box properties dialog box

16. In the **Detail** section, double-click the **Retail Price** text box to open its properties dialog box. Click the **All** tab, if necessary.

17. Click in the **Control Source** text box, delete the existing text, and key **=[Retail Price]*.90**. Click the arrow on the **Format** property text box and select **Currency**. Then, close the dialog box.

18. In the **Category Footer** section, double-click the **Min ([Discount Price])** box to open its properties dialog box. Click the **All** tab, if necessary.

19. Click in the **Control Source** text box, and change the word *Discount* to **Retail**. Close the dialog box.

20. In the **Category Footer** section, double-click the **Max ([Discount Price])** box to open its properties dialog box. Click the **All** tab, if necessary.

21. Click in the **Control Source** text box and change the word *Discount* to **Retail**. Close the dialog box.

22. Click the **View** button to switch to **Print Preview**. If a message appears asking if you want to save changes, click **Yes**.

23. If necessary, scroll to the right to see your name on the report. Choose **Print** on the **File** menu. In the Print dialog box, click **Pages** from the Print Range options. Specify that you want to print only page 1 by keying **1** in the From box and **1** in the To box. Click **OK**.

24. Close the report. Click **Yes** if you are asked if you want to save the report. Leave the database open for the next Step-by-Step.

Hot Tip

To delete a text box, click on the text box and press the **Delete** key or choose **Delete** on the **Edit** menu. To move a text box, click inside the box and drag. To resize a text box, click on the edge of the text box and drag.

Macros

One of the nice features of database management systems such as Access is the ability to automate tasks that are performed often. This is done by creating an object called a macro. A macro is a collection of one or more actions that Access can perform on a database. You can think of a macro as a computer program you create to automate some task you perform with the database.

Creating macros can be challenging, and there are many details to learn before you can become an expert. In this book you will get a taste of how macros work by creating a macro and running it.

Creating a Macro

To create a macro, click Macros on the Objects bar, and click the New button. The Macro window appears, allowing you to specify the actions to be performed by the macro. Figure 5-19 shows a macro in Design view with an example of actions that a macro can perform. The macro will perform the actions specified in the Action list.

FIGURE 5-19
Macro in Design view

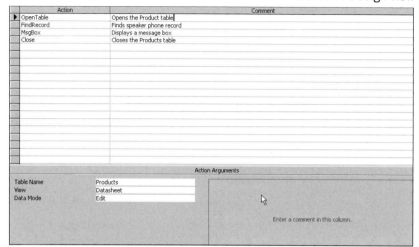

Action	Comment
▶ OpenTable	Opens the Product table
FindRecord	Finds speaker phone record
MsgBox	Displays a message box
Close	Closes the Products table

Action Arguments

Table Name	Products
View	Datasheet
Data Mode	Edit

Enter a comment in this column.

STEP-BY-STEP ▷ 5.8

1. Click **Macros** on the Objects bar.

2. Click **New**. A blank macro window appears. Leave the window open for the next Step-by-Step.

Adding Actions to a Macro

You can choose an action by clicking the down arrow in the Action column cells. There are many available actions, some of which perform advanced operations. You can key an explanation of the action into the Comment column. The lower portion of the Macro window shows the action arguments for the chosen action. Action arguments contain detailed information that Access needs in order to perform the specified action. For example, if you choose the OpenTable action in the Action column, specify which table to open, such as the Products table, in the Action Arguments section.

Different actions require different detailed information in the Action Arguments section, as you will see in the next Step-by-Step. You will create a macro that will open the Products table, find the first speaker phone in the table, present a message box and beep, and close the table.

STEP-BY-STEP ▷ 5.9

1. Click the arrow in the **Action** column of the first blank row to display the list of available actions.

2. Scroll down and choose **OpenTable** from the menu.

3. In the **Comment** section, key **Opens the Products table**.

4. In the Action Arguments section, place the insertion point in the **Table Name** box. An arrow appears. Notice that the box to the right of the Action Arguments contains an explanation of the data to be specified.

5. Click the arrow and choose **Products** from the list.

6. Leave the remaining Action Arguments at the default settings.

7. Place the insertion point in the second row of the **Action** column. Click the drop-down list arrow.

8. Scroll down and choose **FindRecord** from the list.

9. In the **Comment** section, key **Finds speaker phone record**.

10. In the **Action Arguments** section, key **Speaker Phone** into the **Find What** box.

11. In the **Match** box, choose **Any Part of Field** from the drop-down list.

12. Leave the next two action arguments at the default setting. In the **Search As Formatted** box, choose **Yes** from the drop-down list.

13. In the **Only Current Field** box, choose **No** to search all the fields in each record.

14. In the **Find First** box, choose **Yes**, if it's chosen already. Your screen should look similar to Figure 5-20.

15. Place the insertion point in the third row of the **Action** column, scroll down, and choose **MsgBox** from the list.

16. Key **Displays a message box** into the **Comment** section.

17. In the **Action Arguments** section, key **Record Found** in the **Message** box.

18. Choose **Yes** in the **Beep** box, if it is not already chosen.

19. Choose **Information** in the **Type** box.

20. Key **Results:** in the **Title** box.

21. Place the insertion point in the fourth row of the **Action** column and choose **Close** from the list.

22. Key **Closes the Products table** in the **Comment** section.

23. In the **Action Arguments** section, choose **Table** in the **Object Type** box.

24. Choose **Products** in the **Object Name** box. Leave the window open for the next Step-by-Step.

FIGURE 5-20
Specifying Action Arguments

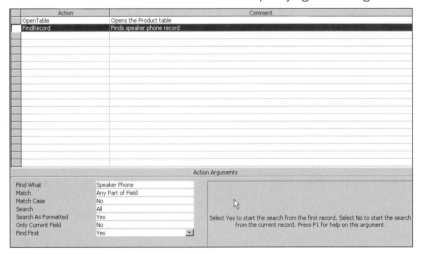

Saving and Running a Macro

After creating a macro, you will need to name and save it. This process is similar to the way you named and saved other database objects. Choose Save As on the File menu and key a name. To close the macro, choose Close on the File menu. When you want to run a macro, highlight it in the Database window and click Run.

STEP-BY-STEP ▷ 5.10

1. Choose **Save As** on the **File** menu. The Save As dialog box appears.

2. In the first box, key **Speaker Phone**, as shown in Figure 5-21. Click **OK**.

3. Choose **Close** on the **File** menu to close the macro window. You are returned to the Database window.

4. Select **Macros** on the Objects bar, if necessary. Highlight the **Speaker Phone** macro, if it is not already highlighted. Click the **Run** button. The Products table opens, the computer beeps, and the message box generated by the macro appears, as shown in Figure 5-22.

5. Click **OK** to close the message box. The table closes because of the Close action in the macro.

6. Open the **Speaker Phone** macro in Design view.

7. Highlight the row with the **MsgBox** action and choose **Delete** on the **Edit** menu.

8. Choose **Rows** on the **Insert** menu to insert a row.

9. Click the down arrow in the **Action** column of the inserted row. Scroll down to choose the **PrintOut** action.

10. Key **Prints speaker phone record** in the **Comment** section.

11. In the **Action Arguments** section, choose **Selection** from the **Print Range** drop-down list.

12. Choose **Save** on the **File** menu to save the design changes.

13. Close the macro window.

14. Highlight the **Speaker Phone** macro, if it is not already highlighted. Click the **Run** button.

15. The Products table opens, the Speaker Phone record prints, and the table closes. Close the database.

FIGURE 5-21
Save As dialog box

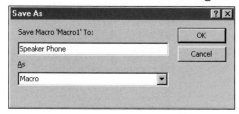

FIGURE 5-22
Macro message box

 Extra Challenge

Modify the Speaker Phone macro to find the scientific calculator record. Save and run the macro.

 Did You Know?

You can also run a macro by double-clicking on it in the Database window.

Summary

In this lesson, you learned:

■ Database reports allow you to organize, summarize, and print all or a portion of the data in a database. Database reports are compiled by creating a report object.

■ The easiest way to create a report object is to use the Report Wizard. When using the Report Wizard, first choose the table on which you want to base the report and the fields of that table you want to include in the report. You can also choose to group the records and sort them.

■ The Report Wizard also allows you to choose a style for your report. The style can give a report a casual or formal look.

■ Reports are modified using Design view. Each report is divided into sections. Each section controls a different part of the report and can be modified.

■ Macros automate tasks you perform often. The Macro window allows you to create a macro object.

VOCABULARY REVIEW

Define the following terms:

Database report   Grouping   Macro

LESSON 5 REVIEW QUESTIONS

TRUE/FALSE

Circle T if the statement is true or F if the statement is false.

T F   1. Database reports are prepared by creating a report object.

T F   2. The Report Wizard always includes all fields in a report.

T F   3. Like filenames, report names can contain only eight characters.

T F   4. Action arguments contain detailed information about an action.

T F   5. To run a macro, highlight it in the Database window and click Run.

WRITTEN QUESTIONS

Write a brief answer to the following questions.

1. What are the two ways to create a report?

2. How does sorting affect a group?

3. List three possible sections in a report.

4. How do you use the Label tool to add text to a report?

5. When creating a macro, what action displays a message box?

LESSON 5 PROJECTS

PROJECT 5-1

1. Open **IA Project5-1** from the data files.

2. Use the Report Wizard to create a report using all the fields in the **Products** table. Group the report by **UnitsInStock** and sort it by **ProductName**.

3. Choose the **Block** layout, **Portrait** orientation, and **Compact** style.

4. Title the report **Products by Units in Stock**. Select the option to preview the report.

5. Close the report after previewing.

6. Modify the report in Design view. Use the label tool to insert your name in the Report header. Save the changes.

7. Print the report.

8. Close the report and the database.

PROJECT 5-2

1. Open **IA Project5-2** from the data files.

2. Use the Report Wizard to create a report. Use the **Employee Information** table and choose the **Last Name**, **First Name**, **Department**, and **Salary** fields.

3. Group the records by **Department** and sort by **Last Name**.

4. Choose the **Stepped** layout, **Portrait** orientation, and **Corporate** style.

5. Title the report **Employees by Department**. Select the option to preview the report.

6. Save the report.

7. Print and close the report. Leave the database open for the next project.

PROJECT 5-3

1. With the **IA Project5-2** database open, create a new macro that will open the **Employee Birthdays** form in Form view and find the **Shapiro** record. For the FindRecord Action Arguments, select **Any Part of Field** in the Match box, **No** in the Match Case box, **All** in the Search box, **Yes** in the Search As Formatted box, **No** in the Only Current Field box, and **Yes** in the Find First box. Then have the macro print the Shapiro record only (*Print Range = Selection*), and close the Employee Birthdays form.

2. Save the macro as **Print Form Record** and close it.

3. Run the macro. Leave the database open for the next project.

PROJECT 5-4

1. Create a new macro in the **IA Project5-2** database that will open the **Managers** query in Datasheet view and find the **Marketing** record. (For the FindRecord Action Arguments, select **Any Part of Field** in the Match box, **No** in the Match Case box, **All** in the Search box, **Yes** in the Search As Formatted box, **No** in the Only Current Field box, and **Yes** in the Find First box. Then, have the macro print the Marketing record (Selection) only, and close the **Managers** query.

2. Save the macro as **Print Marketing Manager** and close it.

3. Run the macro. Close the database.

CRITICAL THINKING

ACTIVITY 5-1

Using the **IA Activity5-1** database file in the data files and the **Houses** table, create a report listing all of the information in the table. Also, create a macro that will open the **2 Bedrooms** query, find all of the two- bedroom houses, print the results (*Print Range = All*), and close the query. Save the macro as **2 Bedroom Houses for Sale**. Run the macro and close the database.

ACTIVITY 5-2

Using the Help feature, look up the definition of a *subreport*. In your own words, write a brief essay that defines a subreport and provide an example of when you might use a subreport. For your example, assume you have a database containing tables on customers and product sales.

ACTIVITY 5-3

A *switchboard* is a form in a database that contains buttons representing macros you've created to open, close, and manage the objects in a database. Use the Help system to find out more about switchboards and how to create them. Write a brief essay explaining how you would use a switchboard in a database that you maintain.

LESSON 6

INTEGRATING ACCESS

Importing and Exporting Data

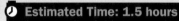

Because Office is an integrated suite of programs, you can easily import and export data between applications. You can export an Access table to an Excel worksheet or you can merge records in a table with a Word document. In this lesson, you'll learn how to share data between Access and other applications.

Word to Access

Suppose you have been given a list of names and addresses in a Word file. The names need to be entered into a database. You can easily paste or import the information into an Access table, where you can then edit and sort it, and create forms, queries, reports, and pages from it. If the text from Word is set up as a table or is separated by tabs, Access will automatically create the fields and enter the data as records. If the text is in a single block, all of the text will be pasted into the currently highlighted field.

Access to Word

You can also export table records from an Access database into a Word document. The data is formatted with tabs when it enters the Word document. This feature could be used to create a table in Word, based on data from Access. Merging database records with a Word document to create a form letter is another method for integrating Access and Word, and is discussed later in this lesson.

Access to Excel

There are times when you might want to export Access data into an Excel worksheet. Excel provides powerful calculation and data analysis features that can easily be applied to database records that are exported to an Excel workbook file. Each record in the table appears as a row in the worksheet, and each field is converted to a column.

Excel to Access

You can also import data from an Excel worksheet into an Access database table. A worksheet is set up as columns and rows, much like a database table. The cells cut or copied from the worksheet will appear in the database beginning with the highlighted entry.

You could also use the Import Spreadsheet Wizard to insert Excel data into an Access table. Open the database file, select the Get External Data command on the File menu, and then select Import on the submenu. An Import dialog box opens, where you can select the file you want to import. The Wizard then guides you through the process of placing the spreadsheet data in a table.

S TEP-BY-STEP ▷ 6.1

1. Open the **IA Step6-1** database from the data files.

2. Choose **Get External Data** on the **File** menu, and select **Import** on the submenu. The Import dialog box appears, similar to that shown in Figure 6-1. From the Look in drop-down list, select the folder containing the data files for this course.

3. Click the down arrow in the Files of type box and choose **Microsoft Excel** from the list.

4. Select the **New Products** Excel workbook from the data files.

5. Click **Import**. The Import Spreadsheet Wizard opens, as shown in Figure 6-2. Notice the data from the New Products worksheet appears in the grid.

6. Click **Next** and a second wizard dialog box opens, asking if the first row of the spreadsheet contains the column headings.

FIGURE 6-1
Import dialog box

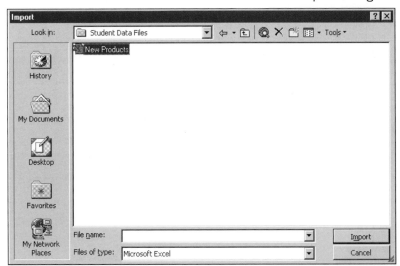

7. Click **Next** since the first row does contain the column headings and the option is already selected. A third wizard dialog box appears asking where you would like to store your data.

8. If not already selected, choose the **In a New Table** option. Click **Next** and a fourth wizard dialog box appears as shown in Figure 6-3.

9. Scroll to the right in the grid to view all the field columns in the table. Then click **Next**.

This wizard dialog box asks you to let Access add a primary key to the table.

10. Choose **No primary key** and click **Next**.

11. Key **New Products** in the Import to Table box. Click **Finish**.

12. A message appears stating that the wizard is finished importing the file. Click **OK**.

FIGURE 6-2
Import Spreadsheet Wizard dialog box

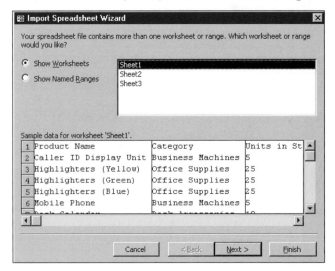

FIGURE 6-3
Import Spreadsheet Wizard lets you tailor Excel data

13. The New Products table should be listed in the Database window. Open the table in Datasheet view. Print the table.

14. Close the table and the database.

Form Letters

Another way to integrate Access and Word is through form letters. A *form letter* is a word processor document that uses information inserted from a database in specified areas to personalize a document.

For example, you might send a letter to all of the members of a professional organization using a form letter. In each letter, the information is the same but the names of the recipients will be different. One letter may begin Dear Mr. Hartsfield and another Dear Ms. Perez.

Creating a Form Letter

To create form letters, export information from a data source, such as an Access database, to a document in Word, called the main document. The *main document* contains the information that will stay the same in each form letter. The *data source* contains the recipient information, such as names and addresses, that will vary in each form letter. You can insert the field names, or *merge fields*, in the main document where you want to print the recipient information from the data source. The merge fields you place in the Word document are enclosed in angle brackets (<< Field Name >>). When the main document and the data source are merged, the merge fields in the main document are replaced with the individual recipient information from the data source to create personalized form letters.

Word provides a Mail Merge task pane that makes it easy to create a form letter. To access the Mail Merge task pane, as shown in Figure 6-4, choose the Letters and Mailings command on Word's Tools menu. Select Mail Merge Wizard from the submenu and the Mail Merge task pane appears on the right side of the screen, as shown in Figure 6-4. You will complete six steps in the Mail Merge task pane to

> **Hot Tip**
>
> Backing up files on your computer should be a regular practice. To back up a database, you must close it first and make sure that no other users have it open. Using Windows Explorer, My Computer, Microsoft Backup, or other backup software, copy the database file to a backup medium, such as a floppy disk, a zip disk, a tape, etc. To restore the database, simply copy the backup database file to the appropriate folder or disk.

FIGURE 6-4
Mail Merge task pane

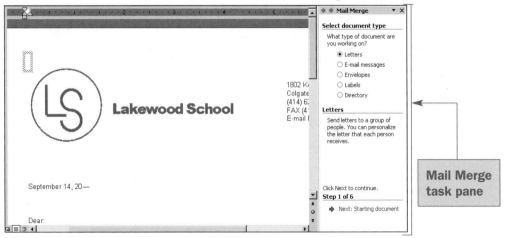

Mail Merge task pane

create a form letter. To specify the main document, click Letters in Step 1 and then select the starting document in Step 2. To specify a data source, click *Use an existing list* in Step 3, and click Browse. When the Select Data Source dialog box appears, choose the file you want to use as the data source. To insert the merge fields in Step 4, position the insertion point in the main document and choose the merge field or item, such as an Address Block, to be inserted. Insert all of the merge fields until your main document is complete. In Step 5, you can preview the letters and edit the recipients to be included in the merge. To edit the recipients, click *Edit recipient list* and the Mail Merge Recipients dialog box will appear, as shown in Figure 6-5. You can then choose which recipients you want to merge, and print. When ready, complete the merge and print the letters.

STEP-BY-STEP ▷ 6.2

C

1. Open **Word** and the **Lakewood letter** document from the data files.

2. Save the file as **Fourth Grade letter**, followed by your initials.

3. Choose **Letters and Mailings** on the **Tools** menu, and select **Mail Merge Wizard** on the submenu. The Mail Merge task pane appears on the right side of the screen, as shown in Figure 6-4.

4. If not already selected, choose **Letters** in the Select document type section of the task pane.

5. Click **Next: Starting document** at the bottom of the task pane. The second Mail Merge task pane appears.

6. If not already selected, choose **Use the current document** in the Select starting document section.

7. Click **Next: Select recipients** at the bottom of the task pane. The third Mail Merge task pane appears.

8. If not already selected, choose **Use an existing list** in the Select recipients section.

9. Click **Browse** in the Use an existing list section. The Select Data Source dialog box appears.

10. Click the down arrow on the **Look in** box to find and select the **Lakewood parents** database in the data files. Click **Open**. The Mail Merge Recipients dialog box appears with the data from the Fourth Grade table, as shown in Figure 6-5. Click **OK**.

FIGURE 6-5
Mail Merge Recipients dialog box

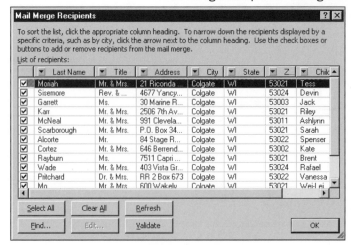

11. Click **Next: Write your letter** at the bottom of the task pane.

12. Within the *Lakewood letter* document (on the left side of the screen), place the insertion point on the second line after the date.

13. Click **Address block** in the Write your letter section of the task pane. The Insert Address Block dialog box appears, as shown in Figure 6-6. (The Address Block is a predefined layout of an address that automatically links the data source with the merge fields.)

14. Click **OK** and the Address Block merge field is inserted.

15. Within the letter, place the insertion point between *Dear* and the semi-colon(;). Add a blank space.

16. Click **More items** in the task pane. The Insert Merge Field dialog box appears, as shown in Figure 6-7.

17. If not already selected, choose **Title** from the list of fields and click **Insert**. The Title is inserted as a merge field. Click **Close** to close the dialog box.

18. Insert the **Last Name** and **Child's Name** fields, as shown in Figure 6-8, using the same method. (Be sure to add spaces where necessary.)

19. When finished, click **Next: Preview your letters** at the bottom of the task pane. The data from the Lakewood parents database is inserted into the merge fields to create the form letters.

20. Click the scroll buttons in the Preview your letters section of the task pane to see the other form letters.

21. Save the file. Leave the document open for the next Step-by-Step.

FIGURE 6-6
Insert Address Block dialog box

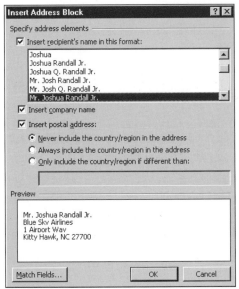

FIGURE 6-7
Insert Merge Field dialog box

FIGURE 6-8
Inserted merge fields

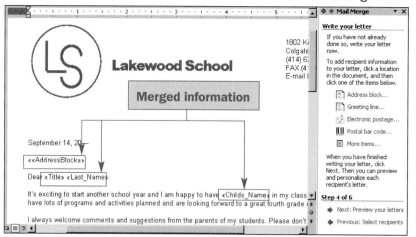

Editing the Recipient list and Printing Form Letters

After the form letters have been created, they are ready to print. If you don't want to print every letter, you can click Edit recipient list in the Make changes section of the task pane. The Mail Merge Recipients dialog box will reappear and you can choose which recipients you want to merge and print.

S TEP-BY-STEP ▷ 6.3

1. The **Fourth Grade letter** document should be open on your screen. Save it as **Fourth Grade letter 2**, followed by your initials.

2. Click **Edit recipient list** in the Make changes section of the task pane. The Mail Merge Recipients dialog box appears, as shown in Figure 6-5.

3. Click the **Clear All** button to remove the check marks.

4. You want to print only the letters to the parents of Devin Sisemore and Kate Cortez. Click the check boxes to select their information, as shown in Figure 6-9. Click **OK.**

5. Click the scroll buttons in the task pane to see the two form letters.

6. Click **Next: Complete the merge** at the bottom of the task pane. The last Mail Merge task pane appears.

7. Click **Print** in the Merge section of the task pane. The Merge to Printer dialog box appears, as shown in Figure 6-10.

8. If not already selected, choose **All**. Click **OK** and the Print dialog box appears.

9. Click **OK**. Save and close the file.

FIGURE 6-9
Mail Merge Recipients dialog box

FIGURE 6-9
Mail Merge Recipients dialog box

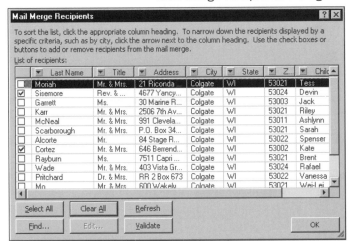

FIGURE 6-10
Merge to Printer dialog box

Mailing Labels

Creating mailing labels is very similar to creating form letters. The main difference is that mailing labels place information from more than one record on the same page. This is because mailing labels usually come in sheets that have as many as 30 labels per page.

To create mailing labels, you will be using the Mail Merge task pane again. This time, choose Labels as the starting document. After specifying a main document and a data source, you can choose the label options you want, insert merge fields that contain the address information, and print your mailing labels.

STEP-BY-STEP ▷ 6.4

1. Open a new Word document.

2. Save the file as **Fourth Grade labels**, followed by your initials.

3. Choose **Letters and Mailings** on the **Tools** menu, and select **Mail Merge Wizard** on the submenu. The Mail Merge task pane appears on the right side of the screen.

4. Choose **Labels** in the Select document type section of the task pane.

5. Click **Next: Starting document** at the bottom of the task pane. The second Mail Merge task pane appears.

6. Choose **Label options** in the Change document layout section of the task pane. The Label Options dialog box appears, as shown in Figure 6-11.

7. From the Printer information option, be sure the correct type of printer is chosen (either **Laser and ink jet** or **Dot Matrix**) is chosen, and then select the Tray option that you wish to use with your printer. (Typically, if you are printing out only one sheet of mailing labels you would manually feed that sheet into the printer.)

FIGURE 6-11
Label Options dialog box

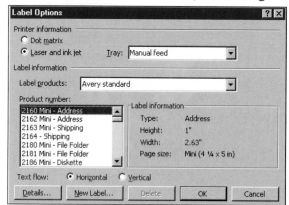

8. For our example, the Label products box should have **Avery standard** chosen. In the Product number box, scroll down to highlight **5160 – Address**. (There are many different company's products available from which to choose.)

9. Click **OK**. A page of blank labels appears on the screen.

10. Click **Next: Select recipients** at the bottom of the task pane. The third Mail Merge task pane appears.

11. If not already selected, choose **Use an existing list** in the Select recipients section.

12. Click **Browse** in the Use an existing list section. The Select Data Source dialog box appears.

13. Click the down arrow in the **Look in** box and find the **Lakewood parents** database in the data files. Click **Open**. The Mail Merge Recipients dialog box appears with the data from the Fourth Grade table. Click **OK**.

14. Click **Next: Arrange your labels** at the bottom of the task pane.

15. Be sure the insertion point appears within the first label. (If you cannot see the individual labels, click **Show Gridlines** on the **View** menu.)

16. Click **Address block** in the Arrange your labels section of the task pane. The Insert Address Block dialog box appears.

17. Click **OK** and the Address Block merge field in inserted.

18. Scroll down to the bottom of the task pane. Click **Update all labels** in the Replicate labels section of the task pane. The layout of the first label is copied to the other labels on the page, as shown in Figure 6-12.

FIGURE 6-12
Inserted merge fields

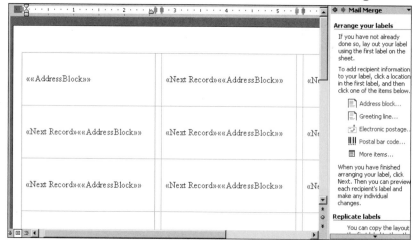

19. Click **Next: Preview your labels** at the bottom of the task pane. The data from the Lakewood parents database is inserted into the merge fields to create the mailing labels.

20. Click the scroll buttons within the document to view the other labels.

21. When finished, click **Next: Complete the merge** at the bottom of the task pane. The last Mail Merge task pane appears.

22. Click **Print** in the Merge section of the task pane. The Merge to Printer dialog box appears.

23. If not already selected, choose **All**. Click **OK** and the Print dialog box appears.

24. Click **OK**. Save and close the file. Close Word.

Data Access Pages

A *data access page* is an object created in a database that lets you publish other objects, such as tables, forms, and reports to the Web. You can then view the database using the Web.

Creating a Data Access Page

As with other Access objects, you can create a data access page manually or use the Page Wizard. The Page Wizard will ask you detailed questions about the fields, format and layout, and then create a page based on your answers. In this lesson, you will create a data access page using the Page Wizard.

Hot Tip

Most of the same features of forms and reports, such as grouping and sorting, are also used in the design of a data access page.

STEP-BY-STEP ▷ 6.5

1. Open **Access** and the **IA Step6-5** database from the data files.

2. Click **Pages** on the **Objects** bar.

3. Click **New**. The New Data Access Page dialog box appears, as shown in Figure 6-13.

4. Choose **Page Wizard** from the list.

5. Click the down arrow and choose the **Products** table from the drop-down list. Click **OK**. The Page Wizard dialog box appears, as shown in Figure 6-14.

6. Click **>>** to move all of the Available Fields to the Selected Fields box.

7. Click **Next**. The Page Wizard now gives you the option to group the data.

8. Click **Next**. For this data access page, you will not group the data. The Page Wizard asks you which fields you want to sort by, as shown in Figure 6-15.

9. Click the down arrow next to the number 1 box and choose **ProductName** as the first sort field. For this data access page, you will have an ascending sort by one field only.

FIGURE 6-13
New Data Access Page dialog box

FIGURE 6-14
Page Wizard dialog box

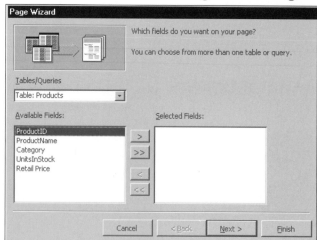

FIGURE 6-15
Sorting a data access page

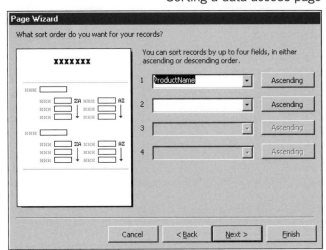

10. Click **Next**. The final Page Wizard dialog box appears, as shown in Figure 6-16.

11. Key **Products Page** as the title of the page.

12. Choose the option to **Open the page** and click **Finish**.

13. The data access page appears, as shown in Figure 6-17.

14. Click the **Next** button to scroll through the data until you find the Disk Storage Box in the Product Name box.

15. Choose **Print** on the **File** menu. The Print dialog box appears.

16. Click **Print**. The product information for the Disk Storage Box will print.

17. Choose **Close** on the **File** menu. A message will appear asking if you want to save changes to the data access page. Click **Yes**.

18. The Save As Data Access Page dialog box appears, as shown in Figure 6-18.

FIGURE 6-16
Naming the data access page

19. Click the down arrow in the Save in box to find the location in which to save the file.

20. Key **Products Page** in the File name box and click **Save**. A message may appear asking if you want this folder as the default folder for data access pages. Click No. A message will appear warning you that the page might not be able to connect to data through the network.

21. Click **OK**. The Products Page is now listed as a Pages object in the Database window.

22. Close the database.

Did You Know?

To display a data access page as it will appear to users on the Web, choose **Web Page Preview** on the **File** menu. This will start Internet Explorer and display the page. Note that users using other Web browsers may see the pages differently. You should test your page in several browsers.

FIGURE 6-17

The Products data access page

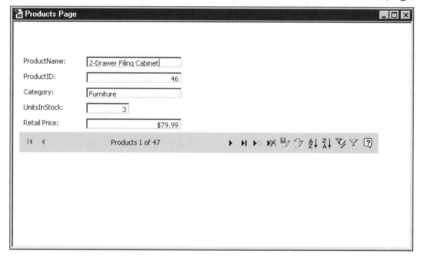

FIGURE 6-18

Save As Data Access Page dialog box

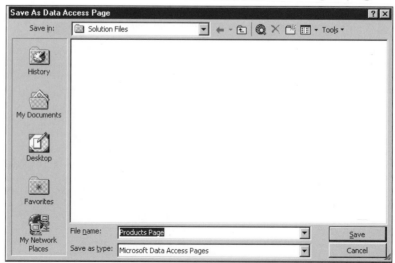

Summary

In this lesson, you learned:

■ Because Office is an integrated suite of programs, you can easily import and export data between applications. No matter which applications you are using, the data is automatically formatted so that it can be used in the destination file.

■ A form letter is a word processor document that uses information from a database in specified areas to personalize a document. To create form letters, you insert merge fields in the main document that are replaced with information from the data source.

■ Creating mailing labels is very similar to creating form letters. The Mail Merge task pane makes it easy to create form letters or mailing labels.

■ A data access page is an object created in a database that lets you publish other objects, such as tables, forms, and reports to the Web. You can then view the database using the Web.

VOCABULARY REVIEW

Define the following terms:

Data access page	Form letter	Merge fields
Data source	Main document	

LESSON 6 REVIEW QUESTIONS

TRUE/FALSE

Circle T if the statement is true or F if the statement is false.

T F 1. A merge field is a field name in the main document where you want to print the information from the data source.

T F 2. When moving and copying data with the Office suite of programs, the data is automatically formatted so that it can be used in the destination file.

T F 3. The data source contains the information that stays the same in each form letter.

T F 4. A data access page is an object that allows you to view a database using the Web.

T F 5. You can use the Mail Merge task pane to create mailing labels.

WRITTEN QUESTIONS

Write a brief answer to the following questions.

1. What option do you click to choose the records you want to merge and print in a form letter?

2. Creating mailing labels involves integrating which two Office applications?

3. What is the Main Document in a form letter?

4. After opening a new Word document, what option do you choose on the Tools menu to create mailing labels?

5. What is a form letter?

LESSON 6 PROJECTS

PROJECT 6-1

1. Open **Word** and the **InfoTech letter** document from the data files.

2. Save the file as **Employee Dinner letter**, followed by your initials.

3. Using the Mail Merge task pane, create a form letter by merging the **Employee Dinner letter** document with data from the **Employee Information** table in the **IA Project6-1** database.

4. Insert the merge fields as shown in Figure 6-19.

5. Preview the letters.

6. Save the file and leave it open for the next project.

FIGURE 6-19

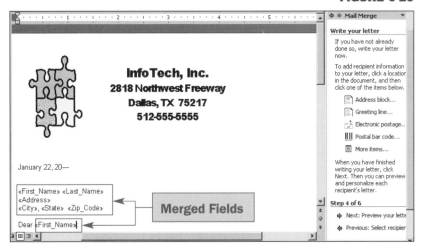

PROJECT 6-2

1. The Employee Dinner letter should be open on your screen. Save it as **Employee Dinner letter 2**, followed by your initials.

2. In the Mail Merge task pane, click **Edit recipient list** and select only the employees in the Public Relations department.

3. When finished, preview the form letters.

4. Merge and print the form letters.

5. Save and close the file.

PROJECT 6-3

1. Open a new Word document.

2. Save the file as **Employee Dinner labels**, followed by your initials.

3. Use the Mail Merge task pane to create mailing labels. Merge the **Employee Information** table from the **IA Project6-1** database.

4. In the Label Options dialog box, be sure **Laser and ink jet** is chosen as the Printer information. Select the Tray option that you wish to use with your printer. Choose **Avery standard** as the Label product. Highlight **5160 – Address** as the Product number.

5. Insert the **Address block** merge field within the first label. Be sure to copy the layout of the first label to the other labels on the page, as shown in Figure 6-20.

6. When finished, merge and print the labels.

7. Save and close the file.

FIGURE 6-20

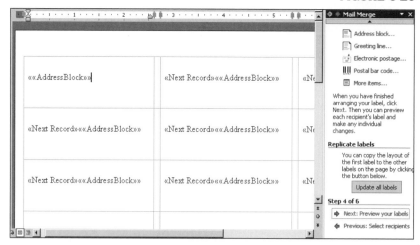

PROJECT 6-4

1. Open **Access** and the **IA Project6-4** database from the data files.

2. Using the **Page Wizard**, create a data access page for the **Employee Information** table.

3. Select all of the available fields. Do not group the data. Sort by the **Last Name** field in ascending order.

4. Key **Employee Page** as the title of the page and choose to **Open the page**.

5. Scroll through the data until you find the employee information on **Alex Pharr**.

6. Print the information.

7. Save the new data access page as **Employee Page**, followed by your initials. (Click **OK** if a message appears warning you that the page might not be able to connect to data through the network.)

8. Close the database.

CRITICAL THINKING

ACTIVITY 6-1

Teachers need to send consent forms to each student's parents at the beginning of the year. This allows the students to participate in field trips or special activities away from the school. Create a consent form letter by merging the **Consent letter** with data from the **Third grade** table in the **Washington parents** database. The letter and database are stored in the data files. Save the new document as **Third Consent letter**. Merge and print letters for only the students with last names of **Davis**, **Hope**, **Shihab**, and **Ellis**. Save the new document as **Third Consent letter 2**.

ACTIVITY 6-2

Using the Help feature, look up the steps for adding a hyperlink to a form or report in a database. Write down the basic steps. Give an example of why you might add a hyperlink to either an Inventory, Customer, or Vendor database.

Introductory Microsoft Access

COMMAND SUMMARY

FEATURE	MENU COMMAND	TOOLBAR BUTTON	LESSON
Close	File, Close	☒	1
Close a Table	File, Close	☒	1
Column Width	Format, Column Width		2
Compact and Repair a Database	Tools, Database Utilities, Compact and Repair Database		2
Copy Record	Edit, Copy	🖺	2
Cut Record	Edit, Cut	✂	2
Database (create)	File, New		1
Datasheet View		🎛	1
Design View		☒	1
Delete Record	Edit, Delete Record	☒	2
Delete Row	Edit, Delete Rows	☒	1
Design View	Highlight name of Object, Design	☒	1
Exit Access	File, Exit		1
Field Properties	Tables, Design	☒	2
File, create	File, New	☐	1
Filter, apply	Filter, Apply Filter/Sort	▽	3
Filter, create	Records, Filter		3
Filter, remove	Filter, Remove Filter/Sort	▽	3
Find Data	Edit, Find	🔍	3
First Record		⏮	2
Form, create	Forms, New		2
Form, modify	Forms, Design	☒	2
Freeze Column	Format, Freeze Columns		2
Index Field	Tables, Design	☒	
Insert Hyperlink	Highlight name of Object, Design, Insert, Hyperlink	🔗	3
Insert Row	Insert, Rows	☒	1
Last Record		⏭	2
Macro, create	Macro, New		5

FEATURE	MENU COMMAND	TOOLBAR BUTTON	LESSON
Mailing Labels, create	Tools, Letters and Mailings, Mail Merge Wizard		6
Mail Merge Wizard	Tools, Letters and Mailings, Mail Merge Wizard		6
New Record		▶✳	2
Next Record		▶	2
Open Existing Database	File, Open		1
Paste Record	Edit, Paste	📋	2
Previous Record		◀	2
Primary Key, create	Tables, Design, Hightlight name of field	🔑	4
Print	File, Print	🖨	1
Query, create	Queries, New		4
Relationships, define	Tools, Relationships	🔗	4
Relationships, print	File, Print Relationships		4
Report, create	Reports, New		5
Report, modify	Reports, Design	📐	5
Row Height	Format, Row Height		2
Save	File, Save	💾	1
Sort Ascending	Records, Sort, Sort Ascending	↕	4
Sort Descending	Records, Sort, Sort Descending	↕	4
Start Access	Start, Programs, Microsoft Access		1
Subdatasheet, Insert	Insert, Subdatasheet		3
Table, create	Tables, New		1
Table, modify	Highlight name of Table, Design	📐	1
Toolbox, display		🛠	3
Undo Changes in Cell	Edit, Undo Typing	↩	2
Undo Changes in Previous Cell	Edit, Undo Current Field/ Record or Esc key		2
Unfreeze All Columns	Format, Unfreeze All Columns		2

TRUE/FALSE

Circle T if the statement is true or F if the statement is false.

T F 1. A record appears as a column in Datasheet view.

T F 2. The navigation buttons are used to move around the datasheet.

T F 3. Queries allow the most complex searches.

T F 4. Sections are shown in Modify Report view.

T F 5. In the Label Options dialog box, you choose the data source you will be using for the mailing labels.

WRITTEN QUESTIONS

Write a brief answer to the following questions.

1. What data type is used to store dollar amounts?

2. What option makes Access choose the width of a column?

3. What button displays the results of a filter?

4. What is a macro?

5. In what document are merge fields inserted?

PROJECTS

PROJECT 1

1. Open the **IA Project1** database from the data files.

2. Open the **Stores** table in Datasheet view.

3. Move the **Hours** column between the **Specialty** and **Credit Cards** fields.

4. Move record **4** to the bottom of the table.

5. Close the table. Click **Yes** if prompted to save changes to the table.

6. Open the **Stores** table in Design view.

7. Insert a field between the **Hours** and **Credit Cards** fields. Name the field **Last Visit** with the **Date/Time** data type, and **Date of last visit** in the description field.

8. Choose **Medium Date** for the format of the **Last Visit** field.

9. Change the field size of the **Specialty** field to **25**.

10. Make the **Name** field **Required**.

11. Save the table design. A message may appear asking if you want to continue. Click **Yes**. Another message may appear asking if you want to test the changes. Click **Yes**.

12. Switch to Datasheet view and print the table in landscape orientation.

13. Close the table and the database.

PROJECT 2

1. Open **IA Project2** from the data files.

2. Create a new form with the Form Wizard using the **Stores** table.

3. Add the **Name**, **Specialty**, **Credit Cards**, and **Hours** fields.

4. Use the **Tabular** layout and the **Standard** style.

5. Title the form **Store Form**.

6. Using the **Store Form**, add the following record:

Name	Specialty	Credit Cards	Hours
Sports Authority	Sporting Goods	Yes	9am to 9pm

7. Print all the records in the form.

8. Close the form and the database.

PROJECT 3

1. Open **IA Project3** from the data files.

2. Open the **Employee Information** table in Datasheet view.

3. Sort the table so that the employees's salaries are listed from lowest to highest.

4. Change the left and right margins to **.5"** and print the results of the sort in landscape orientation.

5. Create a query that displays the employees with a title of manager. Have the query display only the **Last Name**, **First Name**, **Department**, **Title**, and **Salary** fields. Save the query as **Managers**.

6. Run the query and print the results. Close the query. If prompted, save the changes and then close the database.

PROJECT 4

1. Open **IA Project4** from the data files.

2. Open the **Employee Information** table, and use the Find command to locate the employees with a title of Account Executive.

3. Create a Filter by Selection to display only the employees in the **Sales** department.

4. Change the left and right margins to **.5"** and print the results of the filter in landscape orientation.

5. Show all the records in the table.

6. Close the table and the database.

PROJECT 5

1. Open **IA Project5** from the data files.

2. Use the Report Wizard to create a report. Use the **Products** table and choose the **ProductName**, **Category,** and **RetailPrice** fields.

3. Group the report by **Category** and sort by **RetailPrice** in descending order. (Click the **Ascending** button to change the sort to Descending.)

4. Choose **Stepped** layout, **Portrait** orientation, and **Bold** style.

5. Title the report **Products by Retail Price**. Select the option to preview the report.

6. Print the report.

7. Close the report and the database.

PROJECT 6

1. Open the **IA Project6** database from the data files.

2. Create a macro to open the **Products** table in Datasheet view, print all the pages, and close the table.

3. Save the macro as **Print Products Table**.

4. Run the macro.

5. Close the database.

SIMULATION

You work at the Java Internet Café, which has been open a short time. The café serves coffee, other beverages, and pastries, and offers Internet access. Seven computers are set up on tables along the north side of the store. Customers can come in, have a cup of coffee and a Danish, and explore the World Wide Web.

All membership fees for March were due on March 1. A few members have not paid their monthly dues. Your manager asks you to write a letter to the members as a reminder.

JOB 1

1. Open **Word** and the **Payment Late Letter** from the data files.

2. Save the document as **Payment Late Merge Letter**, followed by your initials.

3. Open **Excel** and the **Computer Prices** workbook from the data files.

4. In the spreadsheet, copy the range **A1** through **B11**, and paste it between the first and second paragraphs of the **Payment Late Merge Letter**. Make sure there is one blank line before and after the spreadsheet data.

5. Close **Computer Prices** without saving, and exit Excel.

6. Open **Access**, open the **Java members** database from the data files, and then open the **Membership** table.

7. Scott Payton just paid his membership fee. Key **$10.00** into the March Paid field of his record.

8. Add the following new member to the end of the database:

Ms. Halie Shook, 1290 Wood Crest Apt. 224, Boulder, CO 80302, March Paid = $10

9. Close the table and save changes. Close the database and Access. The Payment Late Merge Letter document should be displayed.

10. Use the Mail Merge task pane to create form letters by merging the **Payment Late Merge Letter** document with the **Membership** table in the **Java members** database. Leave a blank line after the date, and then insert a merge field for *Name* on the next line, a merge field for *Address* on the next line, and merge fields for *City*, *State*, and *Zip* on the next line below the address.

11. When finished, preview the letters.

12. In the Mail Merge task pane, click **Edit recipient list** and select only the members with **0** in the **March Paid** field. (There should be three form letters.)

13. Merge and print the three form letters.

14. Save and close **Payment Late Merge Letter**. Leave Word open for the next job.

JOB 2

You need to create mailing labels for the form letters you printed yesterday.

1. Open a new Word document.

2. Save the file as **Java labels.**

3. Use the Mail Merge task pane to create mailing labels.

4. In the Label Options dialog box, be sure **Laser and ink jet** is chosen as the Printer Information. Select the Tray option that you wish to use with your printer. Choose **Avery standard** as the Label Product. Highlight **5160 – Address** as the Product number.

5. Merge the **Membership** table from the **Java Members** database.

6. Insert the merge fields **Name**, **Address**, and **City_State_Zip** within the first label. Be sure to copy the layout of the first label to the other labels on the page.

7. When finished, merge and print the labels.

8. Save and close **Java labels.** Exit **Word.**

INTRODUCTORY MICROSOFT® POWERPOINT®

UNIT

Estimated Time for Unit: 7 hours

PowerPoint Basics

OBJECTIVES

Upon completion of this lesson, you should be able to:

- Start PowerPoint.
- Open an existing presentation.
- Save a presentation.
- Navigate through a presentation, and use the menus and toolbars.
- Use the Slides and Outline tabs in Normal view.
- Use the task pane, slide pane, and notes pane.
- Change views.
- Delete a slide.
- Print a presentation.
- Exit PowerPoint.

⏱ **Estimated Time: 1.5 hours**

VOCABULARY

Notes pane

Outline tab

Slide sorter

Slides tab

Task pane

Introduction to PowerPoint

PowerPoint is an Office XP application that can help you create a professional presentation by helping you illustrate your ideas using slides, outlines, speaker's notes, and audience handouts. A presentation can include text, clip art, graphs, tables, charts, and even sound or video clips. PowerPoint presentations are usually viewed using a projector on a screen, but you can also use a television monitor or an additional monitor connected to your computer. PowerPoint provides features such as design templates and wizards that help make creating a presentation easier.

Starting PowerPoint

Like other Office XP applications, you start PowerPoint by clicking the Start button, selecting Programs, and clicking Microsoft PowerPoint. The PowerPoint program opens, as shown in Figure 1-1.

FIGURE 1-1
PowerPoint's opening screen

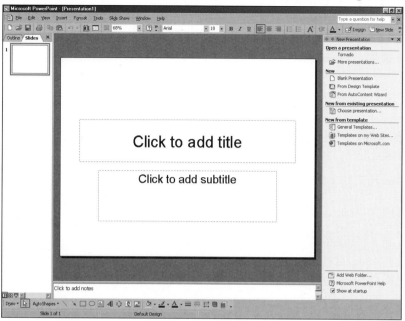

STEP-BY-STEP 1.1

1. Click the **Start** button to open the Start menu.

2. Point to **Programs**, then choose **Microsoft PowerPoint**.

3. The PowerPoint opening window appears (Figure 1-1). Leave the program on the screen for the next Step-by-Step.

Opening and Viewing an Existing Presentation

When you want to open an existing presentation, choose the presentation from the list in the PowerPoint task pane under the heading Open a presentation. This list shows recently opened presentations. Click the presentation you want to open.

If the presentation you want to open is not in the list, click the More presentations folder (see Figure 1-1). This option displays the Open dialog box as shown in Figure 1-2. Locate the presentation you want to open, click the file name, and click the Open button. The presentation you selected appears on the screen as shown in Figure 1-3.

Hot Tip

In addition to the Standard and Formatting toolbars, the PowerPoint screen contains the task pane, located on the right side of the screen. The task pane includes some features that are related to the task on which you are currently working. PowerPoint displays these features on the task pane so you do not have to search for them on the toolbars. If the task pane is not displayed, right-click the Standard toolbar and click **Task Pane** to display it.

FIGURE 1-2
Open dialog box

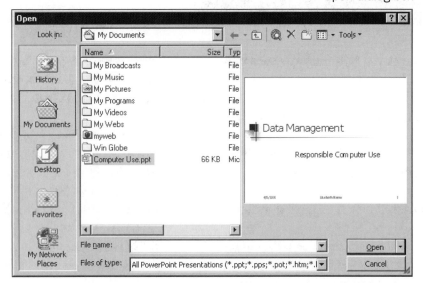

FIGURE 1-3
Opening a presentation

To view the presentation, select View Show from the Slide Show menu on the menu bar. The presentation opens on the screen and you can view it as you would when you present it. You can use the right arrow key on the keyboard to advance the slides and the left arrow key to review a previous slide. You can also click your mouse to advance a slide.

Some slides include animation, which is text or pictures that have motion. You can format a slide to automatically advance through the animation or to pause to let the user trigger the animation. You can advance the animation by right-clicking your mouse or pressing the right arrow key.

S TEP-BY-STEP ▷ 1.2

1. In the task pane, click the **More presentations** link.

2. In the Open dialog box, display the disk drive and/or folder containing the data files for this course, click **IP Step1-2,** and then click **Open.** The file appears as shown in Figure 1-3.

3. Click **View Show** from the **Slide Show** menu.

4. Press the right arrow key or click the mouse to trigger the animation on the first slide. A picture of a tornado appears on the screen and the word *Tornadoes* becomes animated. If you have a sound card and speakers you should also hear a thunderstorm.

5. Click your mouse to advance to the next slide. Notice that the animation on the slide advances automatically.

6. Click your mouse again to advance to the next slide. The title of this slide appears automatically. Click your mouse again to trigger the next text line. Continue to click to advance through the presentation. As the presentation continues, notice the different examples of animation. Leave the presentation open for the next Step-by-Step.

Saving a Presentation

To save a new presentation, choose Save As from the File menu or click the Save button on the toolbar to display the Save As dialog box, as shown in Figure 1-4. Click the down arrow to the right of the Save in box and click the drive where you will save your presentation. Select the contents of the File name box, key a filename, and choose Save.

FIGURE 1-4
Save As dialog box

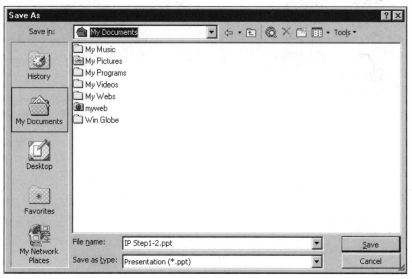

The next time you want to save changes to your presentation, click the Save button on the toolbar or choose Save from the File menu. These commands update the file and do not open the dialog box.

STEP-BY-STEP ▷ 1.3

1. Choose **Save As** on the **File** menu. The Save As dialog box appears.

2. Click the down arrow to the right of the **Save in** box and choose the drive on which you want to save the presentation.

3. In the File name box, key **Tornado,** followed by your initials.

4. Click **Save**. Leave the program on the screen for the next Step-by-Step.

Changing Views

You can view a presentation four different ways using options on the View menu: Normal, Slide Sorter, Slide Show, and Notes Page. You can also change the view quickly by clicking one of the buttons on the bottom-left of the screen, shown in Figure 1-5.

FIGURE 1-5
View buttons

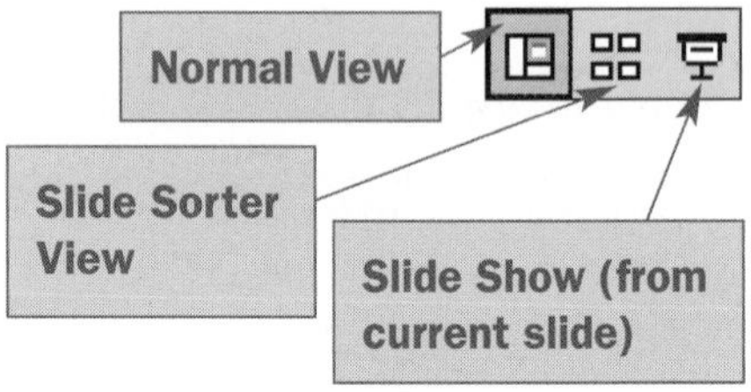

Normal View
Slide Sorter View
Slide Show (from current slide)

Normal View

You have been working in Normal view. This view has four panes, the Slides pane, the task pane, the Outline pane, and the notes pane.

USING THE SLIDE PREVIEW AND OUTLINE PANE

To easily work with the slides in a presentation, PowerPoint displays all your slides in the Slides pane on the left side of your screen. This pane has two tabs at the top, the Outline tab and the Slides tab. The Outline tab displays all the text on your slides in outline form. The Slides tab displays your slides as small pictures or thumbnails. To move between the slides, click the thumbnail in the Slides mode or click on the text in the Outline mode. The Outline mode allows you to edit text in the outline; changes are automatically made on the slide. You can also view the slides in your presentation by scrolling up and down. You can close the Slides and Outline pane by clicking the Close button in the top-right corner of the pane. Choose Normal on the View menu to restore this pane.

STEP-BY-STEP 1.4

1. If it is not already selected, click the **Outline** tab on the left side of the window.

2. Click on slide **7**. Your screen should appear as shown in Figure 1-6.

3. Highlight the number **75,000** in the second bullet point. Key **80,000**.

4. Click the **Slides** tab. Leave the presentation on the screen for the next Step-by-Step.

Hot Tip

You can also press the **Page Down** key to view the next slide or press **Page Up** to view the previous slide.

FIGURE 1-6
Text edit box

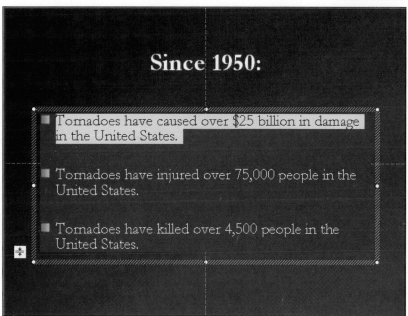

USING THE TASK PANE

The task pane on the right side of the screen contains common tasks that you use frequently when creating a presentation. It is located conveniently so you can use the commands while still working on your files. The task pane contains tasks to help you create a new presentation, select a layout, choose a design template, choose a color scheme, choose an animation scheme, create a custom animation, set slide transitions, search for files, copy and paste text or pictures, as well as access Microsoft PowerPoint Help at any time. The task pane defaults to open when you start PowerPoint. You can turn this option off at the bottom of the task pane. You can close the task pane by clicking its Close button.

1. Click the **Design** button on the Formatting toolbar. (This opens the task pane if it is not already open.) The Slide Design task pane opens.

2. Scroll to view the different design templates.

3. Click **Color Schemes** and **Animation Schemes** to view the templates available for your use. Close the task pane by clicking the **Close** button. Leave the program on the screen for the next Step-by-Step.

USING THE SLIDE PANE

The Slide pane is the workbench for PowerPoint presentations. It displays one slide at a time and is useful for adding text or modifying the slide's appearance. It displays your slides in an area large enough to work on your slide easily. You can also view the slides in your presentation by scrolling up and down. The slides appear on the screen as you move the scroll bar.

1. Use the scroll bar to scroll down to slide **7** if it is not already displayed in the Slide pane.

2. Click the first bullet on the slide. A text edit box appears around the text. Leave the program on the screen for the next Step-by-Step.

Notes Page View

The Notes Page view displays your slides on the top portion of the page, with the speaker notes for each slide in the notes pane on the bottom of the page. To add speaker notes, click in the notes pane and begin keying. You can use these notes to guide you as you make a presentation, or as a handout to your audience to help guide them through your presentation. You will learn more about the notes pane and how to use it effectively in Lesson 2.

Slide Sorter View

Slide Sorter view, as shown in Figure 1-7, displays miniature versions of the slides on screen so that you can move and arrange slides easily by dragging. A Slide Sorter toolbar that helps you with timings, transitions, and animation appears when you switch to this view.

1. Click the **Slide Sorter View** button. The screen appears as shown in Figure 1-7.

2. Click slide **7** so that it is outlined in bold.

3. Click and drag slide **7** between slide 4 and slide 5. A line appears between the two slides. Release the mouse button. Slide 7 moves to become slide 5 and all other slides move down and are renumbered.

4. Click slide **1**.

5. Click the **Slide Show** button on the bottom left corner of the screen. Slide 1 appears on the screen.

6. Click the mouse to advance through all the slides.

7. Once you've advanced through all the slides, a black screen displays. Click to exit the presentation and return to the PowerPoint Slide Sorter screen.

8. Save the presentation and leave it open for the next Step-by-Step.

FIGURE 1-7
Slide Sorter view

Slide Show View

In the Slide Show view, you can run your presentation on the computer as if it were a slide projector and preview how it will look.

Using Menus and Toolbars

When you first use PowerPoint, the short menu displays only the basic commands. To see an expanded menu with all the commands, click the arrows at the bottom of the menu. As you work, PowerPoint adjusts the menus to display the commands you use most frequently, adding a command when you choose it and dropping a command when it hasn't been used recently.

Hot Tip

You can press the Esc key anytime during a presentation to return to the view displayed prior to viewing the show.

In Normal view, the three toolbars displayed on the screen by default are Standard, Formatting, and Drawing, shown in Figures 1-8, 1-9, and 1-10. The Standard and Formatting toolbars generally share the same row. To see additional buttons, click the Toolbar Options button on the toolbar and choose from the list that appears. When you use a button from the list, it is added to the toolbar. If you haven't used a button recently, it is added to the Toolbar Options list.

FIGURE 1-8
Standard toolbar

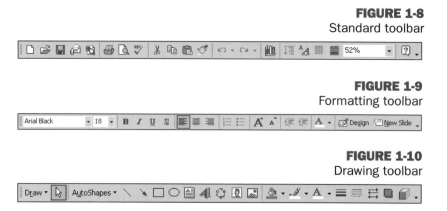

FIGURE 1-9
Formatting toolbar

FIGURE 1-10
Drawing toolbar

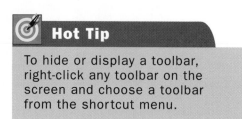

The status bar, shown in Figure 1-11, appears at the bottom of your screen. The area on the left side of the status bar shows which slide is displayed. The second area indicates the design currently in use. You can double-click it to bring up the Apply Design Template dialog box. The third area displays a spell-check icon or the currently loaded language dictionary.

> **Hot Tip**
>
> To hide or display a toolbar, right-click any toolbar on the screen and choose a toolbar from the shortcut menu.

FIGURE 1-11
Status bar

| Slide 1 of 4 | Clouds | English (U.S.) |

Deleting Slides

C

A presentation you create using the AutoContent Wizard includes a predetermined number of slides based on the type of presentation you choose. If you decide that a slide does not fit your presentation, you can easily delete it. With that slide displayed, choose Delete Slide from the Edit menu. If you accidentally delete the wrong slide, immediately choose Undo Delete Slide from the Edit menu to restore the slide or click the Undo button on the toolbar.

> **Hot Tip**
>
> If you make a mistake while using an Office program, you can press Ctrl+Z to undo the last entry. By default, you can undo up to 20 entries in PowerPoint. You can change the number of actions you can undo by selecting **Options** from the **Tools** menu and clicking the **Edit** tab.

STEP-BY-STEP ▷ 1.8

1. If necessary, click the **Slide Sorter View** button.

2. Right-click slide **8** so that it is outlined in bold and a shortcut menu appears.

3. Click **Delete Slide** from the shortcut menu.

4. Click slide **6**.

5. Click the **Slide Show** button. Slide 6 appears on the screen.

6. Click the mouse button to advance through all the slides. Notice that slide 8 has been deleted from the presentation.

7. Save and leave the presentation open for the next Step-by-Step.

Printing a Presentation

PowerPoint offers several print options that can enhance your presentation to an audience. You can print handouts that contain small pictures or thumbnails of your slides and an area for taking notes. You can also use the print feature to create transparencies if you are using an overhead projector to make your presentation. Choose Print from the File menu and the Print dialog box appears, as shown in Figure 1-12. From the Print what drop-down list box, you can choose to print your presentation as slides using the Slides option, with notes using the Notes Pages option, or as an outline using the Outline View option. Using the Handouts option, you can print handouts with two, three, four, six, or nine slides per page and choose whether they are ordered horizontally or vertically.

You can choose to print all the slides, only the current slide, or any combination of slides in your presentation. If you aren't printing your presentation in color, you can choose either the Grayscale or Pure black and white option. To make sure the slides print on the page correctly, there is a Scale to fit paper option. With the Frame slides option, you can choose whether the border of the slides appears when printed.

Computer Concepts

You can preview what your presentation will look like when printed in black and white by choosing **Black and White** from the **View** menu.

FIGURE 1-12
Print dialog box

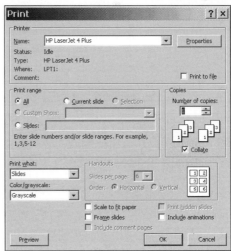

STEP-BY-STEP ▷ 1.9

1. Choose **Print** from the **File** menu. The Print dialog box appears (Figure 1-12).

2. Click the arrow on the **Print what** box, and click **Outline View.**

3. Click the **Scale to fit paper** option.

4. Click **OK**. The presentation prints as an outline on one page.

5. Open the Print dialog box again.

6. In the Print what box, choose **Handouts**.

7. In the Handouts section, click the down arrow on the **Slides per page** box and choose **9**.

8. Choose **Horizontal** as the order, if it is not already chosen.

9. Click **OK.** The presentation prints as a handout. Leave the presentation open for the next Step-by-Step.

 Hot Tip

You do not have to switch views to print a view different from the one you are currently using.

Closing a Presentation and Exiting PowerPoint

When you want to close a presentation, choose Close from the File menu or click the presentation's close window button. To exit PowerPoint, choose Exit from the File menu or click the PowerPoint close box in the upper-right corner of the screen. If there are any unsaved changes to a presentation you have been working on, you will be asked if you want to save them before exiting.

STEP-BY-STEP ▷ 1.10

1. Choose **Close** from the **File** menu to close the presentation. Click **Yes** if prompted to save your changes.

2. Click the **Close** box in the upper right corner of the screen to exit PowerPoint.

Summary

In this lesson, you learned:

■ PowerPoint is an Office XP application that can help you create a professional presentation. When you start PowerPoint, you have the choice of opening an existing presentation or creating a new one.

■ You can view your presentation four different ways: Normal view, Notes Page view, Slide sorter view, and Slide show. Each view has its own advantages.

■ Using the Print dialog box, you can print your presentation as slides using the Slides option, with notes using the Notes Pages option, or as an outline using the Outline View option. You can also choose to print handouts with two, three, four, six, or nine slides per page.

■ To exit PowerPoint, choose Exit from the File menu.

VOCABULARY REVIEW

Define the following terms:

Notes pane	Slide sorter	Task pane
Outline tab	Slides tab	

LESSON 1 REVIEW QUESTIONS

MULTIPLE CHOICE

Select the best response for the following statements.

1. When an existing file you want to open is not shown in the PowerPoint dialog box, choose
   A. Open Another File.
   B. Search.
   C. More Presentations.
   D. Browse.

2. Which toolbar is not displayed by default in Normal view?
   A. Outlining
   B. Standard
   C. Formatting
   D. Drawing

3. Which of the following is not one of the presentation views?
   A. Outline
   B. Notes Page
   C. Slide Show
   D. Slide Sorter

4. What button do you click to display the task pane?
    A. New Slide
    B. Outline
    C. Design
    D. Pane

5. Which option in the Print dialog box lets you choose whether the border of the slide appears when printed?
    A. Grayscale
    B. Print border
    C. Scale to fit
    D. Frame slides

FILL IN THE BLANK

Complete the following sentences by writing the correct word or words in the blanks provided.

1. The list under the heading _____ shows recently opened presentations.

2. Use the _____ key to advance and the _____ key to review slides in a presentation.

3. The _____ tab displays all of the text on your slides in outline form.

4. _____ view displays miniature versions of the slides on screen so that you can move and arrange slides easily by dragging.

5. You can print _____ that contain small pictures or thumbnails of your slides.

LESSON 1 PROJECTS

PROJECT 1-1

1. Open **IP Project1-1** from the data files.

2. Save the presentation as **Networking** followed by your initials.

3. Run the presentation as a slide show.

4. Leave the presentation open for the next project.

PROJECT 1-2

1. Select and delete slide number **6**.

2. Print the presentation as audience handouts with 4 slides per page.

3. Run the presentation as a slide show.

4. Save and close the presentation.

PROJECT 1-3

1. Search the Internet for a PowerPoint project about a subject that interests you.

2. Save the project to disk.

3. Run the presentation as a slide show.

4. Print the presentation as audience handouts with 4 slides per page.

5. Save and close the presentation.

CRITICAL THINKING

SCANS

ACTIVITY 1-1

You can change the way that PowerPoint displays when you initially open the program. Use PowerPoint Help to find out how to change the default view.

SCANS

ACTIVITY 1-2

It is helpful to plan a presentation before you actually create it on the computer. Sketch out ideas on paper for a presentation on one of the topics below or make up your own. The presentation should have at least four slides. Include a title slide and indicate where you would put clip art.

■ Help start a community campaign to keep your city clean.

■ Encourage people to donate blood in the blood drive campaign next week.

■ Explain the procedure for some safety technique (performing CPR, fire prevention, how to baby-proof a house, performing first-aid).

■ Offer the opportunity to be involved in a community project or volunteer organization.

■ Explain the advantages of adopting an animal from the local shelter.

■ Provide information about a new class that will be available in the fall.

ENHANCING A POWERPOINT PRESENTATION

OBJECTIVES

Upon completion of this lesson, you will be able to:

- Create a new presentation.
- Format slides.
- Work with text on slides.
- Use the slide master.
- Add multimedia to slides.
- Add a slide.
- Add a header or footer.
- Use slide transitions.
- Format a single slide.

🕐 **Estimated Time: 2 hours**

VOCABULARY

Animate

AutoContent Wizard

Design template

Effects options

Hyperlink

Motion path

Placeholder

Show Advanced Timeline

Slide master

Slide transitions

Creating a Presentation

When you start PowerPoint, the task pane displays four choices for creating a presentation: Open a presentation, New, New from existing presentation, and New from template. The Open a presentation feature contains the recently used files list, which by default contains the last four opened files. You can change that number by selecting Options from the Tools menu, clicking the General tab, and changing the number. If the presentation you want to open is not in the list, click the More presentations icon.

The New feature has three options: Blank Presentation, From Design Template, and From AutoContent Wizard. The Blank Presentation feature lets you create a presentation from scratch, using whatever layout, format, colors, and styles you prefer. If you decide to create a presentation using the Design Template option, you can choose a design template that is right for the presentation you have planned. The design templates that come with PowerPoint are already formatted with certain colors, fonts, and layouts. The AutoContent Wizard guides you through

Computer Concepts

Unless you have a particular reason for creating a presentation from a blank document, it is easier to use the wizard or a design template. You can always modify the presentation as you go along.

a series of questions about the type of presentation, output options, presentation style, and presentation options. The Wizard offers ideas and an organization for a new presentation based on your answers.

STEP-BY-STEP ▷ 2.1

1. Start PowerPoint. From the task pane choose **From AutoContent Wizard**. Remember, if the task pane is not displayed, you can show it by right-clicking the Standard toolbar and clicking **Task Pane.** The AutoContent Wizard dialog box appears, as shown in Figure 2-1.

2. Read the screen and click **Next**.

3. This screen displays the types of presentations in categories that the AutoContent Wizard can help create. The wizard defaults to the General category. Click the **All** button and view all of the categories.

4. Select **Training** as the type of presentation you are going to give. Click **Next**.

5. Choose **On-screen presentation** as the output. Click **Next**.

6. In the Presentation title box key **Creating a Web Site with FrontPage**.

7. In the Footer box key **Caprock Internet Services, INC.**

8. Click the **Date last updated** box to remove the check mark. Click **Next**.

9. Click **Finish**. Your presentation appears on the screen, similar to Figure 2-2.

10. Save the presentation as **Web Site** followed by your initials and leave it open for the next Step-by-Step.

Note

On the opening slide, PowerPoint automatically inserts the name that is entered in User Information. This information can be changed by selecting **Options** from the **Tools** menu, and clicking the **General** tab.

FIGURE 2-1
Starting AutoContent Wizard

FIGURE 2-2
AutoContent presentation

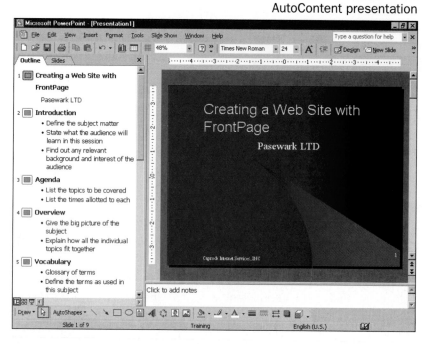

Applying a Design Template

FIGURE 2-3
Drop-down menu

Y ou can use a design template to change the appearance of your slides without changing the content. ***Design templates*** are pre-designed graphic styles that you can apply to your slides. You can change the color scheme, font, formatting, and layout of your slides in a design template to create a different look.

To use a design template, click Design Templates in the task pane. If the Design Templates option is not visible, click the list arrow to the right of the title bar in the task pane and select Design Templates from the drop-down menu. This menu displays all the available design templates. When you hover over (place your mouse pointer over an object without clicking) each design template, the name of the template appears and an arrow for a drop-down menu (Figure 2-3) appears on the right side of the design template. The menu options apply the template to all of the slides in your presentation or to only select slides. There is also an option to view the templates in the large or small format. Choose Apply from the drop-down menu to change all your slides to the new design.

S TEP-BY-STEP ▷ 2.2

1. Select **Design Templates** from the task pane drop-down menu if it is not already selected.

2. In the task pane, scroll down and hover over the design template named **Refined.pot**. When the list arrow appears, click **Apply to**

All Slides. The current presentation is displayed on your screen with a new design. Your screen should look like Figure 2-4.

3. Save and leave the presentation open for the next Step-by-Step.

FIGURE 2-4
Opening slide with new design template applied

Creating a Web Site
with FrontPage

Pasewark LTD

 Caprock Internet Services, INC

Changing Color Scheme

To apply a different color scheme to your presentation, click Color Schemes in the task pane, hover over the color scheme you want to apply, and click the drop-down arrow. To apply the scheme to all of your slides, click Apply to All Slides.

You can apply the color scheme to only specific slides by selecting the slides from the Slide Preview pane. You can select more than one slide by holding down the Ctrl button while clicking the slides. To apply color schemes to only the selected slides, click Apply to Selected Slides from the drop-down menu.

Adding or Changing Slide Animation

When you *animate* an object or text, you add a sound effect or visual effect. Animation enhances your presentation and increases audience interest. To add or change slide animation, click Animation Schemes in the task pane. You can apply an animation to the current (displayed) slide or to

Hot Tip

You can use different colors to show a change of topics in your presentation.

IP-19

all slides. This feature applies animation to all text items on the slide. You can also individually animate text boxes, pictures, and transitions into the slide. You will learn how to do this later in the lesson. The two buttons at the bottom of the task pane allow you to preview the animation. Play activates the animation in the current screen. The Slide Show button shows the slide in full screen, as it would appear in a slide show.

S TEP-BY-STEP ▷ 2.3

1. Click **Animation Schemes** in the task pane.

2. In the task pane, scroll down and click **Title arc** as shown in Figure 2-5.

3. Click **Apply to All Slides.**

4. Click **Play** to view the slide animation.

5. Save and leave the presentation open for the next Step-by-Step.

FIGURE 2-5
Animation schemes

Format a Single Slide

Y ou can use a design template to change the appearance of a single slide without changing the rest of the slides in the presentation. Click the Design button to display the Slide Design dialog box in the task pane. Previously, you learned how to apply these features to an entire presentation. In this Step-by Step you apply these features to a single slide.

S TEP-BY-STEP ▷ 2.4

1. Select slide **9**. Click **Design Templates** in the task pane (if it is not already selected).

2. Scroll down and hover over the design template named **Globe.pot**. When the list arrow

appears, click **Apply to Selected Slides.** The current slide is displayed on your screen with a new design.

3. Click **Color Schemes** in the task pane. Select the fourth color scheme down.

4. Click **Animation Schemes** in the task pane.

5. Select **Grow and Exit** from the **Animation Schemes** menu. Do *not* click the Apply to

Master button or the Apply to All Slides buttons, because you are applying the animation only to this slide.

6. View the presentation to see your additions. Save and leave the presentation open for the next Step-by-Step.

Use the Slide Master

The *slide master* controls the formatting for all the slides in the presentation. You can use the slide master to change such items as the font, size, color, style, alignment, spacing, and background. Changing the slide master affects the appearance of all of the slides and gives them a consistent look. You can add headers and footers to slides and also place an object, such as a logo or graphic, on every slide by placing the object on the slide master. To access the master title slide, shown in Figure 2-6, choose Master from the View menu, then Slide Master from the submenu. When you have finished making changes to the slide master, click Close on the Master toolbar.

FIGURE 2-6
Slide master

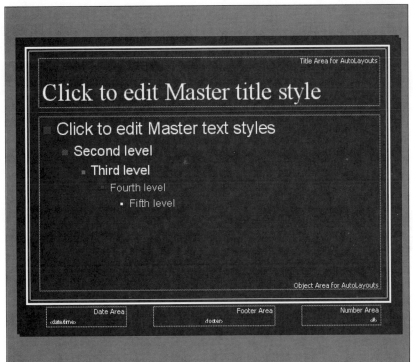

PowerPoint has other masters that work like the slide master. Use the title master to format the first slide of your presentation. The handout master lets you add items that you want to appear on all your handouts, such as a logo, the date, the time, and page numbers. On the notes master, include any text or formatting that you want to appear on all your speaker notes. Choose Master from the View menu and choose the master you want from the submenu.

Computer Concepts

You can override the formats applied to the presentation by the slide master by making changes directly to individual slides.

STEP-BY-STEP ▷ 2.5

1. Click slide 1. Choose **Master** from the **View** menu and **Slide Master** from the submenu. Select the presentation slide (called *Refined Slide Master*). It looks like that shown in Figure 2-6.

2. Choose **Picture** on the **Insert** menu and **From File** on the submenu. The Insert Picture dialog box appears as shown in Figure 2-7. Locate the file labeled **Caprock Logo** in the data files. Click the file to select it, and then click **Insert**. The logo appears on the slide.

3. Click and drag the logo to the bottom-right corner of the text box, as shown in Figure 2-8.

4. Click **Close Master View** on the Master toolbar. Scroll through the presentation to see that the logo appears on all slides except for the first and last slides.

5. Save and leave the presentation open for the next Step-by-Step.

Hot Tip

You can easily display a master by pressing **Shift** and clicking the **Normal View**, **Slide Sorter View**, or the **Slide Show** buttons in the bottom left corner of your screen.

FIGURE 2-7
Insert Picture dialog box

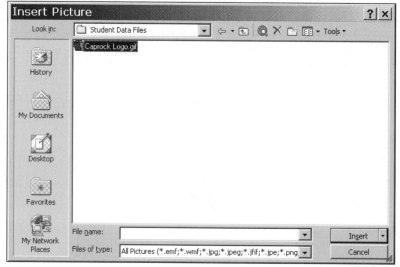

FIGURE 2-8

Positioning the Caprock logo on the slide master

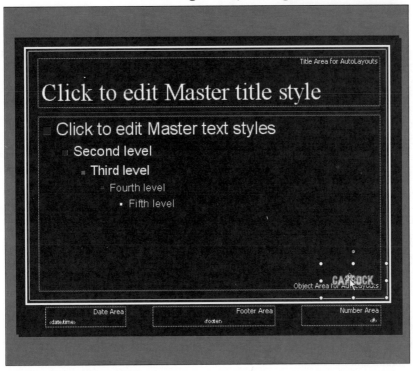

Working with Text

Adding Text to Slides

When the AutoContent Wizard helps you create a presentation, it creates placeholders on each slide that tell you what kind of information might go there. A *placeholder* reserves a space in the presentation for the type of information you want to insert. To replace a text placeholder, click the text. A box with a hashed-line border appears around the text. You can then select the existing text and key in whatever you like.

If you cannot see the text clearly, it is helpful to use the Zoom feature. Click the arrow next to the Zoom box on the

Computer Concepts

To find and replace text, choose **Replace** from the **Edit** menu. Key the text you want to find and the text you want to replace it with. Click **Find Next** to find the next occurrence, **Replace** to replace the next occurrence, and **Replace All** to replace all occurrences.

toolbar. The menu contains preset percentages so you can enlarge or reduce the size of the presentation on screen or you can choose Fit to allow PowerPoint to display the slide at an optimal size.

1. Display slide **2**. Highlight the words **Define the subject matter**. A box appears around all of the text. Key the following:

   ```
   FrontPage is a tool that can be
   used for authoring and publishing
   Web pages.
   ```

2. Highlight the next line of text, *State what the audience will learn in this lesson*, and key:

   ```
   You will learn the basics of
   creating a Web page using
   FrontPage.
   ```

3. Select and delete the rest of the text on the slide. Your slide should look like Figure 2-9. You have learned how to change the text by editing it directly on the slide. You will edit the rest of the presentation using the Outline mode.

4. Click the **Outline** tab in the Slide Preview pane. Click the slide icon for slide **3**. Notice that the text for the entire slide is highlighted in the outline area.

5. Open the **Edit** menu and select **Delete Slide** to delete the slide. Each of the slides moves up to replace the deleted slide.

6. On the new slide **3**, replace the word *Overview* with **General Guidelines**. Highlight all the text below the title and key the following:

   ```
   All of these guidelines are
   important to consider when
   creating a Web site.
   ```

7. Under *Vocabulary* on slide **4**, replace the existing text with the following:

   ```
   Web Page — Combines text with
   audio, video, and animation in
   graphical format that can be
   viewed on the Internet.
   Hyperlinks — Connects Web pages
   so that the user can jump from
   ```

   ```
   one Web page to another.
   Hypertext Markup Language (HTML)
   — Computer language used for doc-
   uments that are shared among
   users on the World Wide Web.
   ```

8. Notice that the text is too large to fit on the slide. If PowerPoint does not automatically change the text size, select the text in the body of the slide. Change the font size to **24**.

9. Replace *Topic One* on slide **5** with **Create a Web Site with a Template**. Replace the rest of the text with:

   ```
   FrontPage provides templates that
   help you to quickly and easily
   create a Web page. These tem-
   plates provide a structure of
   themes, styles, and colors to
   which you can add your text and
   pictures.
   ```

10. Replace *Topic Two* on slide **6** with **Create a Web Site From Scratch**. Replace the rest of the text with the following:

    ```
    FrontPage offers the flexibility
    of creating a Web site from
    scratch. You can use your own
    themes, and create your own
    styles for your Web site.
    ```

Computer Concepts

You can add text to the top or bottom of a slide by inserting a header or footer. You can also add the slide number, date, or time in a header or footer. Choose **Header and Footer** from the **View** menu. Select the options and key the text you want.

11. On slide **7** replace the text under *Summary* with:

FrontPage is a tool that allows you to create Web sites by using a template, or from scratch. FrontPage will help you publish your Web pages to the Internet.

12. On slide **8** replace the text under *Where to Get More Information* with the following:

Caprock Internet Services offers FrontPage classes on Mondays, Wednesdays, and Fridays at 6:00 PM at our Mesa

Mall location. Phone (806) 555-9919 for reservations.

13. Choose **View Show** from the **Slide Show** menu. Click the mouse to advance through the presentation.

14. Save and leave the presentation open for the next Step-by-Step.

 Hot Tip

To move a text box, click to select it and drag. To resize, click the handles and drag.

FIGURE 2-9
Slide 2 with edited text

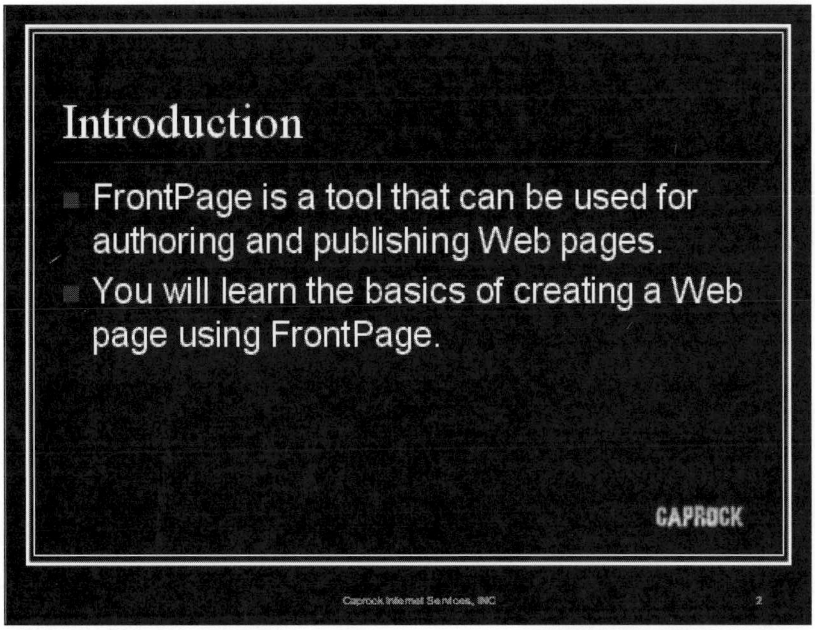

Introduction

■ FrontPage is a tool that can be used for authoring and publishing Web pages.
■ You will learn the basics of creating a Web page using FrontPage.

CAPROCK

Caprock Internet Services, INC

2

 Computer Concepts

If you want to add text to a slide that does not have a text place-holder, click the **Text Box** button on the **Drawing** toolbar or click **Text Box** from the **Insert** menu.

C > **Adding Notes to a Slide**

To add speaker notes, click in the notes pane below the slide and begin keying. A good PowerPoint presentation generally contains brief, main points of the subject. Use the speaker notes to remind yourself of any additional information you need to include in your speech.

S TEP-BY-STEP ▷ **2.7**

1. Click **Normal View** if it is not already selected.

2. On slide **3**, click in the area below the slide that reads *Click to add notes*.

3. Key the following in the notes pane. Adjust the notes pane by dragging the bar above the pane up.

   Learn from other Web sites. Spend some time on the Internet looking at sites that might be similar to the one you want to create.

   Plan your site in advance. Work out what you want to convey to your visitors.

   Set goals. Goal setting is important or you might get lost along the way.

   Plan your layout in advance. Give your site an appealing look. Use exciting colors for a jazzy site, or softer colors for more subtlety.

   Content. Be brief, but include enough to make your point.

   Navigate. Make sure your site can be easily navigated. Include links to your other pages on every page. Don't forget to include a link for your home page.

   Edit your site. Make sure that everything is correct before publishing your Web site to the Internet. Have someone else check your page after you publish it.

   Speed. Make sure that your pages download quickly. Large pictures that take a long time to download will frustrate visitors and they may move on to another site.

   Above all, have fun.

4. Select **Print** on the **File** menu, choose to print slide **3** only, and select **Notes Pages** from the Print what list box.

5. Save the presentation and leave open for the next Step-by-Step.

C > **Change Alignment, Spacing, Case, and Tabs**

To change text alignment, select the text and click one of the alignment buttons on the toolbar. To change spacing, select the text, choose Line Spacing from the Format menu, and make changes in the Line Spacing dialog box. To change the case of text, select the text, choose Change Case from the Format menu, then choose one of the five options in the Change Case dialog box. To set or clear tabs, display the ruler by choosing Ruler from the View menu. Set a tab by selecting the text and clicking the tab button at the left of the horizontal ruler. Clear a tab by dragging the tab marker off the ruler.

S TEP-BY-STEP ▷ **2.8**

1. Select the text below the slide title *Vocabulary* on slide **4**.

2. Click the **Center** button on the toolbar.

3. Choose **Line Spacing** from the **Format** menu. The Line Spacing dialog box appears. In the Line Spacing section, click the up arrow until it reads **1.2**. Click **OK**.

4. Highlight the words *Web Page* in the first sentence. Choose **Change Case** from the **Format** menu. The Change Case dialog box appears. Choose **UPPERCASE** and click **OK**.

5. Repeat these steps for the word *Hyperlink* in the second sentence and *Hypertext Markup Language (HTML)* in the third sentence.

6. Save the presentation and leave it open for the next Step-by-Step.

Working with Bullets

If you want bullets on a slide, you can add them by selecting the text or placeholder and clicking the Bullets button on the toolbar. You can customize a bulleted list after it has been created. You can change the appearance of the bullets—such as their shape, size, or color—and you can also adjust the distance between the bullets and the text. To change the appearance of the bullets throughout the presentation, make the changes on the slide master. You cannot select a bullet to make changes; you must select the associated text.

Computer Concepts

If your list is numbered rather than bulleted, choose the **Numbered** tab in the Bullets and Numbering dialog box to customize the list.

To change all the bullets in a bulleted list, select the entire list. When you choose Bullets and Numbering from the Format menu, the Bullets and Numbering dialog box appears as shown in Figure 2-10. On the Bulleted tab, you can select a preset bullet or add a graphical bullet by clicking the Picture button. You can also change the color or the bullet size in relation to the text.

FIGURE 2-10
Bullets and Numbering dialog box

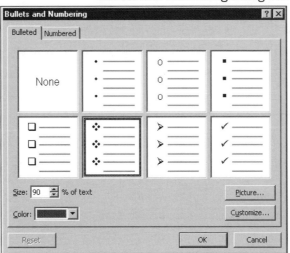

1. Display the slide master by selecting **Master** from the **View** menu and **Slide Master** from the submenu.

2. Highlight **Click to edit Master text styles**.

3. Choose **Bullets and Numbering** from the **Format** menu.

4. Choose the **Bulleted** tab (if it is not already selected), as shown in Figure 2-10.

5. Select the bullet style shown in Figure 2-10 with the box around it. (Your bullet choices may not match the figure exactly). If that bullet is not available, click another appropriate one. Click the up arrow in the Size box until it reads **90**. Click **OK**.

6. Close the Slide Master and advance through the presentation to view the changes.

7. Save and leave the presentation open for the next Step-by-Step.

 Extra Challenge

Change the bullets in your presentation to arrows, dots, starts, check marks, or some other character by choosing **Bullets and Numbering** from the **Format** menu.

C Changing Text Appearance

If you use a design template, the format of the text on your slides is predetermined so that the layout, color scheme, font, size, and style are consistent throughout the presentation. You can alter the format by making changes to individual slides. You change the font, font style, size, effects, and color in the Font dialog box, shown in Figure 2-11, which you access by choosing Font from the Format menu.

FIGURE 2-11
Font dialog box

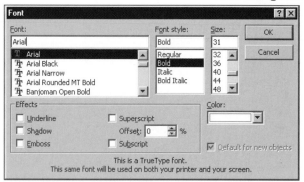

You can also use the Formatting toolbar as a shortcut to changing the font, font size, font style, and font color as shown in Figure 2-12. The Increase Font Size and Decrease Font Size buttons allow you to change the font size quickly in preset increments.

Hot Tip

Press **Tab** to demote a bullet one level.

FIGURE 2-12
Formatting toolbar

| Font | Font Size | | Increase Font Size | Decrease Font Size | Font Color |

STEP-BY-STEP ▷ 2.10

1. Display slide **8** and highlight the text below the title.

2. Choose **Font** from the **Format** menu.

3. In the Font box of the Font dialog box, choose

Arial Narrow. In the Size box, choose **28**. Click **OK**.

4. Save and leave the presentation open for the next Step-by-Step.

Check Spelling and Style

Automatic spell-checking identifies misspellings and words that are not in its dictionary by underlining them with a wavy red line immediately after you key them. To correct a misspelled word, position the pointer on the underlined word and click with the right mouse button. A shortcut menu appears with a list of correctly spelled words. Click the suggestion that you want with the left mouse button and PowerPoint replaces the misspelled word. You can turn the automatic spell checker on, off, or change the way that it checks your document, by accessing the Spelling & Style tab of the Options dialog box through the Tools menu.

You can also check the spelling in a presentation after it is complete by clicking the Spelling button on the Standard toolbar. The Spelling dialog box contains options for ignoring words, making changes, or adding words to your own custom dictionary.

An effective presentation should be consistent, error-free, and visually appealing. PowerPoint helps you determine if your presentation conforms to the standards of good style. For instance, title text size should be at least 36 points and the number of bullets on a slide should not exceed six. A light bulb appears, as shown in Figure 2-13, to alert you to problems with visual clarity such as appropriate font usage and legibility, inconsistent capitalization, and end punctuation. To make changes, click the light bulb and choose an option from the menu.

FIGURE 2-13
Style checker dialog box

Capitalization

Text in this placeholder should be title case.

● Change the text to title case

● Ignore this style rule for this presentation only

● Change style checker options for all presentations

☐ Don't show me this tip again

In the Style Options dialog box you can customize what PowerPoint considers style errors or inconsistencies. Choose Options from the Tools menu and in the Spelling & Style tab, click the Style Options button to access the Style Options dialog box. Make any changes you want or click the Defaults button to restore the original settings.

S TEP-BY-STEP ▷ 2.11

1. Select **Spelling** from the **Tools** menu.

2. Scroll through the presentation to view each slide and make any corrections.

3. Save and leave the presentation open for the next Step-by-Step.

Hot Tip

If the light bulb is not visible choose **Show the Office Assistant** from the Help menu to display it.

Adding a Slide

You can add a slide to a presentation by clicking the New Slide button on the toolbar or by choosing New Slide from the Insert menu. In the Normal view, PowerPoint places the new slide after the currently displayed slide. Choosing New Slide displays the Slide Layout dialog box in the task pane, which allows you to choose a layout for the new slide. The Slide Layout dialog box has 27 layouts. Choose a layout and apply it to the slide as you did above.

Another way to add a slide is to copy it from another presentation. Choose Slides from Files from the Insert menu. Locate the presentation from which you want to copy a slide and click Display. Select the slide you want to copy and click Insert. PowerPoint inserts the slide after the one displayed on the screen.

S TEP-BY-STEP ▷ 2.12

1. Display slide **6** titled *Create a Web Site from Scratch*. The area on the left of the status bar should read Slide 6 of 8.

2. Click the **New Slide** button on the toolbar. The Slide Layout dialog box appears in the task pane.

3. Click the third layout in the column named *Title and Text*, if it is not already chosen.

4. Highlight and replace the text that reads *Click to add title* with *Create a Web Page from an*

Existing Page. Click between the words *from* and *an* and press the **Enter** key to distribute the text evenly in the title.

5. Click where it reads *Click to add text*.

6. Key **FrontPage allows you to create a new Web page, using an existing Web page as a template.**

7. Save and leave the presentation open for the next Step-by-Step.

Formatting Slides

FIGURE 2-14
Slide Layout pane

Slide Layouts

When you want to change the layout of text or graphics on slides easily, you can use the program's preset layouts. PowerPoint includes 27 Auto-Layouts you can choose from to create a new slide or change the layout of an existing slide. The different layouts include placeholders for text, columns, bulleted lists, clip art, tables, organization charts, objects, graphs, and media clips. Just click a placeholder and replace it with your own information. You can choose the layout that best fits the need of a particular slide.

To change the layout for an existing slide, scroll to display the slide you want to change. Then, choose Slide Layout from the Format menu or click the down arrow on the task pane toolbar and choose Slide Layout from the menu. The Slide Layout pane is divided into four categories, Text Layouts, Content Layouts, Text and Content Layouts, and Other Layouts. Each category contains small diagrams of the AutoLayouts, as shown in Figure 2-14. When you hover over each layout template, the name of the template appears and an arrow for a drop-down menu appears on the right side of the layout template.

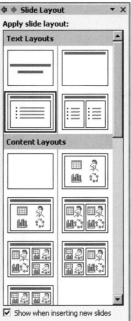

STEP-BY-STEP ▷ 2.13

1. In the Slide Preview pane, click slide **9**.

2. Click the **Design** button on the toolbar to display the task pane. Click the down arrow on the task pane toolbar to display the common tasks and choose **Slide Layout** from the menu. The Slide Layout pane appears, as shown in Figure 2-14.

3. Hover your mouse pointer over the first layout below the *Text and Content Layouts* divider bar. The box that appears as you hover should say *Title, Text & Content*. Click the layout to apply it to the slide. The slide should appear as shown in Figure 2-15.

4. Save and leave the presentation open for the next Step-by-Step.

FIGURE 2-15
Slide layout Title, Text and Content

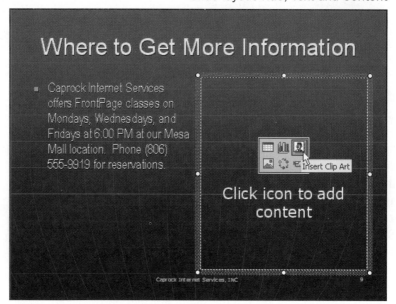

Using Multimedia

Working with Clip Art

FIGURE 2-16
Microsoft Clip Gallery

If there is already a content placeholder on the slide (see Figure 2-15) you can choose from the six options on the Content icon, each of which allows you to insert a different medium. For this lesson you will work with the Clip Art icon in the top-right corner of the Content icon. When you click the Clip Art icon the Microsoft Clip Gallery appears, as shown in Figure 2-16, with numerous categories from which to choose. You can also import clips from other sources into the Clip Gallery and connect to the Web to access more clips. Key a word that describes the item you want in the Search text box. Click the Search button to show the results.

If there is no placeholder, choose Picture from the Insert menu and Clip Art from the submenu and Insert ClipArt appears in the task pane. This task pane offers several options for finding the item you want to insert. To find an item, type one or more words into the Search text box that might help identify the item. You can narrow your search by selecting from the two drop-down menus under Other Search Options. The first menu enables you to narrow your search by selecting the areas that you want to search. Clicking the plus sign next to an item allows you to further narrow your search. In the second menu, notice that in addition to clip art, you can also search for photographs, movies, and sounds. You can narrow this search by clicking the plus sign and selecting from the list of the typical formats for each category. Once you have determined the search filters, click the Search button to show the results.

The results appear in the task pane. An arrow for a drop-down menu appears to the right of the item. Click the Insert option to insert the image in your document at the location of your insertion point. Click Preview/Properties to view the image and its properties without adding it to your document. To see similar clips, click the Find Similar Style.

Hot Tip

When you hover over a picture a label appears with information about it.

STEP-BY-STEP ▷ 2.14

1. On slide **9**, click the **Clip Art** button in the top-right corner of the **Content** icon as shown in Figure 2-15. The Microsoft Clip Gallery dialog box appears, as shown in Figure 2-16.

2. In the Search text box, key **Computer**. Click the picture shown in Figure 2-16 with a box around it. (Your clip art choices might not match the figure exactly.) If that picture is not available, click another appropriate one.

3. Click **OK** to insert the picture.

4. The clip art you chose is displayed on slide 9. Click the clip art and resize or move it to place it attractively on the slide.

5. Save and leave the presentation open for the next Step-by-Step.

Hot Tip

To move clip art, click the object and drag. To resize, click the handles and drag.

Custom Animation

You can add select animation effects to any of the objects on a slide by choosing Custom Animation from the Slide Show menu. The Custom Animation dialog box appears in the task bar. Each animated object is assigned a number on the slide and the corresponding number is listed in the task pane. The objects that are not assigned an animation effect do not have numbers. When you click an object in the task bar, the properties assigned to that object display in the three menu boxes above the objects and the Change and Remove buttons are highlighted, as shown Figure 2-17. You can select how an object is animated, arrange animation order, determine whether to display the animation manually or automatically, and adjust the speed of the animation. If an object is already animated you can change or remove the animation by clicking the object listed in the task pane, and then clicking the Change or Remove button.

FIGURE 2-17
CustomAnimation
task pane

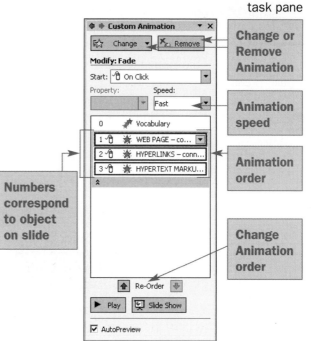

To the right of each animated object there is an arrow that accesses the animation drop-down menu, which contains the commands that determine how you want to trigger that animation of the object. You can set the object to animate three ways: When you click your mouse; with the previous object; or after the previous object. You may also make adjustments to the effects by clicking Effects Options. This displays the dialog box shown in Figure 2-18. In this dialog box, you can select the text to enter the screen in various ways. If you like, you can choose a sound to accompany it. You have the option of dimming the object after it has been animated. You can choose to have the text appear all at once, by the word, or by the letter, and choose to increase or decrease the delay percentage. The Timing tab allows you to adjust the timing of the animation, and determine the trigger for the animation. The Text Animation Tab allows you to animate the text as a group, or by individual levels. The **Show Advanced Timeline** feature displays the time of the animation as a horizontal line graph. This allows you to easily see the timing of each object all at once.

FIGURE 2-18
Setting effects

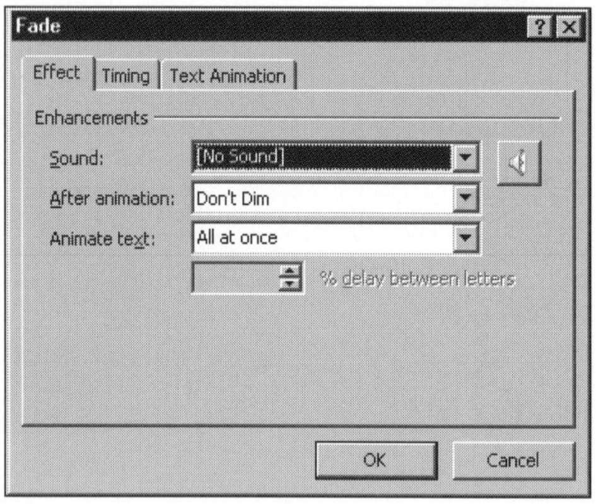

If an object is not animated you can click the object and then click the Add Effect button. The Effects menu appears as shown in Figure 2-19. This menu contains four options: Entrance, Emphasis, Exit, and Motion Paths. Entrance and Exit define the animation for the entry and exit of an object. Emphasis defines the animation of an object that is already placed in the slide. **Motion Path** allows you to use predefined paths for the movement of an object. You can also draw a customized path for an object. As you hover over each option a new menu appears with the last nine animations used. You can click the More Effects option on any of the submenus to display a dialog box containing all the animation features, as shown in Figure 2-20.

FIGURE 2-19
Effects menu

FIGURE 2-20
Add Entrance Effect dialog box

STEP-BY-STEP ▷ 2.15

1. Display slide **3** and choose **Custom Animation** from the **Slide Show** menu. The Custom Animation dialog box appears in the task pane.

2. Click **Play** in the task pane to preview the current animation.

3. Use the Zoom feature to increase the workspace to 150%.

4. Highlight the word *Text* in the top-left corner section of the clip art as shown in Figure 2-21. Change the font size to 14. Key **Learn**, then bold and center the text.

5. Click **Add Effect** in the task pane, then select **Magnify** from the **Entrance** menu. Leave the animation to be triggered *On Click*, because as you are making the presentation you want the clip art objects to animate one at a time so you can talk about each feature. Change the speed to **Fast**.

6. Repeat steps 4 and 5 for the remaining eight pieces of clip art. Insert the following words in place of the word *Text* in the respective pieces:

   `Plan`

   `Goal`

   `Layout`

   `Content`

   `Navigate`

   `Edit`

   `Speed`

   `Have Fun`

7. Double-click the section of the clip art that reads *Learn*. The Format AutoShape dialog box appears. Change the color of the clip art from black to grey. Change the sections labeled *Content* and *Have Fun*.

8. Use the Zoom feature to resize the slide to fit the workspace. Click the **Play** button to view the animation you added to the slide.

9. Save the presentation and leave it open for the next Step-by-Step.

FIGURE 2-21
Highlighted text in clip art

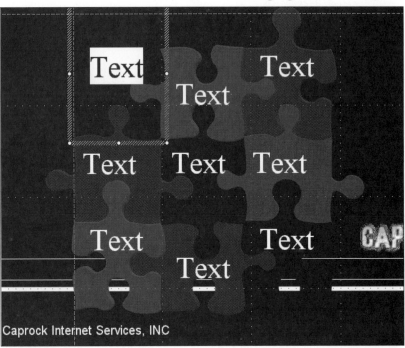

Caprock Internet Services, INC

Insert a Hyperlink

A hyperlink allows you to jump to another location. For example, you can add a hyperlink to go to another slide within your presentation, a different presentation, another Office document, a Web site, or an e-mail address. To insert a hyperlink in a presentation, select the text you want to make a hyperlink and choose Hyperlink from the Insert menu. The Insert Hyperlink dialog box appears, as shown in Figure 2-22. In the Link to section, choose where you want the link to go. When you click OK, a hyperlink is inserted in the document. The text you selected is displayed in blue with a blue underline. Click it to go to the linked location.

Computer Concepts

When you key an e-mail address on a slide, PowerPoint automatically creates a hyperlink.

FIGURE 2-22
Hyperlink dialog box

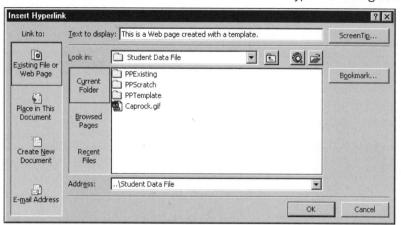

STEP-BY-STEP ▷ 2.16

1. Display slide **5** titled *Create a Web Site with a Template*. The area on the left of the status bar should read Slide 5 of 9. At the end of the last sentence, add

    This is a Web page created with a
    template.

2. Highlight the text you just entered and choose **Hyperlink** from the **Insert** menu. The Insert Hyperlink dialog box appears, as shown in Figure 2-22. In the Link to section, click **Existing File or Web Page** if it is not already selected. Locate the file named **PPTemplate.html** in the **PPTemplate** folder in the data files and click **OK**.

3. The text is underlined in the presentation indicating that it is a hyperlink.

4. Display slide **6** titled *Create a Web Site from Scratch*. Add **This is a Web page created from scratch** to the end of the text. Create a hyperlink to the file named **PPScratch.html** in the **PPScratch** folder in the data files.

5. Do the same for slide **7**, titled *Create a Web Site With a Template,* adding **This is a Web page created from an existing Web page** to the end, and creating a hyperlink to the file **PPExisting.html** in the **PPExisting** folder in the data files.

6. Select **View Show** from the **Slide Show** menu. Click through the presentation until you reach slide 5. As you hover over the hyperlink, your arrow pointer changes to a hand pointer indicating that you are pointing at a link. Click the link to open your Web browser and display the Web page.

7. Close your Web browser. Exit the slide show.

8. Save the presentation and leave it open for the next Step-by-Step.

Adding a Sound

You can add select sound effects to any of the objects on a slide by choosing Custom Animation from the Slide Show menu. The Custom Animation dialog box appears in the task pane. The objects that are animated are assigned a number on the slide and the corresponding number is listed in the task pane. When you want to add a sound to an existing object, click the number that corresponds to an object. To the right of each animated object there is an arrow that drops down the animation menu. You can add a sound to an effect by clicking Effects Options. This displays the Effects dialog box. In this dialog box, you can choose a sound from the existing sounds, or add a sound from another file location.

STEP-BY-STEP ▷ 2.17

1. Display slide **9** titled *Where to Get More Information*.

2. Click the picture of the computer.

3. Click **Add Effect** in the task pane, and then select **Magnify** from the **Entrance** menu. Change the speed to **Fast**.

4. Select **Effect Options** from the drop-down menu. Click the **Effect** tab if it is not already selected.

5. Click **Chime**. Click **OK**.

6. With the picture still selected in the task pane, click the **Reorder** up arrow until the selected item is at the top of the Custom Animation list.

7. Click the item below that reads *Where to Get More Information*. Select the down arrow and change the selection to **Start after Previous**.

8. View the presentation to see your additions.

9. Save and leave the presentation open for the next Step-by-Step.

Adding a Header or Footer

You can add a header or footer on the Slide Master or by selecting Header and Footer from the View menu. The AutoContent Wizard automatically creates a footer during the setup process.

When you select Header and Footer, the Header and Footer dialog box appears on the screen as shown in Figure 2-23. You can add the date and time, slide number, and any text you want to the footer of the slide. When you click the Notes and Handouts tab you also have the option of creating a header. Some items that you might include in a header or footer are the presenter's name, e-mail address, Web site address, or phone number.

FIGURE 2-23

Header and Footer dialog box

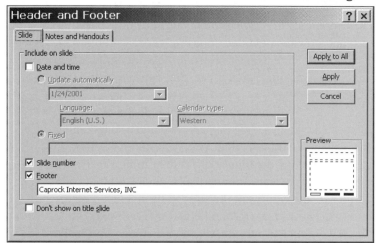

S TEP-BY-STEP ▷ 2.18

1. Select **Header and Footer** from the **View** menu. The Header and Footer dialog box appears on the screen.

2. Click in the Footer text box and key **PetersonM@CIS.com** behind the existing text, Caprock Internet Services, INC.

3. Click the **Notes and Handouts** tab.

4. Click the **Date and Time** option if it is not already selected.

5. Click **Update automatically**.

6. In the Header text box, key **Mike Peterson, Technical Instructor**.

7. In the Footer text box, key **Caprock Internet Services, INC PetersonM@CIS.com**.

8. Click **Apply to All**.

9. View the presentation to see your changes.

10. Save and leave the presentation open for the next Step-by-Step.

Use Slide Transitions

FIGURE 2-24
Slide Transition
dialog box

When you run a presentation, *slide transitions* determine how one slide is removed from the screen and how the next one appears. You can set the transitions between slides by choosing Slide Transition from the Slide Show menu and making choices in the Slide Transition dialog box that appears in the task pane as shown in Figure 2-24.

The Apply to selected slides portion of the dialog box displays a list of effects. You can select the speed at which a slide displays and add a sound under Modify transition. In the Advance slide section you determine whether to advance the slides manually by clicking the mouse or set the timing to advance slides automatically. To set slides to advance automatically, click Automatically after and enter the number of seconds you want the slide to be displayed on the screen. In the Sound section you can choose a sound effect that will play while the slide transition occurs. If you click Apply to All, the selections you made affect all slides in the presentation.

STEP-BY-STEP ▷ 2.19

1. Select slide **1**. Choose **Slide Transition** from the **Slide Show** menu. The Slide Transition dialog box appears in the task pane as shown in Figure 2-24.

2. Choose **Newsflash** in the list box. Choose **Fast** as the speed. In the Advance slide section, **On mouse click** should be chosen and no sound should be selected in the Sound section.

3. Select slide **2**. Choose **Wedge** in the list box. Choose **Fast** as the speed.

4. Select slide **3**. Choose **Cover Down** from the list box. Choose **Slow** as the speed.

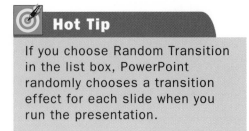

Hot Tip

If you choose Random Transition in the list box, PowerPoint randomly chooses a transition effect for each slide when you run the presentation.

5. Continue changing the transitions for the rest of the slides. Use the transitions of your choice. View the presentation to see your additions.

6. Save and leave the presentation open for the next Step-by-Step.

Extra Challenge

Explore some of the other slide transitions by changing the transitions in your presentation.

Saving a Presentation as Rich Text Format

Saving a presentation as Outline/RTF (Rich Text Format) creates a Word document with the text—but not the graphics—from your presentation. This is useful when you are giving a presentation and you want the audience to have the text, but not the slides.

STEP-BY-STEP ➩ 2.20

1. Choose **Save As** from the **File** menu. The Save As dialog box appears.

2. Click the down arrow on the **Save as type** box and choose **Outline/RTF**.

3. Choose the location where you want to save the file in the Save in box.

4. Save the file as **Web Page** followed by your initials.

5. Click **Save** and print and close your presentation.

Summary

In this lesson, you learned:

■ You can use PowerPoint to create a new presentation and apply Design Templates, Color Schemes, Slide Animations, and Text.

■ You can change a presentation in PowerPoint by applying Slide Layouts, adding Clip Art, and Custom Animation.

■ You can add notes to a slide in PowerPoint.

■ You can change text appearance and bullet appearance in PowerPoint.

■ You can add a slide to an existing PowerPoint presentation.

■ You can insert a hyperlink or a header or footer in a PowerPoint presentation.

VOCABULARY REVIEW

Define the following terms:

Animate	Hyperlink	Show Advanced Timeline
AutoContent Wizard	Motion path	Slide master
Design template	Placeholder	Slide transitions
Effects options		

LESSON 2 REVIEW QUESTIONS

MATCHING

Write the letter of the term in the right column that best matches the description in the left column.

____ 1. Controls formatting for all slides in a presentation

____ 2. Allows you to make adjustments to an effect

____ 3. Adding sound effects or special visuals

____ 4. Determines how one slide is removed from the screen and the next one appears

____ 5. Predesigned graphic styles that can be applied to your slides

A. AutoContent Wizard

B. slide transition

C. Effect Options

D. slide master

E. design template

F. Outline view

G. animate

H. slide layout

WRITTEN QUESTIONS

Write a brief answer to the following questions.

1. What option would you use to create a presentation from scratch using the layout, format, colors, and style you prefer?

2. What four categories define the Slide layout pane?

3. How do you insert clip art if a placeholder for clip art is included on the slide?

4. What three ways can you trigger an object to be animated?

5. How do you display the Outlining toolbar?

PROJECT 2-1

1. Start PowerPoint.

2. Open the presentation **IP Project2-1.rtf** from the data files.

3. Save the presentation as **Web Page Revised** followed by your initials.

4. In Slide view on slide **2**, change the slide layout to **Title Content and Text**.

5. Replace the clip-art placeholder with a piece of clip art that appears when you search using the words *World Wide Web*.

6. Switch to **Slide Sorter** view. Move slide **4** so that it appears between slides 2 and 3.

7. Display slide **1**. Animate the title so it swivels and is accompanied a clapping sound.

8. Set the slide transition for all slides so the effect is Box Out and the speed is Slow.

9. Switch to **Slide Show** view and run the presentation on your computer.

10. Save the presentation and print it as handouts with 4 slides on a page. Leave the presentation open for the next project.

PROJECT 2-2

1. Switch to **Outline** view.

2. Insert a new slide after slide 9 with the layout Title and Text.

3. On slide **10**, key **Prices** as the title.

4. Below Prices, key the following:
   ```
   Beginning Class -- $100
   Intermediate Class -- $125
   Advanced Class -- $150
   ```

5. Print slide **10**, using the Notes Pages print option and so that it fits on one page. Leave the presentation open for the next project.

PROJECT 2-3

1. In Slide view, delete the slide with the title *Vocabulary*.

2. In Normal view, go to slide 1 and key the following in the notes pane: **Be sure everyone has a handout.**

3. Print slide **1** using the Notes Pages print options.

4. Save and print the entire presentation as handouts with 6 slides on a page.

5. Close the presentation and exit PowerPoint.

CRITICAL THINKING

ACTIVITY 2-1

Use the AutoContent Wizard and the skills you learned in this lesson to create a home page for an organization to which you belong. Create the presentation to be viewed as a Web presentation.

ACTIVITY 2-2

Create a presentation using the ideas you organized in Critical Thinking Activity 1-2 in Lesson 1. Choose a design template and clip art. Include slide transitions and animation. Run the presentation for your class.

WORKING WITH VISUAL ELEMENTS

Upon completion of this lesson, you will be able to:

- Build and modify an organization chart.
- Build and modify charts.
- Create and modify tables within PowerPoint.
- Draw an object.
- Add shapes and apply formatting.
- Rotate and fill an object.
- Scale and size an object.
- Create a text box.

⏱ **Estimated Time: 1.5 hours**

Charts (graphs)

Datasheet

Grouping

Handles

Organization charts

Shift-clicking

Working with Organization Charts

Organization charts are useful for showing the hierarchical structure and relationships within an organization. To add an organization chart to a slide, you can use the Diagram or Organization Chart slide layout. This layout contains a placeholder for an organization chart. Double-click the placeholder to open the Diagram Gallery dialog box, which displays different diagram options, as shown in Figure 3-1. Click the Organization Chart icon and then click OK.

To fill in the chart, click in a box and key text. Use the box tools on the icon bar to add more boxes to the organization chart. Click the tool on the icon bar for the box you want to create and then click the box in the chart to which you want to attach it. Add a chart title by replacing the text placeholder. When you are ready to return to the presentation, click the close box and choose to update the object when a message box appears.

FIGURE 3-1
Diagram Gallery dialog box

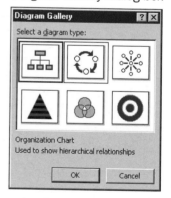

INTRODUCTORY MICROSOFT POWERPOINT

STEP-BY-STEP ▷ 3.1

1. Open **IP Step3-1** from the data files.

2. Save the presentation as **Buffalo** followed by your initials.

3. Display slide 2 and click the **Design** button on the Formatting toolbar.

4. Choose **Slide Layout** from the drop-down menu in the Slide Design task pane. The Slide Layout dialog box appears in the task pane.

5. Under Other Layouts, select the layout named **Title and Diagram or Organization Chart** and click it to apply it to the slide. The slide displays with a placeholder for a diagram or an organization chart. Double-click the placeholder.

6. The Diagram Gallery appears. Click the **Organization Chart** icon if necessary and click **OK**. The chart template appears on the slide and the Organization Chart toolbar appears, as shown in Figure 3-2.

7. Click in the top box, and key **Citizens**.

8. Click in the first text box on the second level, and key **Mayor**.

9. Click in the middle text box on the second level and key **City**. Press **Enter** and then key **Council**.

10. Click in the last text box on the second level and key **Citizen**. Press **Enter** and then key **Commissions**.

11. Click the text box that contains Mayor, click the arrow on the **Insert Shape** button on the Organization Chart toolbar, and then click **Assistant**. Notice that a new level is added to the chart.

12. In the box you just added, key **City**, press **Enter**, and then key **Manager**.

13. Click the **Mayor** box again, click the **Insert Shape** list arrow, and then click **Subordinate** to add a box on the next level.

14. In the box you just added, key **City**, press **Enter**, and then key **Secretary**.

FIGURE 3-2
Chart template and Organization Chart toolbar

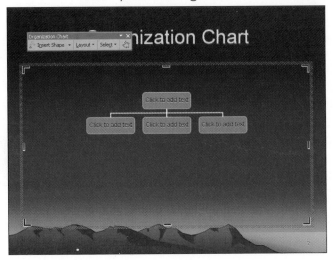

15. Click the **Citizen Commissions** box, click the **Insert Shape** list arrow, and click **Subordinate**. With the Citizen Commissions box still selected, click the **Insert Shape** button twice. Two more text boxes are added to the same level.

16. In the first box you just added, key **Strategic**, press **Enter**, and then key **Planning**. In the second box, key **Zoning**. In the last box, key **Public**, press **Enter**, and then key **Relations**. Your screen should look like Figure 3-3.

17. Save the presentation and leave it open for the next Step-by-Step.

Computer Concepts

Close the task pane to make your working area larger.

FIGURE 3-3
Organization chart

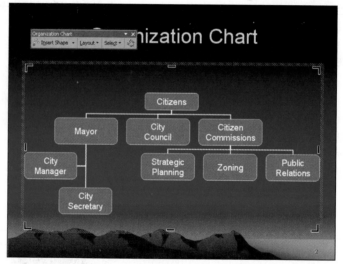

Modifying an Organization Chart

To modify an organization chart, click the chart to activate it. To reorganize the arrangement of boxes in the chart, select a box and drag it over another box to attach it to the second box. You can change text or box formatting, including font, font style, font size, alignment, color, shadows, and

Computer Concepts

Remember that you can press **Crtl+Z** to undo your previous actions.

borders by double-clicking the outer edge of a box and choosing a command from the Format AutoShape dialog box. To change the background color of the chart, double-click the background and choose a command from the Format Organization Chart.

STEP-BY-STEP ▷ 3.2

1. Select the word **Citizens** in the top box of the chart. On the Formatting toolbar change the font to Tahoma. Change the font style to bold and the font size to 24**.**

2. Click the **City Manager** box and drag it over top of the Citizens box. A dotted outline appears around the box. Release the mouse button. The box is now an assistant below the Citizens box.

3. Double-click the **Citizens** box to open the Format AutoShape dialog box.

4. Choose the **Color and Lines** tab, if not already selected. In the Fill section, click the **Color** list

arrow, choose **Red**, and then click **OK**. The box changes to red, as shown in Figure 3-4.

5. Save the presentation and print slide **2**. Leave the presentation open for the next Step-by-Step.

 Hot Tip

To make formatting changes to more than one box, click and drag a selection box around all the boxes you want to change.

FIGURE 3-4
Changing the color of a box

Working with Charts

Charts, also called *graphs*, provide a graphical way to display statistical data in a presentation. When you create a chart in PowerPoint, you are working in a program called Microsoft Graph. When you are building and modifying a chart, Microsoft Graph menus, commands, and toolbar buttons become available to help you.

 Did You Know?

The first row of colors you see displayed on the Color palette on the Color and Lines tab are the same colors used in the scheme applied to the current slide.

Building a Chart

To include a chart in a presentation, choose one of the slide layouts that contains a placeholder for a chart. Double-click the placeholder to open a graph and display a chart with sample data, as shown in Figure 3-5. Click the ***datasheet*** (a table that appears with the chart) and replace the sample data with your own. The chart changes to reflect the new data. When you are ready to return to the presentation, click outside the chart on the PowerPoint slide.

FIGURE 3-5
Chart with sample data

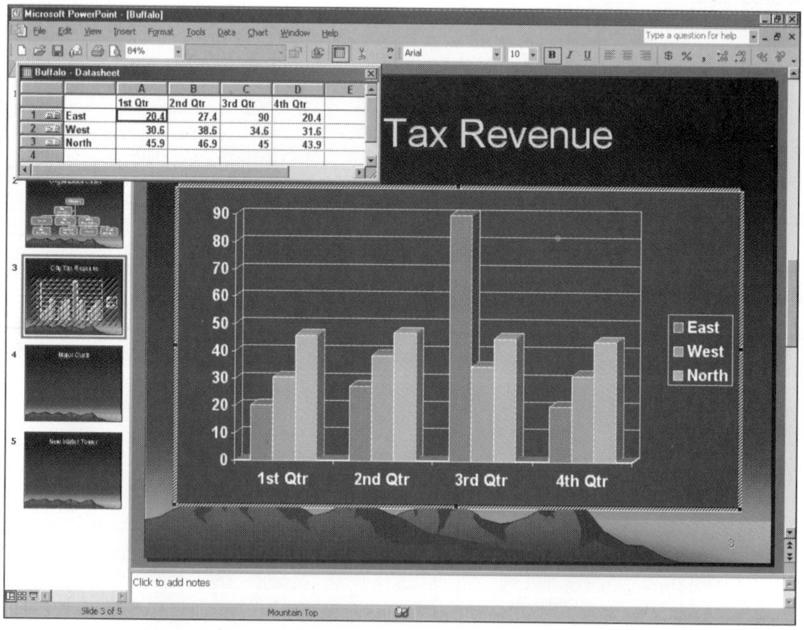

STEP-BY-STEP 3.3

1. Click slide **3** and access the Slide Layout dialog box.
2. From the Other Layouts options, change the slide layout to the one named **Title and Chart.**
3. Double-click the placeholder. Microsoft Graph opens and your screen looks similar to Figure 3-5.
4. Delete the data in row 3 by clicking the row number to select the entire row and choosing **Delete** from the **Edit** menu.
5. Change the sample data in the datasheet to look like Figure 3-6. The chart changes to reflect the new data.

FIGURE 3-6
Inserting new chart data

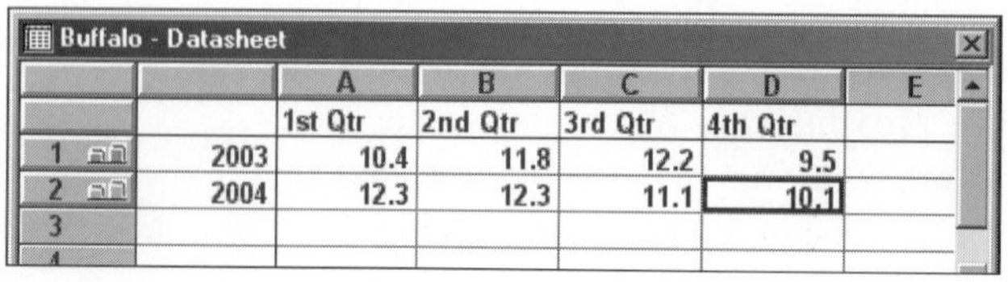

Buffalo - Datasheet

		A	B	C	D	E
		1st Qtr	2nd Qtr	3rd Qtr	4th Qtr	
1	2003	10.4	11.8	12.2	9.5	
2	2004	12.3	12.3	11.1	10.1	
3						
4						

6. Click outside the chart area on the slide to close Microsoft Graph and return to the presentation.

7. Save the presentation and leave it open for the next Step-by-Step.

Modifying a Chart

If you need to modify a chart, double-click it to open it. You can change the type of chart by choosing Chart Type from the Chart menu. The Chart Type dialog box appears, as shown in Figure 3-7. Choose a chart type and subtype. To see what the data will look like in a different type of chart, click and hold down the Press and Hold to View Sample button.

To add a chart or axis title, choose Chart Options from the Chart menu. Click the Titles tab in the Chart Options dialog box and key a chart or axis title. To apply a texture or pattern, or to change color or border style, click the chart item you want to change. The Format dialog box appears for that item.

Computer Concepts

You can animate a chart just as you do other slide objects by choosing **Custom Animation** from the **Slide Show** menu and clicking the **Add Effect** button. Choose how to you want to introduce the chart elements, entry animations and sound by selecting **Effect Options** form the drop-down menu.

S TEP-BY-STEP ⟹ 3.4

1. Double-click the chart to activate it. If the datasheet is displayed, close it by clicking its Close button.

2. Choose **Chart Type** from the **Chart** menu. The Chart Type dialog box appears, as shown in Figure 3-7.

FIGURE 3-7
Chart Type dialog box

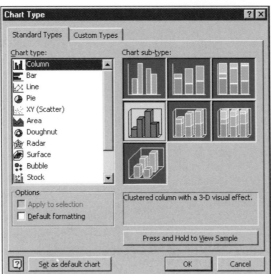

3. In the Chart type section, choose **Line**.

4. In the Chart sub-type section, choose the first type on the second row.

5. Click and hold the **Press and Hold to View Sample** button to see what the chart will look like.

6. Release the mouse button and then click **OK**. The chart changes to a line chart.

7. Choose **Chart Options** from the **Chart** menu. The Chart Options dialog box appears.

8. In the Chart title box, key **Tax Revenue**. The title is added to the sample chart as you key.

9. In the Category (X) axis box, key **Quarter**.

10. In the Category (Y) axis box, key **In Millions of Dollars**.

11. Click **OK**.

12. Click outside the chart on the slide to close Microsoft Graph and return to the presentation.

13. Save the presentation and print slide **3**. Leave the presentation open for the next Step-by-Step.

Working with Tables

Tables are useful when you need to include large amounts of data. The data can be displayed in rows and columns so that it is easier to read.

Creating Tables

To include a table on a slide, you can use the slide layout that has a placeholder for a table. When you double-click the placeholder, the Insert Table dialog box appears. Choose the number of columns and rows you want and a table is inserted on your slide. Key text in the table; you can move between cells by pressing the Tab key.

Computer Concepts

If you want to create a more complex table, use the Draw Table feature on the Tables and Borders toolbar.

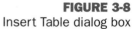 TEP-BY-STEP ⇒ 3.5

1. Display slide **4** and access the Slide Layout dialog box.

2. Change the slide layout to the one named **Title and Table**.

3. Double-click the placeholder. The Insert Table dialog box opens, as shown in Figure 3-8.

FIGURE 3-8
Insert Table dialog box

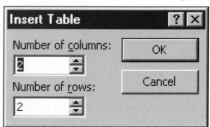

4. In the Number of columns box, key **3**.

5. In the Number of rows box, key **6**. Click **OK**. PowerPoint inserts a table with three columns and six rows on the slide.

6. Click in the first cell of the first row and key **(In Millions)**. Press **Tab** to move to the next cell. Key the data as shown in Figure 3-9.

7. Save the presentation and leave it open for the next Step-by-Step.

FIGURE 3-9
Major Costs slide

(In Millions)	2003	2004
New Water Tower		1.9
New Park		
Renovate Civic Center	.5	1.1
Construction on Bell Street	.85	
New Police and Fire Vehicles	.25	.15

Modifying Tables

To modify a table's borders, fill, or text boxes, choose Table from the Format menu. The Format Table dialog box appears, an example of which is shown in Figure 3-10.

FIGURE 3-10
Format Table dialog box

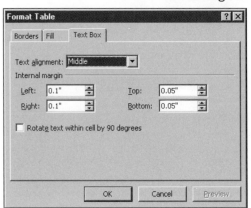

When you are modifying a table, it is helpful to display the Tables and Borders toolbar, shown in Figure 3-11. If it is not displayed, you can display it by right-clicking the Standard toolbar and choosing the toolbar you want from the menu. Using the Tables and Borders toolbar, you can insert columns and rows, merge or split cells, change the alignment and fill color, and format the borders.

To change the width of a column or row, click and drag a border. To insert or delete a column or row, click the Table button on the Tables and Borders toolbar and choose the appropriate command.

FIGURE 3-11
Tables and Borders toolbar

S TEP-BY-STEP ⊳ 3.6

1. Click and drag the column borders to enlarge the first column so all text fits on one line. Reduce the last two columns and size them equally, as shown in Figure 3-12.

2. Select all the text in the chart and then click the **Center** button on the toolbar.

3. Place the insertion point in the cell with the words *New Park*.

4. Display the **Tables and Borders** toolbar, shown in Figure 3-11, if it is not already displayed.

5. Click the **Table** button on the toolbar and choose **Delete Rows** from the menu.

6. Select all of the text in the table. Choose **Table** from the **Format** menu. The Format Table dialog box appears.

7. Click the **Text Box** tab, as shown in Figure 3-10.

8. Click the down arrow in the Text alignment box, choose **Middle**, and click **OK**.

9. Save the presentation and print slide **4**. Leave the presentation open for the next Step-by-Step.

FIGURE 3-12
Adjusting the width of columns

Major Costs

(In Millions)	2003	2004
New Water Tower		1.9
New Park		
Renovate Civic Center	.5	1.1
Construction on Bell Street	.85	
New Police and Fire vehicles	.25	.15

Creating Shapes and Objects

You can add shapes and other drawing objects to your presentation by using the AutoShapes and drawing tools on the Drawing toolbar. Auto shapes are pre-made such as circles, cones, and stars that you can include in your presentation to add interest to a slide.

Drawing an Object

The Drawing toolbar, shown in Figure 3-13, displays by default when you start PowerPoint. It contains buttons for drawing objects such as lines, circles, arrows, and squares. Click the corresponding button to activate the tool. The Rectangle tool draws rectangles and squares. The Oval tool draws ovals and circles. To use a tool, click and hold the mouse button, then drag to draw. To create a perfect circle or square, hold down the Shift key as you drag.

FIGURE 3-13
Drawing toolbar

Adding a Shape

There are also a variety of other shapes you can add by clicking the AutoShapes tool on the Drawing toolbar. A menu appears that has lines, connectors, arrows, and other kinds of objects to help draw the shape you want. Click the slide to insert the shape with a predefined size.

Selecting an Object

When you click an inserted object to select it, little squares appear at the edges of the graphic, as shown in Figure 3-14. These small squares are called *handles*. They indicate that the object is selected and they allow you to manipulate the object. When you choose another tool, the selection handles around an object disappear. You will learn more about selecting objects later in the lesson.

STEP-BY-STEP 3.7

1. Display slide **5**.

2. Click the **Oval** button on the Drawing toolbar.

3. Click in the upper-left corner of the slide and drag to draw an oval about 2" x 1½". When you release the mouse button, handles appear on the object, as shown in Figure 3-14.

4. Click the **Rectangle** button and draw a rectangle next to the oval that's about the same size as the oval.

5. Click the **AutoShapes** button on the Drawing toolbar. Choose **Basic Shapes** from the menu and click the **Can** icon on the submenu. Click below the oval and drag to draw a can whose top is about the same size as the oval.

6. Click the **AutoShapes** button and choose **Block Arrows** from the menu.

FIGURE 3-14
Oval on slide

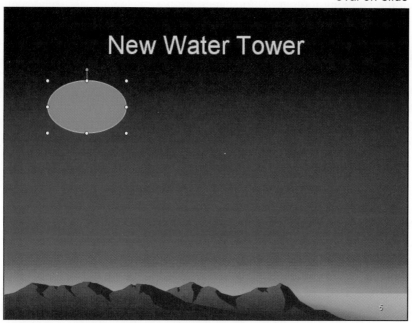

7. Click the **Right Arrow Callout** icon on the sub-menu and click below the rectangle to draw a right arrow callout about the same size as the rectangle.

8. Click **AutoShapes**, **Block Arrows**, and click the **Right Arrow** icon.

9. Draw an arrow to the left of the oval. Your slide should look similar to Figure 3-15.

10. Save the presentation and leave it open for the next Step-by-Step.

FIGURE 3-15
Arrow on a slide

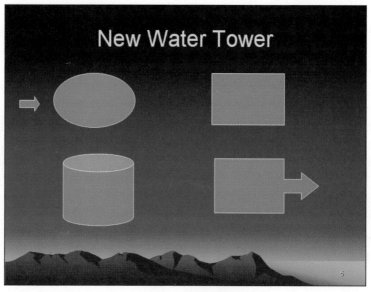

Manipulating Objects

Once you have created an object, there are many ways of manipulating it to achieve the final effect your want. You can rotate, fill, scale, or size an object, as well as change its color and position.

Selecting an Object

As you learned earlier in the lesson, when you select an object square handles surround it. To select an object, be sure the Select Objects tool is chosen on the toolbar, position the insertion point over the object and click. The selection handles appear around the object and you can manipulate

Hot Tip

To delete an object, select it and press the **Delete** or **Backspace** key.

the object. A four-sided arrow appears with the arrow pointer. To deselect an object, click another object or anywhere in the window.

Selecting More Than One Object

Sometimes you will want to select more than one object. PowerPoint gives you two ways to select more than one object. The first method is *Shift-clicking*. The second is to draw a selection box around a group of objects.

SHIFT-CLICKING

To Shift-click, hold down the Shift key and click each of the objects you want to select. Use this method when you need to select objects that are not close to each other or when the objects you need to select are near other objects you do not want to select. If you select an object by accident, click it again to deselect it—still holding down the Shift key.

DRAWING A SELECTION BOX

Using the Select Objects tool, you can drag a selection box around a group of objects. Use a selection box when all of the objects you want selected are near each other and can be surrounded with a box. Be sure your selection box is large enough to enclose all the selection handles of the various objects. If you miss a handle, the corresponding item will not be selected.

COMBINING METHODS

You can also combine these two methods. First, use the selection box and then Shift-click to include objects that the selection box might have missed.

Grouping Objects

As your drawing becomes more complex, you might find it necessary to "glue" objects together into groups. *Grouping* allows you to work with several items as if they were one object. To group objects, select the objects you want to group and choose Group from the Draw menu on the drawing toolbar. You can ungroup objects using the Ungroup command.

Rotating an Object

One way of modifying an object is to rotate it. The three rotate commands are Rotate Right, Rotate Left, and Free Rotate. The Rotate Right command moves a graphic in 90-degree increments to the right. The Rotate Left command rotates the graphic in 90-degree increments to the left. The Free Rotate command lets you rotate a graphic to any angle. When you choose the Free Rotate command, the object is surrounded with green handles that you click and drag to rotate the object.

**Computer Concepts**

You can flip an object by choosing the Flip Horizontal or Flip Vertical commands on the Rotate or Flip submenu.

To rotate an object, select it, click Draw on the drawing toolbar and choose Rotate or Flip from the menu. Choose the command you want from the submenu.

STEP-BY-STEP ▷ 3.8

1. Draw a left arrow in the middle of the screen about twice as long as the one you drew in the last Step-by-Step.

2. With the arrow selected, click the **Free Rotate** button.

3. Click any green dot and drag in a counter-clockwise direction until the arrow points to the can, as shown in Figure 3-16.

FIGURE 3-16
Arrow pointing at can

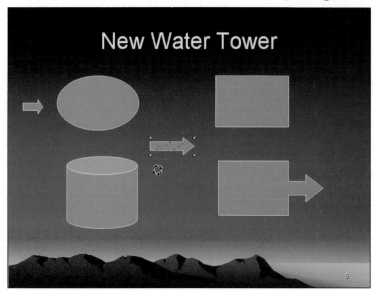

4. Select the arrow before the oval.

5. Click the **Draw** button on the Drawing toolbar.

6. Choose **Rotate or Flip** from the menu and **Rotate Left** from the submenu. The arrow is now pointing up.

7. Click the **Draw** button; choose **Rotate or Flip**, then **Rotate Right**. The arrow points to the right again.

8. Save the presentation and leave it open for the next Step-by-Step.

Applying Formatting

The Drawing toolbar contains various ways to apply formatting to visual elements in a presentation. You can change the fill, line, or font color. You can also change the line, dash, or arrow style, add shadows, and make an object 3D.

FILLING AN OBJECT

Filling an object can help add interest to your drawing objects. Select the object you want to fill and click the Fill Color button on the Drawing toolbar. When you click the down arrow, a box appears, as shown in Figure 3-17.

To change an object back to the default fill color, click Automatic. To choose a color in the color scheme, click one of the eight choices below Automatic. Your selected object becomes filled with the color you click. To fill an object with a color not in the presentation's color scheme, click More Fill Colors. To fill an object with a gradient, texture, pattern, or picture, click Fill Effects. The Fill Effects dialog box appears, as shown in Figure 3-18.

FIGURE 3-17
Color Fill dialog box

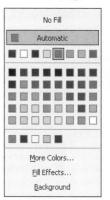

FIGURE 3-18
Fill Effects dialog box

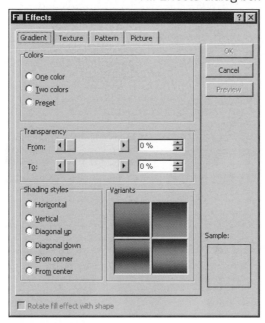

CHANGING LINE COLOR

Another way to apply formatting to a drawing object is to change the line color. Click the arrow next to the Line Color button on the Drawing toolbar and click an option in the Line Color box that appears. The Line Color box looks very similar to the Fill Color box.

1. Double-click the rectangle. Click the arrow next to **Fill Color**. A box appears, as shown in Figure 3-17.

2. Click the color labeled **Blue-Gray**. The rectangle changes to a gray color. Click **OK** to close the Format AutoShape dialog box.

3. Double-click the can. Click the down arrow next to the **Fill Color** button and then click **Fill Effects**. The Fill Effects dialog box appears, as shown in Figure 3-18.

4. Click the **Gradient** tab if necessary. In the Shading styles box, click **Diagonal up**. Click **OK** to close the Fill Effect dialog box. Click **OK**

to close the Format AutoShape dialog box. The can is filled with gradient shading.

5. Select the right arrow callout. Access the **Fill Effects** dialog box and click the **Texture** tab.

6. Click the **Sand** texture, as shown in Figure 3-19.

7. Click **OK** twice. The right arrow callout is filled with a sand texture.

8. Select the oval. Access the Fill Effects dialog box and click the **Pattern** tab.

9. Click the second pattern on the last row (90%), as shown in Figure 3-20.

FIGURE 3-19
Sand texture

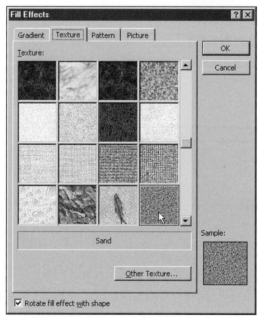

FIGURE 3-20
90% pattern

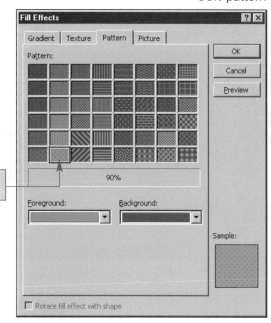

Select this pattern

10. Click **OK** twice. The object is filled with a dotted pattern.

11. Select the rectangle and click the arrow next to the **Line Color**.

12. Click the color **Yellow**. The line around the rectangle changes to yellow. Change the weight of the line to 6 pt.

13. Change the line around the oval, can, and right arrow callout to yellow and 6 pt. Your slide should look similar to Figure 3-21.

14. Save the presentation and leave it open for the next Step-by-Step.

FIGURE 3-21
Textures and patterns applied to shapes

Scaling and Sizing an Object

Handles do more than indicate that an object is selected. They make it easy to resize an object that is too large or too small. Select the object to make the handles appear and then drag one of the handles inward or outward to make the object smaller or larger, as shown in Figure 3-22.

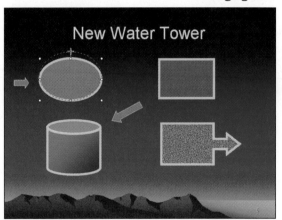

FIGURE 3-22
Enlarging oval

To scale an object, hold down Shift and drag a corner handle. This maintains an object's proportions. You scale and size ClipArt graphics just as you do objects. Many AutoShapes have a yellow diamond adjustment handle that you can drag to change the appearance of the object.

Computer Concepts

You can size an object more precisely by choosing **AutoShape** from the **Format** menu. Click the **Size** tab and specify a height and width.

Copying or Moving an Object

To move an object, first select it and then drag it into place. You can cut, copy, and paste objects the same way you do text. The Cut and Copy commands place a copy of the selected image on the Office Clipboard. Pasting an object from the Office Clipboard places the object in your drawing. You can then move it into position.

S TEP-BY-STEP ▷ 3.10

1. Select the oval. Move the pointer over the top middle handle until it becomes a two-headed vertical arrow.

2. Click and drag the handle up to enlarge the oval, as shown in Figure 3-22.

3. Select the rectangle. Move the pointer over the top right corner handle until it becomes a two-headed diagonal arrow and enlarge the rectangle.

4. Select the can. Hold down **Shift** as you click and drag upward to slightly enlarge the can while maintaining the same proportions.

5. Select the right arrow callout. Three yellow diamond adjustment handles appear in addition to the regular handles. Move the pointer to the middle handle. Click and drag upward and to the right. The arrow part of the object becomes wider, as shown in Figure 3-23.

FIGURE 3-23
Wider arrow

New Water Tower

6. Select the arrow to the left of the oval. Choose **Copy** from the **Edit** menu. A copy of the arrow is pasted on the Office Clipboard.

7. Choose **Paste** from the **Edit** menu. The arrow is pasted from the Office Clipboard into the presentation.

8. Place the pointer over the arrow. Click and drag it to a new position in between the oval and the rectangle.

9. Paste another arrow between the can and the right arrow callout.

10. Save the presentation and leave it open for the next Step-by-Step.

Extra Challenge

Fill the arrows with a different color, gradient, or texture.

Create a Text Box

If you want to add text on a slide that does not have a placeholder for it, you can create a text box. Click the Text Box tool on the Drawing toolbar. Click the mouse button and drag to create a text box the size you want, as shown in Figure 3-24. To move the box, click and drag it to a new location. To resize the box, click and drag one of the handles. To insert text, click inside the text box and begin keying.

FIGURE 3-24
Text box inside oval

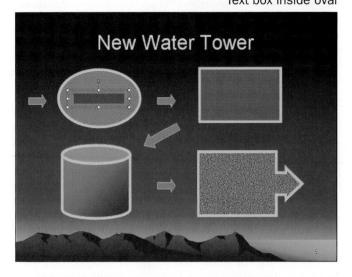

To place text inside a shape, simply create a text box on top of the shape. You can wrap text in a text box by choosing Text Box from the Format menu and then clicking the Text Box tab in the Format Text Box dialog box, as shown in Figure 3-25. The Word wrap text in AutoShape box should be checked.

STEP-BY-STEP ▷ 3.11

1. Click the **Text Box** tool on the Drawing toolbar.

3. Choose **Text Box** from the Format menu and click the **Text Box** tab in the Format Text Box dialog box, as shown in Figure 3-25.

2. Click inside the oval and drag to draw a text box that fits inside, as shown in Figure 3-24.

FIGURE 3-25
Format Text Box dialog box

4. If necessary, check the **Word wrap text in AutoShape** box. Click **OK**.

5. Key **Water Source** inside the text box. Notice how the text wraps.

6. Select the text you just keyed in the text box. Center and bold it.

7. Create a text box in the rectangle and key **Water Processing Plant**. Bold and center the text.

8. Create a text box on the can and key **Water Tower**. Bold and center the text.

9. Create a text box on the right arrow callout object and key **Final Filtration**. Bold and center the text. The slide should look similar to Figure 3-26.

10. Save the presentation, print the entire presentation as a handout with 6 slides per page, and then close it.

FIGURE 3-26
Completed slide

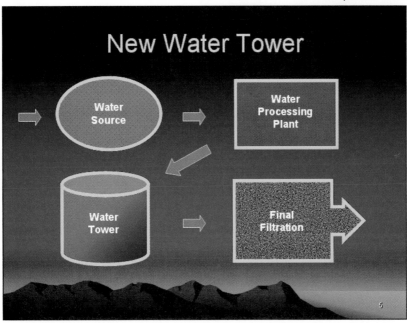

Summary

In this lesson, you learned:

- You can create and modify organization charts in a presentation.

- You can create and modify graphs in a presentation using Microsoft Graph

- You can insert a table on a slide using the Insert Table dialog box and then modify it using the Tables and Borders toolbar.

- You can add shapes and objects to your presentation using the AutoShapes and drawing tools on the Drawing toolbar. You can rotate, fill, scale, or size an object as well as changing its fill or line color.

- You can add text on a slide or inside a shape by creating a text box. You can wrap text inside a text box.

VOCABULARY REVIEW

Define the following terms:

Charts (Graphs)   Handles   Shift-clicking
Grouping   Organization charts

LESSON 3 REVIEW QUESTIONS

TRUE/FALSE

Circle T if the statement is true or F if the statement is false.

T   F   1. The background color of an organization chart must be the same as the color of the slide.

T   F   2. When you double click a table placeholder on a slide, the Insert Table dialog box appears.

T   F   3. Using the Select Objects tool, you can drag a selection box around a group of objects.

T   F   4. To change an object back to the default fill color, click Default in the Fill Color box.

T   F   5. To place text inside a shape, choose Insert Text from the Draw menu.

MULTIPLE CHOICE

Select the best response for the following statements.

1. Pie, line, bar, and column are types of
   A. charts.
   B. textures.
   C. tables.
   D. effects.

2. The small squares surrounding a selected graphic are called
   A. buttons.
   B. tabs.
   C. handles.
   D. boxes.

3. Which command do you use to rotate a graphic to any angle?
   A. Rotate Left
   B. Rotate Right
   C. Free Rotate
   D. None of the above

4. You can fill an object with
   A. gradients.
   B. texture.
   C. patterns.
   D. all of the above.

5. Which key do you hold down to maintain an object's proportions when resizing?
   A. Ctrl
   B. Shift
   C. Alt
   D. Tab

LESSON 3 PROJECTS

PROJECT 3-1

1. Open the **Buffalo** presentation you created in this lesson. Save it as **Buffalo2** followed by your initials.

2. Display slide **2** and click the **Strategic Planning** box.

3. Add an assistant box and key **Community Liaison** in it.

4. Click the **Zoning** box. Add a subordinate box named **Streets**.

5. Print slide **2**. Save the presentation and leave it open for the next project.

PROJECT 3-2

1. Display slide **3** and double-click the chart to open the datasheet.

2. In the cell to the right of *4th QTR,* key **Total**.

3. Add the four quarters for 2003 and key the sum in the cell below Total (Cell E1).

4. Add the four quarters for 2004 and key the sum in the cell in the Total column (Cell E2).

5. Save the presentation as **Buffalo3**, followed by your initials, and print it as a handout with six slides per page. Close the presentation.

CRITICAL THINKING

ACTIVITY 3-1

Use the Internet to do research on a company. Use the information you find to create a presentation about the company that includes an organization chart, a graph, a table, and drawing objects.

ACTIVITY 3-2

You want to make some changes to some text boxes. Use the Help system to find out how to do the following:

■ Change the shape of a text box to an AutoShape.

■ Display text vertically instead of horizontally in a text box.

■ Change the margins around the text in a text box.

EXPANDING ON POWERPOINT BASICS

OBJECTIVES

Upon completion of this lesson, you should be able to:

- Integrate PowerPoint with other Office programs.
- Work with multiple presentations.
- Replace text fonts in an entire presentation.
- Use the Format Painter.
- Deliver a presentation.
- Change the output format.
- Publish a presentation to the Web.
- Send a presentation via e-mail.

🕐 Estimated Time: 2 hours

VOCABULARY

Embed

Format Painter

Grid settings

Guide settings

Pack and Go

Snap to

Route

Integrating PowerPoint with Other Office Programs

You can import text from Word to create a new presentation or add slides to an existing presentation. A Word outline is the easiest kind of document to import because it is formatted with styles and each heading level is translated into a corresponding level of text in PowerPoint. For example, Heading 1 text is converted to slide titles. If the Word document does not have heading styles applied, PowerPoint uses the paragraph indentations to create an outline structure.

1. Start Word and then open **IP Step4-1** from the data files. Notice how the document is formatted as an outline.

2. Close the file and exit Word.

3. Open PowerPoint and choose **Open** on the File menu. The Open dialog box appears.

4. From the Files of type drop-down list box, choose **All Outlines**.

5. Locate **IP Step4-1** in the data files and choose **Open**. PowerPoint imports the Word document text into a presentation and formats it as slides.

6. Save the presentation as **Solar System** followed by your initials.

7. Change the design template to **Orbit**.

8. Display slide **1**, if necessary. Key the following at the end of the second item (delete the period following the word *second*):

—faster than any other planet.

9. Save and leave the presentation open for the next Step-by-Step.

Embedding Data

In the previous lesson you edited a document that originated in Microsoft Word. When you move data among applications by cutting or copying and pasting, Office changes the format of the information you are moving so that it can be used in the destination file. When it is easier to edit the information using the original application, you can *embed* the information as an object by accessing the Insert Object dialog box, shown in Figure 4-1.

FIGURE 4-1
Insert Object dialog box

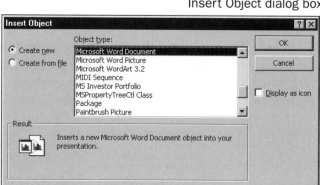

The embedded information becomes part of the new file, but as a separate object that can be edited using the application that created it. For example, if you insert a table from a Word document into a PowerPoint presentation, PowerPoint enables Word to edit the document instead of PowerPoint.

STEP-BY-STEP 4.2

1. Minimize the PowerPoint file.

2. Start Word and open the file named **IP Step4-2** from the data files.

3. Select all of the text in the document. Choose **Copy** from the **Edit** menu to copy the text to the Clipboard. Close the Word document.

4. Maximize the PowerPoint file that you minimized in Step 1.

5. Switch to **Slide Sorter** view, if that is not the current view. You may want to close the task pane to see more of the slides on your screen.

6. Click in front of slide 1 as shown in Figure 4-2.

7. Insert a new slide with a blank layout.

8. Double-click the new slide **1** to display it.

9. Choose **Object** from the **Insert** menu and click **Microsoft Word Document** in the Insert Object dialog box (see Figure 4-1). Click **OK**.

10. Click inside the Word document placeholder and choose **Paste** from the **Edit** menu. Click outside the document. Center the text box on the slide. Your slide should look similar to Figure 4-3.

11. Save and leave the presentation open for the next Step-by-Step.

FIGURE 4-2
Insert new slide

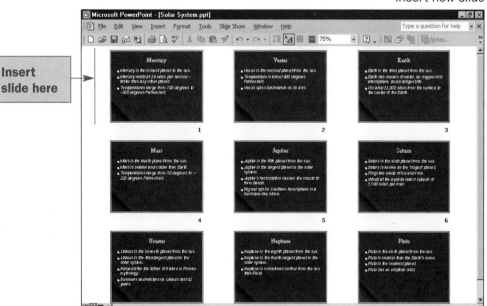

FIGURE 4-3
Embed a Word Document

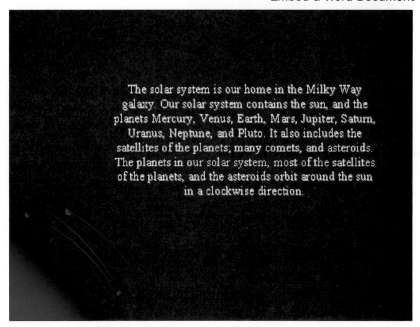

The solar system is our home in the Milky Way galaxy. Our solar system contains the sun, and the planets Mercury, Venus, Earth, Mars, Jupiter, Saturn, Uranus, Neptune, and Pluto. It also includes the satellites of the planets; many comets, and asteroids. The planets in our solar system, most of the satellites of the planets, and the asteroids orbit around the sun in a clockwise direction.

Editing Embedded Data

To make changes to the Word file embedded in the PowerPoint presentation, double-click the text you want to edit. Word, the application in which the file was created, opens so that you can edit the text. When you finish and return to PowerPoint, the presentation includes the changes you made to the text.

S TEP-BY-STEP ▷ 4.3

1. Display slide **1** if it is not already displayed.

2. Double-click on the text to enable the Word edit feature. Click in front of the word *clockwise*, and key **counter-**, so the sentence reads: *The planets in our solar system, most of the satellites of the planets, and the asteroids orbit around the sun in a counter-clockwise direction.*

3. Click outside the placeholder again to exit Word. Notice the changes you made are now part of the presentation.

4. Save and leave the presentation open for the next Step-by-Step.

Import Excel Charts into a Presentation

In Lesson 3 you learned how to build and modify a chart on a slide. You can also create a chart by importing data from an existing Excel worksheet.

STEP-BY-STEP ▷ 4.4

1. Switch to **Slide Sorter** view, if that is not the current view. Click between slide 1 and slide 2. Insert a new slide with a blank layout.

2. Double-click the new slide **2** to display it.

3. Choose **Object** from the **Insert** menu and click **Microsoft Excel Chart**. Click **OK**. Your screen should look similar to Figure 4-4.

4. Click the tab at the bottom of the chart named **Sheet 1**. Click cell **A1** and drag to cell **E8**. Notice that cells A1:D7 are filled with sample text. Press the **Delete** key to delete the sample text.

5. Minimize the Solar System file.

6. Open **IP Step4-4** (Excel file) from the data files.

7. Select all of the text in the worksheet. Choose **Copy** from the **Edit** menu to copy the text to the clipboard. Close the Excel workbook.

8. Maximize the PowerPoint file that you minimized in Step 7.

9. Click in cell A1 again and choose **Paste** from the **Edit** menu. Adjust the columns so you can read all of the text.

FIGURE 4-4
Embedded Excel chart

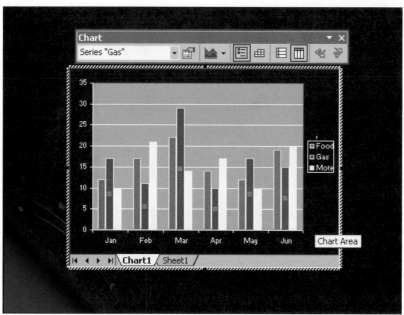

10. Click the **Chart 1** tab to display the chart again.

11. Right-click in the chart area to display the Chart menu as shown in Figure 4-5. Click **Source Data**. The Source Data dialog box appears (Figure 4-6).

FIGURE 4-5
Chart menu

Format Chart Area...
Chart Type...
Source Data...
Chart Options...
Location...
3-D View...
Chart Window
Clear

12. If necessary, click the **Series** tab. Delete the two items in the series column named Blank Series by highlighting them and clicking the **Remove** button.

13. Click the **Collapse Dialog** button to the right of the *Name* series. Highlight cell **B1**. Click the **Collapse Dialog** button to display the Source Data dialog box again.

14. Click the **Collapse Dialog** button to the right of the *Values* series. Highlight cells **B2:B10**. Click the **Collapse Dialog** button to display the Source Data dialog box again.

15. Click the **Collapse Dialog** button to the right of the Category (X) axis labels box. Highlight cells **A2:A10**. Click the **Collapse Dialog** button to display the Source Data dialog box again. Click **OK**.

16. Right-click in the chart area to display the Chart menu as shown in Figure 4-5. Click **Chart Options**. The Chart Options dialog box appears. Click the **Legend** tab and remove the check mark next to *Show legend*. Click **OK**.

17. Click outside the chart boundaries. Center the chart box on the slide. Your slide should look similar to Figure 4-7.

18. Save and leave the presentation open for the next Step-by-Step.

FIGURE 4-6
Source Data dialog box

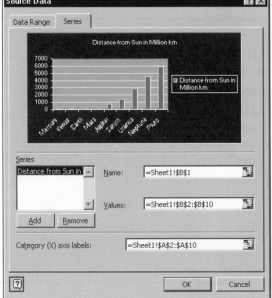

FIGURE 4-7
Embedded Excel chart

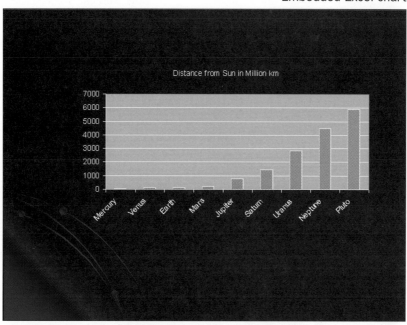

Insert Word Tables on Slides

Earlier in this lesson you learned how to embed a Word file on a slide. You can also insert tables from Word.

STEP-BY-STEP ⟹ 4.5

1. Switch to **Slide Sorter** view if that is not the current view. Insert a new slide with a Blank layout between slides 2 and 3.

2. Double-click the new slide **3** to display it.

3. Choose **Object** from the **Insert** menu and click **Microsoft Word Document**. Click **OK**.

4. Click inside the Word document placeholder, then click the **Tables and Borders** button on the toolbar. The Table and Borders dialog box appears. Click the **Insert Table** button. The Insert Table dialog box appears. In the Table size area, change the number of columns to **2**

and the number of rows to **10**. Click **OK**. Enter the data into the new table as it appears below.

Planet	Time to Rotate around Sun (Year)
Mercury	88 Earth days
Venus	224.7 Earth days
Earth	365.3 days
Mars	687 Earth days
Jupiter	12 Earth years
Saturn	29.5 Earth years
Uranus	84 Earth years
Neptune	165 Earth years
Pluto	248 Earth years

5. Change the text size to 24 and bold it. Change the text color to Blue and center it.

6. Center the text box on the slide. Click outside the table boundaries. Your screen should look similar to Figure 4-8.

7. Print the presentation with 6 slides per page. Save and close the presentation.

FIGURE 4-8
Embed a Word document

Send a Presentation to Word

You can send a presentation to Word to use as a handout or create other documents using the text and slides from the presentation.

To send the presentation to Word, choose Send To from the File menu and Microsoft Word from the submenu. The Send To Microsoft Word dialog box appears as shown in Figure 4-9. The options in the dialog box send your presentation to Word in several different formats.

FIGURE 4-9
Send To Microsoft Word
dialog box

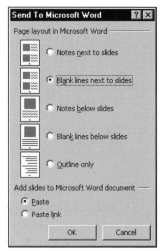

S TEP-BY-STEP ▷ 4.6

1. Open the data file **IP Step4-6**.

2. Choose **Send To** on the **File** menu and **Microsoft Word** on the submenu. The Send To Microsoft Word dialog box appears.

3. Click **Blank lines next to slides** in the dialog box, if necessary.

4. Click **OK**. The presentation is exported into Word and formatted as a document as shown in Figure 4-10.

5. Save the document as **Web Site 2** followed by your initials. Print the document and close it.

FIGURE 4-10
Web Site 2 as a Word document

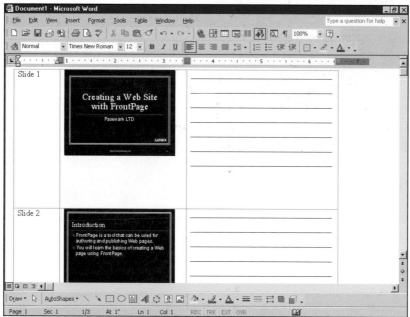

Working with Multiple Presentations

PowerPoint can combine presentations or add slides from another presentation. This saves time if you need to include information from one presentation in a different one. Open the presentation upon which you want to base a new presentation. Make changes to the existing slides, such as applying a different design template, adding or deleting slides, formatting text differently, and making changes to the slide master. When you are finished, choose Save As from the File menu, key a new name for the presentation, and click Save.

You can also add a slide to your new presentation by copying it from another presentation. Choose Slides from Files from the Insert menu. The Slide Finder dialog box appears, as shown in Figure 4-11. Click Browse, locate the presentation you want to copy a slide from, and click Display. Select the slide you want to copy and click Insert. If you want to insert the entire presentation, click Insert All. The slide(s) are inserted after the one displayed on the screen.

FIGURE 4-11
Slide Finder dialog box

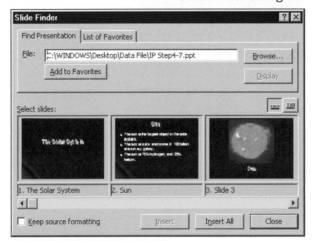

STEP-BY-STEP ▷ 4.7

1. Open the file named **Solar System** that you last saved in Step-by-Step 4.5. Switch to **Slide Sorter** view if that is not the current view.

2. Click to the right of slide 12.

3. Choose **Slides from Files** on the **Insert** menu. The Slide Finder dialog box appears.

4. Click **Browse** and locate the **IP Step4-7** file.

5. Click the box labeled **Keep source formatting**.

6. Click **Insert All**. The slides are inserted after slide 12 in the presentation.

7. Click **Close** to close the Slide Finder dialog box.

8. Drag slide **13** so that it is in front of slide 1.

9. Drag the current slide **14** (titled *Sun*) to place it between slides 4 and 5.

10. Drag the current slide **15** (picture of the sun) to place it between slides 5 and 6.

11. Continue to place the slides with the pictures of each planet after the slide that describes it. The last slide in the presentation should be a picture of the moon.

12. View the presentation.

13. Save the presentation and leave it open for the next Step-by-Step.

Formatting Text and Objects

In earlier lessons you learned the basics of formatting text and objects. PowerPoint has several helpful features to make formatting easier.

Replace Text Fonts

You can change a font throughout your presentation by choosing Replace Fonts on the Format menu. The Replace Font dialog box appears, as shown in Figure 4-12. In the Replace box choose the font you want to replace. In the With box, choose the font you want to use as a replacement, then click Replace.

FIGURE 4-12
Replace Font dialog box

Use the Format Painter

If you format an object with certain attributes, such as fill color and line color, then want to format another object the same way, use the *Format Painter* feature. Select the object whose attributes you want to copy, click the Format Painter button, then click the object you want to format. You can use the same process to copy text attributes, such as font, size, color, or style to other text. To copy attributes to more than one object or section of text, double-click the Format Painter button, click the objects or text you want to format, and click the Format Painter button when you are finished.

STEP-BY-STEP ▷ 4.8

1. Choose **Replace Fonts** from the **Format** menu. The Replace Fonts dialog box appears.

2. The labels on the pictures of the planets are in Times New Roman font. In the Replace box, choose **Times New Roman** if necessary.

3. In the With box, choose **Arial**, if necessary, as shown in Figure 4-12. Click **Replace**. All the text in Times New Roman font throughout the presentation is replaced with the Arial font.

4. Click **Close** to close the Replace Fonts dialog box.

5. Display slide **6**. Select the word **Sun**.

6. Change the font color to orange, 60-point, bold.

7. With *Sun* still selected, click the **Format Painter** button. The pointer changes to an I-beam with a paintbrush next to it.

8. Display slide **8** (Mercury). Click and drag the pointer over the word **Mercury**. The format changes so it is the same as *Sun*. Use the same process to format the rest of the slides with pictures.

9. View the presentation.

10. Save the presentation and leave it open for the next Step-by-Step.

> **Computer Concepts**
>
> To apply one slide's color scheme to another slide, switch to **Slide Sorter** view, select the slide with the color scheme you want to copy, click **Format Painter**, and then click the slide to which you want to apply the color scheme.

Aligning Text and Pictures

A good presentation uses short phrases, pictures, and graphs to convey its point. Presentations that contain out-of-alignment text or pictures can distract from the point of the presentation. To align a text box or picture, you can add grid lines and picture guides to the slide as you are creating it. Choose Grid and Guides from the View menu. The Grid and Guides dialog box appears as shown in Figure 4-13. The **Snap to** area of the dialog box moves an object to the closest gridline on a slide. The **Grid settings** section sets the spacing between the intersections of the gridlines. You can also choose to display the grid from this area as shown in Figure 4-14. The **Guide settings** area displays a set of crosshairs on the screen to help you align an object in the center, left, right, top, or bottom of the slide as shown in Figure 4-15.

FIGURE 4-13
Grid and Guides dialog box

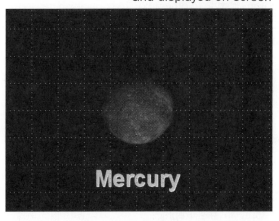

FIGURE 4-14
Grid displayed on screen

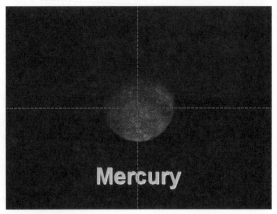

FIGURE 4-15
Guides displayed on screen

STEP-BY-STEP ▷ 4.9

1. Display slide **6** (picture of the sun).

2. Choose **Grid and Guides** from the **View** menu. The Grid and Guides dialog box appears.

3. Click the boxes next to **Display grid on screen** and **Display drawing guides on screen**. Click **OK**.

4. Select **Sun** so that the text box is highlighted.

5. Drag the text box so that the top handles rest on the second gridline from the bottom of the slide.

6. Now drag the text box so that the center handles rest on the center gridline of the slide.

7. Use the same process to format the rest of the slides with pictures. When you have finished aligning the text on the slides, choose **Grid and Guides** from the **View** menu to turn off the grid and drawing guides.

8. View the presentation to make sure the changes look correct.

9. Save the presentation and leave it open for the next Step-by-Step.

Delivering a Presentation

To start a presentation, click the Slide Show view button. You can start the slide show on any slide by displaying or selecting the slide you want to begin with before clicking the Slide Show view button. If you want a particular slide to be hidden when you run your presentation, select the slide in Slide Sorter view and choose Hide Slide from the Slide Show menu.

There are on-screen navigation tools you can use to control a presentation while presenting it. When you run the presentation, a triangle appears in the bottom left of the screen. Click the triangle and a menu displays, as shown in Figure 4-16.

When you click the mouse, the slides advance in order. You can choose Previous or Next from the menu to display the slide before or after the current one. To go to another slide, choose Go from the menu that is displayed and Slide Navigator from the submenu. The Slide Navigator dialog box appears, as shown in Figure 4-17. Choose the slide you want to display and click the Go To button. To exit the slide show, choose End Show from the menu.

FIGURE 4-16
On-screen navigation tools

 Did You Know?

When using overheads or running a presentation, make the text size at least 24 points so it can be easily read.

 Hot Tip

You display a hidden slide by choosing it in the Slide Navigator dialog box. Parentheses around the slide number indicate that it is hidden.

FIGURE 4-17
Slide Navigator
dialog box

When you move your mouse, an arrow appears so that you can point out parts of the slide. Choose Hidden on the Pointer Options menu to hide the pointer. Choosing Pen from the Pointer Options menu changes the mouse pointer to a pen so you can draw or write on the screen. To change the pen color, choose Pen Color on the Pointer Options menu and select a color. To erase what you have written, choose Screen from the on-screen navigation tools, Erase Pen on the submenu.

Computer Concepts

To display your speaker notes, choose **Speaker Notes** from the on-screen navigation tools. To blank the screen, choose **Black Screen** from the **Screen** menu.

S TEP-BY-STEP ▷ 4.10

1. Switch to **Slide Sorter** view and select slide **25**.

2. Choose **Hide Slide** from the **Slide Show** menu. Repeat this process for slide **26**.

3. Select slide **5** and click the **Slide Show** view button. The presentation begins on slide 5.

4. Click the triangle on the bottom left of the screen. A menu appears, as shown in Figure 4-16.

5. Choose **Go** from the menu and **Slide Navigator** from the submenu. The Slide Navigator dialog box appears, as shown in Figure 4-17.

6. In the Slide titles box, select **(1.) The Solar System**. Click the **Go To** button. Slide 1 displays.

7. Click to advance to slide **5**.

8. Right-click your mouse and choose **Pointer Options** from the on-screen navigation tools menu. Choose **Pen Color** from the submenu and **Yellow** from the next submenu.

9. Underline the phrases **75% hydrogen** and **25% helium**.

10. Choose **Pointer Options** from the on-screen navigation tools menu and **Automatic** from the submenu. The pen shape changes to a pointer.

11. Choose **End Show** from the menu to exit the slide show. Leave the presentation on the screen for the next Step-by-Step.

Teamwork

Form small groups and take turns running the slide presentation for the other members of your group.

Set Up a Slide Show

PowerPoint has many features to help make a presentation interesting and effective. There are several options for delivering a presentation. A presentation can be set up as a self-running presentation that can be viewed, for example, at a trade show booth. An individual can view a presentation over a company Intranet or on the Web. However, the most common method is to run a presentation with a speaker who directs the show.

To set up the slide show, choose Set Up Show from the Slide Show menu. The Set Up Show dialog box appears (Figure 4-18), which has six sections:

- *Show type* determines how the show will be viewed.

- *Show slides* allows you to choose which slides you are showing.

- *Show options* allows you to choose features that you want to include when making your presentation.

- *Advance slides* determines whether you advance the slides manually or automatically.

- *Multiple monitors* sets up your computer when you are using a secondary monitor or projector.

- *Performance* adjusts your computer's settings to give the best picture at the fastest speed.

FIGURE 4-18
Set Up Show dialog box

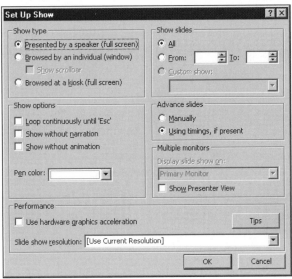

STEP-BY-STEP ▷ 4.11

1. Choose **Set Up Show** from the **Slide Show** menu. The Set Up Show dialog box appears, as shown in Figure 4-18.

2. In the Show type section, click **Presented by a speaker** if it is not already selected.

3. In the Show slides section, click **From.** The first box should be left as 1. Change the second box to read 24.

4. In the Advance slides section, click **Using timings, if present**, if it is not already selected.

5. Click **OK**.

6. View the presentation to see the changes. Leave the presentation on the screen for the next Step-by-Step.

Rehearse Timing

PowerPoint can automatically advance the slides in your presentation at preset time intervals. This is helpful in the case of an unattended presentation at a kiosk or sales booth or if you must make a presentation within a specific time limit.

To rehearse timing for a presentation, choose Rehearse Timings from the Slide Show menu. The slide show automatically starts, and the Rehearsal toolbar with a timer for the slide and a timer for the presentation appears on the screen, as shown in Figure 4-19. When you finish a slide, click on the Next button. The presentation advances to the next slide and the slide timer starts over. You can pause the timer by clicking on the Pause button. The Repeat button resets the slide timer back to zero and the presentation timer back to the time that had elapsed through the previous slide. When you get to the end of the show, a dialog box appears asking if you want to keep the slide timings for the presentation.

FIGURE 4-19
Rehearsal toolbar

To view rehearsal times for each slide, view the presentation in the Slide Sorter view. The time allotted to each slide is listed to the lower-left of each slide. You can further edit the timing of each slide by opening the slide transition dialog box and changing the time below the Advance slide area of the dialog box.

STEP-BY-STEP ▷ 4.12

1. Switch to **Slide Sorter** view.

2. Choose **Rehearse Timings** from the **Slide Show** menu. The slide show starts and the timers for the slide and the slide show begin.

3. Click the **Next** button every four to five seconds. Don't worry if you make a mistake.

4. When you reach the end of slide show, a dialog box appears asking if you want to keep the timings. Click **Yes**. The presentation returns to the Slide Sorter view.

5. Click the **Transition** button on the toolbar. The Slide Transition dialog box appears in the task pane. Correct the timing of any slides if needed by adjusting the time below Advance slide.

6. Choose **View Show** from the **Slide Show** menu.
The slides will automatically advance at the rate
you set for each slide. Leave the presentation
on the screen for the next Step-by-Step.

Embedding Fonts

Not all computers have every font style installed on them. If you are giving
your presentation on a computer other than your own, your presentation text
might not look exactly as it did when you created it. PowerPoint can embed fonts
into your presentation so that your text appears exactly as you originally created
it. You do not have to embed common fonts, such as Times New Roman, Arial, or
Courier New, that are installed with Windows.

To embed fonts in your presentation choose Save As from the File menu.
Click Tools on the toolbar. The Tools menu appears, as shown in Figure 4-20. Click
Save Options, and the Save Options dialog box appears as shown in Figure 4-21.
Click on Embed True Type Fonts, and then click on Embed characters in use only.

FIGURE 4-20
Tools menu

S T E P - B Y - S T E P ▷ 4.13

1. Choose **Save As** from the **File** menu.

2. Click **Tools** on the toolbar. The
   Tools menu appears as shown
   in Figure 4-20.

3. Click **Save Options**. The Save Options dialog
   box appears, as shown in Figure 4-21.

FIGURE 4-21
Save Options dialog box

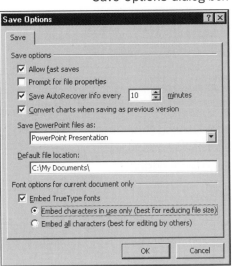

4. Click the check box **Embed TrueType fonts**.

5. Choose **Embed character in use only**.

6. Click **OK**.

7. Click **Save** to finish saving the file. Leave the presentation on the screen for the next Step-by-Step. If a dialog box appears asking if you want to replace a file that already exists, click **Yes**.

Use Pack and Go

If you are giving your presentation on another computer, you can use the *Pack and Go* Wizard to compact all your presentation files into a single, compressed file that fits on a floppy disk. You can then unpack the files when you reach your destination computer.

To use this feature, choose Pack and Go from the File menu. The Pack and Go Wizard appears, as shown in Figure 4-22. The first window is an introduction to the wizard and outlines the steps of the process. As the wizard progresses, select the presentation you want to package, choose the destination of your files, and choose the linked files and fonts you want to package. If the computer on which you are giving your presentation does not have PowerPoint installed, the wizard also allows you to download a PowerPoint Viewer.

FIGURE 4-22
Pack and Go Wizard

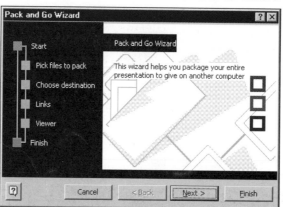

1. Minimize the presentation to display your desktop. Create a new folder on your desktop by right-clicking on the desktop. Choose **New** from the menu and **Folder** from the submenu. Name this new folder **Solar System** followed by your initials.

2. Maximize the presentation and choose **Save As** from the File menu. Choose the folder you just created and click **Save**.

3. Choose **Pack and Go** from the File menu. The Pack and Go Wizard appears, as shown in Figure 4-22.

4. Read the information on this window and click **Next**.

5. Click the **Active presentation** box, if it is not already selected, to package the open presentation. Click **Next**.

6. Click **Choose destination** and then click the **Browse** button. Choose the folder you created and click **Next**.

7. Since this presentation does not include any linked files and you embedded the fonts in the previous Step-by-Step, deselect both the linked files and embedded fonts boxes. Click **Next**.

8. Choose **Don't include the Viewer**, if it is not already selected. Click **Next**.

9. Click **Finish** to compress the file and save it to the destination disk.

10. Minimize the presentation again to view the desktop. Open the **Solar System** folder. Highlight the file named **Solar System** and check the file size in the description on the left side of the screen. Highlight the file that you created using Pack and Go; notice that the file size is much smaller.

11. Close the window and delete the **Solar System** folder by right-clicking it and selecting **Delete** from the menu.

12. Maximize the presentation and leave it on the screen for the next Step-by-Step.

Publishing Presentations to the Web

Similar to other Office applications, PowerPoint also helps you easily create Web documents, either by creating a new presentation for the purpose or converting an existing presentation. If you are creating a new presentation for the Web, you can use the AutoContent Wizard. If you are converting an existing presentation to a Web page, choose Save as Web Page from the File menu. The Save As dialog box appears, as shown in Figure 4-23.

Computer Concepts

Making a presentation available on the Web is also known as "publishing a presentation."

FIGURE 4-23
Save a presentation as a Web page

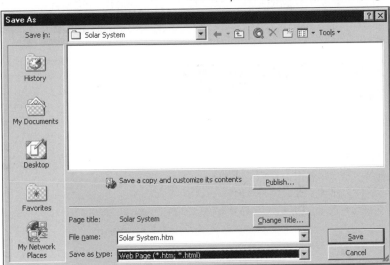

When you choose Publish in the Save As dialog box, the Publish as Web Page dialog box appears, as shown in Figure 4-24. To preview a presentation in your browser, choose Web Page Preview from the File menu. The browser opens and displays your presentation as a Web page.

FIGURE 4-24
Publish as Web Page dialog box

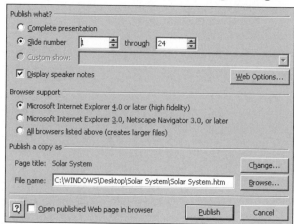

STEP-BY-STEP ▷ 4.15

1. Choose **Save as Web Page** from the **File** menu. The Save As dialog box appears, as shown in Figure 4-23.

2. Click the **Publish** button in the middle of the dialog box as shown in Figure 4-23. The Publish as Web Page dialog box appears, as shown in Figure 4-24.

3. In the Publish what? box, choose **Complete Presentation** if it is not already selected.

4. Click **Publish**.

5. Choose **Web Page Preview** on the **File** menu. Your browser opens and the presentation displays as a Web page. Your screen should look similar to that in Figure 4-25.

6. Click the titles in the left frame to go to each slide. When you are finished, close the browser, but leave the presentation on the screen for the next Step-by-Step.

FIGURE 4-25
View your presentation in a browser

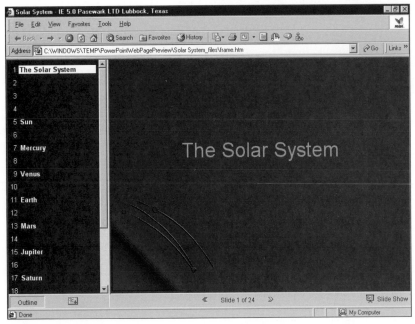

Scheduling and Delivering Web Broadcasts

PowerPoint allows you to broadcast your presentation over the Internet or an intranet, to an audience as close as the next room or in a city across the country. If you want to include narration with your presentation so that the audience can see and hear you as if you were presenting in the same room, Online Broadcast requires a video camera and microphone.

Online Broadcast has three options for broadcasting a presentation.

■ *Record and Save a Broadcast* saves your presentation in a Web format so that you can publish it to the Web.

■ *Schedule a Live Broadcast* uses Microsoft Outlook to set up a meeting request so that you can schedule a meeting time for your audience.

■ *Start Live Broadcast Now* broadcasts your saved presentation to your audience as soon as you are ready to start.

To set up your presentation for later broadcast, choose Online Broadcast on the Slide Show menu and choose Record and Save a Broadcast from the submenu. The Record Presentation Broadcast dialog box containing information about your presentation appears. Click the Settings button to set your Broadcast Settings and choose the Presenter tab. If you have audio or video capabilities, choose the corresponding box in the Audio/Video section. Choose where you want to save your files in the File Location section.

C

1. Choose **Online Broadcast** from the **Slide Show** menu and **Record and Save a Broadcast** from the submenu. The Record Presentation Broadcast dialog box appears.

2. Click the **Settings** button. Choose **None** in the Audio/Video section, and choose where you want to save your presentation under File Location. Click **OK**.

3. Click **Record**. PowerPoint begins processing your files.

4. Click **Start** to preview your presentation. PowerPoint shows your presentation as it will appear when you publish it to the Internet. When the presentation is finished running, a dialog box appears. Choose **Continue** and leave the presentation open for the next Step-by-Step.

C

Sending a Presentation via E-mail

There are several ways you can use e-mail in conjunction with PowerPoint. You can send a presentation as an e-mail attachment or to a recipient for review.

Open the presentation you want to send and choose Send To from the File menu and Mail Recipient (as Attachment) from the submenu. PowerPoint automatically opens your e-mail editor, and the presentation is inserted into the e-mail as an attachment, as shown in Figure 4-26.

Hot Tip

A presentation attached to e-mail is sent in HTML format and can be viewed by any e-mail program that can read HTML.

FIGURE 4-26
E-mail with Solar System attachment

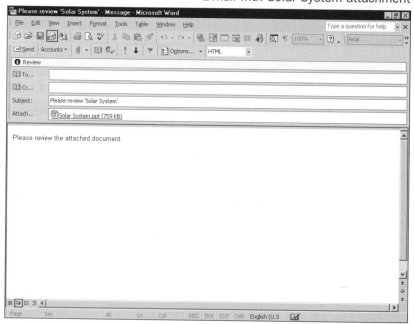

Fill in the recipient information, key a message, and click Send. A copy of the presentation is e-mailed, but the original stays open so you can continue working on it.

To *route* a presentation is to send it via e-mail for others to review that allows the recipient to make changes to the presentation. A routed presentation is sent as an e-mail attachment. First you must create a routing slip. Open the presentation you want to route, choose Send To on the File menu and Routing Recipient on the submenu. The Add Routing Slip dialog box opens, as shown in Figure 4-27.

Computer Concepts

To send a slide as a message, choose **Mail Recipient** on the submenu. To send the presentation as an attachment, choose **Mail Recipient (as Attachment)** on the submenu.

FIGURE 4-27
Add Routing Slip dialog box

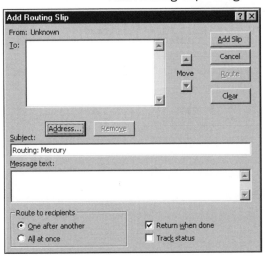

Click Address to open your address book and choose recipients. Choose whether you want to route the presentation to recipients all at once or sequentially. Key your message text and click Route to route the presentation immediately. To route it later, click Add Slip and when you are ready, choose Send To on the File menu and Next Routing Recipient on the submenu.

STEP-BY-STEP ▷4.17

1. Choose **Send To** from the **File** menu and **Mail Recipient (for Review)** from the submenu. Your e-mail editor appears with the presentation as an attachment and *Please review the attached document* in the body of the e-mail.

2. Choose a partner and exchange your presentations. Key your partner's e-mail address in the To box and click the **Send** button to send the presentation. Close the presentation.

Extra Challenge

Create a routing slip for a presentation and route it to two people in your class one after another.

Review Presentations

You might want to send your presentation to another person so they can make corrections or additions. PowerPoint has a feature that allows another person to make corrections and marks the changes so the original author can easily identify them. To review a presentation that you have received, double-click the presentation attachment to open it and make the changes to the presentation. Choose Toolbars from the View menu, and click Reviewing on the submenu. The Reviewing toolbar appears, as shown in Figure 4-28. You can use the icons on the toolbar to add, edit, or delete comments to the presentation. When you have finished, choose Send To from the File menu and Original Sender from the submenu.

FIGURE 4-28
Reviewing Toolbar

S TEP-BY-STEP ▷ 4.18

1. Open Outlook (or another e-mail program) and double-click on the presentation attachment that your partner sent to you in the last Step-by-Step to open it. The PowerPoint program opens and the attached presentation displays.

2. Choose **Toolbars** from the **View** menu and click on **Reviewing** to place a check mark next to it.

3. View your partner's presentation and look for any mistakes he or she might have made. If you find a mistake, click the **Insert Comment** button on the Reviewing toolbar and write a short note to your partner describing the mistake. If you do not find any mistakes, click on slide **1** and insert a comment saying that there were no mistakes.

4. When you have finished inserting the comments, Choose **Send To** from the **File** menu and **Mail Recipient (as Attachment)** from the submenu. Mail the presentation back to your partner. Close the presentation without saving.

Creating Output

You can alter the output format of your presentation by choosing Page Setup from the File menu. The Page Setup dialog box appears, as shown in Figure 4-29. You can change the orientation of your slides or notes, handouts, and outline. You can choose the type of output from the menu in the *Slides sized for* box. For example, to print a slide as an overhead transparency, choose Overhead.

FIGURE 4-29
Page Setup dialog box

![Step-by-step 4.19]

S TEP-BY-STEP ▷ 4.19

1. Open the file named **Solar System** that you created earlier.

2. Choose **Page Setup** from the **File** menu. The Page Setup dialog box appears.

3. In the Notes, handouts & outline section, click **Landscape**.

4. Click **OK**.

5. Print the presentation as handouts with 6 slides per page. Save and close the presentation.

Summary

In this lesson, you learned:

- You can create a new presentation from existing slides and you can copy a slide from one presentation into another.

- To replace fonts throughout an entire presentation, choose Replace Fonts from the Format menu. You can change the formatting of an object or text by clicking the Format Painter button.

- When delivering a presentation, you can start the slide show on any slide. To navigate through a presentation while it is running, click the triangle in the corner of the screen and choose from the menu.

- You can use your pointer as a pen to draw or write on a slide while running a presentation. To change the color of the pen, choose Pen Color from the Pointer Options menu and choose a color.

- You can e-mail a copy of a presentation as an attachment or route a presentation for others to review.

- You can create a presentation for the Web using the AutoContent Wizard. To convert any presentation to a Web page, choose Save as Web Page from the File menu.

- You can import text from Word to create a new presentation or add slides. It is easiest for PowerPoint to convert the text to slides when the Word document is in outline form.

- Embedding is another way to integrate data between applications. Information is embedded as an object so that it can be edited using the original application.

- To make changes to an embedded object, double-click on it to open the application that created it. Changes made when editing are reflected in the destination file.

VOCABULARY REVIEW

Define the following terms:

Embed   Guide settings   Snap to
Format Painter   Pack and Go   Route
Grid Settings

LESSON 4 REVIEW QUESTIONS

FILL IN THE BLANK

Complete the following sentences by writing the correct word or words in the blanks provided.

1. When running a presentation, click the _____ in the bottom-left corner of the screen to display a menu of navigation tools.

2. If you format an object with certain attributes, such as fill color and line color, then want to format another object the same way, use the _____ feature.

3. When importing text from Word, a(n) _____ is the easiest document for PowerPoint to convert.

4. To _____ a presentation is to send it to others for review.

5. To preview a published presentation in your browser, choose _____ on the File menu.

MATCHING

Write the letter of the term in the right column that best matches the description in the left column.

____ 1. Dialog box you use to copy a slide from another presentation

____ 2. View button you click to start a presentation

____ 3. Dialog box where you alter the output format of a presentation

____ 4. Copy attributes of text or objects

____ 5. Dialog box you access to embed information

A. Format Painter

B. Insert Hyperlink

C. Page Setup

D. Slide Finder

E. Insert Object

F. Slide Navigator

G. Slide Show

LESSON 4 PROJECTS

PROJECT 4-1

1. Start PowerPoint and open the **Solar System** file you worked on earlier in this lesson. Save the presentation as **Solar System 2** followed by your initials.

2. Change the output format so that handouts print in landscape.

4. Replace the Arial font throughout the presentation with Tahoma. (If that font is not available, choose another appropriate one.)

5. Select the title **The Solar System** on slide 1.

6. Change the font to Impact, 48-point.

7. Use the Format Painter to apply that title format to the rest of the titles in the presentation.

8. Publish the presentation as a Web page and preview it in a browser.

9. Save, print the presentation as handouts with 4 slides per page, and close.

PROJECT 4-2

1. Open the **Solar System** presentation.

2. Save the presentation as **Solar System 3**.

3. Insert a new slide with a blank layout between slides 24 and 25.

4. Insert a Word table that contains the following information:

```
Planet          Number of Moons
Mercury         0
Venus           0
Earth           1
Mars            2
Jupiter         16
Saturn          18
Uranus          15
Neptune         8
Pluto           1
```

5. Change the text size to 24 and bold it. Change the text color to blue and center it.

6. Center the text box on the slide.

7. View the presentation.

8. Save, print, and close the presentation.

CRITICAL THINKING

SCANS

ACTIVITY 4-1

Your supervisor wants you to insert a chart into the presentation you are editing for him. You decide to use a Microsoft Excel chart that you have already created. Use the Help system to find out how to insert an Excel chart into a presentation.

SCANS

ACTIVITY 4-2

Create an outline in Word using heading styles. Use at least three Heading 1 styles so your presentation has at least three slides. Import the text into PowerPoint to create a new presentation. Convert the presentation into a Web page and view it with your browser.

COMMAND SUMMARY

FEATURE	MENU COMMAND	TOOLBAR BUTTON	LESSON
Align	Format, Alignment		2
Animation Effects	Slide Show, Custom Animation		2
AutoShapes	Insert, Picture, AutoShapes	AutoShapes ▾	3
Bold	Format, Font	B	2
Bulleted List	Format, Bullets and Numbering, Bulleted		2
Can			3
Clip Art	Insert, Picture, Clip Art		1
Close	File, Close		1
Copy	Edit, Copy		3
Collapse dialog box			3
Create a New Presentation	File, New		2
Cut	Edit, Cut		3
Design	Format, Slide Design		1
Delete a Slide	Edit, Delete Slide		2
E-mail			4
Find	Edit, Find		2
Font	Format, Font	PMingLiU	2
Font Color	Format, Font	A	2
Font Size	Format, Font	32	2
Format Painter			4
Free Rotate			3
Header and Footer	View, Header and Footer		2
Hyperlink	Insert, Hyperlink		4
Insert Table	Insert, Table		3
Italic	Format, Font	I	2
Line Color	Format, Colors and Lines		3
New Slide	Insert, New Slide		1
Next			1
Numbered List Numbered	Format, Bullets and Numbering		2

FEATURE	MENU COMMAND	TOOLBAR BUTTON	LESSON
Office Assistant	Help, Show the Office Assistant		1
Open Existing Document	File, Open		1
Oval			3
Paste	Edit, Paste		3
Print	File, Print		1
Rectangle			3
Replace	Edit, Replace		2
Replace Fonts	Format, Replace Fonts		4
Save	File, Save		1
Slide Show			1
Spell Check	Tools, Spelling		2
Text Box	Insert, Text Box		3
Underline	Format, Font		2
Undo	Edit, Undo		2
View Datasheet	View, Datasheet		3
Views	View, desired view		1
Web Page	File, Save as Web Page		4
Web Page Preview	File, Web Page Preview		4

REVIEW QUESTIONS

TRUE/FALSE

Circle T if the statement is true or F if the statement is false.

T F 1. If the presentation you want to open is not in the task pane, click the More presentations folder for more options.

T F 2. A slide transition allows you to change the speed of an effect.

T F 3. It is not possible to cut and copy objects the way you do text.

T F 4. Changing the slide master affects the appearance of all the slides.

T F 5. To navigate through a running presentation, click the triangle in the screen corner and choose from the menu.

MULTIPLE CHOICE

Select the best response for the following statements.

1. Which of the following features does not allow you to create a new presentation?
   A. Blank Presentation
   B. More presentations
   C. From Design Template
   D. From AutoContent Wizard

2. Which of the following reserves space in the presentation for the type of information you want?
   A. Master
   B. Object box
   C. Template
   D. Placeholder

3. Slide design allows you to change all of the following parts of a slide except:
   A. Design templates
   B. Color schemes
   C. Animation schemes
   D. Effects

4. Which of the following do you use to best show hierarchical structure and relationships in a company?
   A. Table
   B. Graph
   C. Text box
   D. Organization chart

5. You can apply changes to the entire presentation using all of the following, except
   A. Slide Master
   B. Handout Master
   C. Design Template Master
   D. Notes Master

PROJECTS

PROJECT 1

1. Use the AutoContent Wizard to create a Generic presentation (in the General category). The type of output will be an on-screen presentation.

2. Key **Data Management** as the presentation title.

3. Include your name as the footer on each slide.

4. Save the presentation as **Computer Use** followed by your initials.

5. Apply the **Blends** design template.

6. Change the subtitle on slide **1** to **Responsible Computer Use**.

7. Delete slides **2** (**Introduction**), **3** (**Topics of Discussion**), **7** (**Real Life**), **8** (**What This Means**), and **9** (**Next Steps**).

8. Switch to **Normal** view if necessary and key text on the remaining slides as shown in Figures UR-1, UR-2, and UR-3.

9. Insert a new slide 5 and create objects to make it look like Figure UR-4.

10. Save and leave the presentation open for the next project.

FIGURE UR-1
Passwords slide

Passwords

- Every morning you will log on to your computer with your username and a 5-10 character password.
- Choose a password that is easy to remember, but not easy for someone to guess.
- Change your password periodically to keep it confidential.

3/28/2001   Student's Name   2

FIGURE UR-2
Authorized Use slide

Authorized Software Use

- The software installed on your computer is licensed under specific terms of agreement.
- Please do not delete, install, copy, or move any software without permission.

3/28/2001   Student's Name   3

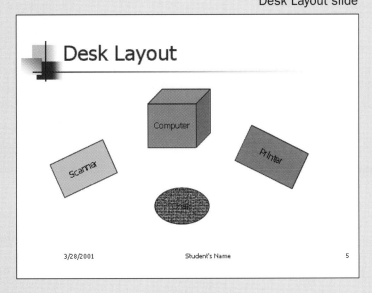

PROJECT 2

1. Save the presentation with the new name **Computer Use 2** followed by your initials.

2. Change the layout of slide **3** to **Title, Text and Clip Art**.

3. Replace the clip art placeholder with a picture of a floppy disk. If a picture of a floppy disk is not available, make another computer-related selection.

4. Add this speaker's note to slide **4**: **Hand out employee ethics agreements. Be sure they are signed and returned by Friday.**

5. Print slide **4** in Notes Pages view.

6. On slide **1**, animate the title to Faded Zoom accompanied by a Laser sound.

7. Set the slide transitions for all slides to **Checkerboard Across** at medium speed.

8. Run the presentation as a slide show.

9. Change the output format so the handouts print in landscape orientation.

10. Print the presentation as audience handouts with 6 slides per page.

11. Save and close the presentation.

PROJECT 3

1. Open **IP Project3** from the data files.

2. Save the presentation as **Hong Kong** followed by your initials.

3. Add a slide to the end of the presentation titled **Food**.

4. In Outline or Normal view, key the rest of the slide in bulleted list format:
   - The basic food is rice and is often prepared with fish, pork, chicken, and vegetables.
   - Chopsticks are used with most meals.
   - When you eat, it is good manners to hold the rice bowl close to your mouth.

5. In Slide Sorter view, move slide 4 so it becomes slide 2.

6. Replace the current font with PMingLiU (or another similar font) throughout the presentation.

7. Change the font of the title on slide **2** to Century Gothic, 48 point, bold.

8. Use the Format Painter to copy the format to the title of slides 3 and 4.

9. Print the presentation in Outline view.

10. Save and leave the presentation open for the next application.

PROJECT 4

1. In Normal view, display slide **3**. Delete the words **Population and** from the title.

2. Delete the first bullet on the slide.

3. Change the slide layout to **Title, Text and Clip Art**.

4. Insert a clip art picture with mountains.

5. Size the clip art and text boxes to make everything fit well on the slide.

6. On slide **1** animate the title to **Rise Up**, and the subtitle to **Ease In**.

7. Apply a Random Transition set at slow speed to all slides and choose a Chime sound to accompany the transitions.

8. Insert a hyperlink on the last slide using the words Hong Kong in the first bullet to jump to slide 1.

9. Start a slide show on the last slide.

10. Click the hyperlink to go to the first slide. Advance through the presentation to slide 3.

11. Use the red pen to underline **tropical climate**.

12. Exit the slide show.

13. Save the presentation as **Hong Kong 2** followed by your initials and print it as audience handouts with 2 slides per page.

14. Save the presentation as a Web page. Preview it in your browser. Close the browser.

15. Save and close the presentation. Exit PowerPoint.

SIMULATION

Your manager asks you to create a presentation to show to all new members.

1. Start PowerPoint and open **IP Job1** from the data files. Save the presentation as **Internet Basics** followed by your initials.

2. Change the layout of slide **3** to **Title, Text and Clip Art** and insert a clip-art picture relevant to the slide.

3. Start Word and open **Table** from the data files. Save the document as **Computer Table** followed by your initials.

4. Center all headings in the table.

5. Close the table (saving your changes), exit Word, and switch to PowerPoint.

6. Insert a new slide after slide 11 with a Title and Content layout.

7. Key **Computer Equipment** as the title.

8. Embed the **Computer Table** document as the object.

9. Adjust the text by resizing, bolding, and changing the font to make the text easy to read.

10. Double-click the table. Change the yes to no in the first cell of the Scanner Access column.

11. Click the slide to return to the presentation.

12. Delete the three vocabulary slides (currently slides 5–7)

13. Save and print **Internet Basics** as handouts with 9 slides per page. Close the presentation and exit PowerPoint.

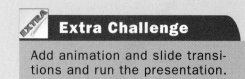

Extra Challenge

Add animation and slide transitions and run the presentation.

INTRODUCTORY MICROSOFT® OUTLOOK

OUTLOOK BASICS AND E-MAIL

OBJECTIVES

Upon completion of this lesson, you should be able to:

- Start Outlook.
- Create a list of contacts and add contacts.
- View, sort, and print the Contacts list.
- Use e-mail to send and receive messages.
- Create and use an Address Book.
- Insert a signature.
- Attach documents to e-mails.
- Create, move, and archive folders.
- Print and save e-mail messages.
- Search and delete e-mail messages.

⏱ **Estimated Time: 1 hour**

VOCABULARY

Address Book

Archive

Contact

Distribution list

E-mail

Outlook Bar

Introducing Outlook

Outlook is a desktop information manager that helps you organize information, communicate with others, and manage your time. You can use the various features of Outlook to send and receive e-mail, schedule events and meetings, record information about business and personal contacts, make to-do lists, record your work, and create reminders. You can organize all this information into categories for viewing and printing. For example, you might group all the information on your most important customers into the Key Customer category. You can also create a new category for a specific group of information. For example, you could put all the information on your customers located in Texas into a *Texas Customers* category.

Because Outlook is integrated, you can use it easily with all other Office programs. For example, you can send and receive e-mail messages in Outlook and you can move a name and address from a Word document into your Outlook Contacts list.

Starting Outlook

To start Outlook, click the Start button, select Programs, and then choose Microsoft Outlook. When you click the Inbox icon on the Outlook Bar, the Inbox view appears as shown in Figure 1-1. You send and receive e-mail messages from the Inbox view if your computer is set up for this.

FIGURE 1-1
Inbox view

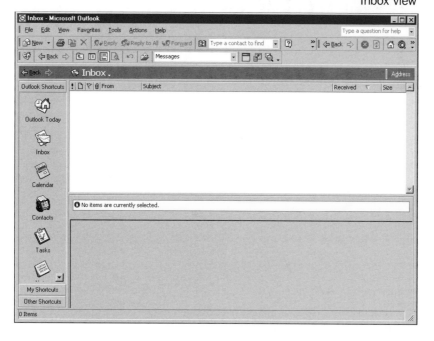

The ***Outlook Bar*** is located on the left side of the Outlook window and includes groups and short-cuts so you can quickly access information and folders. The Outlook Bar has three categories: Outlook Shortcuts, My Shortcuts, and Other Shortcuts. The Outlook Shortcuts category contains icons you can use to access many of Outlook's features, as listed in Table 1-1. The My Shortcuts category displays icons you can use to draft, send, receive, and organize e-mail messages. You will learn more about e-mail later in this lesson. The Other Shortcuts category allows you to view the contents of any folder on your computer.

TABLE 1-1
Outlook Bar icons

ICON	NAME	DESCRIPTION
	Outlook Today	Lists today's activities from Calendar, Tasks, and Inbox and summarizes in one view.
	Inbox	Contains e-mail messages you've received.
	Calendar	Schedules your appointments, meetings, and events.
	Contacts	Lists information about those with whom you communicate.
	Tasks	Creates and manages your to-do lists.
	Journal	Records entries to document your work.
	Notes	Keeps track of anything you need to remember.
	Deleted Items	Stores files deleted from other folders.

1. Choose **Start**, **Programs**, and **Microsoft Outlook**. If the Choose Profile dialog box appears, click **OK**.

2. Leave Outlook open for use in the next Step-by-Step.

Computer Concepts

You can customize the Outlook Bar by right-clicking on it and making your choices from the menu that appears.

Creating a Contacts List

Y ou can use the Contacts view in Outlook to create and use your Contacts list. A *contact* is any person or company in your Address Book. Your Contacts list contains mail, phone, and other information about your contacts. Click the Contacts icon on the Outlook Bar to display the Contacts view, similar to Figure 1-2.

FIGURE 1-2
Contacts view

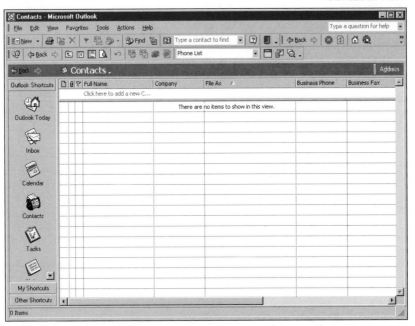

Adding a Contact

To add a contact, click the New Contact icon on the toolbar. The Contact dialog box appears, as shown in Figure 1-3. When you finish adding information about the contact, click Save and Close to return to the Contacts view or click the Save and New button to add another contact.

Notice the five tabs at the top of the Contact dialog box. The General tab includes mailing, phone, and other information, such as the contact's job title and the company name. To help keep track of your contacts, you can assign categories to the contacts. You store additional information about a contact, such as department, nickname, or birthday, on the Details tab. You track all journal entries related to a contact on the Activities tab. You will learn more about the Journal in Lesson 3. The Certificates tab allows you to send a secure message over the Internet. The All Fields tab allows you to create custom fields.

Computer Concepts

To edit information about a contact, double-click the contact's name in the Contacts list.

FIGURE 1-3
Contact dialog box

S TEP-BY-STEP ▷ 1.2

1. Click the **Contacts** icon on the Outlook Bar. The Contacts view appears, similar to Figure 1-2.

2. Click the **New Contact** button on the toolbar. The Contact dialog box appears as shown in Figure 1-3. Click the **General** tab, if it is not already chosen.

3. In the Full Name box, key **Mary Daly**.

4. Press **Tab**. The contact's name appears as *Daly, Mary* in the File as box.

5. In the Job title box, key **Sales Manager** and press **Tab**.

6. In the Company box, key **Northstar, Inc**. and press **Tab**.

7. For the remaining boxes, key the information as shown in Figure 1-4. If necessary, enlarge the Contact dialog box to see all your data entries.

8. After completing the information, click the **Save and New** button located on the toolbar. Save and New is also located on the File menu.

9. Add two more contacts using the information shown in Figure 1-5. When you finish with the last contact, click **Save and Close** to return to the Contact view. Leave the Contacts list open for the next Step-by-Step.

Extra Challenge

Add five more contacts to your Contacts list.

FIGURE 1-4
Your first contact

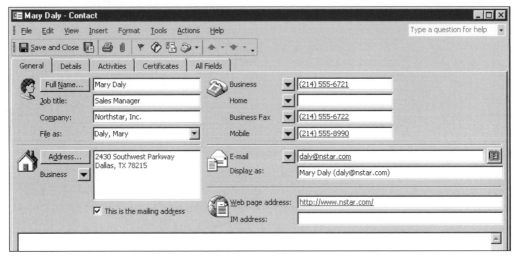

FIGURE 1-5
Add two more contacts

McGinnis, Paul		Worthington, Zela	
Full Name:	Paul McGinnis	Full Name:	Zela Worthington
Job Title:	Vice President	Job Title:	Director of Marketing
Company:	McGinnis Enterprises	Company:	Monark Company
Business:	4552 Oakland Ave. Austin, TX 78746	Business:	5688 Fillmore Blvd. Beaumont, TX 77703
Business:	(512) 555-7824	Business:	(409) 555-6776
Home:	(512) 555-6634	Home:	(409) 555-2331
Business Fax:	(512) 555-7825	Business Fax:	(409) 555-6778
E-mail:	pmcginnis@mcenter.com	E-mail:	zworthington@monark.com
Web Page:	http://www.mcginnis.com	Categories:	Suppliers
Categories:	Key Customer		

Viewing, Sorting, and Printing the Contacts List

To change how you view your contacts, choose Current View from the View menu and then choose from the list of view options, which are described in Table 1-2. Address Cards is the default view.

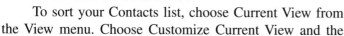
Computer Concepts

When using Address Cards view, you can click a letter on the bar on the right to quickly display contacts beginning with that letter.

To sort your Contacts list, choose Current View from the View menu. Choose Customize Current View and the View Summary dialog box appears. When you click the Sort button, the Sort dialog box appears showing the available sorting options for the Contacts list, including sorting by full name, last name, company, mailing address, and job title.

To print your Contacts list, choose Print from the File menu. The Print dialog box opens. The Print style box provides different options depending on the view you are using. For example, you can choose to print your contacts as cards, booklets, or a phone list.

TABLE 1-2
View options for Contacts list

VIEW	DESCRIPTION
Address Cards	Default view displays general information on individual cards.
Detailed Address Cards	Displays detailed information about contacts on individual cards.
Phone List	Lists contacts in a table with all phone numbers included.
By Category	Groups contacts in a list according to category.
By Company	Groups contacts in a list according to company.
By Location	Groups contacts in a list according to country.
By Follow-Up Flag	Groups contacts in a list according to follow-up dates.

S TEP-BY-STEP ▷ 1.3

1. With the Contacts view displayed, choose **Current View** from the **View** menu, then select **Detailed Address Cards**. Your screen should look similar to Figure 1-6.

2. Choose **Current View** from the **View** menu and select **Phone List**.

3. Choose **Current View** from the **View** menu, and then select **Customize Current View**.

4. In the View Summary dialog box, click the **Sort** button. The Sort dialog box appears. Your screen should look similar to Figure 1-7.

5. In the Sort items by box, click the down arrow to view the available sorting options and then click **Company**. Click **OK** in both the Sort dialog box and the View Summary dialog box. Your contacts are now sorted by company in ascending order.

6. Choose **Print** from the **File** menu. The Print dialog box appears.

7. In the Print style box, **Table Style** should already be highlighted. Click **OK**. The Contacts list will print as a phone list. Leave Outlook open for the next Step-by-Step.

Computer Concepts

Creating a Contacts list makes it easy to communicate with others. To send an e-mail message to a contact, choose New Message to Contact from the Actions menu, key the message, then click Send. You will learn more about sending e-mail messages later in this lesson.

FIGURE 1-6
Contacts view in Detailed Address Cards view

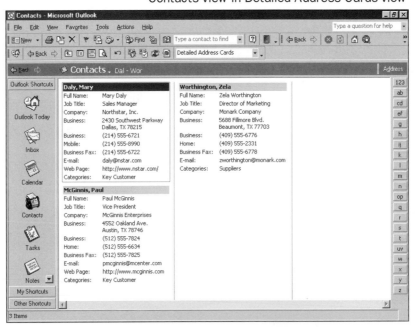

FIGURE 1-7
Sort dialog box

Using E-mail

One of the most common and most useful Internet services is *e-mail* (electronic mail), using a computer network to send and receive messages. The value of e-mail is that it is faster than the United States Postal Service's traditional method of delivering letters. It is also less expensive and more efficient, since it allows you to send a message to more than one person at the same time. E-mail is global and it is environment-friendly, since it does not require paper.

To use electronic mail, you need an e-mail address that includes your name; your host, server, or domain name; and an extension that tells whether the account is at a school, business, government location, or in another country. No one has your unique e-mail address. E-mail addresses look like this:

dateline@nbc.com

president@whitehouse.gov

Using Outlook, you can send e-mail messages to others connected by your intranet. If you have an Internet connection, you can send messages to anyone around the world who also has an Internet connection. E-mail has transformed business and personal communication and, in many cases, has become the preferred way to communicate with clients, co-workers, friends, and family. Your software needs to be configured with the appropriate profile and service settings to send and receive e-mail.

Hot Tip

It is important to manage your e-mail. You should save and delete messages as necessary, since everyone who has an e-mail account has a limited amount of space available for messages.

Setting E-Mail Options and Assigning Categories to Messages

To help you manage your e-mail messages, Outlook has provided several defaults settings for sending and receiving messages. By changing these defaults, you can choose the way you want your messages to be sent or received. By clicking the New Message button, an Untitled Message dialog box appears as shown in Figure 1-8. Click the Options button and the Message Options dialog box appears similar to Figure 1-9. There are three main sections on this screen: Message settings, Voting and Tracking options, and Delivery options. The default setting for Message settings is "normal" for both Importance and Sensitivity. There are no defaults set in the Voting and Tracking options section. The Delivery options section has a check beside Save sent message to. You can access both the Contacts list and the Categories dialog box through the Message Options dialog box.

1. Click the **Inbox** icon on the **Outlook Bar**.

2. Double-click the message from Microsoft or another message if you have one in your Inbox. Scroll through and read the message. Notice all the formatting features used in the message.

3. Choose **Close** from the **File** menu. The message closes.

4. Click the **New Mail Message** button. The Untitled Message dialog box appears similar to Figure 1-8.

5. Click the **Options** button and the Message Options dialog box appears similar to Figure 1-9.

6. In the Message settings section, click the **Importance** down arrow and change the setting to **Low**.

7. In the Voting and Tracking options section, click the box beside **Use voting buttons** and a check appears.

8. In the Delivery options section, click the boxes to change where replies are sent. Your name and e-mail address will appear in the field.

9. Click the **Categories** button. The Categories dialog box appears. Click the **Business** box and click **OK**.

10. Change the settings back to the original defaults, using Figure 1-9 as your guide. (*Note:* The Encoding default might not be the same as Figure 1-9.)

11. Close the Message Options dialog box and the Untitled Message dialog box appears. Click **No** and leave Outlook open for the next Step-by-Step.

FIGURE 1-8
Untitled Message dialog box

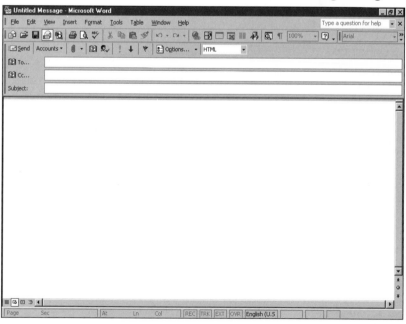

FIGURE 1-9
Message Options dialog box

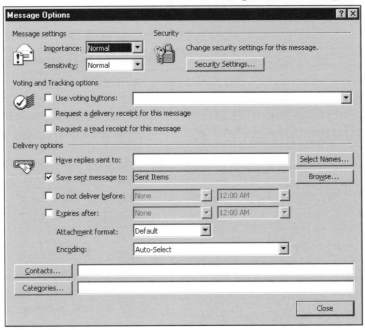

Sending and Printing Messages

When you click the My Shortcuts button at the bottom of the Outlook bar, a group of icons is displayed. Each icon represents a folder, such as the Drafts folder in which unsent items are stored. The Outbox stores outgoing mail and Sent Items stores the e-mail messages you've sent. Click an icon to view its contents.

If you return to the Inbox and double-click a message, the message is opened. After reading a message, you can send a reply to the author of the message by clicking the Reply button on the toolbar. You can also print the message or read your next message.

To send e-mail, choose New Mail Message from the Actions menu or click the New Mail Message button on the toolbar. A blank e-mail message appears, like that shown in Figure 1-8. In the To box, key the e-mail address of the person to whom you are sending the message. You can send a copy of the message to someone by keying his or her e-mail address in the Cc box. Key the subject of your message in the Subject box and key your message in the message window.

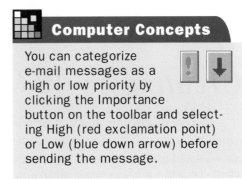

Computer Concepts

You can categorize e-mail messages as a high or low priority by clicking the Importance button on the toolbar and selecting High (red exclamation point) or Low (blue down arrow) before sending the message.

Just as you did in other Office programs, you can use the buttons on the Formatting toolbar to change the font, size, color, style, and alignment of text in your message. You can also save the message and check its spelling. By clicking the Print button on the toolbar, your message can be printed. It is even possible to attach a file to an e-mail message. When you're finished writing your message, you can send it by clicking the Send button on the toolbar.

1. Click the **New Mail Message button**. A blank e-mail message form appears, as shown in Figure 1-8.

2. Key your e-mail address, or one provided by your instructor, in the **To** box.

3. Key **Test** in the Subject box.

4. In the message window, key **This is a test.**

5. Click the **Send** button. Your mail is sent, and if Outlook is set up correctly for intranet e-mail, you should receive the message in a few moments. (If you have only Internet e-mail, you'll need to choose **Remote Mail** from the **Tools** menu and **Connect** from the submenu.)

6. Double-click the e-mail with the subject *Test* to open the message.

7. Click the **Print** button to print the message.

8. From the **File** menu, click **Close** to close the message.

9. Click the **My Shortcuts** button on the Outlook Bar to display the mail icons.

10. Click the **Sent Items** icon on the Outlook Bar. The message you sent should be there. (*Note:* It might take a few minutes for your message to display.)

11. Click the **Outbox** icon on the Outlook Bar. If the message you sent wasn't in your Sent Items folder, it is here. Leave Outlook open for the next Step-by-Step.

Did You Know?

Clicking the Reply to All button sends your message to all the addresses listed in the original message. To forward the message to someone new, click the Forward button, insert the new address, and click the Send button.

Creating an Address Book

Most of the time you will be sending e-mail messages to the same people. To make sending an e-mail message easier, you can access names and addresses from an ***Address Book,*** a program that stores personal and professional contact information. Outlook creates Address Book information automatically when you add a new contact with an e-mail address to your contacts list. The Address Book includes the contact's name, e-mail address, and phone numbers.

To display the Address Book from the Inbox view, choose Address Book from the Tools menu or click the Address Book button on the toolbar. The Address Book dialog box appears, as shown in Figure 1-10. To add a new contact, click the New Entry button and the New Entry dialog box appears, as shown in Figure 1-11. Select New Contact and click OK. The Untitled Contact dialog box appears as shown in Figure 1-12. When you are done adding information about the contact, click Save and Close to return to the Address Book dialog box. The new contact should display in the Address Book.

To display the more detailed information about a contact listed in the Address Book, click the contact's name and wait for a box to display with the information.

FIGURE 1-10

Address Book dialog box

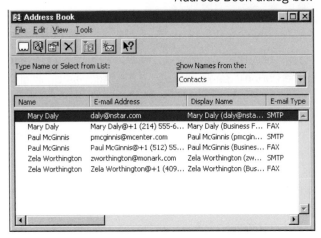

FIGURE 1-11

New Entry dialog box

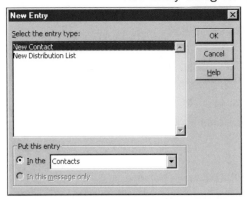

FIGURE 1-12

Untitled–Contact dialog box

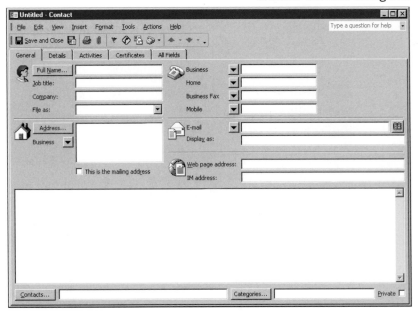

1. Click the **Inbox** icon on the Outlook Shortcuts section of the Outlook Bar to display the Inbox contents.

2. Display the Address Book by clicking the **Address Book** button on the toolbar. The Address Book dialog box displays, as shown in Figure 1-10.

3. Click the **New Entry** button and choose **New Contact** from the New Entry dialog box. Click **OK**. The Untitled - Contact dialog box displays, as shown in Figure 1-12.

4. In the Full Name box, key your full name. The File as box should show your first and last names.

5. In the E-mail box, key your e-mail address or one provided by your instructor.

6. Click the **Save and Close** button. The Address Book dialog box reappears with your name added to the list.

7. Double-click either listing for **Zela Worthington** and wait for a box to display the more detailed information added earlier.

8. When finished viewing, choose **Close** from the **File** menu to return to the Address Book dialog box.

9. Choose **Close** from the **File** menu to return to the Inbox view. Leave Outlook open for the next Step-by-Step.

Using an Address Book

To display the Address Book from a new e-mail message form, click the Address Book icon beside the To dialog box. The Select Names dialog box appears with names from your Contacts list, as shown in Figure 1-13. Choose the contact to receive the message and click To. The contact appears in the Message Recipients box. Click OK and the contact's name appears in the To box as the recipient of the e-mail message. When you finish your e-mail message, click the Send button on the toolbar.

FIGURE 1-13
Select Names dialog box

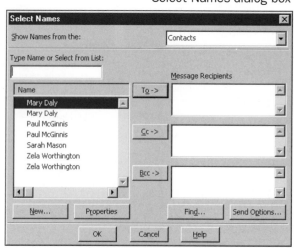

1 Lesson Outlook 2002   Page 14   A4371 23740   07/25/01-CI

STEP-BY-STEP ▷ 1.7

1. From the Inbox view, create an e-mail message by clicking the **New Mail Message** button on the toolbar. A blank e-mail message form appears.

2. Click the **Address Book** button. The Select Names dialog box appears as shown in Figure 1-13.

3. Highlight your name from the list of contacts and click the **To** box. Your name appears in the Message Recipients box.

4. Click **OK**. The untitled message reappears and you are the recipient of the e-mail message.

5. Key **Tomorrow's meeting** in the Subject box.

6. In the message window, key **Don't forget tomorrow's meeting at 1:30.**

7. Click the **Send** button.

8. Click the **My Shortcuts** button on the Outlook Bar to display the icons.

9. Click the **Sent Items** or the **Outbox** icon on the My Shortcuts Bar to see the sent message. Leave Outlook open for the next Step-by-Step.

Developing Distribution Lists

You can use your time more efficiently by designing distribution lists. *Distribution lists* are collections of contacts that provide an easy way to send messages to everyone within a group or department.

From the Inbox, click the Address Book button and the Address Book dialog box appears. Click the New Entry button and the New Entry dialog box appears. In the Select the entry type box, select New Distribution List and click OK. The Untitled-Distribution List dialog box appears. Click the Members tab and name the distribution list. The Select Members button allows you to select members for your distribution list from your Contacts list. After you create your distribution list, you can type the name of a distribution list in the To box of a new e-mail message and the message automatically goes to all the contacts on the list.

STEP-BY-STEP ▷ 1.8

1. From the Inbox, click the **Address Book** button on the toolbar. The Address Book dialog box appears.

2. In the *Show Names from the* box, click the down arrow and select **Contacts**.

3. Click the **New Entry** button and the New Entry dialog box appears.

4. In the Select the entry type box, select **New Distribution List** and click **OK**. The Untitled-Distribution List dialog box appears. Enlarge the box, if necessary.

5. In the Name box, key **Northstar Project**.

6. Click the **Select Members** button. The Select Members dialog box appears.

7. Select **Mary Daly** and **Zela Worthington** from the Name box and click the **Members** button to add these names to the distribution list.

8. Click **OK**. The Northstar Project-Distribution List dialog box appears with Mary Daly and Zela Worthington listed as the members.

9. Click the **Print** button to print the distribution list.

10. Click the **Save and Close** button on the tool-bar to return to the Address Book dialog box. The Northstar Project Distribution list now appears in the Address Book.

11. From the File menu, click **Close** to return to the Inbox. Leave Outlook open for the next Step-by-Step.

Inserting a Signature

Through the Tools menu you can design a signature to end each of your documents. To design this signature, choose Options from the Tools menu. Click the Mail Format tab and click the Signatures button at the bottom right-hand corner of the Options dialog box. In the Create Signature dialog box, key the signature of your choice. If you click the Edit button, you can design your own style in the Edit Signature dialog box.

1. From the Inbox view, click **Tools** on the menu bar and select **Options**. The Options dialog box appears.

2. Click the **Mail Format** tab in the Options dialog box.

3. Click the **Signatures** box in the bottom right-hand corner in the Options dialog box. The Create Signature dialog box appears.

4. Click **New** and the Create New Signature dialog box appears.

5. In the Enter a name for your new signature box, key your name. Click **Next**. The Edit Signature dialog box appears, similar to Figure 1-14. In the signature text box key your name.

6. Click **Finish**. Close all signature option boxes to return to the Inbox. Leave Outlook open for the next Step-by-Step.

FIGURE 1-14
Edit signature dialog box

Composing Documents within Outlook and Attaching Documents to E-mails

One useful feature of Outlook enables you to attach a variety of documents to e-mails and send these documents to others. From the Inbox, click the File menu, select New, and click Office Document. The New Office Document dialog box appears. Double-click the icon for the type of document you wish to create. After you have the new Office document, create and address a new e-mail. Click the Insert File button. The Insert File dialog box showing a list of your documents appears similar to Figure 1-15. Select a document and click the Insert button in the bottom right-hand corner of the dialog box. The window returns to your new e-mail and you can now send both the attached document and the e-mail.

FIGURE 1-15
Insert File dialog box

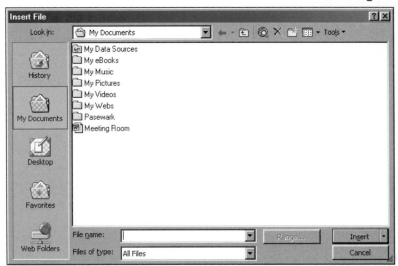

STEP-BY-STEP ▷ 1.10

---

1. From the Inbox view, create a new Word document by selecting **New** from the **File** menu.

2. Click **Office Document** and the New Office Document dialog box appears.

3. Double-click the **Microsoft Word Document** icon and a new Microsoft Word document appears.

4. Key **The meeting will be held in Room 317.**

5. Click **Save As** from the **File** menu, name the file **Meeting Room**, and click **Save**.

6. From the **File** menu, close the document and exit Microsoft Word. You will return to the Inbox view.

7. From the Inbox view, create a new e-mail by clicking the **New Mail Message** button on the toolbar. A blank e-mail message form appears.

8. Click the **Address Book** button. The Select Names dialog box appears.

9. Highlight your name from the list of contacts and click the **To** box. Your name appears in the Message Recipients box.

10. Click **OK**. Your name appears as the recipient in the new e-mail.

11. In the Subject box, key **See attachment**.

12. Click the **Insert File** button and the Insert File dialog box appears.

13. Select the **Meeting Room** Word document and click the **Insert** button in the bottom right-hand corner. A new *Attach* box appears in your e-mail with the selected document showing.

14. Click **Send**. You are the recipient of the e-mail and the attachment. Leave Outlook open for the next Step-by-Step.

Did You Know?

From the Insert File dialog box, you can insert the highlighted document in text form by clicking on the Insert down arrow located in the bottom right-hand corner.

Creating, Moving, and Archiving Folders

At times it is necessary to clean off your desk and discard accumulated documents. There will be times when your Outlook mailbox also needs to be reorganized. The process of organizing, storing, and saving old documents is called *archiving*. Outlook can archive all items, even Excel or Word documents, as long as they are stored in mail folders.

You can create new folders to organize documents from the Inbox view. From the drop-down menu in the New Mail Message button, click Folder. The Create New Folder dialog box appears similar to Figure 1-16. In the Name box, key the name of the folder you want to create. In the Folder contains box, select Mail and Post Items. In the Select where to place the folder, highlight where you want to place the new folder. Click OK and the Add shortcut to Outlook Bar? dialog box appears. Click Yes and a new folder appears on the My Shortcuts Bar.

You can transfer old files to a storage file by clicking Archive from the File menu. The Archive dialog box appears as shown in Figure 1-17. Click Archive this folder and all subfolders and highlight the folder to be archived. In the Archive folders older than: box, click the down arrow to select a date from the calendar. Click OK and your folder is archived to the date selected.

FIGURE 1-16
Create New Folder dialog box

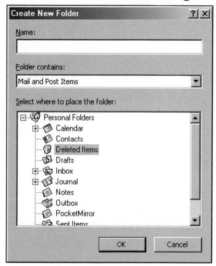

FIGURE 1-17
Archive dialog box

STEP-BY-STEP ▷ 1.11

1. From the Inbox view, click the **New Mail Message** button's list arrow. A drop-down menu appears.

2. Click **Folder** and the Create New Folder dialog box.

3. In the Name box, key **Test.** In the Folder contains box, select **Mail and Post Items** and click **OK**. The Add shortcut to Outlook Bar? dialog box appears. Click **Yes** and the Inbox view appears with the new Test folder in the My Shortcuts Bar.

4. In the Inbox, highlight the message named **Test**. Place the pointer on the highlighted message, and click and drag the message to the Test folder located in the My Shortcuts Bar. Double-click the **Test** folder to view its contents.

5. Click **Sent Items** in the My Shortcuts Bar. Sent messages appear in the window. Highlight the **Test** message you sent to yourself.

6. From the **File** menu, click **Archive**. The Archive dialog box appears and Sent Items will be highlighted. Select **Archive this folder and all subfolders** if it is not already chosen.

7. Click the list arrow on the **Archive items older than** box and a calendar appears. Choose a date approximately three months prior to today's date and click **OK**. Messages are archived and you can retrieve them through the Archive folder.

8. Click the **Outlook Shortcuts** button and click the **Inbox** icon. Leave Outlook open for the next Step-by-Step

Searching, Saving, and Deleting E-mail Messages

Many times e-mails are important enough that you want to print or save them for further reference. To print a message from the Inbox, highlight the message and click the Print button. To save a message as a document or HTML (Web page) file, click Save As from the File menu. Click the Save In box and highlight the location at which you want the message to be saved. To delete a message, highlight the message to be deleted in the Inbox. Click the Delete button and the message is sent to the Deleted Items folder.

 Hot Tip

Another way to visually organize your e-mail is by color-coding messages you send or receive. From the toolbar, click Tools and then Organize to open the Ways to Organize Inbox dialog box. Click Using Colors and the options for color-coding both messages sent and messages received appear.

STEP-BY-STEP ▷ 1.12

1. Click the **Inbox** icon on the Outlook Shortcuts Bar to display the Inbox contents.

2. Click the **New Mail Message** button. A blank e-mail message form appears.

3. Key your e-mail address, or one provided by your instructor, in the To box.

4. Key **Delete** in the Subject box.

5. In the message window, key **Delete this message**.

6. Click the **Send** button. Your mail is sent and, if Outlook is set up correctly for intranet e-mail, you should receive the message in a few moments. (If you have only Internet e-mail, you'll need to choose **Remote Mail** from the **Tools** menu and **Connect** from the submenu.)

7. Double-click on the message titled *Delete* and the message appears. Click the **Print** button to print the message.

8. To save this message as a document, click **Save As** on the **File** menu. The Save As dialog box appears.

9. Click the list arrow on the **Save In** box and highlight **My Documents**. My Documents appears in the Save In box.

10. The title of the e-mail message appears in the File name box. Click the **Save** button and the message is saved as a document in the My Documents folder.

11. To save this message as an HTML document, click **Save As** on the **File** menu. The Save As dialog box appears.

12. Click the list arrow on the **Save In** box and highlight **My Documents**. My Documents appears in the Save In box.

13. The title of the e-mail message appears in the File name box. Click the **Save as type** list arrow and click **Web Page (*.htm; *.html)**.

14. Click the **Save** button and the message is saved as an HTML document in the My Documents folder. Close the e-mail message. The Inbox appears and you can still view the message as an e-mail document.

Extra Challenge

Open the two documents you just saved in My Documents. Note that one opens in Microsoft Word and one opens in Internet Explorer.

15. Click **Find** from the Tools menu. The Find box appears under the Inbox toolbar.

16. Key your e-mail address in the Look for box. Click **Find Now** and your e-mail appears highlighted.

17. Click the **Delete** button on the toolbar. The message is sent to the Deleted Items folder.

18. Choose **Exit** from the **File** menu to close Outlook. The Outlook window closes and the Microsoft Windows desktop appears.

Computer Concepts

You can customize your Inbox view by clicking and dragging the selected field to a different area on the toolbar.

Summary

In this lesson, you learned:

■ Outlook is a desktop information manager that helps you organize information, communicate with others, and manage your time. The Outlook Bar contains icons you can use to access many of Outlook's features.

■ The Contacts list is a useful tool in which to store mail, phone, and other information about people and companies. You can view or print your contacts in several ways including as address cards or as a phone list.

■ The value of e-mail is that it is faster, less expensive, and more efficient than the United States Postal Service's traditional method of delivering mail. Electronic mail allows you to send a message to one or more persons. E-mail is global and it is environment-friendly, since it does not require paper.

■ Most of the time you will be sending e-mail messages to the same people. To make sending an e-mail message easier, you can use an Address Book listing the addresses that you use most often.

■ Using Outlook, you can send e-mail messages to others connected to your network or to anyone around the world with Internet connection. E-mail messages can also be sent with Word or other documents attached to them. You can view and organize your messages in a variety of ways, as well as archive them and save them as documents.

VOCABULARY REVIEW

Define the following terms:

Address Book	Contact	E-mail
Archive	Distribution list	Outlook Bar

LESSON 1 REVIEW QUESTIONS

TRUE/FALSE

Circle T if the statement is true or F if the statement is false.

T F 1. The Outlook Bar contains the Inbox, Calendar, Notes, and Tasks icons, among others.

T F 2. The default view for Contacts is Phone List.

T F 3. The General tab in the Contacts dialog box is where you can store additional information about a contact, such as department, nickname, or birthday.

T F 4. The Address Book information is automatically created when you add a new contact and e-mail address to your Contacts list.

T F 5. In Outlook, the Inbox displays your new mail.

Write a brief answer to the following questions.

1. What is a contact?

2. What are the advantages of e-mail over the United States Postal Service's traditional method of delivering mail?

3. Name three types of contact information included under the General tab.

4. Explain the importance of creating distribution lists.

5. What information is contained in an Address Book?

LESSON 1 PROJECTS

PROJECT 1-1

You recently met two people to add to your Contacts list.

1. Display the Contacts view.

2. Add the two contacts using this information. Save and close when you finish.

    Name: **Todd McKee**   Name: **Claire Hunter**
    Job Title: **Associate Professor**   Job Title: **Head Pro**
    Company: **Clark Junior College**   Company: **Litchfield Tennis Club**
    Address: **1880 Holst-Grubbe Road**   Address: **34 Segalla Lane**
        Berkshire, VT 53217   **Litchfield, PA 60211**
    Business Phone: **(420) 555-7642**   Home Phone: **(709) 555-0901**
    Business Fax: **(420) 555-7644**   E-mail: **hunter@spoloc.org**
    E-mail: **t_mckee@cjc.edu**   Category: **Personal**
    Category: **Personal**

3. View the Contacts list as Address Cards.

4. View the Contacts list as a Phone List.

5. Choose **Print** from the **File** menu and print a copy of your Contacts list.

6. Delete the contacts you keyed.

7. Leave Outlook open for the next project.

PROJECT 1-2

Create and send an e-mail message to your staff concerning the monthly staff meeting.

1. Display the Inbox view.

2. Create a new mail message and key your e-mail address or the e-mail address of a classmate in the *To* box.

3. Key **Monthly Staff Meeting** as the subject.

4. In the message window, key **Meeting held in Conference Room A from 2:00 to 3:30 p.m. Be prepared to give an update on projects.**

5. Click the **Importance** button and click **High** to identify the message as high priority.

6. Send the message.

IO-23

7. Choose **Sent Items** or **Outbox** on the My Shortcuts Bar. The message should be listed in either folder.

8. Open the message to read and then print it.

9. Delete this e-mail message.

10. Leave Outlook open for the next project.

PROJECT 1-3

Create and send an e-mail message to yourself about the promotion of a staff member.

1. Open the **Address Book** from the Inbox view.

2. Create a new e-mail message and send it to yourself. Access your e-mail address from the Address Book.

3. Key **Congratulations to Amy Jenkins** as the subject.

4. In the message window, key **Please join me in congratulating Amy Jenkins who has been promoted to Sales Department Manager. This promotion is well deserved!**

5. Insert your signature at the bottom of this e-mail.

6. Send the message.

7. Choose **Sent Items** or **Outbox** on the My Shortcuts Bar to see the sent message.

8. Choose **Print** from the **File** menu and print a copy of this e-mail message.

9. Delete this e-mail message.

10. Choose **Exit** from the **File** menu to close Outlook.

CRITICAL THINKING

ACTIVITY 1-1

Use the Help system to find out how to drag and drop a name and address from a Word document into the Outlook Contacts list. Write down the basic steps. After you have completed this activity, delete the name from the Contacts list.

CALENDAR

OBJECTIVES

Upon completion of this lesson, you should be able to:

- View Calendar.

- Apply conditional formats to Calendar.

- Schedule and change appointments.

- Schedule, change, and delete events.

- Schedule a meeting, and respond to meeting requests.

- Print a calendar.

⏱ **Estimated Time: 1 hour**

VOCABULARY

Appointment

Appointment Book

Date Navigator

Event

Meeting

Resources

Introducing Calendar

Outlook Calendar is designed to help you stay organized and coordinate your activities with others. Calendar will document activities different ways. One way is with *appointments*, activities that have a set time and date but do not involve inviting other people or reserving resources. Another way is with *meetings*, which are appointments for which you invite people and/or reserve resources. *Resources* are materials and/or equipment needed for meetings. The last way Calendar can help you stay organized is by allowing you to schedule *events*, activities that occur on a weekly, monthly, or yearly basis and do not have a set time. Events usually last an entire day or occur over a period of several days. To help you anticipate and prepare for upcoming appointments, meetings, and events, Calendar can create reminders and categorizing your appointments, meetings, and events so you can view them quickly and easily. Meetings can be scheduled through Calendar and, because Outlook is an integrated program, you can receive responses to planned meetings through e-mail.

Viewing the Calendar

The Calendar, shown in Figure 2-1, allows you to enter your appointments, meetings, and events. You can display the Calendar by clicking the Calendar icon on the Outlook Bar.

You can view the Calendar in various ways. Choose the Current View option from the View menu to see a list of options. In Figure 2-1, the Calendar is displayed in Day/Week/Month view that shows appointments, meetings, and tasks scheduled for a given time frame. You can click buttons on the toolbar to see a daily, weekly, or monthly calendar, or to display the calendar for today. If you do not see the buttons on your toolbar, click the Toolbar Options button on the toolbar to add them.

Use the *Date Navigator*, the monthly calendars at the top right of the window, to change dates by clicking directly on the date you want to view. You can change months by clicking the arrows next to the month names. A boldface date on the Date Navigator means an activity is scheduled for that day.

The *Appointment Book* displays appointments for the time frame you choose. The TaskPad in the Calendar view displays the task list, which you learn about in Lesson 3.

Hot Tip

You can also change months by clicking the name of the month and choosing a month from the menu that appears.

FIGURE 2-1
Viewing the Calendar

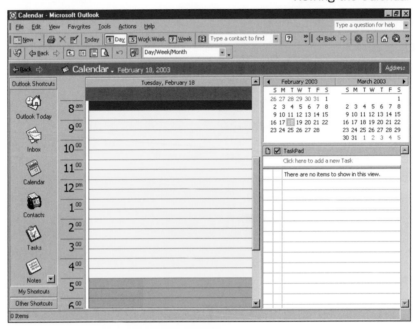

 TEP-BY-STEP ▷ 2.1

1. Click the **Calendar** icon on the Outlook Bar. The Calendar appears, similar to Figure 2-1.

2. Using the **Date Navigator**, click tomorrow's date. Notice that the date automatically changes at the top of the Appointment Book. If you have appointments scheduled, they appear in the appointment area.

3. Click the **Week** button on the toolbar to display the current week's schedule.

4. Click the **down arrow** on the scroll bar to display next week's schedule. Notice that the highlighted week in the Date Navigator changes as you scroll to the next week.

5. Click the **20th of this month** on the Date Navigator monthly calendar to display the schedule for the 20th.

6. Click the **Today** button on the toolbar to move to today's date.

7. Click the **Month** button on the tool- bar to display the current month's schedule.

8. Click the **Day** button on the toolbar to display the daily schedule once again. Leave the Calendar open for the next Step-by-Step.

Applying Conditional Formats to Calendar

Calendar comes with specific defaults, but you can add conditional formats and change the defaults so Calendar is formatted to meet your needs. From the Tools menu, click Options and the Options dialog box appears. The Options dialog box displays the defaults and allow you to make any changes you want to apply.

STEP-BY-STEP ⟹ 2.2

1. From the Calendar view, click **Options** from the **Tools** menu. The Options dialog box appears.

2. Click the **Calendar Options** button and the Calendar Options dialog box appears similar to that shown in Figure 2-2.

3. In the Calendar work week section, place checks in the boxes for **Tuesday, Wednesday, Thursday**, and **Friday**.

4. In the Start time box, select **6:00 AM**.

5. In the End time box, select **5:00 PM**.

6. Click **OK** twice to return to Calendar.

7. Click the **Work Week** button to view the new workweek format.

8. Click **Options** from the **Tools** menu and return to the Calendar Options dialog box.

9. In the Calendar work week section, place checks in the boxes for **Monday, Tuesday, Wednesday**, and **Thursday**.

10. In the Start time box, select **8:00 AM**.

11. In the End time box, select **5:00 PM**.

12. Click **OK** twice to return to Calendar.

13. Click the **Week** button to view the week format. Leave the Calendar open for the next Step-by-Step.

FIGURE 2-2
Calendar Options dialog box

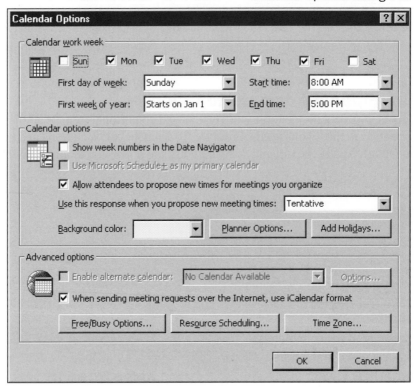

Scheduling an Appointment

To add an appointment to your Calendar, use the Date Navigator to choose the date. In the Appointment book, click on the time the appointment will begin and drag down to the end time. Then choose New Appointment from the Actions menu or click the New Appointment button on the toolbar. The Appointment dialog box appears, as shown in Figure 2-3.

Key the subject and location of the appointment in the appropriate boxes. Click the up and down arrows to change the Start time or End time, if necessary. Select the All day event option if the appointment is scheduled for the entire day. In the text box at the bottom, you can key any additional information about the appointment.

You can choose the Reminder option to have Outlook notify you a certain number of minutes, hours, or days before the appointment. A bell icon appears next to the appointment on the calendar indicating that a reminder is set. A dialog box displays when it is time for the reminder. At that time, you can dismiss the reminder, click the snooze button to be reminded again later, or open the appointment to remind yourself of the details.

The Show time as box lets you decide how to display the scheduled time on your calendar and the Label box color-codes your appointment. The Categories box allows you to organize your appointments. The Private option prevents other users on an intranet from viewing your appointment information. A key icon appears next to the appointment on the calendar when the private option is in use.

Hot Tip

You can type words such as *this Friday* or *midnight* in the date and time fields and Outlook's AutoDate feature converts them for you.

When you have entered all the necessary information about the appointment, click Save and Close to return to the Calendar. You'll see the information in the appointment area next to the appointment time.

FIGURE 2-3

Appointment dialog box

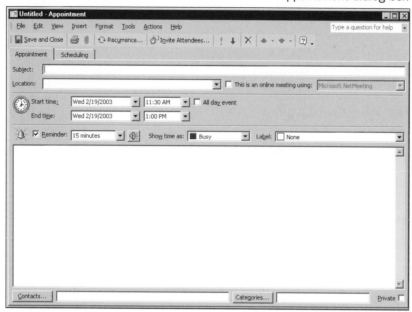

STEP-BY-STEP ▷ 2.3

1. Click tomorrow's date in the Date Navigator.

2. Highlight the appointment time by clicking on **11:30 a.m.** and dragging through to **1:00 p.m.**

3. Click the **New Appointment** button on the toolbar. The Appointment dialog box appears as shown in Figure 2-3.

4. In the Subject box, key **Lunch with Mark Anderson**.

5. In the Location box, key **Lakeview Cafe**.

6. Click the **Reminder** box to insert a checkmark if it isn't chosen already.

7. Click the down arrow in the **Reminder** box and choose 30 minutes from the menu.

8. In the Show time as box, click the down arrow and choose **Out of Office**.

9. In the Label box, click the down arrow and choose **Business**.

10. In the text box, key **Bring latest draft of proposal**.

11. Click the **Categories** box and choose **Key Customer**. Click **OK**. (*Note:* If you do not see the Categories and Private boxes, increase the window size by clicking the maximize button in the top right-hand corner of the window.)

12. Click the **Private** box.

13. Click the **Save and Close** button on the toolbar. The appointment information and icons appear in the appointment area. The key icon indicates the appointment is private. The bell icon indicates that a meeting reminder has been set. Leave the Calendar open for the next Step-by-Step.

Changing an Appointment

To edit an appointment, double-click the appointment. The Appointment dialog box appears for you to make changes. To reschedule an appointment, click the border and drag the appointment to a new time. To delete an appointment, right-click the border and choose Delete.

STEP-BY-STEP ▷ 2.4

1. Double-click the **Mark Anderson** appointment. The Appointment dialog box appears.

2. Change the location to **Trotsky's Deli**.

3. In the text box, key the following:

```
Have Carolyn make reservations
and call Mark about time and
location changes.
```

4. Click **Categories** and the Categories dialog box appears.

5. In the Available categories box, click **Key Customer** to remove the check.

6. Click **Master Category List** at the bottom of the dialog box.

7. In the New category box, key **Anderson Consulting Co.** and click **Add**.

8. Click **OK** to return to the Categories dialog box.

9. Choose **Anderson Consulting Co.** as the new category and click **OK**. The Appointment dialog box appears.

10. Remove the check from the **Private** box.

11. Click **Save and Close**.

12. Reschedule the Mark Anderson appointment by clicking the border and dragging down until it

appears between 12:00 and 1:30, as shown in Figure 2-4. (Your window might show 13:30 and might show the entire appointment message.)

13. Double-click the **Mark Anderson** appointment. The Appointment dialog box appears.

14. Click **Categories** and the Categories dialog box appears.

15. In the Available categories box, click **Key Customer** to place a check in the box and click **Anderson Consulting Co.** to remove the check in the box.

16. Click **Master Category List** at the bottom of the dialog box.

17. Highlight **Anderson Consulting Co.** and click **Delete**.

18. Click **Reset** and **OK** in the dialog box that appears. The Master dialog box appears.

19. Click **OK** to return to the Categories dialog box. Anderson Consulting Co. will remain in the Categories dialog box until it is closed.

20. Click **OK** to return to the Appointment dialog box.

21. Click **Save and Close** to return to Calendar. Leave the Calendar open for the next Step-by-Step.

FIGURE 2-4
Rescheduled appointment

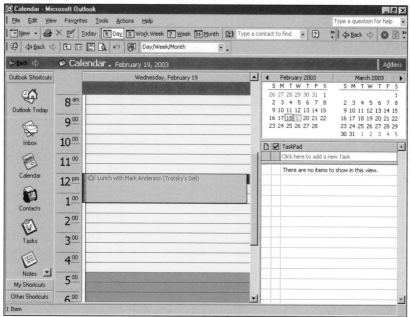

Scheduling an Event

An *event* is an activity that usually lasts an entire day and does not necessarily have a set time assigned. An annual event occurs every year on the same date, such as a birthday. A recurring event occurs every so many days, weeks, or months, such as a day-long stockholder's meeting scheduled every quarter (every three months). You can use your Calendar to schedule any type of event.

Use the Date Navigator to locate the date of the event, then choose New All Day Event from the Actions menu. The Event dialog box appears, as shown in Figure 2-5. Provide information about the event such as subject, location, and description. Choose the Reminder option if you would like to be reminded of the event. For example, you could set a two-day notice to buy a birthday card for someone. Select the Private option to prevent other users on an intranet from viewing the event.

If it is an annual event, click the Recurrence button on the toolbar in the Event dialog box to bring up the Appointment Recurrence dialog box, shown in Figure 2-6. You can choose a recurrence pattern and your event will appear on the calendar every day, week, month, or year. Key a range of recurrence or a beginning and end date for how long the event should appear in the Calendar. Choose OK to return to the Event dialog box. Choose Save and Close when you are finished. The event information will be shown at the top of your daily schedule.

S **TEP-BY-STEP** ⇒ **2.5**

1. Click **July 4** in the Date Navigator.

2. Choose **New All Day Event** from the **Actions** menu. The Event dialog box appears.

3. Key the event information as shown in Figure 2-5.

4. Click **Save and Close**.

5. Click **June 10** in the Date Navigator.

6. Choose **New All Day Event** from the **Actions** menu.

7. In the Event dialog box, key **Brittany's Birthday** in the Subject box.

8. Click the **Recurrence** button on the toolbar. The Appointment Recurrence dialog box appears, similar to that shown in Figure 2-6.

9. Click **Yearly** in the Recurrence pattern box.

10. Click **OK**.

11. In the Reminder box, choose **1 day**.

12. In the Label box, choose **Birthday**.

13. Click **Save and Close**. The event appears at the top of the appointment area. Leave the Calendar open for the next Step-by-Step.

Extra Challenge

Add five more annual events to your Calendar, such as birthdays and anniversaries of family members and friends.

FIGURE 2-5
Event dialog box

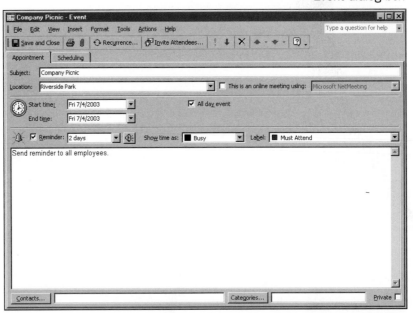

Hot Tip

You can use your Tab key to move around a dialog box.

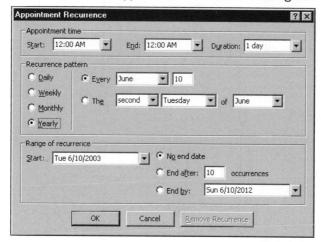

FIGURE 2-6
Appointment Recurrence dialog box

Changing and Deleting an Event

To edit an event, double-click the event listed at the top of the calendar. If the event is marked as one that is recurring, the Open Recurring Item dialog box will appear as shown in Figure 2-7. Choose the option *Open this occurrence* to open only a selected occurrence and not a series of recurring events. Choose the option *Open the series* to update every occurrence of the event. The Event dialog box appears for you to make changes. To delete an event, right-click the event at the top of the daily calendar and choose Delete from the menu.

STEP-BY-STEP ▷ 2.6

1. You realize that you confused Brittany's birthday with a co-worker's. Change the date of Brittany's birthday by double-clicking the event **Brittany's Birthday**. The Open Recurring Item dialog box appears as shown in Figure 2-7.

2. Click **Open the series**, then click **OK**. The Recurring Event dialog box appears.

3. Click the **Recurrence** button on the toolbar.

4. In the Recurrence pattern box, change the date to **Every May 22**. Click the down arrow next to the Range of recurrence box and change the date to **May 22**. Click **OK**. If necessary, click **OK** in the dialog box that appears. The Recurring Event dialog box reappears with the new recurrence date in the middle of the box.

5. Click **Save and Close**.

FIGURE 2-7
Open Recurring Item dialog box

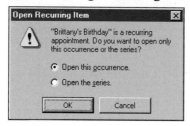

6. Using the Date Navigator, click **May 22.** Brittany's Birthday should appear at the top of the calendar.

7. Right-click **Brittany's Birthday** and click **Delete** in the drop-down menu that appears. In the Confirm Delete dialog box, click **Delete**

the series and click **OK.** Brittany's Birthday is removed from the Calendar program.

8. Click the **Today** button on the toolbar to go back to today's date. Leave the Calendar open for the next Step-by-Step.

Scheduling a Meeting and Responding to Meeting Requests

If you and your co-workers use Outlook and are connected by an intranet, you can use your Calendar to schedule meetings and resources. A *meeting* is an appointment to which you invite people and schedule resources. *Resources* are materials and/or equipment needed in a meeting, such as a conference room, computer, or projector.

Use the Date Navigator to choose a date for the meeting. In the appointment area, choose the meeting time by clicking on the start time and dragging to the end time. Choose Plan a Meeting from the Actions menu and the Plan a Meeting dialog box appears, as shown in Figure 2-8.

In the All Attendees list, key the names of people you want to attend the meeting. Set the date, make any necessary changes to the start and end times, and then click Make Meeting. The Meeting dialog box appears. You can use this dialog box to include more details about the meeting, such as subject and location. Send invitations over the intranet to the attendees by clicking the Send button.

Once attendees receive an invitation, they can accept or decline the invitation, or propose a new time for the meeting. The responses to the meeting requests appear in your Inbox.

STEP-BY-STEP ⟹ 2.7

1. Choose a date from the Date Navigator.

2. Select **Plan a Meeting** from the **Actions** menu and the Plan a Meeting dialog box appears, as shown in Figure 2-8.

3. Click the **Add Others** box and select **Add from Address Book**. The Select Attendees and Resources dialog box appears, as shown in Figure 2-9.

4. Hold down the **Ctrl** key, select several names, and click **Required**.

5. Click in the Resources box and key **Conference Room 2**.

6. Click **OK.** The Plan a Meeting dialog box appears showing the invited attendees and the resources requested for the meeting.

7. Click **Make Meeting** and a new e-mail message appears with the selected names and Conference Room 2 in the To box. (An administrator is assigned to each resource, so the administrator for Conference Room 2 receives the meeting request.) Key the information as shown in Figure 2-10 making sure to include the subject in the Subject box.

8. On the Actions menu, click **Request Responses** so a check appears.

9. Click **Send** and Outlook sends the e-mail message to you and the attendees. The Plan a Meeting dialog box appears with the meeting times highlighted.

10. Click **Close** and return to the Calendar window.

11. Click the **Inbox** icon on the Outlook Bar to see the e-mail you received. Double-click to open your e-mail and the Meeting dialog box appears.

12. Check the Inbox to see the e-mail. Double-click to open your e-mail and the Meeting dialog box appears.

13. Click **Accept Proposal** and click **Send Update**.

14. Click the **Calendar** icon to return to the Calendar program and view the proposed meeting. Leave the Calendar open for the next Step-by-Step.

FIGURE 2-8
Plan a Meeting dialog box

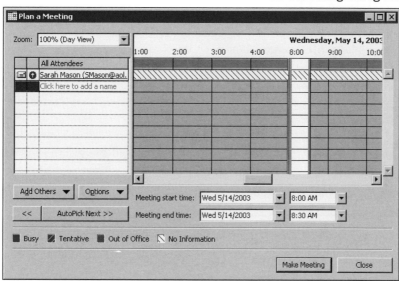

FIGURE 2-9
Select Attendees and Resources dialog box

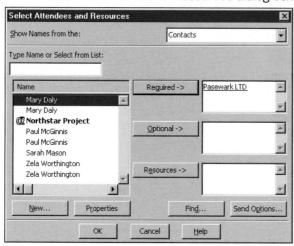

Did You Know?

Icons are placed beside the names of each meeting attendee to help easily identify those who are Required Attendees, Optional Attendees, Resources, and/or the Meeting Organizer.

FIGURE 2-10
Meeting dialog box

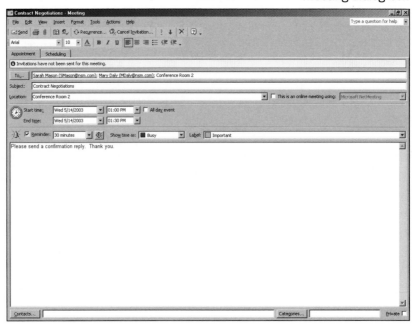

Printing a Calendar

You have several options for printing your Calendar. You can print a daily schedule, a weekly schedule, a monthly schedule, a tri-fold style, or a calendar details style that includes the daily calendar, tasks list, and weekly calendar. Choose Print from the File menu. The Print dialog box appears, as shown in Figure 2-11. Choose from the options in the Print style section and click OK. You can print a more specific range of dates by choosing Start and End dates in the Print range section.

To preview a Calendar before printing, choose Print Preview from the File menu or click the Preview button in the Print dialog box. The mouse pointer changes to a magnifying glass that you can click to zoom in or out when previewing the page.

Extra Challenge

Choose a month and add some personal appointments, events, and a meeting. When you finish, print a monthly schedule.

STEP-BY-STEP 2.8

1. Using the Date Navigator, click the date with the contract negotiations meeting. (In Step-by-Step 2.7, you added the contract negotiations meeting to Calendar.)

2. Choose **Print** from the **File** menu. The Print dialog box appears as shown in Figure 2-11.

3. If necessary, click **Daily Style** in the Print Style box.

4. Click **OK** to print a daily calendar.

5. Choose **Print** from the **File** menu. The Print dialog box appears.

6. Click **Weekly Style** in the Print Style box.

7. Click **OK** to print a weekly calendar.

8. Choose **Print** from the **File** menu. The Print dialog box appears.

9. Click **Monthly Style** in the Print Style box.

10. Click **OK** to print a monthly calendar.

11. When you finish printing, highlight the Contract negotiations appointment and click **Delete**. The appointment is deleted from Calendar.

12. Choose **Exit** from the **File** menu to close Outlook. The Outlook window closes.

FIGURE 2-11
Print dialog box

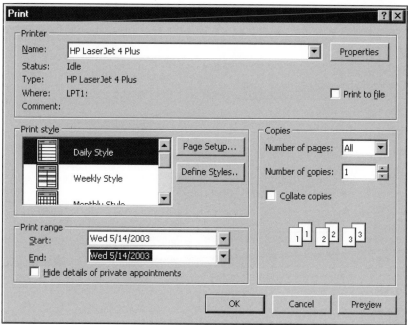

Summary

In this lesson, you learned:

- The Calendar is used to schedule appointments, events, and meetings. You can view the Calendar in daily, weekly, or monthly format. If you use the Reminder option, Outlook notifies you before each activity.

- Using Calendar, you can schedule a meeting, invite other people to the meeting, and reserve resources for the meeting. You can also use Calendar to send a response to meeting requests.

- The Appointment Recurrence dialog box makes it easy to schedule events that occur annually.

- You can print the Calendar information in a daily, weekly, or monthly schedule. Calendar can also be printed in a tri-fold style or a calendar details style that includes the daily calendar, task list, and weekly calendar.

VOCABULARY REVIEW

Define the following terms:

Appointment	Date Navigator	Meeting
Appointment Book	Event	Resources

LESSON 2 REVIEW QUESTIONS

TRUE/FALSE

Circle T if the statement is true or F if the statement is false.

T F 1. It is possible to customize the work week to view different days of the week.

T F 2. You can set a reminder option to notify you before an appointment.

T F 3. It is impossible to make changes to an appointment once it is placed into Calendar.

T F 4. Calendar allows you to set appointments and events on a recurring basis.

T F 5. An appointment is an activity that does not have a set time.

WRITTEN QUESTIONS

Write a brief answer to the following questions.

1. Which button do you click in the Date Navigator to return to today's date?

2. What does the Categories box allow you to do with the information added to Outlook?

3. What is the difference between an appointment and an event?

4. How does Calendar help you track recurring events?

5. What is the process used to change the default settings in Calendar?

PROJECT 2-1

1. Display the Calendar window in Day view.

2. Use the Date Navigator to select tomorrow's date for a new appointment.

3. Highlight the appointment time from **9:00 a.m.** to **11:00 a.m**.

4. Add an appointment with **Training Session with Staff** as the subject.

5. Add the location of the appointment, **Training Room 5**.

6. Set a reminder for one hour before the appointment.

7. In the text box, key **Request a TV and VCR**. Save and close the Appointment dialog box.

8. Add another appointment from **8:00 a.m.** to **8:30 a.m.** with **Coffee with Greg** as the subject and **Daybreak Coffee Shop** as the location.

9. Do not set a reminder. Show the time as **Out of Office** and use the **Private** option.

10. In the text box, key **Ask him about tennis this weekend**. Save and close the Appointment dialog box.

11. Leave the Calendar open for the next project.

PROJECT 2-2

1. Move the time of the Training Session with Staff appointment to **10 a.m.** to **noon**.

2. Change the location to **Conference Room 3**.

3. In the text box, add **Make copies of new office policies**.

4. Add a new category called **Staff**.

5. Assign the Training Session with Staff appointment to the new category.

6. Use the Date Navigator to select this Sunday for an event.

7. Add **My Anniversary** as an annual event.

8. Set a reminder for one day before the event date. Save and close the Event dialog box.

9. Leave Calendar open for the next project.

PROJECT 2-3

1. Display the Calendar in Day view.

2. Create a new appointment for today from **2:00** to **3:30 p.m.**

3. Key the subject **Staff Meeting** and the location **Conference Room A**.

4. Do not set a reminder.

5. In the text box, key **Take 15 copies of agenda**.

6. Assign the appointment to category **Staff Meeting**. Save and close the appointment.

7. The new appointment should display in the Day view.

8. Leave Calendar open for the next activity.

CRITICAL THINKING

SCANS

ACTIVITY 2-1

Create your personal calendar for this month. Be sure to include class activities, recurring music or sports/exercise activities, medical/dental appointments, and work schedules. When you are finished, delete all the entries for this activity.

3

WORKING WITH OTHER OUTLOOK TOOLS

OBJECTIVES

Upon completion of this lesson, you should be able to:

- Use Outlook Today.
- Create a tasks list.
- Manage tasks.
- Assign and delegate tasks.
- View and print a tasks list.
- Use the Journal.
- Use Notes.
- Exit Outlook.

⏱ **Estimated Time: 1 hour**

VOCABULARY

Categories

Journal

Notes

Tasks

Using Outlook Today

Outlook Today gathers information about the day's activities from Calendar, Tasks, and Mail and summarizes the information in one window. You can display the Outlook Today screen, shown in Figure 3-1, by clicking the Outlook Today icon on the Outlook Bar. The Outlook Bar contains the icons that are shortcuts to your local folders.

FIGURE 3-1
Outlook Today view

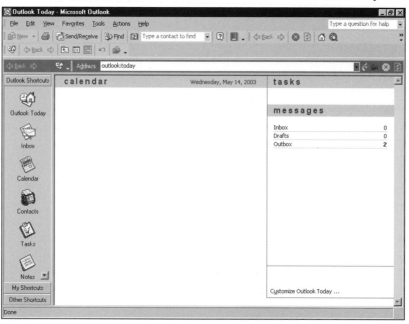

In the Outlook Today view, the Calendar section displays the appointments for the day. The next appointment is flagged with an arrow and appointments earlier in the day display in a lighter type. The Tasks section lists previously entered tasks. When you finish a task, click the check box to add a check mark. The task displays with a strike through the text. The Messages section contains the number of messages in the Inbox, Drafts, and Outbox. To move around Outlook quickly, simply click on the heading to each section or click the icon on the Outlook Bar.

To customize the Outlook Today view, click Customize Outlook Today at the top of the window. A list of options for customizing will display as shown in Figure 3-2. Click the check box next to *When starting, go directly to Outlook Today* to automatically display the Outlook Today view every time you start Outlook. You can also choose the message folders and how many days of your Calendar to display. In your tasks list, you can sort and display all the tasks or only the tasks for the day. Different styles for the Outlook Today view are also available.

FIGURE 3-2
Customize Outlook Today view

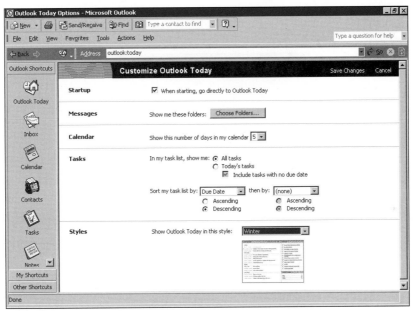

S TEP-BY-STEP ▷ 3.1

1. Click the **Outlook Today** icon on the Outlook Bar. The Outlook Today view appears, similar to Figure 3-1. Your screen might appear different, depending on items that have been previously added or deleted.

2. Click **Customize Outlook Today** at the right side of the Outlook Today date banner. The Options window for Outlook displays as shown in Figure 3-2.

3. Click to insert a check in the box next to **When starting, go directly to Outlook Today** if it is not already checked. The Outlook Today view will automatically appear every time Outlook is started.

4. Click **Save Changes** at the right side of the Custom Outlook Today banner to go back to the Outlook Today view.

5. Click the **Tasks** heading to display the Tasks view.

6. Click **Current View** from the View menu and, if necessary, click **Simple List** in the drop-down menu. A check appears as shown in Figure 3-3.

7. Click the **Outlook Today** icon on the Outlook bar to return to the Outlook Today view.

8. Click the **Calendar** heading at the top of the Outlook Today screen to display the Calendar window.

9. Create a new appointment using today's date and the information shown in Figure 3-4.

10. Click **Save and Close** to return to the Outlook Today view. The new appointment displays in the Calendar section. Leave Outlook open for the next Step-by-Step.

FIGURE 3-4
Add an appointment

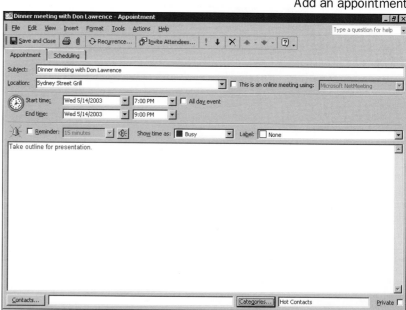

FIGURE 3-3
View menu

Creating a Tasks List

You can use the Tasks view in Outlook to create and manage your tasks. A *task* is any activity you want to perform and monitor to completion. You can assign tasks to *categories* to specify start and due dates, check the status of tasks, prioritize, and set reminders.

Click the Tasks icon on the Outlook Bar to display the Tasks screen. To add a task, click the New Task button on the toolbar. The Task dialog box appears, as shown in Figure 3-5. When you are done creating the task, click Save and Close.

Computer Concepts

If you and your co-workers are connected by an intranet, you can assign a task to someone else by choosing New Task Request from the Actions menu. After keying the request, click the Send button to e-mail it.

FIGURE 3-5
Task dialog box

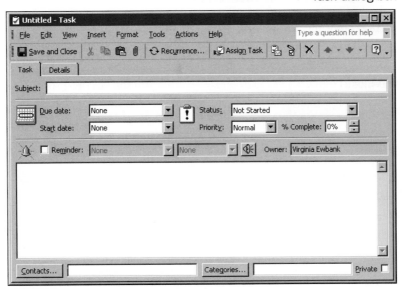

STEP-BY-STEP ▷ 3.2

1. Click the **Tasks** icon on the Outlook Bar. The Task view appears. If necessary, delete the default **Welcome to Tasks!** by right-clicking the task and choosing **Delete** from the menu.

2. Click the **New Task** button on the toolbar. The Task dialog box appears, as shown in Figure 3-5.

3. In the Subject box, key **Buy supplies**.

4. In the Due date section, click the down arrow and choose the next Thursday from the calendar.

5. In the Start date box, click the down arrow and choose last Friday from the calendar.

6. In the Status box, click the down arrow and choose **In Progress**.

7. In the Priority box, click the down arrow and choose **High**.

8. In the % Complete box, click the up arrow until **75%** appears.

9. Check the **Reminder** box if it is not already selected, then click the down arrow and choose the next Wednesday from the calendar. Set the reminder time for 10:00 a.m.

10. In the text box key **Purchase trees, bushes, ground cover, flowers, root starter, edging, and mulch. Already have shovels, spade, hoe, and wheelbarrow.**

11. Click the **Categories** button and click **Personal** in the Available categories box. Click **OK**.

12. Click the **Private** button. Your Task dialog box should appear similar to Figure 3-6.

13. Click **Save and Close**.

14. Create three more tasks using the information shown in Figures 3-7, 3-8, and 3-9. (Key your own dates.) Leave the Tasks view open for the next Step-by-Step.

FIGURE 3-6
Create a task

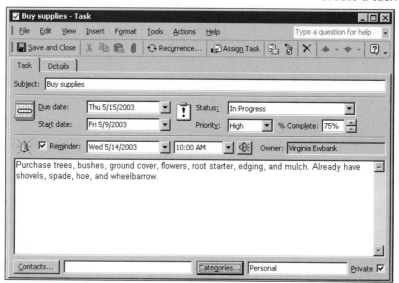

FIGURE 3-7
Create a task using this information

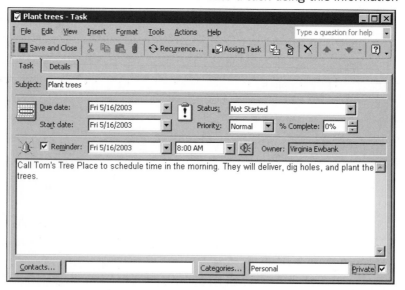

FIGURE 3-8
Create a task using this information

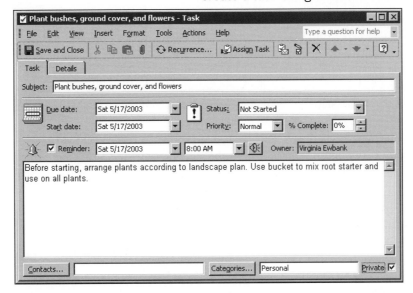

FIGURE 3-9
Create a task using this information

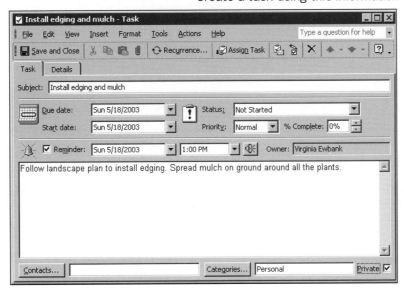

Managing Tasks

You can sort and group tasks, move tasks up and down the list, add and delete tasks, edit a task, or mark a task off when you complete it.

To sort or group tasks, choose Current View from the View menu, then click Customize Current View. The View Summary dialog box appears, as shown in Figure 3-10. Click the Sort button to display the Sort dialog box. In the Sort Items By box, click the down arrow and choose the fields you want to sort. To group tasks, click the Group By button in the View Summary dialog box and

 Hot Tip

You can quickly sort tasks by subject by clicking the Subject bar at the top of the tasks list. To quickly sort by due date, click the Due Date bar at the top of the tasks list.

follow the same steps. When finished, your tasks list should appear sorted and/or grouped according to your selections.

To move a task, be sure the Sort and Group By settings are cleared. Choose Current View from the View menu, then click Customize Current View. The View Summary dialog box appears, as shown in Figure 3-10. Click the Group By button and choose Clear All. Click OK to return to the View Summary dialog box. Follow the same steps to clear the Sort settings. When finished, highlight the task you want to move. Drag until the red arrows and line appear where you want the task, as shown in Figure 3-11, and release the mouse button.

To quickly add a new task, click the top of the list where it says Click here to add a New Task and key the task. Click the Due Date box, then click the arrow and choose from the calendar to include a due date for the task.

You can mark a task as complete by clicking the completed task check box. A line appears through the task. To delete a task, right-click the task and choose Delete from the shortcut menu that appears. Edit a task by double-clicking the task. Make your changes in the Task dialog box that appears and then choose Save and Close.

FIGURE 3-10
View Summary dialog box

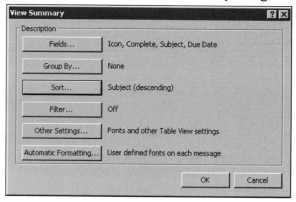

FIGURE 3-11
Move a task by clicking and dragging

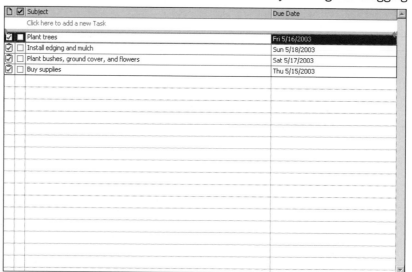

S TEP-BY-STEP ▷ 3.3

1. Click the **Due Date** bar at the top of the tasks list to sort the list by due date.

Computer Concepts

Clicking the Due Date bar once reverses the Due Date order.

2. Choose **Current View** from the **View** menu.

3. Choose **Customize Current View** from the submenu. The View Summary dialog box appears, as shown in Figure 3-10.

4. Click the **Sort** button and the Sort dialog box appears.

5. Click **Clear All** and then click **OK**. The View Summary dialog box returns.

6. Click **OK** to return to the tasks list.

7. Click the **Plant trees** task and drag up until the red arrows and line are at the top of the list, as shown in Figure 3-11.

8. Release the mouse button. *Plant trees* becomes the first task on the list.

9. Click the top row of the list where it says *Click here to add a New Task* and key **Fertilize trees and plants**.

10. Click the **Due Date** box on the same line. Click the down arrow and choose next Monday's date from the calendar.

11. Click the box to the left of the **Buy supplies** task to mark it as complete. A line appears through the task. (Note: If the box is not in view, choose **Current View** from the **View** menu and click **Simple List**.)

Hot Tip

To mark a task completed, you can also right-click the task and select **Mark Complete** from the shortcut menu.

12. Double-click the **Plant bushes, ground cover, and flowers** task to open the Task dialog box for editing.

13. Remove the check mark from the **Reminder** box and click **Save and Close**.

14. Right-click the **Install edging and mulch** task. A shortcut menu appears.

15. Choose **Delete**. Your screen should appear similar to Figure 3-12. Leave the tasks list on the screen for the next Step-by-Step.

Extra Challenge

Create a tasks list that includes at least five things you need to do in the next week.

FIGURE 3-12
Tasks list

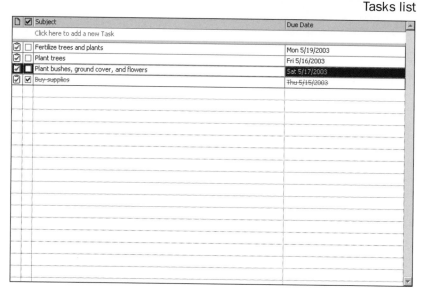

	☑	Subject	Due Date
		Click here to add a new Task	
☑	☐	Fertilize trees and plants	Mon 5/19/2003
☑	☐	Plant trees	Fri 5/16/2003
☑	☐	Plant bushes, ground cover, and flowers	Sat 5/17/2003
☑	☑	~~Buy supplies~~	~~Thu 5/15/2003~~

Assigning and Delegating Tasks

At times, you need to delegate tasks to others. To assign a new task to someone else, click the down arrow next to the New Task button and click Task Request. The Task dialog box appears. From the task dialog box, click the To box and the Select Task Recipient dialog box appears. From the Name box, choose the task recipients (the people you want to handle the task) and click OK. The Task dialog box appears with the recipients in the To box. Identify the task in the Subject box and select the Due dates. Click Send to deliver the task to the recipient.

If a task has already been created, you can delegate the task to someone else by double-clicking the task to open the dialog box. Click the Assign Task button and the To box. The Select Task Recipient dialog box appears. From the Name box, choose the task recipient and click OK. The Task dialog box appears with the recipients in the To box. Click Send to deliver the task to the recipient.

S TEP-BY-STEP ▷ 3.4

1. Click the down arrow next to the **New Tasks** button and click **Task Request**. The Task dialog box appears.

2. In the dialog box, click the **To** box and select two classmates' names.

3. In the Subject box, key **Task Assignment**.

4. Click the down arrow next to the **Due date** box. From the calendar, select the date for next Friday. Next Friday's date will appear in the Due date box.

5. Click the **Send** button to send the message to your classmates.

6. From the tasks list, double-click the **Plant trees** task. The Plant Trees – Task dialog box appears.

7. Click the **Assign Task** button. In the dialog box, click the **To** box and select a classmate's name.

8. Click the **Send** button and, if necessary, click **OK** in the dialog box that appears. The message is sent to your classmate. Your classmate should be sending you a task at this time.

9. Click the **Inbox** and the task request from your classmate should appear. Double-click this message to open it.

10. Below the toolbar is the Accept and Decline box. Click **Decline** and the Decline Task box appears.

11. Click **Edit the response before sending** button and click **OK**.

12. The message opens with the cursor in the text box. Key **I will be out of town this week**.

13. Click the **Send** button and, if necessary, click **OK** in the dialog box that appears. The message is sent to your classmate. Close the Tasks icon and leave the Tasks window open for the next Step-by-Step.

Viewing and Printing the Tasks List

To change how you view your tasks, choose Current View from the View menu. Choose from the list of view options. The view options are shown in Figure 3-13 and described in Table 3-1. Simple List is the default view.

To print your tasks list, choose Print from the File menu. The Print dialog box opens. The Print style box displays various options depending on what view you are using. You can choose to print your tasks in a table or memo style.

FIGURE 3-13
View options for a
task list

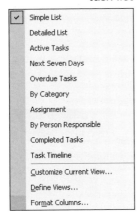

Computer Concepts

By default, the current day's tasks appear in the TaskPad when you are in Calendar view. To view all tasks on the TaskPad click View, TaskPad View, All Tasks.

TABLE 3-1
View options for a tasks list

VIEW	DESCRIPTION
Simple List	Lists tasks, completed check box, and due date
Detailed List	Lists details about each task including priority and status
Active Tasks	Lists tasks that are still in progress
Next Seven Days	Lists tasks due in the next seven days
Overdue Tasks	Lists only overdue tasks
By Category	Lists tasks grouped by category and sorted by due date
Assignment	Lists tasks assigned to others
By Person Responsible	Lists tasks according to the person responsible for completing
Completed Tasks	Lists only completed tasks
Task Timeline	Tasks are displayed in chronological order according to start date

S TEP-BY-STEP ▷ 3.5

1. Choose **Current View** from the **View** menu.

2. Choose **Detailed List** from the submenu. (Note: Adjust the columns so you can read your entries in the Subject, Status, Due Date, % Complete, and Categories columns.)

3. Choose **Print** from the **File** menu. The Print dialog box appears. Click the **Page Setup** button. The Page Setup Table Style dialog box

appears. Click the **Paper** tab. If it is not already selected, click the **Portrait** option in the orientation section. Click **OK**.

4. In the Print style box, **Table Style** should already be highlighted. Click **OK**. The task list prints in a table format, portrait orientation. Leave Outlook open for the next Step-by-Step.

Using the Journal

Y ou can use *Journal* to record entries and document your interactions with contacts. You can create journal entries manually to keep track of phone calls and other activities, or you can choose to automatically record e-mail, requests, and responses.

Click the Journal icon on the Outlook Bar to display the Journal screen. To add an entry manually, click the New

Computer Concepts

To automatically record entries, choose Options from the Tools menu. Under Contacts, select Journal Options to view the Journal Options dialog box. Click the items, contacts, and record files that you want to have recorded automatically.

Journal Entry button on the toolbar. The Journal Entry dialog box appears, as shown in Figure 3-14. When you are finished making the journal entry, click Save and Close.

The default view is By Type, which displays information as icons on a timeline, grouped by type. To change how you view your journal entries, choose Current View from the View menu. Choose from the list of view options. Choose Phone calls to display a list of phone calls recorded in your journal. Choose AutoPreview from the View menu to preview an entry.

S TEP-BY-STEP ▷ 3.6

1. On the Outlook Bar, click the **Journal** icon. If a message appears, click **No**. The Journal view displays.

2. Click the **New Journal** button on the toolbar. The Journal Entry dialog box appears, as shown in Figure 3-14. (Note: The entries in your dialog box might not be the same as in the figure.)

3. In the Subject box, key **Decide topics and attendees for meeting on Tuesday.**

4. In the Entry type box, choose **Phone call**, if it is not already selected.

5. In the Contacts box, key **David Powell**.

6. In the Duration box, choose **15 minutes**.

7. In the text box key **He will fax finalized agenda and list of attendees on Monday.**

8. Click **Save and Close**.

9. Choose **Current View** from the **View** menu. If it is not already selected, choose **Phone Calls** from the submenu. Your screen should appear similar to Figure 3-15. Leave Outlook open for use in the next Step-by-Step.

Computer Concepts

You can use the Start Timer and Pause Timer buttons like a stopwatch to record the actual time of your phone calls.

FIGURE 3-14
Journal Entry dialog box

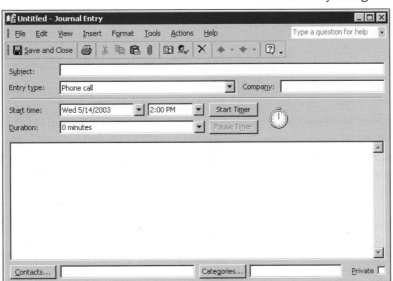

FIGURE 3-15
Preview a journal entry

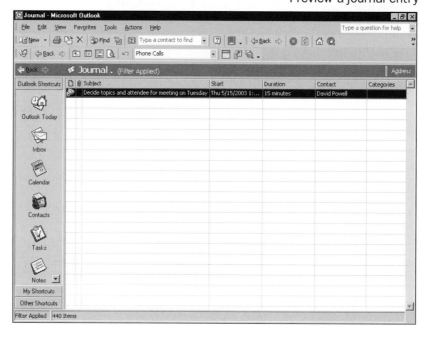

Using Notes

The *Notes* program is the electronic equivalent of using paper sticky notes as reminders. You can use Notes to key anything you need to remember, such as errands to run, birthday gift ideas, or a question to ask a co-worker. You can assign contacts from your Address Book to your notes, and just as you did with e-mail and calendar, you can also assign categories to notes.

Click the Notes icon on the Outlook Bar to display the Notes view. To add a note, click the New Note button on the toolbar. A blank note appears, as shown in Figure 3-16. Outlook automatically adds the date and time. Click the Close button on the note to save and close it.

Computer Concepts

You can change the font, font style, size, and color of the text on your notes by choosing Options from the Tools menu and then clicking the Note Options button.

The Icons view is the default view for Notes. In this view, an icon represents each note. To change how you view your notes, choose Current View from the View menu. Choose from the list of view options.

The default color of a note is yellow, but you can change it by clicking the note icon on an open note. Choose Color from the menu that appears and pick a color from the submenu, as shown in Figure 3-17. If you have different color notes, you can then display them according to color by choosing By Color from the Current View box in the View menu.

FIGURE 3-16
Use Notes to key important reminders

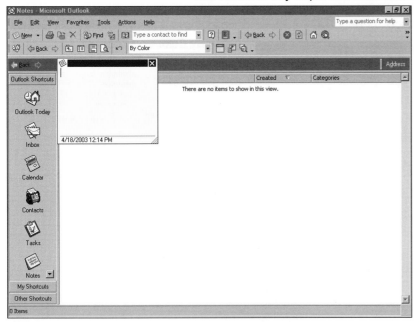

FIGURE 3-17
Changing the
color of a note

STEP-BY-STEP ▷ 3.7

1. Click the **Notes** icon on the Outlook Bar. (It might be necessary to click **Outlook Shortcuts** first.) The Notes view is displayed. If necessary, right-click the default note and choose **Delete** to remove it from your window.

2. Click the **New Note** button on the toolbar. Your screen should appear similar to Figure 3-16.

3. Key **Fax tax information to accountant**.

4. Click the **Note** icon in the upper-left corner of the note. A drop-down menu appears.

5. Choose **Color**. A submenu appears, as shown in Figure 3-17.

6. Click **Green**. The note color changes to green.

7. Click the **Close** button to close the note. Notice that your note now appears in the Notes window.

8. Open a new note and key **Order supplies from OfficePro salesman.**

9. Click the **Notes** icon in the upper-left corner of the note. A drop-down menu appears.

10. Click **Categories** and select **Business** and **Suppliers** from the Available Categories box.

11. Click **OK** to return to the note. Close the note.

12. Open a new note and key **Deposit payroll check into bank account**.

13. Click the **Notes** icon in the upper-left corner of the note. A drop-down menu appears.

14. Click **Contacts** and the Contacts for Note dialog box appears.

15. Click the **Contacts** box and the Select Contacts dialog box appears. In the Items box, highlight **Daly, Mary** (or another contact) and click **OK**. Close the Contacts for Note dialog box and close the note.

16. Open a new note and key **Call PrinterPlus about repair: 555-7822**. Close the note.

17. Choose **Current View** from the View menu. Choose **By Color** from the submenu.

18. Click the plus sign (**+**) to the left of each Color label to sort your notes by color. Your screen should appear similar to Figure 3-18.

19. Choose **Current View** from the **View** menu. Choose **Icons** from the submenu to return to the default view. Leave Outlook open for use in the next Step-by-Step.

FIGURE 3-18
Notes sorted by color

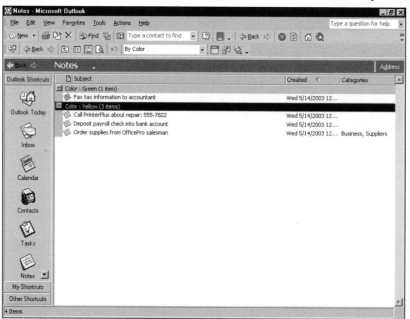

Exiting Outlook

You can exit Outlook by choosing Exit from the File menu.

S TEP-BY-STEP ⟹ 3.8

1. Choose **Exit** from the **File** menu.

2. The Outlook window closes.

Summary

In this lesson, you learned:

■ Outlook Today gathers information about today's activities from Calendar, Tasks, and Mail and summarizes the information in one window. You can display the Outlook Today window by clicking the Outlook Today icon on the Outlook Bar.

■ The Tasks view is where you create and manage tasks. You can assign categories, specify start and end dates, check the status of tasks, prioritize, and set reminders. You can also move tasks up and down the list, sort by subject or due date, add or delete tasks, edit a task, assign or delegate a task, or mark a task off when you complete it.

■ The Journal view is used to record entries and document your work. You can have Outlook automatically record entries or use the Journal Entry dialog box to record entries manually.

■ The Notes view is similar to using paper sticky notes as reminders. The date and time are automatically added. You can change the color of a note and view them according to color.

VOCABULARY REVIEW

Define the following terms:

Categories	Notes	Tasks
Journal		

LESSON 3 REVIEW QUESTIONS

TRUE/FALSE

Circle T if the statement is true or F if the statement is false.

T F 1. Using Notes in Outlook is similar to using sticky paper notes.

T F 2. Choose Current View from the View menu to preview an entry.

T F 3. Using Journal entries is the best way to remember errands that you need to do.

T F 4. You can customize Outlook to automatically display the Outlook Today view every time Outlook is started.

T F 5. A task is any activity you want to perform and monitor to completion.

WRITTEN QUESTIONS

Write a brief answer to the following questions.

1. Outlook Today summarizes information about today's activities from what three areas of Outlook?

2. What is the default view for your tasks list?

3. What Outlook view do you use to record entries and document your work?

4. Explain the benefits of color-coding your Notes.

5. List five different Entry Types that can be used when listing Journal Entries.

LESSON 3 PROJECTS

PROJECT 3-1

1. Display the Tasks view.

2. Mark all existing tasks as complete.

3. Add a new task with **Paint bathroom** as the subject and due this Saturday.

4. Set a reminder at 5 p.m. on Friday.

5. In the text box, key **Get another drop cloth**. Save and close the Task dialog box.

6. Add another new task with **Pick up carpet samples** as the subject and due this Friday.

7. Set a reminder at 10 a.m. on Friday. Set the priority as **High**. Save and close the Task dialog box.

8. View the tasks in Detailed List view.

9. Sort the tasks by Due Date. Leave Outlook open for the next project.

PROJECT 3-2

1. Display the Journal view.

2. Create a new journal entry with **Phone interview** as the subject.

3. Use **Phone call** as the Entry type.

4. Key **Clay Sipowitz** as the Contact and **Rocky Mountain Journal** as the Company.

5. Choose a duration of **30 minutes**.

6. In the text box, key **Will send photographer Monday**.

7. Assign the journal entry to the category called **Phone Calls**. Save and close the Journal Entry dialog box. Leave Outlook open for the next project.

PROJECT 3-3

1. Display the Notes view.

2. Add a pink note that says **Order flowers for Aunt Mollie's birthday**.

3. Add a green note that says **Buy stamps**.

4. Add a yellow note that says **Call Tracey (555-2208) about summer trip**.

5. View the notes by color.

6. Exit Outlook.

CRITICAL THINKING

ACTIVITY 3-1

SCANS

Pick a type of small business that you would like to own. Describe how you would use the Calendar, Tasks, and Journal features of Outlook to organize information, communicate with others, and manage time. Also, list four or more categories for grouping all of the information.

ACTIVITY 3-2

Your supervisor asks you to change the default settings for Journal tracking or the automatic recording of Outlook activities. Use the Help system to search for the steps to change the defaults.

ACTIVITY 3-3

SCANS

Design an Outlook Today view for your supervisor using the customizing options. Explain in a short paragraph why you chose the particular options.

IO-59

COMMAND SUMMARY

FEATURE	MENU COMMAND	TOOLBAR BUTTON	LESSON
Accept a Task Request		✓ Accept	3
Add a Contact	Actions, New Contact	New	1
Add a Journal Entry	Actions, New Journal Entry	New	3
Add a Meeting	Actions, Plan a Meeting		2
Add an All Day Event	Actions, New All Day Event		2
Add an Appointment	Actions, New Appointment	New	2
Add a Note	Actions, New Note	New	3
Add a Task	Actions, New Task	New	
Address Book	Tools, Address Book		1
Assign a Task	File, New, Task Request	Assign Task	3
Change Views	View, Current View		1
Daily Calendar View	View, Day	Day	2
Decline a Task Request		✗ Decline	3
Delete an Appointment/ Event	Edit, Delete	✗	2
Go to Today		Today	2
Group Tasks	View, Current View, Customize Current View, Group By		3
Monthly Calendar View	View, Month	Month	2
New Mail Message	Actions, New Mail Message	New	1
Print	File, Print		1
Print Preview	File, Print Preview		1
Recurring Appointment	Actions, New Recurring Appointment		2
Save and Close		Save and Close	1
Sort Tasks	View, Current View, Customize Current View, Sort		3
Weekly Calendar View	View, Week	Week	2
Work Week Calendar View	View, Work Week	Work Week	2

TRUE/FALSE

Circle T if the statement is true or F if the statement is false.

T   F   1.   A boldface date in the Date Navigator means an activity is scheduled for that day.

T   F   2.   Resources are people you invite to a meeting.

T   F   3.   Choose Current View from the View menu to change how you view your contacts.

T   F   4.   Use the Journal Entry dialog box to record entries manually.

T   F   5.   Exit Outlook by choosing Quit from the File menu.

WRITTEN QUESTIONS

Write a brief answer to the following questions.

1.   What option do you use in the Appointment dialog box to prevent others from viewing the information?

2.   How do you change an appointment?

3.   What button on the Outlook Bar do you click to display the mail icons?

4.   How do you mark a task as complete?

5.   How do you change the color of a note?

PROJECTS

PROJECT 1

Add the following tasks to prepare for an upcoming sales conference.

1. Display the **Tasks** screen.

2. Create a new task with **Create agenda for sales conference in July** as the subject and due this Friday.

3. Set a reminder for 3:00 p.m. on Friday. Set the priority as **High**.

4. In the text box, key **Call Dave Lowry for conference schedule and planned activities.** Save and close the Task dialog box.

5. Add a new category called **Sales Conference** and assign the task to it.

6. Create another task. Key **Write memo to send with the agenda** as the subject. Make it due the following Monday.

7. Set a reminder for 1:00 p.m. on Monday. Set the status as **In Progress**.

8. Set the percent complete as **50%**.

9. In the text box, key **Ask Molly to create labels from the sales mailing list.**

10. Assign the task to the category Sales Conference. Save and close the Task dialog box.

11. View the tasks in Detailed List view.

12. Leave Outlook open for the next project.

PROJECT 2

You work for a local advertising agency during the day and attend classes at Southwest University in the evenings. Add an appointment with your advisor to discuss your classes for next semester. Also, add a friend's birthday so you don't forget it.

1. Display the **Calendar** screen.

2. Create a new appointment for tomorrow from 5:00 p.m. to 5:30 p.m.

3. In the subject box, key **Meet with advisor at school**.

4. In the location box, key **Business Education building, Room 2c**.

5. Set a reminder for 30 minutes before the appointment.

6. Show the time as **Out of Office**.

7. In text box, key **Take class schedule for next semester**.

8. Assign the appointment to the **Personal** category. Save and close the Appointment dialog box.

9. Use the Date Navigator to select **September 12** of next year.

10. Create a new all-day event and key **Sarah's birthday** in the subject box.

11. Choose a yearly recurrence pattern and set a reminder for one day before the birthday.

12. Assign the event to the **Personal** category. Save and close the Event dialog box.

13. Leave Outlook open for the next project.

PROJECT 3

After attending a sales convention in Austin, Texas, you have two new contacts to add to your Contacts list and Address Book.

1. Display the **Contacts** screen.

2. Add the two contacts using this information.

```
Name: Brad Gatlin                    Name: Rebecca McInturf
Job Title: Sales Manager             Job Title: Design Specialist
Company: Software Specific, Inc.     Company: Office Concepts
Address: 2190 Metric Blvd.           Address: 610 W. Broadway
         Austin, TX 78712                     Lubbock, TX 79412
Business Phone: (512) 555-9267       Business Phone: (806) 555-8844
Business Fax: (512) 555-9269         Home Phone: (806) 555-9241
E-mail: b_gatlin@softspec.com        E-mail: rmcinturf@offcon.com
```

3. View the Contacts list as Address Cards.

4. View the Contacts list as a Phone List.

5. When finished, display the Address Book to view the contacts.

6. Leave Outlook open for the next project.

PROJECT 4

1. Display the **Outlook Today** screen.

2. Click **Calendar** and add your birthday as a recurring event.

3. Click **Tasks** and add a task to today that you need to complete for school or for yourself.

4. When finished, go back to the Outlook Today screen and mark all tasks as completed.

5. Exit Outlook.

You work at the Java Internet Café, which has been open a short time. The café serves coffee, other beverages, and pastries, and offers Internet access. Seven computers are set up on tables along the north side of the store. Customers can come in and have a cup of coffee and a bagel, and explore the World Wide Web.

Your manager asks you to write a letter to Mary Daly, a new contact recently added to the contact list. The message should include an invitation to the shop for a free specialty drink.

JOB 1

1. Open Outlook and display the **Inbox** screen. Click the **New Mail Message** button to open the Message dialog box.

2. In the **To** box, key Mary Daly's e-mail address. (*Hint*: Refer to your Contacts list for the address.)

3. In the Subject box, key **Java Internet Café**.

4. In the Text box, key the following:

```
Mary,
    I enjoyed visiting with you at the last meeting of the Small Business
Owners Association. Please let me know if I can be of any help in your new
position as leader of the School Volunteer Project.
    Also, I am sending you an invitation to visit the Java Internet Café
located at Highway 45 and Loop 210 in the Oakdale Shopping Center.
    The Java Internet Café is a coffee shop with a twist. While enjoying one of
our specialty drinks such as a Café au lait and a bagel, you can access the
Internet and explore the World Wide Web on one of our seven high-speed computers.
    Visit us soon and bring a copy of this e-mail message with you for a free
specialty drink. I hope you enjoy your visit at the Java Internet Café.
```

5. Do not send the message. Choose **Close** from the **File** menu. Click **No** when prompted to save your changes.

6. Exit Outlook.

INTRODUCTORY MICROSOFT® PUBLISHER & MICROSOFT® FRONTPAGE

UNIT

lesson 1
Publisher Basics

1.5 hrs.

lesson 2
FrontPage Basics

2.5 hrs.

Estimated Time for Unit: 4 hours

PUBLISHER BASICS

OBJECTIVES

Upon completion of this lesson, you will be able to:

- Start Publisher and identify parts of the Publisher screen.
- Create a project using a wizard.
- Modify a logo.
- Create a project using the By Design Sets option.
- Open and edit an existing Publisher project.
- Create your own Publisher project.

⏱ **Estimated Time 1.5 hours**

VOCABULARY

Blank publication

Design set

Personal information set

Wizard

Introduction to Publisher

Publisher is a desktop publishing program that you can use to create a wide assortment of documents, such as business cards and restaurant menus. Publisher contains hundreds of predesigned templates you can use as the basis for professional-looking projects. All you have to do is add your own custom touches.

Starting Publisher

To start Microsoft Publisher, click the Start button, click Programs, and then choose Microsoft Publisher. Publisher starts and the screen appears, as shown in Figure 1-1, with the New from Existing Publication task pane displayed on the left.

FIGURE 1-1
Microsoft Publisher screen

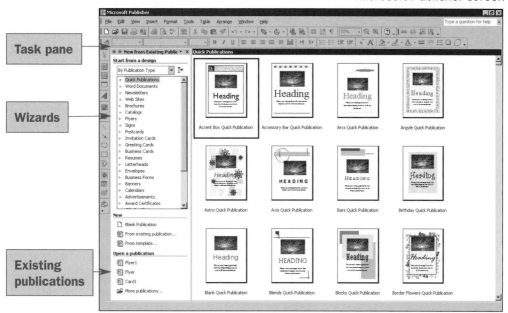

Task pane

Wizards

Existing
publications

STEP-BY-STEP ▷ 1.1

1. Click the **Start** button to open the **Start** menu.

2. Click **Programs** to open the **Programs** menu.

3. Click **Microsoft Publisher** to start the program. The screen appears, as shown in Figure 1-1, with the task pane displayed on the left.

4. Leave the program running for the next Step-by-Step.

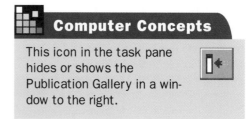

Computer Concepts

This icon in the task pane hides or shows the Publication Gallery in a window to the right.

Starting a Project

Using the task pane, you can start a publication project in a variety of ways.

Start from a Design

You can choose to create a publication with a publication wizard or from a design set. *Wizards* use predesigned templates that provide the framework for various types of publications. Publisher comes with more than 25 wizards.

When By Publication Type is selected in the task pane, the available wizards are listed in the box below it. When you select a wizard from the list, the available designs for that type of publication are shown in the pane on the right.

In Figure 1-1, notice that there are diamonds or triangles next to the wizards listed in the task pane. When you select a wizard with a triangle next to it, a list of subcategories appears. These subcategories represent more specific publications. Wizards with diamonds do not have additional subcategories.

When you select By Design Sets in the task pane, the window to the right shows the available publications grouped according to the type of design you want to use. A *design set* is a series of documents (letterheads, business cards, envelopes, etc.) that incorporate the same design. There are also design sets that offer specific layouts for special events, holidays, and fund raising.

New

The New section of the task pane contains several more options for starting a new publication, including Blank Publication. A *blank publication* is one you use to create a document from scratch using whatever format, colors, and designs you prefer. You can also choose to create a new publication based on an existing one or start a new publication using a template that you have previously created as a starting point.

Open a Publication

This section of the task pane lists recently saved publications. To open an existing publication that is not listed, choose More Publications. The Open Publication dialog box appears so you can open a file you have previously saved.

Personal Information Sets

A helpful feature of Publisher is the personal information sets. You can use a *personal information set* to store information about your businesses, other organizations, or your home and family. Then, when you are creating a publication, Publisher will automatically insert the information you have stored, such as names, addresses, phone numbers, and logos. If you have not yet created a personal information set, Publisher will prompt you to do so when you start a publication, but you can view the Personal Information dialog box (see Figure 1-2) at any time by choosing Personal Information from the Edit menu. To make changes to the information, click Update.

FIGURE 1-2
Personal Information dialog box

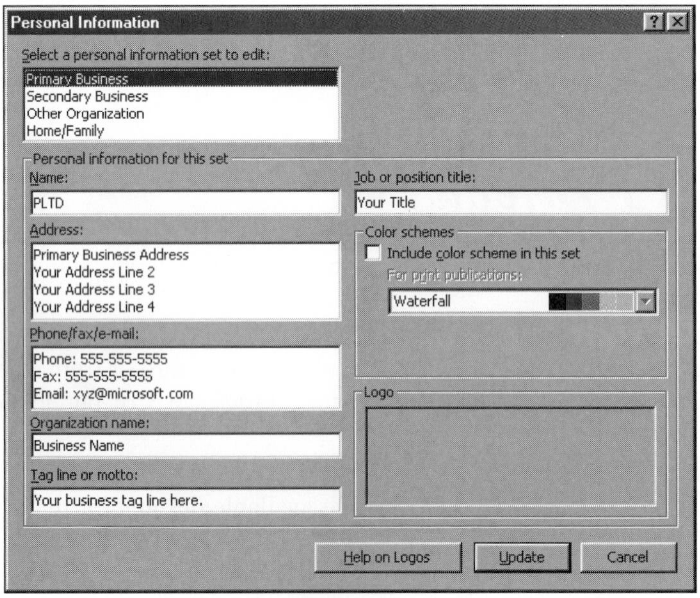

STEP-BY-STEP 1.2

1. Choose **By Publication Type** in the task pane if it is not already selected. Click **Business Cards** in the list of wizards. A variety of designs appear on the right (see Figure 1-3).

2. Click the **Accent Box Business Card** template, as shown in Figure 1-3, if necessary. The Business Card Options task pane appears on the left side of the screen (see Figure 1-4) and the Accent Box template appears on the right.

FIGURE 1-3
Business Card wizard

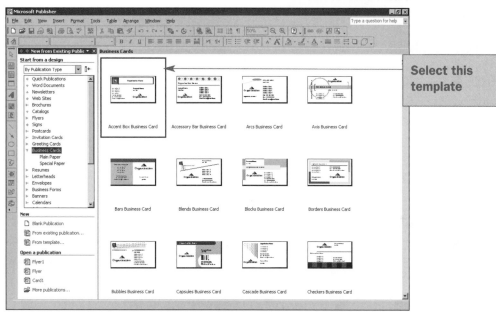

FIGURE 1-4
Business Card Options task pane

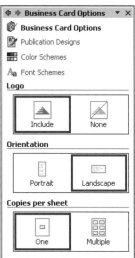

3. If you have not created a personal information set, a message appears prompting you to tell the wizard about yourself. Click **OK** to display the Personal Information dialog box (see Figure 1-2). If a message does not appear, choose **Personal Information** from the **Edit** menu to display it.

4. In the **Select a personal information set to edit** box, select **Primary Business**, if necessary.

5. In the Name box, key **Miriam Lockhart**.

6. In the Address box, key the following:

```
1218 Albany
Anderson, IN 46011
```

7. In the Phone/fax/e-mail box, key the following:

```
Phone: 812-555-9213
Fax: 812-555-9211
Email: mlockhart@lawsoncomp.com
```

8. In the Organization name box, key **Lawson Computers**.

9. In the Tag line or motto box, key **Hardware & Software Solutions**.

10. In the Job or position title box, key **Technician**.

11. Click the **Update** button to close the Personal Information dialog box.

12. Your card should look like the one in Figure 1-5.

13. Save the file as **Card** followed by your initials. Leave the file open for the next Step-by-Step.

FIGURE 1-5
Finished business card

Adding a Logo

Y ou can make changes to your card by clicking on the item directly in the window. For example, if you wanted to change the title of Technician, you simply click on the item, and a blinking insertion point appears so that you can key a new title.

To create a new logo for the card, simply click on the existing logo. A Wizard icon appears. When you click the icon, the task pane on the left displays designs and options you can use to customize a logo. You can apply a different design, create a logo with Publisher, or insert an existing picture file as a logo. You also have the option of removing the graphic from the logo or adding lines of text.

STEP-BY-STEP ▷ 1.3

1. Click the logo portion of your business card to select it, as shown in Figure 1-6.

2. Click the Wizard icon. The Logo Designs task pane appears, as shown in Figure 1-7.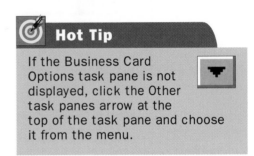

3. The Apply a design section of the task pane lists the different types of designs available. Click the **Foundation Bar** design. Notice that the logo design changes.

4. Click anywhere on the business card outside the logo to close the Wizard.

5. Select the word **Organization** in the logo part of your business card. The thick box around the text indicates that you are able to edit it.

6. Key **Lawson Computers**. Click outside the text box to close it.

7. Save the file by clicking the **Save** button on the toolbar. A message appears asking if you want to save the new logo to the Primary Business personal information set. Click **Yes**.

Hot Tip

If the Business Card Options task pane is not displayed, click the Other task panes arrow at the top of the task pane and choose it from the menu.

FIGURE 1-7
Logo Options and Logo Designs task pane

FIGURE 1-6
Editing the logo

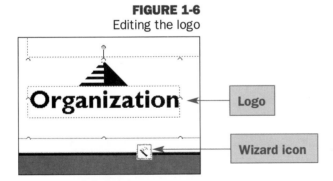

8. Your business card should look similar to the one in Figure 1-8.

9. In the Business Card Options task pane, under Copies per sheet, choose **Multiple**.

10. Choose **Print** on the **File** menu. In the Print dialog box, click **OK** to print your business card.

11. Save and close the file.

FIGURE 1-8
Modified business card

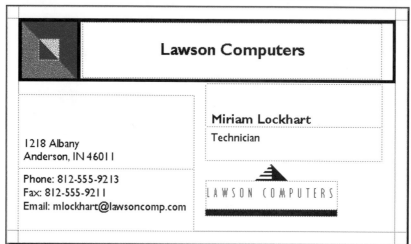

By Design Sets

The By Design Sets option allows you to design an entire series of documents that include the same design, information, and logo. This way you can maintain a consistent format throughout all the documents you produce.

STEP-BY-STEP ▭ 1.4

1. In the Start from a design section of the New Publication task pane, click the down arrow to choose **By Design Sets**. In the Master Sets list, click the Accent Box design. The Accent Box templates are displayed on the right side of the screen.

2. Scroll down through the Accent Box templates, and click **Accent Box Special Offer Flyer**.

3. The Flyer Options task pane appears, as shown in Figure 1-9. In the Tear-offs section, scroll down if necessary and click **Coupon**. Your flyer is updated to include a coupon.

4. Choose **Personal Information** from the **Edit** menu and verify that the data entered in Step-by-Step 1.2 is correct.

5. Save the file as **Flyer**, followed by your initials. Leave the publication open for the next Step-by-Step.

FIGURE 1-9
Flyer Options task pane

You can also make changes to the flyer using the same methods you applied on your business card.

S TEP-BY-STEP ▷ 1.5

1. Click the Promotion Title portion of the flyer. This allows you to edit the title.

2. Key **Annual Clearance Sale**.

3. In the **Date of Sale** box, key in next Saturday's date. You may need to click on the **Zoom In** button on the toolbar once or twice to enlarge your editing area.

4. In the **Time of Sale** box, key **8 a.m. – 6 p.m.**

5. Click in the box that asks you to describe your location, and key **Located next to Willow Park Mall**.

6. Click to select the **Free Offer** logo. Click the **Wizard** icon. The **Attention Getter Design** task pane appears, as shown in Figure 1-10.

7. In the task pane, scroll and click the **Double Slant** design. Notice that the logo design changes. Click outside the logo to close the wizard.

8. Click on the **Free Offer** logo, and key **FREE** and press **Enter**. Key **Mouse** and press **Enter**. Key **Pad** and press **Enter**.

FIGURE 1-10
Attention Getter
Design options

9. Click on the picture in your flyer to select it. Click on the picture again so the selection handles change color and have x's in them. The Picture toolbar appears.

10. Choose **Picture** from the **Insert** menu and choose **Clip Art** on the submenu.

11. In the Search text box in the Insert Clip Art task pane, key **Computer** and click the **Search** button.

12. In the results that are displayed, double-click a computer-related picture that you like to insert it in the flyer.

13. Click in the box that contains the phone number and key **812-555-9213**.

14. Click in the tag line (motto) box and select the text **Hardware & Software Solutions**.

15. Change the font size of the tag line to **20**.

16. Click in the text box under the picture to select all the text. Key the following:

> Everything that your computer needs is now on sale! From audio cards to disk drives, we can meet your every computer need. We provide the latest technology, great pricing, and continuous service to keep yoursystem running at peak performance.
> With any purchase of hardware or software over $25, you will receive a free Lawson Computers mouse pad. Receive 15% off any purchase over $100 when you present the coupon below.

17. Click in the box that contains the text List items here, and key the following text:

> Computers
> Printers
> Monitors
> Wide Selection of Software
> Service & Support

18. Click the Name of Item or Service text box on the coupon. Key **Any Purchase Over $100**.

19. Click the 00% OFF text box. Key **15% OFF**.

20. Click in the box that asks you to describe your location, and key **Located next to Willow Park Mall**. You may need to click the **Zoom In** button again to enlarge your edit area.

21. Click in the box that contains the phone number. Key **812-555-9213**.

22. Click in the box that contains the expiration date and key the date for the Saturday following the next one. (So that the coupon expires one week after the sale date.)

23. Your flyer should look similar to the one in Figure 1-11.

24. Save, print, and close the flyer.

FIGURE 1-11
Flyer with Attention Getter

Other Types of Publications

Using Publisher, you can create many different types of publications using the process you have learned so far in this lesson.

S TEP-BY-STEP ⇨ 1.6

1. In the New Publication task pane, choose **By Design Sets** if necessary.

2. With the Accent Box design selected, click **Accent Box Calendar.** The Calendar Options task pane appears, as shown in Figure 1-12.

3. In the Orientation section of the task pane, click **Portrait.** The calendar changes to portrait orientation.

4. In the Month or year section of the task pane, select **Yearly.**

5. Your calendar should look similar to Figure 1-13.

FIGURE 1-12
Calendar Options task pane

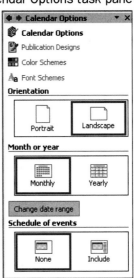

6. Save the file as **Calendar**, followed by your initials.

7. Print your calendar and close the file.

Hot Tip

To change the dates on the calendar, click the **Change date range** button in the Month or year section of the task pane.

FIGURE 1-13
Completed calendar

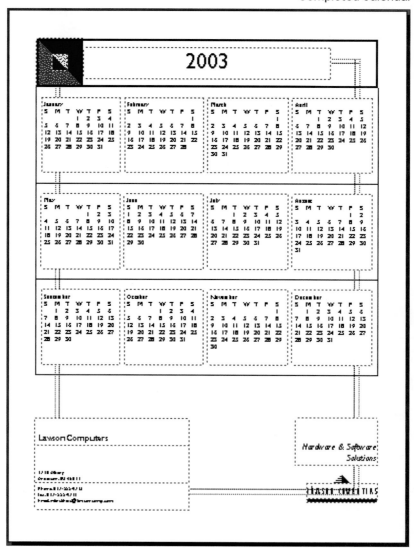

Summary

In this lesson, you learned:

- Microsoft Publisher is a program that allows you to produce professional-looking documents in almost any format imaginable. Publisher makes this process even easier with the use of wizards and design sets.

- You can choose to create a publication with a publication wizard. Wizards use predesigned templates that provide the framework for various types of publications.

- By using design sets, you can create a series of documents that include the same design, information, and logo. This helps you maintain a consistent format throughout all the documents you produce.

- With Publisher, you can easily add a logo, clip art, or make changes to your publication once it has been created. By updating the Personal Information dialog box you can personalize the publication with your information.

VOCABULARY REVIEW

Define the following terms:

Blank publication	Personal information set	Wizard
Design set		

LESSON 1 REVIEW QUESTIONS

TRUE/FALSE

Circle T if the statement is true or F if the statement is false.

T F 1. To start a new publication, choose the Open a publication option.

T F 2. By choosing Blank Publication, you can create a new publication based on an existing one.

T F 3. You can use design sets to create a series of documents with the same design.

T F 4. Logo options include removing the graphic and adding lines of text.

T F 5. You cannot use the Personal Information dialog box to customize your publication with business information.

WRITTEN QUESTIONS

Write a brief answer to the following questions.

1. List the three options that are listed in the New section of the task pane.

2. When does the logo wizard button appear?

3. Which option in the task pane allows you to create a series of documents (letterheads, business cards, and envelopes) with the same design?

4. What option would you select in the task pane to retrieve any files you have saved?

5. What does it mean when a wizard category has a triangle next to it?

LESSON 1 PROJECTS

PROJECT 1-1

1. Start Publisher, if necessary.

2. In the Open a publication section of the New Publication task pane, click **More publications** and locate **PF Project1-1** in the data files.

3. Save the file as **Card1** followed by your initials.

4. Use the logo wizard button to change the logo design from Foundation Bar to a Crossed Corner design.

5. Use the Logo Options task pane to add another line of text to the logo.

6. For the second line of text, key **Hardware & Software**.

7. Choose multiple copies per sheet if necessary, and print the business cards.

8. Save the file. Click **Yes** if asked whether to save the new logo to the Primary Business personal information set. Close the file.

PROJECT 1-2

1. Open the **PF Project1-2** file.

2. Save the file as **Flyer1** followed by your initials.

3. Use the Flyer Options task pane to remove the coupon.

4. Edit the text to remove the sentence about the coupon.

5. Change the attention getter graphic to the **Chevron** design.

6. Add **Scanners** to the list of bulleted items after *Monitors*.

7. Change the time of sale to **9 a.m. – 5 p.m.**

8. Save the file and print the flyer. Close the file.

CRITICAL THINKING

ACTIVITY 1-1

Use the By Publication Type Wizard to create a business card that includes your name and a company or organization with which you are affiliated. When you design your card, think about the impression you want the public to have about you and your organization.

ACTIVITY 1-2

You are asked to change the color scheme and the font scheme of the Flyer file you created in this lesson. Use the Help system to find information on color schemes and font schemes and how to change them in a publication. Write a paragraph that defines font and color schemes and explains the procedure for changing them. Modify your publication by changing the color scheme and font scheme of the Flyer document. Save the file as **Flyer Scheme** followed by your initials.

FRONTPAGE BASICS

OBJECTIVES

Upon completion of this lesson, you should be able to:

- Start FrontPage.
- Identify parts of the Page view screen.
- Create a new Web page, add pages to a Web, and save pages.
- Use Navigation view and name pages.
- Add a theme, banner, and navigation bars.
- Add shared borders and a photo gallery.
- Use FrontPage views.
- Add text, a picture, and other formatting features.
- Add hyperlinks and create an image map.
- Work with graphic and dynamic elements.
- View, print, and publish Web pages.

⏱ **Estimated Time 2.5 hours**

VOCABULARY

Hotspot

Hyperlinks

HyperText Markup
Language (HTML)

Themes

Web page

Introduction to FrontPage

FrontPage is an Office XP application that can help you create professional-looking Web pages. A ***Web page*** combines text with audio, video, and animation in a graphical format that can be viewed on the Internet. Web pages are connected by ***hyperlinks*** that a user can click to jump from one Web page to another.

Starting FrontPage

To start FrontPage, click the Start button, select Programs, and then choose Microsoft FrontPage. A blank page appears in Page view, as shown in Figure 2-1.

Computer Concepts

You may see a message box if FrontPage is not your default editor. Click Yes to make it the default editor or No so it will not be the default editor.

FIGURE 2-1
FrontPage opening screen

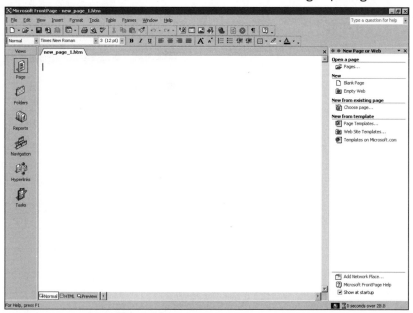

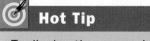

1. Click the **Start** button to open the Start menu.

2. Click **Programs**, then choose **Microsoft FrontPage**.

3. FrontPage starts and your screen appears in normal Page view.

4. Leave FrontPage open for the next Step-by-Step.

Hot Tip

To display the screen in Page view at any time, click **Page** from the **View** menu or from the Views bar.

Identifying Parts of the Screen

When you start FrontPage, a blank page appears in Page view where you can edit Web pages. Buttons for other views are displayed in the Views bar on the left of the screen. To learn the purpose of each view, position the mouse pointer over a button and a ScreenTip appears with a description. To switch to another view, click the button. In this lesson, you will work in two views; Page and Navigation.

There are three buttons at the bottom of the Page view window. The Normal button displays your pages graphically and is what you will typically use to make changes. The *HTML* (short for *HyperText Markup Language* - the computer language for creating Web pages) button displays your page in HTML code so you can edit it directly. The Preview button shows how your Web page will look when viewed by a Web browser. Click the button to select it.

The title bar, menu bar, and standard and formatting toolbars are familiar parts of the screen that you have used in other Office applications. The status bar across the bottom of the screen displays information and messages. For example, in Page view the status bar gives an estimate of how long the page will take to download at a particular modem speed.

New Page or Web Task Pane

The New Page or Web task pane on the right of the screen offers several options for beginning to work.

Hot Tip

Choosing **New** from the **File** menu and **Page or Web** from the submenu will display the New Page or Web task pane if it is not visible.

OPEN A PAGE

If you have already created Web pages, you can open them by clicking Pages under this section to display the Open File dialog box.

NEW

To create a new page, click the Blank Page option in this section. To create a new Web site with nothing in it, click Empty Web. The Web Site Templates dialog box appears with the Empty Web option chosen, as shown in Figure 2-2. You can specify a location for the new Web site or accept the default.

FIGURE 2-2
Web Site Templates dialog box

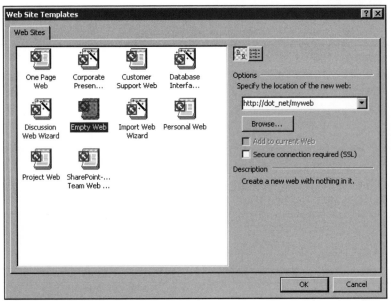

NEW FROM EXISTING PAGE

Click Choose page in this section to create a new publication based on an existing one.

NEW FROM TEMPLATE

To create a new page using a template as a starting point, click the Page Templates option. This opens the Page Templates dialog box, as shown in Figure 2-3, where you can choose from a selection of general, frame page, and style sheet templates. A description and a preview of the option are shown when you click it. Clicking the Web Site Templates option opens the same dialog box shown in Figure 2-2. If you are connected to the Internet, you can click Templates on *Microsoft.com* for more templates.

FIGURE 2-3
Page Templates dialog box

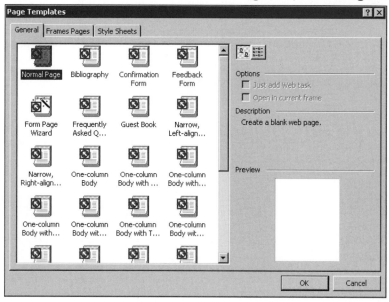

Creating a New Web Site

When you create a new Web site by choosing an option in the Web Site Templates dialog box and clicking OK, a Create New Web dialog box briefly appears, as shown in Figure 2-4. This occurs as FrontPage is creating folders for your Web. These folders then appear in the Folder List, which is displayed on the screen, as shown in Figure 2-5.

FIGURE 2-4
Create New Web dialog box

FIGURE 2-5
Folder List

Adding Pages

You can add more pages to your Web site whenever you need them. When more than one page is open at once, you can move from one to another by clicking on the page tabs at the top of the screen in Page view. This allows you to easily switch between pages to edit them.

 Hot Tip

You can hide or display the Folder List by choosing Folder List from the View menu or Folders on the Views bar.

Saving Pages

When you save a page, it is added to the list of files in the Folder List. Your home page should always be saved as *index.htm* or *default.htm*. FrontPage does this for you (or prompts you to do so) when you use a Web Site template to create a Web site.

STEP-BY-STEP ▷ 2.2

1. In the New section of the task pane, click **Empty Web**. The Web Site Templates dialog box appears, as shown in Figure 2-2.

2. Choose a location for the new Web site or accept the default and click OK. A Create New Web dialog box briefly appears (see Figure 2-4).

3. Click the **Folders** icon in the **Views** bar, on the left side of the screen, to display the folders created for your Web site, as shown in Figure 2-5.

4. Choose **New** from the **File** menu, and then **Page or Web** from the submenu.

5. In the New section of the task pane, click **Blank Page**. The Index page is added to your

Web site. This is the default filename for your home page.

Hot Tip

If the task pane is not displayed, choose **Task Pane** from the **View** menu.

6. Choose **New** from the **File** menu, and **Page or Web** from the submenu.

7. In the New section of the task pane, click **Blank Page** to add the first page to your Web site. Leave the Web site open for the next Step-by-Step.

Using Navigation View

You can design your Web site's structure and organize the pages using Navigation view. To switch to Navigation view, click the Navigation button on the Views bar. To add an existing page to the structure in Navigation view, click the file in the Folder List and drag it to the position you want. To create a page in Navigation view, click the Create a new normal page button on the toolbar.

Naming Pages

To name a page in Navigation view, click on it. The page color changes from yellow to blue to indicate it is selected. Click the text to select it and key a new name. You can also move from page to page by clicking the Tab key.

Computer Concepts

Changing a page name in Navigation view does not change the page's filename.

1. Click the **Navigation** button on the Views bar. The page that is displayed is your home page (index.htm).

> **Hot Tip**
>
> To easily rename a page, right-click the page and select Rename from the menu.

2. Click the page. The color changes from yellow to blue to indicate that it is selected. Click the text to select it, as shown in Figure 2-6.

FIGURE 2-6
Naming a page

3. Key **Home Page** and click outside the page to deselect it.

4. In the Folder List, rename the current **new_page_1.htm** to **adoption.htm**.

5. Add the adoption page to the navigation structure by clicking it in the Folder List and dragging it into position under the home page.

6. Click the **adoption.htm** page in the navigation structure and rename it **Adoption**.

7. Select the Home Page again. Add a new page by clicking the **Create a new normal page button** on the toolbar. A new page appears in the navigation structure. Name it **Contributions**.

8. Add another new page the same way and name it **Links**.

9. Click the **Refresh** button on the toolbar for your new pages to appear in the Folder List. Your screen should look similar to Figure 2-7.

10. In the Folder List, double-click the index.htm file to open it in Page view.

FIGURE 2-7
Navigation view

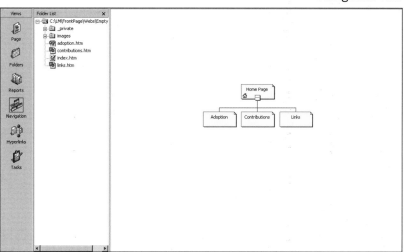

11. Switch back to Navigation view and double-click the **adoption.htm** file to open it in Page view. Open the **contributions.htm** and **links.htm** files the same way. You can tell which pages are open in Page view by the page tabs, as shown in Figure 2-8

12. Leave all pages open for the next Step-by-Step.

FIGURE 2-8
Page tabs in Page view

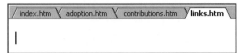

Adding a Theme

FrontPage contains preset *themes* that allow you to apply designs and color schemes to either a single page or to your entire Web site. The Theme feature alsos allow you to change the colors, graphics, and text to give your Web pages a consistent and professional appearance. To apply themes to your Web site, choose Theme from the Format menu. The Themes dialog box appears (see Figure 2-9).

FIGURE 2-9
Themes dialog box

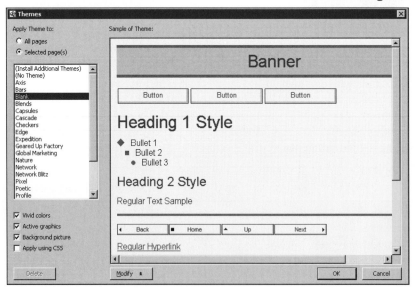

Choose the theme that you want to apply to All pages or Selected page(s). You can change aspects of the theme to suit your needs by clicking the Modify button. You are given the choice of modifying the colors, graphics, or text. When you choose one, the Modify Theme dialog box appears where you can make changes (see Figure 2-10).

FIGURE 2-10
FIGURE 2-10
Modify Theme dialog box

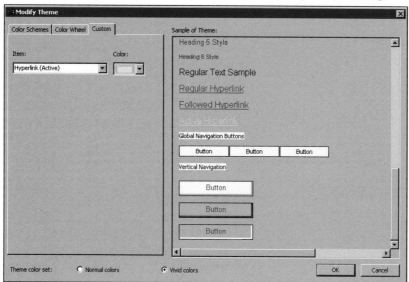

TEP-BY-STEP ▷ 2.4

1. Click the **index.htm** page tab to display the home page in Page view.

2. Choose **Theme** from the **Format** menu. The Themes dialog box appears, allowing you to select from a variety of themes for your Web page.

3. Choose **Blank**. The Sample of Theme section shows the Blank theme elements, as shown in Figure 2-9.

Hot Tip

If the Blank theme is not available, choose another.

4. Click **Selected page(s)** if necessary. If they are not already checked, click the check boxes next to **Vivid Colors, Active Graphics,** and **Background Picture.**

5. Click **OK**. If a message appears asking if you want to apply the theme, click **Yes**. The theme is applied to the index page.

Computer Concepts

The effects of applying a theme may not be evident until you start adding elements to a page.

6. Display the Themes dialog box again. Click **All pages** and then click **OK** to apply the Blank theme to all of your Web pages. Click **Yes** if a message appears asking if you want to apply the theme.

7. Display the Themes dialog box again. Click the **Modify** button and then click **Colors**. The Modify Theme dialog box is displayed.

8. Click the **Custom** tab. In the Item box, choose **Hyperlink (Active)**. In the Color box, choose **Yellow**. The dialog box should look like Figure 2-10.

9. Click **OK** to return to the Themes dialog box. Click **All pages** and then click **OK** to make the modification on all pages.

10. A message appears asking if you want to save changes to the Blank theme. Click **Yes**. A Save Theme dialog box appears, as shown in Figure 2-11.

FIGURE 2-11
Save Theme dialog box

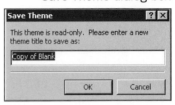

11. Key **Blank** followed by your initials and click **OK**. Click **Yes** if a message appears asking if you want to apply the theme. Leave the Web site open for the next Step-by-Step.

Adding Banners

Most Web pages begin with a banner, which is a title or description of the content on the page. If you have set up a navigation structure, the page title that appears in a banner is the same one that appears in Navigation view. This name is also the one that will be displayed in the title bar when viewed in a Web browser.

Display the page you want to construct and choose Page Banner from the Insert menu. The Page Banner Properties dialog box appears as shown in Figure 2-12. If you want the banner to include the picture of the banner (not text only), click Picture. Key the page title in the Page banner text box if you want to change it, then click OK.

FIGURE 2-12
Page Banner Properties dialog box

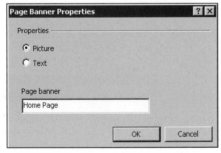

Computer Concepts

Changing the name of the page title on a banner also changes it on buttons if you have created a navigation bar.

STEP-BY-STEP ▷ 2.5

1. Click the page tab to display the index page if necessary.

2. Choose **Page Banner** from the **Insert** menu. The Page Banner Properties dialog box appears as shown in Figure 2-12.

3. Picture is selected and Home Page is displayed in the Page banner text box. Click **OK.** The banner appears on the page.

4. Click the **Center** button on the Fomatting toolbar to center the banner. Save the page.

5. Click the **adoption.htm** page tab in Page view to switch to the Adoption page. Choose **Page Banner** from the **Insert** menu. Key **Animals for Adoption** in the Page banner text box and click **OK.** Center the banner and save the page.

6. Switch to the contributions page and add a page banner with the title **Contributions**. Center the banner and save the page.

7. Switch to the links page and add a banner with the title Links. Center the banner and save the page. Leave the Web site open for the next Step-by-Step.

Adding a Navigation Bar

If your Web site contains more than one page, you will want your visitors to be able to go from one page to another. A navigation bar will allow the visitor to jump from page to page using links. To add a navigation bar, choose Navigation from the Insert menu. The Insert Web Component dialog box appears as shown in Figure 2-13.

FIGURE 2-13
Insert Web Component dialog box

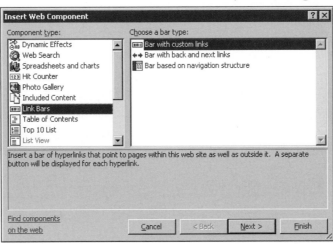

With Link Bars selected as the component type, choose a bar type in the Choose a bar type list in the pane on the right. Click Next and choose a bar style. Click Next and choose an orientation. Click Finish to add the navigation bar to your Web page. The Link Bar Properties dialog box appears, as shown in Figure 2-14.

FIGURE 2-14
Link Bars Properties dialog box

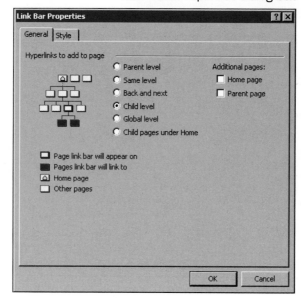

Select the hyperlink level that you want to add. Notice that the map next to the hyperlink levels changes to reflect whatever pages you have selected. You can choose to add the home page or parent page as additional links on the navigation bar.

STEP-BY-STEP ▷ 2.6

1. Switch to the index page. Press **Enter** twice to move the insertion point below the page banner.

2. Choose **Navigation** from the **Insert** menu. The Insert Web Component dialog box appears, as shown in Figure 2-13.

3. Links Bars is selected in the Component type box. Click **Bar based on navigation structure** in the Choose a bar type box. Click **Next**.

4. Use Page's Theme is selected in the Choose a bar style box. Click **Next**.

5. The horizontal orientation is selected in the Choose an orientation box. Click **Finish**. The Link Bar Properties dialog box appears, as shown in Figure 2-14.

7. Child level is selected. The Home Page box should not be selected. Click **OK**. The navigation bar appears on the page, which should look similar to Figure 2-15. Save the page.

8. Switch to the **adoption** page. Press **Enter**.

9. Insert a navigation bar as you did on the index page. In the Link Bar Properties dialog box, choose **Same level** and click **Home page**. Click **OK**. A navigation bar with four buttons appears on the page. Save the page.

10. Click on the navigation bar to select it. Choose **Copy** from the **Edit** menu.

11. Switch to the contributions page. Press **Enter**. Choose **Paste** from the **Edit** menu. Save the page. Leave the Web site open for the next Step-by-Step. (*Note:* You are not adding the navigation bar to the links page. You will be placing something different—an image map—on the links page in Step-by-Step 2.10.)

FIGURE 2-15
Page banner and navigation bar

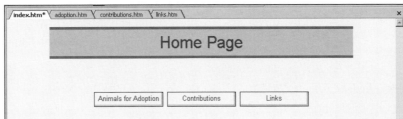

Adding and Formatting Text

You can add text to a page by keying or by copying it from another application. When keying text, press Shift+Enter to move to the next line and press Enter to start a new paragraph. You can apply formatting to text by using the buttons on the Formatting toolbar.

STEP-BY-STEP ⇒ 2.7

1. Switch to the index page and place the insertion point between the page banner and the navigation buttons.

2. Click the **Style** arrow list button on the Formatting toolbar, then select **Heading 1**. Key **Plains Animal Welfare Shelter**. Press **Enter**.

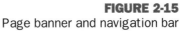

3. Key **(PAWS)**. Highlight the text you just keyed. Click the **Style** arrow list button on the Formatting toolbar and select **Heading 1**. Center the heading if necessary. Click to the right of the text to deselect it and press **Enter**.

4. Key the following text (press **Shift+Enter** after each line):

```
149 Knibloe Hill Road
Edmond, OK 73013
(405) 555-1285
```

5. Highlight the text you keyed in step 4. Click the **Style** arrow list button on the Formatting toolbar and select **Heading 3**. Center the text if it is not already. Deselect the text, move the insertion point to the line after the phone number, and press **Enter**.

6. Key the following text:

```
We maintain a lost and found list
for animals in the Edmond area. I
f you lose or find an animal,
please contact PAWS and provide
information about your animal. We
receive new animals every day, so
call daily to see if your pet has
been located.
```

7. Select text you just keyed and left align it. Click the font size down arrow on the Formatting toolbar and choose **2 (10 pt)**. Save the page.

8. Open the Word document **PF Step2-7** from the data files.

9. Choose **Select All** from the **Edit** menu. Choose **Copy** from the **Edit** menu. Close Word.

10. Switch to the contributions page. Move the insertion point between the page banner and the navigation bar.

11. Choose **Paste** from the **Edit** menu.

12. Select the list in the text you just pasted (from *Exercise and groom the animals* through *Maintain Web Site*) and click the **Bullets** button on the Formatting toolbar.

13. Save the page. It should look similar to Figure 2-16. Leave the Web open for the next Step-by-Step.

FIGURE 2-16
Formatted Web page text

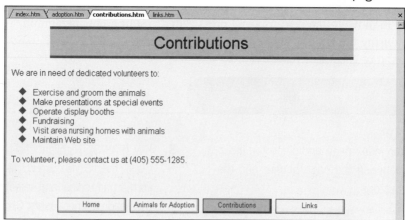

Adding Shared Borders

Shared borders is the area that a Web page has in common with other pages in the Web site. Shared borders makes it possible to put text, graphics, or other elements, like the current date, on all pages at once rather than editing each page individually. Add a shared border by choosing Shared Borders from the Format menu. The Shared Borders dialog box appears, as shown in Figure 2-17. Choose whether you want the shared borders applied to the current page or all pages and specify the location on the page. The area on your page designated as shared borders is indicated by a dotted line.

FIGURE 2-17
Shared Borders dialog box

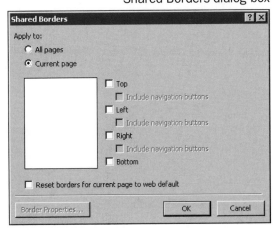

S TEP-BY-STEP ▷ 2.8

1. Switch to the **index** page. Place the insertion point below the navigation bar.

2. Choose **Shared Borders** from the **Format** menu. The Shared Borders dialog box appears, as shown in Figure 2-17.

3. Click **All pages** and **Bottom**. Click **OK**. A dotted line appears at the bottom of the page.

4. Click the Comment text in the shared border to select it.

5. Key the following text: **This page was last updated on:** making sure to include a space after the colon.

6. Choose **Date and Time** from the **Insert** menu. The Date and Time dialog box appears, as shown in Figure 2-18.

7. Click **OK** to insert the current date.

8. Select the text and the date and change the font size to **1 (8pt)**. Save the page.

9. Switch to the other pages to see that the shared border was inserted on them as well. Leave the Web site open for the next Step-by-Step.

FIGURE 2-18
Date and Time dialog box

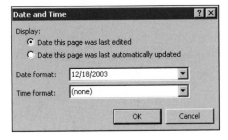

Adding a Photo Gallery

A photo gallery is used to display a series of photos or other images on a page. Choose Picture from the Insert menu and New Photo Gallery from the submenu. The Photo Gallery Properties dialog box appears, as shown in Figure 2-19. Click the Add button and you can choose to add pictures from files or from scanners or cameras. You can add captions and descriptions to your photos and change the order of images and their sizes. Click the layout tab to choose the layout.

FIGURE 2-19
Photo Gallery Properties dialog box

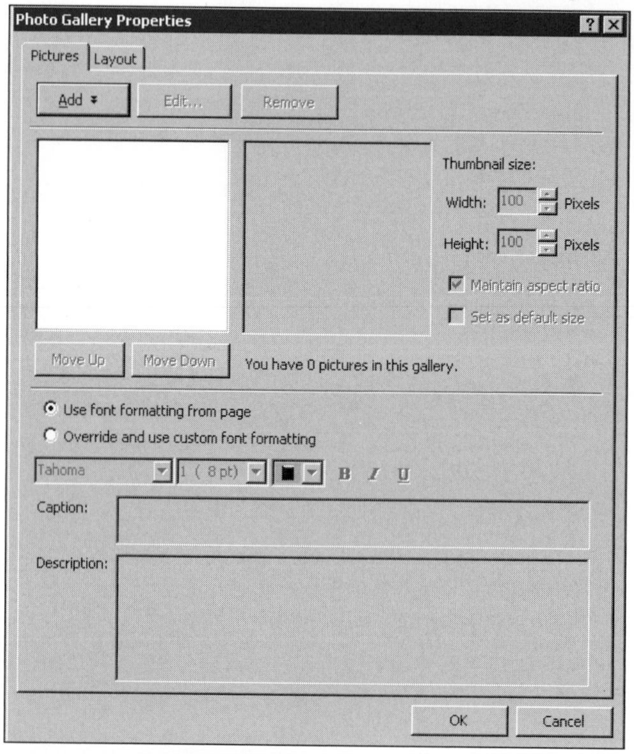

STEP-BY-STEP 2.9

1. Switch to the **adoption** page. Place the insertion point between the banner and the navigation bar. (Press **Enter** if necessary to insert a blank line.)

2. Choose **Picture** from the **Insert** menu and **New Photo Gallery** from the submenu. The Photo Gallery Properties dialog box appears, as shown in Figure 2-19.

3. Click the **Add** button and choose Pictures from Files. The File Open dialog box appears.

4. Locate **Beta.jpg** in the data files and click **Open**.

5. In the Caption box, key **Beta**.

6. In the Description box, key **Beta is a friendly Samoyed/Golden Retriever mix.**

7. Using the same method (repeating steps 3–6), add the following photos (the name of the file is the same as the caption name):

Caption: **Blake**
Description: **Blake is an independent cat of unknown origin.**

Caption: **Duke**
Description: **Duke is a sports-loving Collie.**

Caption: **Gizmo**
Description: **Gizmo is a kitten that was found in a parking lot.**

Caption: **Mohican**
Description: **Mohican is a German Shepherd/Chow mix puppy.**

Caption: **Ranger**
Description: **Ranger is a three-year-old Brittany Spaniel/Border Collie mix.**

8. Click the **Layout** tab. In the Choose a layout box, click **Vertical Layout**. In the Number of pictures per row box, click the down arrow and choose **3**. Click **OK**. Your page should look similar to Figure 2-20.

9. Save the page. The Save Embedded Files dialog box appears. Click the **Change Folder** button to display the Change Folder dialog box. (If the dialog box does not appear, just click **OK** and skip to step 11.)

10. Double-click the **images** folder to open it. Click **OK** and then click **OK** again.

Computer Concepts

If you insert a file from an outside source such as the Internet or a disk, FrontPage will save or embed that file into your current Web page.

11. Center the photo gallery, save the page, and leave the Web site open for the next Step-by-Step.

FIGURE 2-20
Page with Photo Gallery

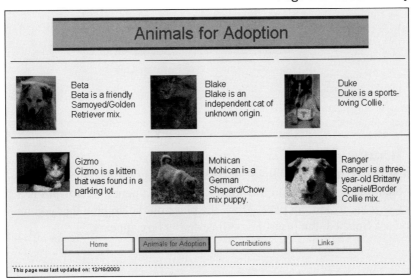

Adding a Table

Adding a table to a page is a good way to help lay out your page. It makes it much easier to align text or place a graphic where you want it on a page. By eliminating the table border you can even provide an invisible structure.

Choose Insert from the Table menu and Table from the submenu. The Insert Table dialog box appears, as shown in Figure 2-21. Cells can be inserted, deleted, or merged using the Table menu.

Adding Hyperlinks

A hyperlink allows you to jump from page to page within your Web site, or jump to another Web site. To insert a hyperlink on your page, select the text or graphic and choose Hyperlink from the Insert menu. The Insert Hyperlink dialog box appears on your screen, as shown in Figure 2-22. You can link to an existing file or Web page, to a place in the current document, or to an e-mail address. Click on a file or page and click OK. Or, if you know a page address, you can key it into the Address text box. You can also search for a page on the Internet by clicking on the Browse the Web button.

Computer Concepts

By choosing Rows or Columns, you can insert multiple cells at once.

FIGURE 2-21
Insert Table dialog box

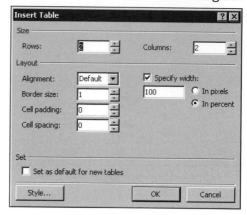

FIGURE 2-22
Insert Hyperlink dialog box

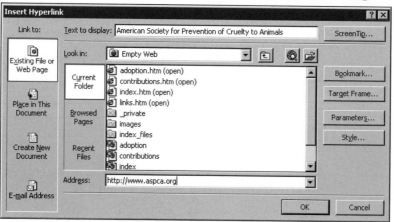

Adding an Image Map

An image map can be used to add links to a graphic. Select the graphic to display the Pictures toolbar. Click one of the hotspot buttons and the pointer becomes a pencil. A *hotspot* is a place on an image map that you click to jump to another page. Draw the place on the graphic that you want to be the hyperlink and when you are finished, the Insert Hyperlink dialog box appears.

1. Switch to the **links** page. Place the insertion point after the banner. (Press **Enter**, if necessary, to add a blank line.)

2. Choose **Insert** from the **Table** menu and **Table** from the submenu. The Insert Table dialog box appears, as shown in Figure 2-21.

3. In the Rows box, click the up arrow to display **3**. In the Alignment box, click the down arrow and choose **Center**. In the Specify width box, key **500** and click the **In pixels** button. In the Border size box, click the down arrow to display 0. Click **OK**.

4. Select the second column and right-click on the selected cells to display a shortcut menu. Choose **Cell Properties** and the Cell Properties dialog box appears.

Hot Tip

To select a column, drag to highlight it or place the insertion point in a cell and choose **Select** from the **Table** menu and **Column** from the submenu. You can also move your pointer to the top of the column where you will see it become a thick black down arrow and then click. The same process can be used for selecting rows.

5. Click the **Specify width** box, key **450**, and click **In pixels**. Click **OK**.

6. Select the first row spanning both columns and choose **Merge Cells** from the **Table** menu. The two cells are merged into one.

7. In the first row, key **Organizations** and bold it. In the second cell of the second row, key **American Society for Prevention of Cruelty to Animals**. In the second cell of the third row, key **American Pet Association**.

8. Place the insertion point in a cell on the bottom row. Choose **Insert** from the **Table** menu and **Rows or Columns** from the submenu. The Insert Rows or Columns dialog box appears, as shown in Figure 2-23.

FIGURE 2-23
Insert Rows or Columns dialog box

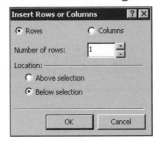

9. **Rows** and **Below selection** should be selected. In the Number of rows box, click the up arrow to display **9**. Click **OK**. Nine more rows of cells are added to the table.

10. Key the text in the rest of the table, merging the heading rows, as shown in Figure 2-24.

FIGURE 2-24
Completed Table

Organizations	
	American Society for Prevention of Cruelty to Animals
	American Pet Associations
Health	
	Pet Education
	Care for Pets
General	
	Pet City
	The Pet Channel

PF-33

11. Select the last row. Choose **Delete Cells** from the **Table** menu to delete the cells.

12. Select the text **American Society for Prevention of Cruelty to Animals**. Choose **Hyperlink** from the **Insert** menu to display the Insert Hyperlink dialog box.

13. In the Address box, key **www.aspca.org** as shown in Figure 2-22. Click **OK**. (Note that you do not need to type *http://* because it is automatically entered for you.)

14. Continue to add hyperlinks to the text as follows:

Text	Hyperlink
American Pet Association	www.apapets.com
Pet Education	www.peteducation.com
Care for Pets	www.avma.org/care4pets
PetCity	www.petcity.com
The Pet Channel	www.thepetchannel.com

Hot Tip

These are actual Web addresses; however, Web sites frequently change, and these may not be available when you publish your Web site.

15. Place the insertion point below the table. Insert the **imagemap** graphic from the data files. Click on the graphic to select it. The Pictures toolbar appears.

16. Click the **Rectangular Hotspot** button and the pointer turns to a pencil. Draw a square around the picture of a home (it does not have to be precise). When you are finished the Insert Hyperlink dialog box appears.

17. Click the **index.htm (open)** file in the list and click **OK**. The home picture on the graphic is now a link to the home page.

18. Using the same method, draw a hotspot around the animals and link it to the **adoption** page. Link the piggy bank to the **contributions** page and the computer to the **links** page.

19. Save the page. If the Save Embedded Files dialog box appears, click **OK**. Leave the Web site open for the next Step-by-Step.

Working with Graphic and Dynamic Elements

FrontPage contains many features that allow you to make your Web pages more interesting to view. You can insert an Office drawing, AutoShapes, and WordArt using the Drawing toolbar, just as you learned in Word. These graphics can be edited to fit your needs.

You can insert Web components such as hover buttons, hit counters, and marquees on your page by choosing Web Components from the Insert menu and choosing a component type in the Web Components dialog box. Some Web components will only be displayed properly once the page is published to a Web server.

1. Switch to the index page. Select the **(PAWS)** text.

2. Choose **Toolbars** from the **View** menu and **Drawing** from the submenu to display the Drawing toolbar at the bottom of the screen.

3. Click the **Insert WordArt** button on the toolbar to display the WordArt Gallery dialog box.

4. Click on the style three rows down and three columns over. Click **OK**. The Edit WordArt Text dialog box appears, as shown in Figure 2-25.

5. Click **OK**. The WordArt appears in the document with the WordArt toolbar displayed.

6. Click the **Format WordArt** button. The Format WordArt dialog box appears.

7. Click the down arrow in the Color box of the Line section and choose **Dark Blue**. Click **OK**.

8. Click the **Edit Text** button. The Edit WordArt Text dialog box appears.

9. In the Font box, choose **Arial** and click **OK**. Your screen should look similar to Figure 2-26.

10. Click the **Close** button (**X**) on the WordArt toolbar to close it.

11. Place the insertion point between the navigation bar and the shared border. Press **Enter** if necessary to enter a new line. Key **This page has been accessed times**.

12. Place the insertion point between the words *accessed* and *times*. Choose **Web Component** from the **Insert** menu to open the Insert Web Component dialog box.

13. In the Component type dialog box, choose **Hit Counter**. Click **Finish**. The Hit Counter Properties dialog box appears. Click **OK**. The [Hit Counter] placeholder is inserted.

14. Select the sentence you keyed, including the [Hit Counter] placeholder. Change the font size to **2 (10 pt)**.

15. Save the page and leave the Web site open for the next Step-by-Step.

FIGURE 2-25
Edit WordArt Text dialog box

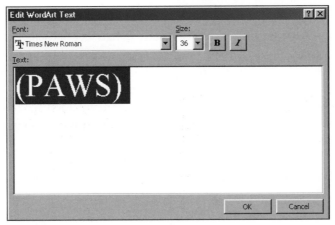

FIGURE 2-26
Edited graphic

Using FrontPage Views

FIGURE 2-27
New Task dialog box

You have already used Navigation and Page views in this lesson. Other views available on the Views bar are Folders, Reports, Hyperlinks, and Tasks. Folders view is used to organize files and folders. You can rename a file easily in this view. Reports view helps you analyze your Web site and manage its contents. Using Hyperlinks view, you can view hyperlinks to and from any page. Creating and managing tasks is done in Tasks view. To create a task, choose Tasks from the Edit menu and Add Task from the submenu. The New Task dialog box appears, as shown in Figure 2-27.

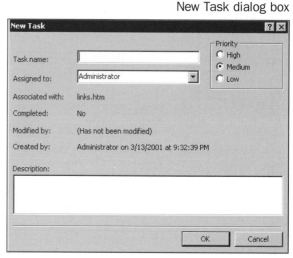

S TEP-BY-STEP ▷ 2.12

1. Click the **Folders** button on the Views bar. The files and folders in your Web site are displayed.

2. Right-click the **adoption** file in the Contents of list. Choose **Rename** from the menu that appears. Rename the page by keying **animals.htm** in the box and then click anywhere on the page. A message appears to let you know that there are pages that have hyperlinks to this page and asking if you want to update these pages so that the hyperlinks

are not broken. Click **Yes**. A brief message appears, as shown in Figure 2-28, showing that the file is being renamed.

FIGURE 2-28
Rename message

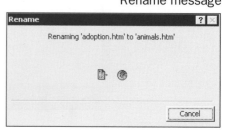

3. Double-click the **links** file to display it in Page view.

4. Click the **Hyperlinks** button on the View bar. All the links to and from the index page are displayed.

5. Click on the **links** file in the folder list to see the links to and from the links page, as shown in Figure 2-29.

6. Click the **Reports** button on the View bar. A site summary is displayed so you can manage your files.

7. Click the **Reports** arrow list button on the Reporting toolbar. Choose **Problems**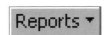

from the menu and **Broken Hyperlinks** from the submenu. If a message appears asking if you want FrontPage to verify your links, click **Yes**.

8. Choose **Save As** from the **File** menu. The Save As dialog box appears. Click **Save** to save the report in your Web site as **Broken Hyperlinks**.

FIGURE 2-29
Links View

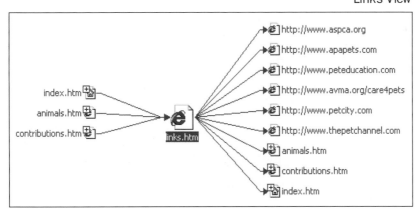

Lesson ② FrontPage Basics

9. Open up your browser and browse to locate the file you just saved. Choose **Open** from the **File** menu to see the report, as shown in Figure 2-30.

10. Choose **Print** from the **File** menu and then click **OK** to print the report. Close the browser.

11. Switch back to FrontPage in Page view and display the **links** page. Choose **Tasks** from the **Edit** menu and **Add Task** from the sub-menu. The New Task dialog box appears, as shown in Figure 2-27.

12. In the Task name box, key **Add links**. In the Assigned to box, key **Margaret Crawford**. In the Description box, key **Search Internet for new Web sites to add to the Links page**. In the Priority box, click **Low**. Click **OK**.

Hot Tip

When you create a task while editing a page in Page view, the task is automatically associated with that page.

13. Switch to the animals page and add another task with the following information.

Task name: **Update photo gallery.**

Assigned to: **Karen Ballinger**

Description: **Add photos of new animals and delete pictures of animals that were adopted.**

Priority: **High**

14. Click the **Tasks** Button. The tasks are displayed. Right-click the first task to display a shortcut menu. Choose **Mark Complete**. Notice the Status column changes for that task. Leave the Web site open for the next Step-by-Step.

FIGURE 2-30
Broken Hyperlinks Report

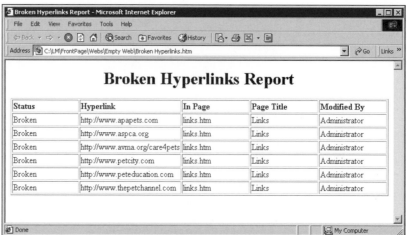

Publishing Webs

To view your completed Web page, click the Preview in Browser button on the toolbar. FrontPage will load your pages into the default browser on your computer, which allows you to see how your pages will look when they are published. To print a page, display it in the browser then choose Print from the File menu. To publish your pages to the Internet choose Publish Web from the File menu. The Publish Web dialog box appears and prompts you for the location to publish your Web pages.

S TEP-BY-STEP ▷ 2.13

1. Your Web pages are ready to be published. To view your pages as they will appear on a browser, click the **Preview in Browser** button on the toolbar. (Depending upon how your browser is set up, you may need to select the Web page you want to open from Windows Explorer.)

2. View all the pages of your Web site by clicking the Navigation Bar buttons. Click the **Home** button to return to the home page. Click each of the hyperlinks you created on the Links page to view them.

3. Print each page by displaying it and then choosing **Print** from the **File** menu in your browser. The Print dialog box appears. Click **OK**. Choose **Close** from the **File** menu to close your browser.

4. You may, following your instructor's directions, publish your Web pages by choosing **Publish Web** from the **File** menu and specifying the destination. Click **OK** to save your pages to your Web site.

5. Choose **Close Web** from the **File** menu in FrontPage to close your Web pages. Save any changes. Choose **Exit** from the **File** menu in FrontPage to exit the program.

Summary

In this lesson, you learned:

- FrontPage is an Office XP application that can help you create professional-looking Web pages. When you start FrontPage, a blank page appears in Page view.

- In Page view you can create a Web site, add pages, and edit your Web site. In Navigation view you can see the structure of your Web site and name pages.

- To add a theme to your Web pages, choose Theme from the Format menu. Click the Modify button to modify a theme. To add a banner to a Web page, choose Page Banner from the Insert menu.

- A navigation bar allows visitors to switch to another page in your Web site. Choose Navigation from the Insert menu.

- Text can be added to pages by keying or copying it from another application.

- Shared borders make it possible to put text or graphics on all pages at once. Choose Shared Borders from the Format menu.

- A photo gallery displays a series of images on a page. Choose Picture from the Insert menu and New Photo Gallery from the submenu.

- Tables can help organize your page. You can add, delete, or merge cells using the Table menu.

- Hyperlinks allow you to move around your Web site. To create hyperlinks, choose Hyperlinks from the Insert menu.

- Use the Pictures toolbar to turn a graphic into an image map. The hotspots you create become links to other pages.

- You can insert dynamic elements by choosing Web Components from the Insert menu.

- FrontPage views available to create, edit, organize, manage, and analyze your Web site are Page, Folders, Navigation, Reports, Hyperlinks, and Tasks.

- You can view your Web pages as they will look on the Internet by selecting the Preview in Browser button on the toolbar. To publish your Web pages to the Internet, select Publish Web from the File menu and key the destination.

VOCABULARY REVIEW

Define the following terms:

Hotspot	HyperText Markup Language	Themes
Hyperlinks	(HTML)	Web page

LESSON 2 REVIEW QUESTIONS

TRUE/FALSE

Circle T if the statement is true or F if the statement is false.

T F **1.** You can jump from one Web page to another by using hyperlinks.

T F **2.** A page banner can be added by clicking on the Insert menu.

T F **3.** Page view allows you to view the hierarchy of your Web pages.

T F **4.** Shared borders display a series of photos on a page.

T F **5.** Creating and managing tasks is done in Folders view.

WRITTEN QUESTIONS

Write a brief answer to the following questions.

1. List four of the ways to view your Web site in FrontPage.

2. Describe how to apply themes to your Web pages.

3. Which option do you choose in the New Page or Web task pane to create a new page?

4. What is the purpose of a navigation bar?

5. How do you view your Web page in a browser?

LESSON 2 PROJECTS

PROJECT 2-1

1. Start FrontPage and open the **PF Project2-1** Web site from the data files.

2. Switch to Navigation view. Add a new page to the Web site titled Mission.

3. Open the Mission page in Page view. Add a banner with the page title Our Mission and center it.

4. Add the following text, formatted as you wish:

   ```
   To offer medical care, nourishment, and refuge to animals in our community.
   To protect them from suffering because of cruelty, carelessness, or neglect;
    or accidents through education, example, and enforcement.
   To encourage neutering and spaying to prevent overpopulation.
   To maximize community resources (financial contributions and volunteers) for
    the prevention of animal abuse.
   ```

5. Insert a horizontal navigation bar after the text that includes the home page.

6. Save the page, view it in your browser, and print it.

7. Switch to the links page. Add a new row of cells to the bottom of the table. Key PetsHub.com and link it to www.petshub.com. Save the page.

8. Leave the Web site open for the next project.

PROJECT 2-2

1. Change the theme on all the pages to Expedition.

2. Open the contributions page in Page view. Place the insertion point after the last line of text.

3. Open **PF Project2-2** from the data files. Copy the text and paste it on the contributions page. Select the list items and format them as a bulleted list.

4. Save the page, view it in your browser, and print it.

5. Switch to the links page. Delete the image map and replace it with a horizontal navigation bar that includes the home page.

6. Open the home page and add a new task with this information:

   Task name: Replace logo

   Assigned to: Kirby Wells

   Description: Replace logo on home page with new PAWS logo.

   Priority: High

7. Save the page, close all pages, and exit FrontPage.

CRITICAL THINKING

SCANS

ACTIVITY 2-1

Create a Web site about yourself or an organization to which you belong that has at least three pages. Include at least two of the following features: navigation bar, page banners, image map, table, theme, Web component, or photo gallery.

ACTIVITY 2-2

Use Microsoft FrontPage Help to learn how to insert a marquee on a Web page. Write a brief paragraph explaining the process, and then insert a marquee on a page of the Web site you just created.

COMMAND SUMMARY

Publisher

FEATURE	MENU COMMAND	TOOLBAR BUTTON	LESSON
Enlarge documents	View, Zoom		1
Open existing files	File, Open		1
Print file	File, Print		1
Save file	File, Save		1

FrontPage

FEATURE	MENU COMMAND	TOOLBAR BUTTON	LESSON
Align Left			2
Apply theme	Format, Theme		2
Banners	Insert, Page Banner		2
Bold		**B**	2
Bullets	Format, Bullets and Numbering		2
Center			2
Create a Web page	File, New, Page or Web		2
Folder List	View, Folder List		2
Folders View	View, Folders		2
Font Size	Format, Font	2 (10 pt)	2
Hyperlinks	Insert, Hyperlinks		2
Hyperlinks View	View, Hyperlinks		2
Navigation View	View, Navigation		2
Open existing Web pages	File, Open		2
Page View	View, Page		2
Preview pages	File, Preview in Browser		2
Print Web pages	File, Print		2
Publish Web pages	File, Publish Web		2
Reports View	View, Reports		2
Save Web pages	File, Save		2
Start FrontPage	Start, Programs, Microsoft FrontPage		2
Tasks View	View, Tasks		2

TRUE/FALSE

Circle T if the statement is true or F if the statement is false.

T F   1.   To add a picture to a Publisher project, click the + key on the View menu.

T F   2.   In Publisher, you should use the By Design Sets option to create a layout for special events, such as holidays.

T F   3.   Using the From existing publication option allows you to create a series of documents that include the same design, information, and logo.

T F   4.   Web pages are connected by hyperlinks that allow you to move around a Web site.

T F   5.   In FrontPage, it is best to add new Web pages in Tasks view.

WRITTEN QUESTIONS

Write a brief answer to the following questions.

1.   List at least three documents that you can create with Publisher.

2.   What type of information can be updated in Publisher's Personal Information dialog box?

3.   Describe how to add a banner to a FrontPage Web page.

4.   What is the purpose of a shared border?

5. Describe how to add a hyperlink to a Web page.

PROJECTS

PROJECT 1

1. Start Microsoft Publisher and create a business card with the **Bars** design.

2. Save the publication as **AppCard** followed by your initials.

3. Use the Business Card Wizard to change the design from **Bars** to **Checkers**.

4. Change the logo design to **Suspended Rectangle.**

5. Change the Orientation to **Portrait.**

6. Click on the items in the new business card and adjust the text layout and font sizes if necessary to make the card easier to read.

7. Save the publication, print multiple copies of the card per sheet, and close the file.

PROJECT 2

1. Create a thank you card for a new customer. Open Microsoft Publisher, and select the Greeting Cards Wizard.

2. Choose **Accent Box Thank You Card.**

3. Save the publication as **Thanks** followed by your initials.

4. Click **Select a Suggested Verse.** The Suggested Verse dialog box appears.

5. In the Suggested Verse dialog box, click **Thanks for your business.** Notice that the message will be applied to the front and an accompanying message will appear in the inside of your card. Click OK.

6. Click **page 2 or page 3** icon in the Page Navigation buttons at the bottom of the screen.

7. Click on the Thank You text on page 2 to highlight it.

8. Click the **Center** button, and change the font size to 16.

9. Key the following text in the text placeholder:

   ```
   We appreciate your recent purchase from Computer Solutions. Remember that
   all of our sales and services are backed by a 100% guarantee. We are open
   from 8:00 a.m. to 6:00 p.m., Monday — Saturday, to serve you.
   ```

10. Click the page navigation buttons at the bottom of the screen to view your card.

11. Save, print, and close the file.

SIMULATION

Your employer at Java Internet Café has created a Web page to advertise the store on the Internet. You are asked to create a postcard mailer for customers announcing the Web address.

JOB 1

1. Open Publisher, and click the **Postcards Wizard.**

2. Select **Informational,** and then choose **Marquee Informational Postcard.**

3. In the Size section of the task pane, Quarter-page should be chosen. In the Side 2 information section, Address only should be chosen. In the Copies per sheet section, One should be chosen.

4. Save the publication as **Postcard** followed by your initials.

5. Choose **Personal Information** from the **Edit** menu to open the Personal Information dialog box. Delete the data already in the boxes and key the following information in the appropriate text boxes.

   ```
   Java Internet Café
   2001 Zephyr
   Boulder, CO
   Phone: 303-555-JAVA
   E-mail: JavaCafe@Cybershop.com
   ```

6. Click **Update** to close the dialog box.

7. Click the Computer Solutions logo to select it. Choose **Delete Object** on the **Edit** menu.

8. Double-click the picture of pears on your postcard. In the Insert Clip Art section of the task pane, search for coffee and insert any resulting clip you want. (If there are no coffee pictures in the Clip Art archives, insert the coffee picture from the data files.)

9. Click in the text box underneath the coffee picture, and key the following text (you may have to reduce the font size to make it fit).

Relax with friends, enjoy a great cup of coffee, and surf the net at
the Java Internet Café. We now have seven new computers with broadband
Internet access.

We are pleased to announce our new Web site. Check us out at:
www.JavaCafe.Cybershop.com

10. Center the text you just keyed.

11. Save the postcard, print, and close the file.

JOB 2

Your employer at Java Internet Café has asked you to add a page to the store's current Web site that includes the prices of the coffee served and the membership prices. The page should include a banner and the pages should be linked together.

1. Open FrontPage. Using the task pane, open the Web folder labeled **Job 2** from the data files, and then open the index file.

2. Change to Navigation view and change the name of the **index.htm** page to Home Page.

3. Add a new page named Prices. Display it in Page view.

4. Add the Pixel theme to all pages.

5. Insert and center a banner on the Prices page called **Menu and Prices**.

6. Insert a horizontal navigation bar below the banner that links to the home page. Center the bar.

7. Under the navigation bar, insert a centered table 600 pixels wide with 4 columns and no border, and then key the following text. Add rows and merge cells as needed.

Coffee Prices

House coffee	$1.50	Café breve	$3.25
Café au lait	$2.50	Café latte	$3.25
Cappuccino	$2.75	Con panna	$3.50
Espresso	$3.00	Espresso doppio	$3.75

Access Prices

Membership fee	includes own account with personal ID, password, and e-mail address	$10 per month
Internet access	includes World Wide Web, FTP, and IRC plus e-mail	$12 per hour
Color Scanner	includes Internet access, use of software, and the CD-ROM library	$7 per 1/2 hour
Laser printer	inquire about copying capabilities	$.35 per page

8. Switch to the home page and insert a navigation bar at the bottom of the page that links to the Prices page.

9. Save both pages and preview them in your browser. Print both pages and close the Web site.

CAPSTONE SIMULATION

Introduction

Throughout this book, you have learned to use Word, Excel, Access, PowerPoint, and Outlook. In this business simulation, you will utilize the skills learned in each Office XP application.

First, you will modify a presentation in PowerPoint. Then you will use Word to create a form letter that will advertise Great Day Lawn Care Service. A calendar will be generated with Outlook. Access will be used to maintain address and billing information for customers. Excel will be used to calculate and maintain data on earnings and expenses. You will integrate Access and Word to create a billing form and form letter that will be sent to customers. In addition, you will create a Web page.

BACKGROUND

You started Great Day Lawn Care Service last spring. You spent the warm months of the year (mid-May to mid-September) caring for ten lawns in the neighborhood. You offered the following services:

- Lawn mowing
- Edging
- Hedge clipping
- Watering

In September, several customers asked you about continuing your services the following year. In addition, a few neighbors of your current customers inquired about care for their lawns for the next year.

As the summer approaches, you are making plans to continue the lawn care business. You know that if you increase the number of lawns you mow and edge, you will need some extra help. In fact, with two more workers, you could finish each job faster. Since you own two mowers and one edger, all machines could be operated simultaneously and each job would be completed in approximately one-third the time.

MAY 1

You are thinking of asking two friends, Tracy and Jordan, to help you with Great Day Lawn Care Service. You have been working on a PowerPoint presentation to show them the business.

1. Open PowerPoint and the **Presentation** file from the data files.

2. Save the file as **GDPresentation** followed by your initials.

3. Insert a new slide after slide 6 with the Title and Text layout. Key the title and text as shown in Figure 1-1. (After keying the Advantages, press **Shift+Tab** to move the text back one level.)

FIGURE 1-1

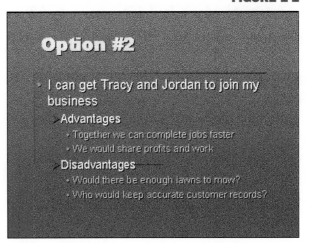

4. Change the title of slide 8 to **Option #3**.

5. Change the title of slide 6 to **Option #1**.

6. Display the first slide and then use Slide Show view to show the presentation.

7. Print the presentation as handouts with six slides per page.

8. Save, close, and exit PowerPoint.

Tracy and Jordan agree to join you in business. The three of you agree to work together and split the profits (giving you a greater share since everyone will be using your equipment). You begin a brainstorming session to solve the anticipated problems of the new business and all decide that Microsoft Office can help generate business, bill customers, and monitor profits.

MAY 3

The three of you compile the addresses that appear in Figure 1-2. Names are available for some of the addresses because they were your customers the previous year. Other names are taken from mailboxes. If names are unavailable, the word "Resident" is used. All addresses are in the city of Smyrna, GA 30080.

FIGURE 1-2

Title	Last Name	First Name	Address	City, State, ZIP	Fee
Mr.	Dye	Allen	200 Thistle	Smyrna, GA 30080	$15.00
Mr.	Dunsten	A.	201 Thistle	Smyrna, GA 30080	$20.00
Mr.	Mata	Ricardo	203 Thistle	Smyrna, GA 30080	$15.00
Mr.	Neman	John	204 Thistle	Smyrna, GA 30080	$22.00
Mr.	Rigby	Eddy	205 Thistle	Smyrna, GA 30080	$22.00
Mr.	Wolfe	James	206 Thistle	Smyrna, GA 30080	$22.00
Mr.	Carter	John	207 Thistle	Smyrna, GA 30080	$15.00
Ms.	Sanchez	Christina	208 Thistle	Smyrna, GA 30080	$15.00
Ms.	Marcus	Lois	209 Thistle	Smyrna, GA 30080	$20.00
Ms.	Lake	Jasmine	210 Thistle	Smyrna, GA 30080	$20.00
Mr.	Torres	Ruben	211 Thistle	Smyrna, GA 30080	$20.00
Ms.	Mueller	Anne	212 Thistle	Smyrna, GA 30080	$15.00
Resident			213 Thistle	Smyrna, GA 30080	$15.00
Mr.	Roberts	Chad	214 Thistle	Smyrna, GA 30080	$15.00
Ms.	Johnson	Virginia	215 Thistle	Smyrna, GA 30080	$15.00

FIGURE 1-2
(continued)

Title	Last Name	First Name	Address	City, State, ZIP	Fee
Ms.	Novack	D. K.	216 Thistle	Smyrna, GA 30080	$15.00
Mr.	Keung	Y.	217 Thistle	Smyrna, GA 30080	$15.00
Mr.	Schultz	Jason	218 Thistle	Smyrna, GA 30080	$15.00
Mr.	Robinson	T.J.	219 Thistle	Smyrna, GA 30080	$15.00
Ms.	Estes	Jaunita	220 Thistle	Smyrna, GA 30080	$15.00
Mr.	Reynolds	Clay	200 Kilt	Smyrna, GA 30080	$22.00
Ms.	Richards	Della	201 Kilt	Smyrna, GA 30080	$22.00
Mr.	Malcolm	R.J.	202 Kilt	Smyrna, GA 30080	$22.00
Ms.	Patel	Nina	203 Kilt	Smyrna, GA 30080	$22.00
Mr.	Cash	H. J.	204 Kilt	Smyrna, GA 30080	$22.00
Ms.	Phillips	Paula	205 Kilt	Smyrna, GA 30080	$22.00
Mr.	Moody	Mark	206 Kilt	Smyrna, GA 30080	$22.00
Mr.	Harper	G.H.	207 Kilt	Smyrna, GA 30080	$22.00
Mr.	Montoya	E. B.	208 Kilt	Smyrna, GA 30080	$22.00
Resident			209 Kilt	Smyrna, GA 30080	$22.00
Ms.	Strawser	L. T.	210 Kilt	Smyrna, GA 30080	$22.00
Mr.	Piper	Nate	211 Kilt	Smyrna, GA 30080	$20.00
Mr.	Williams	R. B.	212 Kilt	Smyrna, GA 30080	$20.00
Mr.	Hix	Jordan	213 Kilt	Smyrna, GA 30080	$20.00
Mr.	Guy	D. P.	214 Kilt	Smyrna, GA 30080	$20.00
Mr.	Carver	Alton	215 Kilt	Smyrna, GA 30080	$20.00
Ms.	Ellis	J. B.	216 Kilt	Smyrna, GA 30080	$20.00
Ms.	Liu	Lini	217 Kilt	Smyrna, GA 30080	$20.00
Mr.	Lauer	Corey	218 Kilt	Smyrna, GA 30080	$20.00
Mr.	Aslam	Ritu	219 Kilt	Smyrna, GA 30080	$20.00
Ms.	Gibb	H. T.	220 Kilt	Smyrna, GA 30080	$20.00
Mr.	Leon	Steven	200 Plaid	Smyrna, GA 30080	$15.00
Mr.	Gold	Richard	201 Plaid	Smyrna, GA 30080	$15.00
Mr.	Edge	A. V.	202 Plaid	Smyrna, GA 30080	$15.00
Mr.	Shell	Charles	203 Plaid	Smyrna, GA 30080	$15.00
Mr.	Valdez	Robert	204 Plaid	Smyrna, GA 30080	$20.00
Mr.	Yarbrough	Frank	205 Plaid	Smyrna, GA 30080	$20.00
Mr.	Sims	Trevor	206 Plaid	Smyrna, GA 30080	$20.00
Mr.	Terrell	Kevin	207 Plaid	Smyrna, GA 30080	$20.00
Resident			208 Plaid	Smyrna, GA 30080	$20.00
Ms.	Johnson	Veronica	209 Plaid	Smyrna, GA 30080	$20.00
Ms.	Levine	Heather	210 Plaid	Smyrna, GA 30080	$20.00
Mr.	Womack	David	211 Plaid	Smyrna, GA 30080	$15.00
Resident			213 Plaid	Smyrna, GA 30080	$15.00
Ms.	Yapp	B. J.	214 Plaid	Smyrna, GA 30080	$15.00
Ms.	Page	Misha	215 Plaid	Smyrna, GA 30080	$15.00
Ms.	Taylor	Vicky	216 Plaid	Smyrna, GA 30080	$15.00
Mr.	Sutton	Forrest	217 Plaid	Smyrna, GA 30080	$15.00
Mr.	Smith	Charles	218 Plaid	Smyrna, GA 30080	$15.00
Ms.	Ruff	Keesha	219 Plaid	Smyrna, GA 30080	$15.00

Use these addresses to create a database that will supply addresses for the advertising letter and the billing form.

The three partners estimate a charge for their services based on the size of the lawn.

1. Create a new Access database named **Neighbors**. Create a new table using Design view. Define the following fields.

Field	Data type	Description
Title	Text	Title
Last Name	Text	Customer's Last Name
First Name	Text	Customer's First Name
Address	Text	Customer's Address
City, State, ZIP	Text	Customer's City, State, and ZIP
Fee	Currency	Amount to charge for this customer's lawn

2. Save and name the table **Potential Customers**. (No primary key is needed.)

3. Open the table in Datasheet view and enter the data shown in Figure 1-2. Adjust the widths of the fields appropriately. (*Hint*: You may use the Copy and Paste commands to enter Smyrna, GA 30080 in the City, State, ZIP field of each record.)

4. Save the table and the database file.

MAY 4

Tracy writes a form letter, shown in Figure 1-3, to advertise the services of Great Day Lawn Care Service. You design a letterhead template. The letter will be personalized by merging the names and addresses of potential customers in the database with the form letter.

FIGURE 1-3

May 4, ----

«Title» «First_Name» «Last_Name»
«Address»
«City_State_ZIP»

Dear «Title» «Last_Name»

Great Day Lawn Care Service is a partnership of friends. We would like to care for your lawn on a weekly basis and perform the following services:

Lawn Mowing
Edging
Hedge Clipping
Watering

We are prepared to offer these services to you at a cost of «Fee» per week, billed monthly. We are conscientious, guarantee all of our work, and will provide references in your neighborhood.

If you would like to employ our services or if you have any questions, please contact us at 555-3894.

Sincerely

Student's name   Tracy Ruthart   Jordan Perry

1. Open Word.

2. Design a letterhead template for Great Day Lawn Care Service to be used with the letter in Figure 1-3. Include in the letterhead the name of the company, as well as the following address and telephone number:
   221 Kilt Avenue
   Smyrna, GA 30080
   404-555-3894

   You should add a graphic to the letterhead using Clip Art or the Drawing tools. Save the document as a template in the Office XP templates folder (your program directory may be named something else). Name it **Letterhead Template**. Close the file.

3. Open the **Letterhead Template** file as a Word document. Save it as **Form Letter**. Key in the form letter as shown in Figure 1-3. Do not key the merge fields. Later you will put the merge fields in the form letter to pull data from the database file into the word processing file.

4. Save and leave the document open.

MAY 5

You need to print the form letters only for those for whom you don't have names so you can distribute them door-to-door.

1. The Form Letter document should be on your screen. Save it as Resident Letters. Use the Mail Merge task pane to merge the Resident Letters document with data from the Potential Customers table in the Neighbors database.

2. Edit the Recipient list to merge only those with Resident in the Title field. (There should be four records.)

3. Insert the merge fields as shown in Figure 1-3.

4. Merge and print Resident Letters.

5. Save and close the file.

MAY 6

Anticipating a response to the letters, Jordan suggests that the billing information for the month of May be set up.

Create a worksheet to figure and track billing. Columns will be created to show the amount owed by each customer for each week. For example, 3-May will contain the amount owed for the third week in May. May Bill will contain the total amount owed by the customer for the month of May, and May Paid will contain the amount paid by the customer for the month of May.

1. Open a new Excel worksheet.

2. Save the worksheet as **Billing** followed by your initials.

3. In A1, key **3-May**.

4. In B1, key **4-May**.

5. In C1, key **May Bill**.

6. In D1, key **May Paid**.

7. Enter a formula in C2 to total the bill for May. It should contain the sum of the amounts in the 3-May and 4-May fields.

8. Copy the formula down to C61.

9. Save and close the document.

MAY 7

The three of you decide to create a Web page announcing your services. Use FrontPage, the Web Page Wizard in Word, or create a Web presentation and save it as HTML. Use the logo and some of the text from the form letter on your page. Print and close the document.

MAY 8

The following people (mostly former customers) have notified you that they would like to employ the services of Great Day Lawn Care Service:

Carver, Alton   Phillips, Paula
Cash, H. J.   Piper, Nate
Guy, D. P.   Strawser, L. T.
Harper, G. H.   Williams, R. B.

In addition, the residents of 209 Kilt, Mr. Tom Alfreds, and 213 Thistle, Ms. Lillian Spears, have employed Great Day Lawn Care Service.

1. Switch to Access.

2. Insert the following new fields in the Potential Customers table of the Neighbors database.

Field	Data Type	Description
Cust	Yes/No	Is this a customer?
May Bill	Currency with 2 decimal places	Amount owed for May

3. The residents of 209 Kilt and 213 Thistle were not known when the database was created. Edit the Title, Last Name, and First Name fields to show their correct names.

4. Indicate the people who are now customers by clicking to insert a check mark in the Cust field box of your Access database. Since the database is large, you may want to use the Find command or sort the database alphabetically by last name to help you find customers.

5. Save the table.

MAY 9

In anticipation of billing new customers, Jordan drafts a billing form to be put in a word processing file. A copy of the draft is in Figure 1-4.

FIGURE 1-4

Great Day Lawn Care Service

221 Kilt Avenue
Smyrna, GA 30080
404-555-3894

June 2, ——

Charges for the Month of May

«Title» «First_Name» «Last_Name»
«Address»
«City_State_ZIP»

We have calculated your May bill based on our agreed amount of «Fee» per week.
The total charge for May is «May_Bill».

Please make your check payable to "Great Day Lawn Care Service." Payment is
due by June 10.

Thank you for your business.

1. Switch to Word.

2. Open the **Letterhead Template** file as a document. Save the file as **Bill form**.

3. Key the billing form from Figure 1-4 into the file. Do not insert the merge fields yet.

4. Save and close the file.

MAY 10

Several more people have notified you that they would like to employ the services of Great Day
Lawn Care Service for the summer:

Mata, Ricardo	Gold, Richard
Sanchez, Christina	Edge, A. V.
Lake, Jasmine	Valdez, Robert
Mueller, Anne	Yarbrough, Frank
Novack, D. K.	Johnson, Veronica
Robinson, T. J.	Yapp, B. J.
Lauer, Corey	Page, Misha

Switch to Access and indicate that these people are customers by inserting a check mark in the Cust
field of the Potential Customers table.
Save the table.

MAY 11

For planning purposes, you decide to create a calendar.

1. Open Outlook.

2. Use the Date Navigator to go to **May 2003**.

3. View the entire month by choosing **Month** from the **View** menu.

4. Insert appointments on the days shown in Figure 1-5 by clicking on the day and keying the tasks.

FIGURE 1-5

Calendar					May 2003
Monday	Tuesday	Wednesday	Thursday	Friday	Sat/Sun
April 28	29	30	May 1	2	3
					4
5	6	7 / Income Stmt	8	9 / Service Equipment	10
					11
12	13	14	15 / Get Gas/Ice / Mow Lawns	16 / Get Gas/Ice / Update Billing	17
					18
19 / Mow Lawns / Update Billing	20	21	22 / Get Gas/Ice / Mow Lawns	23 / Mow Lawns / Update Billing	24
					25
26 / Mow Lawns / Update Billing	27	28	29	30	31
					June 1

5. Print the monthly calendar. Be sure to choose the dates 5/1/03 to 5/31/03 in the print range.

6. Exit Outlook without saving.

MAY 12

An income statement will be prepared each month to report the profits of Great Day Lawn Care Service. Figure 1-6 is a draft of the income statement for the month of May. All three partners agree that the income statement will give them the information needed to evaluate the progress of their business venture.

1. Switch to Excel and set up an income statement, as shown in Figure 1-6, for the month of May.

2. Save the file as **Income Statement**. Computed fields and amounts will be added to the income statement later.

FIGURE 1-6

	A	B	C	D
1	GREAT DAY LAWN CARE SERVICE			
2	INCOME STATEMENT			
3	FOR THE MONTH ENDING MAY 31,——			
4				
5	REVENUES			
6				
7	Collected Lawn Care Revenues			
8	Uncollected Lawn Care Revenues			
9				
10	TOTAL REVENUES			
11				
12	EXPENSES			
13				
14	Gasoline			
15	Mower Repair and Maintenance			
16	Trailer Repair and Maintenance			
17	Refreshments and Ice			
18	Computer Supplies			
19	Misc. Expenses			
20				
21	TOTAL EXPENSES			
22				
23	NET INCOME			
24				

MAY 14

More residents have notified you that they want the services of Great Day Lawn Care for the summer:

Dye, Allen   Liu, Lini
Richards, Della   Gibb, H. T.

The residents of 208 Plaid, Mr. Reginald Hinkle, and 213 Plaid, Ms. Misty Lobo, have also employed the service.

1. Switch to Access.

2. The residents of 208 Plaid and 213 Plaid were not known when the database was originally created. Edit the fields to show their correct names.

3. Indicate that these people are customers by inserting a check mark in the Cust field of the Potential Customers table.

4. Save the table.

MAY 16

You want to be sure your equipment is in good shape before the summer begins. You take your lawn care equipment into the mower repair shop for servicing. The cost of servicing is $105.34. You also buy a new tire and brake light for the trailer. The total cost for these items is $89.75.

1. Switch to Excel and the **Income Statement** file. Record the expense for Mower Repair and Maintenance in column B. Record the trailer costs as Trailer Repair and Maintenance.

2. Format column B for accounting with 2 decimal places and $ as the symbol.

3. Save the file.

MAY 21

The lawns of the following customers have been serviced.

Dye	Gold
Mata	Edge
Sanchez	Valdez
Lake	Yarbrough
Mueller	Johnson
Novack	Yapp
Robinson	Page

1. Switch to Access and create a filter to show only those customers with a check mark in the Cust field. (*Hint*: Key **Yes** in the *Criteria* field. Do not use quotes.)

2. Sort the Last Name field in ascending order. Save the table.

3. Switch to Excel and open the **Billing** file. Insert three new columns to the left of column A.

4. Switch to Access and the Potential Customers table. Copy the Last Name, Address, and Fee columns from the filter to the three new columns in the Billing file in that order. (If you get the message: "Data on the Clipboard is not the same size and shape as the selected area, paste anyway?" click **OK**.)

5. Adjust field widths in the Billing file as needed.

6. In the **Billing** file, enter the amounts (listed in the Fee column) owed by the customers listed above in the 3-May column. Format C2:D31 for accounting with 2 decimal places and $ as the symbol.

7. In row 1, center and boldface the headings and change the cell color to No Color. Remove the borders from A1 through C31.

8. Save the file.

9. Switch to the **Income Statement** file and enter **$10.13** in column B for gasoline. Enter **$15.12** in column B for refreshments and ice.

10. Save the file.

MAY 24

The lawns of the following customers have been serviced.

Richards	Carver
Cash	Liu
Phillips	Lauer
Harper	Gibb
Strawser	Alfreds
Piper	Hinkle
Williams	Lobo
Guy	Spears

1. Switch to the **Billing** file and enter the amounts owed by each customer in the 3-May field.

2. Save the file.

3. Switch to the **Income Statement** file and add $6.33 to the existing amount in the Gasoline expense column. The $10.13 in the gasoline account should be replaced with the formula =10.13+6.33. Add $6.56 to the existing amount in the Refreshments and Ice column. The $15.12 in the refreshments and ice account should be replaced with the formula =15.12+6.56.

4. Save the file.

MAY 28

The lawns of the following customers have been mowed and edged.

Dye	Sanchez
Mata	Lake
Richards	Mueller
Cash	Spears
Gold	Hinkle
Edge	Johnson
Valdez	Lobo
Yarbrough	Page

1. Switch to the **Billing** file and enter the amounts owed by the customers in the 4-May column.

2. Format E2:G31 for accounting with 2 decimal places and $ as the symbol. Save the file.

3. Switch to the **Income Statement** file and add $10.18 for gasoline, and $6.78 for refreshments and ice to the previously recorded amounts in the expense column.

4. Save the file.

MAY 30

During May, $30.15 was spent on printer paper, and $20.51 of miscellaneous expenses were incurred.

1. Record the amount for computer supplies and miscellaneous expenses to the **Income Statement** file under the appropriate account names.

2. Save the file.

MAY 31

The lawns of the following customers have been serviced.

Novack	Liu
Robinson	Lauer
Phillips	Gibb
Harper	Yapp
Alfreds	Strawser
Piper	Williams
Guy	Carver

1. Switch to the **Billing** file and enter the amounts owed by the customers in the 4-May column. Save the file.

2. Switch to the **Income Statement** file and add $9.76 for gasoline and $6.90 for refreshments and ice to the previously recorded amounts in the expenses column.

3. Save the file.

JUNE 2

The three partners decide to prepare the bills for the month of May. The bills are printed and distributed door-to-door.

1. Switch to Access and the **Neighbors** database.

2. With the Customers filter still in effect, sort by Last Name in ascending order if necessary.

3. Switch to Excel. Copy the amounts in the May Bill column (F2 through F31) of the Billing file. Switch to Access. Click the **May Bill** field name of the **Potential Customers** table to highlight the entire field. Paste the data into the May Bill field. You will get the message: "You are about to paste 30 records. Are you sure you want to paste these records?" Click **Yes**.

4. Open **Bill form** in Word. Save it as **SNBills**.

5. Use the Mail Merge Task Pane to merge the SNBills document with data from the Potential Customers table in the Neighbors database. Edit the Recipient list to merge only the billing forms for Spears and Novack.

6. Insert the merge fields as shown in Figure 1-4.

7. Merge and print **SNBills**.

8. Save and close the file. Exit Word.

JUNE 3

The following customers were at home when the bills were distributed and promptly paid the amounts due.

Dye	Guy
Mata	Lauer
Lake	Gold
Novack	Valdez
Robinson	Yarbrough
Cash	Hinkle
Alfreds	Lobo
Piper	Yapp
Williams	Page

Switch to Excel and record the collection of these amounts in the May Paid column of the Billing worksheet. Save the file.

JUNE 8

The following customers have delivered checks to Great Day Lawn Care Service.

Phillips   Harper
Strawser   Liu
Sanchez   Gibb
Spears   Johnson

1. Record the collection of these amounts in the Billing worksheet in the *May Paid* column.

2. Save the file.

JUNE 9

Tracy wonders about the unpaid bills. Calculate the amounts billed to the customers and the amounts actually received.

1. In the **Billing** file, clear F32 through F63.

2. In A33, key **Totals**.

3. Enter a formula in F33 to sum the May Bill column. Format the cell for accounting with 2 decimal places and $ as the symbol.

4. Copy the formula to G33.

5. In A35, key **Uncollected**.

6. In B35, enter a formula to subtract the total May Paid from the total of May Bill. Format the cell for accounting with 2 decimal places and $ as the symbol.

7. Boldface A33, A35, B35, F33, and G33.

8. Save, print, and close the file. (Print only A1 through G35).

JUNE 10

Great Day Lawn Care Service has now compiled the data for the first month of operations. The partners want to know if they made a profit during May. They want copies of the May income statement to assess their progress.

1. Switch to the file **Income Statement**. This file already contains updated expenses for May.

2. In B7, key **960** and in B8, key **144**.

3. In C10, enter a formula to total the Collected Lawn Care Revenues and the Uncollected Lawn Care Revenues.

4. In C21, enter a formula to total all the expenses.

5. In C23, enter rmula to find the difference between the *Total Revenues* and *Total Expenses*.

6. Format column C for accounting with 2 decimal places and $ as the symbol.

7. Save, print, and close the file. Exit Excel.

8. Close all other open Office applications.

APPENDIX A

THE MICROSOFT® OFFICE USER SPECIALIST PROGRAM

What Is Certification?

The logos on the cover of this book indicate that the book is officially certified by Microsoft Corporation at the **core** user skill level for Office XP in Word, Excel, Access, Outlook, and FrontPage, and at the **core** and **expert** levels for PowerPoint. This certification is part of the **Microsoft Office User Specialist (MOUS)** program that validates your skills as knowledgeable of Microsoft Office.

The following grids outline the various skills and where they are covered in this book.

MICROSOFT WORD 2002 CORE

	Skill Set and Skills Being Measured	Lesson #	Page #(s)	Exercise #
W2002-1	**Inserting and Modifying Text**			
W2002-1-1	Insert, modify, and move text and symbols	1, 2, 3, 7, 8	IW–6, 24, 25, 33, 47, 49, 163	SBS1.2, 2.5, 2.6 P2–3, P2–4, SBS2.6, P2–1, SBS3.1, SBS3.10, SBS3.11, P3–1, P3–2, SBS7.2, P7–1, SBS8.16
W2002-1-2	Apply and modify text formats	4	IW–55, 56, 57, 58, 59	SBS4.1, P4–1, P4–4, SBS4.2, SBS4.3
W2002-1-3	Correct spelling and grammar usage	3	IW–38, 39, 40, 41, 42, 43, 45	SBS3.5, SBS3.6, SBS3.7, P3–2, SBS3.9 P3–1, P3–3
W2002-1-4	Apply font and text effects	4, 8	IW–60, 61, 158	SBS4.4, P4–1, P4–3, SBS4.5, P4–2, P4–4, SBS8.13
W2002-1-5	Enter and format Date and Time	3	IW–44	SBS3.8
W2002-1-6	Apply character styles	4	IW–55, 56, 57, 58, 59, 63, 64	SBS4.1 SBS4.2 SBS4.3 P4–1, P4–4

	Skill Set and Skills Being Measured	Lesson #	Page #(s)	Exercise #
W2002-2	**Creating and Modifying Paragraphs**			
W2002-2-1	Modify paragraph formats	5, 6	IW–69, 70, 74, 92	SBS5.2, P5.3, SBS5.3, P5–2, P5–4, SBS5.5, P5–3, SBS6.2, SBS6.3, P6–1, P6–3
W2002-2-2	Set and modify tabs	5	IW–75	SBS5.7, P5–2
W2002-2-3	Apply bullet, outline, and numbering format to paragraphs	5, 7	IW–77, 79, 132	SBS5.8, P5–1, P5–4, SBS5.9, P5–5, SBS7.16, SBS7.18, P7–4
W2002-2-4	Apply paragraph styles	7	IW–126	SBS7.10, P7–2
W2002-3	**Formatting Documents**			
W2002-3-1	Create and modify a header and footer	7	IW–121	SBS7.7, P7–1, P7–2
W2002-3-2	Apply and modify column settings	6	IW–90	SBS6.1, P6–1
W2002-3-3	Modify document layout and Page Setup options	1, 5, 7	IW–13, 67, 116, 123	SBS1.8, P1–2, P1–4, SBS5.1, P5.1, SBS7.3, P7–1
W2002-3-4	Create and modify tables	7	IW–127, 128, 129, 130, 131	SBS7.11, P7–3, SBS7.12, SBS7.13, P7–3, SBS7.14, SBS7.15, P7–3
W2002-3-5	Preview and Print documents, envelopes, and labels	1, 8	IW–10, 12, 152, 154	SBS1.6, P1–2, P1–4, SBS1.7, P1–3, SBS8.9, SBS8.10, P8–2
W2002-4	**Managing Documents**			
W2002-4-1	Manage files and folders for documents	1	IW–8	SBS1.4
W2002-4-2	Create documents using templates	8	IW–141, 142, 143, 144, 145	SBS8.1, SBS8.2, SBS8.3, P8–1
W2002-4-3	Save documents using different names and file formats	1	IW–8, 17, 18	SBS1.4, P1–2, P1–3, P1–4
W2002-5	**Working with Graphics**			
W2002-5-1	Insert images and graphics	6	IW–96, 97, 98, 99, 100, 101, 102, 103	SBS6.4, P6–1, P6–3
W2002-5-2	Create and modify diagrams and charts	6	IW–104, 105, 106, 110	SBS6.11, SBS6.12, SBS6.13, P6–4

	Skill Set and Skills Being Measured	Lesson #	Page #(s)	Exercise #
W2002-6	**Workgroup Collaboration**			
W2002-6-1	Compare and Merge documents	8	IW–151	SBS8.8
W2002-6-2	Insert, view, and edit comments	8	IW–147, 148, 149	SBS8.5
W2002-6-3	Convert documents into Web pages	8	IW–157, 159	SBS8.12, SBS8.13, P8–3

MICROSOFT EXCEL 2002 CORE

	Skill Set and Skills Being Measured	Lesson #	Page #(s)	Exercise #
EX2002-1	**Working with Cells and Cell Data**			
EX2002-1-1	Insert, delete, and move cells	2, 3	IE–26, 46, 47	SBS3.5, P3–2, P3–5, P3–7, SBS3.4, P3–4
EX2002-1-2	Enter and edit cell data including text, numbers, and formulas	1, 2, 4, 5	IE–9, 11, 30, 64, 82	SBS1.5, P1–2, P1–3, P1–4, SBS1.6, SBS4.1, SBS4.2, SBS4.3, SBS4.4, SBS4.5, P4–2, P4–3, P4–4, P4–5, CT4–1, CT4–2
EX2002-1-3	Check spelling	3	IE–54	SBS3.9, P3–3
EX2002-1-4	Find and replace cell data and formats	1, 2	IE–7, 13, 34	SBS1.7, P1–4, SBS1.3, SBS2.11
EX2002-1-5	Work with a subset of data by filtering lists	6	IE–103	SBS6.2, P6–3
EX2002-2	**Managing Workbooks**			
EX2002-2-1	Manage workbook files and folders	1	IE–5, 14	SBS1.2
EX2002-2-2	Create workbooks using templates	6	IE–114	SBS6.8, P6–5, CT6–1
EX2002-2-3	Save workbooks using different names and file formats	1, 6	IE–5, 118	SBS1.8, P1–2, P1–3, P1–4, SBS6.8, SBS6.10
EX2002-3	**Formatting and Printing Worksheets**			
EX2002-3-1	Apply and modify cell formats	2	IE–30	0SBS2.6, SBS2.7, SBS2.8, P2–2, P2–3, P2–4, P2–5
EX2002-3-2	Modify row and column settings	3, 6	IE–47, 48, 105	SBS3.5, P3–2, P3–5, P3–7, SBS6.3, P6–4, SBS3.6 P3–3, P3–5

	Skill Set and Skills Being Measured	Lesson #	Page #(s)	Exercise #
EX2002-3-3	Modify row and column formats	2	IE–22, 26	SBS2.1, P2–2, P2–3, P2–5, P2–6, SBS2.3, SBS2.4, SBS2.5, P2–4
EX2002-3-4	Apply styles	2	IE–32	SBS2.9
EX2002-3-5	Use automated tools to format worksheets	2	IE–33	SBS2.10
EX2002-3-6	Modify Page Setup options for worksheets	3	IE–50, 52	SBS3.7, P3–3, P3–4, P3–5, P3–6
EX2002-3-7	Preview and print worksheets and workbooks	3, 7	IE–52, 53, 135	SBS3.8, SBS7.2, P7–1, P7–2, P7–3, P7–4, SBS7.3
EX2002-4	**Modifying Workbooks**			
EX2002-4-1	Insert and delete worksheets	7	IE–131	SBS7.2
EX2002-4-2	Modify worksheet names and positions	7	IE–130, 131	SBS7.2, P7–1, P7–2, P7–3, P7–4
EX2002-4-3	Use 3-D references	7	IE–132	SBS7.3, P7–1, P7–2, P7–3, P7–4
EX2002-5	**Creating and Revising Formulas**			
EX2002-5-1	Create and revise formulas	4	IE–66, 67, 69	SBS4.3, SBS4.5, P4–3, P4–4, SBS4.1, SBS4.6, SBS4.4, P4–5
EX2002-5-2	Use statistical, date and time, financial, and logical functions in formulas	5	IE–84	SBS5.1, SBS5.2, SBS5.3, SBS5.4, SBS5.5, P5–2, P5–3, P5–4, P5–5, P5–6
EX2002-6	**Creating and Modifying Graphics**			
EX2002-6-1	Create, modify, position, and print charts	8	IE–146, 147	SBS8.1, SBS8.2, SBS8.3, SBS8.4, SBS8.5, SBS8.6, SBS8.7, SBS8.8, P8–1, P8–2, P8–3, P8–4, P8–5, P8–6, P8–7, P8–8, CT8–1, SBS8.9, SBS8.10

	Skill Set and Skills Being Measured	Lesson #	Page #(s)	Exercise #
EX2002-6-2	Create, modify, and position graphics	6	IE–106	SBS6.4, SBS6.5, SBS6.6, SBS6.7, P6–6, CT6–2
EX2002-7	**Workgroup Collaboration**			
EX2002-7-1	Convert worksheets into Web pages	6	IE–119	SBS6.10
EX2002-7-2	Create hyperlinks	6	IE–117	SBS6.9
EX2002-7-3	View and edit comments	6	IE–120, 121	SBS6.11, P6–7, SBS6.12

MICROSOFT ACCESS 2002 CORE

	Skill Set and Skills Being Measured	Lesson #	Page #(s)	Exercise #
AC2002-1	**Creating and Using Databases**			
AC2002-1-1	Create Access databases	1	IA–9	ExtraChallenge, SBS1.4
AC2002-1-2	Open database objects in multiple views	1	IA–6, 10, 16	SBS1.3, SBS1.5, SBS1.9
AC2002-1-3	Move among records	1, 2	IA–16, 26	SBS1.9, SBS2.1
AC2002-1-4	Format datasheets	2	IA–30, 31, 32, 38, 39	SBS2.5, SBS2.6, SBS2.7, SBS2.8, P2–1, P2–2, P2–3
AC2002-2	**Creating and Modifying Tables**			
AC2002-2-1	Create and modify tables	1	IA–10, 12, 14, 21, 22, 23, 24	Hot Tip, CT1–1, SBS1.5, SBS1.6, SBS1.8, P1–2, P1–3, P1–4
AC2002-2-2	Add a pre-defined input mask to a field	2	IA–35	SBS2.9
AC2002-2-3	Create Lookup fields	1	IA–12	SBS1.6
AC2002-2-4	Modify field properties	2	IA–35, 38, 39	SBS2.9, P2–1, P2–3
AC2002-3	**Creating and Modifying Queries**			
AC2002-3-1	Create and modify Select queries	4	IA–66	SBS4.4, SBS4.3, P4–1, P4–4
AC2002-3-2	Add calculated fields to select queries	4	IA–64	SBS4.3
AC2002-4	**Creating and Modifying Forms**			
AC2002-4-1	Create and display forms	3	IA–42, 43, 44, 46, 58, 59	SBS3.1, SBS3.2, SBS3.3, SBS3.4, P3–1, CT3–1, SBS3.5, P3–3

	Skill Set and Skills Being Measured	Lesson #	Page #(s)	Exercise #
AC2002-4-2	Modify form properties	3	IA–50, 53, 58	SBS3.7, SBS3.8, P3–2
AC2002-5	**Viewing and Organizing Information**			
AC2002-5-1	Enter, edit, and delete records	1, 2, 3	IA–16, 21, 23, 26, 28, 29, 38, 39, 40, 58	SBS1.9, P1–1, P1–2, P1–4, P2–3, CT2–1, SBS3.6, SBS2.1, SBS2.3, SBS2.4, SBS3.6, P2–1, P2–2, CT2–1, P3–1
AC2002-5-2	Create queries	4	IA–64, 66	SBS4.4, SBS4.3
AC2002-5-3	Sort records	4	IA–71, 82	SBS4.6, P4–2
AC2002-5-4	Filter records	4	IA–69, 82	SBS4.5, P4–2, P4–3
AC2002-6	**Defining Relationships**			
AC2002-6-1	Create one-to-many relationships	4	IA–74	SBS4.10
AC2002-6-2	Enforce referential integrity	4	IA–74	SBS4.10
AC2002-7	**Producing Reports**			
AC2002-7-1	Create and format reports	5	IA–85, 102, 103, 104	SBS5.1, SBS5.2, SBS5.3, SBS5.4, SBS5.5, P5–1, P5–2, CT5–1
AC2002-7-2	Add calculated controls to reports	5	IA–93	SBS5.7
AC2002-7-3	Preview and print reports	5	IA–91, 93, 102	SBS5.6, SBS5.7, P5–1
AC2002-8	**Integrating with Other Applications**			
AC2002-8-1	Import data to Access	6	IA–106	SBS6.1
AC2002-8-2	Export data from Access	6	IA–109, 111, 112, 119, 120, 121	SBS6.2, SBS6.3, SBS6.4, P6–1, P6–2, P6–3, CT6–1
AC2002-8-3	Create a simple data Access page	6	IA–115, 121	SBS6.5, P6–4

MICROSOFT POWERPOINT 2002 COMPREHENSIVE

	Skill Set and Skills Being Measured	Lesson #	Page #(s)	Exercise #
PP2002-1	**Creating Presentations**			
PP2002-1-1	Create presentations (manually and using automated tools)	2	IP–17	SBS2.1, SBS2.2
PP2002-1-2	Add slides to and delete slides from presentations	2, 4	IP–30, 79	SBS2.12, SBS4.7

	Skill Set and Skills Being Measured	Lesson #	Page #(s)	Exercise #
PP2002-1-3	Modify headers and footers in the Slide Master	2	IP–39	SBS2.18
PP2002-2	**Inserting and Modifying Text**			
PP2002-2-1	Import text from Word	4	IP–70	SBS4.1
PP2002-2-2	Insert, format, and modify text	2, 4	IP–24, 26, 71, 96	SBS2.6, SBS2.8, SBS2.10
PP2002-3	**Inserting and Modifying Visual Elements**			
PP2002-3-1	Add tables, charts, clip art, and bitmap images to slides	2	IP–33, 43, 97	SBS2.14, SBS3.1
PP2002-3-2	Customize slide backgrounds	2	IP–20	SBS2.4
PP2002-3-3	Add OfficeArt elements to slides	2	IP–33	SBS2.14
PP2002-3-4	Apply custom formats to tables	4	IP–67, 75	SBS3.6
PP2002-4	**Modifying Presentation Formats**			
PP2002-4-1	Apply formats to presentations	4	IP–70	SBS4.1
PP2002-4-2	Apply animation schemes	2	IP–20	SBS1.3
PP2002-4-3	Apply slide transitions	2	IP–40, 43	SBS2.19
PP2002-4-4	Customize slide formats	4	IP–70	SBS3.2
PP2002-4-5	Customize slide templates	4	IP–75	SBS4.5
PP2002-4-6	Manage a Slide Master	2	IP–22	SBS2.5
PP2002-4-7	Rehearse timing	4	IP–85	SBS4.12
PP2002-4-8	Rearrange slides	4	IP–43, 79	SBS4.7
PP2002-4-9	Modify slide layout	2	IP–20, 31	SBS2.4, SBS2.13
PP2002-4-10	Add links to a presentation	2	IP–37	SBS2.16
PP2002-5	**Printing Presentations**			
PP2002-5-1	Preview and print slides, outlines, handouts, and speaker notes	2	IP–26, 96, 97	SBS1.9, SBS2.7
PP2002-6	**Working with Data from Other Sources**			
PP2002-6-1	Import Excel charts to slides	4	IP–73	SBS4.4
PP2002-6-2	Add sound and video to slides	2	IP–38, 43	SBS2.17
PP2002-6-3	Insert Word tables on slides	4	IP–75, 97	SBS4.5
PP2002-6-4	Export a presentation as an outline	2, 4	IP–41, 77	SBS2.20 SBS4.6
PP2002-7	**Managing and Delivering Presentations**			
PP2002-7-1	Set up slide shows	4	IP–85	SBS4.11
PP2002-7-2	Deliver presentations	4	IP–83	SBS4.10
PP2002-7-3	Manage files and folders for presentations	4	IP–87	SBS4.14
PP2002-7-4	Work with embedded fonts	4	IP–86	SBS4.13
PP2002-7-5	Publish presentations to the Web	4	IP–89, 96	SBS4.15, P4–1
PP2002-7-6	Use Pack and Go	4	IP–87	SBS4.14
PP2002-8	**Workgroup Collaboration**			
PP2002-8-1	Set up a review cycle	4	IP–92	SBS4.17
PP2002-8-2	Review presentation comments	4	IP–93	SBS4.18
PP2002-8-3	Schedule and deliver presentation broadcasts	4	IP–91	SBS4.16
PP2002-8-4	Publish presentations to the Web	4	PI–89, 96	SBS4–15, P4–1

MICROSOFT OUTLOOK 2002 CORE

	Skill Set and Skills Being Measured	Lesson #	Page #(s)	Exercise #
OL2002-1	**Creating and Viewing Messages**			
OL2002-1-1	Display and print messages	1	IO–10, 23	SBS1.4, P1–2
OL2002-1-2	Compose and send messages to corporate/workgroup and Internet addresses	1	IO–15, 16	SBS1.7, SBS1.8
OL2002-1-3	Insert signatures and attachments	1	IO–16, 17, 24	SBS1.8, SBS1.9, P1–3
OL2002-1-4	Customize views	1	IO–7	SBS1.3
OL2002-2	**Scheduling**			
OL2002-2-1	Add appointments, meetings, and events to the Outlook calendar	2	IO–29, 33, 41, 42, 43	SBS2.2, SBS2.5, P2–1, P2–3, CT2–1
OL2002-2-2	Apply conditional formats to the Outlook calendar	2	IO–29, 42	SBS2.2, P2–2
OL2002-2-3	Respond to meeting requests	2	IO–36	SBS2.7
OL2002-2-4	Use categories to manage appointments	2	IO–29, 31	SBS2.2, SBS2.3
OL2002-2-5	Print calendars	2	IO–38	SBS2.8
OL2002-3	**Managing messages**			
OL2002-3-1	Move messages between folders	1	IO–19	SBS1.11
OL2002-3-2	Search for messages	1	IO–20	SBS1.12
OL2002-3-3	Save messages in alternate file formats	1	IO–20	SBS1.12
OL2002-3-4	Use categories to manage messages	1	IO–10	SBS1.4
OL2002-3-5	Set message options	1	IO–10	SBS1.4
OL2002-4	**Creating and Managing Contacts**			
OL2002-4-1	Create and edit contacts	1	IO–4, 23	SBS1.1, P1–1
OL2002-4-2	Organize and sort contacts	1, 3	IO–5, 24, 60	SBS1.2, CT1–1, CT3–2
OL2002-4-3	Link contacts to activities and journal entries	1, 3	IO–4, 53	SBS1.1, SBS3.5
OL2002-5	**Creating and Managing Tasks and Notes**			
OL2002-5-1	Create and update tasks	3	IO–44, 46, 59	SBS3.1, SBS3.2, P3–1
OL2002-5-2	Modify task organization and Task view	3	IO–46, 50	SBS3.2, SBS3.3
OL2002-5-3	Accept, decline, or delegate tasks	3	IO–51	SBS3.4
OL2002-5-4	Create and modify notes	3	IO–54, 60	SBS3.6, P3–3
OL2002-5-5	Use categories to manage tasks and notes	3	IO–44, 46	SBS3.1, SBS3.2

MICROSOFT FRONTPAGE 2002 CORE

	Skill Set and Skills Being Measured	Lesson #	Page #(s)	Exercise #
FP2002-1	**Creating and Modifying Web Sites**			
FP2002-1-1	Create and manage a FrontPage Web	2	PF–20	SBS2.2
FP2002-1-2	Create and Preview Web pages	2	PF–38	SBS2.2, P2–1
FP2002-1-3	Open, view, and rename Web pages	2	PF–22	SBS2.3
FP2002-1-4	Rename a Web page	2	PF–36	SBS2.12

	Skill Set and Skills Being Measured	Lesson #	Page #(s)	Exercise #
FP2002-1-5	Change the title for a Web page on banners and buttons	2	PF–25	SBS2.5
FP2002-2	**Importing Web Content**			
FP2002-2-1	Insert text and images	2	PF–27	SBS2.7
FP2002-2-2	Insert Office Drawings, AutoShapes, and WordArt	2	PF–34	SBS2.11
FP2002-3	**Formatting Web Pages**			
FP2002-3-1	Apply text and paragraph formats	2	PF–27	SBS2.7, P2–1
FP2002-3-2	Insert hyperlinks	2	PF–32	SBS2.10
FP2002-3-3	Insert a date using shared borders	2	PF–29	SBS2.8
FP2002-3-4	Create and edit tables	2	PF–32	SBS2.10
FP2002-3-5	Apply Web themes	2	PF–24	SBS2.4, P2–2
FP2002-4	**Formatting Web Pages**			
FP2002-4-1	Edit graphic elements	2	PF–35	SBS2.11
FP2002-4-2	Create image maps	2	PF–33	SBS2.10
FP2002-4-3	Add a FrontPage Web component to a Web page	2	PF–35	SBS2.11
FP2002-4-4	Add a Photo Gallery	2	PF–30	SBS2.9
FP2002-5	**Organizing and Viewing FrontPage Web Sites**			
FP2002-5-1	Use FrontPage views	2	PF–36	SBS2.12
FP2002-5-2	Manage Web structures	2	PF–22	SBS2.3
FP2002-5-3	Organize Web files	2	PF–36	SBS2.12
FP2002-5-4	Manage tasks	2	PF–37	SBS2.12, P2–2
FP2002-6	**Managing Web sites**			
FP2002-6-1	Publish a Web page	2	PF–38	SBS2.13
FP2002-6-2	Create Custom Reports	2	PF–38	SBS2.12

Key: SBS = Step-by-Step   CT = Critical Thinking Activity   P = Project

APPENDIX B

WINDOWS BASICS

This appendix is designed to familiarize you with the Windows 98, Windows Me and Windows 2000 operating systems. It provides you with the basic information you need to move around your desktop and manage the files, folders, and other resources you work with on a daily basis. It also covers the Windows Help system.

Starting Windows

If Windows is already installed, it should start automatically when you turn on the computer. If your computer is on a network, you may need some help from your instructor.

STEP-BY-STEP ▷ B.1

1. Turn on the computer.

2. After a few moments, Microsoft Windows 98, Windows Me, or Windows 2000 appears.

The Mouse

A mouse is a device that rolls on a flat surface and has one or more buttons on it. The mouse allows you to communicate with the computer by pointing to and manipulating graphics and text on the screen. The *pointer*, which appears as an arrow on the screen, indicates the position of the mouse. The four most common mouse operations are point, click, double-click, and drag. These operations are outlined below:

Point–Moving the mouse pointer to a specific item on the screen.

Click–Pressing the mouse button and quickly releasing it while pointing to an item on the screen. (The term *click* comes from the noise you hear when you press and release the button.)

Double-click–Clicking the mouse button twice quickly while keeping the mouse still.

Drag–Pointing to an object on the screen, pressing and holding the left mouse button, and moving the pointer while the button is pressed. Releasing the button ends the drag operation.

The Desktop

When Windows starts up, the desktop displays on the screen. The *desktop* is the space where you access and work with programs and files. Figure B-1 illustrates a typical desktop screen. Your screen may vary slightly from those shown in the figures. For example, your screen may display icons that were installed with Windows or shortcut icons you've created. You can customize and organize your desktop by creating files, folders, and shortcuts.

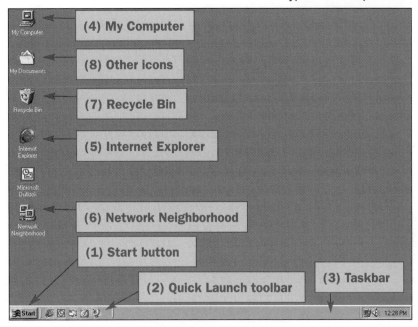

The main features of the desktop screen are labeled and numbered on the figure and discussed below:

1. The *Start* button brings up menus that give you a variety of options, such as starting a program, opening a document, finding help, or shutting down the computer.

2. The *Quick Launch* toolbar to the right of the Start button contains icons so you can display the desktop or quickly start frequently used programs.

3. The *taskbar*, located at the bottom of the screen, tells you the names of all open programs.

4. *My Computer* is a program that allows you to see what files and folders are located on your computer.

5. *Internet Explorer* is a Web browser that allows you to surf the Internet, read e-mail, create a Web page, or download your favorite Web sites right to your desktop.

6. *Network Neighborhood* (Windows 98) and *My Network Places* (Windows Me and Windows 2000) show all the folders and printers that are available to you through the network connection, if you have one.

7. The *Recycle Bin* is a place to get rid of files or folders that are no longer needed.

8. Other *icons*, or small pictures, represent programs waiting to be opened.

Windows makes it easy to connect to the Internet. Just click the Launch Internet Explorer Browser button on the Quick Launch toolbar. The Quick Launch toolbar also has buttons so you can launch Outlook Express, view channels, and show the desktop.

With Windows you can incorporate Web content into your work by using the Active Desktop, an interface that lets you put "active items" from the Internet on your desktop. You can use *channels* to customize the information delivered from the Internet to your computer. By displaying the Channel bar on your desktop you can add, subscribe to, or view channels.

1. Click the **Launch Internet Explorer Browser** button on the Quick Launch toolbar.

2. Click the **Show Desktop** button on the Quick Launch toolbar to display the Windows desktop.

3. Click the **Internet Explorer** button on the taskbar to return to the browser window.

4. Choose **Close** on the **File** menu to close Internet Explorer.

5. Point to the **Start** button.

6. Click the left mouse button. A menu of choices appears above the Start button as shown in Figure B-2.

7. Point to **Settings**, and then click **Control Panel** on the submenu. A new window appears. The title bar at the top tells you that Control Panel is the name of the open window. Leave this window on the screen for the next Step-by-Step.

FIGURE B-2
Start menu in Windows Me

Using Windows

Many of the windows you will work with have similar features. You can work more efficiently by familiarizing yourself with some of the common elements, as shown in Figure B-3, that are explained below.

1. A *title bar* is at the top of every window and contains the name of the open program, window, document, or folder.

2. The *menu bar* lists available menus from which you can choose a variety of commands.

3. The *standard toolbar*, located directly below the menu bar, contains commands you can use by simply clicking the correct button.

4. The *Address bar* tells you which folder's contents are being displayed. You can also key a Web address in the Address bar without first opening your browser.

5. At the bottom of the window is the *status bar* that gives you directions on how to access menus and summarizes the actions of the commands that you choose.

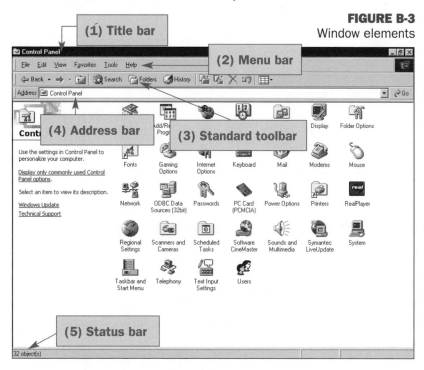

FIGURE B-3
Window elements

Moving and Resizing Windows

Sometimes you will have several windows open on the screen at the same time. To work more effectively, you may need to move or change the size of a window. To move a window, click the title bar and drag the window to another location. You can resize a window by dragging the window borders. When you position the pointer on a horizontal border, it changes to a vertical two-headed arrow. When you position the pointer on a vertical border, it changes to a horizontal two-headed arrow. You can then click and drag the border to change the width or height of the window. It is also possible to resize two sides of a window at the same time. When you move the pointer to a corner of the window's border, it becomes a two-headed arrow pointing diagonally. You can then click and drag to resize the window's height and width at the same time.

S TEP-BY-STEP ▷ B.3

1. Move the Control Panel window by clicking on the title bar and holding the left mouse button down. Continue to hold the left mouse button down and drag the Control Panel until it appears to be centered on the screen. Release the mouse button.

2. Point anywhere on the border at the bottom of the Control Panel window. The pointer turns into a vertical two-headed arrow.

3. While the pointer is a two-headed arrow, drag the bottom border of the window down to enlarge the window.

4. Point to the border on the right side of the Control Panel window. The pointer turns into a horizontal two-headed arrow.

5. While the pointer is a two-headed arrow, drag the border of the window to the right to enlarge the window.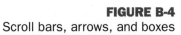

6. Point to the lower right corner of the window border. The pointer becomes a two-headed arrow pointing diagonally.

7. Drag the border upward and to the left to resize both sides at the same time until the window is about the same size as the one shown in Figure B-4.

8. Leave the window on the screen for the next Step-by-Step.

FIGURE B-4
Scroll bars, arrows, and boxes

Scroll Bars

A *scroll bar* appears on the edges of windows any time there is more to be displayed than a window can show at its current size (see Figure B-4). A scroll bar can appear along the bottom edge (horizontal) and/or along the right side (vertical) of a window. Scroll bars appeared in the last step of the preceding Step-by-Step because the window was too small to show all the icons at once.

Scroll bars are a convenient way to bring another part of the window's contents into view. On the scroll bar is a sliding box called the *scroll box*. The scroll box indicates your position within the window. When the scroll box reaches the bottom of the scroll bar, you have reached the end of the window's contents. *Scroll arrows* are located at the ends of the scroll bar. Clicking on a scroll arrow moves the window in that direction one line at a time.

1. On the horizontal scroll bar, click the scroll arrow that points to the right. The contents of the window shift to the left.

2. Press and hold the mouse button on the same scroll arrow. The contents of the window scroll quickly across the window. Notice that the scroll box moves to the right end of the scroll bar.

3. You can also scroll by dragging the scroll box. Drag the scroll box on the horizontal scroll bar to the left.

4. Drag the scroll box on the vertical scroll bar to the middle of the scroll bar.

5. The final way to scroll is to click on the scroll bar. Click the horizontal scroll bar to the right of the scroll box. The contents scroll left.

6. Click the horizontal scroll bar to the left of the scroll box. The contents scroll right.

7. Resize the Control Panel until the scroll bars disappear. Leave the window open for the next Step-by-Step.

Other Window Controls

Three other important window controls, located on the right side of the title bar, are the Maximize button, the Minimize button, and the Close button (see Figure B-5). The Maximize button enlarges a window to the full size of the screen. The Minimize button shrinks a window to a button on the taskbar. The button on the taskbar is labeled and you can click it any time to redisplay the window. The Close button is used to close a window.

When a window is maximized, the Maximize button is replaced by the Restore button (see Figure B-6). The *Restore button* returns the window to the size it was before the Maximize button was clicked.

FIGURE B-5
Maximize, Minimize, and Close buttons

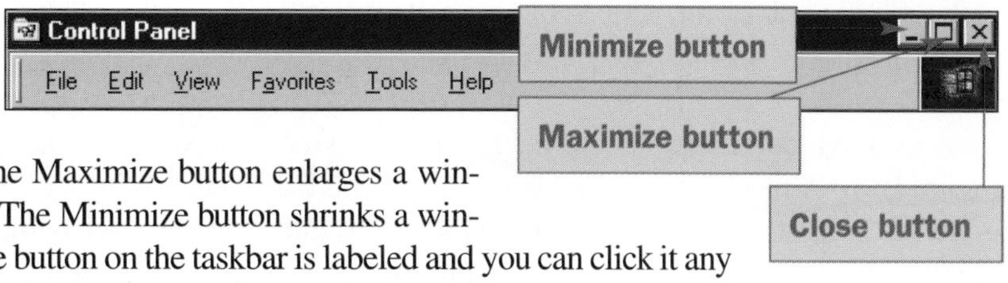

FIGURE B-6
Restore button

1. Click the **Maximize** button. The window enlarges to fill the screen.

2. Click the **Restore** button on the Control Panel window (see Figure B-6).

3. Click the **Minimize** button on the Control Panel window. The window is reduced to a button on the taskbar.

4. Click the **Control Panel** button on the taskbar to open the window again.

5. Click the **Close** button to close the window.

Menus and Dialog Boxes

To find out what a restaurant has to offer, you look at the menu. You can also look at a *menu* on the computer's screen to find out what a computer program has to offer. Menus in computer programs contain options for executing certain actions or tasks.

When you click the Start button, as you did earlier in this appendix, a menu is displayed with a list of options. If you choose a menu option with an arrow beside it, a submenu opens that lists additional options. A menu item followed by an ellipsis (…) indicates that a dialog box will appear when chosen. A *dialog box*, like the Shut Down Windows dialog box shown in Figure B-7, appears when more information is required before the command can be performed. You may have to key information, choose from a list of options, or simply confirm that you want the command to be performed. To back out of a dialog box without performing an action, press Esc, click the Close button, or choose Cancel (or No).

STEP-BY-STEP ▷ B.6

1. Click the **Start** button. A menu appears.

2. Click **Shut Down**. The Shut Down Windows dialog box appears, as shown in Figure B-7.

3. Click **Cancel** to back out of the dialog box without shutting down.

In a Windows application, menus are accessed from a menu bar (see Figure B-8). A menu bar appears beneath the title bar in each Windows program and consists of a row of menu names such as File and Edit. Each name in the menu bar represents a separate pull-down menu, containing related options. Pull-down menus are convenient to use because the commands are in front of you on the screen, as shown in Figure B-8. Like a menu in a restaurant, you can view a list of choices and pick the one you want.

You can give commands from pull-down menus using either the keyboard or the mouse. Each menu on the menu bar and each option on a menu is characterized by an underlined letter called a mnemonic. To open a menu on the menu bar using the keyboard, press Alt plus the mnemonic letter shown on the menu name. To display a menu using the mouse, simply place the pointer on the menu name and click the left button.

Just as with the Start menu, pull-down menus also have items with right-pointing arrows that open submenus, and ellipses that open dialog boxes. Choosing an item without an ellipsis or a right-pointing arrow executes the command. To close a menu without choosing a command, press Esc.

1. Open the Notepad accessory application by clicking **Start**, **Programs**, **Accessories**, and then **Notepad** (see Figure B-9).

2 Click **Edit** on the menu bar. The Edit menu appears.

3. Click **Time/Date** to display the current time and date.

4. Click **File** on the menu bar. The File menu appears (see Figure B-10).

5. Click **Exit**. A save prompt box appears.

6. Click **No**. The Notepad window disappears and you return to the desktop.

FIGURE B-9
Opening menus in an application

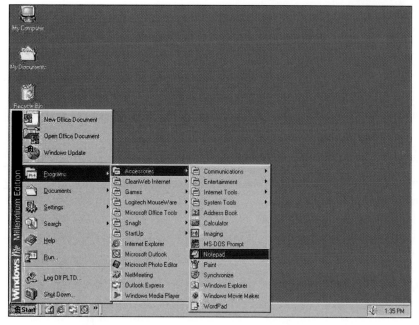

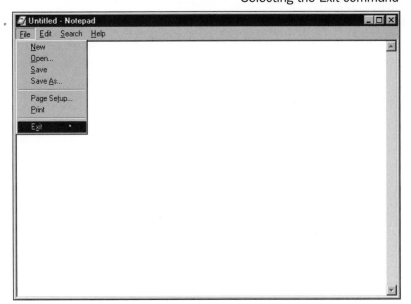

Windows Help

This appendix has covered only a few of the many features of Windows. For additional information, Windows has an easy-to-use Help system. Use Help as a quick reference when you are unsure about a function. Windows Help is accessed through the Help option on the Start menu. Then, from the Windows Help dialog box, you can choose to see a table of contents displaying general topics and subtopics, or to search the Help system using the Index or Search options. If you are working in a Windows program, you can get more specific help about topics relating to that program by accessing help from the Help menu on the menu bar.

Many topics in the Help program are linked. A *link* is represented by colored, underlined text. By clicking a link, the user "jumps" to a linked document that contains additional information.

Using the buttons on the toolbar controls the display of information. The Hide button removes the left frame of the Help window from view. The Show button will restore it. Back and Forward buttons allow you to move back and forth between previously displayed Help entries. The Options button offers navigational choices, as well as options to customize, refresh, and print Help topics.

The Contents tab is useful if you want to browse through the topics by category. Click a book icon to see additional Help topics. Click a question mark to display detailed Help information in the right frame of the Help window.

STEP-BY-STEP ▷ B.8

1. Open the Windows Help program by clicking the **Start** button, and then **Help**.

2. If you're using *Windows 98* or *Windows 2000*, click the **Hide** button on the toolbar to remove the left frame, if necessary. If you're using *Windows Me*, go to step 5.

3. Click the **Show** button to display the left frame again, if necessary.

4. Click the **Contents** tab if it is not already selected.

5. *Windows 2000 users*: Click **Introducing Windows 2000 Professional** and then click **How to Use Help**. Your screen should appear similar to Figure B-11A.

Windows 98 users: Click **Introducing Windows 98** and then click **How to Use Help**. Your screen should appear similar to Figure B-11B.

Windows Me users: Click **Using Windows Millennium Edition**. Your screen should appear similar to Figure B-11C.

FIGURE B-11A
Windows 2000 Help program

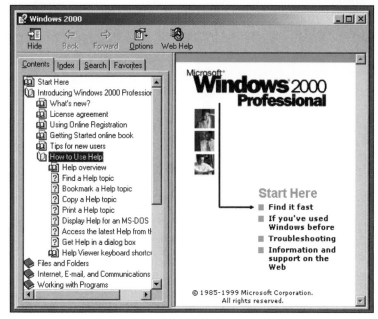

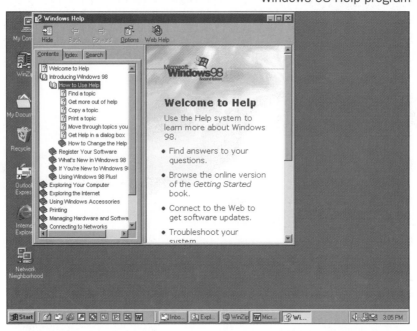

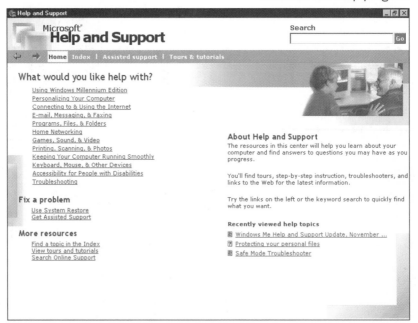

STEP-BY-STEP ⟹ B.8 **CONTINUED**

6. *Windows 2000* users: Click **Find a Help Topic.**
   Windows 98 users: Click **Find a Topic**.
   Windows Me users: Click **Getting Started with Windows Me**.

7. Read the Help window and leave it open for the next Step-by-Step.

B-11

When you want to search for help on a particular topic, use the Index tab and key in a word. Windows will search alphabetically through the list of Help topics to try to find an appropriate match, as shown in Figure B-12. Double-click a topic to see it explained in the right frame of the help window. Sometimes a Topics Found dialog box will appear that displays subtopics related to the item. Find a subtopic that you'd like to learn more about and double-click it.

STEP-BY-STEP ▷ B.9

1. Click the **Index** tab.

2. *Windows 2000* users: Begin keying **printing** until *printing* is highlighted in the list of index entries.

   Windows 98 users: Begin keying **printing** until *printing* is highlighted in the list of index entries.

   Windows Me users: Begin keying **help** until *Help* is highlighted in the list of index entries.

3. *Windows 2000* users: Click **printing Help topics** and then **from a Server** to display information in the right frame as shown in Figure B-12A.

   Windows 98 users: Double-click the **Help topics** subtopic to display information in the right frame as shown in Figure B-12B.

   Windows Me users: Double-click the **new features in Windows** subtopic to display information in the right frame as shown in Figure B-12C.

FIGURE B-12A
Using the Windows 2000 Help index

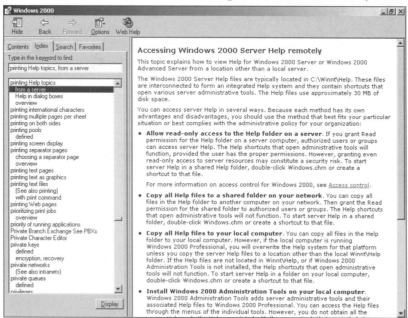

Using the Windows 98 Help index

Using the Windows Me Help index

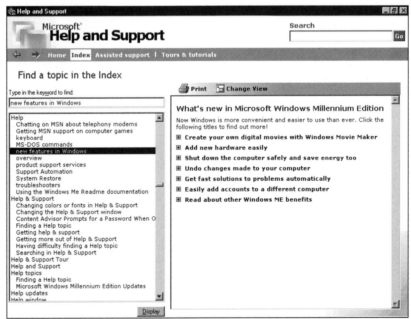

4. *Windows 2000* users: Read the Help window, and then print the information by following the instructions you read.

   Windows 98 users: Read the Help window, and then print the information by following the instructions you read.

   Windows Me users: Read the Help window, and then print the information by clicking the **Print** button on the toolbar.

5. *Windows 2000* users: Click **Back** to return to the previous Help entry.

   Windows 98 users: Click **Back** to return to the previous Help entry.

   Windows Me users: Click the **Back** arrow to return to the previous Help entry.

6. *Windows 2000* users: Click **Forward** to advance to the next help entry.

   Windows 98 users: Click **Forward** to advance to the next help entry.

   Windows Me users: Click the **Forward** arrow to advance to the next Help entry.

7. Close the Help program by clicking the **Close** button.

The Search tab (Search box in Windows Me) is similar to the Index tab, but will perform a more thorough search of the words or phrases that you key. By using the Search option, you can display every occurrence of a particular word or phrase throughout the Windows Help system. Double-click on the topic most similar to what you are looking for and information is displayed in the Help window.

If you need assistance using the Windows Help program, choose *Introducing Windows, How to Use Help* from the Contents tab, or *Using Windows Millennium Edition* from the Home tab and then *How to use Help* if you are using Windows Me.

If you are using an Office application, you can also get help by using the Office Assistant feature. These features are covered in the *Office XP Basics and the Internet* lesson.

Other Features

One of Windows' primary features is its file management capabilities. Windows comes with two file management utilities: My Computer and Windows Explorer. The Recycle Bin utility also helps you manage files. When open, these utilities display a standard toolbar like the one shown in Figure B-13. Your toolbar may look different from Figure B-13 depending on the customization. To customize your toolbar, choose Toolbars on the View menu, and Customize on the submenu.

FIGURE B-13
Standard toolbar

The Back and Forward buttons let you move back and forth between folder contents previously displayed in the window. The Up button moves you up one level in the hierarchy of folders. You can use the Cut, Copy, and Paste buttons to cut or copy an object and then paste it to another location. The Undo button allows you to reverse your most recent action. The Delete button sends the selected object to the Recycle Bin. The Properties button displays a Properties dialog box with information about the selected object. The View button lists options for displaying the contents of the window.

My Computer

As you learned earlier, there is an icon on your desktop labeled My Computer. Double-clicking this icon opens the My Computer window, which looks similar to the one shown in Figure B-14. The My Computer program is helpful because it allows you to see what is on your computer. First double-click the icon for the drive you want to view. That drive's name appears in the title bar and the window displays all the folders and files on that drive.

FIGURE B-14
Windows Me My Computer window

Because computer disks have such a large capacity, it is not unusual for a floppy disk to contain dozens of files or for a hard disk to contain hundreds or thousands of files. To organize files, a disk can be divided into folders. A *folder* is a place where files and other folders are stored. They help keep documents organized on a disk just the way folders would in a file cabinet. Folders group files that have something in common. You can also have folders within a folder. For example, you could create a folder to group all of the files you are working on in computer class. Within that folder, you could have several other folders that group files for each tool or each chapter.

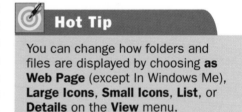

Hot Tip

You can change how folders and files are displayed by choosing **as Web Page** (except In Windows Me), **Large Icons**, **Small Icons**, **List**, or **Details** on the **View** menu.

When you double-click a folder in My Computer, the contents of that folder are displayed—including program files and data files. Double-clicking a program file icon will open that program. Double-clicking a data file icon opens that document and the program that created it.

To create a new folder, double-click a drive or folder in the My Computer window. Choose New on the File menu and then choose Folder on the submenu. A folder titled *New Folder* appears, as shown in Figure B-15. You can rename the folder by keying the name you want. Once you have created a folder, you can save or move files into it.

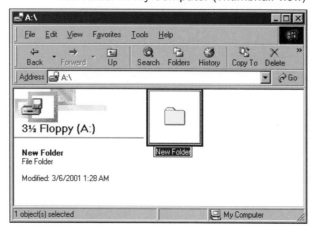

STEP-BY-STEP ▷ B.10

1. Double-click the **My Computer** icon on your desktop.

2. Double-click the drive where you want to create a new folder.

3. Choose **New** on the **File** menu and then choose **Folder** on the submenu. A folder titled *New Folder* appears.

4. Name the folder by keying **Time Records**. Press **Enter**.

5. Choose **Close** on the **File** menu to close the window.

Windows Explorer

Another way to view the folders and files on a disk is to use the Windows Explorer program. To open it, click Start, Programs, and then Windows Explorer for Windows 98 and Start, Program, Accessories, and then Windows Explorer for Windows Me and Windows 2000. The Explorer window is split into two panes, as shown in Figure B-16. The left pane shows a hierarchical, or "tree" view of how the folders are organized on a disk; the right side, or Contents pane, shows the files and folders located in the folder that is currently selected in the tree pane. Explorer is a useful tool for organizing and managing the contents of a disk because you can create folders, rename them, and easily delete, move, and copy files.

STEP-BY-STEP ▷ B.11

1. *Windows 2000* users: Open Windows Explorer by clicking **Start**, **Programs**, **Accessories**, and then **Windows Explorer**.

   Windows 98 users: Open Windows Explorer by clicking **Start**, **Programs**, and then **Windows Explorer**.

   Windows Me users: Open Windows Explorer by clicking **Start**, **Programs**, **Accessories**, and then **Windows Explorer**.

2. In the tree pane, double-click the drive where the *Time Records* folder you just created is located.

3. Select the **Time Records** folder in the Contents pane of the Explorer window.

4. Choose **Rename** on the **File** menu.

5. Key **Finance**. Press **Enter**.

6. Leave Windows Explorer open for the next Step-by-Step.

Recycle Bin

Another icon on the desktop that you learned about earlier is the Recycle Bin. It looks like a wastebasket and is a place to get rid of files and folders that you no longer need. Items that have been "thrown away" will remain in the Recycle Bin from which they can be retrieved until you empty the Recycle Bin.

1. Right-click the **Finance** folder.

2. Choose **Delete** on the shortcut menu. The Confirm Folder Delete dialog box appears, as shown in Figure B-17.

3. Click **Yes**. The folder is removed.

4. Choose **Close** on the **File** menu to close Windows Explorer.

FIGURE B-17
Confirm Folder Delete dialog box

Summary

In this appendix, you learned:

■ The desktop organizes your work. Clicking the Start button displays options for opening programs and documents, and shutting down the computer. You can connect to the Internet using the Explorer browser and you can use the Active Desktop and channels to incorporate Web content into your work.

■ Windows can be moved, resized, opened, and closed. If all the contents of a window cannot be displayed in the window as it is currently sized, scroll bars appear to allow you to move to the part of the window that you want to view. Windows can be maximized to fill the screen or minimized to a button on the taskbar.

■ Menus allow you to choose commands to perform different actions. Menus are accessed from the Start button or from a program's menu bar near the top of the window. When you choose a menu command with an ellipsis (…), a dialog box appears that requires more information before performing the command. Choosing a menu option with an arrow opens a submenu.

■ The Windows Help program provides additional information about the many features of Windows. You can access the Help program from the Start button and use the Contents, Index, or Search tabs to get information. You can also get help from the Help menu within Windows programs.

■ Folders group files that have something in common. To organize a disk, it can be divided into folders where files and other folders are stored. Other useful features of Windows include My Computer, which lets you see what is on your computer; Windows Explorer, which helps organize and manage your files; and the Recycle Bin for deleting unneeded files or folders.

APPENDIX C

COMPUTER CONCEPTS

What Is a Computer?

A computer is a mechanical device that is used to store, retrieve, and manipulate information (called data) electronically. You enter the data into the computer through a variety of input devices, process it, and output it in a number of ways. Computer software programs run the computer and let you manipulate the data.

Hardware

The physical components, or parts, of the computer are called hardware. The main parts are the central processing unit (CPU), the monitor, the keyboard, and the mouse. Peripherals are additional components like printers and scanners.

Input Devices. You enter information into a computer by typing on a keyboard or by using a mouse, a hand-held device, to move a pointer on the computer screen. Other input devices include a joystick, a device similar to the control stick of an airplane that moves a pointer or character on the screen, and a modem, which receives information via a telephone line. Other input devices include scanners, trackballs, and digital tracking. You can use scanners to "read" text or graphics into a computer from a printed page or to read bar codes (coded labels) to keep track of merchandise in a store or other inventory. Similar to a mouse, a trackball has a roller ball you turn to control a pointer on the screen. Digital tracking devices let you press a finger on a small electronic pad on the keyboard of a laptop to control the pointer on the screen, instead of using a trackball or a mouse.

Processing Devices. The CPU is a silicon chip that processes data and carries out instructions given to the computer. The data bus includes the wiring and pathways by which the CPU communicates with the peripherals and components of the computer.

Storage Devices. The hard drive is a device that reads and writes data to and from a round magnetic platter, or disk. The data is encoded on the disk much the same as sounds are encoded on magnetic tape. The hard drive is called hard because the disk is rigid, unlike a floppy disk drive, which reads and writes data to and from a removable non-rigid disk, similar to a round disk of magnetic tape. The floppy disk is encased in a plastic sleeve to protect its data. The floppy disk's main advantage is portability. You can store data on a floppy disk and transport it to another computer to use the data there.

At one time, the largest hard drive was 10 MB, or 10,000,000 bytes of data. A byte stands for a single character of data. At the current time, typical hard drives range from 10 gigabytes to 80 gigabytes.

The most recent storage device is the CD, or compact disk, which is a form of optical storage. Information is encoded on the disk by a laser and read by a CD-ROM drive in the computer. These disks have a great advantage over floppies because they can hold vast quantities of information—the entire contents of a small library, for instance. However, most computers cannot write (or save) information to these disks; CD-ROMs are Read-Only Memory (ROM) devices. Drives are now available that write to CDs. Although these drives used to be very expensive and therefore were not used widely, they are becoming more affordable. The great advantage of CDs is their ability to hold graphic information— including moving pictures with the highest quality stereo sound.

Similar to a CD, the digital video drive (DVD) can read high-quality cinema-type disks. A DVD is a 5-inch optical disk and it looks like an audio CD or a compact disk. It is a high-capacity storage device that contains 4.7 GB of data, which is a seven-fold increase over the current CD-ROMs. There are two variations of DVDs that offer even more storage, a 2-layer version with 9.4 GB capacity and double-sided disks with 17 GB. These highest-capacity disks are designed to eventually replace the CD-ROM to store large databases. A DVD disk holds 133 minutes of data on each side, which means that two two-hour movies could be held on one disk.

Another storage medium is magnetic tape. This medium is most commonly used for backing up, making a copy of files from a hard drive. Although it is relatively rare for a hard drive to crash (that is, to have the data or pointers to the data be partially or totally destroyed), it can and does happen. Therefore, most businesses and some individuals routinely back up files on tape. If you have a small hard drive, you can use floppy disks to back up your system.

Output Devices. The monitor on which you view your work is an output device. It provides a visual representation of the information stored in or produced by your computer. The monitor for today's typical system is the SVGA (super video graphics array). It provides a very sharp picture because of the large number of tiny dots, called pixels, which make up the display as well as its ability to present the full spectrum of colors. Most laptop computers use a liquid crystal display (LCD) screen that is not as clear a display because it depends on the arrangement of tiny bits of crystal to present an image. However, the latest laptops use new technology that gives quality near or equal to that of a standard monitor.

Printers are another type of output device. They let you produce a paper printout of information contained in the computer. Today, most printers are of the laser type, using a technology similar to a photocopier to produce a high-quality print. Like a copy machine, the laser printer uses heat to fuse a powdery substance called toner to the page. Ink jet printers use a spray of ink to print. Laser printers give the sharpest image. Ink jet printers provide nearly as sharp an image, but the wet printouts can smear when they first come out. However, most color printers are ink jet; these printers let you print information in its full array of colors as you see it on your SVGA monitor. Laser color printers are available but are more costly.

Modems are another output device, as well as an input device. They allow computers to communicate with each other by telephone lines. Modems convert information in bytes to sound media to send data and then convert it back to bytes after receiving data. Modems operate at various rates or speeds; typically today, a computer will have a modem that operates at 33.6 Kbps to 56 Kbps baud (a variable unit of data transmission) per second or better.

Local telephone companies currently offer residential ISDN services that provide connection speeds up to 128 Kbps and digital subscriber line technologies (DSL), which can provide speeds beyond 1.5 Mbps. Other alternatives include fast downstream data connections from direct broadcast satellite (DBS), fixed wireless providers, and of course, high-speed cable modems.

Laptops and Docking Stations. A laptop computer is a small folding computer that literally fits in a person's lap. Within the fold-up case is the CPU, data bus, monitor (built into the lid), hard drive (sometimes removable), a 3.5-inch floppy drive, a CD-ROM drive, and a trackball or digital tracking device. The advantage of the laptop is its portability—you can work anywhere because you can use power either from an outlet or from the computer's internal, rechargeable batteries. The drawbacks are the smaller keyboard, liquid crystal monitor, smaller capacity, and higher price. The newer laptops offer full-sized keyboards and higher quality monitors. As technology allows, storage capacity on smaller devices is making it possible to offer laptops with as much power and storage as a full-sized computer. The docking station is a device into which you slide a closed laptop that becomes the desktop computer. Then you can plug in a full-sized monitor, keyboard, mouse, printer, and so on. Such a setup lets you use the laptop like a desktop computer while at your home or office.

Personal Digital Assistants (PDA). A Personal Digital Assistant is a pocket-sized electronic organizer that helps you to manage addresses, appointments, expenses, tasks, and memos. This information can be shared with a Windows-based or Macintosh computer through a process called synchronization. By placing your PDA in a cradle that is attached to your computer, you can transfer the data from your PDA's calendar, address, or memo program into your computer's information manager program such as Outlook. The information is updated on both sides, making your PDA a portable extension of your computer.

Functioning

All of the input, processing, storage, and output devices function together to make the manipulation, storage, and distribution of data and information possible.

Data and Information Management. Data is information entered into and manipulated in a computer. Manipulation includes computation, such as adding, subtracting, and dividing; analysis planning, such as sorting data; and reporting, such as presenting data for others in a chart. Data and information management runs software on computer hardware.

Memory. There are two kinds of memory in a computer—RAM and ROM. RAM, or Random Access Memory, is a number of silicon chips inside a computer that hold information as long as the computer is turned on. RAM is what keeps the software programs up and running and keeps the visuals on your screen. RAM is where you work with data until you "save" it to a hard or floppy disk. Early computers had simple programs and did little with data, so they had very little RAM—possibly 4 or fewer megabytes. Today's computers run very complicated programs that "stay resident" (remain available to the user at the same time as other programs) and run graphics. Both of these tasks take a lot of memory; therefore, today's computers have at least 64 or more megabytes of RAM. ROM, or read-only memory, is the small bit of memory that stays in the computer when it is turned off. It is ROM that lets the computer "boot up," or get started. ROM holds the instructions that tell the computer how to begin to load its operating system software programs.

Speed. The speed of a computer is measured by how fast the drives turn to reach information to be retrieved or to save data. The measurement is in megahertz (MHz). Early personal computers worked at 4.77 to 10 megahertz; today, machines run at 1000 MHz or more. Another factor that affects the speed of a computer is how much RAM is available. Since RAM makes up the work area for all programs and holds all the information that you input until you save, the more RAM available, the quicker the machine will be able to operate.

One other area of speed must be considered, and that is how quickly the modem can send and receive information. As mentioned earlier, modem speed is measured in baud. The usual modem runs at 33,600 or 56,000 baud per second or more.

Communications. Computers have opened up the world of communications, first within offices via LANs (local area networks that link computers within a facility via wires) and, later, via the Internet. Using the Internet, people can communicate across the world instantly with e-mail and attach files that were once sent by mailing a floppy disk. Also, anyone with a modem and an access service can download information from or post information to thousands of bulletin boards.

Software

A program is a set of mathematical instructions to the computer. Software is the collection of programs and other data input that tells the computer how to operate its machinery, how to manipulate, store, and output information, and how to accept the input you give it. Software fits into two basic categories: systems software and applications software. A third category, network software, is really a type of application.

Systems Software. Systems software refers to the operating system (OS) of the computer. The OS is a group of programs that is automatically copied in RAM every couple of seconds from the time the computer is turned on until the computer is turned off. Operating systems serve two functions: they control data flow among computer parts and they provide the platform on which application and network software work—in effect, they allow the "space" for software and translate its commands to the computer. The most popular operating systems in use today are the Macintosh operating system, and a version of Microsoft Windows, such as Windows 98, Windows Me, or Windows NT.

Macintosh has its own operating system that has evolved over the years since its introduction. From the beginning, Macintosh has used a graphical user interface (GUI) operating system since its introduction in the mid-1970s. The OS is designed so users "click" with a mouse on pictures, called icons, or on text to give commands to the system. Data is available to you in WYSIWYG (what-you-see-is-what-you-get) form; that is, you can see on-screen what a document will look like when it is printed. Graphics and other kinds of data, such as spreadsheets, can be placed into text documents. However, GUIs take a great deal of RAM to keep all of the graphics and programs operating.

The OS for IBM and IBM-compatible computers (machines made by other companies that operate similarly) originally was DOS (disk operating system). It did not have a graphical interface. The GUI system, Windows™, was developed to make using the IBM/IBM-compatible computer more "friendly." Users no longer had to memorize written commands to make the computer carry out actions, but could use a mouse to point and click on icons or words. Windows 3.1, however, was a translating system that operated on top of DOS—not on its own.

Windows 3.1 was a GUI system that operated on top of DOS; Windows 3.1 was not an operating system by itself. It allowed you to point and click on graphics and words that then translate to DOS commands for the computer. Data was available to you in WYSIWYG (what-you-see-is-what-you-get) form. Graphics and other kinds of data, such as spreadsheets, could be placed into text documents by Object Linking and Embedding (OLE). However, Windows 3.1, because it was still using DOS as its base, was not really a stay-resident program. In other words, it did not keep more than one operation going at a time; it merely switched between operations quickly. Using several high-level programs at the same time, however, could cause problems, such as memory failure. Therefore, improvements were inevitable.

Windows 98 and Windows Me are their own operating systems, unlike the original Windows 3.1. Windows has DOS built in but does not operate on top of it—if you go to a DOS prompt from Windows, you will still be operating inside a Windows system, not in traditional DOS. Windows is the logical evolution of GUI for IBM and IBM-compatible (now more commonly known as "Windows-based") machines. It is a stay-resident, point-and-click system that automatically configures hardware to work together. With all of its ability comes the need for more RAM or this system will operate slowly. Newer versions of Windows continue to be released.

Applications Software. When you use a computer program to perform a data manipulation or processing task, you are using applications software. Word processors, databases, spreadsheets, desktop publishers, fax systems, and online access systems are all applications software.

Network Software. Novell™ and Windows NT are two kinds of network software. A network is a group of computers that are hardwired (hooked together with cables) to communicate and operate together. One computer acts as the server, which controls the flow of data among the other computers, called nodes, on the network. Network software manages this flow of information. Networks have certain advantages over stand-alone computers. They allow communication among the computers; they allow smaller capacity nodes to access the larger capacity of the server; they allow several computers to share peripherals, such as one printer, and they can make it possible for all computers on the network to have access to the Internet.

History of the Computer

Though various types of calculating machines were developed in the nineteenth century, the history of the modern computer begins about the middle of this century. The strides made in developing today's personal computer have been truly astounding.

Early Development

ENIAC, designed for military use in calculating ballistic trajectories, was the first electronic, digital computer to be developed in the United States. For its day, 1946, it was quite a marvel because it was able to accomplish a task in 20 seconds that took a human three days to do. However, it was an enormous machine that weighed more than 20 tons and contained thousands of vacuum tubes, which often failed. The tasks that it could accomplish were limited, as well.

From this awkward beginning, however, the seeds of an information revolution grew. Significant dates in the history of computer development are the first electronic stored program in 1948, the first junction transistor in 1951, the replacement of tubes with magnetic cores in 1953, the first high-level computer language in 1957, the first integrated circuit in 1961, the first minicomputer in 1965, the invention of the microprocessor (the silicon chip) and floppy disk in 1971, and the first personal computer in 1974 (made possible by the microprocessor). These last two inventions launched the fast-paced information revolution in which we now all live and participate.

The Personal Computer

The PC, or personal computer, was mass marketed by Apple, beginning in 1977, and by IBM, beginning in 1981. It is this desktop device with which people are so familiar and which, today, contains much more power and ability than did the original computer that took up an entire room. The PC is a small computer (desktop size or less) that uses a microprocessor to manipulate data. PCs may stand alone, be linked together in a network, or be attached to a large mainframe computer.

Computer Utilities and System Maintenance

Computer operating systems let you run certain utilities and perform system maintenance. When you add hardware or software, you might need to make changes in the way the system operates. Beginning with the Windows 95 version, most configuration changes are done automatically; however, other operating systems might not, or you might want to customize the way the new software or hardware will interface (coordinate) with your system. Additionally, you can make alterations such as the speed at which your mouse clicks, how fast or slow keys repeat on the keyboard, and what color or pattern appears on the desktop or in GUI programs.

You need to perform certain maintenance regularly on computers. You should scan all new disks and any incoming information from online sources for viruses. Some systems do this automatically; others require you to install software to do it. From time to time, you should scan or check the hard drive to see that there are no bad sectors or tracks and to look for corrupted files. Optimizing or defragmenting the hard disk is another way to keep your computer running at its best. You can also check a floppy disk if it is not working properly. Programs for scanning a large hard drive could take up to half an hour to run; checking programs run on a small hard drive or disk might take only seconds or minutes. Scanning and checking programs often offer the option of "fixing" the bad areas or problems, although you should be aware that this could result in data loss.

Society and Computers

With the computer revolution have come many new questions and responsibilities. There are issues of responsibility and ethics, access control, and privacy and security.

Responsibility and Ethics

When you access information—whether online, in the workplace, or via purchased software—you have a responsibility to respect the rights of the creator of that information. You must treat electronic information in a copyrighted form the same way as you would a published book or article or a patented invention. For instance, you must give credit when you access information from a CD-ROM encyclopedia or a download from an online database. Also, information you transmit must be accurate and fair, like that printed in a book. When you use equipment that belongs to your school, a company for which you work, or others, the following ethical guidelines apply:

1. You must not damage computer hardware and must not add or remove equipment without permission.

2. You must not use an access code or equipment without permission.

3. You must not read others' electronic mail.

4. You must not alter data belonging to someone else without permission.

5. You must not use the computer for play during work hours or use it for personal profit.

6. You must not access the Internet for nonbusiness use during work hours.

7. You must not add to or take away from the software programs and must not make unauthorized copies of data or software.

8. You must not copy software programs to use at home or at another site in the company without multisite permission.

9. You must not copy company files or procedures for personal use.

10. You must not borrow computer hardware for personal use without asking permission.

Internet Access and Children

Children's access to the Internet is another matter to consider. Many of the online services allow parents or guardians to control what areas of the service users can access. Because there are some discussion topics and adult information that are inappropriate for younger computer users, it is wise to take advantage of this access-limiting capability. Families using direct Internet access can purchase software for this purpose. If this software is not available, the solution must be very careful monitoring of a child's computer use.

Privacy and Security

Not only are there issues of privacy in accessing work on another's computer, there are also issues that revolve around privacy in communicating on the Internet. Just as you would not open someone else's mail, you must respect the privacy of e-mail sent to others. When interacting with others online, you must keep confidential information confidential—such as the address of a new friend made online. You must think, too, about the information that you are providing. You do not want to endanger your privacy, safety, or financial security by giving out personal information to someone you do not know. A common scam (trick) on some online services is for someone to pretend to work for the service and ask for your access code or password, which controls your service account. Never give this out to anyone online because the person can use it and charge a great deal of costly time to your account. Also, just as you would not give a stranger your home address, telephone number, or credit card number if you were talking on the street, you should take those same precautions online.

Career Opportunities

In one way or another, all of our careers involve the computer. Whether you are a grocery checker using a scanner to read the prices, a busy executive writing a report on a laptop on an airplane, or a programmer creating new software—almost everyone uses computers in their jobs. Everyone in a business processes information in some way. There are also specific careers available if you want to work primarily with computers.

Schools offer computer programming, repair, and design degrees. The most popular jobs are systems analysts, computer operators, and programmers. Analysts figure out ways to make computers work (or work better) for a particular business or type of business. Computer operators use the programs and devices to conduct business with computers. Programmers write the software for applications or new systems.

There are courses of study in using CAD (computer-aided design) and CAM (computer-aided manufacturing). Computer engineering and architectural design degrees are now available. Scientific research is done on computers today, and specialties are available in that area. There are positions available to instruct others in computer software use within companies and schools. Also, technical writers and editors must be available to write manuals on using computers and software. Computer-assisted instruction (CAI) is designing a system of teaching any given subject on the computer. The learner is provided with resources, such as an encyclopedia on CD-ROM, in addition to the specific learning program with which he or she interacts on the computer. Designing video games is another exciting and ever-growing field of computer work.

What Does the Future Hold?

The possibilities for computer development and application are endless. Things that were dreams or science fiction only 10 or 20 years ago are a reality today. New technologies are emerging. Some are replacing old ways of doing things; others are merging with those older devices. We are learning new ways to work and play because of the computer. It is definitely a device that has become part of our offices and our homes.

Emerging Technologies

The various technologies and systems are coming together to operate more efficiently. For instance, since their beginnings, Macintosh and Windows-based systems could not exchange information well. Today, you can install compatibility cards in the Power Macintosh and run Windows, DOS, and Mac OS on the same computer and switch between them. Macs (except for early models) can read from and write to MS-DOS and Windows disks. And you can easily network Macintosh computers with other types of computers running other operating systems. In addition, you can buy software for a PC to run the Mac OS and to read Macintosh disks. New technology in the works will allow you to incorporate both systems and exchange information even more easily.

Telephone communication is also being combined with computer e-mail so users can set a time to meet online and, with the addition of new voice technology, actually speak to each other. The present drawbacks are that users must e-mail and make an appointment to meet online rather than having a way just to call up each other, and speaking is delayed rather than in real-time. Although not perfected, this form of communication will certainly evolve into an often-used device that will broaden the use of both the spoken and written word.

Another emerging technology is the CUCME (see you, see me) visual system that allows computer users to use a small camera and microphone wired into the computer so, when they communicate via modem, the receiver can see and hear them. This technology is in its infancy—the pictures tend to be a bit fuzzy and blur with movement; however, improvements are being made so sharp pictures will result. For the hearing impaired, this form of communication can be more effective than writing alone since sign language and facial expression can be added to the interaction. CUCME is a logical next step from the image transfer files now so commonly used to transfer a static (nonmoving) picture.

A great deal of research and planning has gone into combining television and computers. The combined device has a CPU, television-as-monitor, keyboard, joystick, mouse, modem, and CUCME/quick-cam. Something like the multiple communications device that science fiction used to envision, this combined medium allows banking, work, entertainment, and communication to happen all through one piece of machinery—and all in the comfort of your home. There are already printers that function as a copier, fax machine, and scanner.

Trends

One emerging trend is for larger and faster hard drives. Twenty- and forty-gigabyte hard drives have virtually replaced the 540-megabyte drives, and 80-gigabyte drives are appearing on the scene. RAM today is increasing exponentially. The trend is to sell RAM in units of 8 or 16 megabytes to accommodate the greater purchases of 32, 64, and larger blocks of RAM. All of these size increases are due to the expanding memory requirements of GUIs and new peripherals, such as CUCME devices and interfaces with other devices. Although the capacities are increasing, the actual size of the machines is decreasing. Technology is allowing more powerful components to fit into smaller devices—just as the 3½-inch floppy disk is smaller and holds more data than the obsolete 5¼-inch floppy.

Another trend is the increased use of computers for personal use in homes. This trend is likely to continue in the future.

Home Offices. More and more frequently, people are working out of their homes—whether they are employees who are linked to a place of business or individuals running their own businesses. Many companies allow workers to have a computer at home that is linked by modem to the office. Work is done at home and transferred to the office. Communication is by e-mail and telephone. Such an arrangement saves companies workspace and, thus, money. Other employees use laptop computers to work both at home and on the road as they travel. These computers, in combination with a modem, allow an employee to work from virtually anywhere and still keep in constant contact with her or his employer and customers.

With downsizing (the reduction of the workforce by companies), many individuals have found themselves unemployed or underemployed (working less or for less money). These people have, in increasing numbers, begun their own businesses out of their homes. With a computer, modem, fax software, printer, and other peripherals, they can contract with many businesses or sell their own products or services. Many make use of the Internet and World Wide Web to advertise their services.

Home Use. As the economy has tightened, many people are trying to make their lives more time- and cost-efficient. The computer is one help in that search. Having banking records, managing household accounts, and using electronic banking on a computer saves time. The games and other computer interactions also offer a more reasonable way of spending leisure dollars than some outside entertainment. For instance, it might not be feasible to travel to Paris to see paintings in the Louvre Museum; however, it might be affordable to buy a CD-ROM that lets you take a tour of that famous facility from the comfort of your chair in front of your computer. This can be quite an educational experience for children and a more restful one for those who might tire on the trip but can easily turn off the computer and come back to it later. Young people can benefit enormously from this kind of education as well as using the computer to complete homework, do word processing, create art and graphics, and, of course, play games that sharpen their hand-to-eye coordination and thinking skills.

Purchasing a Computer

Once you decide to take the plunge and purchase a computer, the selection of a new computer system should be a careful and meticulous one to ensure that your needs are fulfilled. This section will help you evaluate what computer is best suited for you and help you select a new computer for purchase.

Choosing a Computer System

This is perhaps the most critical step in your quest for the ultimate computer system. It is generally best to buy a computer with an operating system and format you know. It is also important to consider what kinds of tasks you wish to perform on your computer. Windows-based machines have more available software and are more common in businesses, whereas Macintosh computers excel at desktop publishing and graphics. After you decide which type of computer you will buy, you must decide whether to buy a desktop or laptop. Your pocketbook will probably decide this for you. Laptops generally cost more than desktop computers. If you need the portability a laptop has to offer and can afford the additional cost, then it might be the choice for you. Otherwise, desktops are very suitable for use in business, home, and school.

Outlining Your Needs

After you decide what kind of computer you will buy, it is time to confirm the details. When purchasing a computer, you should consider several specific components. The recommended minimum of a few of these are noted in Table C–1.

Depending on what you plan to do with your computer, you might need different components. For instance, if you plan to do a large amount of video and graphical analysis and manipulation, you probably want at least 128 MB of RAM rather than 32 MB. High-powered gaming requires a faster video card with more RAM, as would any emerging technologies such as MPEG and virtual reality. If your office plans to do a large amount of online publishing and commerce via the Internet, a faster modem connection is a necessity.

TABLE C-1
Recommended computer components

	WINDOWS-BASED	MACINTOSH
Processor	Pentium/Celeron	PowerPC G3
Speed	600	500
Memory (RAM)	96	64
Hard Drive Size	10	10
CD Speed[1]	40X	24
Modem/Fax[2]	56Kbps	56Kbps
Expansion Slots	5	2 to 6
Operating System	Windows ME	Mac OS X
Video Card	32	16
Sound Card	64	64
Zip Drive	100	100

[1]Other choices include CDRW and DVD.
[2]Other choices include ISDN, DSL, and CableComparative Shopping.

Next comes the most challenging task: finding your computer system. Perhaps the most effective way of doing this is to make a spreadsheet similar to the one in Table C–2. This lets you directly compare different systems from different companies while saving time. Using what you have learned in this book, you could even create charts to show how the different computer systems relate to each other graphically.

Before you begin comparison shopping, it is important to be aware of hidden costs. For instance, many large chain stores offer computer packages that might not include a monitor. If a system does not include a monitor, you must add this cost. In addition to your system, you might need a printer or extra software. If your system will be mailed to you, then you must also consider shipping and handling costs. Sales tax, when applicable, is another hidden cost. On large purchases such as a computer, tax can rapidly add up, so it is important to figure this in before making the final decision.

Making the Final Decision

After you complete the chart, it is time to purchase your computer. Resist the temptation to buy the cheapest or most powerful system. The cheapest computer might be of lesser quality and might not have the features you desire. It is important to get a system powerful enough to last you at least three years but still be within your budget. The most powerful system might contain more features than you need and could be too expensive. Also, remember that the most expensive does not necessarily guarantee superior quality. Sometimes the most expensive system contains "free" software or other extras that you do not need. It is good to consider the manufacturer's reputation when deciding where to purchase your system. Some good unbiased sources for this information include the Internet, where customers who have purchased computers often voice their opinions, and consumer magazines. Other points to consider include financing, warranty, available training, and technical support and service.

TABLE C-2
Comparing computer systems

FEATURES	PREFERRED FEATURES	SYSTEM 1	SYSTEM 2	SYSTEM 3
Manufacturer				
Model				
Processor	Pentium 4			
Speed	1400			
Memory (RAM) **Price**	256			
Hard Drive Size **Price**	20 GB			
CD/DVD **Price**	DVD			
Modem/Fax **Price**	56 Kbps			
Expansion Slots **Price**	5			
Video Card **Price**	32MB			
Sound Card **Price**	320MB			
Zip Drive **Price**	250MB			
Printer **Price**				
Software **Price**				
Subtotal				
Sales tax				
Shipping				
Total Price				

USING MICROSOFT® OFFICE XP SPEECH RECOGNITION

Training Your Speech Software

Welcome to Microsoft Office XP Speech Recognition. Speech recognition is an emerging technology that promises to increase productivity, lower risk for keyboard-related injuries (like carpal tunnel syndrome), and make using computers a more natural experience. After you complete this initial training, you will be able to use your voice to perform many Microsoft Office tasks that normally require a keyboard or a mouse.

FIGURE D-1
A sound card style headset
(©2000 Plantronics, Inc.)

Connecting and Positioning Your Microphone

Start your speech recognition experience by setting up your microphone. There are several microphone styles used for speech recognition. Figure D-1 shows an example of a sound card compatible headset. The most common headset microphone connects to your computer's sound card. Connect the microphone end to your computer's microphone audio input port. Connect the speaker end into your speech output port.

USB (Universal Serial Bus) speech microphones (see Figure D-2) are becoming very popular because they bypass the sound card and input speech with less distortion to your system, thus increasing performance and accuracy.

USB microphones are plugged into the USB port found in the back of most computers. Windows will automatically install the necessary USB drivers after you start your computer with the USB microphone plugged into its slot.

FIGURE D-2
A USB Headset
(©2000 Plantronics, Inc.)

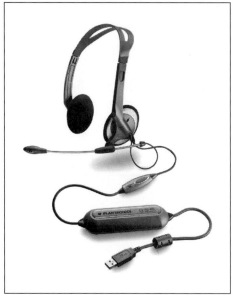

After your headset has been installed, put your headset on and position it comfortably. Remember these two important tips:

Place the speaking side of your microphone about a thumb's width away from the side of your mouth as shown in Figure D-3.

Keep your microphone in the same position every time you speak. Changing your microphone's position can decrease your accuracy.

Installing Microsoft Speech Recognition

Open Microsoft Word. If speech software is installed, you should see either the floating Language bar (Figure D-4) or the Language bar icon in the Windows taskbar tray (Figure D-5). You can click the Language bar icon and select *Show the Language bar* to open the Language bar. (Note: If Microsoft Speech Recognition is already installed on your system, skip to Step-by-Step D.2.)

FIGURE D-3

Position your headset within an inch of the side of your mouth

FIGURE D-4

The Floating Language bar

FIGURE D-5

Click the Language bar icon and choose Show the Language bar

S TEP-BY-STEP ▷ D.1

1. To install Microsoft Speech Recognition, open Microsoft Word by choosing **Start**, **Programs**, and then **Microsoft Word**.

2. Choose **Tools**, then **Speech** from the menu bar as shown in Figure D-6.

FIGURE D-6

Choose Speech from the Tools menu

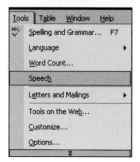

3. You will be prompted through the installation procedure. Follow the on-screen instructions to install the feature.

4. After the installation has been completed, you can begin training your system. The training process will create a profile that remembers how you speak. Because you're the first (or default) user of your software on this computer, the Microsoft Office XP Speech Recognition Wizard will quickly walk you through the training process as explained in the next section.

Training Your System

Microsoft Speech Recognition can accommodate many different voices on the same computer. In order to work properly, your Speech Recognition software must create a user profile for each voice it hears, including your voice.

If you are the first user and have just installed your speech software, the system will automatically begin prompting you through these essential training steps. Follow the instructions on your screen and skim read steps 4-6 below for helpful hints as you continue.

However, if you are the second or later user of the system, you will need to create a new profile. Carefully follow the next few steps, starting with step 1.

S TEP-BY-STEP ▷ D.2

1. To create your own personal speech profile, click the **Tools** button on the Language bar and select **Options**. The Speech Properties dialog box opens, as shown in Figure D-7.

2. In the Speech Properties dialog box, click **New** as shown in Figure D-7.

FIGURE D-7
The Speech Properties dialog box

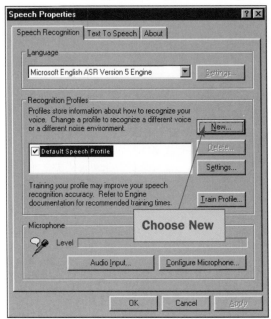

3. Enter your name in the Profile Wizard as shown in Figure D-8 and click **Next** to continue. (*Note*: If you accidentally click **Finish** instead of **Next**, you must still train your profile by choosing **Train Profile** in the Speech Properties dialog box.)

4. Adjust your microphone as explained in the Microphone Wizard Welcome screen shown in Figure D-9. Click **Next** to begin adjusting your microphone.

FIGURE D-8
The Profile Wizard dialog box

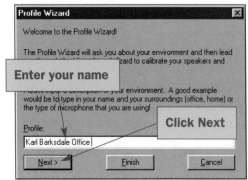

FIGURE D-9

Correctly position your microphone

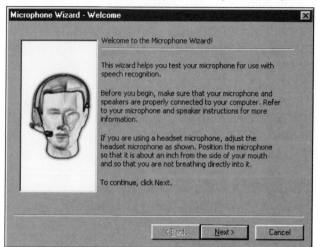

5. In the next dialog box (see Figure D-10), read the test sentence as instructed until the volume adjustment settings appear consistently in the green portion of the volume adjustment meter. Your volume settings will be adjusted automatically as you speak. Click **Next** to continue.

6. In the next dialog box, the output of your speakers is tested. Read the test sentence and listen. If you can hear your voice, your speakers are connected properly. Click **Finish**.

FIGURE D-10

Read the sample sentences to adjust the volume settings

Training Your Software

In this next step you'll be asked to train your software. During the training session you'll read a training script for ten to fifteen minutes. As you read, your software will gather samples of your speech. These samples will help your speech software customize your speech recognition profile to your way of speaking. As you read, remember to:

Read clearly.

Use a normal, relaxed reading voice. Don't shout but don't talk softly either.

Read at your normal reading pace. Do not read slowly and do not rush.

Speech Recognition

Microsoft Office Speech Recognition will tell you if your microphone is not adequate for good speech recognition. You may need to try a higher-quality microphone, install a compatible sound card, or switch to a USB microphone. Check the Microsoft Windows Help files for assistance with microphone problems.

STEP-BY-STEP ▷ D.3

1. Microsoft Office Speech Recognition will now prepare you to read a script. Read the instruction screens as they appear and click **Next** to continue.

2. Enter your gender and age information (as shown in Figure D-11) to help the system calibrate its settings to your voice. Choose **Next** to continue.

3. Click the **Sample** button and listen to a short example of how to speak clearly to a computer (see Figure D-12). After the recording, read the instructions and continue clicking **Next** to continue.

4. Begin reading the training session paragraphs. Text you have read will be highlighted as shown in Figure D-13. The Training Progress bar will let you know how much reading is left to do. If you get stuck on a word, use the **Skip Word** button to move past the problem spot.

FIGURE D-11
Enter your gender and age information

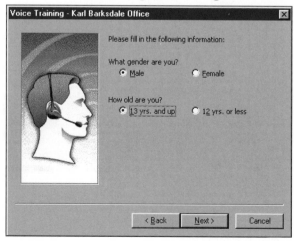

FIGURE D-12
Listen to the speech sample

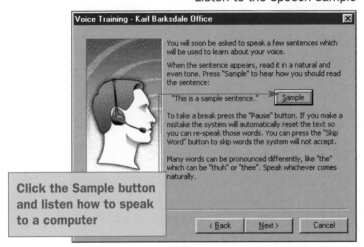

Click the Sample button and listen how to speak to a computer

FIGURE D-13
The software keeps track of your progress

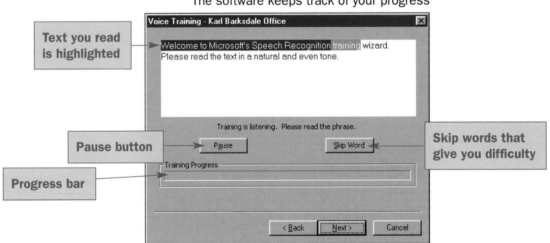

Text you read is highlighted

Pause button

Progress bar

Skip words that give you difficulty

5. The screen shown in Figure D-14 will appear after you have finished reading the entire training session script. You can click the **More Training** button and continue reading additional scripts or you can click **Finish** and begin using your software. (*Note*: Skip to step 7 if you choose **Finish**.)

6. If you chose **More Training** in step 5, you have made a smart decision! To increase the accuracy of your speech recognition software, select and read another training session story from the list as shown in Figure D-15.

7. At the end of the training process, Microsoft Office Speech Recognition will show you a multimedia training tutorial. Enjoy the tutorial before continuing!

Speech Recognition

Your user file will remember your microphone settings from session to session. However, if others use the system before you, you may need to readjust the audio settings by choosing **Tools**, **Options**, and then **Configure Microphone**.

FIGURE D-14
Congratulations! You've finished your first training script

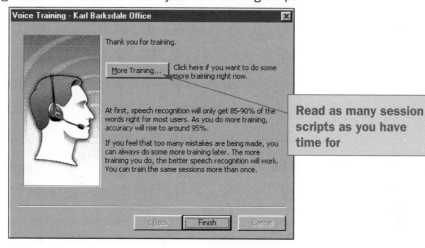

Read as many session scripts as you have time for

FIGURE D-15
Choose another training story to read

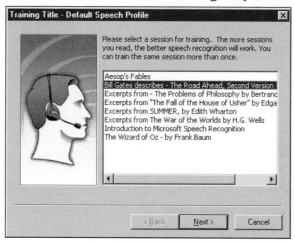

Using Voice Commands

You can begin using Microsoft Office Speech Recognition immediately after you train your software. Because Microsoft Word is probably where you'll do most of your heavy-duty voice writing, it makes sense to begin using speech with this word-processing program. Using speech with other Office applications will be a snap after you master the basic commands in Word.

If more than one person is using speech recognition on the same computer, you must choose your user profile from the Current Users list. Display this list by clicking Tools on the Language bar and then Current User, as shown in Figure D-16.

Hot Tip

Never touch any part of your headset or microphone while speaking. Holding or touching the microphone will definitely create errors.

FIGURE D-16
Choose your name from the Current Users list

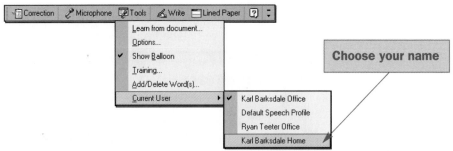

Choose your name

Switching Modes and Moving the Language Bar

Microsoft Office Speech Recognition works in two modes: Dictation and Voice Command. In Dictation mode, you simply dictate words that the software automatically inputs for you. In the Voice Command mode, you give commands to your computer, much like you would do with your mouse.

When using Voice Command mode, simply say the menu items, icons, and buttons you see on the screen or in dialog boxes.

Speech Recognition

You'll be required to read until Microsoft Office Speech Recognition has a large enough sample of your voice to process. Processing allows your speech software to adjust to your unique way of speaking. Click **Pause** if you need to take a break. However, it is best to read the entire session training script in one sitting.

STEP-BY-STEP ▷ D.4

1. Open **Microsoft Word**, if necessary. If the Language bar is not displayed, select **Tools** and then **Speech** from the Microsoft Word menu bar, or click the **Language bar** icon in the taskbar tray and choose **Show the Language bar**.

2. The Language bar can be collapsed (see Figure D-17) or expanded (see Figure D-18). You can switch between the two by clicking the **Microphone** button. Click the **Microphone** button. This will turn the microphone on and expand the Language bar.

FIGURE D-17
Collapsed Language bar

Microphone button

FIGURE D-18
Expanded Language bar

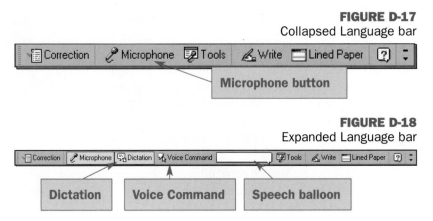

Dictation   Voice Command   Speech balloon

3. Compare the tools found on the expanded Language bar with those in the collapsed bar. You will see several new features including the Dictation, Voice Command, and Speech Balloon options.

4. Switch between Dictation mode (used for dictating words) and Voice Command mode (used for giving commands) by saying the following commands clearly. (*Note*: Make sure you pause momentarily after saying each command.)

   Voice Command <pause>

   Dictation <pause>

Voice Command <pause>

Dictation <pause>

5. Practice turning the microphone off with your voice (thereby collapsing the Language bar) by saying **Microphone.**

6. Click and drag the Language bar to various parts of the screen by clicking the marker on its left edge as shown in Figure D-19. (*Note*: When you position the pointer on the marker, it changes to the shape of a four-headed arrow, letting you know you can move the Language bar.)

FIGURE D-19
Move the Language bar to a convenient spot

Click and drag the marker

Giving Menu Commands

Before you begin issuing commands, take a few seconds to review Figure D-20. The toolbars you will be working with in the next few exercises are identified.

Speech Recognition

The more scripts you read the better. Users with thick accents or accuracy below 90 percent must read additional scripts. You can read additional training session scripts at any time by clicking **Tools** and then **Training** on the Language bar.

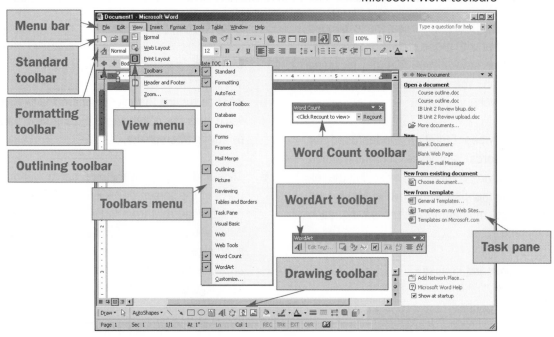

STEP-BY-STEP D.5

1. Click the **Microphone** button on the Language bar.

2. Switch to Voice Command mode by saying **Voice Command**.

3. Open and close several menus by repeating the following commands. (Remember to pause briefly between commands.)

File

Escape

Edit

Cancel

View

Escape

4. Say the following commands to hide toolbars or, if they are already hidden, to display them.

View

Toolbars

Standard

View

Toolbars

Formatting

View

Toolbars

Drawing

D-10

5. Speak the following commands to redisplay the toolbars or, if they are already displayed, to hide them.

View

Toolbars

Drawing

View

Toolbars

Formatting

View

Toolbars

Standard

6. Practice giving voice commands by opening and closing the task pane and WordArt toolbar. Experiment with displaying and hiding other toolbars. When you are done, turn the microphone off and collapse the Language bar by saying **Microphone.** Remain in this screen for the next Step-by-Step.

> **Speech Recognition**
>
> After you have selected your user profile, you may wish to refresh your audio settings by selecting **Tools**, **Options**, and then **Configure Microphone**. This will help adjust the audio settings to the noise conditions in your current dictation environment.

Navigating Dialog Boxes

Opening files is one thing you will do nearly every time you use Microsoft Office. To open files you will need to display and execute commands in the Open dialog box, shown in Figure D-21. For example, in the Open dialog box you can switch folders and open files by voice.

> **Speech Recognition**
>
> Your Language bar can float anywhere on the screen. Move your Language bar to a spot that is convenient and out of the way. Most users position the Language bar in the title bar or status bar.

STEP-BY-STEP ▷ D.6

1. Turn on the **Microphone** and access the Open dialog box by saying the following:

   Voice Command

   File

   Open

2. Notice the options in the left pane of the Open dialog box (History, My Documents, Desktop, and Favorites). Say the following voice commands to switch between folder locations. (*Note:* Remember to pause slightly after saying each command.)

   Desktop

   My Documents

   History

   Desktop

   Favorites

   My Documents

3. You can change how your folders and files look in the Open dialog box by manipulating the Views options, as shown in Figure D-22. Say the following voice commands to change the view:

   Views

   Small Icons

   Views

   List

   Views

   Details

   Views

   Thumbnails

   Views

   Large icons

   Views

   List

FIGURE D-22
Change the way folders and files display

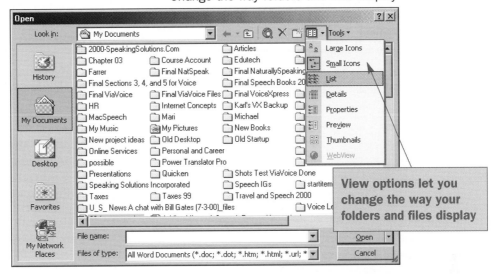

View options let you change the way your folders and files display

4. Close the Open dialog box by saying the following:

Cancel

Microphone

Remain in this screen for the next Step-by-Step.

Speech Recognition

In Voice Command mode you can say almost any command you would normally execute with your mouse, and the result will be the same. For the most part, simply say the menu items, commands, and buttons you see on the screen. Voice commands are very easy to learn.

Open and Count the Words in a Document

In the next Step-by-Step, you will combine your traditional mouse skills with voice skills to accomplish tasks more conveniently.

Speech Recognition

The Escape and Cancel commands are like pressing the Escape key on your keyboard. These commands cancel whatever menu you have voice-selected.

1. Turn your **Microphone** on. Using your voice, say **Voice Comand**, **File**, **Open**. If necessary, change the view in the Open dialog box to **List**.

2. Using your mouse, locate and select the **Prevent Injury** document in the data files. Then say **Open**.

3. As the file opens you will notice that the title of the article is *PREVENT INJURY WITH SPEECH*. Speech recognition can help you avoid serious keyboarding and mouse injuries. Count the words in the article. Open the Word Count toolbar by saying the following:

   View

   Toolbars

   Word Count

4. With the Word Count toolbar open, say **Recount** to count the words.

5. How many words are contained in the article? Leave the document open for the next Step-by-Step.

Speech Recognition

Any time a button in a dialog box appears dark around the edges, it means the button is active. Active buttons can be accessed at any time by saying the name of the button or by saying **Enter**. You can also move around dialog boxes using the **Tab** or **Shift Tab** voice commands, or move between folders and files by saying **Up Arrow**, **Down Arrow**, **Left Arrow**, and **Right Arrow**.

Save a Document and Exit Word

Saving a file will give you a chance to practice manipulating dialog boxes. Switching from the keyboard and mouse to your voice has several benefits. For example, have you heard of carpal tunnel syndrome and other computer keyboard-related injuries caused by repetitive typing and clicking? By using your speech software even part of the time, you can reduce your risk for these long-term and debilitating nerve injuries.

In the next set of steps, you will change the filename *Prevent Injury* to *My Prevent Injury File* using the Save As dialog box.

1. Open the Save As dialog box by saying **File**, **Save as**.

2. Using your mouse, select the location to which you want to save the file. Then, click in the **File name** box and key **My Prevent Injury File**.

3. Save your document and close the Save As dialog box by saying **Save**.

4. Close the Word Count toolbar using the commands you learned in Step-by-Step D.5.

5. Close Microsoft Word and collapse the Language bar with the following commands (when asked to save other open documents say **No**):

File

Exit

Voice Dictating, Editing, and Formatting

It is common for people to dictate 130 to 160 words per minute with their speech software—much faster than almost anyone can type. However, Microsoft Office XP Speech Recognition is not made for complete hands-off use. You will still need to use your keyboard and the mouse to do many things. But, if you're willing to put in some effort, you can improve your speech accuracy to the point that you will be able to effectively dictate and format much of your writing.

Dictating

Microsoft Office Speech Recognition allows you to work in Dictation mode when voice-typing words into your documents. To switch from Voice Command mode to Dictation mode, simply say Dictation.

In Dictation mode, don't stop speaking in the middle of a sentence, even if your words don't immediately appear. Your software will need a few seconds to process what you're saying. You will know that Microsoft Speech Recognition is working by the appearance of a highlighted bar with dots in your document, as shown in Figure D-23. Think about the following as you begin voice writing:

Speak naturally without stopping in the middle of your sentences.

Don't speak abnormally fast or unnaturally slow.

Say each word clearly. Don't slur your words or leave sounds out.

You'll need to dictate punctuation marks. Say the word *period* to insert a (.), *comma* to insert a (,), *question mark* for a (?), *exclamation point/mark* for (!), and *colon* for (:). Be sure to pause slightly before and after you issue a punctuation command. In the following Step-by-Step exercises, don't be concerned about making mistakes. You will learn how to correct them later in this appendix.

> ### Speech Recognition
>
> The best way to improve dictation accuracy is to read additional training session stories to your computer. You should read about three to five stories. Do this by selecting **Tools**, **Current User**, and double-checking to see if your user profile name has a check mark by it. Next choose **Tools**, then **Training** from the Language bar and follow the on-screen instructions.

Continue talking even if your words don't instantly appear

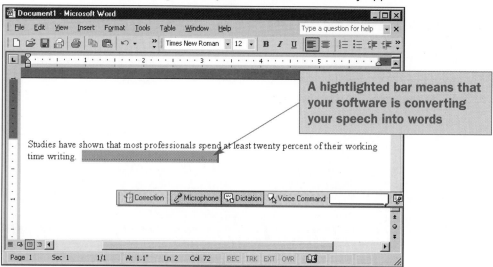

A hightlighted bar means that your software is converting your speech into words

STEP-BY-STEP ▷ D.9

1. Open Word and the Language bar if necessary. Don't forget to select your user profile.

2. Click the **Microphone** button on the Language bar, and say the following:

   Dictation

   Studies have shown that most professionals spend at least twenty percent of their working time writing <pause> **period** <pause> **You can use speech recognition software to help you in any career you choose** <pause> **period** <pause> **Microsoft speech can be used in the medical** <pause> **comma** <pause> **legal** <pause> **comma** <pause> **financial** <pause> **comma** <pause> **and educational professions** <pause> **period**

   Microphone

3. Examine your paragraph. How well did you do? Count the mistakes or word errors. How many errors did you make?

4. Turn on the microphone, and delete all the text on your screen with the following commands (remember to pause briefly after each command):

   Voice Command

   Edit

   Select All

   Backspace (or you may also say **Delete**)

5. Repeat the dialog from step 2. This time, say any word that gave you difficulty a little more clearly. See if your computer understands more of what you say this time around. Did you improve?

6. Delete all the text on your screen again using the same voice commands that you used in step 4. Remain in this screen for the next Step-by-Step.

Using the New Line and New Paragraph Commands

You can use the *new line* and *new paragraph* commands to start text on a new line or in a new paragraph, as shown in Figure D-24. When you use these commands in your dictation, be sure to pause before and after saying them, as in *<pause> new line <pause>* and *<pause> new paragraph <pause>*.

FIGURE D-24

Starting new lines and paragraphs with voice commands

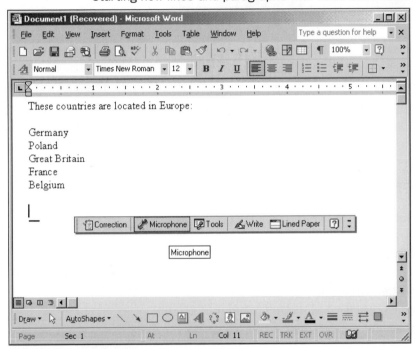

STEP-BY-STEP ▷ D.10

1. Dictate the following list of European countries. Turn the **Microphone** on and say:

   Dictation

   These countries are located in Europe <pause> **colon**

   <pause> **new paragraph**<pause>
   Germany <pause> **new line**
   Poland <pause> **new line**
   Great Britain <pause> **new line**
   France <pause> **new line**
   Belgium <pause> **new paragraph**

2. Save the file by saying the following:

   Voice Command

   File

   Save As

3. Click in the **File name** box and key **Countries of Europe** as the filename.

4. Close the Save As dialog box with the **Save** command, then clear your screen by saying **Edit**, **Select All**, **Backspace.** Remain in this screen for the next Step-by-Step.

Using "Scratch That"

Microsoft Office Speech Recognition offers powerful ways to make corrections and dictate difficult words so they appear correctly when you say them. For example, erasing mistakes is easy with the "scratch that" command. All you need to do is pause slightly after you've made a mistake and say *scratch that.*

STEP-BY-STEP ▷ D.11

1. Say the name of the following academic subjects, and then erase them immediately with the scratch that command. Remember to pause briefly before saying *scratch that.*

    Dictation

    Biology \<pause\> **scratch that**

    French \<pause\> **scratch that**

    American history \<pause\> **scratch that**

2. The scratch that command will delete the last continuous phrase you have spoken. Practice using the Scratch That command more by reciting:

    To infinity and beyond \<pause\> **scratch that**

The check is in the mail \<pause\> **scratch that**

Money isn't everything \<pause\> **scratch that**

Microphone

Remain in this screen for the next Step-by-Step.

Speech Recognition

A key to speech recognition accuracy is to talk in complete phrases and sentences. This makes it easier for your software to guess what you're trying to say. Your software makes adjustments based on the context of the words that commonly appear together. The more words you say as a group or phrase, the more words your software has to work with.

Correcting Errors and Formatting

Because speech recognition software recognizes phrases better than individual words, an effective way to correct a mistake is to choose the phrase where the mistake occurs with your mouse and then repeat the phrase. For example, if you want to correct the sentence: *You sound very share of yourself* to be *You sound very sure of yourself,* you would select the portion of the sentence: *very share of yourself,* and then repeat that portion using the correct word *sure* instead of *share.*

If you still make a mistake, choose the misspoken word with your mouse and take advantage of the power of the Correction button on the Language bar. When you issue the Correction command, a list will display giving you options to replace the incorrect word with.

When you correct a mistake using the Correction button, Microsoft Office Speech Recognition plays back what you said and remembers any corrections that you make. This ensures that the same mistake is less likely to be made the next time you say the same word or phrase. Use the Correction button as often as you can. This will help improve your speech recognition accuracy.

After you dictate text you can format it, copy it, paste it, and manipulate it just like you would with a mouse. In the next Step-by-Step exercise you'll dictate a few sentences and then you'll change the font styles and copy text.

STEP-BY-STEP ▷ D.12

1. Dictate the following using the **new paragraph** command after each line. Do not pause in the middle of any of the lines. If you make more than one mistake in each sentence, say **scratch that** and repeat the phrase. If you still have mistakes, correct them using the **Correction** button.

Dictation

A place for everything and everything in its place.

It's the thought that counts.

How did you know?

What time is it?

Ready or not, you shall be caught!

I would absolutely love to come!

2. With your mouse, choose the first two sentences. Make them bold with the following commands:

Voice Command

Bold

3. Select the two questions using your mouse, and italicize them by saying **Italic**.

4. Select the final two exclamatory sentences using your mouse, and underline them by saying **Underline.**

5. Copy all the text and paste it at the bottom of the document by saying:

Edit

Select All

Copy

Down Arrow

Paste

6. Print the document by giving the following commands (remember to pause between commands):

File

Print

OK

7. Close your document without saving by using the **File, Close** command and say **No** when you are asked to save.

8. Open a new document by saying **File, New, Blank Document** and then turn off your **Microphone**. Remain in this screen for the next Step-by-Step.

Adding and Training Names

Your speech software can remember what you teach it. Select the Add/Delete Word(s) command on the Language bar's Tools menu to open the Add/Delete Word(s) dialog box, as shown in Figure D-25. You can enter a name or any other word or phrase in the dialog box, click the Record pronunciation button, and record your pronunciation of the word or phrase.

S TEP-BY-STEP ▷ D.13

1. Choose **Tools**, and then **Add/Delete Word(s)** from the Language bar.

2. Enter your name in the Word box as shown in Figure D-25.

FIGURE D-25
Enter your name in the Word box

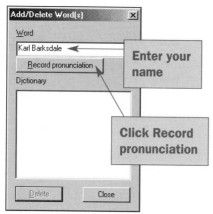

3. Click the **Record pronunciation** button and say your name.

4. Your name will appear in the Dictionary list. Double-click your name to hear a digitized voice repeat your name.

5. Close the Add/Delete Word(s) dialog box by clicking the **Close** button.

6. Turn on your **microphone** and switch to Dictation mode. Say your name several times and see if it appears correctly.

7. Exit Microsoft Word without saving.

Speech Recognition

If your speech recognition software doesn't hear you properly, the name will not appear in the Dictionary. If this happens, try again. When the system has accepted your pronunciation of the word, the name will appear in the Dictionary.

Speech Recognition

If your name doesn't appear properly when you say it, return to the Add/Delete Word(s) dialog box, choose your name, then click the **Record pronunciation** button and re-record the correct pronunciation of your name. Close the Add/Delete Word(s) dialog box.

Turning Microsoft Speech Recognition On and Off

You may have a number of reasons for wanting to stop using Microsoft Office Speech Recognition. Perhaps your computer isn't fast enough to process your speech. Maybe your headset isn't performing properly, or maybe you just want to type instead of talk to your computer.

There are two ways to turn off Microsoft Office Speech Recognition: You can minimize the Language bar and place it aside temporarily, or you can turn it off entirely. As you learned earlier, when you minimize the Language bar, the Language bar icon representing it appears in the taskbar system tray. Right-click the icon, and choose the Close the Language bar option to turn off the Speech Recognition feature.

STEP-BY-STEP ▷ D.14

1. Open Microsoft Word and the Language bar if necessary.

2. Click the **Minimize** button on the Language bar.

Minimize

3. When you minimize for the first time, a message box opens, as shown in Figure D-26, explaining what is going to happen to your Language bar. Read this box carefully the first time you see it, then click **OK**.

4. Right-click the **Language bar** icon. A shortcut menu opens, as shown in Figure D-27. Click the **Close the Language bar** option.

5. The Language bar dialog box opens. It explains a process you can follow for restoring your speech operating system after you have turned it off. If you click **OK**, the system will be turned off and your language tools will disappear.

6. Close Microsoft Word.

FIGURE D-26
Read this message box carefully

FIGURE D-27
Click the Language bar icon and choose
Close the Language bar

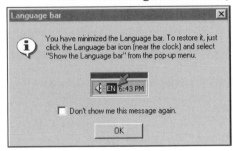

To turn Microsoft Office Speech Recognition back on, simply select start Word, and select Speech on the Tools menu. If your speech software does not restore itself, you may need to do something more drastic: Open the Control Panel and select Text Services. Click Language bar in the Text Services dialog box. In the Language Bar Settings dialog box, place a check mark in the *Show the Language bar on the desktop* box. Click OK, exit the Control Panel, and restart your computer.

GLOSSARY

A

Absolute cell reference Worksheet cell reference that does not adjust to the new cell location when copied or moved.

Active cell Highlighted worksheet cell ready for data entry.

Active sheet Worksheet that appears on the screen.

Address bar Displays the name of the folder whose contents are being displayed.

Address Book A program that stores personal and professional contact information, including names, e-mail addresses, street addresses, phone numbers, and other data.

Alignment How text is positioned between margins.

And operator Used to find records that meet more than one criteria.

Appointment In Outlook, an activity that has a set time and date, but does not involve inviting other people or reserving resources.

Appointment book In Outlook, displays appointments for the time frame you choose.

Archive A program that allows you to organize, store, and save old documents.

Argument In Excel, value, cell reference, range, or text that acts as an operand in a function formula.

Ascending sort Sort that arranges records from A to Z or smallest to largest.

AutoComplete Suggests the entire word after keying the first few letters.

AutoCorrect Corrects common spelling and grammatical errors.

AutoFilter Displays a subset of the data in a worksheet that meet certain criteria.

AutoFilter arrows Appear at the lower right corner of the worksheet's column headings. By clicking the arrow, a drop down list will appear that allows you to display a specific row, the top ten items in the column, a customized search, or restore all the data in the worksheet.

AutoFormat Collection of font, patterns, and alignments that can be applied to a range of data.

AutoFormat As You Type Automatically applies built-in formats to the text you type.

Automatic Spelling and Grammar Check Identifies spelling and grammatical errors as you key your text.

AutoText Stores frequently used text so you do not have to re-key it each time.

Axis Line that identifies the values in a chart; most charts have a horizontal (or X axis) and a vertical (or Y axis).

B

Blank publication In Publisher, used to create a document from scratch using whatever format, colors, and designs are preferred.

Borders Lines that are placed around text for emphasis or decoration.

Bound control Control on a database form or report that is connected to a field in a table. Can be used to display, enter, and update data.

Bullet A character or symbol placed before text, usually in a list, to add emphasis.

C

Calculated control Control on a database form or report that uses an expression to generate the data value for a field.

Categories Helps you keep track of items so you can easily find and group them.

Cell Intersection of a row and column in a worksheet or table.

Cell reference Identifies a worksheet cell by the column letter and row number (for example, A1, B2, C4).

Channels Means of customizing the information delivered from the Internet to your computer.

Chart A graphical representation of data.

Chart sheet Area separate from the Excel worksheet in which a chart is created and stored; the chart sheet is identified by a tab near the bottom of the screen.

Chart Wizard Four-step, on-screen guide that aids in preparing a chart from an Excel worksheet.

Clip art Graphics that are already drawn and available for use in documents.

Clipboard A temporary storage place in the computer's memory.

Clips Online A clip art collection maintained by Microsoft on the Internet.

Close Removing a document or window from the screen.

Close button "X" on the right side of the title bar that you click to close a window.

Column chart Chart that uses rectangles of varying heights to illustrate values in a worksheet.

Columns Appear vertically in a worksheet and are identified by letters at the top of the worksheet window.

Comment Message that provides information concerning data in a cell.

Contact A person or company in your Address Book.

Copy A copy of the selected text is placed on the clipboard while the original text remains in the document.

Cut Removes selected text from the document and places it on the Clipboard.

D

Data access page An object created in a database that lets you publish to the Web other objects, such as tables, forms, and reports.

Data labels Values depicted by the chart objects (such as columns or data points) that are printed directly on the chart.

Data series Group of related information in a column or row of a worksheet that is plotted on a worksheet chart.

Data sheet In PowerPoint, a table that contains sample data and automatically appears when you create a chart.

Data source A file that contains information that will vary in a form letter.

Database management system Any system for managing data.

Database report A report that allows you to organize, summarize, and print all or a portion of the data in a database.

Datasheet view In a database, a form similar to a spreadsheet that allows records to be entered directly into a table.

Date Navigator The monthly calendar at the top right of Outlook's Calendar window. Date Navigator offers a quick and easy way to view a specific date or see which day has an activity scheduled.

Default Setting used unless another option is chosen.

Descending sort Sort that arranges records from Z to A or largest to smallest.

Design set In Publisher, a series of documents (letterheads, business cards, envelopes, etc.) that incorporate the same design.

Design view Where you design and modify tables in a database.

Desktop Space where you access and work with programs and files.

Desktop publishing The process of combining text and graphics to create attractive documents.

Detail Section in a database form or report that displays the records.

Diagram A graphical illustration for organizing data.

Dialog box A message box that "asks" for further instructions before a command can be performed.

Discussion server A Web server that accomodates discussion of an Office file on the Internet.

Distribution list A group of contacts that provides an easy way to send messages.

Drag and Drop A quick method for copying and moving text a short distance.

Drawing tools Tools to use to insert lines and objects that help make a worksheet more informative.

E

E-mail The use of a computer network to send and receive messages.

Embed Information that becomes part of the current file, but is a separate object that can be edited using the application that created it.

Embedded chart Chart created within a worksheet; an embedded chart may be viewed on the same screen as the data from which it is created.

Endnote Printed at the end of your document, it is used to document quotations, figures, summaries or other text you do not want to include in your text.

Event In Outlook, an activity that occurs on a weekly, monthly, or yearly basis and does not have a set time associated with it.

F

Field A category of data that make up records.

Field name Name that identifies a field in a database table.

Field properties Specifications that allow you to customize a database table field beyond choosing a data type.

Field selectors Located at the top of a database table, they contain the field name.

Filling Copies data into the cell(s) adjacent to the original.

Filter Simpler form of a database query that cannot be saved and that displays all fields.

Filter Arrows When using the AutoFilter in Excel, filter arrows appear at the lower right corner of the column headings. By clicking the arrow, a drop down list will appear that allows you to display a specific row, the top ten items in the column, a customized search, or restore all the data in the worksheet.

Financial functions Functions such as future value, present value, and payment which are used in worksheets to analyze loans and investments.

Folder A place where files and other folders are stored on a disk.

Font size Determined by measuring the height of characters in units called points.

Font style Formatting feature that changes the appearance of text such as bold, italic, and underline.

Fonts Designs of type.

Footer Text that is printed at the bottom of the page.

Footnote Printed at the bottom of each page, it is used to document quotations, figures, summaries or other text that you do not want to include in your text.

Form footer Section of a database form that displays information that remains the same for every record. Appears once at the end of the form.

Form header Section that displays information that remains the same for every record. Appears once at the beginning of the form.

Form letter A word processor document that uses information from a database in specified areas to personalize a document.

Format Painter Used to format an object with the same attributes as another object.

Formatting Arranging the shape, size, type, and general make-up of a document.

Formula Equation that calculates a new value from values currently on a worksheet.

Formula bar Appears directly below the toolbar in the worksheet; displays a formula when the cell of a worksheet contains a calculated value.

Formula palette Specifies the elements to be included in the function formula of a worksheet.

Freezing Keeps row or column titles on the screen no matter where you scroll in the worksheet.

Function formula Special formulas that do not use operators to calculate a result.

G

Graphics Pictures that help illustrate the meaning of the text or that make the page more attractive.

Graphs See **Charts**.

Gridlines Lines displayed through a worksheet chart that relate the objects (such as columns or data points) in a chart to the axes.

Grouping Allows you to work with several objects as though they were one object. In Access, organizing records into parts or groups based on the contents of a field.

Guide settings A set of crosshairs that help you align an object in the center, left, right, top, or bottom of a slide.

H

Handles Small boxes that appear around an object when it is selected. You can drag the handles to resize the object.

Header Text that is printed at the top of the page.

Hiding Temporarily removes a worksheet row or column from the screen.

Highlight Entry point of a worksheet; a highlighted cell is indicated by a dark border; to shade text with color to emphasize important text or graphics.

Home page First page that appears when you start your Web browser.

Hotspot Place on an image map that you click to jump to another page.

HTML See **Hypertext Markup Language**.

Hyperlink Words or objects that may be clicked to move from page to page within a Web site, to jump to another Web site, or to go to a different location within a document.

Hypertext Markup Language The language or format for creating Web pages.

I

Icon Small pictures that represent an item or object.

Image handles See **Handles**.

Indent The space placed between text and a document's margins.

Indexing Feature of databases that allows a field to be more quickly searched.

Integrated software package Computer program that combines common tools into one package.

Internet Vast network of computers linked to one another.

Internet Explorer Office XP's browser for navigating the Web.

Intranet A company's private network.

J

Journal An Outlook program to record entries and document interactions with contacts.

L

Landscape orientation Page orientation where the document is wider than it is long.

Leader A line of periods or dashes that precedes a tab.

Line chart Chart that is similar to a column chart except columns are replaced by points connected by a line.

Line spacing The amount of space between lines of text.

Link See **Hyperlink**.

Logical function Function used to display text or values if certain conditions exist.

M

Macro Collection of one or more actions that automate certain routine tasks.

Mail merge Combining a document with information that personalizes it.

Main document The document with information that does not change in a form letter.

Margins Blank spaces around the top, bottom, and sides of a page.

Mathematical function Function that manipulates quantitative data in the worksheet using operators such as logarithms, factorials, and absolute values.

Maximize button Button at the right side of the title bar that you click to enlarge a window to fill the screen.

Media clips A collection of clip art that may be placed on your hard disk when Office is installed.

Meeting In Outlook, an appointment for which people are invited and/or resources are needed.

Menu List of options from which to choose.

Menu bar A bar normally at the top of the screen that lists the names of menus, each of which contains a set of commands.

Merge fields Fields in a main document where you want to print the information from a data source.

Minimize button Button at the right side of the title bar that you click to reduce a window to a button on the taskbar.

Mixed cell reference Cell reference containing both relative and absolute references.

Mnemonic An underlined letter that is pressed in combination with the Alt key to access items on the menu bar, pull-down menus, and dialog boxes.

Multitable query Database query that searches related tables.

My Computer Program to help you organize and manage your files.

N

Name box Area on the left side of the worksheet formula bar that identifies the cell reference of the active cell.

Network Neighborhood Displays all of the folders and resources that are available to you through the network connection, if you have one.

Normal view screen Simplified layout of the page so you can quickly key, edit, and format text.

Notes The electronic equivalent of using paper sticky notes as reminders.

Notes pane Area in a PowerPoint presentation where you include speaker notes that you want to include with your presentation.

O

One-to-many relationship In Access, a relationship in which a record in table A can have a number of matching records in table B, but a record in table B has only one matching record in table A.

Open Process of loading a file from a disk onto the screen.

Operand Numbers or cell references used in calculations in the formulas of worksheets.

Operator Tells Excel what to do with operands in a formula.

Or operator Used to find data that meet one criteria or another.

Organization charts Show the hierarchical structure and relationships within an organization.

Outline numbered list A list with two or more levels of bullets or numbering.

Outline tab Displays all of the text in a PowerPoint slide show in outline form.

Outlook Bar The column on the left side of the Outlook screen that includes groups and shortcuts to quickly access information and folders that you create.

Overtype mode Allows you to replace existing text with the new text that is keyed.

P

Pack and Go Compacts all of the files required by your presentation into a single, compressed file that will fit on a floppy disk.

Page break Separates one page from the next.

Pane An area of a split window that contains separate scroll bars that allow you to move through that part of the document.

Paste Text is copied from the Clipboard to the location of the insertion point in the document.

Paste Special Command that allows you to link data among files created in different Office programs.

Personal information set In Publisher, used to store information about your businesses, other organizations, or your home and family.

Pie chart Chart that shows the relationship of a part to a whole.

Point-and-click method Constructs a cell formula in Excel by clicking on the cell you want to reference rather than keying the reference.

Portrait orientation Page orientation where the document is longer than it is wide.

Primary key Field in a database table that contains a value which uniquely identifies each record.

Print preview Allows you to view a document as it will appear when printed.

Pull-down menu A list of commands that appears below each menu name on the menu bar.

Q

Query A search method that allows complex searches of a database.

Quick Launch toolbar Contains icons you can click to quickly display the desktop or start frequently used programs.

R

Range Selected group of cells on a worksheet identified by the cell in the upper left corner and the cell in the lower right corner, separated by a colon (for example, A3:C5).

Read-only file File that can be viewed but not changed.

Record Complete set of database fields.

Record pointer The pointer that Access uses internally to keep track of the current record.

Record selectors Located to the left of a database table record's first field.

Recycle Bin Place to get rid of files or folders that are no longer needed.

Referential integrity Rules that ensure valid relationships between database tables and prevent invalid data from being entered.

Relationship Link between database tables that have a common field, allowing you to create forms, queries, and reports using fields from all tables in the relationship.

Relative cell reference Worksheet cell reference that adjusts to a new location when copied or moved.

Resources In Outlook, materials and/or equipment needed for meetings.

Restore button Button at the right side of the title bar that you click to resize a maximized window to its previous size.

Rotated text Displays text at an angle within a cell of a worksheet.

Rows Appear horizontally in a worksheet and are identified by numbers on the left side of the worksheet window.

S

Save Process of storing a file on disk.

Scale Resizing a graphic so that its proportions are precise.

Scatter chart Chart that shows the relationship of two categories of data.

Scroll arrows Drag to move the window in the corresponding direction one line at a time.

Scroll bar Appears at the bottom and/or right side of a window to allow user to view another part of the window's contents.

Scroll box Box in the scroll bar that indicates your position within the contents of the window.

Search criteria In a query, it's the information for which you are searching.

Section A part of the document where you can create different layouts within one document.

Selecting Highlighting a block of text.

Selection rectangle The box that appears around a graphic when you select it.

Shading Adding colors or grays to emphasize text.

Sheet tabs Label that identifies a worksheet in a workbook.

Shift-clicking Allows you to select objects that are not close to each other or when the objects you need to select are near other objects you do not want to select.

Sizing handles See **Handles**.

Slide sorter Displays miniature versions of slides in a presentation and allows you to arrange them.

Slides tab Displays slides in a presentation as small pictures or thumbnails.

Snap to Moves an object to the closest gridline on a slide.

Sorting Arranges a list of words or numbers in ascending order (A to Z; smallest to largest) or in descending order (Z to A; largest to smallest).

Spelling and Grammar Checker Used to check the spelling and grammar of a document after you finish keying.

Spreadsheet Grid of rows and columns containing numbers, text, and formulas; the purpose of a spreadsheet is to solve problems that involve numbers.

Standard toolbar Toolbar that is normally near the top of the screen and which contains buttons used to perform common tasks.

Start Button on the taskbar that you click to display menus with a variety of options.

Statistical function Function used to describe large quantities of data such as the average, standard deviation, or variance of a range of data.

Status bar Bar normally at the bottom of a screen that contains information summarizing the actions of the commands that you choose.

Style A predefined set of formatting options that have been named and saved.

Subdatasheet In database tables that are related, you can show records from one table in the related record in the primary table.

T

Table An arrangement of data in rows and columns, similar to a spreadsheet.

Tabs Mark the place the insertion point will stop when the Tab key is pressed.

Task pane Separate window on the right hand side of the opening screen that contains commonly used commands.

Taskbar Bar normally at the bottom of a screen that displays the Start button and the names of all open programs.

Tasks Any activity you want to perform and monitor to completion.

Template A file that contains page and paragraph formatting and text that you can customize to create a new document similar to but slightly different from the original.

Themes Allow users to apply design and color schemes to either a single page or to an entire Web site.

Thesaurus A feature for finding a synonym, or a word with a similar meaning for a word in your document.

Three dimensional cell reference Formula references that incorporate data from worksheets in an active worksheet.

Title bar Bar at the top of a window that contains the name of the open program, document, or folder.

Toggling Clicking a toolbar button to turn a feature on or off.

Toolbar Bar at the top or bottom of the screen that displays buttons you can click to quickly choose a command.

Track Changes Keeps a record of changes made in a document by one or more reviewers.

Trigonometric function Function that manipulates quantitative data in the worksheet using operators such as sines, cosines, and tangents.

U

Unbound control Control on a database form or report that is not connected to a field in a table.

Uniform Resource Locators (URLs) Internet addresses that identify hypertext documents.

V

Vertical alignment How text is positioned between the top and bottom margins of a document.

W

Web browser Software used to display Web pages on your computer monitor.

Web discussion A forum that permits several worksheet users to view and comment on an Excel worksheet that has been posted on the Internet.

Web page A document created with HTML that can be viewed by a Web browser.

Web site A collection of related Web pages connected with hyperlinks.

Wizard A program that asks you questions and creates a document, similar to a template, based on the answers. In Publisher, pre-designed templates that provide the framework for various types of publications.

Word processing The use of a computer and software to produce written documents such as letters, memos, forms, and reports.

Word wrap A feature that automatically wraps words around to the next line when they will not fit on the current line.

Workbook Collection of related worksheets in Excel.

Worksheet Computerized spreadsheet in Excel; a grid of rows and columns containing numbers, text, and formulas.

World Wide Web System of computers that share information by means of hypertext links.

Wrapped text Begins a new line within the cell of a worksheet when the data exceeds the width of a column.